231.00 set

ETHICS

Volume II
Freedom of Expression – Personal Relationships

A Magill Book
from the Editors of Salem Press

Consulting Editor

John K. Roth
Claremont McKenna College

Salem Press, Inc.
Pasadena, California   Englewood Cliffs, New Jersey

Library of Congress Cataloging-in-Publication Data

Ethics / consulting editor, John K. Roth
       p. cm. — (Ready reference)
  "A Magill Book"
  Includes bibliographical references and index.
  ISBN 0-89356-395-1 (set : alk. paper). — ISBN 0-89356-397-8 (v. 2 : alk. paper).
  1. Ethics—Encyclopedias. I. Roth, John K. II. Title: Ready reference, ethics. III. Series
BJ63.E54 1994
170' .3—dc20
                                                 94-3995
                                                 CIP

First Printing

PRINTED IN THE UNITED STATES OF AMERICAN

CONTENTS

ALPHABETICAL LIST OF ENTRIES

Volume I

Volume III

Freedom of expression

TYPE OF ETHICS: Civil rights

DATE: Fifth century B.C.E. to present

DEFINITION: The philosophical belief that assumes that every individual has an inherent right to freedom of expression

SIGNIFICANCE: Views the individual right to express opinions as having priority over a society's desire to inculcate particular beliefs in its members

The modern belief in freedom of speech is assumed to include all other forms of free expression. These forms include the right to speak freely in political assemblies, the right to petition those assemblies, the right to relate and publish debates of the assemblies, and freedoms of correspondence, of teaching, of worship, of publishing newspapers and books, and freedom of expression in the arts. Freedom of expression is all-inclusive, but it is epitomized in freedom of speech. It is from freedom of speech that all other individual expressions take their distinctive forms. Understood to accompany the freedom of expression are freedom of thought (spiritual freedom) and the right to criticize—to inquire or to research old dogmas.

History. The language, theory, and practice of freedom of expression in the modern, Westernized world is linked to Greek and Latin ideas and institutions. Freedom of expression was born in Athens in the archaic period (c. 800-600 B.C.E.), when the aristocratic rulers allowed certain classes to voice their opinions without fear of reprisal. This freedom was increased under the reforms of Solon (c. 594 B.C.E.), and it reached a high point in the golden age of Pericles (c. 507 B.C.E.) and Cleisthenes (c. 443-429 B.C.E.). The citizens of Athens were granted freedom of expression in the political processes, including the council, the assembly, the courts, and in society at large, and also in the areas of philosophy and the arts. Freedom of speech is excellently illustrated by the dramatist Aristophanes' criticism of Cleonymus, an Athenian politician of considerable power, as a "glutton," a "perjurer," and one who throws away his shield in battle (a coward).

Despite the broad latitude permitted in Athens for freedom of expression, such freedom was by no means absolute. Restrictions were placed upon the speakers, the content of the speech, and the time and place of utterance. The leaders of the assembly restricted freedom of speech to the citizen class; those individuals who were considered "unworthy" or "dishonorable" were punished by having their right to speak taken away.

In Republican Rome, freedom of expression differed markedly from the variety found in Athens. The representative democracy of Rome was established on the basis of the idea that all political authority came from the people. The notions of liberty (*libertas*) and of the political process (*civitas*) were considered inseparable. Therefore, there was no basic clash between the individual and the state, for the free and responsible citizen had certain rights that the state could legitimately support so long as they furthered *civitas*.

Roman law did not support legal guarantees for freedom of expression, but a tradition of tolerance evolved in Rome that permitted and encouraged freedom of expression. Both orators and writers freely criticized public and private figures by name. Some controls were exercised regarding who could speak and what could be said. The government also established theaters and exercised censorship over them.

The right to speak and speech content in the assembly were controlled by procedures. The republican constitution provided that the assembly serve as the principal legislature and as the supreme court. The ordinary citizen who participated in the assembly did not have a right to speak but did have a right to listen to debates by magistrates, senators, and juriconsults (lawyers). They also had the right to vote. The right to speak was controlled by the governing class.

The Twelve Tablets, Rome's first written law, which was codified in 451 B.C.E., provided for the punishment of seditious libel or defamation. Nevertheless, orators often engaged in defamation and invective. Cicero attacked his opponent Piso, calling him a "beast," "funeral pyre of the state," "mud," "donkey," "hog," and a "piece of rotten flesh." Libelous expression was constrained, although the record is not clear about the existence or enforcement of specific laws governing sedition or defamation in the assembly and the senate. Defamation, however, was actionable if it occurred on the stage or in the courts.

In the Roman Empire, government control mutated from democratic institutions to one-man rule. Free expression was commonly tolerated on an ad hoc basis, depending on the emperor. Augustus was moderately tolerant of dissent, Tiberius allowed a considerable degree of freedom of expression, and Caligula started with a policy of leniency but soon turned toward brutal repression that included having one writer burned alive in the amphitheater. Claudius suspended the law of treason, but his successor, Nero, reinstated it; Vespasian and Domitian applied the law of high treason vigorously, including having the historian Hermogenes Tarsus put to death and his secretaries crucified.

The late classical world's pattern of constraints on freedom of expression formed the basis for the emergent practices in the West for more than seventeen centuries. During this lengthy period, no Western nation extended to its citizens a legal guarantee of freedom of expression. The Christian Church fervently persecuted those whom it thought unorthodox or heretical. Inquisitions of various kinds were carried out by the Church from the thirteenth century through the eighteenth century.

During this dark period for human liberty, England moved quietly but unquestionably toward establishing a tradition of civil liberty. In June, 1215, King John, a tyrant, was forced to sign the Magna Carta, which is now recognized as the foundation of constitutional liberty for both England and the

United States. This charter did not mention freedom of expression, but it did claim that no free man could be deprived of life or property except by peer judgment and by the law of the land. The word "liberty" appears several times in the document.

The regal Magna Carta gave support, through its transformation, to political liberty, including freedom of expression. While there is no direct line of descent from antiquity to Western Europe and England of freedom of expression, the West had to learn the principles and practice of freedom of expression reflexively and by intentional emulation. Once the idea of freedom of expression took hold, its growth was assured by an increasingly mobile and rational society that was beginning to debate and test everything.

The Renaissance, the Scientific Revolution, the Reformation, the Enlightenment, and the two great revolutions of the eighteenth century imbued views of freedom of expression with much of their modern implications and tone. The debate and testing of worldviews blossomed in the United States in 1791 with the ratification of the Bill of Rights. In the meantime, following King John's signing of the Magna Carta, church and state in England continued for centuries to restrain the development of liberty of speech by controlling the content of speech and the medium of speech—the printing press.

The Early Modern Era. John Milton (1608-1674) was the first to decry prior restraint of the press. Milton published his argument in *Areopagitica*. Milton's essay states in cautious prose four arguments against prior restraint or press censorship by Parliament: First, prior restraint was conceived and used by the Catholic church to suppress the Protestant Reformation. Second, prior restraint, according to Milton, weakens character, since individuals do not have the chance to determine the truth for themselves. Third, prior restraint does not work; the censored ideas will inevitably become known. Fourth, prior censorship discourages learning and the search for truth (it replaces the pursuit of truth with unquestioned authority), which injures society. Milton had many reservations about extending freedom of expression to everyone (for example, Milton did not believe that freedom of expression should be extended to Catholics). Nevertheless, his work was a milestone in the development of civil liberties in the West and Westernized societies.

John Stuart Mill (1806-1873), an English philosopher and economist, went much further than Milton in his argument in support of freedom of expression. In his work *On Liberty,* Mill asserts three basic reasons for government to permit freedom of expression. First, the "hated ideas" may be true and the orthodox ideas may be false. Second, truth is powerful enough to triumph over falsehood without the artificial protection of government, and the continual challenging of truth prevents it from becoming dead dogma. Third, there is probably some degree of truth in all ideas or opinions; therefore, to suppress any idea is to endanger possible truth.

Mill's argument for freedom of expression is that it is socially useful. Freedom of expression must have purpose beyond itself. Mill maintains that "absolute certainty" is not available to human beings, and therefore the suppression of any idea "is an assumption of infallibility"; such an assumption is unwarranted. Mill's espousal of freedom of expression is best exemplified in one of his quotations: "If all mankind minus one, were of one opinion, and only one person were of the contrary opinion, mankind would be no more justified in silencing that one person, than he, if he had the power, would be justified in silencing mankind."

The American Synthesis. The next leap forward in the progression of human rights occurred in America. It took its most complete development in the First Amendment to the U.S. Constitution. The framers of the Constitution placed freedom of conscience first, and then freedom of speech and the press. James Madison, Thomas Jefferson, and the others who inspired the First Amendment were inheritors of the Enlightenment and its antecedents. They believed in the power of reason, in the search for truth, in progress, and in the inevitable perfectibility of humankind. Freedom of expression was considered essential to the discovery and advancement of truth, for only by constant testing in a public forum could falsehood be uncovered.

The twentieth century, especially its last third, was a high point for freedom of expression. Alexander Meiklejohn, a foremost constitutional scholar, maintained that a teacher's freedom to pursue knowledge (academic freedom) may be curtailed in certain circumstances; political speech, however, enjoys "an absolute, preferred position" in the Constitution. James Madison, author of the First Amendment, said, "If we *examine* the nature of Republican Government, we shall find the censorial power is in the people over the Government, and not in the Government over the people." It is only by freedom of expression that the people can voice their grievances and aspire to redress them. It is principally by exercising free speech that people can build without molestation political power that can counter recurrence of excesses by government.

The Judiciary. The Supreme Court, as the final decipherer of the Constitution, has acted as the guardian of freedom of expression. In *Garrison v. Louisiana* (1964), Justice Joseph Brennan declared: "Speech concerning public affairs is more than self-expression; it is the essence of self-government."

The primacy of freedom of expression has never been absolute in the United States, and it has been even more circumscribed in Western Europe. In times of war or similar crisis, for example, some publications that may threaten the national security are prohibited. Other forms of expression are restrained on certain occasions by the courts, since they may unfairly assail the communal interest in public morality. Picketing, parades, and even words, if permitted at a particular time and place, may threaten public safety or order despite the constitutionality of the information or ideas.

The Court employed the bad-tendency test, or the "nip it in the bud" approach, to judging expression. This approach stops or punishes speech that the Court believes has a tendency to create a serious danger at some point in the future if it is allowed to continue. The principal statement of this position was in *Gitlow v. United States* (1925), in which the Supreme Court upheld the sedition conviction of Benjamin Gitlow: "A single revolutionary spark may kindle a fire that, smoldering for a time may burst into a sweeping and destructive conflagration"; therefore, it is reasonable and expected for the state to seek to extinguish the spark to protect the public peace and safety.

The Supreme Court began to inquire into the limits of freedom of expression only in 1919. The first landmark case decided by the Court was *Schenck v. United States* (1919). In more than seven decades, the Court assembled a body of constitutional law, but it did not formulate a theoretical basis for interpreting the First Amendment. The Court has consistently held that freedom of expression, especially of speech and of the press, assures the survival of the American political system. The chief purpose of the First Amendment, in the eyes of the Court, is to serve the political needs of an open and democratic society. Such political needs also include the right of the people to alter by lawful means the political process itself. Justice Felix Frankfurter's famed pronouncement reflects the Court's consistent opinion that freedom of expression is a means to better the political system: "Winds of doctrine should freely blow for the promotion of good and the correction of evil." Justices Hugo Black and William O. Douglas reiterated the contention that freedom of expression exists to preserve American democracy: "It is the purpose of the First Amendment to preserve an uninhibited marketplace of ideas in which truth will ultimately win."

Before the mid-twentieth century, the Court and political philosophers argued for freedom of expression in general terms. Zechariah Chafee, Jr., writing in the 1940's, discussed problems of preserving the peace, defamation, and obscenity. His emphasis was on political expression and seditious libel. Chafee's theory recognizes two types of expression: that which serves an individual interest and that which serves a more broad social interest. Chafee tries to balance freedom of expression in searching for truth against public safety. Every effort, Chafee says, should be made to maintain both interests unimpaired. Free expression should be only sacrificed when the interest in public safety is really imperiled, not when it is narrowly affected. Chafee espoused the doctrine of a clear and present danger test. Profanity and defamation, to Chafee, were socially "worthless" activities that were unprotected by the First Amendment.

Thomas Emerson, another constitutional scholar, wrote in the 1960's. Emerson argued that freedom of expression includes the right to form and hold beliefs on any subject and to communicate those beliefs to others by whatever medium one chooses—whether through speech or by other means, including art or music. Freedom of expression, according to Emerson, includes the right to hear the opinions of others, the right to inquire, reasonable access to information, and the rights of assembly and association. Freedom of expression, Emerson declares, operates in four ways: first, individual self-fulfillment; second, discovering truth; third, democratic decision making, and fourth, finding a balance between healthy strife and necessary consensus. Emerson tried to fashion a theory that would determine where the line should be drawn between expression and action in the many cases involving freedom of expression. Speech, ideally, should not be punishable at all; however, in certain situations, actions, if they are pernicious and unlawful, can and must be punishable.

Franklyn Haiman wrote in the 1980's and argued for a free marketplace of ideas. The law is an inappropriate tool for dealing with "hated" speech. The remedy for such speech is more speech, never (or nearly never) the repression of speech. Even in cases of defamation, the remedy is a right of reply, except when the alleged defamer refuses to provide for such a reply or when time is inadequate to permit a reply. Haiman is even tolerant of speech that incites unlawful actions. Haiman insists that those who allegedly incite others to illegal conduct should not be held accountable themselves for the actions of their listeners, unless the audience is deceived, coerced, or is mentally impaired. Haiman also argues for a wide dissemination of all ideas. The law should be used to enrich and expand communications and to ensure that the marketplace of ideas remains free. Even the views of nonconformists should be distributed, Haiman concludes. Also, the scheduling of the time and place of speech should be done in a content-neutral way. Owners and managers of quasi-public private property (such as shopping centers and airports) should make provisions for nondisruptive communications with the public by any individual. Haiman further emphasizes that government in a free society is the servant and should not inhibit, distort, or dominate public discourse.

Most constitutional scholars agree that the freedom of American citizens to participate in governing themselves is best protected by the First Amendment. Free people, who govern themselves, must not be shielded from any idea that is considered unwise, or unfair, or dangerous; it is they, the American people, who must judge any idea. Freedom of expression is not a law of nature or a principle of abstract reason, but a basic American agreement that public issues shall be decided by the people. A general theory may be stated in the following way: The people's suffrage in a democracy must always be couched broadly in terms of freedom of expression in the political process; however, government interference in personal conduct must be rarely permitted or not permitted at all.   —*Claude Hargrove*

See also Bill of Rights, English; Civil Rights Act of 1964; Commission on Civil Rights, U.S.; *Dronenburg v. Zech*; First Amendment; *Goss v. Lopez*; *Griswold v. Connecticut*; Immigration Reform and Control Act; *Miranda v. Arizona*; Poll tax; Poona Pact; U.N. Covenant on Civil and Political Rights.

BIBLIOGRAPHY

Bonner, Robert J. *Aspects of Athenian Democracy*. New York: Russell & Russell, 1967. Reprint. A lucidly written work on various aspects of freedom of expression. The author examines the constraint of free expression and the procedures that those in power use to control public speech.

Britton, Karl. *John Stuart Mill*. 2d ed. New York: Dover, 1969. An excellent study of Mill's *On Liberty*. Mill's absolutist views were very modern and were nearly a definitive position of absolutism.

Chafee, Zechariah, Jr. *Free Speech in the United States*. Cambridge, Mass.: Harvard University, 1942. The author himself is a constitutional scholar who has had a major influence on American constitutional law and the theory of balancing free speech against unlawful conduct.

Emerson, Thomas I. *The System of Freedom of Expression*. New York: Random House, 1970. A solid work that attempts to establish a theory that delineates speech and action. Holds that the speaker is not responsible for the unlawful action of his audience.

Haiman, Franklyn S. *Speech and Law in a Free Society*. Chicago: University of Chicago Press, 1981. The author expounds a view of wide dissemination of ideas in quasi-public places; he holds that even slanderous speech should be tolerated.

Meiklejohn, Alexander. *Political Freedom: The Constitutional Powers of the People*. New York: Oxford University Press, 1965. The author is a constitutional scholar who helped to give direction to constitutional theory. He argues that speech should hold a preferred position with reference to other considerations, such as public morality.

Schauer, Frederick. *Free Speech: A Philosophical Enquiry*. New York: Cambridge University Press, 1982. A composite work that surveys the theoretical basis of the freedom of expression.

Freedom of Information Act

TYPE OF ETHICS: Media ethics

DATES: 1966; amended in 1974, 1976, and 1986

ASSOCIATED WITH: Movement toward "open government"; public access to records and information in the possession of federal government agencies

DEFINITION: An act mandating that every record possessed by federal agencies must be made available to the public upon request, except to the extent that the records are covered by the Act's nine exemptions or excluded from its coverage

SIGNIFICANCE: Strengthens the public's right to know, reaffirming the view that an informed citizenry is vital to the functioning of a democratic society

Historical Background. Before the enactment of the U.S. Freedom of Information Act (FOIA) in pre-Watergate 1966, the public's "right to know" was merely a slogan coined by journalists, not a legal right. The press led the fight for "open government" and cited numerous instances of random and unexplained denials of access to information about crucial governmental decisions. Claims of executive privilege without any requirement of justification shielded the nondisclosure of materials to Congress for legislation and supervision. Government records were required to be revealed only to persons properly and directly concerned with them. Any records could be kept secret if such policy was in the public interest or if the records related solely to the internal management of an agency.

The Act. The rights conferred on the people by the FOIA are not specifically protected in the Constitution. Its goals, however—the elimination of secrecy and preservation of government accountability—were familiar even to the nation's founding fathers (James Madison, Alexander Hamilton, and Thomas Jefferson), who viewed excesses of power in the seat of big government with alarm.

Under the FOIA, all individuals have an equal right of access to information. The Act provides that "any person" (citizen or noncitizen, partnership, corporation, association, foreign or domestic government) may file a request for an agency record for any reason. The requester does not have to be a party in an agency proceeding, and no showing of relevancy or involvement in litigation is required. The purpose for which the request is made has no bearing on its merits. The FOIA specifies only that requests must reasonably describe the documents sought and must comply with agencies' published procedural regulations. The agency must provide the document unless it falls within one of the nine exemptions contained in the Act. If the agency refuses to produce the record, the requester may go to court, where the agency must prove that the documents in question are exempt under the law and that its refusal to produce them is justified. Courts determine the propriety of agency action without deference to agency opinion and expertise, unlike the course of action followed in other matters.

The FOIA establishes two categories of information that must be disclosed. The first requires publication in the Federal Register of basic information regarding the transaction of agency business; descriptions of the organization, including its functions, procedures, and rules; and policy statements of the agency. The second requires the availability for inspection and copying of so-called "reading room" materials: final adjudicatory opinions, specific policy statements, and administrative staff manuals. These materials must be indexed to facilitate public access, to help any citizen involved in a controversy with an agency, and to guard against the development of internal agency secrets. Records not covered by the foregoing are subject to disclosure upon an agency's receipt of a request by any person.

The FOIA applies only to "records" maintained by "agencies" within the federal government. Not included are records maintained by state and municipal governments, courts, Congress, or private citizens. Many states have counterparts to the FOIA. The Supreme Court has developed a basic two-pronged test for determining what constitutes an "agency record" under the FOIA: documents that must be (1) either created or obtained by an agency and (2) under agency control at the time of the request.

Exemptions. Release of information contained in nine categories of exemptions is not required. These include national security and foreign policy matters, internal personnel rules and practices, exemptions specified by other federal statutes, privileged or confidential trade secrets and commercial or financial information, interagency or intraagency memoranda, personnel and medical files constituting an unwarranted invasion of privacy, investigatory records compiled for law enforcement purposes (including protecting the identity of confidential sources and information furnished to authorities), financial institution reports, and geological and geophysical information and data. It should be noted, however, that the exemptions are discretionary rather than mandatory. When challenged, therefore, their application to particular records and situations must be determined on a case-by-case basis and may be subject to varying interpretations by the courts.

Significant Amendments. As a reaction to the abuses of Watergate and widespread concern over excessive government secrecy, the FOIA was substantially amended in 1974. The overall scope of the Act's law enforcement and national security exemptions was narrowed and its procedural aspects broadened. The 1974 amendments included a provision whereby a court could conduct an *in camera* (behind closed doors) inspection of withheld information in order to determine the propriety of nondisclosure and classification and whether certain portions of otherwise withheld records could be segregated and released. A time limit of ten working days for agency response to a request was also established, as was a provision for the disciplining of persons responsible for arbitrary and capricious withholding of information, and the awarding of court costs and attorney's fees to a plaintiff who prevails in an FOIA case.

As part of the Anti-Drug Abuse Act of 1986, the FOIA was amended to provide broader exemption protection for law enforcement information, special law enforcement record exclusions, and new fee and fee waiver provisions. The 1990's brought discussions about the need to implement refinements to the FOIA to accommodate technological advances such as electronic record-keeping. Numerous treatises and legal journal articles contain references to the Freedom of Information Act. —*Marcia J. Weiss*

See also Confidentiality; Constitutional government; Democracy; Information, access to; Inside information; Journalistic ethics; Privacy.

BIBLIOGRAPHY

Citizen's Guide to the Freedom of Information Act. Chicago: Commerce Clearing House, 1987.

Sherick, L. G. *How to Use the Freedom of Information Act.* New York: Arco, 1978.

United States, Dept. of Justice, Office of Information and Privacy. *Freedom of Information Act Guide and Privacy Act Overview.* Washington, D.C.: Government Printing Office, 1992.

Freud, Sigmund (May 6, 1856, Freiburg, Moravia—Sept. 23, 1939, London, England): Psychoanalyst

TYPE OF ETHICS: Psychological ethics

ACHIEVEMENTS: Founder of psychoanalysis; author of *Die Traumdeutung* (1900; *The Interpretation of Dreams*, 1913) and *Das Unbehagen in der Kultur* (1930; *Civilization and Its Discontents*, 1930)

SIGNIFICANCE: Freud advocated a rational and secular basis for ethics that was free from many of the unrealistic constraints of religion and conventional morality

Although Sigmund Freud has had a powerful impact on the field of ethics, he did not initially set out to study moral questions. Freud's original interest was medical research, and he was trained in Vienna as a physician. Financial constraints, however, forced Freud to abandon his chief interest in pure research, and he began to practice during the 1880's as a neurologist. In 1884, Freud was introduced to Josef Breuer, a Viennese physician, who had developed a "cathartic" method for the treatment of hysterical symptoms. This method involved encouraging patients to talk in a completely free and unencumbered manner about the development of their symptoms. The talking alone seemed to produce a surprising improvement in patients' conditions. This discovery was the starting point of what later became the field of psychoanalysis. Freud and Breuer collaborated on *Studies in Hysteria* (1895), in which they described their groundbreaking work in this area.

The Development of Psychoanalysis. Freud continued this work alone, publishing such seminal volumes as *The Interpretation of Dreams* (1900), *Three Essays on the Theory of Sexuality* (1905), and *The Origin and Development of Psychoanalysis* (1910). In all these works, Freud developed a new way of examining the structure, nature, and diseases of the human mind. Freud's original focus was on the understanding and treatment of emotional disorders, but as the field of psychoanalysis rapidly progressed, Freud's ideas gradually took a broader perspective. Freud eventually left his followers with a theory of the human psyche, a therapy for the relief of its ills, and a method for the interpretation of culture and society. It was in his later works, such as *Totem and Taboo* (1913), *The Future of an Illusion* (1927), and *Civilization and Its Discontents* (1930), that Freud spoke most directly to ethical and social issues.

Ethical Implications. In many ways, Freud rejected the conventional ethics of his era. His focus on the egoistic, narcissistic, and aggressive roots of human behavior led some readers to conclude that Freudian psychoanalysis was an amoral discipline that left no room for either a philosophical or a practical theory of morality. It is true that Freud rejected many traditional religious values. He believed that a number of central religious beliefs were merely a misguided human effort to overcome infantile feelings of helplessness and dependence. In *The Future of an Illusion*, Freud argued that the belief in God is a mythic attempt to overcome the human sense of powerlessness. Like an idealized

tics have often celebrated as the most fundamental of all religious experiences. Freud believed that the origin of this feeling was the desire to re-create the undifferentiated infant's profound sense of fusion with its mother. By attempting to debunk such central aspects of religious belief, Freud called into question many religious notions of moral right and wrong.

Sigmund Freud (Library of Congress)

parent, the concept of God is, for Freud, the projection of childish wishes for an omnipotent protector. In *Civilization and Its Discontents*, Freud again argued that religious phenomena were merely the reflection of unresolved psychological needs from the early years of life. In the opening chapter of the book, Freud described the oceanic feeling, or sense of indissoluble oneness with the universe, which mys-

In addition to his rejection of religious morality, Freud also disagreed with Kant's position that reason and duty should be the central grounds for morality. While Freud believed that reason must play a part in the development of ethical guidelines, he also saw a place in ethics for the promotion of human happiness and welfare. Freud advocated a practical form of ethics that was designed to promote the general welfare of society while simultaneously allowing individuals a sufficient degree of instinctual gratification.

Freud's View of Human Nature. For Freud, this position grew logically from his rather mixed view of human nature. Freud believed that most individuals possessed powerful aggressive and egoistic tendencies, along with a capacity for self-observation and altruistic behavior. Freud consistently maintained that theorists who saw human nature as inherently good were seriously deluded. For this reason, Freud believed that the golden rule—to love one's neighbor as oneself—was a destructive and unrealistic goal. Freud also suggested that utopian schemes such as communism were destined to failure, because they called for humans to give more than they were capable of giving. According to Freud, the best course for humanity was to establish civilizations in which the more destructive elements of instinctual drives were prohibited, in order to promote the common social good. People will be able to tolerate the rules of such social organizations if nondestructive outlets for aggressive and narcissistic wishes can be developed. This will not be an easy task, and Freud believed that individual and group needs will generally be in conflict. Freud's hope was that society would adopt a realistic view of human nature and gradually learn more effective ways to manage the individual's need for instinctual gratification. —*Steven C. Abell*

See also Jung, Carl Gustav; Psychology; Therapist-patient relationship.

BIBLIOGRAPHY

Freud, Sigmund. *Letters.* Edited by Ernst L. Freud. Translated by Tania Stern and James Stern. New York: Basic Books, 1960.

_____. *The Standard Edition of the Complete Psychological Works of Sigmund Freud.* Translated by James Strachey. London: Hogarth Press, 1953-1974.

Hartmann, Heinz. *Psychoanalysis and Moral Values.* New York: International Universities Press, 1960.

Marcuse, Herbert. *Eros and Civilization: A Philosophical Inquiry Into Freud.* Boston: Beacon Press, 1955.

Ricour, Paul. *Freud and Philosophy: An Essay on Interpretation.* Translated by Denis Savage. New Haven, Conn.: Yale University Press, 1970.

Rieff, Philip. *Freud: The Mind of the Moralist.* Garden City, N.Y.: Doubleday, 1961.

Roazen, Paul. *Freud: Political and Social Thought.* New York: Knopf, 1968.

Wallwork, Ernest. *Psychoanalysis and Ethics.* New Haven, Conn.: Yale University Press, 1991.

Friendship

TYPE OF ETHICS: Personal and social ethics
DATE: Fourth century B.C.E. to present
ASSOCIATED WITH: Moral philosophers from Plato, Aristotle, and Cicero down to modern times
DEFINITION: Attachment to another person, characterized by mutually acknowledged affection, esteem, and goodwill

SIGNIFICANCE: Since entering the vocabulary of ethical philosophy in the dialogues of Plato, the concept of friendship has been seen as closely related to those of love and goodness

Friendship in the Greek World. Friendship became a topic of Western philosophical discussion in Plato's early dialogue *Lysis* (early fourth century B.C.E.). Because this work belongs to a type of inquiry called aporetic, meaning that the author was interested in raising difficult questions about the topic, it is irritatingly inconclusive, but the questions Plato raises are ones that later Greek and Roman philosophers energetically set about discussing. He also touches upon friendship in many of his later works; in the *Laws* (middle fourth century B.C.E.) for example, he describes love as a "vehement" form of friendship, and love, one of Plato's favorite topics, is the subject of his celebrated *Symposium* (early fourth century B.C.E.).

Not surprisingly, Aristotle, who defined man as a "political animal" (the adjective carries the wider meaning of "social"), devotes the eighth and ninth books of his *Nicomachean Ethics* (c. 330 B.C.E.), to friendship. He allows that friendship may be based on the relatively selfish motives of utility and pleasure but finds that the highest and most permanent form of friendship derives from a perception of goodness. All friends wish one another well, but a good person will value a friend not for a mere advantage but also for the friend's sake, and for the sake of the goodness in that friend.

Aristotle is one of many thinkers who point out that friendship does not, on the surface, appear to be necessary. It is neither a preliminary to the creation of new life, like erotic love, nor a condition of civil order. People cannot exist without water or food or shelter from the elements, and they normally crave human companionship, but they can and do exist without friends. To the question of why the happy person, presumably in possession of the good and essential things, would need friends, Aristotle applies another of his basic ideas, that of happiness as virtuous *activity*. The virtuous actions of one's own friend will be a delight, even a need, in one's own pursuit of happiness.

Cicero's Practical Ethic of Friendship. Of all the treatises on friendship from the ancient world, Marcus Tullius Cicero's *Laelius on Friendship* (44 B.C.E.) has had the most pervasive influence. From its composition through the Middle Ages and into the Renaissance, Cicero's was by far the discussion most often cited and reiterated. His philosophy is eclectic and unsystematic, drawing upon Platonic, Aristotelian, Stoic, and Epicurean thought. An accessible authority as well as a practical one, Cicero offered the medieval and Renaissance eras guidance on such questions as: How far should the love of a friend extend? Cicero's answer: As far as is honorable. Accepting the common Greek idea that virtue induces friendship, he argues that virtue cannot be forsaken for the sake of friendship. For Cicero, the obligations of friendship include the avoidance of hypocrisy and suspicion, but he acknowledges that even good friends can go wrong. Therefore, it is one's duty not only to advise but also to rebuke one's friend if necessary.

Christianity and Friendship. If friendship is a type or degree of love, as several of these ancient philosophers have claimed, Christianity has tended to see friendship as one of the manifestations of charity—or love for the sake of God. Thus argued Saint Thomas Aquinas, the greatest of the medieval Scholastics, who also incorporated much Aristotelian thought into his *Summa Theologica* (1266-1272). It is difficult to reconcile the disinterestedness of charity with the exclusiveness of friendship (for the Greco-Roman philosophers had pointed out that one's circle of true friends cannot be large), but Christianity has generally held that all true love is divine at its core.

Modern Views of Friendship. Modern philosophers have concerned themselves little with friendship, and Freudian psychology, which argues that expressed motives are often not the real underlying ones, has complicated later discussions of friendship. One modern advocate of classical and Christian thought, C. S. Lewis, in his *The Four Loves* (1960), deplores the modern habit of equating friendship with the nonethical concept of companionship. Lewis also vigorously rejects the tendency to regard friendships between those of the same sex as homoerotic. He recognizes that friendships can, and frequently do, turn into erotic love; his strong disapproval of homosexual love, however, detracts somewhat from his noteworthy attempt to reaffirm traditional moral dimensions of friendship.

Unresolved Ethical Questions. It remains unclear whether friendship should be regarded as distinct in kind or only different in degree from erotic love. While exclusive, it does not nearly so often foment the jealousies that afflict the latter. A friendship of two can grow into a circle. For Cicero, the fact that *amicitia* derives from *amor* proves that friendship is a version of love, but in many other languages, English among them, the characteristic terms for the two concepts are etymologically distinct.

It is also not clear to what extent friendship is a human need. Though it is obviously a need for some people, it now seems presumptuous to argue, as does Aristotle, that those who feel the greatest need for it are the *best* people; that is, the people most desirous of cultivating goodness. The great moral philosophers agree, however, that the motivation for friendship cannot be *merely* satisfaction of a need. If friendship were primarily a need, Cicero remarks, then the weakest and most deficient people would make the best friends.

—*Robert P. Ellis*

See also Goodness; Loyalty; Platonic ethics; Trustworthiness.

BIBLIOGRAPHY
Aristotle. *Nicomachean Ethics*. Edited by G. Ramsauer. London: Garland, 1987.
Bloom, Allan. *Love and Friendship*. New York: Simon & Schuster, 1993.
Cicero, Marcus Tullius. *Laelius De Amicitia (Laelius on Friendship)*. Edited by Clifton Price. Cincinnati: American Book, 1902.
Lewis, C. S. *The Four Loves*. New York: Harcourt Brace Jovanovich, 1960.
Plato. *Lysis*. Translated by W. R. M. Lamb. Cambridge, Mass.: Harvard University Press, 1975.

Future generations

TYPE OF ETHICS: Beliefs and practices

DATE: Began to be discussed actively in the 1960's and 1970's

ASSOCIATED WITH: The environmental movement

DEFINITION: The idea that, in making decisions whose consequences may affect persons as yet unborn, decision makers should take into account the interests of those persons

SIGNIFICANCE: The theoretical issue concerns whether people have obligations to the unborn; practical issues include whether the existing population may pollute the earth and exhaust scarce natural resources

Since the time of the Stoics, most mainstream Western philosophers have agreed that people have some ethical obligations toward human beings in general, simply because they are human. Thus, Immanuel Kant wrote that the moral law commands one to "treat humanity, whether in one's own person or that of another, always as an end, and never as a means only"; and John Stuart Mill prescribed that one ought to maximize the happiness of all who will be affected by what one does.

These traditional philosophers did not specify, however, whether unborn future generations are to be included in this mandate. It did not occur to them to confront this issue, because the ethical problems with which they were preoccupied concerned transactions among contemporaries only.

The environmental movement has alerted people to the possibility that the profligate treatment of nature may leave to future generations a despoiled planet much less suited to human life. In the economic sphere, lavish public spending may saddle future generations with a crushing burden of debt. Here, the theoretical question of whether individuals have ethical obligations to those who do not yet exist becomes linked with large practical questions of public policy relating to intergenerational equity.

There are three ways of answering the central theoretical question. The narrowest answer holds that people can have obligations only toward persons who are now in existence. Those advocating this answer seek to justify it by arguing that analysis of locutions of the form "x has an obligation toward y" shows that these cannot be true unless y exists at the time of utterance. Such reasoning is sophistical, however, and the conclusion drawn is morally repugnant in its selfishness.

The broadest answer is that people ought to give equal consideration to all human beings who may be affected by their actions, regardless of when they exist. This answer is troublingly radical, because it goes so far in imposing obligations to promote the well-being of merely potential persons who are very remote in time.

An in-between answer would say that the interests of those as yet unborn ought not to be disregarded, yet that what consideration they are given should be less, other things being equal, the greater their distance in time from the present. Those favoring this answer presumably see temporal distance as generating a type of moral distance that diminishes obligations. They might mention that one's obligations toward contemporary persons vary, depending on how close one's genetic and social links with these persons are (for example, one has stronger obligations toward close relatives than toward strangers). The idea would be that separation in time tends to generate moral distance; hence, the amount of ethical consideration one owes to future persons will tend to be less, the more remote in time they are from one.

In modern times, birth rates have been declining sharply in most advanced nations and family lines have been dying out at an increasing rate. As a result, individuals of each successive generation have had less and less reason to suppose that distant generations will include direct descendants of theirs. Many people regard direct biological descent as a particularly important tie creating ethical obligations. If they are right, the dwindling of that tie will tend to diminish ethical obligations. It would seem to follow that in modern times the ethical obligations of people of a given generation toward unborn future generations have been decreasing.

When one tries to decide which of the three theoretical answers concerning obligations to future generations to accept, one's reflection tends to be severely obstructed by the uncertainty of predictions about the future. No one knows with certainty what the needs and abilities of future people will be, how well they will be able to adapt to a changing environment, how much need they will have of natural resources that the present population contemplates exhausting, or even whether human life will endure into future centuries. Moreover, one not only cannot be sure that any human successors will be one's biological descendants but also cannot be sure that any such descendants will be persons whom one would wish to benefit.

People usually believe, for example, that ingratitude on the part of others lessens their obligations toward them; and if it should be that the persons of the future are not going to feel gratitude for any consideration that the present population shows them, then the present population perhaps owes them considerably less than would otherwise be the case. Thus, in trying to assess specific obligations to future generations, it is easy to become lost in a fog of speculations. Uncertainty concerning the theoretical issue about how much, in principle, the living owe to the unborn tends to be smothered by myriad other uncertainties concerning what sort of future lies ahead, and decisive answers become difficult to reach. —*Stephen F. Barker*

See also Environmental ethics; Environmental movement.

BIBLIOGRAPHY

Cooper, David E., and Jay A. Palmer, eds. *The Environment in Question: Ethics and Global Issues.* New York: Routledge, 1992.

DeGeorge, Richard T. "The Environment, Rights, and Future Generations. In *Ethics and Problems of the Twenty-first Century,* edited by K. E. Goodpaster and K. M. Sayre. Notre Dame, Ind.: Notre Dame University Press, 1979.

Dower, Nigel, ed. *Ethics and the Environmental Responsibility.* Brookfield, Vt.: Avebury, 1989.

Regan, Tom, ed. *Earthbound: New Introductory Essays in Environmental Ethics.* New York: Random House, 1984.

Scherer, Donald, ed. *Upstream/Downstream: Issues in Environmental Ethics.* Philadelphia: Temple University Press, 1990.

Future-oriented ethics

TYPE OF ETHICS: Politico-economic ethics

DATE: Eighteenth century to present

DEFINITION: A discipline devoted to understanding the implications of current actions on future conditions and future generations

SIGNIFICANCE: Concerns the welfare of future generations of people rather than solely those currently living

Future-oriented ethics concerns the influence of current decisions on the future. Some decisions affect people who are not yet living and who therefore have no voice in the decisions. Some choices, in fact, will influence which people will be alive in the future.

In some senses, future-oriented ethics began when humans first acquired the ability to reason and choose. Many religions discuss the possibility of an afterlife, with behavior during this life determining an individual's fate in the afterworld. Development of future-oriented ethics as a guide to political and social policy in addition to individual action developed slowly. During the eighteenth century, philosophers such as Adam Smith and Thomas Robert Malthus began to explore formally the implications of various types of social, political, and economic behavior. Malthus is famous for his theories of population, which state that human populations are destined to experience cycles of prosperity and famine because population will grow more rapidly than will food supplies until there is insufficient food and people starve.

Population Control. Malthus' theories, based on agricultural economies, in general have proved to be overly pessimistic. The Industrial Revolution allowed production to increase more rapidly than did population, allowing rising standards of living.

Many less-industrialized countries, however, face Malthusian cycles of poverty. In these countries, agricultural production serves as a check on population: If there is not enough food produced, possibly because the population has grown too rapidly, people do starve to death. Nature thus controls population if people do not do so consciously.

Ethical issues of population control concern whether policy planners are willing to let nature take its course. Many of the wealthier countries step in, providing food and other supplies, when famine or other disasters threaten populations. Some population theorists argue that this type of aid perpetuates the problem, allowing populations to survive and grow even though the natural environment cannot support them.

Wealthier nations face similar, though less desperate, questions. Welfare programs of various sorts provide a better standard of living, or perhaps even survival itself, for those less able to support themselves. These programs may create a cycle of poverty in which parents who are unable to support themselves have children who in turn are unable to support themselves.

Medicine. Population also can be controlled through various medical means. Birth control is one example. Some countries—China is a prominent example—actively promote birth control as a means of keeping their populations at sustainable levels. Many religions, however, prohibit artificial means of birth control, ruling out that option of poverty alleviation for some countries.

As life extension through medical technology becomes possible, societies must decide the value of a human life. The fact that it is possible to prolong or save a life does not mean that it is beneficial or ethical to do so. Medical care costs money that could be spent on something or someone else. Saving one life could mean failing to save (or improve) others. Furthermore, money spent on research to delay or even prevent future deaths could be spent on care for current populations.

Medicine also has increasing power to determine and control life chances of infants and even fetuses. The theory of eugenics proposes that people should be bred so as to improve the genetic pool, creating "better" children. Medical technology can determine some characteristics of fetuses and can abort those fetuses found to be "undesirable." Ethical questions surround the choices of which characteristics should be promoted and the circumstances under which such abortions should be performed. Medical technology literally has the ability to determine the characteristics of future generations. That ability will increase as scientists learn better how to manipulate genes.

Education. Education provides a nonmedical means of ending the cycle of poverty. Through education, people can learn how better to provide for themselves. Education, however, has real costs. The starkest cases again are in poorer nations. A day spent in school can mean a day not spent out in the fields producing food. Even in wealthier countries, money spent on education, which will benefit people in the future, must be taken away from programs that benefit people today.

Investment. A basic problem of future-oriented ethics is the tradeoff, illustrated by education, of present versus future. People can improve their abilities to produce and earn a living through investment in education; similarly, a society can increase its ability to produce through investment in various types of infrastructure and through research and development. A power supply system, railroad network, or a factory, for example, can significantly increase future productive capacity. Building or purchasing these things, however, takes money. Poorer nations may be unable to pay the cost without endangering current populations.

The development of financial markets offered one solution to this dilemma. Nations (or individuals) can borrow to pay for the means to improve their productivity; these loans can be repaid through higher earnings now possible in the future. Such borrowing is rational for loans that will be repaid within an individual's lifetime by his or her own earnings; ethical questions come up, however, concerning loans of longer duration. Policymakers today must decide whether to borrow money to invest in projects that will have benefits for generations to come.

The debt incurred may have to be repaid by future generations. The question is whether it is ethical to force generations of the future to pay the debts incurred in the present. The issue is less troublesome if the debt is incurred for the benefit of those who will repay it; for example, in the case of research that benefits future generations. It is more troublesome if the debt is incurred to increase standards of living for those currently alive. Borrowing is a way of forcing one's children to finance one's own well-being.

Investment in technology poses other questions. The type of investment made will determine the types of jobs available in the future. Increasing sophistication of technology creates the possibility of a small number of skilled, high-paying jobs existing alongside a large number of unskilled, low-paying jobs. Technological advance thus presents the possibility of creating a technological elite at the expense of the majority of workers.

The Environment. Many methods of producing goods involve the exhaustion of nonrenewable resources such as oil and metals. Any of these resources used today simply will not be available for the people of the future. In addition, production processes often involve pollution of the environment. There is a clear tradeoff between producing more today (possibly by producing through processes that are cheaper in dollar terms but use more resources or pollute more) and being able to produce more tomorrow.

—*A. J. Sobczak*

See also Environmental ethics; Genetic engineering; Malthus, Thomas; Politics; Public interest.

BIBLIOGRAPHY

Gabor, Dennis. *The Mature Society*. New York: Praeger, 1972.

Hine, Thomas. *Facing Tomorrow: What the Future Has Been, What the Future Can Be*. New York: Alfred A. Knopf, 1991.

Jungk, Robert. *The Everyman Project: Resources for a Humane Future*. New York: Liveright, 1976.

Rosen, Stephen. *Future Facts: A Forecast of the World as We Will Know It Before the End of the Century*. New York: Simon & Schuster, 1976.

Rosenbaum, Robert A. *The Public Issues Handbook: A Guide for the Concerned Citizen*. Westport, Conn.: Greenwood Press, 1983.

Schumacher, Ernst Friedrich. *Small Is Beautiful*. New York: Harper & Row, 1973.

Gaia

TYPE OF ETHICS: Environmental ethics

DATE: Coined 1979

ASSOCIATED WITH: British geochemist and inventor James Lovelock, U.S. biologist Lynn Margulis, and the environmental movement

DEFINITION: A theory stating that the earth is a living entity whose biosphere is self-regulating and is able to maintain planetary health by controlling its chemical and physical environment

SIGNIFICANCE: The Gaia theory holds that the entire earth is a living being and that the human race is simply one part of that being; the theory is biocentric rather than anthropocentric, requiring the maintenance of balanced relationships between humans and other forms of life

While working on a project that would send a space probe to determine whether life exists on Mars, Lovelock theorized that one could answer the question by observing the activity in the planet's lower atmosphere. His thinking culminated in the book, *Gaia: A New Look at Life on Earth* (1979), which presented his hypothesis that life and its natural environment have coevolved and that the lower atmosphere provides the raw materials for life to exist on the planet. The original title of the theory was the Biocybernetic Universal System Tendency (BUST), but novelist William Golding suggested that the theory be named for Gaia, the Greek Earth goddess who is also called Ge (from which root the words "geography" and "geology" are derived).

Although the Gaia hypothesis did not generate much scientific activity until the late 1980's, it was supported by both industrialists (who believed that it supplied a justification for pollution, since the earth could theoretically counteract any harmful effects) and some environmentalists. Other environmentalists, however, believe that the theory argues against any attempt by humans to try to correct environmental degradation.

See also Environmental ethics.

Gandhi, Mohandas Karamchand (Oct. 2, 1867, Porbandar, India—Jan. 30, 1948, New Delhi, India): National and spiritual leader

TYPE OF ETHICS: Modern history

ACHIEVEMENTS: Leader of nonviolent resistance against British rule in India; author of *An Autobiography: Or, The Story of My Experiments with Truth* (1927)

SIGNIFICANCE: Gandhi inspired millions of people around the world, including Martin Luther King, Jr., and many other practitioners of nonviolence, by following the ethics of the Bhagavad Gītā, one of the Hindu scriptures of India, which advocates doing one's duty without thinking about the consequences

Gandhi incorporated the teachings of the Bhagavad Gītā, a Hindu scripture, and the Sermon on the Mount of the Christian New Testament into a philosophy of nonviolence that he used as an ethical standard. Gandhi's message to the world was that

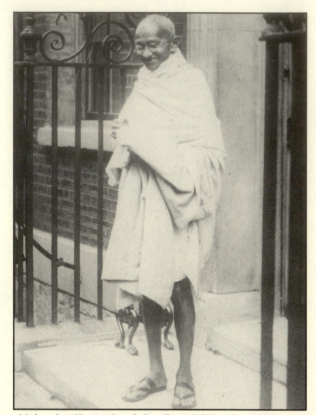

Mohandas Karamchand Gandhi (AP/Wide World Photos)

nonviolence is truth and love in action. The ethics of the Bhagavad Gītā, which Gandhi followed and which he urged others to follow, held that one has a duty to fight against evil or injustice by persuading one's opponents to do good. One should not hate a person who does evil, because human beings are basically good. One should hate the action that the person performs and, through noncooperation, resist that action. If one is ready to experience suffering, eventually the evildoer will realize the injustice and make an attempt to change it. One must hold on to truth no matter what. Gandhi's way of life is a discipline that must be practiced. Gandhi used the term *satyagraha*, or truth-force, which is sometimes translated as passive resistance, for this method of nonviolence.

See also Poona Pact.

Gangs

TYPE OF ETHICS: Personal and social ethics

DATE: Late nineteenth century to present

ASSOCIATED WITH: Frederic Thrasher and James Vigil

DEFINITION: A structured subculture of individuals organized primarily by socioeconomic and ethnic status and promoting actions that deviate from the laws and morality of the culture

SIGNIFICANCE: Gangs exhibit, despite their deviant behavior, traits that are central to many moral theories; for example, *commitment*, *responsibility*, and the development of *character*

In the eyes of many, the violence and drug-related activities of many late-twentieth century gangs appear to be anything but ethical; however, as Plato pointed out in *Republic*, even the individuals in a gang of thieves must cooperate and be just among themselves if they are to achieve their ends. Many researchers on twentieth century gangs have made this same point. For example, Frederic Thrasher, in his landmark study *The Gang: A Study of 1,313 Gangs in Chicago* (1927), claims that the members of gangs are highly committed to protecting each other, and James Vigil, in his article "Group Processes and Street Identity: Adolescent Chicano Gang Members"

and a sense of power and security. Others argue that individuals join gangs primarily as a means of securing a sense of self, or as a way of expressing who they are. Despite these differences, most scholars agree that gangs develop and emerge on the margins of traditional mainstream culture and that they often mimic and mock that culture. The reason for this, as Thrasher has argued, is that gangs generally appear in what he calls a "zone in transition." That is, gangs usually surface in communities that are removed from the stability of both urban central business districts and working-class neighborhoods.

Members of the rival Los Angeles gangs the Bloods and the Crips tie their gang bandanas together to symbolize the truce that they called after the Los Angeles riots of 1992. (AP/Wide World Photos)

(1988), argues that gang members' sense of self is motivated and affirmed by their commitment to the gang.

The nature of this commitment and the way in which it is motivated have received much attention, but there are two primary interpretations. Some scholars argue that people join gangs on the basis of rational self-interest. They join in order to achieve goals that they believe they would not otherwise be able to accomplish, such as acquiring money, sex, friends,

More recent research, however, has shown that gangs do thrive in some neighborhoods or places that are stable; as Vigil argues, however, it is true that individuals are more likely to join gangs when they come from an environment that suffers what he calls "multiple marginality." Vigil claims that family, school, work, the ethnic majority of the culture, and other mainstream institutions and values are each elements with which an individual gang member, like a geographical "zone in transition" that is only marginally assimilated by stable urban centers and suburban neighborhoods, may be only marginally associated. The more an individual is marginally related to one or more of these elements, the more "multiple" is that person's marginality and the more "stressors" that person will experience. It is as a response to these stressors that the values and ethics of a gang, and the marginal and deviant nature of these values and ethics, are to be understood.

As a response to the stressors of "multiple marginality," individuals who join a gang attempt to compensate for these marginal attachments. The result is that these individuals tend to overcompensate. For example, juvenile males who join a gang often have had little or no caretaking from their parents, the father in particular, and these juveniles overcompensate for this lack by adopting stereotyped and oversimplified masculine values that honor being tough and violent. In addition, individuals who join gangs also attempt to compensate for the ambiguous and weak sense of self that results from being marginally attached to those institutions that can give them a sense of who they are. By joining a gang, they overcompensate for this weak sense of self by identifying solely with the gang. Sigmund Freud discussed this phenomenon in *Group Psychology and the Analysis of the Ego* (1921), arguing that a result of this phenomenon is that other groups appear as threats not only to gang members' territory but also to their very sense of self. This explains why gang members often say that "you're either with the group or against it"; this, in turn, explains why real or imagined enemies are such an extremely important focal point for gangs.

Since a gang member's self-identity is defined in terms of the group and other groups are seen as a threat to this identity, it is not surprising that most of what is valued and honored by gang members concerns the ability to defend, violently if necessary, the gang and its territory. Being and acting tough, Vigil argues, is the "focal value" of most gangs of the late twentieth century. One must be able to protect and defend the gang and its members. In return, one will also be protected, but only, as many researchers have noted, if one proves that one is dependable and loyal to the gang.

The morality of the gang, therefore, although in many respects deviating greatly from mainstream society, is nevertheless a morality—a morality that can be most clearly understood if placed in the context of the group. To this extent, the morality of gangs could be given a relativistic interpretation: That is, as Ruth Benedict argued in "Anthropology and the Abnormal" (1934) and Gilbert Harman later argued in "Moral Relativism Defended" (1975), moral claims are about the practices of the sociocultural group (for example, a gang) and nothing else. The moral claims of gangs, likewise, such as those that value violence, commitment, dependability, and the development of a "tough" character, are themselves expressive of the group dynamics and processes of the gang and its members' "marginal" relationship to traditional culture and morality.   —*Jeff Bell*

See also Anthropological ethics; Character; Ethnocentrism; Loyalty.

BIBLIOGRAPHY

Benedict, Ruth. "Anthropology and the Abnormal." *Journal of General Psychology* 10 (January, 1934): 58-82.

Freud, Sigmund. *Group Psychology and the Analysis of the Ego*. Translated by James Strachey. New York: W. W. Norton, 1959.

Harman, Gilbert. "Moral Relativism Defended." *Philosophical Review* 84 (January, 1975): 3-22

Thrasher, Frederic M. *The Gang: A Study of 1,313 Gangs in Chicago*. Chicago: University of Chicago Press, 1927.

Vigil, James. "Group Processes and Street Identity: Adolescent Chicano Gang Members." *Ethos* 16, no. 4 (December, 1988): 421-45.

Gay rights

TYPE OF ETHICS: Sex and gender issues

DATE: June 28, 1969, to present

ASSOCIATED WITH: David Mixner, Human Rights Campaign Fund, ACT-UP, Queer Nation, National Gay & Lesbian Task Force, and *The Advocate*

DEFINITION: The extension to the homosexual community of the fundamental rights of life, liberty, and the pursuit of happiness that are guaranteed to all Americans by the U.S. Constitution

SIGNIFICANCE: Gay rights raises three issues: denial of basic rights and opportunities, public exposure of homosexuality by other homosexuals ("outing"), and attempts to encourage or force homosexuals to give up their homosexuality

Homosexuality as a Sin. Ronald Bayer (1981) has observed that despite periods of relative tolerance, homosexuality has been considered an abomination in the West for the past two thousand years. Homosexuality has been a target of repression, oppression, disenfranchisement, and discrimination by political and religious institutions as well as by individuals and groups. Condemnation of homosexual behavior and the threat of death are found in the Bible. The Vatican Declaration on Sexual Ethics of 1976 stated that "Homosexual acts are intrinsically disordered and can in no way be approved of." Homosexuality was considered a mental disorder by the American Psychiatric Association until the early 1970's. The firing of homosexuals has been upheld in court. Homosexuals have long been prohibited from employment in certain federal jobs (military, intelligence). Prominent citizens have periodically urged punitive action against homosexuals (in 1978, Anita Bryant urged prison sentences of up to twenty years), and various citizen interest groups have placed measures on ballots that would deny homosexuals protection of rights and opportunities. In 1992, Colorado voters approved an initiative that abolished city gay rights bills ensuring equal opportunity access to housing, employment, and social services. In 1986, the Supreme

Court ruled that the Constitution did not protect homosexual acts. Justice Lewis Powell wrote that it could not be a "fundamental right" to engage in sexual behavior "that for centuries has been recognized as deviant."

This repression and condemnation of homosexuality has occurred against a backdrop of steadily accumulating scientific evidence that suggests that sexual orientation exists on a natural continuum. Thus, by definition, heterosexual, homosexual, and bisexual orientations are all normal expressions of sexuality. The evidence suggests that sexual orientation is independent of mental health and adjustment. The same frequencies of normal behavior and mental disorders appear in all sexual orientations. Thus, sexual orientation is independent of any impairment in personal, social, or occupational functioning.

Given this evidence and the fundamental belief in equal rights for all Americans, a credible case can be made that homophobia in all its forms is unethical, immoral, and illegal. Therefore, over the years, an active and increasingly powerful and influential Gay Rights Movement has evolved.

The Gay Men's Chorus of Los Angeles is one of many organizations that promote gay rights. (Gay Men's Chorus of Los Angeles)

that sexual orientation has significant biological determinants and that one's sexuality is not malleable or reversible. It is not a preference, personal choice, or lifestyle. It is neither chosen nor changeable. It is an orientation or imperative. In extreme cases, hysterectomies and estrogen injections have been forced upon lesbians in order to change their sexual orientation, to no effect. Gays have been subjected to transorbital lobotomies, electroshock, castration, aversion therapy, psychotherapy, and psychoanalysis. In addition to several of these procedures and their imposition upon homosexuals being wholly unethical, these procedures were utterly ineffective in altering sexual orientation.

Also, the social sciences have convincingly demonstrated

The Gay Rights/Gay Liberation Movement. The watershed moment for gay rights was the "Stonewall Rebellion" of June 28, 1969. New York City police staged a routine raid on the Stonewall Inn, a bar frequented by homosexuals. Instead of allowing themselves to be passively arrested as in the past, however, the homosexuals resisted and threw bottles and bricks at the police. Within weeks the Gay Liberation Front was formed in New York. By the first anniversary of the Stonewall Rebellion, dozens of similar organizations were in place across the country.

The ensuing years have seen the gay rights movement become increasingly powerful and influential. This power and influence are manifested in four areas:

Politics. The relative affluence of homosexuals has made them a significant source of campaign contributions. Their concentration in pivotal states with huge Electoral College numbers makes them a sought-after constituency. Their political savvy and active lobbying efforts have resulted in eight states and more than 135 local jurisdictions specifically protecting them against discrimination. Increasing numbers of homosexuals have attained political office at all levels.

The Arts. Homosexual themes and advocacy of gay rights have become increasingly prominent in literature, drama, and cinema. First-rate works of art are being created that are reaching a wide audience.

Media Events. To take one example, the 1993 March on Washington for Lesbian, Gay, and Bi Equal Rights and Liberation was an effective plea for political respect and a celebration of victory that attracted thousands of participants and spectators and widespread media coverage.

Radical Gay Rights Groups. These groups are perceived as an internal problem and headache by the mainstream gay rights movements. The radicals, in turn, see the mainstream players as "Uncle Toms." ACT-UP and Queer Nation are the two most prominent groups. Among their more radical acts has been the ethically questionable practice of "outing"—publishing the names of closeted gays and lesbians on the grounds that to deny one's homosexuality is hypocritical and detrimental to the movement.

It remains to be seen what the ultimate outcome of the gay rights movement will be. The weight of scientific evidence and the effectiveness of the movement in various spheres of American life have put the gay rights movement on an upward power curve, but it is doing battle against a long history of opposition from many influential and powerful organizations. The issue has moved above the level of sloganeering, however, and now involves genuine debate, discussion, and analysis. —*Laurence Miller*

See also Homophobia; Homosexuality; National Gay and Lesbian Task Force; Stonewall Inn Riots.

BIBLIOGRAPHY

Bayer, Ronald. *Homosexuality and American Psychiatry.* New York: Basic Books, 1981.

Burr, Chandler. "Homosexuality and Biology." *The Atlantic* 271 (March, 1993): 47-65.

Shilts, Randy. *And the Band Played On.* New York: Viking-Penguin, 1988.

Signorile, Michelangelo. *Queer in America.* New York: Random House, 1993.

Sullivan, Andrew. "The Politics of Homosexuality." *The New Republic* 208, no. 19 (May 10, 1993): 24-37.

Generosity

TYPE OF ETHICS: Personal and social ethics
DEFINITION: Generosity is a virtue based on benevolent interest in others
SIGNIFICANCE: Certain unique characteristics distinguish generosity from other giving-related virtues

A virtue can be briefly defined as a form of moral excellence, goodness, or righteousness. Generosity clearly fits into this definition.

The term "generosity" is often used interchangeably with benevolence, altruism, charity, or kindness, and it is linked to the concepts of sympathy and forgiveness. All these virtues are associated with giving, but each is distinct.

There are four prerequisite conditions that distinguish generosity from the other virtues that are associated with giving. Generosity must arise from an awareness of circumstances, it must be based on a desire to benefit the recipient and be free of any other underlying motive, what is given must be of value to the giver, and what is given must be more than would be considered necessary under the circumstances.

In addressing the issue of awareness, Elizabeth Pybus states, "Being aware of the world around us is necessary for us to exercise our agency well and helpfully towards other people." In other words, those people (agents) who lack awareness of the needs of others cannot be generous.

Lack of awareness takes different forms. There is simple want of information, which, once it is provided, promotes generous behavior. Charitable organizations base their appeals on educating the public about the needs of others in order to stimulate contributions. There may be a lack of awareness because of a high degree of self-interest. Very young children exhibit such a lack of awareness. So do people with sociopathic personalities. Regardless of the cause, the result is the same. Without awareness of the circumstances of others, the agent cannot express generosity. This, then, lends a certain weight of moral obligation to awareness.

It is true that one cannot know everything. Individuals and societies are morally obligated, however, to try to be informed about the circumstances that others are experiencing. It can be very difficult to obtain information about some topics, especially when there is an organized effort to suppress truth or to spread disinformation. In these cases, it is even more important than usual to be aggressive in searching out the facts. Lack of awareness allows Holocausts to happen. While most situations that people face are not that extreme, the premise is the same: People are morally obligated to be as aware as possible.

Generosity is an other-oriented behavior. It flows freely from goodwill without the weight of other obligations. It must not be linked with motives such as reciprocity or duty. The only motive that can be involved is the desire to benefit the recipient. This does not mean, however, that all self-interest must be disregarded. To value the other above the self in a benevolent act is not generosity but altruism.

Generosity requires that there be no motive of personal gain. That is, one who gives must not expect anything in return. Generosity precludes even a minimal degree of the attitude, "You scratch my back, and I'll scratch yours." Likewise, there must not be any expectation on the part of the agent of gratitude or recognition from the recipient for generous acts. While the agent may derive pleasure from giving, the anticipation of that pleasure cannot be the motive for the act, or it will not be generosity.

To give because one feels obligated is not generosity but charity. Generosity involves free choice, and the decision can be based on a rational or emotional basis. The campaign presented by a charitable organization is factual, but its appeal is emotional. Some people respond out of duty, because it is morally correct to give to those in need, and they will feel guilty if they do not give. Others give out of generosity because they decide that they want to, because they are persuaded by the facts or are moved by sympathy.

What a person gives is an important factor in generosity. It does not necessarily have to be anything material. It must, however, be something of value to the giver. Time is quite valuable to most people, and those who are given the gift of someone's time have often been given a treasure. There are those, however, who feel that they have much spare time, and therefore to give it may not mean very much. They may choose to use that time to share their particular talents. This, then, could be an act of generosity, if they did it purely for the benefit of the recipient and not just to fill up their hours with activity. Although it is usually so, what is given does not necessarily have to be valuable to the recipient. Its value in terms of generosity is in the intent of the giver.

In order for an act to be considered generosity, what is given should exceed what might be considered reasonable under the circumstances. This factor can be viewed from the context of either the giver or the situation. If two people—one wealthy and one earning minimum wage—each decided to donate a day's wages to some cause, the one with low income might be considered to be giving more than was required by his financial circumstances, and that contribution would be considered truly generous. In another situation, if a person's shoes were worn out and someone gave him three new pairs, that also would be an act of generosity.

James Wallace states that a virtue such as generosity tends "to foster good feelings based on mutual good will." In some cases, however, the recipient may not appreciate a generous act in his behalf and may even be harmed rather than benefited. These results may not be possible to anticipate. If the agent is acting in the recipient's best interest and with compassionate awareness, however, the generosity that is offered is authentic.
—*Marcella T. Joy*

See also Altruism; Aristotelian ethics; Benevolence; Charity; Duty; Goodness; Integrity; Kant, Immanuel; Moral responsibility; Needs and interests; Social justice and responsibility; Supererogation; Virtue; Virtue ethics.

BIBLIOGRAPHY

Attfield, Robin. *A Theory of Values and Obligation.* New York: Croom Helm, 1987.

Butler, Joseph. *Fifteen Sermons.* London: G. Bell & Sons, 1964.

Pybus, Elizabeth. *Human Goodness.* London: Harvester Wheatsheaf, 1991.

Spaemann, Robert. *Basic Moral Concepts.* Translated by T. J. Armstrong. New York: Routledge, 1989.

Wallace, James. *Virtues and Vices.* Ithaca, N.Y.: Cornell University Press, 1978.

Genetic counseling

TYPE OF ETHICS: Bioethics

DATE: 1960 to present

DEFINITION: Genetic counseling uses family histories and clinical tests to identify deleterious genes, both to assess risks to those being tested and to facilitate informed reproductive decisions by estimating the likelihood that offspring will inherit the defect

SIGNIFICANCE: Genetic counseling, although not in itself an ethical concept, raises serious ethical questions in clinical practice, since reproductive decisions are central to conventional morality and the identification of inherited defects carries the possibility of discrimination

Although it has roots in the eugenics movements of the early twentieth century, which have been justly criticized as being hampered by imperfect understanding of inheritance and tainted by racial and class prejudice, genetic counseling relies on landmark genetic discoveries of the 1950's—the elucidation of the structure of DNA and of the specific biochemical bases for a number of inherited disorders, including Tay-Sachs syndrome, sickle-cell anemia, and hemophilia. Beginning in 1960, specialists in medical centers began advising couples who had already had a child with such a disorder or had close relatives who were affected. The availability of these services and the number of conditions amenable to testing have risen steadily, although access is not universal even in the developed world. Most severe genetic diseases are recessive; carriers with one defective gene may or may not be identifiable. Gross chromosomal abnormalities and some metabolic disorders can be diagnosed *in utero* through amniocentesis.

United States government guidelines for genetic testing and counseling caution against using the process for perceived societal good and stress that the impetus for testing and reproductive decisions must come from the affected individuals, without outside compulsion. Nevertheless, many people perceive that a genetically abnormal individual places a burden on society and believe that it is immoral to bear a defective child; this attitude is seen by others as providing a justification for abandoning the handicapped. Voluntarily abstaining from conceiving children is morally acceptable to most people in Western society, but objections to abortion are widespread. Some heritable abnormalities are commonest among small, inbred ethnic minorities, in which case refraining from having children and marrying outside the group, the most prudent courses of action from a medical standpoint, have genocidal overtones. Not all genetic disorders are equally debilitating, and it is uncertain whether genetic counseling is appropriate for less-severe conditions. Finally, there are many disorders (alcoholism, for example) that may be at least partially heritable, whose genetic basis is unknown, and for which the scientific basis for genetic counseling is tenuous.

Tests exist for some genetically transmitted conditions (for example, certain cancers) that manifest themselves late in life, and more are continually being developed. Although knowing of their existence is helpful to medical professionals, there is real concern that this information could be used to deny employment or insurance coverage to those who are affected. Maintaining confidentiality and respecting the rights of individuals are paramount in genetic counseling.

See also Abortion; Birth defects; Eugenics; Genetic engineering; Genocide.

Genetic engineering

TYPE OF ETHICS: Bioethics

DATE: 1970's to present

ASSOCIATED WITH: Genetics research laboratories, the Asilomar Conference, the Human Genome Project, and the National Institutes of Health

DEFINITION: The cloning of specific genes and their insertion into cells or organisms

SIGNIFICANCE: Genetic engineering has led to genetic testing, which in turn can lead to discrimination in hiring and health insurance policies; serious ethical questions are raised by its potential use for biological warfare and altering the human genome

Since the 1970's, advances in genetics have led to the revolutionary technology of genetic engineering. It is now possible to clone genes and to insert them into different organisms. Genes are the hereditary material of an organism. Composed of deoxyribonucleic acid (DNA), they are the blueprint from which all proteins are made. Various methods of gene cloning exist, but a simplified copying procedure, called the polymerase chain reaction (PCR), now has made it possible to manufacture millions of copies of a gene in an afternoon. The copied gene then can be manipulated so that it recombines with the DNA of other organisms. In a certain percentage of cases, the newly inserted gene is active, and the organism starts making the corresponding gene product.

These recombinant DNA procedures have been used to insert genes such as the human insulin gene into bacteria, causing them to become minifactories of commercially and therapeutically valuable products. Because this is a relatively inexpensive method of making an extremely pure product, it has been used by the pharmaceutical industry to develop products such as interferons for fighting cancer, factors VIII and IX, the blood-clotting factors needed by hemophiliacs, and human growth hormone for treating children with dwarfism. The technology has also been used in gene therapy. A person with a disease caused by a defective gene can have cells from his or her body engineered to carry correct copies of the gene. Gene therapy is already being used for diseases such as cystic fibrosis, hypercholesterolemia, and severe combined immunodeficiency (SCID).

The potential for the beneficial use of genetic engineering seems limitless, but the potential for misuse is also glaring. Just as bacteria can be engineered to produce beneficial products, so they can be engineered for the malevolent purposes of biological warfare by increasing their resistance to antibiotics, enhancing their virulence, or causing them to produce deadly toxins. Treaties such as the Geneva Protocol (1925) and the Biological Warfare Convention (1972), signed by all the major powers, are meant to protect against such abuses, but they cannot protect against terrorists or other subversive groups, and they do not protect against the development of toxins with therapeutic use that subsequently could be adapted to biological warfare.

When the potential hazards of genetic engineering were being realized in the 1970's, there was a torrent of reaction. The Asilomar Conference in California, in 1975, was the first major scientific reaction. Primarily a gathering of geneticists, this international conference attempted to outline the problems of and appropriate restrictions for recombinant DNA research. By 1976, Britain and the United States had issued recombinant DNA guidelines, and those from the United States, the National Institutes of Health (NIH) Guidelines for Research Involving Recombinant DNA Molecules, are now generally accepted by all European nations. In the United States, an enforcement committee, the Recombinant DNA Advisory Committee (RAC), oversees research in genetic engineering and approves all clinical trials of gene therapy.

Recombinant DNA technology has led to the controversial possibility of altering genes in the unborn. It is already possible, through in vitro fertilization techniques, to manipulate a fertilized egg in the laboratory before it is implanted in a woman. Should genetic screening be done on this embryo and genetic defects corrected before it is implanted? Could this lead to children being "made to order"? The ethics of this technique is very controversial. It can be argued that improving the quality of life is valuable, but the narrow boundary between eliminating deleterious genes and practicing eugenics renews horrifying visions of a "brave new world" and the Nazi experiments in ethnic purity. Guidelines are not yet clearly delineated on experiments that would alter the human genome.

The medical uses of genetic engineering are truly in their infancy. With the advent in 1990 of the Human Genome Project, an international effort to map and sequence all human genes, the ability to identify genetic diseases by looking at a DNA analysis of a person is greatly enhanced. The fallout from this is complex. Who has the right to access this information? If someone is diagnosed as having a particular gene that makes her or him more likely to contract cancer, should a health insurance company or potential employer be allowed to know? Will "genetic discrimination" become a major problem? A portion of the Human Genome Project's budget (about 5 percent) has been set aside to study the ethical, legal, and social implications (ELSI program) of the project.

The specter of plagues and monsters that had been raised in the 1970's in the wake of genetic engineering technologies has not become fact, but the potential for abuse certainly remains. It is imperative, as scientists boldly forge into this new knowledge, that the formulation of policy keep step with scientific advances. —*Mary S. Tyler*

See also Bioethics; Diagnosis, ethics of; Genetic counseling; Health care allocation; Insurance, medical; Privacy.

BIBLIOGRAPHY

Jordan, Elke. "Invited Editorial: The Human Genome Project: Where Did It Come From, Where Is It Going?" *The American Journal of Human Genetics* 51, no. 1 (July, 1992): 1-6.

Joyce, Christopher. "Your Genome in Their Hands." *New Scientist* 127, no. 1729 (August, 1990): 52-55.

Tabor, John M., ed. *Genetic Engineering Technology in Industrial Pharmacy*. New York: Marcel Dekker, 1989.

Verma, Inder M. "Gene Therapy." *Scientific American* 263, no. 5 (November, 1990): 68-85.

Zilinskas, Raymond A., and Burke K. Zimmerman, eds. *The Gene-Splicing Wars*. New York: Collier Macmillan, 1986.

Geneva conventions

TYPE OF ETHICS: Modern history

DATE: 1863-1977

DEFINITION: A series of meetings that codified the rules of warfare

SIGNIFICANCE: In a world that consists of sovereign states often at war with one another, the Geneva conventions and their rules encourage the humanitarian treatment of the enemy

The background for the Geneva conventions can be found in European diplomatic and military development since the sixteenth century. The breakup of the medieval Christian outlook during the Reformation era and the devastating religious and dynastic wars that resulted led to the growth of international law. During the eighteenth century Enlightenment, several philosophers applied these rules with some success to the conduct of war. The French Revolution and the wars of national liberation that resulted broke the comparative calm of the Age of Reason and introduced a new note of savagery into armed conflict. Writing in the wake of the revolutionary age, Carl Von Clausewitz (1780-1831) advocated the concept of total war—that is, the necessity to push conflict to the utmost bounds of violence in order to crush the enemy. These teachings were widely accepted in the Western world, and the nineteenth century Industrial Revolution made it possible to produce the various weapon systems that could carry out Von Clausewitz's dictum.

The new attitude of "efficiency" and ferocity in warfare led to a strong humanitarian reaction. During the Crimean War, Florence Nightingale (1820-1910) and her colleagues worked with the wounded and drew public attention to the scandalously inadequate arrangements made for them by the armies. A few years later a Genevan businessman, Henri Dunant (1828-1910), was traveling in north Italy and happened upon the battlefield at Solferino (1859). Encouraged by the example of hospital work in the Crimea and moved by the tragic plight of the wounded and dying, he organized groups to help the unfortunate soldiers. For Dunant, this was such a traumatic experience that he dedicated his life to helping soldiers, a category of poor who seemed to be neglected by their employers. In 1862, he published a moving account of his reminiscences of the Italian experience which, along with his personal contacts, aroused the sympathy of the rulers of Europe and led to the Geneva Conference of 1863. The meeting had two results; a decision to create Red Cross societies and a decision to provide a set of rules for the humane treatment of those who were incapacitated. The second of these decisions led to the Geneva Convention of 1864. Attended by representatives from sixteen states, it did not give official recognition to the Red Cross societies as such but did lay down a series of rules that were to be followed in time of war. These rules provided for the care of sick and wounded soldiers, the neutrality of the medical corps, the humane treatment of prisoners, and the display of a distinctive emblem, such as the Red Cross, by persons and places involved in medical work. The Conventions were signed by twelve states and were open to acceptance by others whenever they wished. By the early twentieth century, they were ratified by forty-eight nations, including even the non-Western powers of China, Japan, Siam, and the Ottoman Empire. The Red Cross movement flourished more or less under the direction of the entirely Swiss leadership of an international committee yet was made up of a series of nationally controlled societies. The articles of 1864 were extended in a series of meetings held at The Hague in 1899 and 1907 and at Geneva in 1906, 1929, 1949, and 1977.

The Hague meeting of 1899, called at the suggestion of Czar Nicholas II of Russia, was attended by delegates from twenty-six nations. The Geneva rules commanded such respect that there was a strong desire among the major powers to extend them to naval conflict and to limit the use of new, more horrible weapons. At The Hague conference, conditions regulating a state of war were defined and the use of asphyxiating gases, expanding bullets (dumdums), and aerial bombardment (dropping projectiles from balloons) was forbidden. The conference also established a permanent court of arbitration to encourage the peaceful settlement of disputes between nations. The second Geneva Conference (1906) revised the decisions of the first meeting, based upon the war experiences of the intervening years. It provided for the policing of battlefields, the identification of the dead, the protection of the name and sign of the Red Cross, and the dissemination and enforcement of the Convention's decisions through military penal codes.

A second meeting (1907) was suggested by President Theodore Roosevelt and called by the Czar. Attended by delegates from forty-four nations, it passed a series of acts

GENEVA CONVENTIONS				
A chart of the treaties concluded in Geneva, Switzerland (and at The Hague), for the purpose of ameliorating the effects of war on soldiers and civilians				
1864	1906	1929	1949	1977
Convention for the Amelioration of the Wounded in Time of War	Second Geneva Convention	Third Geneva Convention	Fourth Geneva Convention	Fifth Geneva Convention
Initiated by Henri Dunant. Provided for: (1) the immunity from capture and destruction of all establishments for the treatment of wounded and sick soldiers and their personnel (2) the impartial reception and treatment of all combatants (3) the protection of civilians rendering aid to the wounded (4) recognition of the Red Cross symbol as a means of identifying persons and equipment covered by the agreement.	Amended and extended the provisions of the first convention.	Amended and extended the provisions of the first two conventions. Introduced the convention relating to the treatment of prisoners of war. Provisions included: (1) belligerents must treat prisoners humanely (2) they must supply information about them (3) they must permit visits to prison camps by representatives of neutral states.	More than 150 nations have become parties to this agreement. Following the horror of World War II, this was the most complete of the treaties and included the following provisions: (1) provision for care of the wounded and sick in land warfare (2) rules for the care of those who were injured or shipwrecked at sea (3) laws guaranteeing the just treatment of prisoners of war (4) provisions that protected citizens of occupied territories by condemning suchpractices as deportation, the taking of hostages, torture, collective reprisals, wanton destruction of property, and discrimination based on race, religion or nationality.	Only slightly more than half of the nations who signed the Fourth Convention have signed the 1977 protocols (the United Kingdom and the United States have not). Supplemented the provisions of the previous conventions with two additional protocols that extended the protection of international law to wars of liberation and to civil wars.

that provided for the enforcement of contracts, the recognition of rights of neutrality, the prohibition of submarine contact mines, the limitation of bombardment by naval forces, and restriction on aerial warfare. Ominously, when one looks back on the meeting after the experience of World War I, it did not renew the 1899 prohibitions against the use of gas or dumdum bullets. The third Geneva Convention's (1929) most original contributions concerned prisoners of war. They

THE HAGUE CONVENTIONS	
A series of international treaties from international conferences held at The Hague in The Netherlands that concerned issues similar to those defined in Geneva	
1899	1907
The First Conference	The Second Conference
Convened at the invitation of Count Mikhail Nikolayevich Muravyov, Minister of Foreign Affairs of Nicholas II of Russia. Twenty-six nations were present. It defined the conditions of a state of belligerency and other customs relating to war on land and sea. Declarations were passed (1) prohibiting the use of asphyxiating gases, (2) prohibiting the use of expanding bullets (dumdums), (3) prohibiting the discharges of projectiles or explosives from balloons. Also adopted the Convention for the Pacific Settlement of International Disputes, which created the Permanent Court of Arbitration.	Proposed by U.S. President Theodore Roosevelt, convened by Nicholas II. Forty-four nations attended. Conventions adopted reemployment of force for recovery of contract debts; rights and duties of neutral powers and persons in war on land and sea; laying of automatic submarine contact mines; status of enemy merchant ships; bombardment by naval forces in wartime; establishment of an international prize court. Renewed declaration prohibiting discharge of projectiles from balloons. Did not reaffirm declarations prohibiting asphyxiating gas and expanding bullets.

were to be dealt with in a humane manner, information about them was to be supplied to their governments, and their treatment was to be monitored by neutral observers.

Probably the most important of the Geneva meetings was held in 1949 in response to the horror of World War II. It drew up the most complete of the Geneva Conventions, including: (1) provision for care of the wounded and sick in land warfare; (2) rules for the care of those who were injured or shipwrecked at sea; (3) laws guaranteeing the just treatment of prisoners of war; and (4) provisions that protected citizens of occupied territories by condemning such practices as deportation, the taking of hostages, torture, collective reprisals, wanton destruction of property, and discrimination based on race, religion, or nationality. In 1977, another conference supplemented these provisions with two additional protocols that extended the protection of international law to wars of liberation and civil wars. More than one hundred fifty nations have signed the 1949 conventions, but far fewer have agreed to the 1977 protocols.

—*Robert G. Clouse*

See also Biological warfare; Chemical warfare; International law; League of Nations; Military ethics; Scorched-earth policies; War and peace.

BIBLIOGRAPHY

Best, Geoffrey. *Humanity in Warfare.* New York: Columbia University Press, 1980.

Bordwell, Percy. *The Law of War Between Belligerents; A History and a Commentary.* Chicago: Callaghan, 1908.

Davis, Calvin D. *The United States and the Second Hague Peace Conference.* Durham, N.C.: Duke University Press, 1976.

Forsythe, David P. *Humanitarian Politics: The International Committee of the Red Cross.* Baltimore: The Johns Hopkins University Press, 1977.

Roberts, Adam, and Guelff Richard, eds. *Documents on the Laws of War.* New York: Oxford University Press, 1982.

Genocide

TYPE OF ETHICS: Race and ethnicity
DATE: From antiquity
ASSOCIATED WITH: Adolf Hitler
DEFINITION: The deliberate and systematic attempt to annihilate an entire human population
SIGNIFICANCE: The act of genocide, which is based on hatred, bigotry, prejudice, and misconceptions of superiority and inferiority, is opposed to the concepts of human rights, civil rights, and basic freedoms

Genocide is the deliberate and systematic attempt to annihilate an entire human population. Perpetrators of this unjustifiable and heinous practice direct their actions against groups that differ from their own in religious belief, race, ethnic affiliation, nationality, or sexual orientation. The extermination of any human group has no ethical, moral, or legal justification. It is wrong because it extends to an entire group some presumed guilt that is associated with a small segment of that group or their ancestors. Even worse,

A few of the millions who died during Hitler's campaign of genocide against the Jews. (National Archives)

it falsely asserts that such groups have inherent characteristics that make them unworthy of existence.

Brutal massacres of entire Jewish populations were ordered by Adolf Hitler as his "final solution" to the "Jewish question" in Germany and throughout Europe. Hitler argued that many of Germany's problems stemmed from the fact that Jews formed a separate, degenerate race. To Hitler, each race inherited certain qualities through its blood and genes; the Aryans were thus a naturally superior race, while Jews were sinister and devious. Hitler accused the Jews of secretly forming an "international Jewish conspiracy" aimed at dominating the globe economically and politically by cheating everyone else. He argued that because Jews were a lower and undesirable form of life, the only real solution to the "Jewish question" was total extermination. As a result, he ordered the extermination of more than six million Jews. Hitler's Nazi Party used the Holocaust to cover up its theft of Jewish families' valuable art treasures, life savings, and property. The Nazi Party used the term *Judenrein*, meaning to clean an area of Jews, as a euphemism for genocide. Hitler applied the same flawed reasoning to gypsies, the mentally retarded, and homosexuals. All were to be exterminated because they were inherently inferior and unworthy of life. The heinous extermination carried out by Hitler and the Nazi Party has been condemned by every sane nation on Earth.

History provides numerous examples of genocide. When the Australian government wanted land on the island of Tasmania, the native population refused to sell it or give it away. Ultimately, the Tasmanians' water supply was poisoned. Every native Tasmanian man, woman, and child perished, and white settlers from Australia subsequently claimed the land.

Turkey offers another example of this crime against humanity. Sultan Abdul Hamid II encouraged Kurdish depredations against Armenian villages. By 1894, these actions had grown into full-scale war, and the Turkish army assisted in the massacre of Armenians. Initially, an estimated 200,000 Armenians were killed. During World War I, the Turks sided with Germany, but the Armenians sided with Russia and Britain. As a result, the Turks did not trust the Armenians and viewed them as subversives. To secure its border with Russia, Turkey forcibly removed millions of Armenians and forced them to march south without adequate food or shelter. Armenians claim that the result was a holocaust and that more than one million Armenians died in Turkey in 1915. To add insult to injury, the Turks took more than 90 percent of the Armenians' land. Even today, many Armenians live in constant fear of a return to these contemptible practices. Unlike the German government, the Turkish government has never admitted guilt and claims that the Armenians killed just as many Turks during World War I. Turkey claims that it merely acted in self-defense.

William Shockley has proposed a theory of "dysergenics" that states that African Americans are biologically inferior to whites. To him, education cannot change this condition, therefore he has proposed making America more competitive globally by the forced sterilization of all African Americans living in the United States. Within one generation, there would be no race problem because the black race would die out. Aside from the callousness of this theory, it ignores growing African, Caribbean, Hispanic, and Asian immigration. Shockley has been barred from speaking in Britain because the British consider his theory outrageous. World history is replete with examples of human willingness to violate moral and ethical codes, yet genocide constitutes the gravest violation of ethical principles on record. Genocide has no ethical justification or moral defense. —*Dallas L. Browne*

See also Anti-Semitism; Apartheid; Bigotry; Genocide, cultural; Native American genocide; Racial prejudice; Racism.

BIBLIOGRAPHY

Bauman, Zygmunt. *Modernity and the Holocaust*. Ithaca, N.Y.: Cornell University Press, 1989.

Chalk, Frank, and Kurt Jonassohn. *The History and Sociology of Genocide: Analyses and Case Studies*. New Haven, Conn.: Yale University Press, 1990.

Cherny, Israel W. *How Can We Commit the Unthinkable? Genocide: The Human Cancer*. New York: Hearst, 1982.

Haas, Peter. *Morality After Auschwitz*. Philadelphia: Fortress Press, 1988.

Kuper, Leo. *The Prevention of Genocide*. New Haven, Conn.: Yale University Press, 1985.

Porter, Jack Nusan, ed. *Genocide and Human Rights*. Lanham, Md.: University Press of America, 1982.

Genocide, cultural

TYPE OF ETHICS: Race and ethnicity
DATE: From antiquity
DEFINITION: The deliberate and systematic destruction of a particular culture

SIGNIFICANCE: Acts of cultural genocide raise various ethical questions regarding such issues as human rights, civil rights, equality, and sovereignty

Cultural genocide is the deliberate and systematic destruction of a culture. Absent harm, it is not ethical to destroy the culture of another group of human beings or change it without their consent. Each culture should be judged by its own standards of excellence and morality, unless its cultural practices threaten to harm others physically or mentally.

The Canadian government outlawed many indigenous customs of the Kwakiutl Indians of the Northwest Coast of Canada in an effort to convert them into pale imitations of Europeans. The Kwakiutl were renowned for a unique custom that they called the *potlatch*. Kwakiutl chiefs competed

One of the results of the conquest of Mexico by Hernán Cortéz (1485-1547) was the complete destruction of various indigenous cultures. (Library of Congress)

with one another for status and power through this custom. It involved accumulating vast wealth in the form of artistic items known as "coppers," blankets, and food. After accumulating a fortune, a chief would invite his rival and the rival's followers to a feast. During this feast, the host would wine and dine all of his guests lavishly. Dancers would entertain them. At a prearranged time, the host would conspicuously destroy the valuable coppers and other treasures to demonstrate that he could afford to do so. He would challenge his guest to top this feat or accept inferior status. Upon leaving the feast, guests were given many blankets and food to take home with them. The Canadian government viewed this practice as a wanton and savage destruction of valuable property and a waste of labor, so they outlawed the *potlatch*.

Anthropologists have argued that, in addition to serving the overt function of leveling individuals, the *potlatch* served a covert or hidden function by redistributing wealth from areas that had accumulated a surplus to areas that had experienced shortages during bad years. The destruction of this and other pivotal institutions caused the Kwakiutl culture to collapse, leaving in its wake a vacuum that was soon filled by alcoholism, dysfunctional families, and other social problems.

Another example of cultural genocide comes from Africa. In 1884, at the Berlin Conference, European powers unilaterally carved up the African continent into territories that they claimed for themselves. Africans were not invited to this meeting. These European powers pledged to support the "civilizing" of Africans by Christian missionaries, which was "calculated to educate the natives and to teach them to understand and appreciate the benefits of civilization." The missionaries immediately declared traditional religions "devil worship." They collected all indigenous statues, relics, and artifacts and destroyed them. They fought to outlaw clitoridectomy, polygyny, and other native customs that they found "repugnant." These acts led to a clash of cultures and to an identity crisis for many Africans.

The classic example of cultural genocide in North America grew out of slavery. Plantation owners feared that allowing African slaves to speak their own languages, use African names to identify themselves, or practice African culture would encourage slave revolts. Consequently, every effort was made to stamp out African culture in the United States. The people survived, but much of their culture was destroyed. Today, African Americans are culturally more like other Americans than they are like Africans, despite strong physical similarities and a common ancestry.

The assumption that one's own culture is better for others than theirs is constitutes the ultimate cultural arrogance. It assumes that one's own culture is superior and that one has the right to impose one's values on others. This imposition is unfair and unethical. Cultures, like individuals, have a right to life unless their customs threaten the lives of others, as in the case of head hunting and cannibalism.

See also Bigotry; Genocide; Racial prejudice; Racism.

Genocide, frustration-aggression theory of

TYPE OF ETHICS: Theory of ethics
DATE: Formulated in the late 1930's
ASSOCIATED WITH: John Dollard and Neal Miller
DEFINITION: According to the frustration-aggression theory of genocide, genocidal behavior is the result of hostility and frustration caused by the blockage or interruption of goal-directed behavior
SIGNIFICANCE: Attempts to determine the psychological impetus behind genocidal behavior, which has been manifested throughout the history of humankind

John Dollard and Neal Miller's frustration-aggression theory asserts that the blockage or interruption of goal-directed behavior can cause frustration and hostile feelings. Often, these cannot be directed at the source of the frustration, which may be either unknown or too powerful to confront. Consequently, a person may displace this hostility onto an unrelated scapegoat.

Following World War I, the Allied nations imposed harsh economic conditions upon Germany for "causing" the war.

As a result, Germans experienced severe hardships. Defeated and too weak to lash out at the Allied powers, Germany turned against its Jewish population. According to the frustration-aggression theory, between 1920 and 1945 Germans scapegoated the Jewish population and persecuted them instead of hitting back at Britain and France, who were causing their suffering. The Jews were too weak to fight back. When a German bought a loaf of bread, he paid a Jewish merchant, not a French capitalist, so the Jewish merchant became the target for his anger.

Adolf Hitler took advantage of this popular anti-Jewish resentment, which was widespread in Poland, Russia, France, and England as well as in Germany and Austria, to help him rise to power. Hitler accused the German Jews of subversion and of making deliberate attempts to sabotage the German people in order to further selfish Jewish economic interests. Nazi propaganda films compared Jews to rats and suggested that the only true means of ridding Germany of either pest was extermination. The Nazi Party wanted to deport all German Jews to Madagascar, but this plan proved to be impractical because Allied submarines were sinking many German ships, and the Vichy regime in France, which controlled Madagascar, did not relish the idea. Therefore, soon after the German conquest of Poland in 1939, the Nazis ordered the extermination of all known Jews. More than six million Jews were exterminated between 1939 and 1945. This horrific act did not, however, relieve the German sense of frustration. Instead, it created a false consciousness, because Britain, France, and a weak economy—not the Jews—were the real sources of Germany's problems.

The Jews had been treated as scapegoats for centuries throughout Europe and elsewhere before Hitler and the Nazi Party attempted to exterminate them. They were herded into segregated ghettos and became the target of frequent pogroms in Russia and elsewhere. Because the frustration-aggression theory of genocide fails to account for this long history of abuse prior to the rise of Hitler and the Nazi Party, the theory has limited explanatory value.

Despite the fact that scapegoating is based on misconceptions, aggression aimed at a scapegoat has been alleged to have a cathartic effect because it temporarily relieves frustrations. Regrettably, this temporary effect only reinforces negative behavior. In theory, the release of such tension onto a third party should promote mental health. Thus, games such as football have been thought to be cathartic and actually to help to reduce the probability of war. In fact, however, such games may increase the likelihood of aggression by reinforcing antisocial violent behavior. Once set in motion, a vicious self-perpetuating cycle can be created. A wiser course of action is to teach people to control negative thoughts and behavior rather than vent them.

The frustration-aggression model and the accompanying scapegoating and oppression of another group produce behavior that is ethically deplorable. Members of the persecuted group receive prejudicial treatment and may become targets of genocide. Flawed and rigid thinking encourages people to adopt this model of behavior. Insecurity feeds it. Once such attitudes are formed, they are difficult to change unless society can force prolonged contact with members of the other group on a frequent basis, under conditions in which neither group is superior to the other and competition is minimal. Under such conditions, people find that it is easier to abandon prejudices and to adopt healthier attitudes that view others as equals deserving of whatever rewards their talents earn them. Ethically, society has a social and moral obligation to create the sustained contact and minimal competition that will be required to reduce or stamp out the prejudice, bigotry, stereotyping, racism, and discrimination that breed the human tragedy of genocide.

See also Anti-Semitism; Apartheid; Bigotry; Genocide; Genocide, cultural; Racial prejudice; Racism.

al-Ghazâlî, Abû Ḥâmid (1058, Tus, Khurasan, northeastern Iran—Dec. 18, 1111, Tus, Khurasan, Iran): Philosopher

TYPE OF ETHICS: Religious ethics

ACHIEVEMENTS: Author of *Iḥyâ' 'Ulûm al-Dîn* (c. 1103; *The Revival of Religious Sciences*, 1964), *Mishkât al-Anwâr* (*The Niche for Lights*), *al-Tahâfut al-Falâsifa* (*The Incoherence of the Philosophers*, 1958), and an influential spiritual autobiography, *al-Munqidh Min al-Dalâl*

SIGNIFICANCE: His works on ethics are extremely widely read, both academically and popularly; his mysticism also made Sufism more acceptable to conservatives

Abû Ḥâmid al-Ghazâlî (not to be confused with his younger brother, Aḥmad Ghazâlî) is best known for his writings on ethics, the proper foundations for ethics, and mysticism (which is, for al-Ghazâlî, continuous with ethics). His work enjoys widespread respect, earning him the honorific title "the scholar among the inhabitants of the world." Unlike many other philosophers, who were happy to begin their reflections with reason or sense experience, al-Ghazâlî placed great emphasis on the importance of the Qur'ân and the *ḥadîth* (traditions) of the life of Muḥammad.

Al-Ghazâlî was a successful and respected professor of theology at the most important college in the Seljuk empire, the Nizâmiyya, in Baghdad. In 1095, however, he suffered a severe personal crisis, left the Nizâmiyya, traveled throughout the Middle East, and eventually resettled in his ancestral home, Tus. There, he wrote the many treatises that secured his enduring, central place in Islamicate thought.

The crisis of 1095 was focal to al-Ghazâlî's later thought. A superb logician, he was not only able to construct impressive systematic theology but also was aware that intellectual argumentation about that which transcends the abilities of argumentation is built on a foundation of sand. Furthermore, the scholarly endeavors of orthodox legalists and theologians came to seem arid, even

spiritually sterile, to al-Ghazâlî, who appears to have felt an increasing sense of loss of the presence of God in these scholarly religious investigations. After carefully studying the works of numerous Sufis and understanding their principles intellectually, he appears to have had an epiphany in which those principles became experiential.

The Incoherence of the Philosophers. *The Incoherence* and the reply by Averroës (*The Incoherence of the Incoherence*) constitute one of the most famous philosophical exchanges in the Islamicate world and were also very widely discussed in medieval and Renaissance Europe. Al-Ghazâlî attacked Avicenna, al-Fârâbî, and Aristotle for logical inconsistencies in their work and for basing their systems of thought on rational argument alone, denying a central role for revelation and for the direct experience of God. Al-Ghazâlî did not reject wholesale the conclusions of these philosophers, and he did not deny an important role for Aristotelian logic. Some of his conclusions about practical ethics, for example, do not differ from those of Aristotle. Further, although he did reject Neoplatonic emanation schemes entirely, he did so by perspicuously demonstrating their logical impossibility. Nevertheless, al-Ghazâlî argued that the work of these philosophers was not built on a sound foundation; would lead the faithful astray in many matters; and, hence, ought to be abandoned in favor of an ethical system based on Qur'ân, *ḥadîth*, and experiential knowledge of God—a system that he provided in the *Revival*.

Revival of the Religious Sciences. Written in forty (the number symbolic of patient effort) chapters, the first section of the *Revival* concerns '*Ibâdât*, or worship. The second section, on customs, might seem mundane to Western readers. It offers very practical guidance in such areas as diet, ways to serve food, child-rearing, and so forth. (Much of al-Ghazâlî's advice on child-rearing strikes the modern reader as far ahead of its time.) In Islam, however, all aspects of life, even the most mundane, should be infused with reminders of Divine Will, and therefore these practical matters are part of religious sciences. The central chapter celebrates the Prophet and emphasizes the importance of the traditions of Muḥammad's life as the "good example" (Qur'ân, *sûra* 33:21) for ethical conduct. The third section examines vices and their sources, and the final section examines those things that lead to salvation (including virtues and their sources, as well as mystical love and longing).

Although Western modernity might see the topics of the *Revival* as diverse, al-Ghazâlî clearly saw them as continuous, as necessary training in one's gradual development toward the highest possible perfection. The ultimate goal is experiential knowledge of God, which "can be reached only when the barriers in the heart precluding such achievement are removed." This essentially mystical goal requires practical ethical training so that the passions and excessive attachment to bodily pleasures can be curbed, and so that wisdom can be developed.

The Niche for Lights. The relationship of this text to al-Ghazâlî's other works has been highly controversial. The *Niche* is a commentary on the "Sûra of Light" (Qur'ân, 24:35), in which Allah is indicated as the purest Light, which inspired al-Ghazâlî to develop a metaphysics of light that has remarkably strong affinities with Illuminationist Sufi doctrines. One refers to Light properly only when one indicates God, al-Ghazâlî argued, and one uses "light" only analogically in all other instances. Only the Divine Light exists, and all in this phenomenal world is but a shadow cast by that light (comparison with Plato's allegory of the cave would not be far-fetched). The ultimate good in human life is attainment of direct apprehension of Light and complete immersion in Light.   —*Thomas Gaskill*

See also Averroës; Avicenna; al-Fârâbî, Muḥammad ibn Muḥammad ibn Ṭarkhân; *Ḥadîth*; Islamic ethics; Sufism.

BIBLIOGRAPHY
al-Ghazâlî, Abû Ḥâmid. *The Faith and Practice of Al-Ghazali* [*al-Munqidh Min al-Dalâl*]. Translated by W. Montgomery Watt. London: George Allen & Unwin, 1967.

_____. *Imam Gazzali's Ihya ulum-id-din.* Translated by Fazlul Karim. Lahore, Pakistan: Sind Sagar Academy, 1978.

Umaruddin, Muhammad. *The Ethical Philosophy of al-Ghazzâlî.* Lahore, Pakistan: Muhammad Ashraf, 1970.

Gideon v. Wainwright

TYPE OF ETHICS: Civil rights
DATE: 1963
ASSOCIATED WITH: U.S. Supreme Court
DEFINITION: The Court held that felony defendants are entitled to legal representation regardless of the crime with which they are charged, and that if such a defendant cannot afford an attorney, the court must appoint one
SIGNIFICANCE: By successfully petitioning the Court to hear his claim that his constitutional right to a fair trial had been violated, Clarence Earl Gideon wrought a historic change in American trial procedure and judicial ethics

Because of a 1942 Supreme Court decision, *Betts v. Brady*, the state was not required to appoint an attorney for Clarence Earl Gideon at the time of his first trial for robbery in Panama City, Florida, in 1961. Following the dictates of *Betts*, Florida provided counsel only to defendants accused of capital offenses, and Gideon, an impoverished individual of limited education, was forced to act as his own attorney. He was found guilty and sent to prison. While there, he penciled a petition to the Supreme Court to hear his claim that his constitutional rights had been violated. The Court agreed that, because he had been forced to appear without benefit of counsel, Gideon had been denied a fair trial. The Court ordered that Gideon be allowed a new trial and a court-appointed attorney. At his second trial, Gideon was acquitted of all charges. He had demonstrated the power of a single individual to change the entire legal establishment.

See also Constitution, U.S.; Due process.

Global warming

TYPE OF ETHICS: Environmental ethics
DATE: 1950's to present
ASSOCIATED WITH: National Resources Defense Council
DEFINITION: A secular increase in the earth's temperatures
SIGNIFICANCE: Raises the question of whether human activity should change to prevent global warming

The earth's average surface temperature increased about 0.5 degree Celsius in the last hundred years, arguably as a result of concurrent human generation of "greenhouse" gases. Furthermore, some environmental modeling indicates 0.7 to 2 degrees Celsius of more warming after the oceans reach equilibrium, plus a further 2 to 5 degrees by the year 2020 if no action is taken. Even greater changes, however, have occurred many times in the past without any human activity. Repeated glaciation and deglaciation in the last million years repeatedly exceeded the hypothesized changes without human influence, and the causes of glaciation are not thoroughly understood. The major environmental effects of global warming include the poleward shift of climatic belts, the sea level's rising as much as 6 meters by 2020, and drastically changed atmospheric and oceanic circulation. All these occurrences will disrupt present human activity. Thus, regulation or abolition of activities that may be responsible for warming, such as the burning of fossil fuels, is an ethical issue that has provoked proposed action at both national and international levels. The prohibition of combustible fuels, for example, entails massive social and economic changes, which should not be undertaken lightly in view of substantial lack of consensus regarding the cause and future course of currently observed global warming.

See also Earth, human relations to; Greenhouse effect.

Gluttony

TYPE OF ETHICS: Personal and social ethics
DATE: From antiquity
ASSOCIATED WITH: Medieval theology
DEFINITION: Overindulgence in food and drink to the detriment of the individual and, sometimes, of society
SIGNIFICANCE: Focuses on the conflict between the biological limits of a natural function and the good of the individual and society

Since classical antiquity, gluttony has been regarded as a reprehensible individual choice; however, both the motivation and the degree of social censure have varied. In ancient Rome, the vomitoria were viewed as the ultimate symbol of decadence (the *Satyricon* of Petronius), but in general, overindulgence for sheer hedonistic pleasure inspired more envy than disdain. In the Middle Ages, gluttony came under heavy censure, partly because the overindulging individual was incapacitated, but primarily because of the awareness that excessive consumption by a few denied food to those in need. Gluttony was counted among the Seven Deadly Sins on the strength of Paul's censure of "those whose god is their belly" (Phil. 3:19). From the Renaissance onward, the religious and social censure of gluttony gradually became muted; gluttony even received an ironic apology from François Rabelais in the course of his overall attack on the vestiges of medieval philosophy and ethics (*Gargantua*, 1552). In the eighteenth and nineteenth centuries, gluttony became increasingly regarded as a purely medical problem, and by the late twentieth century, the term "gluttony" was generally replaced by "eating disorder," "compulsive eating," "compulsive drinking," and "alcoholism," reflecting a sense that overindulgence in food and drink (including alcohol) is involuntary and is thus outside the sphere of moral or ethical choice.

See also Hedonism; Psychology; Temperance.

God

TYPE OF ETHICS: Religious ethics
DATE: From antiquity
DEFINITION: The supreme supernatural being(s) is involved with human life in such a way as to influence the nature of morality
SIGNIFICANCE: For those who take the referent of the concept of God as real rather than imaginary, God is in some way fundamental for all human behavior

All persons of sound mind have in some way answered, though few may have asked, the question "Why be moral?" The typically philosophical question is "What is the good?" The answers to both questions have attempted to lay the cornerstone for a moral life. One common answer centers on humanity within the context of the world. "The good," or "being moral," is defined in terms of the natural world. Here, natural sciences and anthropocentric disciplines are used to discover the moral life. A second response to the seldom-asked question "Why be moral?" is God, solely God. God is good. God's acts are moral acts. God's acts define morality. From this perspective, theology and philosophy are the primary disciplines that provide insight into the moral life. A third customary response maintains that there is no fundamental contradiction between God and God's creation. Many believers in God, therefore, combine the first two answers to one of life's most fundamental questions. God is good. God has created a good world. God has created humanity as part of the world in such a way that humans are to live in the manner that God has required of them. Consequently, the natural sciences, social sciences, philosophy, and theology can all contribute to the moral life. Though this more unified approach to morality is most inclusive, avoiding both the abstractions of an intellectually isolated theology and a narrow thoroughgoing naturalism, the remainder of this article focuses on the concept of God and the moral life.

There are at least three ways in which God's actions can be relevant for human morality. These three relationships constitute the main theological theories of ethical objectivism. First, God's actions and commandments define what is right. Whatever God commands is moral simply because God commands it. The weakness of this view is that whatever a person understands God to do or to command would be considered moral, including, for example, war, infanti-

cide, and human sacrifice. This would magnify God's power, but at great cost to God's morality. Another way in which God and ethics might be related is for morality to be determined independently of God. All of God's actions and commandments would still be morally correct, but their morality would be determined externally to God. The problem with this view is that morality is determined prior to and separately from God. Thus, God is rendered dependent and limited. Moreover, the identity and nature of this unrivaled moral power is unknown. The third view holds that God's actions correspond to the good. It is not that any arbitrary act of God defines moral actions or that the good is externally delimited, but that every act of God reveals God's character as the good God who created the good world and continues to act without self-contradiction. God has revealed God's own nature in creating and sustaining a moral world. The difficulty with this view is that one must explain how persons who believe that there is no God, and how persons with radically divergent ideas about God, can nevertheless lead highly moral lives. This complaint appears answerable, however, by the third response to the initial question: Humans should be moral because God has created them in the cosmos in such a way that they are to live in the manner for which they have been created. Thus, the sciences, philosophy, and theology can all contribute to the moral life that builds upon God as the source and foundation of morality.

Different notions of God lead to different moral decisions. According to the priestly theology of the Pentateuch, Moses justifies many of ancient Israel's civil laws by citing the acts of Yahweh, the God of Israel. At Yahweh's direction Moses taught, "You shall be holy, for I the LORD your God am holy. . . . When you reap the harvest of your land, you shall not reap to the very edges of your field, or . . . strip your vineyard bare; . . . you shall leave them for the poor and the alien: *I am the LORD your God.* . . . You shall not cheat in measuring length, weight, or quantity. You shall have honest balances and honest weights: *I am the LORD your God, who brought you out of the land of Egypt. You shall keep all my statutes: . . . I am the LORD*" (Lev. 19). Though it is the case that many of Israel's laws are related to other religions and nations, its ethical justifications are not cultural, political, or philosophical but historical and, preeminently, theological.

Though not identified as God, Plato's "form of the good" functions in his ethics as God. At the pinnacle of his philosophical hierarchy rests "the good" in relation to which all other objects exist (both ideals and sensible objects) and must properly live. The good is the source of all moral principles. This functional apotheosis of the good conjoined with the primacy of his ideals or forms (they are nonphysical, nonspatial, nontemporal, and beyond the sensible world), leads Plato to distrust the material world even to the point of rejecting most physical pleasures and advocating a philosopher king rather than a popularly chosen ruler.

In another example, according to the Gospel of Luke, Jesus of Nazareth understands God as generous and forgiving toward all persons. Jesus consciously roots his moral teachings in his concept of God. "Bless those who curse you, pray for those who abuse you. . . . If you love those who love you, what credit is that to you? For even sinners love those who love them. . . . But love your enemies, do good, and lend, expecting nothing in return. Your reward will be great, and you will be children of the Most High; for he is kind to the ungrateful and the wicked. Be merciful, just as your Father is merciful" (Luke 6:27-36).

By definition, beliefs about God influence the ethics of those who believe that God exists. Nevertheless, a system of ethics and human behavior are not identical. Research has shown that behavior is less predicated upon theological beliefs than upon perceived threats and authority, and upon the central object of one's trust and loyalty.

—Paul Plenge Parker

See also Divine command theory; Human nature; Objectivism; Religion.

BIBLIOGRAPHY

Gustafson, James M. *Ethics from a Theocentric Perspective.* Chicago: University of Chicago Press, 1981-1984.

Moltmann, Jurgen. *The Crucified God.* Translated by R. A. Wilson and John Bowden. New York: Harper & Row, 1974.

Niebuhr, H. Richard. *Radical Monotheism and Western Culture.* New York: Harper & Row, 1970.

Plato. *The Republic.* Translated by Allan Bloom. New York: Basic Books, 1968.

Stassen, Glen H. "Social Theory Model for Religious Social Ethics." *Journal of Religious Ethics* 5 (Spring, 1977): 9-37.

Golden mean

TYPE OF ETHICS: Classical history

DATE: 335-323 B.C.E.; Published 60 B.C.E.

ASSOCIATED WITH: Aristotle

DEFINITION: The ethical principle that virtue consists in following a course of action somewhere between the extreme of too much (excess) and that of too little (defect)

SIGNIFICANCE: The golden mean, or moderation in a person's course of life, has had widespread appeal as a practical ethical guide

The ethical doctrines of Aristotle are expounded in three major works: the *Nicomachean Ethics,* the *Eudemian Ethics,* and the *Great Ethics,* or *Magna Moralia.* The *Nicomachean Ethics* is considered to be Aristotle's most mature work on the subject of ethics. In the *Nicomachean Ethics,* a work divided into ten "books" of roughly similar length (approximately 20 pages), Aristotle addresses the issue of human conduct and raises and attempts to answer the question: "What is the good life?" In book 6 of the *Nicomachean Ethics,* Aristotle gives one of the most typically Greek answers to this question of ethics and in so doing makes use of the compromise position that he took in philosophy generally.

The golden mean, which has also been called the "doctrine of the mean" and the "Aristotelian mean," is the ideal that Greeks customarily sought as a guide to their daily lives, both public and private. It followed naturally that Aristotle associated ethics with the state—not with religion, as Christianity subsequently taught. Thus, the *Nicomachean Ethics* has been viewed as a fundamentally political work.

Aristotle argues from the premise that human beings occupy an intermediate position in the hierarchy of living forms: Human lives are not as good as those of gods, but they are (or at least can be) better than the lives of other animals and plants. He seeks a theory of the human good that not only accords with this assumption but also explains it: Humans want to know what it is that makes their lives occupy this intermediate position. The best good for a human being, according to Aristotle, must be something that no other animal or plant can achieve.

To fully understand Aristotle's defense of the virtues of character—the skills that enable humans to listen to reason—it is necessary to see how they are connected to the preeminent virtue: practical wisdom. In book 2 of the *Nicomachean Ethics,* Aristotle states that he undertakes his present project for a practical purpose: for humans not to contemplate truths about what virtue is, but to become good people. In this spirit, Aristotle then introduces the notion of a mean: Such bodily virtues as strength and health are destroyed by deficiency and excess (too much or too little exercise, too much or too little eating), and the same holds of such virtues of the soul as temperance and courage. For example, to be courageous means not to fear everything and avoid every danger, nor must humans be without fear and accept every risk; to be temperate one must not pursue every pleasure, and one must not go to the opposite extreme of pursuing none. Aristotle points out that the mean for one person in one situation will differ from the mean for someone else in a different situation. The idea is that there is not some one correct amount of anger, for example. Instead, when one aims at the mean, one must aim at something that is for him or her neither too great nor too little: It must be the appropriate amount of anger, fear, or appetite at this time, in relation to this person, and so on.

To be virtuous, people must aim their actions and feelings at a mean between deficiency and excess. In the same way that a good craftsman attempts to produce something from which nothing should be taken away and to which nothing need be added, so humans should strive for something equally appropriate to the situations in which they find themselves. Finding this intermediate path is difficult, according to Aristotle, because there are so many different ways to under- or overshoot one's target. Striking the mean in one's actions and feelings is a task that requires practical reason. Thus, when Aristotle defines ethical virtue, he describes it as a state concerned with choice, since a mean is relative to the individual as determined by reason, the reason by which the practically wise person would determine it.

Echoes of this formulation run throughout Aristotle's discussion of the virtues—to exercise the virtues is to follow reason; his doctrine of the mean is the guiding principle behind his classification of virtues and vices. To possess an ethical virtue is to know how to strike the mean. Consequently, there are two kinds of character defects: One may regularly do and feel either too much or too little. Every such virtue is therefore to be understood by comparing it with its corresponding vice.

Whether or not Aristotle's claims are true, it has been argued that they do provide a workable standard for decision making. Nearly the whole of book 6 of the *Nicomachean Ethics* is devoted to the study of two kinds of virtues: practical wisdom and theoretical wisdom. Aristotle is saying that either of these should be the target toward which the reasonable person aims. Thus, the "right" amount in actions and feelings will be whatever amount best contributes to the fullest expression of these two rational skills. Aristotle's entire discussion may be viewed as contributing in one way or another to an understanding of what he maintains are the two highest human virtues.   —*Genevieve Slomski*

See also Aristotelian ethics; Aristotle; Mādhyamaka; *Nicomachean Ethics.*

BIBLIOGRAPHY

Hardie, W. F. R. *Aristotle's Ethical Theory.* 2d ed. New York: Oxford University Press, 1980.

Hutchinson, D. S. *The Virtues of Aristotle.* New York: Routledge & Kegan Paul, 1986.

Kraut, Richard. *Aristotle on the Human Good.* Princeton, N.J.: Princeton University Press, 1989.

Moravcsik, J. M. E., ed. *Aristotle: A Collection of Critical Essays.* Garden City, N.Y.: Anchor Books, 1967.

Urmson, J. O. "Aristotle's Doctrine of the Mean." In *Essays on Aristotle's Ethics,* edited by Amelie O. Rorty. Berkeley: University of California Press, 1980.

Golden rule

TYPE OF ETHICS: Theory of ethics

DATE: Sixth century B.C.E. to present

ASSOCIATED WITH: All major religions and codes of ethics

DEFINITION: The golden rule is an ethical principle that advises that one should treat others as one wants to be treated

SIGNIFICANCE: Emphasizes that the needs of others are on a par with one's own needs and thus guards against the performance of unduly self-directed actions

The injunction that one should treat others as one wants to be treated is known as the "golden" rule because it is often said to be of unparalleled value as a fundamental ethical principle. Testimony to the value that human beings have accorded this principle is found in its long and rich history, a history that includes, but is not limited to, its appearance in Confucianism (sixth century B.C.E.), Buddhism (fifth century B.C.E.), Jainism (fifth century B.C.E.), Zoroastrianism (fifth century B.C.E.), Hinduism (third century B.C.E.), Judaism

(first century B.C.E.), Christianity (first century C.E.), and Sikhism (sixteenth century C.E.).

The golden rule has been formulated both negatively (Do not do to others what you would not want done to yourself) and positively (Do unto others what you would have them do unto you). The negative formulation seems to be the older of the two, being the version endorsed in Confucianism, Buddhism, Jainism, and Zoroastrianism; nevertheless, it has been argued that the positive formulation is superior to the negative formulation because the former includes a call to beneficence that is lacking in the latter. This criticism of the negative version does not withstand scrutiny, however, for neglect is certainly one of the things that an individual might want to avoid and thus—in keeping with the negative formulation—would be something an individual should not do to others.

A more serious problem said to afflict both versions of the golden rule is that neither provides a basis for distinguishing between virtuous and nonvirtuous wants. Thus, an individual who wants to be debased or subjugated is enjoined by the golden rule to debase and subjugate others. For this reason, it has been thought that the golden rule cannot serve as a fundamental principle of morality, since its just application is possible only if one already has some independent means for distinguishing between morally good and morally corrupt behavior.

Because of this concern, it has sometimes been suggested that a close cousin of the golden rule—Love thy neighbor as thyself—is a superior fundamental moral principle. The superiority of the call to love one's neighbor as oneself is thought to reside in the concept of love, a concept that specifies that one's wants should be directed toward the welfare of oneself and others. By virtue of its focus upon the welfare of the beloved, the call to extend the same love to oneself and others prohibits acting upon wants that are unjustifiably damaging. In fairness to the golden rule, however, it should be pointed out that applicability of loving one's neighbor as oneself presupposes both that people do love themselves and that this self-love can be used as a model for attitudes toward others. While these presuppositions might seem reasonable, it is worth noting that the possibility of nonvirtuous self-directed wants that drives the objection against the golden rule poses similar problems for the aforementioned presuppositions of the call to love thy neighbor as thyself.

It was also concern over the problem of corrupt wants that led Immanuel Kant (1724-1804) to distinguish his own first moral principle, the categorical imperative, from the golden rule. One version of Kant's categorical imperative states that one should act only according to that maxim (rule of action) that one can at the same time will to be a universal law. The difference between the golden rule and the categorical imperative is found, according to Kant, in the fact that one can always treat others as if they shared one's wants, corrupt or otherwise; however, it is not possible consistently to will the universalization of corrupt behavior. To illustrate the difference between the two principles, Kant points out that many individuals would gladly agree to receive no assistance from others and thereby—in accordance with the golden rule—be relieved of the duty to assist others. Willing that such mutual neglect be universal would be irrational, however, because it would involve willing that no human being ever render assistance to others, a policy that would undermine the very existence of the human race. In this way, says Kant, the categorical imperative excludes corrupt wants that the golden rule allows to stand.

Even if the problem of nonvirtuous wants and related problems do show that the golden rule cannot generate an ethical system by itself, however, the rule is still deserving of its rich history insofar as it can serve as a ready test of the impartiality of some proposed plan of action.

—*James Petrik*

See also Impartiality; Kant, Immanuel; Sidgwick, Henry; Universalizability.

BIBLIOGRAPHY

Allinson, Robert E. "The Confucian Golden Rule: A Negative Formulation." *Journal of Chinese Philosophy* 12 (Spring, 1985): 305-315.

Blackstone, W. T. "The Golden Rule: A Defense." *The Southern Journal of Philosophy* 3 (Winter, 1965): 172-177.

Gewirth, Alan. "The Golden Rule Rationalized." *Midwest Studies in Philosophy* 3 (1978): 133-147.

Gould, James A. "The Not-So-Golden Rule." *The Southern Journal of Philosophy* 1 (Fall, 1963): 10-14.

Ivanhoe, Philip J. "Reweaving the 'One Thread' of the Analects." *Philosophy East and West* 40 (January, 1990): 17-33.

Kant, Immanuel. *The Moral Law: Kant's "Groundwork of the Metaphysics of Morals."* Translated by H. J. Paton. London: Hutchinson University Library, 1969.

Pike, E. Royston. *Ethics of the Great Religions.* London: C. A. Watts, 1948.

Rost, H. T. D. *The Golden Rule.* Oxford, England: George Ronald, 1986.

Singer, Marcus. "Golden Rule." In *The Encyclopedia of Philosophy*, edited by Paul Edwards. Vol. 3. New York: Macmillan, 1967.

Good samaritan laws

TYPE OF ETHICS: Legal and judicial ethics
DATE: 1980's
DEFINITION: Pertains to the legal aspects surrounding the rendering of aid in an emergency, by emergency medical services personnel and private citizens
SIGNIFICANCE: Allows legal protection to those who follow their human conscience to assist someone who is sick or injured

Some people refuse to stop and help injured accident victims because they fear being sued for improper action. Much of the fear is generated by misunderstanding and by misinterpretation of the laws. Good samaritan laws have helped to alleviate some of these fears. Essentially, good samaritan laws protect from lawsuit emergency medical services personnel (and, in some cases, private citizens), as long as they act in good faith and to the best of their abilities. Mistreatment, gross negligence, and abandonment are not included in this protection.

Thus, these good samaritan laws attempt to ensure that anyone who voluntarily helps an injured or ill person at a scene is not legally liable for error or omissions in rendering good faith emergency care. The provision of the Massachusetts General Law c111C, section 14, which is typical of that of many other states, reads: "No emergency medical technician who in the performance of his duties and in good faith renders emergency first aid or transportation to an injured or incapacitated person shall be personally in any way liable as a result of rendering such aid or as a result of transporting such person to a hospital or other safe place."

See also Bill of Rights, U.S.; Disability rights; Human rights; Right to life.

Goodness

TYPE OF ETHICS: Theory of ethics
DATE: The concept of goodness has been central to ethics since at least the fifth century B.C.E.; the term entered the English language in Old English from Old Norse
ASSOCIATED WITH: Value theory
DEFINITION: Goodness means "that which one ought to do" or, alternatively, gives a substantive answer to the question, "What ought one to do?"
SIGNIFICANCE: The way in which one defines or approaches the good shapes the nature of one's entire ethical thought; furthermore, the nature of the good ultimately ties into questions of free will, moral responsibility, and even theodicy

Plato spoke of a kind of trinity of forms: the good, the true, and the beautiful. Each of these corresponded to the perfection of a faculty in humanity. The beautiful was the perfect object of the faculty of the judgment. The true was the perfect object of the faculty of the intellect, and the good was the perfect object of the faculty of the will.

In Platonic metaphysics, moreover, these three forms enjoy a kind of consubstantiality. In later natural-law thinking, goodness, truth, and beauty were coextensive with being itself.

In the theodicy of Saint Augustine, furthermore, this becomes crucial, since that father of the Church overcame the metaphysical implications of the existence of evil by denying real being to evil: Evil does not enjoy substantial existence but subsists in a kind of parasitic relation to the good. Evil is the absence of a good where a good should be. In the will, this situation amounts to a choice of a lesser good over a greater good.

In these ways, metaphysical notions of goodness interact with ethical conceptions of the good. Classical philosophers as well as patristic and scholastic theologians held that the human will must always will a good; in reality, there are only goods to be willed.

Aristotle analyzed the nature of goods by distinguishing

between intrinsic and nonintrinsic goods (often called instrumental goods). Intrinsic goods are valuable for their own sake, while nonintrinsic goods are sought for the sake of some intrinsic good.

Aristotle further noted that among intrinsic goods, one good will be a *summum bonum*, or ultimate good. The *summum bonum* for Aristotle (and for Saint Thomas Aquinas) was happiness—*eudaimonia*—and the activity/state most associated with the achievement of this end was philosophical contemplation for Aristotle and beatitude (with the attendant beatific vision) for Saint Thomas. On account of this divergence, Aristotelian ethics are designated as natural eudaimonism and Thomistic ethics as supernatural, or theological eudaimonism.

For both Aristotle and Thomas Aquinas, the *summum bonum* served as an architectonic principle that was capable of ordering all other lesser goods in relationship to it.

This Aristotelian-Thomistic approach combines eudaimonism with a natural-law approach that conceives of a fixed and universally shared human essence. Each subordinate faculty of humanity has its own teleology—its specific purpose or end (that is, its own good)—but the ends of these are ordered to the final end of humanity.

This natural-law approach to morality upholds a strict objectivity in ethics, for while a man might pervert his nature by ignoring the promptings of his conscience and his reason, that would in no way alter the nature of his true good.

Ethical pluralists deny that there is a *summum bonum* for humankind; there are only individual choices of goods in accordance with hierarchies of value created by individual tastes and commitments.

The distinction between ethical objectivists and ethical subjectivists in regard to goodness is vital. Subjectivists maintain that there is no activity of persons or state of being that is inherently good unless it produces an appropriate subjective response in the individual. An objectivist, however, claims that some human activities or states of being are inherently good, apart from any subjective response that they may produce in the subject.

Classical hedonism of both the rational school, associated with Epicurus, and the so-called irrationalist school (or Cyrenaic school), associated with Aristippus of Cyrene, claimed pleasure as the inherent good for humanity. In the more sophisticated versions of hedonism, the concept of pleasure is so expanded as to come close to the multifaceted concept of *eudaimonia*.

In modern times, in both the act utilitarianism of Jeremy Bentham and the rule utilitarianism of John Stuart Mill, pleasure is the good for humanity, which position has caused many scholars to treat utilitarianism as a special form of hedonism. Classical hedonism, of course, developed its social aspects by building up its theory from the individual's interests, needs, and desires, while utilitarianism, with its central criterion of "the greatest good for the greatest number" begins with an inherently social perspective.

Both Mill and Bentham defined the good as pleasure, but they differed so radically in their definitions of pleasure that it has been standard practice among philosophers to refer to Bentham's quantitative theory of pleasure as hedonistic utilitarianism and to Mill's qualitative theory of pleasure as eudaimonistic utilitarianism.

There was, perhaps, no more significant development in the modern search for the good than G. E. Moore's demonstration of the so-called naturalistic fallacy. Having demonstrated that no natural property can be designated as the good, Moore went on to claim that goodness must be a nonnatural property inhering in good acts.

Analytical philosophers of the Anglo-American tradition accepted Moore's proof that the good could not be a simple natural property, but they rejected his notion that it constituted a nonnatural property, electing instead to assume that the term was used differently in different contexts, indicating quite different natural properties or combinations of natural properties.

Pragmatists such as John Dewey agreed with the analytical philosophers concerning the nature of the good, but they were led to their conclusions by ontological rather than linguistic considerations. Given his commitment to situational ethics and to the ultimate plasticity of human nature, Dewey envisioned the good as varying with historical circumstances and cultural contexts.

Noncognitivist ethicians have interpreted the good in terms of their special linguistic approaches. Emotivists have held the term "good"—like all positive ethical language—to express a positive emotional response to ethical actions in the world: "Charity is good" is translated as an emotional approval of charity. Imperativists hold that ethical statements are overt or covert commands, and "Charity is good," for them, means "Perform charitable deeds." Finally, emoto-imperativists see a term such as "good" as combining a command function with emotional responses.

David Hume's explication of the is/ought problem also must be seen as vital for an understanding of the difficulties that modern ethical philosophers have had with the concept of the good. With the discovery that prescriptive ("ought") conclusions cannot be derived from descriptive ("is") premises, the conception of the good was put under an inordinate strain. Always implicit in the concept of the good had been the notion of "that which one ought to do." With the is/ought dichotomy, this aspect of the concept of the good was forever divorced from the more substantive contents of its various alternative definitions.

Sir Karl Popper noted that the definition of the good as "that which one ought to do" cannot be expanded to accommodate any substantive content beyond that meaning.

In contrast to the consequentialistic tradition in ethics, the great counter-tradition of formalism arose, defining the good not in view of the consequences of particular acts, but in respect to the form of the ethical judgments that choose those acts.

Perhaps Cicero may be seen as the originator of formalism, with his unique ethical theory that derived from the academics of the late Platonic school, the peripatetics of the late Aristotelian school, and the stoics. In Ciceronian moral philosophy, the *summum bonum* was equated generally with virtue and specifically with the virtue of *honestum*, or right doing.

Immanuel Kant, whose ethical thought seems to have been influenced by Cicero and the stoics, is the very epitome of a formalist ethician. Although Kant believed that a properly virtuous person would ultimately enjoy acting morally and would achieve happiness thereby, these considerations were unnecessary for the essential goodness of his or her actions. The goodness of an action rests in its meeting the formal criterion of the categorical imperative: An action whose implicit maxim can become a universalizable law for all moral agents is a good action. Any action not in accord with that standard is a morally impermissible action.

For Kant, furthermore, it is not meritorious to do the correct action because one desires some benefit from that action. A merchant who keeps honest weights and measures because such a practice is good for his business is not acting in a morally good manner. To be morally virtuous, Kant would maintain, an action must be done for the sake of the moral law. That is why Kant could term his ethical system a "deontology"—a science of duty.

In contrast to the absolutist moral claims of Kantian formalism, the various forms of ethical relativism have descriptive definitions of the good. In individual ethical relativism, nothing is held to be right or wrong for the individual person except that which he or she truly believes to be right or wrong. Cultural ethical relativism holds that good actions are those approved by one's culture and that evil actions are those condemned by one's culture. Finally, the relativism of situational ethics defines the good in terms of the judgments of one's historical era and so forth.

Divine command morality, one of the less fashionable byways of ethical theory, must be acknowledged as having a formalistic account of the good, for the goodness of acts consists in their being done in response to divine command alone.

The history of ethical philosophy may well be said to be the history of the changing notions of goodness, and that history is a tormented one indeed. In the earliest days of ethical theory, Aristotle found it necessary to abandon Plato's form of the good, because, attractive as that concept was, it seemed to bear no real relationship to human ethics. Aside from possible mystical experience, humans do not seem to have access to the form of the good; thus, it could have no real bearing upon ethical theory.

Aristotle's abandonment of the form of the good led to great alterations in agathokakological theory—the philosophy of good and evil. While Plato ascribed evil to ignorance—Socrates stated repeatedly that to know the good is to do the good—Aristotle added *akrasia* (weakness of the will) to the causes of evil. Aristotle did not deny the role that the Socratic/Pla-

tonic concept of evil arose from ignorance, but he held that notion to be inadequate to encompass all evil. Some men know the good, Aristotle believed, but lack the force of will and character to pursue it.

In late Judaism and early Christianity, the concept of the free will (*liberum arbitrium*) and its role in the selection or rejection of the greater good came to play a predominant part. The notion that one may know the good, have the strength of will to do it, and yet deliberately reject it entered theological ethics. Freely chosen evil—the "Mystery of Iniquity"—came not merely to supplement the concepts of ignorance and *akrasia* as wellsprings of evil but to dominate them. Evil done from ignorance or *akrasia* in this view would only be true moral evil if the ignorance or *akrasia* were itself culpable, and that culpability requires that, at the end of the chain of moral causation, a free choice must have been the basis of all else that followed.

In part, concerns of theodicy—the theological/philosophical investigation of Divine justice—fueled the Judeo-Christian development of the concept of freely chosen evil. How is it just that God punishes sin if an individual could not act otherwise? Freely chosen evil was the answer that was proposed. In addition, Judeo-Christian demonology, with the figure of Satan/Lucifer, contributed to the need for a new explanation for the rejection of the good, for by traditional doctrine, Lucifer was the highest of all created minds and, as an angel, lacked a lower nature—thus, ignorance and *akrasia* are excluded as explanations for his evil.

For Kant also, the question of freely chosen evil became a fundamental problem in his ethical theory. In the *Foundations of the Metaphysics of Morals* and the *Critique of Practical Reason*, Kant seemed to speak as if deliberately chosen evil were possible. Already, however, there were problems, for true freedom—the autonomous will—was possible only when the will made a law for itself, and that law could only be the categorical imperative.

Finally, in *Religion Within the Bounds of Reason Alone*, Kant repudiated the notion of freely chosen evil, maintaining that there could be no "devilish minds." Despite Kant's conclusion, however, it is unclear that the notion of human free will—the *liberum arbitrium*, the free choice between good and evil—can be maintained without the concept of freely chosen evil. Furthermore, as hard and soft determinists contest with one another, it is uncertain that moral responsibility can be maintained in the absence of the *liberum arbitrium*. In this way, the very question of the ability freely and knowingly to reject the good ties into the most basic issues in ethics, such as free will and the existence of moral responsibility.

There is, perhaps, no concept so central to every aspect of ethical philosophy as the concept of goodness. What distinguishes ethical philosophies from one another is most often their differing visions of the good. They are further distinguished by their handling of the brute fact of human rejection of the good. What is the good? Why do people find it attractive? How are some able to reject the good? These are among the three most crucial questions in the ethical sphere. —*Patrick M. O'Neil*

See also Intrinsic good; Language; Life, meaning of; Morality; Natural law; Right and wrong; Truth; Virtue.

BIBLIOGRAPHY

Aristotle. *Nicomachean Ethics*. Indianapolis: Hackett, 1985. Aristotle views *eudaimonia* (happiness) as the good for humanity.

Brandt, Richard. *A Theory of the Good and the Right*. Oxford, England: Clarendon Press, 1979. The good is seen as the object of rational desire.

Hobbes, Thomas. *Leviathan*. Edited by Richard Tuck. New York: Cambridge University Press, 1991. Rational prudence is seen as the basis of morality, and ethical egoism is defended as the true moral philosophy.

Kant, Immanuel. *Foundations of the Metaphysics of Morals and What Is Enlightenment*. Translated by Lewis White Beck. 2d ed. New York: Macmillan, 1990. The good will (proper moral intention to obey the moral law) is seen as the source of all ethical good.

Mill, John Stuart. *Utilitarianism and Other Essays*. New York: Penguin Books, 1987. The greatest good—defined as a kind of eudaimonistic pleasure—for the greatest number is seen as the standard of the good action for moral agents.

Oates, Whitney Jennings. *Stoic and Epicurean Philosophers*. New York: Random House, 1940. The stoic notions of virtue and the Epicurean idea of pleasure as the highest good for humanity may be found in a number of different representatives of these schools who have been assembled in this anthology.

Plato. *The Republic*. Translated by A. D. Lindsay. New York: Knopf, 1992. The form of the good is introduced and explicated.

Goss v. Lopez

TYPE OF ETHICS: Civil rights

DATE: 1975

ASSOCIATED WITH: U.S. Supreme Court

DEFINITION: The Court held 5-4 that states must provide some elements of due process of law in school disciplinary proceedings that can result in suspension

SIGNIFICANCE: The decision stands for the proposition that schoolchildren are also entitled to at least some elementary procedural guarantees and evidentiary rules in school disciplinary proceedings

During a period of unrest in the Columbus, Ohio, school system, Dwight Lopez was a student at Central High School. He was suspended from school for ten days for allegedly participating in a demonstration in the school cafeteria. There was some physical damage to the lunch room. Lopez received no hearing prior to his suspension. He later testified that he himself had not participated in the disturbance. The Supreme Court held, in a 5-4 decision written by Justice Byron R. White, that Lopez and the other nine suspended appellants were entitled to a hearing prior to suspension so that the charges against them could be assessed. The state of Ohio's argument that it was constitutionally entitled not to offer public education at all and could thus manage the system as it pleased was rejected by the Court; having established the system and given the public rights in it, Ohio could not deprive people of due process by later depriving them of that right. The dissenting justices in this case argued that the penalty was too insignificant to warrant a hearing.

See also Bill of Rights, U.S.; Due process; *In re Gault.*

Gratitude

TYPE OF ETHICS: Personal and social ethics

DATE: From antiquity

ASSOCIATED WITH: Generosity, grace, humility, reciprocity, gifts, sacrifice, thanks, and social norms

DEFINITION: Appreciation of an unearned gift, considered a moral obligation by some philosophers

SIGNIFICANCE: The appropriate expression of gratitude may be considered a virtue, while ingratitude may be considered a vice

Humankind is constantly preoccupied with equitable exchange. Gratitude is the heart's internal indicator when the tally of gifts outweighs exchanges. Gratitude is a moral value that helps regulate the "give and take" of human encounters. Gratitude is a universally recognized virtue. The Roman poet Cicero called it the "mother of all virtue." Seneca, an ancient Stoic, stated, "There was never any man so wicked as not to approve of gratitude and detest ingratitude." When the ancient Chinese sage Confucius was asked to summarize his ethics in one word, he replied, "Reciprocity." "Reciprocity" implies a sense of gratitude that arises when goods received go beyond what was deserved. The consensus of sages and philosophers is that people have a moral duty to keep fresh the memory of good things done for them.

As is often the case, moral injunctions serve to counter a trend in human nature that would otherwise remain unchecked. Prophets and moralists have found it necessary to counter the selfish and ungrateful tendency in human nature. Social critic Christopher Lasch, in his *Culture of Narcissism* (1978), has called attention to the dangers of a society that fails to maintain an "attitude of gratitude" as a core value. When the individual's "expectation of entitlement" becomes the group norm, gratitude is destroyed and the fabric of society is weakened. Gratitude is imperative for group survival and cohesion.

Many Christian theologians have argued that gratitude is the obligatory response of the believing person to the grace and goodness of God's creation and redemption. Saint Paul writes, "In everything give thanks." One's metaphysical and political commitments may, however, shape one's perceptions of life in such a way that "gratitude," rather than being a virtue, may be judged to be a form of self-deception or even a subtle coalition with one's oppressors. For example, Jean-Paul Sartre argues that life is essentially absurd and inchoate, prompting one who is "authentic" to have a fundamental attitude of "nausea" toward life. Karl Marx, the economic determinist, implied that the individual has a moral obligation to feel ingratitude toward society when that society fails to fairly meet the needs of all.

In many forms of Asian thought, the status of gratitude is ambiguous, since gratitude requires a certain dualism between "benefactor" and "recipient" that may not apply in Asian systems. In much of Asian thought, the goal of life is to transcend the smallness of the finite self. As the devotee comes to identify with the impersonal absolute, the concept of "giving and receiving" becomes vacuous. The enlightened devotee may say, "One to me is loss or gain, One to me is fame or shame, One to me is pleasure, pain." (Bhagavad Gītā) Thus, gratitude may assume a different meaning in Asian thought. Yet even Buddhists, who hold steadfastly to the doctrine of "no-self," staunchly express gratitude to the noble Buddha who taught the path of "no-self." In the Taoist perspective, good and evil lose their absolute character to such a degree that the concept of gratitude may become irrelevant. If both faces of fortune are greeted with equal countenance, the concept of gratitude becomes equivocal.

The book *Twelve Steps and Twelve Traditions* by Bill Wilson, a cofounder of Alcoholics Anonymous, states, "Action expresses more gratitude than words." Retroactively, gratitude is expressed through thankful remembrances, verbal expressions, and thank-you notes. Proactively, gratitude is expressed through charitable deeds that are performed without thought of reward. Alcoholics Anonymous (AA) meetings often focus on the topic of "gratitude" since the inculcation of this attitude is believed to be not only morally desirable but also necessary for peace of mind and high-quality sobriety. AA teaches that gratitude is the key to happiness and recovery, thus implying a moral imperative to be grateful.

Friedrich Nietzsche believed that gratitude was usually a disguise for covert interests. To have a person's gratitude is to have that person's loyalty. Sacrifice to the gods was never purely to express gratitude but to appease or ward off other evils. The "slave" who serves the "master" above the call of duty secretly expects a boon, not merely the master's gratitude. If gratitude is expressed with the motive of eliciting more gifts from God or any other superior agent, it becomes a form of mercantilism or spiritual materialism.

Nietzsche did, however, recognize a higher gratitude that makes possible a noble expression based on strength and true generosity of spirit. Similarly, Fyodor Dostoevski saw a dynamic connection between gratitude and human freedom. In the "Legend of the Grand Inquisitor," in *The Brothers Karamazov*, he allegorized that when God calls to humanity he must do so in an ambiguous form in order to maintain humanity's nobility. If God were to appear to man with all of his power, glory, and gifts, humans would be awed with gratitude and would have no choice but to obey. God, however, wanted human obedience and gratitude to be freely given. Hence the ambiguous nature of God's gifts and

communications. This ambiguity dampens humanity's gratitude while preserving its freedom.

Joseph Amato, in his *Guilt and Gratitude* (1982), argues that the concept of gratitude is based on an older worldview that assumes a "limited good and the age-old struggle against scarcity." This older worldview taught that humankind was dependent on material things. In a world of "scarcity," gifts are deeply appreciated. To give generously was noble. Amato argues that the concept of gratitude requires a worldview based on scarcity of goods. There is a new "worldview" emerging, however, which says that the good is unlimited and that happiness can be achieved on Earth. A new ethics of gratitude is implied in this view. This challenges the old understanding of gratitude as based on sacrifice and limitation. Gratitude no doubt will continue to be a socially desirable attitude but will have high moral value only when intentions to posture, control, or placate the benefactor are absent. Correlatively, the only gift that can evoke the highest form of gratitude is one that is truly given without expectation that the recipient be obliged or perhaps even capable of repaying the gift. —*Paul August Rentz*

See also Cicero, Marcus Tullius; Confucius; Dostoevski, Fyodor; Marx, Karl; Nietzsche, Friedrich.

BIBLIOGRAPHY

Amato, Joseph A. *Guilt and Gratitude*. Westport, Conn.: Greenwood Press, 1982. Through the perspective of "tragic optimism," this work establishes a new ethics of gratitude.

Dostoevski, Fyodor. *The Brothers Karamazov*. New York: W. W. Norton, 1976.

McCloskey, Mary A. "Gratitude." In *Encyclopedia of Ethics*, edited by Lawrence C. Becker. 2 vols. New York: Garland, 1992.

Nietzsche, Friedrich. *The Genealogy of Morals*. New York: Macmillan, 1992.

Gray Panthers

TYPE OF ETHICS: Older persons' rights
DATE: Founded 1970
DEFINITION: Gray Panthers was established to combat discrimination based on age
SIGNIFICANCE: Gray Panthers was the first national organization to bring old and young people together to address discrimination based on age

In 1970, a woman named Maggie Kuhn joined several friends to address two concerns. They wanted to change the laws that permitted forced retirement at age 65, because they knew many people older than 65 who had much to contribute, and they wanted to join younger people in actively opposing the Vietnam War. From these concerns came a group called the Consultation of Older and Younger Adults for Social Change, whose name was later changed to Gray Panthers. The name is a humorous take-off on Black Panthers, a civil rights group for African Americans. Gray Panthers, whose motto is "Age and Youth in Action," is unlike many other advocacy groups for older people in that it does not set up or feed on competition

The Gray Panthers was formed to serve the interests of older people such as this woman, who is protesting rent increases for fixed-income tenants. (Hazel Hankin)

between old and young people. It advises that by valuing its youngest and oldest citizens, society can become more just and humane. Through national publications and local seminars, the members of Gray Panthers work for improved media sensitivity to age, regulation of the nursing-home and hearing-aid industries, affordable and adequate housing for all, innovative concepts for jobs and work emphasizing the involvement of people of all ages, and an increased emphasis on intergenerational association.

See also Ageism.

Greed

TYPE OF ETHICS: Beliefs and practices
DATE: From antiquity
DEFINITION: A defect of character or will in which a person, corporate entity, or government is unwilling to restrain itself from taking more than it is due or is prudent
SIGNIFICANCE: Greed is a sin that results in evil behavior, alienation from God, and possibly ruinous and destructive behavior

Greed Is Pervasive. Greed occurs at all levels of human endeavor, and it can occur at the individual or the group level. Donald Worster (1993) documents the "greed is good" mentality in the rise of agribusiness. In its greed for short-term profits, it has followed a "slash-and-burn" policy of economic development that has wreaked environmental destruction and bequeathed future generations a legacy of worsening soil erosion, water shortage, dust bowl conditions, and extinction of wildlife.

Greed may also characterize the workings of government. Robert Lekachman (1982) stated the liberal argument that the administration of U.S. president Ronald Reagan was motivated by greed. Reagan's administration purportedly engaged in an enthusiastic and massive redistribution of wealth and power that further enriched the already obscenely rich, such as "greedy dabblers in oil, gas and coal properties." All this was at the expense of the working poor, minorities, and welfare families.

The Origins of Greed. Greed is a sin. The biblical concept of Original Sin states that individuals are born as sinners; sin is rooted in human nature.

Rather than viewing greed as an inherent trait or motive, other explanations have looked to the environment. The psychoanalyst Erich Fromm believed that parents are shaped by society to mold their children in a manner consistent with society's values. Fromm viewed American society as passing through a series of stages. One of these was the "hoarding character," which was obsessed with accumulating, holding, and retaining things. In this vein, Ray Porter observed that the noble and virtuous intentions of the Constitution and Bill of Rights, Christian religion, and the capitalist economy actually fostered a mentality of greed that led to widespread destruction of the environment. The right to own and accumulate private property and do with it whatever one wanted was seen as legitimate self-interest. The view that humankind was created in God's image and had a soul led to the view that plants and animals were subordinate to human purposes. The Scriptures and the Protestant ethic encouraged people to control and exploit nature to their profit. Economics contributed the belief that the source of all that was of value was labor. Nature had no intrinsic value until it was exploited for products and wealth—a "greed is good" mentality.

Greed and Ethics. Greed is a sin—that is, a thought, motive, or desire that results in evil behavior because of a wrong attitude toward God. Greed rests in opposition to the eternal law of God and results in alienation from Him and possible ruin and destruction. The Old and New testaments of the Bible contain numerous references to the sinfulness of greed.

The list of the seven deadly sins has been common since the time of Thomas Aquinas. One of these sins is gluttony, which is listed in *Roget's Thesaurus* and *Webster's Collegiate Dictionary* as a synonym for greed. Gluttony/greed and the other sins were considered to be root causes of actions or failures to act that constitute serious sins or which are the inevitable source of other sins. They are considered to be deadly because they are directly opposed to virtue.

Solutions. Both the Bible and contemporary writers agree that greed is bad and potentially destructive to the individual and to society. Both also agree that greed needs to be replaced by contentment with a modest style of living. The Bible extols individuals to "Keep your lives free from the love of money and be content with what you have." (Heb. 13:5). "Godliness with contentment is great gain. For we brought nothing into the world and we can take nothing out of it. But if we have food and clothing we will be content with that" (1 Tim. 6:6-10).

The psychologist Burrhus F. Skinner believed that people must reduce their consumption, especially of nonessential luxuries that are falsely believed to be necessary for a satisfying life. "The assignment is to somehow induce people to take the future into account and live simpler lives, consuming less and moving less . . . we need to arrange immediate consequences which will induce people to act in ways which have consequences that are ultimately constructive."

John A. Nevin believes that it is necessary to emphasize the increasingly aversive conditions under which humankind lives and target those responsible: industries seeking short-term profits at the expense of long-term well-being; religions that encourage overpopulation to maintain and increase their membership; and, ultimately, each overavid consumer.   —*Laurence Miller*

See also Environmental ethics; Exploitation; Selfishness.

BIBLIOGRAPHY

Fromm, Erich. *To Have or To Be?* New York: Harper & Row, 1976.

Lekachman, Robert. *Greed Is Not Enough.* New York: Pantheon Books, 1982.

Nicolaus, Robert H. "B. F. Skinner Talks About Energy." *Behaviorists for Social Action Journal* 3, no. 2 (1982): 22-24.

Schumacher, E. F. *Small Is Beautiful.* New York: Harper & Row, 1973.

Worster, Donald. *The Wealth of Nature: Environmental History and the Ecological Imagination.* New York: Oxford University Press, 1993.

Greenhouse effect

TYPE OF ETHICS: Environmental ethics
DATE: 1896
DEFINITION: An increase in the earth's surface temperature caused by the absorption of reflected, infrared radiation by atmospheric "greenhouse gases"
SIGNIFICANCE: "Greenhouse gas" emission may drastically change global climates, thus creating an ethical environmental issue

The "greenhouse gases"—water vapor and small amounts of carbon dioxide, methane, nitrous oxide, ozone, and chlorofluorocarbons—absorb reflected infrared radiation, thus raising the atmospheric temperature. Without this increase, the earth's mean surface temperature would be about 17.3

degrees Celsius rather than the observed 15 degrees Celsius (approximate); therefore, the "greenhouse effect" makes the earth habitable. The warming primarily results from absorption and restricted diffusion rather than reflection and is more properly referred to as the "atmospheric effect." Human production of carbon dioxide, chlorofluorocarbons, nitrous oxide, and ozone may have caused the global warming that has been noted since industrialization. Atmospheric carbon dioxide is increasing about 0.3 percent annually, an increase closely paralleling rates of fuel consumption. Some scientists predict doubled atmospheric carbon dioxide by the year 2080. Chlorofluorocarbons, which are entirely of industrial origin, are increasing by 5 percent per year. Actions to control greenhouse gas emissions include attempts to restrict fossil fuel combustion, which generates carbon dioxide, and reforestation and forest preservation, which remove carbon dioxide from the atmosphere. An international agreement made in 1987 requires halving chlorofluorocarbon emissions in thirty-one countries by the year 2000.

See also Earth, human relations to; Global warming; Rain forests.

Greenpeace

TYPE OF ETHICS: Environmental ethics
DATE: 1970
ASSOCIATED WITH: Development of the "green" political movement in the 1970's and later
DEFINITION: An international organization dedicated to the protection of the environment
SIGNIFICANCE: Introduced organized interference with governmental and private activities that were considered to be contrary to the environmental ethic

In 1970 Jim Bohlen, Paul Cote, and Irving Stowe formed the Don't Make a Wave Committee, in Vancouver, Canada, which sent a protest vessel, the *Rainbow Warrior*, to Amchitka in the Aleutian Islands to provoke publicity regarding nuclear testing at that site. An attempt to disrupt the test failed, but the resultant publicity established Greenpeace, the new name of the group, as a major factor in environmental activism. Also, no further tests were held at that site. Among the notable continuing campaigns of Greenpeace is the attempted disruption of French nuclear tests at Moruroa in the South Seas. This effort led to violence on the high seas when French agents sank the *Rainbow Warrior* in Auckland Harbor, New Zealand, killing one activist. Beginning in 1973, Greenpeace expanded from antinuclear activity to general environmental protest. Interference with sealing and whaling in the St. Lawrence estuary and on the high seas, also involving physical conflict at sea, became prominent. The organization also spread to Europe, the United States, Argentina, and elsewhere, initiating numerous acts of protest and physical interference with such activities as waste disposal.

See also Earth, human relations to; Greens; Nature, rights of.

Greens

TYPE OF ETHICS: Environmental ethics

DATE: Established in 1980's

DEFINITION: Greens are diverse political parties that are most widely known for promoting environmental issues

SIGNIFICANCE: Greens were the first political parties promoting environmental issues to win seats in national legislatures

Greens, or Green parties, make environmental issues the focus of their political goals. They criticize the social, political, and economic structures and policies of industrialized countries as the causes of the environmental crisis. Greens consider environmental, economic, social, and political problems to be interrelated and global. Because of this relationship, Greens variously espouse grassroots democracy, social justice and equality, peace, and small-scale economics. They often oppose capitalism, the construction of nuclear power plants, and the testing and production of nuclear weapons. Most Green parties were established in the 1980's in industrialized countries, and they are active in every western European country, as well as in Australia and New Zealand. West Germany's Green Party (*die Grünen*), one of the most powerful Green parties, in 1983 became the first to win seats in a national legislature. Support for the Greens was strongly linked with active involvement in social movements. The majority of votes supporting the German Green party in 1983 were active in the ecology, antinuclear, or peace movements. Green parties have also won seats in Austria, Belgium, Finland, Luxembourg, The Netherlands, Romania, Sweden, Switzerland, and the European Parliament.

See also Social justice and responsibility.

Griswold v. Connecticut

TYPE OF ETHICS: Civil rights

DATE: June 7, 1965

ASSOCIATED WITH: U.S. Supreme Court

DEFINITION: The Court's decision affirmed the right of privacy in marriage by striking down a Connecticut law prohibiting both the use of contraceptives and counseling for the use of such

SIGNIFICANCE: This decision prohibits any government from violating the sacred bonds of marriage by regulating the details of such an intimate union

Planned Parenthood League's executive director (Griswold) and medical director (Buxton) knowingly violated a Connecticut statute that prohibited the giving of counsel to any person for the purpose of preventing conception. After being convicted in the Connecticut courts, Griswold and Buxton appealed to the U.S. Supreme Court, which overturned the Connecticut birth control law as unconstitutional. Justice William O. Douglas, writing the majority opinion, held that a right to privacy is implied in the Bill of Rights, that the marriage "right of privacy [was] older than the Bill of Rights . . . ," and that the state could not invade its freedoms. Concurring opinions by the court emphasized that the due process clause of the Fourteenth Amendment incorporated the Bill of Rights against any intrusion by state governments. Justices Hugo Black and Potter Stewart dissented on the grounds that the Bill of Rights does not explicitly list a right of privacy, stating that this law did not violate any specific provision of the Constitution and that the high court had no right to invalidate state laws simply because those laws were "capricious or irrational."

See also Due process.

Group therapy

TYPE OF ETHICS: Psychological ethics

DATE: 1934

ASSOCIATED WITH: Jacob Moreno, founder of psychodrama; the encounter group movement of the 1960's and 1970's

DEFINITION: The simultaneous psychotherapeutic treatment of several clients under the leadership of a therapist (or therapists) who tries to facilitate helpful interactions among group members

SIGNIFICANCE: All group members agree to hold confidential everything that occurs within group sessions; leaders of group therapy are bound by the same ethical strictures that bind all psychotherapists

Typically, therapy groups consist of three to twelve members who meet once per week for twelve to an unlimited number of weeks. Formats of group therapy differ widely depending on the approach taken by the therapist, but all forms provide an opportunity for members to interact with other members and to learn from these interactions with the help of the therapist.

Compared to individual therapy, group therapy provides a fuller social context in which an individual can work out social problems. Thus, group therapy affords a unique laboratory for working out interpersonal relationships. Members interact in a setting that is more representative of real life than is individual therapy.

Group therapy first became popular during World War II, when there were too few therapists available to treat all the psychological casualties of war. Many experienced therapists, however, have come to believe that group therapy has a number of advantages beyond the efficient use of a therapist's time (and lower cost to the individual).

One additional advantage of group therapy is that it encourages members to recognize quickly that they are not the only ones who feel the way they do; it gives them the opportunity to derive comfort, encouragement, and support from others who have similar, perhaps more severe, problems. This recognition tends to raise each member's expectations for improvement, an important factor in all forms of treatment. In addition, members have an opportunity to see themselves as others see them and to obtain more honest feedback about their behavior than they receive elsewhere in everyday life. They receive this feedback not only from the leader but also from other members, whose insights and observations can be very beneficial. Members also have an opportunity to try alternative responses when old ones prove ineffective. Thus, they can actually practice new behaviors in addition to talking about them. Further, members can learn vicariously by watching how others behave and can explore attitudes and reactions by interacting with a variety of people, not only the therapist. Also, members often benefit from feeling that they are part of a group, from getting to know new people, from expressing their own points of view, and from becoming emotionally intimate with others. The group experience may make members less guarded, more willing to share feelings, and more sensitive to other people's needs, motives, and messages. Members may also experience increased self-esteem as a result of helping other members.

Potential disadvantages of group therapy are, first, that some people, because of insecurities or distrustfulness, may be unsuited to group therapy or may need individual therapy before they can function well in a group setting. Second, in some groups, the therapist's attention may be spread too thin to give each member the attention that he or she needs. Third, the pressure to conform to group rules may limit the therapy process. Fourth, some people may desire more confidentiality than a group can afford or may desire individual attention.

Some types of problems are more appropriate for group than individual therapy. Such problems include substance abuse, eating disorders, child abuse, problems with intimacy, compulsive behaviors (such as gambling), hypochondriasis, narcissism, and post-trauma adjustment (such as post-divorce adjustment or recovering from the effects of sexual victimization). Also, group therapy is a popular form of personal growth therapy; thus, groups are often composed of individuals who are essentially normal but who want to grow or develop more fully.

Some forms of group therapy currently in existence are: *sensitivity training* or *encounter groups,* which promote personal growth by encouraging members to focus on their immediate relationships with other members; *assertiveness training,* in which leaders demonstrate specific ways of standing up for one's rights in an assertive but not aggressive manner; *psychodrama,* in which an individual acts out dramatic incidents resembling those that cause problems in real life; *family therapy,* in which two or more family members work as a group to resolve the problems of each individual family member (for example, school phobia in an eight-year-old) and to create harmony and balance within the family by helping each family member better understand the family's interactions and the problems they create; *marriage encounter,* in which couples explore themselves and try to expand and deepen their marriage relationships; and *self-help* groups such as Alcoholics Anonymous, Parents Without Partners, Synanon, and Weight-Watchers, which often function within a specified structure but without a trained or formal leader.

People most likely to benefit from group therapy are those who can communicate thought and feelings and who are motivated to be active participants. Poor candidates are those who are withdrawn, uncommunicative, combative, antisocial, or so depressed or unreachable that they are likely to frustrate other group members. —*Lillian M. Range*

See also Behavior therapy; Family therapy; Therapist-patient relationship.

BIBLIOGRAPHY

Bowen, Murray. *Family Therapy in Clinical Practice.* New York: Jason Aronson, 1978.

Haley, Jay, and Lynn Hoffman. *Techniques of Family Therapy.* New York: Basic Books, 1967.

Lieberman, Morton A., Irvin D. Yalom, and Matthew B. Miles. *Encounter Groups: First Facts.* New York: Basic Books, 1973.

Minuchin, Salvador. *Families & Family Therapy.* Cambridge, Mass.: Harvard University Press, 1974.

Napier, Augustus, with Carl Whitaker. *The Family Crucible.* New York: Harper & Row, 1978.

Satir, Virginia. *Conjoint Family Therapy.* Rev. ed. Palo Alto, Calif.: Science and Behavior Books, 1967.

Yalom, Irvin D. *The Theory and Practice of Group Psychotherapy.* 3d ed. New York: Basic Books, 1985.

Guilt and shame

TYPE OF ETHICS: Personal and social ethics
DATE: From antiquity
ASSOCIATED WITH: Psychological studies of self-evaluation and self-control, anthropological studies of evaluation and control of individuals by groups
DEFINITION: Emotions resulting from self-evaluation either as moral transgressor (guilt) or as morally inadequate in the judgment of others (shame)
SIGNIFICANCE: These emotions of self-assessment play crucial roles in a person's motivation to avoid doing what is regarded as morally wrong

An individual is "objectively" guilty if he or she is responsible for violating a standard of conduct prescribed by an authority, which violation renders the individual liable to compensation for the transgression. The violated standard may be a law, a rule of group morality, or a principle of the individual's own conscience. The subjective condition of "feeling guilty" is the sense of having committed an immoral act for which one is answerable to the authority of one's own conscience. Though the compensation to which one feels bound because of this transgression can take a variety of forms (punishment, repayment, being forgiven, and so forth), subjective guilt always involves the sense that one must do or suffer something in order to rectify a moral wrong that one has committed. As defined, the sense of being guilty is not identical with feeling empathic pain for those harmed by the violation. It is also not fear of repercussion or fear of punishment or the sense of having "made a mistake."

A person may be "objectively" guilty of acting against the law or the morals of others and yet not feel guilty. This occurs when such transgressions are not contrary to personal conscience. A person also may be objectively innocent of violating the law or group morality and yet feel guilty. This occurs if the individual violates the dictates of conscience even though the conduct is allowed by the law or others' morals.

Shame is the sense that one is a failure because one is regarded as such in the eyes of others. In feeling moral shame, one is thinking of and endorsing a moral condemnation by others (either real or imagined) of some specific fault, which occasions a global sense of one's own moral inadequacy. One is "shamed" by others into being "ashamed of" one's whole self. In feeling guilt, one condemns oneself and does so only for a specific misdeed. This difference between shame and guilt is evident in the way each varies in intensity. Guilt varies as a function of the grievousness of the misdeed and the degree of responsibility of the agent. A sense of full responsibility for doing something horribly wrong should elicit a severe sense of guilt. A sense of less responsibility for doing something that is regarded as less grievous should elicit a less severe sense of guilt. Moral shame varies in degree as a function of the esteem in which the others who are condemning the self are held. Those who are held in low regard should elicit little or no shame in the individual whom they morally disparage. Those who are held in high esteem should elicit much shame if they are regarded as being critical (even if what they are morally condemning is regarded by the individual as trivial).

Both guilt and shame play crucial roles in moral motivation. Guilt motivates one to make compensation for wrongs done, by submitting to punishment and/or by making satisfaction for harm caused. Doing either assuages the painful feeling of being guilty by partially "undoing" the wrong. Because guilt is a painful emotion, people are motivated to avoid experiencing it in the first place; that is, to avoid doing the wrongs that cause them to feel guilty. By shame, people are motivated to correct moral defects that they take others to be criticizing in them. This correction serves to assuage the pain of shame by eliminating its cause. It also serves to reestablish good relations with those who are regarded as being critical. Again, because shame is a painful emotion, people are motivated to avoid experiencing it in the first place; that is, to avoid acting in ways that cause them to be ashamed. Thus, people take account of and anticipate the moral judgments of them by others and "adjust" themselves accordingly.

Guilt and shame have closely related origins. When wrongdoing and punishment by parents become sufficiently linked in a child's mind, the mere thought of having done wrong will elicit the associated pain, as in guilt. Parental punishment also establishes a linkage between pain and negative evaluation of the self by others. Hence, they very thought of disapprobation of oneself by "significant" others will come to elicit the associated pain, as in shame.

Whether an individual is more prone to guilt or to shame depends upon whether the wrongs done by the person as a child or the disapproval by others of those wrongs was emphasized by the parents. This emphasis varies across cultures. Some societies emphasize the individual's sense of responsibility for wrongdoing (so-called "guilt societies"), while others emphasize the individual's sense of what others think of the individual's wrongdoing (so-called "shame societies").

Experiencing the appropriate degree of either shame or guilt on the occasion of moral wrongdoing or failure is rational and constitutive of being a moral person. Shame and guilt become irrational, however, when they are unwarranted by the occasion in which they are experienced. Irrational shame and guilt become pathological when they are persistently experienced even after their irrationality is acknowledged.
—*Mark Stephen Pestana*

See also Conscience; Forgiveness; Freud, Sigmund; Jurisprudence; Moral education; Moral responsibility; Punishment.

BIBLIOGRAPHY

Morris, Herbert. *Guilt and Shame*. Belmont, Calif.: Wadsworth, 1971.

_____. *On Guilt and Innocence: Essays in Legal Philosophy and Moral Psychology*. Berkeley: University of California Press, 1976.

Piers, Gerhart, and Milton B. Singer. *Shame and Guilt: A Psychoanalytic and a Cultural Study*. New York: W. W. Norton, 1971.

Taylor, Gabriel. *Pride, Shame, and Guilt: Emotions of Self-Assessment*. New York: Oxford University Press, 1985.

Gulag Archipelago: Book

TYPE OF ETHICS: Modern history

DATE: Published 1973-1975 as *Arkhipelag GULag, 1918-1956*; *Opyt Khudozhestvennogo issledovaniya*

AUTHOR Aleksandr Solzhenitsyn

SIGNIFICANCE: Examined the history of the penal system established in the Soviet Union by the Communist Party after the 1918 revolution and the cruelties inflicted upon millions of political prisoners

GULAG is the Russian abbreviation for the Chief Administration of Collective Labor Camps, which was established in the Union of Soviet Socialist Republics (USSR) after the Russian Revolution of 1918. An archipelago is an extensive group of islands, such as exists in the Arctic Ocean off the coast of Siberia. It is in these bitterly cold regions that collective labor camps were built to house more than ten million inmates. In 1973, Aleksandr Solzhenitsyn, a Russian novelist, began publishing a three-volume history of those camps called *The Gulag Archipelago, 1918-1956: An Experiment in Literary Investigation*. Though banned in his own homeland, Solzhenitsyn's work was smuggled to the West, was translated, became a best-seller, and led to the author's expulsion from Soviet territory in 1974. The three published volumes were based on letters, documents, and the experiences of 227 eyewitnesses, including those of the author, who spent eight years in the camps.

History. Soviet labor camps were first established by Vladimir Lenin, leader of the Russian Communists during the revolution, to reeducate and punish enemies of the Communist Party. After Lenin's death in 1924, Joseph Stalin took power and sent millions of Soviet citizens to the camps for "crimes against the state." In a chapter called "The History of Our Sewage Disposal System," Solzhenitsyn explores Stalin's legal and ethical motivations for carrying out a reign of terror that lasted from 1927 to the dictator's death in 1953. Under the Soviet constitution, written by the dictator himself, any "counterrevolutionary" activity was punishable by ten years of slave labor and even death. Any actions "injurious to the military might" of the Soviet Union, any "intention" to do injury, and any "attempt to weaken state power" could get a citizen thrown into the Gulag. Other crimes included attempts at armed rebellion, providing aid to the "international bourgeoisie" or capitalist class, espionage, suspicion of espionage, and contacts "leading to suspicion to engage in espionage," including more easily witnessed criminal acts such as "subversion of industry, transport, and trade" by failing to achieve and produce as much as was expected of loyal citizens. One could also be punished for failing to denounce people that one suspected of having committed any of these crimes. Solzhenitsyn received an eight-year sentence for violating the law against weakening the state by criticizing its leaders. He had criticized Stalin's military leadership in a "private" letter to a fellow army officer, but since all mail was opened and read by secret police agents, nothing was truly private. The Communist judge sent Solzhenitsyn to a labor camp in Siberia. While in the Gulag, he heard many stories of suffering, death, and other horrors, and he pledged to write about those experiences so that they would never be forgotten.

Ethical Principles. Inside the camps, the most vicious criminals were in charge. According to Stalinist ethics, political prisoners had no human rights because they were inferior beings and enemies of the state. Refusal to obey orders or attempts to avoid work meant immediate death. Millions died from twenty-hour days in gold mines or in clearing forests in 60-degrees-below-zero weather. Inmates were not expected to survive, so they were fed inadequate, miserable food, frequently nothing more than watery potato or "fish" soup and a moldy crust of bread once a day.

The camps were built and maintained according to the ethics of pure force. Stalin's word became law and his only motive became increasing his own power. "To choose one's victims, to prepare one's plans minutely, to slake an implacable vengeance, and then to go to bed . . . there is nothing sweeter in the world," he wrote. The methods of force that

he used included torture and psychological terror. The only way to avoid immediate death at the hands of the police was to confess to everything and to submit to the absolute power of the torturers. Stalinist ethics were based on one principle: Stalin and the Party were right, and everything else was wrong. Even children as young as twelve could be executed for crimes against the state, usually upon no more proof than a confession elicited after the child had been subjected to days of continuous questioning, without sleep, in an isolated cell.

The ethics of the Gulag inmates demanded the destruction of all human feeling and trust. Survival depended upon finding meaning in circumstances that evoked only horror, hatred, and degradation. Yet, as Solzhenitsyn discovered, many inmates did survive. He attributed survival inside the camps to a prisoner's strength of character before he entered the system. The people who surrendered and died or became informers were those who "before camp had not been enriched by any morality or by any spiritual upbringing." Survival demanded a "steadfast faith" in the human spirit or in some religious ethic. People who had found meaning in life before becoming victims of the terrorists could put up with the worst conditions, while those without a philosophy of life surrendered to despair and died horrible deaths. For Solzhenitsyn, this was the lesson of the Gulag: Know how to live and you will survive any conditions within or without the camps.

—*Leslie V. Tischauser*

See also Lenin; Soviet psychiatry; Stalin, Joseph.

BIBLIOGRAPHY

Bullock, Alan. *Hitler and Stalin: Parallel Lives.* New York: Alfred A. Knopf, 1992.

Conquest, Robert. *The Great Terror: Stalin's Purge of the Thirties.* New York: Macmillan, 1968.

_____. *Kolyma: The Arctic Death Camps.* New York: Viking Press, 1978.

Fireside, Harvey. *Soviet Psychoprisons.* New York: W. W. Norton, 1979.

Medvedev, Roy A. *Let History Judge.* Rev. and exp. ed. Edited and translated by George Shriver. New York: Columbia University Press, 1989.

Solzhenitsyn, Aleksandr I. *The Gulag Archipelago, 1918-1956: An Experiment in Literary Investigation.* Translated by Thomas P. Whitney. 3 vols. New York: Harper & Row, 1974-1978.

Tucker, Robert C. *Stalin in Power: The Revolution from Above, 1928-1941.* New York: W. W. Norton, 1990.

Hadîth

Type of ethics: Religious ethics
Date: Beginning early in the Islamic era, c. seventh century
Associated with: Islamic law (*sharî'a*) and ethics
Definition: Traditions of the life and sayings of the Prophet Muhammad
Significance: The actions and decisions of Muhammad are seen as exemplary in Islamic ethics and are, in many traditions, legally binding in those instances in which there are not specific Qur'ânic injunctions

The first source of ethical guidance in Islam is the Qur'ân and its exegesis. One text, however rich, cannot supply guidance in the particulars of all matters, though, and so great importance usually is placed on the traditions of the actions and statements (way of life, or *sunna*) of the Prophet Muhammad. The importance of *hadîth* is further grounded in Qur'ân 33:21, which enjoins the faithful to look to Muhammad's example for guidance. There is a broad range of subjects of *hadîth*, from those which have or are alleged to have mystical import, to those concerned with proper worship, to those which deal with the most everyday matters such as manner of dress.

There has also been a broad range of approaches to the use of *hadîth*. In many Islamic legal traditions, *hadîth* is second only to the Qur'ân in authority and is legally binding. Very often, it is seen as ethically regulative, especially in matters of worship but not always in more mundane matters. There has also been persistent critique of the use of *hadîth* as innovative or unreliable, although such critique tends to be a minority position.

The question of which *hadîth* to accept as authentic became a central concern in Islamic legal and ethical thought because the *hadîth* could determine the community's acceptable range of behavior. Thus arose the science of analysis of isnâd, the chain of transmission of *hadîth*, in which the authenticity and accuracy of each stage of the transmission is examined. The major collections of *hadîth* were assembled in the ninth century, with the collections by Abû 'Abdallâh Muhammad al-Bukhârî and Abû al-Husayn Muslim ibn al-Hallâj most often accepted as authoritative. The elections of *hadîth* were at the core of the curriculum at many of the medieval *madrasas* (roughly equivalent to modern colleges). The importance of *hadîth* was also a major impetus to serious, scholarly research into history in the Islamicate world, since the soundness of the chain of transmission of *hadîth* cannot be determined without accurate facts about the history of the transmitters.

Many Sufis often employ controversial *hadîth* with less concern for *isnâd* than for transcendent or mystical meaning of the *hadîth*. Ibn 'Arabî, for example, reported the *hadîth* that God had revealed to Muhammad that God was a hidden jewel, who created the world so that He could be known. Ibn 'Arabî then argued against the independent reality of the phenomenal world, which is merely a mirror of God.

See also Islamic ethics; Muhammad al Mustafâ; *Sharî'a;* Sufism.

al-Hallâj, al-Husayn ibn Mansûr (c. 858, al-Bayda, west of Shiraz, Iran—Mar. 26, 922, Baghdad, Iraq): Mystic

Type of ethics: Religious ethics
Achievements: Author of *Kitâb al-Tawâsîn*; his execution is a focal point for much of later Sufism
Significance: Central to the development of Sufism

Al-Hallâj has often been called the martyr of mystical love, because he paid the highest price for his devotion to loss of the ego in pure, unconditional love of God. His burning desire for extinction of the self is reflected in his verse, "Kill me, oh, my trustworthy friends." He is best known for proclaiming, in a state of mystical ecstasy, *"anâ'l-haqq."* Al-haqq literally means "the truth" (often in the sense of 'true reality'), but is also one of the names of God. *Ana'* is the first-person singular pronoun. This led many to interpret al-Hallâj as a pantheist (reading anâ'l-haqq as "I am God"), which led to his particularly gruesome execution. Al-Hallâj's surviving works, and the work of Louis Massignon (*The Passion of Hallâj*), make clear that the charge was false. Al-Hallâj's calm and steadfastness in love of God throughout his execution ensured his later role in much of Sufism as a martyr. Following his execution, most of his disciples fled from Iraq to the more tolerant northeast, where they energized Khurasani and Central Asian Sufism.

See also al-Rûmî al-Balkhî, Maulânâ Jalâl al-Dîn; Sufism.

Hammurabi's code

Type of ethics: Legal and judicial ethics
Date: Established between 1792 and 1750 B.C.E.
Associated with: Hammurabi, king of Babylon
Definition: Compiled by the great king, Hammurabi's code consisted of 282 specific laws regulating the social and economic behavior of the people of his kingdom
Significance: The code was one of the earliest and most thorough attempts in history to set up a harmonious social order based on individual rights backed by the gods and the state

Hammurabi (ruled c. 1792-1750 B.C.E.) was the sixth king of an Amorite (Semitic) dynasty ruling over the city-state of Babylon and one of the most important rulers of ancient times. He united all the city-states of Mesopotamia under his rule and, in time, created a huge empire. As an effective, pragmatic administrator, he desired to establish order by setting up standardized rules of moral conduct and ensuring that people would accept decisions made by courts rather than seek to avenge wrongs on the spur of the moment without restraint.

History. In order to establish a uniform system of justice and create something approaching universal law applicable to varying cultures from formerly independent city-states, Hammurabi used existing laws and court decisions, and he added new laws as different situations arose. Earlier Mesopotamian law codes, antedating Hammurabi's code by one to three centuries, indicate that the great Babylonian king consulted precedent and that his code rested on a widespread ancient Near Eastern legal tradition. Three previous Near Eastern codes are the Code Of Ur-nammu (founder of the third dynasty of Ur c. 2060 B.C.E.); the Code of Lipit-Ishtar (c. 1870 B.C.E.); and the Laws of Eshnunna (promulgated c. nineteenth century B.C.E.)

Inscription. After all the laws and judgments had been collected, they were inscribed on several stelae, which were set up in public in various cities of the empire. Officials were appointed by the king to mete out the prescribed penalties to violators of the law.

A single copy of the Code of Hammurabi was first discovered in the winter of 1901-1902 at Susa, the capital of ancient Elam. The recovered stele is an eight-foot-tall block of black diorite. The upper part displays a relief, or carving, depicting Hammurabi receiving the commission to write the law from the god of justice, the sun god Shamash. This commission provided significant legitimization of the code by showing the world that the gods were behind the establishment of the code and that they desired, as well as expected, mortals to behave according to its principles.

There is no hint in the code itself, however, of the concept of *imitatio dei* (the requirement to be holy because God is holy) as the rationale for moral behavior.

The inscription on the stele was divided into three parts: a prologue, the code itself, and an epilogue at the bottom of the stone slab. The epilogue added extra incentive for obedience by reinforcing the promise of rewards to those who obeyed the laws and punishment to those who disobeyed.

Ethical Principles. Hammurabi proclaimed that he issued his code on divine authority in order to "establish law and justice in the language of the land, thereby promoting the welfare of the people." The main ethical principle upon which the code rested was that "the strong shall not injure the weak." Individuals were not permitted to take the law into their own hands.

An important consideration for modern interpreters of the code, however, centers on how one defines such terms as "justice" and "injury to the weak." One striking feature of the code is that it was not strictly egalitarian in its application of punishments; the law differed according to the social status of the offender. Aristocrats were not punished as harshly as commoners, and commoners were not punished as harshly as slaves. Still, slaves had rights and received some protection under the law.

The code also rested on the conviction that punishment should fit the crime. Like the Law of Moses in ancient Israel, Hammurabi's code employed the *lex talionis*, "an eye for an eye, and a tooth for a tooth," and it may be the oldest law code in the ancient Near East to prescribe this system. It operated, however, only among equals. An aristocrat who destroyed the eye of a commoner or slave could pay a fine instead of losing his own eye. As long as the criminal and victim shared the same social status, however, the latter could demand exact retribution.

In an attempt to guarantee a fair trial and a just verdict, the code forbade a judge to change his verdict once a decision had been rendered. Any judge who did so was heavily fined and deposed. There were no public prosecutors in Hammurabi's day, so individuals brought their own complaints before the court and produced supporting documentation or witnesses. In cases of murder, the accuser had to prove the defendant guilty. Any accuser who failed to do so was put to death! This severe measure was designed to prevent frivolous, groundless cases from clogging the courts and wasting the time of defendants.

Hammurabi's code displays an understanding of the difference between accidental deed and malicious intent, but it does not seem to attach to this principle the same importance afforded it by the later Mosaic code.

Civilization and Moral Continuity. Hammurabi's code addressed what it considered to be unethical behavior in a wide variety of situations, demonstrating a significant moral continuity between ancient and modern civilization. The concept of strict accountability is evident in all the laws.

The code mandated consumer protection. Merchants and businessmen had to guarantee the quality of their goods and services. No one was exempt. A house builder whose careless work resulted in the collapse of a house and the death of its inhabitants was himself put to death. A merchant who tried to increase the interest rate on a loan forfeited the entire loan amount. A surgeon whose patient died during an operation was executed. A surgeon whose patient lost an eye during treatment had his fingers cut off—a punishment that no doubt proved inconvenient to his future career.

Crime was a serious problem in Mesopotamian urban life, so the code ordered that exacting measures be taken against criminals. Burglars caught in the act were put to death on the spot. Anyone caught looting a burning building was thrown into the fire. Such penalties were intended to stamp out crime as well as limit the cycle of violence that sometimes resulted from private vengeance.

Hammurabi's code gave careful attention to marriage and family relationships. Proved adultery with a married woman incurred the death penalty for both participants. The wife was expected to be rigorously faithful, and the husband had virtually absolute power over his household. By the standards of the time, however, certain "rights" of women were set forth in this code for the first time. Husbands who abused their wives without cause had to pay a penalty in silver. If a wife proved herself innocent of charges of adultery, she could take her dowry and leave her husband.

Influence. There is debate over how often, if ever, the penalties and provisions of Hammurabi's code were actually carried out. Contemporary legal documents are scanty and silent on the issue, but there is no question that the code greatly influenced the behavior of the civilizations and the people of the Near East long after the fall of Babylonia. It provided the backdrop against which Moses revealed the law to Israel. The Law of Moses contains many similarities and parallels to Hammurabi's code. While it was not the first law code in history, the Code of Hammurabi was the most comprehensive in the world until the Byzantine Emperor Justinian ordered the compilation of the *Corpus Juris Civilis* about 550 C.E.   —*Andrew C. Skinner*

See also Capital punishment; Criminal punishment; Due process; Ethical monotheism; Jewish ethics; Magna Carta; Moses; Ten Commandments.

BIBLIOGRAPHY

Cook, Stanley A . *The Laws of Moses and the Code of Hammurabi.* London: A. and C. Black, 1903.

Driver, Godfrey R., and John C. Miles, eds. *The Babylonian Laws.* 2 vols. Oxford: Clarendon Press, 1952.

Harper, Robert F., ed. *The Code of Hammurabi, King of Babylon About 2250 B.C.* Chicago: University of Chicago Press, 1904.

Hoare, Frederick R. *Eight Decisive Books of Antiquity.* Freeport, N.Y.: Books for Libraries Press, 1969.

Martin, W. J. "The Law Code of Hammurabi." In *Documents From Old Testament Times,* edited by David Winton Thomas. New York: Harper, 1961.

Mendenhall, George E. *Law and Covenant in Israel and the Ancient Near East.* Pittsburgh: Biblical Colloquium, 1955.

Hare, Richard Mervyn (b. Mar. 21, 1919, Backwell, near Bristol, Somerset, England): Philosopher

TYPE OF ETHICS: Modern history

ACHIEVEMENTS: Author of *The Language of Morals* (1952), *Freedom and Reason* (1963), *Applications of Moral Philosophy* (1972), *Moral Thinking* (1981), *Essays in Ethical Theory* (1989), and *Essays on Political Morality* (1989)

SIGNIFICANCE: Hare offers a prescriptivist analysis of moral judgments without wishing to sacrifice their normative force

Hare's moral theory, called "universal prescriptivism," is based on the idea that moral judgments are universalizable prescriptions. Like the noncognitivist, he stresses the commending or evaluating function of value statements. Therefore, at least part of what it means to say "*x* is right" is "*x* is to be commended," or "one ought to do *x*." Hare also thinks, however, unlike the noncognitivist, that moral statements are meant both to guide choices through a veiled appeal to universal principles and to assert on rationally testable grounds that something is the case. He agrees with G. E. Moore that naturalistic theories are fallacious but differs in his account of the reason for this. Hare's work is one of the most eclectic efforts in contemporary moral philosophy, for his view has certain definite affinities with utilitarianism (in the idea that the basic human good is to maximize rational preferences that embody prescriptions), with existentialist ethics (in his suggestion that one makes a "decision of principle" when one chooses a particular action), with Kantian ethics (in connection with his universalizability thesis), and with emotivism (in his focus on the logic of the language of morals). On the practical side of moral philosophy, Hare shows an unusual philosophical interest in problems related to moral education and moral decision making.

See also Cognitivism and noncognitivism; Existentialism; Kantian ethics; Metaethics; Moore, G. E.; Prescriptivism; Universalizability; Utilitarianism.

Hasidism

TYPE OF ETHICS: Religious ethics

DATE: Mid-eighteenth century

ASSOCIATED WITH: Hasidism's Polish founder, the Baal-Shem-Tov (1700-1760), born Israel ben Eliezer

DEFINITION: A form of emotional Jewish mysticism that originated in eighteenth century Poland and spread rapidly throughout eastern Europe and Russia; Hasidism was influenced by the interpretive system of the Kabbala

SIGNIFICANCE: As the focus of rabbinical Judaism grew increasingly intellectual during the eighteenth century, the Baal-Shem-Tov preached a joyous, simple devotion to God

The Baal-Shem-Tov's relatively uncomplicated message of joyful worship appealed to the predominantly uneducated peasant populations of eastern Europe. Many Jews abandoned the rabbinical, intellectual traditions of Talmudic study to embrace Hasidism's emotionalism. Hasidism stressed God's mercy, the goodness inherent in human beings, the universality of God leading to the spiritual unity of God and humanity, and the joyfulness of religious experience, which frequently found expression in music and dance. Despite the opposition of Talmudists who, in 1781, pronounced Hasidism heretical, the popularity of the anti-intellectual movement peaked in the early nineteenth century. While less numerous in the twentieth century, Hasidic communities remain an active force in modern Judaism, and Hasidism has broader influence in both the Jewish and gentile worlds principally through Hasidic com-

Lubavitcher Hasidim celebrate Hanukkah in New York City. (Frances M. Roberts)

posers, artists, and philosophers, including, notably, composer Ernest Bloch (1880-1959) and Yiddish writer Isaac Bashevis Singer (1904-1991). Through the works of philosopher Martin Buber (1878-1965), Hasidism has also influenced twentieth century life, notably, through the adoption of Buber's system of collective farming known as the *kibbutz*.

See also Buber, Martin; *I and Thou*; Jewish ethics; Kabbála.

Hate

TYPE OF ETHICS: Personal and social ethics
DATE: First given philosophical significance by the Greek philosopher Empedocles in the fifth century B.C.E.
DEFINITION: Personal or social antipathy toward others arising from real or imagined injuries, or from racial, ethnic, political, or religious differences
SIGNIFICANCE: A primary cause of conflict between individuals, classes or ethnic groups, and nations

Most people understand hate, or hatred, as an emotion felt by one individual for another that is characterized by animosity and sometimes is accompanied by the desire to see the hated person suffer. This highly personal understanding of hate is, however, relegated almost entirely to lay persons; scholars have given it not only moral but also metaphysical, sociological, psychological, and criminological significance.

For the Greek philosopher Empedocles, hate was a metaphysical reality, one of two forces of change in the universe, the other being love. Empedocles explains all natural objects in terms of four basic material elements—fire, earth, air, and water—which combine and decombine in a cyclical process of production and decomposition. Love is responsible for the attraction between elements and for whatever order and stability the universe possesses. Love is in constant conflict with hate, its cosmic opposite. As the cycle of change unfolds, love is superseded by hate in its turn, and disorder and decay appear in direct proportion to the hate unleashed by the progression of this cycle. The universe is the scene of constant creation and destruction as the dyadic conflict between love and hate proceeds.

Baruch Spinoza gives hate a prominent place in his *Ethics* as a fundamental emotion and determinant of human behavior. People love what arouses joy in them, while they hate what arouses sorrow; likewise, one loves the person who "affects with joy a thing which we love" but hates him if "we imagine that he affects it with sorrow." Love and hate, the respective responses to joy and sorrow, are psychological constants in the deterministic natural order of which humans are a part, acting as the determinants of the nature of all relationships with others, whether they be individuals, classes of individuals, or entire nations. So strong are these emotions that one may hate an entire class or nation of people because one of its members has done one an injury. Hatred induces "anger," the desire to injure those one hates; when one's hatred and anger toward others are mutual and result in an injury being done to one, one develops the desire for vengeance against those who have injured one. Hatred also exists in other forms—"indignation," hatred of those who injure others, and "envy," hatred of another's good fortune.

For Friedrich Nietzsche, hate exists primarily as *ressentiment* (resentment), the vengeful, jealous hatred that reveals the weakness of those who perceive their own self-respect to be threatened by their superiors. The early Christians resented the Romans because of their paganism and their power. Resentment is what was directed by the "herd," the masses of nineteenth century Europeans, who were bound to one another by mediocrity and conformity, against the noble individual who dared to be different, who determined for himself what his values would be, and who used the life-giving energy provided by his animal instincts to create a superior life characterized by the mastery of those instincts. Consequently, resentment of others, according to Nietzsche, is beneath the dignity of the noble man; if he does experience hatred, it spends itself quickly and is over before it "poisons" him. Hatred festers in the souls of the weak and powerless, who spend whatever creative energies they possess cultivating plans for revenge.

The Nietzschean view of hatred as a psychosocial phenomenon is reflected in the attitudes of twentieth century thinkers, who have made it the object of not only philosophical reflection but also psychological, sociological, and criminological research. Samuel Tenenbaum, in *Why Men Hate*, adopts a distinctly Nietzschean view of hatred: "Hate warps and stultifies the soul. It consumes the individual and fills him with suspicion and distrust. . . . The world becomes a giant conspiracy, where men and women, instead of living normal lives, connive and plot." The twentieth century has seen hatred erupt as animosity toward various racial, ethnic, and religious groups, often culminating in open warfare.

Jeffrie Murphy, in *Forgiveness and Mercy*, acknowledges several varieties of hatred: simple hatred, which is dislike for someone for some "non-moral objectionable quality," such as being a bore; moral hatred, which consists of hatred of someone because of the person's association with an immoral cause, such as Nazism; and, finally, malicious hatred, which consists of the desire to injure another for the purpose of gaining some competitive advantage. Only the last variety of hatred is morally objectionable, but Murphy also argues for the existence of "retributive hatred." Retributive hatred is hatred that is motivated by justifiable anger over an unjustifiable wrong, for which the wronged party rightfully expects and is entitled to some form of retribution. No matter how justifiable it is, however, Murphy does not favor acting upon retributive hatred. Moral humility demands that one recognize one's own limitations of knowledge and virtue, lest one's hatred drive one to excessive vengeance. In addition, retribution is often either impossible or too costly, and one's own moral decency imposes constraints upon one's desire for revenge. For these reasons, although retributive hatred is a proper response to a genuine wrong, it can be dangerous and should be subjected to "reflective restraint."

—Barbara Forrest

See also Bigotry; Cruelty; Hitler, Adolf; Racial prejudice; Racism; Revenge; Violence.

BIBLIOGRAPHY

Berrill, Kevin T., and Gregory M. Herek, eds. *Hate Crimes: Confronting Violence Against Lesbians and Gay Men*. Newbury Park, Calif.: Sage, 1992.

Hamm, Mark. *American Skinheads: The Criminology and Control of Hate Crime*. Westport, Conn.: Praeger, 1993.

Kaufmann, Walter, ed. "Empedocles." In *Thales to Ockham*. Vol. 1 in *Philosophic Classics*. Englewood Cliffs, N.J.: Prentice-Hall, 1968.

Murphy, Jeffrie G., and Jean Hampton. *Forgiveness and Mercy*. New York: Cambridge University Press, 1988.

Nietzsche, Friedrich. *On the Genealogy of Morals*. Edited by Walter Kaufmann. New York: Vintage Books, 1967.

Spinoza, Benedictus de. *Ethics*. Edited by James Gutman. 1949. Reprint. New York: Hafner Press, 1974.

Tenenbaum, Samuel. *Why Men Hate*. New York: Beechhurst Press, 1947.

Head Start

Type of ethics: Children's rights
DATE: Founded 1965
ASSOCIATED WITH: Office of Child Development; Administration for Children, Youth and Families; and the Office of Economic Opportunity
DEFINITION: The Economic Opportunity Act of 1964 provided for the establishment of the Head Start Program, a comprehensive developmental program of educational, social, and health services for economically disadvantaged children
SIGNIFICANCE: Head Start was conceived as a program designed to break the cycle of poverty by enabling children from low-income families, as well as their parents, to improve their intellectual development, self-esteem, and physical and mental health

Head Start emerged as a social-action program at a time in history when social and political forces, as well as intellectual traditions in the social sciences, had begun to focus on the problem of poverty. The program developed out of the civil rights era and the War on Poverty, the revival of scientific interest in the role of the environment in human development, and the design of educational-intervention efforts for economically disadvantaged children. The lines of its development converged amid an alliance of child-development experts and social policymakers, under whose auspices Head Start grew from an idea to a proposal and finally to an active program. Head Start provides a broad range of services to children and their families. Play, group, and individual activities with both direct and indirect instruction are offered, as well as medical and dental care.

See also Society for the Prevention of Cruelty to Children, American (ASPCC).

Health care allocation

TYPE OF ETHICS: Bioethics
DATE: Since the 1970's
DEFINITION: The distribution of resources to health care, to specific areas within a health care system, and to certain individuals in need of a particular procedure
SIGNIFICANCE: Raises questions of societal obligation and individual rights to health care, as well as values inherent in specific treatment choices

The allocation of scarce resources is an issue that is central to every political party, every government, every organization and company. Whether to allocate 2 percent or 10 percent of the gross national product to health care, rather than defense, or education, or housing, or whatever other particular need is most pressing, is a decision that is central to the type of government and the values of those in power. Once this health care budget is established, the choices become progressively less global and more oriented to the individual. While the values inherent in the original budget decisions can still be found, they are often less visible than the physician's personal opinions or the assessment of medical or social utility found in specific allocation decisions.

Macroallocation Versus Microallocation. Given a set amount of resources—funding, personnel, equipment, and so forth—to dedicate to health care, a particular system must then determine the allocation to different areas of health care. Preventive medicine, health care promotion, research, medical education, the physical establishment of new facilities, and technological advancement all compete for resources with the treatment of injured and ill patients. This system-wide form of decision making, along with the initial allotment of resources, is usually considered macroallocation. By contrast, the individual determination of eligibility for a given procedure or selection of patients for treatment is called microallocation. Allocation in general is inextricably linked with societal and individual perceptions of justice. A society that considers inequities in health to be unjust, as opposed to unfortunate, will allocate a proportionately greater amount of its resources to mitigate health differences. If a society deems it a pity but not unjust that some people enjoy better health care than others, it will not feel such a societal obligation to correct these differences.

Theories of Justice. There are several theories of justice with regard to health care, some of which overlap, and others of which have different possible methods of distribution applicable to the overall concept. Three of the most general theories are the egalitarian, the libertarian, and the utilitarian.

Egalitarian Theories. Egalitarian theories of distributive justice advocate either the equal distribution of goods and resources to all people or the provision of equality of opportunity in obtaining care. Equal distribution has the major drawback of ignoring differences in health needs in a given population. Treatment appropriate to a reasonably healthy individual would

Type of system	Industrialized countries		Developing countries		Very poor countries		Oil-producing countries	
METHODS OF MICROALLOCATION OF MEDICAL RESOURCES IN SELECTED COUNTRIES								
Entrepreneurial Health Care Systems	United States	Medical prognosis; Ability to pay	Philippines	Medical prognosis; Ability to pay	Ghana	Ability to pay		
			South Korea	Employment status*; Ability to pay				
			South Africa	Ability to pay; Proximity to health care facility; Race				
			Thailand	Ability to pay; Proximity to health care facility				
Welfare-oriented Health Care Systems	Australia	Proximity to health care facility; Queuing can be avoided by ability to pay	Turkey	Ability to pay; Proximity to health care facility	India	Employment status*; Social status/ class; Proximity to health care facility		
	Belgium	Employment status*; Ability to pay						
	Canada	Queuing; First come, first served						
	Japan	Employment status*						
Comprehensive Health Care Systems	Italy	Queuing can be avoided by ability to pay; Need and ability to pay***	Israel	Need**			Kuwait	Need**
	New Zealand	Type of impairment ****					Saudi Arabia	Need**
	Norway	Need and ability to pay***						
	Sweden	Medical prognosis; Age						
	United Kingdom	Medical prognosis; Age; Queuing can be avoided by ability to pay; visibility of illness; social factors *****						
Socialist Health Care Systems			Cuba	Need**	China	Employment status*; Social status/ class		

*	Also insurance class
**	Current funding is adequate to pay for all needed services
***	Approved drugs and services available on need; other services depend on ability to pay
****	Injuries take priority over diseases
*****	Social factors affecting recovery; for example, family support

certainly not be appropriate for someone with diabetes or epilepsy, much less kidney disease or cancer.

Equality of opportunity emphasizes distribution of resources in accordance with what each individual needs in order to function at a "normal" level. "Normal" in this sense is usually taken to mean that level that is species-typical. The assumption made is that no one should be denied medical treatment on the basis of undeserved disadvantaging properties such as social class, ability to pay, or ill health. The questions of what constitutes need and what constitutes an undeserved disadvantage, however, make the application of this theory very complicated. For example, does a person with a disfiguring feature, such as a birthmark or scar, *need* to have plastic surgery in order to enjoy the same social benefits as others?

Problems also arise when a particular system does not have enough resources to provide for all. At what level is it necessary to provide these resources? The range goes from the treatment of common diseases and injuries to the provision (at least theoretically) of heart and liver transplants to anyone who shows a need.

Libertarian Theories. Libertarian theories of justice, when applied to health care, challenge the concept of health care as a right. If something is a right, society has an obligation to provide it to all people. Libertarians contend that justice results from allowing a society to participate in voluntary exchanges to obtain what they need; in other words, a free-market economy. A person is entitled to health care in proportion to his or her ability to exchange that which has been rightfully acquired. Any redistribution of resources, such as taxing the wealthy to fund health care for the poor, is inherently unjust, because it denies the wealthy the right to use that which they fairly gained. These theories tend to ignore the fact that extreme wealth can give the rich the power to deny the poor the ability to exercise their rights freely.

Utilitarian Theories. Utilitarian theories focus on the principle of the greatest good for the greatest number. If *x* dollars could provide food for fifty starving people or open-heart surgery for one, that money should be devoted to food. The problem with utilitarian systems in general is that they tend to lose sight of the individual.

Two-tiered Systems. Many health systems today are the result of a two-tiered philosophy. On the first level, a minimum of health care is provided to every person in a society, without regard to wealth or class. On the second level, goods are obtained on the basis of individual decisions and ability to pay. This is usually considered a fair compromise in the United States' health care system. Debate will always exist regarding where the tiers separate, and what decent minimum should be provided for all.   —*Margaret Hawthorne*

See also Justice; Libertarianism; Utilitarianism.

BIBLIOGRAPHY

Beauchamp, Tom L., and James F. Childress. *Principles of Biomedical Ethics.* 3d ed. New York: Oxford University Press, 1989.

Garrett, Thomas M., Harold W. Baillie, and Rosellen M. Garrett. *Health Care Ethics: Principles and Problems.* Englewood Cliffs, N.J.: Prentice-Hall, 1989.

Greenberg, Warren. *Competition, Regulation, and Rationing in Health Care.* Ann Arbor, Mich.: Health Administration Press, 1991.

Roemer, Milton I. *National Health Systems of the World.* New York: Oxford University Press, 1991.

Veatch, Robert M., ed. *Medical Ethics.* Boston: Jones & Bartlett, 1989.

Hedonism

TYPE OF ETHICS: Theory of ethics
DATE: From antiquity
ASSOCIATED WITH: Epicureans, Jeremy Bentham, and others
DEFINITION: Maintains that pleasure is intrinsically desirable and the highest good
SIGNIFICANCE: Hedonism, with its claim that pleasure is the highest good, is a perennial candidate among moral theories

Ethical Hedonism/Psychological Hedonism. Hedonism, from the Greek *hēdonē*, meaning "pleasure," is the ethical theory that maintains that pleasure is the highest good. The term is also sometimes used to refer to the psychological theory that all human behavior is motivated by the desire for pleasure or the avoidance of pain. This second view is properly designated "psychological hedonism" (a theory about the way things *are*) in order to distinguish it from ethical hedonism (a theory about the way things *ought* to be or about what things are good). Jeremy Bentham, in his *Introduction to the Principles of Morals and Legislation* (1789), espoused both of these views when he wrote, "Nature has placed mankind under the guidance of two sovereign masters, pain and pleasure. It is for them alone to point out what we ought to do, as well as to determine what we shall do."

Many ethical hedonists point to the purported fact of psychological hedonism in support of their ethical position, but is it a fact? Only if an adherent admits the possibility of a human action *not* being motivated by the desire for pleasure can psychological hedonism be a factual or empirical claim. Since the adherent cannot admit an exception because he or she equates motivation with desire for pleasure, however, then the claim is not a factual one; it provides no information.

Philosophers opposed to hedonism have noted that persons who deliberately seek pleasure fail to find it, while, paradoxically, they find pleasure when they seek other things as their end and obtain those other things. This has been called the "hedonistic paradox."

Further, if psychological hedonism is true and all human actions *are* motivated by a desire for pleasure, then the ethical hedonist's admonition that people *ought* to seek pleasure is unnecessary.

Ethical hedonists also support their position in other ways. One of these is by claiming that hedonism is true by definition. Examples of this approach can be seen in John

Locke, who defined "good" as that which "is apt to cause or increase pleasure," and in Baruch Spinoza, who defined it as "every kind of pleasure." John Stuart Mill has also been said to define "good" as the "desirable" and the "desirable" as what is desired, which happens to be pleasure.

This definitional approach is criticized by those who insist that there are things other than pleasure that are intrinsically good and some pleasurable things that are intrinsically bad. Further, G. E. Moore has argued that such attempts to define "good" commit the naturalistic fallacy; that is, they purport to define the indefinable, especially to define a moral entity in terms of a natural one.

Aristippus and the Cyrenaics. Aristippus (c. 435-c. 386 B.C.E.) founded an early school of hedonism known as the Cyrenaics, so named for his birthplace, Cyrene. This Greek philosopher, a follower of Socrates, claimed that one's way of life should be one of as much pleasure as possible, even if followed by pain, but that one should maintain control of the pleasures as opposed to being a slave to them.

Epicurus and the Epicureans. The Greek philosopher Epicurus (341-270 B.C.E.), on the contrary, maintained that practical wisdom weighs pleasures against pains, choosing pleasures that are accompanied by the least pain and pains that are accompanied by the most pleasure. Mental pains were especially to be avoided. The Epicureans believed that the fear of death or fear of the gods could be dispelled by the study of atomistic philosophy.

Jeremy Bentham. The English philosopher Jeremy Bentham (1748-1832) supported his quantitative hedonism (that is, one that claims that all pleasures are sensual and hence comparable quantitatively) with a "hedonistic calculus." The calculus allows the computation of specific values of pleasures in terms of their intensity, duration, certainty (how likely to be realized), propinquity (nearness or remoteness), fecundity (likelihood of being followed by more pleasures), purity (chance of *not* being followed by pain), and extent (number of persons affected by them). Bentham provided his students with a ditty to help them remember:

Intense, long, certain, speedy, fruitful, pure—
Such marks in pleasure and pain endure.
Such pleasures seek if private be thy end;
If it be public, let them wide extend.

John Stuart Mill. John Stuart Mill (1806-1873), Bentham's young friend and protégé, rejected Bentham's quantitative hedonism for a qualitative one, holding that pleasures differ in kind as well as quantity. "Human beings have faculties more elevated than the animal appetites, and when once made conscious of them, do not regard anything as happiness which does not include their gratification." "Better to be a human being dissatisfied than a pig satisfied; better to be a Socrates dissatisfied than a fool satisfied. And if the fool, or the pig, are of a different opinion, it is because

they only know their own side of the question. The other party to the comparison knows both sides."

Mill, in his attempt to raise hedonism from the level of a "pig philosophy," may have espoused a view that abandoned hedonism. If the amount of pleasure ceases to be definitive, and if the only judges qualified to make qualitative judgments must exercise "higher-than-pig" judgments, it seems that Mill is guilty of either circular reasoning (with respect to his choice of judges) or of introducing criteria other than pleasure as being intrinsically good (in his appeal to qualitative differences).

Conclusion. Hedonism has enjoyed a long and continuing history in varied forms. As long as philosophers and others ask questions about what is intrinsically valuable or good, hedonism will no doubt remain a popular answer.

—*Ruth B. Heizer*

See also Bentham, Jeremy; Cyrenaics; Epicurus; Intrinsic good; Mill, John Stuart.

BIBLIOGRAPHY

Broad, C. D. *Five Types of Ethical Theory*. London: Routledge & Kegan Paul, 1930.

Frankena, William K. *Ethics*. Englewood Cliffs, N.J.: Prentice-Hall, 1963.

Sahakian, William S. *Systems of Ethics and Value Theory*. New York: Philosophical Library, 1963.

Taylor, Paul W. *Principles of Ethics: An Introduction*. Encino, Calif.: Dickenson, 1975.

Wheelwright, Philip. *A Critical Introduction to Ethics*. New York: Odyssey, 1935.

Hegel, Georg Wilhelm Friedrich (Aug. 27, 1770, Stuttgart, Württemberg—Nov. 14, 1831, Berlin, Prussia): Philosopher

TYPE OF ETHICS: Politico-economic ethics

ACHIEVEMENTS: Author of *Phänomenologie des Geistes* (1807; *The Phenomenology of Spirit* [also known as *The Phenomenology of Mind*], (1931); *Wissenschaft der Logik* (1812-1816; *Science of Logic*, 1929); and *Encyclopädie der Philosophischen im Grundrisse* (1817; *Encyclopedia of Philosophy*, 1959)

SIGNIFICANCE: Believed that freedom, the goal of world history, is realized in the state, not in the individual

The political and ethical dimensions of Hegel's philosophy grow out of his understanding of *mind* and *dialectic*.

Mind. In Hegel's philosophy, mind (*Geist* in the original German) is defined as "absolute consciousness." "Absolute," in this usage, means "absolved" of relations to objects outside consciousness. As absolute consciousness, mind is consciousness of consciousness itself. The opposite concept, "relative consciousness," is so called because it relates to objects outside itself.

Logic and Dialectic. Logic is traditionally understood to consist of unchanging rules that govern thought. Hegel's logic is different. He sees the rules of thought in terms of mind as absolute consciousness.

Absolute consciousness, as Hegel understands it, is a process in which mind continuously realizes itself, moving from potential to actual self-knowledge. The laws of thinking that concern Hegel are the steps in this process. The resulting "logic in motion" is called *dialectic*. It proceeds in a three-step pattern that repeats itself, in spiral form, on ever-higher levels of consciousness.

Hegel's philosophy is known for its difficulty, but anyone who has entered a hall of mirrors can retrace the basic steps of Hegelian dialectic:

Step 1: I become conscious of some object outside my consciousness, for example a stone.

Step 2: I become conscious of my consciousness of the stone.

Step 3: I become conscious of self-consciousness in my consciousness of my consciousness of the stone.

Step 1 (repeated at higher level): The consciousness of self-consciousness just realized becomes the new object of my consciousness. What was consciousness is now distanced from it, no longer consciousness in immediacy, but its object.

Step 2 (repeated at higher level): I become conscious of my consciousness of this new object.

Step 3 (repeated at higher level): I become conscious of self-consciousness in my consciousness—and so on.

The self-consciousness that keeps appearing in this spiral of self-reflection is occasioned by an object outside consciousness (the stone) but is not dependent on it as a specific object. Any other object would do as well. This self-consciousness is also occasioned by an individual "I" but is not dependent on any specific person. Anyone will do. Consider the hall of mirrors. Each individual sees his or her own image reflected, but the pattern of reflection, determined by the mirrors and the unchanging laws of optics, remains the same no matter who is reflected. Consciousness of consciousness always has the same form and content, regardless of which specific individual happens to be "reflecting."

The pure self-consciousness that appears in this spiraling reflection is the phenomenon Hegel refers to when he speaks of mind. The highest level of consciousness occurs when the individual becomes conscious of the universal aspect of this pure self-consciousness, recognizes it as mind, and realizes that this recognition is not so much an individual recognizing mind as it is mind recognizing itself. The individual is an instrument used by mind to come to itself.

The spiraling steps of Hegelian dialectic have names. The first is called "thesis," the second "antithesis," and the third "synthesis." The movement continues as the synthesis becomes the thesis of the next dialectical round.

Thesis and antithesis oppose but do not destroy each other. The synthesis conserves their opposition at a higher level of awareness, in which the condition that held thesis and antithesis together in opposition is discovered to be their underlying unity.

This can be illustrated by reconsidering the stone used above as an example of an object "outside consciousness."

This object is not left behind in the dialectical steps that follow, but is taken along. What changes is the perception of its nature. At a higher level—from the point of view of absolute consciousness—it is seen that the stone did not enter consciousness through the individual's sense perception, but was in the consciousness from the beginning. What really happened—again, from the Hegelian position of absolute consciousness—is that mind concealed or negated itself with respect to the stone so that the individual consciousness could discover it as an object outside its own consciousness, thus occasioning the dialectical process of progressively greater self-consciousness, as which mind comes to itself.

Ultimately, for Hegel, nothing is truly outside absolute consciousness: All that is, is mind. This is the fundamental tenet of German idealism.

Philosophy of History. The dialectical process in which mind realizes itself as absolute consciousness is, for Hegel, not an abstract principle. It is the meaning of history.

Hegel's concept of history is Eurocentric. He believed that history realized itself more perfectly in Europe than elsewhere. Western history begins, Hegel taught, with the Judaic teaching of monotheism, the first awakening of mind to its own oneness. The rest of Western history is interpreted as a process in which mind achieves progressively higher levels of self-awareness, finally approaching full development in Germanic civilization, Hegel believed, the first to completely exclude slavery and conceive of universal freedom.

Political Philosophy. The bloody revolution in France and slavery in the United States convinced Hegel that democracy would not lead to freedom. History, as the increasing self-realization of mind, must lead to ever-increasing freedom—not for individuals to pursue happiness, but for the state to institute laws integrating culture, religion, and politics into a rational, harmoniously functioning national unity.

Hegel's philosophy influenced conservative and revolutionary political theory. Hegel used it to justify the Prussian State (a centralized monarchy, enlightened, perhaps, in comparison to others, but an authoritarian regime with police-state tactics all the same). His philosophy also, however, provided the background for the theory of socialistic democracy developed by Karl Marx. —*Ted William Dreier*

See also *Phenomenology of Spirit.*

BIBLIOGRAPHY

Heidegger, Martin. *Hegel's Phenomenology of the Spirit.* Bloomington: Indiana University Press, 1988.

Inwood, N. J. *A Hegel Dictionary.* Cambridge, Mass.: Blackwell, 1992.

Kaufmann, Walter, ed. *Hegel: Texts and Commentary.* Garden City, N.Y.: Doubleday, 1966.

Olson, Alan M.: *Hegel and the Spirit.* Princeton, N.J.: Princeton University Press, 1992.

Walsh, W. H. *The Philosophy of Hegel.* New York: Garland, 1984.

Heidegger, Martin (Sept. 26, 1889, Messkirch, Germany—May 26, 1976, Messkirch, West Germany): Philosopher

TYPE OF ETHICS: Modern history

ACHIEVEMENTS: Author of *Sein und Zeit* (1927; *Being and Time*, 1962)

SIGNIFICANCE: Saw the basic questions of ethics as wholly subsumed in the ontological query "What is the meaning of *being*?"

Heidegger studied at the University of Freiburg under Edmund Husserl, whom he succeeded as professor of philosophy in 1928. For Heidegger, the basic questions of ethics, such as "What is good?" and "What is it that one ought to do?" are subsumed in the prior ontological question "What is?" Heidegger found, however, that the traditional formulation of the ontological question "What is being?" failed to explicitly thematize the dimension of *meaning*. The leading question in Heidegger's thought, as opposed to traditional ontology, became "What is the *meaning* of being?" The Greek words used by Plato and Aristotle that are commonly translated as "being" and "truth," had meanings, Heidegger showed, that had been neglected by the tradition. The Greek words for being (*einai*, *ousía*) mean "presence"; the central word for truth (*aletheia*) means "discovered." Discovering these early meanings for being and truth marked the beginning, not the end, of Heidegger's search for the meaning of being. Why was "presence" the first name for being in the Western tradition? Had not this tradition always taught that "presence" was a mode of time, and that being was essentially timeless, outside the real of history? Is time the original and necessary context for asking about the meaning of "being?" This final question was the question of *Being and Time*, Heidegger's first major publication.

See also Existentialism; Sartre, Jean-Paul.

Heroism

TYPE OF ETHICS: Personal and social ethics

DEFINITION: The human virtue that enables one to confront fear-evoking danger and difficulty with reason and resolution and act in a way that benefits the general well-being of others or the common good

SIGNIFICANCE: Heroism is good, noble, virtuous, and beautiful; it is an ethical act in which the essential part of a person's being prevails against the less essential

Anxiety and Heroism. Anxiety is a primary human emotion and is existential; that is, it is a basic, normal part of existence. Anxiety is a pervasive, unpleasant feeling of apprehension, menace, threat, or fear that is produced by a dangerous or difficult situation. Thus, heroism involves the consideration of the advantages and disadvantages of several alternative courses of action that may present a danger or threat to the self and that elicit anxiety and the subsequent choice of a course of action that confronts that danger and anxiety, that is indicated by practical reason, and that promotes the general well-being and common good.

Heroism and Courage. Courage is widely listed as a synonym for heroism. Courage is certainly a necessary component of heroism; heroism could not exist without courage. Yet courage lacks a component that heroism possesses. Courage has been called a "self-regarding" virtue because it may primarily serve the purpose of the courageous individual. Heroism, in contrast, represents an "other-regarding" virtue because the welfare of others and the common good are the central considerations. Heroic acts are noble and virtuous in that they are necessarily intended to promote the general well-being of others or the common good. Because heroic individuals can be relied on when the common good is threatened, heroism is a highly prized commodity.

One can exhibit acts of courage without being heroic, however, if the act does not positively affect the general well-being or the common good. A criminal who executes a daring bank robbery, may be courageous but certainly not heroic.

The Components of Heroism. Several conditions are necessary for an act to be considered heroic (see James D. Wallace, 1973):

1. A particular act is performed rather than another.

2. That act is perceived as risky or dangerous; that is, it threatens the actor's well-being. To perceive no peril in what one does is not to act heroically. The peril may involve injury or death, economic loss, loss of prestige, or ostracism or censure. The act is likely to be accompanied by feelings of fear or anxiety. The danger involved in performing the act may be formidable enough that most people in that situation would find it difficult to perform the act.

3. The actor believes that performing the act is worth the risk that it entails.

4. The decision to perform the act is reasoned and rational. The act is not foolish or reckless. If a person plays Russian roulette but then backs down because he is afraid to pull the trigger, this is not acting cowardly. Fear has saved that person from folly.

5. The actor is not coerced into performing the act by the threat of a punishment that is more feared than is performing the act. If a soldier is ordered to destroy an enemy tank or be summarily executed, and he destroys the tank, his is not an act of heroism.

6. The act has a purpose or goal that is believed to be important and worthwhile. Heroism is a virtue that is exhibited through goal-directed behavior that benefits the general well-being and public good.

Cowardice. Cowardice is the opposite of heroism. The coward is beset by excessive fears that prevent him or her from acting on his or her practical reasoning in situations in which it would be reasonable to act. The coward therefore avoids actions that he or she might otherwise perform and is thus incapacitated.

Heroism and Ethics. Heroism is an ethical act of the highest order. Through it, the actor affirms the essence of his or her being and serves humanity in the face of elements that conflict with this affirmation of the self. Since the beginning of the history of Western thought, heroism has been considered to be noble and virtuous. In Plato's *Republic*, it is the unreflective quest for that which is noble. Aristotle believed that heroism led a person to act for the sake of what was noble, which was the purpose of virtue. Heroism is to be praised because it allows one to achieve one's potential.

Thomas Aquinas continued this thought. Aquinas often refers to courage, but it would seem that what he says describes heroism rather than courage. For Aquinas, courage/heroism was a strong mind that was able to overcome whatever blocked the path to the highest good. Courage/heroism, along with wisdom, temperance, and justice, were the four cardinal virtues.

These themes carry through to contemporary times. A noteworthy example is F. Scott Peck's famous book *The Road Less Travelled* (1978). To Peck, life is difficult because it continually presents problems that demand confrontation and solution. This fact can make life a painful process, but this is also where life achieves meaning. Problems call forth and create the resources that allow people to solve them. By solving problems, people grow mentally and spiritually. In order to foster the growth of the human spirit, it is necessary to solve problems. When this process incorporates actions that serve the common good and general welfare, human mental and spiritual growth attain high levels.

—*Laurence Miller*

See also Courage.

BIBLIOGRAPHY

Cofer, Charles N., and Mortimer H. Appley. *Motivation: Theory and Research*. New York: Wiley, 1964.

Moran, Charles. *The Anatomy of Courage*. Boston: Houghton Mifflin, 1967.

Peck, M. Scott. *The Road Less Travelled*. New York: Simon & Schuster, 1978.

Tillich, Paul. *The Courage To Be*. New Haven, Conn.: Yale University Press, 1952.

Wallace, James D. "Cowardice and Courage." In *Studies in Ethics*. Oxford, England: Basil Blackwell, 1973.

Hindu ethics

TYPE OF ETHICS: Religious ethics

DATE: 2,000 B.C.E. to present

DEFINITION: Derived from the Hindu religion and Vedic texts and mainly practiced in India, Hindu ethics supply a complete moral code to good behavior

SIGNIFICANCE: Postulates the interdependence of personal and spiritual well-being by emphasizing that right action leads to liberation from the need to be reincarnated

Hindu ethics is based on the premise that ethical life is the means to spiritual freedom. Hinduism has behind it a philosophy that is not only a religious doctrine but also a complex web of moral principles. It offers practical guidance, rites, prayers, festivals, and social structures, all aimed at securing social harmony and God realization (direct experience of God). Since God is the embodiment of truth and justice, right action is the means to experience God realization.

Background. Hindu ethical philosophy has been evolving for four thousand years. Its sources are the Vedas, the oldest known literature in the world. Hindu ethics differ from much of Western ethics in perceiving a direct link between social and spiritual life. Greek philosophy is a "pursuit of truth for its own sake," based on reason and the intellect, in which the wise, the lawmakers, direct people to create a moral society. Hindu ethics is primarily concerned with right action as a means to religious fulfillment.

Vedic Literature. The Vedas are hymns and rites that glorify the Vedic gods, who are representatives of the divine power of the Supreme God. They deal with personal issues, universal concerns, and theories of creation. Hinduism teaches that reading or listening to the Vedas enlivens the connection between the individual and the Creator. Vedic writings are fundamental to Hinduism.

The *Ṛg Veda* and the *Atharva Veda*, the hymns of the Vedas, are quite specific about actions that can be seen as righteous and moral. Honesty, rectitude, friendship, charity, nonviolence (*ahiṁsā*, a moral principle that attracted considerable attention when it was espoused by Mohandas K. Gandhi), truthfulness, modesty, celibacy, religious worship, and purity of heart are all listed as desirable and necessary virtues. The *Ṛg Veda* also cites bad intentions, swearing, falsehood, gambling, egoism, cruelty, adultery, theft, and injury to life as sinful actions.

The Bhagavad Gītā, a central text of Hinduism, gives very specific ethical advice. It consists of a dialogue between Lord Kṛṣṇa, an incarnation of one of the three major gods of Hinduism, and Arjuna a noble warrior. Arjuna is unable to go into battle, because his opponents are also his kinsmen. He appeals for help. Lord Kṛṣṇa states that the correctness of the action should be the primary consideration when doing something. He advises Arjuna always to act in accordance with dharma (ethical living). Furthermore, he says, if Arjuna could experience the divine, his actions would spontaneously reflect absolute wisdom and purity, and therefore all dilemmas would evaporate. In this instance, the right course of action is to fight.

There are numerous stories in Hindu literature about morality and how best to behave. Deities advise and guide. In the *Rāmāyana*, the hero, Rāmā, is the embodiment of dharma, teaching the values of obedience, respect, and duty. The later writings of the Purāṇas, specific to Shiva and Viṣṇu, advocate worship and devotion as a means to liberation.

The Upaniṣads embrace the concept of God as an impersonal Supreme Being, Brahman. The verses state that divinity is everywhere, that the individual is indeed Brahman itself—"*Ahum Brahmmasmi*" ("I am the totality"). The

Upaniṣads reaffirm that *mokṣa* ("liberation") is the goal of life. To achieve liberation, it is necessary to follow a strict code of ethical and spiritual discipline. Austerity, chastity, silence, and solitude lead the soul forward, while self-restraint, self-sacrifice, and compassion free one from greed and anger.

Social Life. Hinduism asserts that, just as there is order in the universe, human life can be equally harmonious and orderly. Human society should express the divine purpose. All people belong to social castes determined by character, natural inclinations, and function in society. These castes consist of *brāhmins* (the wise), *kṣatriyas* (the warriors), *vaiśyas* (the merchants), and *śūdras* (the laborers). Within each caste the individual can achieve perfection, and the whole system promotes spiritual progress.

Hindu thought divides life into four twenty-five-year stages, giving specific ethical advice for each. The first stage is for learning, the second is the time of the householder, the third is a time for meditation and study of the scriptures, and the final stage is one of renunciation of the outer life. This sequence should ultimately end in liberation, the goal of life. Members of a family should always follow their duty. Children should respect and obey their parents' wishes. Husbands and wives ought to be loving and respectful, advising their families and teaching moral values.

Many Hindu practices derive from the belief that Brahman, the divine, is all-pervading. If divinity is everywhere, then everything must be respected. Nature is not separate from humanity; therefore, animals are revered, particularly cows. Gandhi defended this as a "practical application of the belief of oneness, and therefore the sacredness of life."

The importance given to spiritual life in India creates the interdependence between the mystical and the practical. Ethics is central to Hinduism, improving the present and ultimately freeing the individual from the cycle of birth and death. Hinduism, with all its complexity, has unity at the heart of its diversity. Its goals are to raise the quality of life, ensure spiritual awakening, and fulfill humanity's destiny.

—*Catherine Francis*

See also Ahiṁsā; Bhagavad Gītā; Gandhi, Mohandas Karamchand; God; Moral status of animals; Nonviolence.

BIBLIOGRAPHY

Berry, Thomas. *Religions of India*. New York: Bruce Publishing, 1971.

Mahesh Yogi, Maharishi. *On the Bhagavad-Gita*. Harmondsworth, England: Penguin Books, 1969.

Radhakrishnan, Sarvepalli. *Eastern Religions and Western Thought*. New York: Oxford University Press, 1959.

Sharma, I. C. *Ethical Philosophies of India*. Edited and revised by Stanley M. Daugert. New York: Harper & Row, 1970.

Shearer, Alaister, and Peter Russell, trans. *The Upanishads*. New York: Harper & Row, 1978.

Hippocrates (c. 460 B.C.E., Greek island of Cos—c. 377 B.C.E., Larissa, in Thessaly): Physician

TYPE OF ETHICS: Bioethics

ACHIEVEMENTS: Traditionally regarded as the author of the Hippocratic treatises, including the Hippocratic oath

SIGNIFICANCE: The medical-ethical treatises of the Hippocratic Corpus both created a standard of professional etiquette for the physician and formed the basis of the Western tradition of medical ethics

Hippocrates. Although Hippocrates has traditionally enjoyed the reputation of being the father of Greek medicine, little is known about him. Only a few references to him by contemporary or near-contemporary authors exist. According to these references, he came from the island of Kos, off

Hippocrates (Library of Congress)

the southwestern coast of Asia Minor, and was a teacher of medicine. He was a member of the Asclepiads, a family or guild of physicians that traced its origins to the god of healing, Asclepius. For reasons that are not clear, Hippocrates came to be idealized after his death, and he became the subject of an extensive biographical tradition. Four short biographies exist, together with a collection of spurious epistles that are attributed to Hippocrates. They assert that Hippocrates learned medicine from his father, who was also a physician. He is supposed to have taught medicine in Cos (which later boasted a famous school of medicine) and to have traveled throughout Greece, dying at an advanced age at Larissa in Thessaly, in northern Greece. Many of the biographical details recorded in these later works must be regarded as legendary.

A large collection of about sixty medical treatises, the Hippocratic Corpus, came to be attributed to Hippocrates after his death. Most were written in the late fifth or fourth centuries B.C.E., but some were composed much later. The works are anonymous and are marked by differences in style. Even in antiquity it was recognized that not all of them were genuine, and attempts were made to determine which were written by Hippocrates. There is no reliable tradition that attests the authenticity of any of the treatises, and the internal evidence is inconclusive. Most modern scholars believe that none of them can be attributed with certainty to Hippocrates.

Hippocratic Medical Ethics. The ethical or deontological treatises of the Hippocratic Corpus (*The Physician, Precepts,* and *Decorum,* dates unknown) constitute the earliest writings on medical etiquette. They define the professional duties that should be expected of Greek physicians. Most of these principles of etiquette are the product of common sense. They recognize that certain types of conduct are inherently detrimental to the practice of medicine. Physicians should behave in a manner that will add dignity to their profession. Thus, they should look healthy and not be overweight. They should be gentlemen, cheerful and serene in their dealings with patients, self-controlled, reserved, decisive, and neither silly nor harsh. They should not engage in sexual relations with patients or members of their households. They are to be sensitive to the fees they charge, should consider the patient's means, and should on occasion render free treatment. Many of these precepts are meant to preserve the reputation of the physician, which (in the absence of medical licensure) was his most important asset in building and maintaining a medical practice.

The Hippocratic Oath. The best-known, though most puzzling, of the Hippocratic writings is the so-called Hippocratic oath. The oath is characterized by a religious tenor. It begins with an invocation of the healing gods Apollo and Asclepius and includes a pledge to guard one's life and art "in purity and holiness." It is divided into two parts: the covenant, which is a contract between the teacher and his pupil; and the precepts, which defines the duty of the physician to his patients. The oath prohibits, among other things, dispensing a deadly drug, performing an abortion, and practicing surgery (or at least lithotomy).

Several stipulations of the oath are not consonant with ethical standards prevalent elsewhere in the Hippocratic treatises, while some practices prohibited by the oath (induced abortion, euthanasia, and surgery) were routinely undertaken by Greek physicians. It is difficult, moreover, to find a context in which to place the oath. Although it was traditionally attributed (like the

other Hippocratic treatises) to Hippocrates, it is anonymous. It has been dated as early as the sixth century B.C.E. and as late as the first century of the Christian era (when it is first mentioned). Most scholars assign it to the fifth or fourth century B.C.E., making it roughly contemporaneous with Hippocrates. It has been suggested that it was administered to students who were undertaking a medical apprenticeship, but there is no evidence that it ever had universal application in the Greek world. Greek and Roman physicians were not required to swear an oath or to accept and abide by a formal code of ethics. To be sure, ethical standards appear in the Hippocratic Corpus, but no one knows how widespread these standards were among medical practitioners in antiquity. The oath appealed to Christian physicians, however, who in late antiquity took over its precepts and infused them with new meaning. It was later adopted by Christian, Jewish,

---

Tʜᴇ Hɪᴘᴘᴏᴄʀᴀᴛɪᴄ Oᴀᴛʜ

I will look upon him who shall have taught me this Art even as one of my parents.

I will share my substance with him, and I will supply his necessities, if he be in need.

I will regard his offspring even as my own brethren, and I will teach them this Art, if they would learn it, without fee or covenant.

I will impart this Art by precept, by lecture, and by every mode of teaching, not only to my own sons but to the sons of him who has taught me, and to disciples bound by covenant and oath, according to the Law of Medicine.

The regimen I adopt shall be for the benefit of my patients according to my ability and judgment, and not for their hurt or for any wrong.

I will give no deadly drug to any, though it be asked of me, nor will I counsel such, and especially I will not aid a woman to procure abortion.

Whatsoever house I enter, there will I go for the benefit of the sick, refraining from all wrongdoing or corruption, and especially from any act of seduction, of male or female, of bond or free.

Whatsoever things I see or hear concerning the life of men, in my attendance on the sick or even apart therefrom, which ought not to be noised abroad, I will keep silence thereon, counting such things to be as sacred secrets.

---

and Moslem physicians as a covenant by which physicians could govern their practices.

There have been a number of attempts to explain away the problem passages of the oath or to attribute it to an author whose views represented those of a group that lay outside the mainstream of medical ethics as described in the Hippocratic Corpus. The most notable is the attempt by Ludwig Edelstein to demonstrate that the oath originated in the

Pythagorean community. Parallels can be found outside Pythagoreanism for even the most esoteric injunctions of the oath, however, and its Pythagorean origin cannot be said to have been conclusively proved.

The Influence of Hippocratic Ethics. The medical-ethical treatises of the Hippocratic Corpus have exercised great influence on the formulation and development of Western medical ethics. In establishing not only guidelines for the physician's deportment but also standards of professional obligation, they created both the basis of Greek medical ethics and an ideal of what the physician ought to be. Even in the rapidly changing field of bioethics, their influence continues to be felt to the present day.

—Anne-Marie E. Ferngren and Gary B. Ferngren

See also Bioethics; Medical ethics; Physician-patient relationship.

BIBLIOGRAPHY

Carrick, Paul. *Medical Ethics in Antiquity: Philosophical Perspectives on Abortion and Euthanasia.* Boston: Reidel, 1985.

Edelstein, Ludwig. *Ancient Medicine: Selected Papers of Ludwig Edelstein.* Edited and translated by Owsei Temkin and C. Lilian Temkin. Baltimore: The Johns Hopkins University Press, 1967.

Hippocrates. *Hippocrates.* Translated by W. H. S. Jones. 4 vols. Cambridge, Mass.: Harvard University Press, 1923-1931.

Sigerist, Henry E. *Early Greek, Hindu and Persian Medicine.* Vol. 2 in *A History of Medicine.* Edited by Ludwig Edelstein. New York: Oxford University Press, 1961.

Temkin, Owsei. *Hippocrates in a World of Pagans and Christians.* Baltimore: The Johns Hopkins University Press, 1991.

Hiring practices

TYPE OF ETHICS: Business and labor ethics

ASSOCIATED WITH: Organizational development, integrity tests

DEFINITION: Techniques used by organizations to attempt to hire honest, ethical employees

SIGNIFICANCE: The cost of employee theft is $40 billion dollars annually; 30 percent of all business failures are caused by dishonesty

Hiring right is a company's first and best defense against business abuses and potential disaster, but it is difficult to implement hiring practices that screen out people whose honesty and integrity are less than acceptable, because the elements of privacy, cost, and time must be taken into account.

What Is Intrusive? What Is Not? At one end of the spectrum are those who feel that many hiring practices are intrusive and violate individuals' right to privacy. Robert Ellis Smith, editor of *The Privacy Journal*, opposes integrity testing and credit checks in all hiring situations. He recommends verifying data on résumés and relying on closer supervision and auditing in the posthiring probation period.

Author and consultant Tom Peters agrees with Smith regarding integrity testing but favors lengthy, in-depth interviewing. Still others, such as Paul Brooks, claim that in-depth interviews often involve invasion of privacy. Brooks, a psychologist with Reid Psychological Systems, which develops integrity tests, counters that in-depth interviews are frequently more intrusive and less effective than is testing, and that they are inherently biased.

In-depth interviews take management's time and can be costly. Some companies believe that the best method is to use a series of in-depth interviews—as many as a dozen, including some with potential peers. Background checks also can be costly. Some companies hire private investigation firms for executive recruitment and for other positions in sensitive areas.

The hiring practices that are utilized must be effective. The challenge is to juggle cost and effectiveness while maintaining respect for the candidates' privacy.

Integrity Tests. In 1988, the Federal Employee Polygraph Protection Act was passed, which prohibits preemployment polygraph testing in the private sector. Federal, state, and local governments and firms doing sensitive work with the Department of Defense, the FBI, or the CIA, however, may use them. Pencil-and-paper "integrity tests" are permitted and have grown in popularity. Although some states have specific laws regarding integrity tests, the general rule is that an employer cannot target any specific group for integrity testing. The tests are especially popular with hotel chains, hospitals, retailers, and fast food restaurants.

Integrity tests are designed to measure an applicant's attitudes toward a wide range of counterproductive behaviors. Based on established psychological theories about attitude and behavior relationships, they seek to discover attitudes that predict honesty and integrity. Two major producers of integrity tests—Reid and London House—explain the testing approach as follows: "Past research has shown that the 'typical' employee-thief is: 1) more tempted to steal; 2) engages in many of the common rationalizations for theft; 3) would punish thieves less; 4) often thinks about theft-related activities; 5) attributes more theft to others; 6) shows more loyalty to other thieves; and 7) is more vulnerable to peer pressure to steal than is an honest employee." Integrity tests attempt to measure those attitudes.

Before using a particular integrity test, a company must evaluate its validation and reliability. Validation studies should conform to standards developed by the Association of Personnel Test Publishers (APTP) and the American Psychological Association (APA). Generally, a validity study consists of administering the test to job applicants, recording their attitudes, and, later, tracking behavior on the job. Validity studies measure "false positives" and "false negatives."

Reliability factors consist of two measures: consistency, based on whether all who failed the test answered the questions consistently; and the test-retest factor, consistency in response when people retake the test in the future.

Proponents of integrity tests believe that traditional screening techniques are comparatively time-consuming and have not produced evidence of high predictive accuracy regarding theft. The APTP states, however, that traditional employment interviews have been reported in the scientific literature as having very low levels of validity.

Both the APTP and the APA have ethics guidelines and guidelines for the development, validation, and use of integrity tests, which are designed to protect the rights of employers and job applicants alike.

Background Checks. As many as 30 percent of job applicants lie on their résumés. A background check should certainly begin with the résumé. References also should be checked. In some situations, it is appropriate to check police records and credit reports. The following criteria hold for background checks: the information must be germane to doing the job effectively and ethically; the job applicant should understand why such a check is necessary and should give permission for it; and the employer should abide by state law.

Michael Maddaloni, writing in *Security Management* (September, 1990), recommends using different types of background checks for various levels of employees. Executives and those in sensitive positions should have detailed background checks on past employment, credit checks, criminal record checks, and verifications of education and detailed references. Other positions require less investigation, in varying degrees.

Interviewing. During the interview, the interviewer should acquaint the interviewee with the values of the organization, discussing what the company stands for and what level of integrity is expected. If the employer has an ethics program or an ethics code, that code should be discussed. It is also advisable for an employer to have several people, especially potential peers of the job candidates, interview those candidates.

Effective hiring practices that do not infringe upon the rights of job candidates require a substantial investment in time and effort on the part of the employer. When such practices are utilized, however, job candidates, employees, and companies all benefit in the long run.

—*Kathleen D. Purdy*

See also Cheating; Lying; Privacy; Professional ethics.

BIBLIOGRAPHY

DeGeorge, Richard T. "Workers' Rights and Duties Within a Firm." In *Business Ethics*. New York: Macmillan, 1990.

Jones, John W., and David W. Arnold. "Integrity Testing: The Debate Continues." *Security Management* 35 (January, 1991): 71.

Lawler, Edmund O. "A Question of Character." *Business Marketing* 75, no. 7 (July, 1990).

Maddaloni, Michael V. "You Can't Afford Not to Do It." *Security Management* 34, no. 9 (September, 1990).

Hiroshima and Nagasaki, bombing of

TYPE OF ETHICS: Military ethics

DATES: August 6, 1945; August 9, 1945

ASSOCIATED WITH: The United States' decision to drop atomic bombs, developed during the war, on the Japanese

DEFINITION: The dropping of single atomic bombs on these two Japanese cities resulted in incomprehensible death and misery, forever obliterating the distinction between civilian and soldier

SIGNIFICANCE: Because of their unparalleled destructive power, atomic weapons have forced humankind to reconsider the uses of science in war and the ethics of atomic warfare

The unleashing of atomic weapons on Hiroshima and Nagasaki profoundly shaped the nature of international relations in the post-World War II era. These bombs, so lethal and used only twice in history, have forced humankind to examine critically the nature of modern warfare, especially within the context of "just war theory."

Brief History. The development of the atomic bomb by the United States government during World War II is generally regarded as one of the greatest technological and engineering achievements of modern times. What was particularly noteworthy about the atomic bomb was the sheer scale of its ability to kill and devastate. Drawing upon the insights and efforts of the most brilliant physicists, mathematicians, and chemists of the nineteenth and twentieth centuries, scientists and engineers were able to liberate the cataclysmic power of the atom, harnessed in a single bomb that had the destructive impact of almost twenty kilotons of conventional explosives.

Ethical Context. Using a weapon of such magnitude raised serious ethical issues, especially as they related to an idea that can be traced back to the ancient Greeks: just war theory. Considered down through the centuries by such thinkers as Aristotle, Cicero, and Saint Augustine, just war theory involves the essential notion that war, though intrinsically evil, can be justified morally if certain conditions exist. Although the theory consists of several components, particularly relevant to the bombing of Hiroshima and Nagasaki are the ideas of proportionality and discrimination.

Proportionality refers to the idea that a warring power should not use any means over and above what is necessary to achieve victory. By late July, 1945, according to most military historians, Japan's military situation was desperate. From March onward, Japan suffered almost daily bombings by American B-29 bombers armed with incendiary bombs. Such bombing runs resulted in almost 190,000 deaths from fires and asphyxiation in six major Japanese cities. In addition, the U.S. Navy was taking steps to implement a full-scale blockade of Japan. After the war, the U.S. Strategic Bombing Survey maintained that such tactics would have eventuated in Japan's surrender by approximately November 1, 1945, without the use of atomic bombs.

Those who advocate that the dropping of atomic bombs was a proportional response in the war make two points. First, while the bomb that fell on Hiroshima immediately killed

78,000 people and the one that fell on Nagasaki killed 70,000 people, the use of the bombs prevented a large-scale land invasion of the Japanese mainland. While estimates vary, some speculate that total American and Japanese casualties would have approached one million because of the determination of the Japanese people. Hence, the atomic bombings, while gruesome, actually prevented more deaths in the immediate future. A second line of argument holds that given the conduct of the Japanese military during the war—for example, the surprise attack on the U.S. fleet at Pearl Harbor, the Bataan "Death March," and the brutal treatment of Allied prisoners-of-war—the dropping of the atomic bombs was a morally justifiable and proportional action.

The concept of discrimination maintains that in the conduct of war, every effort should be made to prevent civilians from suffering the potentially brutal fate of soldiers. The force unleashed by an atomic bomb is such that it devastates everything in its wake: combatants, noncombatants, military outposts, hospitals, crops, and so forth. It must be pointed out, however, that the distinction between civilians and soldiers already had been blurred by more conventional weapons already in use during the war. The fires ignited by incendiaries dropped from American planes over Hamburg and Dresden resulted in tens of thousands of civilian deaths. Moreover, Dresden was bombed although it was primarily a cultural center, not a significant military target. Similarly, toward the end of the war, German V-1 and V-2 rockets fell indiscriminately throughout England, resulting in thousands of civilian casualties.

Also apropos of discrimination, some military strategists argued that since many civilians were engaged in supporting a nation's capacity to wage war through their jobs as farmers, machinists, seamstresses, and technicians, the distinction between civilian and military no longer obtained. Indeed, British pilots were explicitly ordered to bomb working-class neighborhoods during their runs in order to reduce both the Nazi war effort and civilian morale. In the conduct of the war, "civilian" deaths increasingly became a regrettable, but accepted, component of modern warfare.

Ethics of Science. After the detonation of atomic bombs, the avowed neutrality of science was questioned. For example, because something is theoretically and practically possible (nuclear fission), especially something so powerful as atomic energy, must it be developed? If scientists develop something novel, can they guarantee control of its use? After witnessing the awesome energy released in the first explosion of a nuclear device in New Mexico in July, 1945, some of the scientists working on the bomb's development argued that Japanese officials should be privy to a demonstration of the bomb's power rather than experiencing an actual bombing. Their views were summarily dismissed by the military as impractical.

A final aspect of the ethics of the atomic bombing of Hiroshima and Nagasaki concerns utilitarian logic. This model of decision making argues that people must rationally calculate the perceived costs and benefits of pursuing certain actions. From this perspective, the investment of more than $1 billion and four years of intense work by tens of thousands of workers and scientists (the bomb's costs) almost guaranteed that the bomb would be used once it was developed (its perceived benefit, shortening the war). No one could have perceived, however, the immense economic, political, and social costs associated with the Cold War after "The Bomb," and people still debate whether the decision to drop atomic bombs on Hiroshima and Nagasaki was a benefit at all. —*Craig M. Eckert*

See also Atom bomb; Military ethics; War and peace.

BIBLIOGRAPHY

Boyer, Paul. *By the Bomb's Early Light: American Thought and Culture at the Dawn of the Atomic Age.* New York: Pantheon, 1985.

Catholic Church National Conference of Catholic Bishops. *The Challenge of Peace: God's Promise and Our Response.* Washington, D.C.: Office of Public Services, United States Catholic Conference, 1983.

Gilpin, Robert. *American Scientists and Nuclear Weapons Policy.* Princeton, N.J.: Princeton University Press, 1962.

Howard, Michael, ed. *Restraints on War.* New York: Oxford University Press, 1979.

Lackey, Douglas P. *Moral Principles and Nuclear Weapons.* Totowa, N.J.: Rowman & Allanheld, 1984.

Hitler, Adolf (Apr. 20, 1889, Braunau am Inn, Austro-Hungarian Empire—Apr. 30, 1945, Berlin, Germany): Political leader

TYPE OF ETHICS: Politico-economic ethics

ACHIEVEMENTS: Dictator of Germany; initiated Holocaust against European Jews

SIGNIFICANCE: Hitler's system of thought became the predominant one in Germany and continental Europe during parts of the 1930's and 1940's; though crass and unoriginal, his theories of racial and national destiny combined to form a powerfully twisted ethic that continues to attract many people

It does little good to insist that Adolf Hitler and his Nazi party were without a system of ethics; to do so demonizes Hitler and perpetuates the unfortunate myth that the Nazi period may be explained by the German nation having temporarily lost its collective mind. The more difficult truth is that a great many German people identified a system of morality in the Nazi party that corresponded with their own.

Adolf Hitler's system of ethics was based upon the twin foundations of race and nationalism. His combination of these traditions in German political life was both of great help to him in his quest for power and of inestimable force in the drive toward the Holocaust. Believing that might made right, Hitler promoted this ethic within his party—and later his state—with a ruthless zealotry.

Origins. The variety of anti-Semitism that Hitler found in Vienna in the period of 1907 to 1913 was both populist and German nationalist—best described by the German word *volkisch*. Hitler was greatly influenced by the Mayor of Vienna, Karl Lüger, who combined vehement anti-Semitism and the political strength to dominate Viennese politics to a degree that Hitler admired. In fact, Hitler, in an uncharacteristic display of humility, described Lüger in *Mein Kampf* as the last great German born in Austria.

Another great influence on Hitler's intellectual development in Vienna was the leader of the Pan- German movement, Georg von Schönerer. Schönerer's movement appealed to Hitler on both a racial and a national level. Like Hitler, Schönerer believed that the unification of all German-speaking peoples was an imperative and blamed Germans of Jewish extraction for standing in the way of unification.

In German history, as well, there were many influences on Hitler's thought. Figures as diverse as Martin Luther, Frederick the Great, Houston Stewart Chamberlain, and, most famously, Richard Wagner contributed to Hitler's ideas of race and the destiny of the German people. Their ideas about authority, nationalism, race, and the romantic ideals of war, sacrifice, and destiny all influenced Hitler in ways that many historians have identified as seminal.

Race. Essentially, Hitler believed that the German race could only succeed if it were "pure." *Mein Kampf* is filled with statements such as "the originally creative race died out from blood poisoning." Hitler blamed the Jews for the apparent dissipation of "pure German stock," particularly in Austria, where he first was introduced to anti-Semitism. Hitler's variety of anti-Semitism differed from that of Lüger and Shönerer, though, in that Hitler insisted that religion had nothing to do with it; race, not religion, was what made Jews different and dangerous in Hitler's mind. The implications of this idea are grim. If Jews are considered dangerous because of their religion, they can at least convert. This is what happened in a great many cases previous to Hitler. If, as Hitler thought, Jews are dangerous because of their race, there can be no conversion. Extermination is the logical answer in Hitler's convoluted and hateful system of thought. Because he believed that the "parasite" of European Jewry was threatening the strength and virtue (Hitler employed a great deal of sexual imagery in his discussions on this subject) of the German nation, Hitler thought it justifiable to "eradicate the parasite."

Nationalism. The second foundation for Hitler's system of thought was nationalism. Considering himself a student of history, Hitler was influenced by a kind of skewed Hegelianism, identifying cycles of world leadership and seeing a sort of dialectical pattern of struggle and destiny in assuming that leadership. Further influenced by the Franco-German War (1870-1871) and the unification of Germany (1871), and filled with a patriotism that only an envious noncitizen can muster (Hitler was not a German citizen), Hitler came to the conclusion that it was Germany's turn to act as leader of the world. There was no room in the world for Jews, intellectuals, socialists, or liberals.

Much of the intolerance contained in Hitler's nationalism can be traced to the traditions of German Romanticism. The romantic imagery found in Hitler's anti-Semitism was also present in his thought on questions of nationalism (race and nationalism were inexorably tied in his mind). Shunning Christianity as "a religion for cowards," he saw Germany's true heritage in the pagan spectacle of the operas of Richard Wagner. The antirationalism of the Romantic period, as filtered through the German experience, served to create a religion of nationality and race in Hitler's mind, with himself as messiah (Hitler spoke at length about Providence's intentions for him), that was as compelling to the true believer as any other religion could be.

Zealotry. Hitler's religion of blood and nation was compelling to many Germans in large part because of the power it promised. The hate that Hitler felt, his dreams of dominion, could not be fulfilled without both power and an ethic that sanctioned the use of power in ways that most people would describe as morally reprehensible. Hitler worshipped power, and his system of thought relied on it heavily. On reading *Mein Kampf*, one cannot help but be struck by the number of times Hitler wrote the equivalent of "might makes right." Hitler admired the Marxists' tactics of violence and intimidation, preferring to use converted Communists as street fighters because they shared his zealotry. His greatest scorn for the liberal parties of his day concentrated on "the weakness of will inherent in parliamentary government."

Implications. Hitler and his millions of followers believed that his vision allowed, even compelled, them to shun questions of everyday ethics. His vision established a new

Hitler addressing a crowd on April 4, 1938. (Library of Congress)

system of ethics defined by race and the nation, utterly devoid of moral restraint. The outcome of this system of thought was, inevitably, the Holocaust.

—*Robert A. Willingham*

See also Anti-Semitism; Genocide; Hate; Holocaust; Nazi science; Racial prejudice.

BIBLIOGRAPHY

Bullock, Alan. *Hitler: A Study in Tyranny.* Rev. ed. New York: Harper & Row, 1962.

Fest, Joachim C. *Hitler.* Translated by Richard and Clara Winston. New York: Harcourt Brace Jovanovich, 1974.

Flood, Charles B. *Hitler: The Path to Power.* Boston: Houghton Mifflin, 1989.

Heiden, Konrad. *Der Fuehrer: Hitler's Rise to Power.* Translated by Ralph Manheim. Boston: Houghton Mifflin, 1944.

Hitler, Adolf. *Mein Kampf.* Translated by Ralph Manheim. Boston: Houghton Mifflin, 1943.

Kershaw, Ian. *Hitler.* London: Longman, 1991.

Von Maltitz, Horst. *The Evolution of Hitler's Germany.* New York: McGraw-Hill, 1973.

Waite, Robert G. L. *The Psychopathic God: Adolf Hitler.* New York: Basic Books, 1977.

Hobbes, Thomas (Apr. 5, 1588, Westport, Wiltshire, England—Dec. 4, 1679, Hardwick Hall, Derbyshire, England): Political philosopher

TYPE OF ETHICS: Enlightenment history

ACHIEVEMENTS: Author of *De Cive* (1642), *Leviathan: Or, The Matter, Form, and Power of a Commonwealth* (1651), *De Homine* (1658), and *Behemoth: The History of the Causes of the Civil Wars of England* (1682)

SIGNIFICANCE: The most prominent seventeenth century English political philosopher of state sovereignty and political absolutism, Hobbes deduced his theories of morality, including his political ethics, from a mechanistic, materialist understanding of reality

Hobbes was a proponent of natural rights and monarchical absolutism, although he was distrusted by both Cromwellian republicans and supporters of the Stuart monarchy. As a student at Magdalen College, Oxford University, Hobbes rejected the ethics and methodological perspectives of Aristotelianism, medieval Scholasticism, and Christian philosophy. The moral political philosophy expressed in Hobbes's works was grounded in the methodology of mathematical argumentation, empirical science, and secularism. Hobbes's mechanistic and materialist explanation of existence, including political ethics, was sharply criticized by seventeenth century ecclesiastical leaders for having suggested an agnostic or atheistic metaphysical foundation. In Hobbes's political philosophical works, moral behavior was scientifically explained and logically reduced to corporal matter in motion. Moral judgments were made in reference to two types of human movements or endeavors: appetites, or motions toward material objects perceived to be desirable; and aversions, or motions away from material objects perceived to be harmful. Hobbes's pessimistic interpretation of human nature, in conjunction with his "resolutive compositive" method, reduced political morality to an individual's most basic fears and passions (for example, fear of violent death and the desire for possessions). In contrast to classical Greek and medieval Christian moral political philosophy, in Hobbes's thought, reason was not the faculty that guided and constrained the passions. Knowledge (or "scientific reason") and power were the prescribed means to fulfill each individual's subjective desires. Hobbes considered ethics to be an essential field of philosophy and natural rights as the critical subject of ethics. Hobbes's political philosophical works, particularly *Leviathan*, conveyed a moral theory that was focused on the natural right of self-preservation and governmental legitimacy linked to the protection of human life. Although all people were in agreement about the critical value of self-preservation, Hobbes's ethical relativism or nominalism articulated the position that there were no universal objective or absolute moral, political, or spiritual truths. Individuals named or evaluated the moral worth of particular acts based upon the consequences of such acts to their self-interests. *Leviathan* expressed the political theory that sovereign political authority and governmental legitimacy were based on a social contract (government by "institution") or superior physical coercion (government by "acquisition"). The prescribed commonwealth was conceived as the highly centralized rule of an absolute sovereign—preferably, an absolute monarch.

See also *Leviathan*; Locke, John; Machiavelli, Niccolò; Machiavellian ethics; Social contract; *Two Treatises of Government.*

Holistic medicine

TYPE OF ETHICS: Bioethics

DATE: From antiquity

ASSOCIATED WITH: Acupuncture, herbs, homeopathy, macrobiotics, massage, natural foods, naturopathy, osteopathy, vitamins, and yoga

DEFINITION: An approach to medicine that expresses respect for the whole person by practicing health maintenance through patient education and disease curing through noninvasive procedures

SIGNIFICANCE: Advocates of holistic medicine say that it offers a more humane alternative to mainstream medical practice

Holistic health practitioners regard patients as whole persons, teaching health maintenance, offering a wide choice of cure, and freely sharing expert knowledge. Holistic practitioners accept as valid knowledge from prescientific ages, as well as psychological and spiritual knowledge which are accessible to everyone. Therefore, for the holistic practitioner, the best possible health care makes use of ancient as well as modern healing arts from a variety of cultures. It treats people as psychological and spiritual beings as well as bodies, and educates them in the care of their own psychological and physical health. Therefore, holistic health maintenance and disease curing typically involve teaching the patient actively to change habits of nutrition, exercise, and self-reflection. In contrast, mainstream medicine is based on the premise that physical science is the most authoritative field of knowledge, though it can only be understood by trained experts such as medical doctors. Therefore, the mainstream physician offers the best possible care by acting as an expert authority, dispensing diagnoses and treatments of bodily diseases with the help of new technologies that are the fruits of science.

See also Medical ethics; Medical research.

Holocaust

TYPE OF ETHICS: Human rights
DATE: 1933-1945
ASSOCIATED WITH: Adolf Hitler, Nazism, and World War II
DEFINITION: The Holocaust was Nazi Germany's planned total destruction of the Jewish people and the actual murder of nearly six million of them
SIGNIFICANCE: Exemplifies the way that racism can lead to genocide and shows that human rights should never be taken for granted

Referring to their regime as the Third Reich, Adolf Hitler and his Nazi party ruled Germany from 1933 to 1945. The Holocaust happened during those years. It was Nazi Germany's planned total destruction of the Jewish people and the actual murder of nearly six million of them. That genocidal campaign—the most systematic, bureaucratic, and unrelenting the world has seen—also destroyed millions of non-Jewish civilians. They included Gypsies (Roma and Sinti), Slavs, Jehovah's Witnesses, Freemasons, homosexuals, the mentally retarded, the physically handicapped, and the insane. The Nazis believed that their threat to the Third Reich approached, though it could never equal, the one posed by Jews.

In German, this unprecedented destruction process became known euphemistically as *die Endlösung*—the Final Solution. The Hebrew word *Shoah,* which means catastrophe, is also used to name it, but the term "Holocaust" most commonly signifies the event. That word has biblical roots. In the Septuagint, a Greek translation of the Hebrew Bible, the Hebrew word *olah* is translated as *holokauston.* In context, *olah* means that which is offered up. It refers to a sacrifice, often specifically to "an offering made by fire unto the Lord." Such connotations make "Holocaust" a problematic term for the devastation it names. The word's religious implications seem inappropriate, even repulsive, to many people, including many Jews. Still, Holocaust remains the term that is most widely used.

Nazi Germany's system of concentration camps, ghettos, murder squadrons, and killing centers took more than 12 million defenseless human lives. Between 5 and 6 million of them were Jewish, including approximately 1 million children under fifteen. Although not every Nazi victim was Jewish, the Nazi intent was to rid Europe, if not the world, of Jews. Hitler went far in meeting that goal. Although Europe's Jews resisted the onslaught as best they could, by the end of World War II two-thirds of European Jews—and about one-third of Jews worldwide—were dead. The vast majority of the Jewish victims came from eastern Europe. More than half of them were from Poland; there, the German annihilation effort was 90 percent successful. At Auschwitz alone—located in Poland, it was the largest of the Nazi killing centers—more than 1 million Jews were gassed.

How did the Holocaust happen and why? Those questions are both historical and ethical. Their implications are huge. As Elie Wiesel, Jewish survivor of Auschwitz and winner of the 1986 Nobel Peace Prize, has rightly said of Birkenau, the major killing area at Auschwitz: "Traditional ideas and acquired values, philosophical systems and social theories—all must be revised in the shadow of Birkenau."

History. Adolf Hitler became chancellor of Germany on January 30, 1933. He soon consolidated his power through tyranny and terror. Within six months, the Nazis stood as the only legal political power in Germany, Hitler's decrees were as good as law, basic civil rights had been suspended, and thousands of the Third Reich's political opponents had been imprisoned.

Emphasizing the superiority of the German people, Nazi ideology was anti-Semitic and racist to the core. The Nazis affirmed that German racial purity must be maintained. Building on precedents long-established by Christianity's animosity toward Jews, the Nazis went further and vilified Jews as the most dangerous threat to that goal. Here it is important to underscore that Jews are not, in fact, a race but a people unified by memory and history, culture, tradition, and religious observances that are widely shared. Any person of any race can become Jewish through religious conversion. Nevertheless, Nazi ideology defined Jewish identity in biological and racial terms.

German law established detailed conditions to define full and part-Jews. To cite three examples, if one had three Jewish grandparents, that condition was sufficient to make one fully Jewish. If one had only two Jewish grandparents and neither practiced Judaism nor had a Jewish spouse, however, then one was a *Mischlinge* (mongrel) first-class. A person with only a single Jewish grandparent would be a *Mischlinge* second-class. The identity of one's grandparents was determined, paradoxically, not by blood but by their membership in the Jewish religious community. Once these Nazi classifications were in effect, the identity they conferred was irreversible.

Defining Jewish identity was crucial for identifying the population targeted by the Nazis' anti-Semitic policies. Those policies focused first on segregating Jews, making their lives intolerable, and forcing them to leave Germany. Between 1933 and the outbreak of World War II in September, 1939, hundreds of decrees, such as the Nuremberg Laws of September, 1935, deprived the Third Reich's Jews of basic civil rights. When Jews tried to emigrate from German territory, however, they found few havens. In general, doors around the world, including those

NORTH BALTIC SEA

LITHUANIA

GERMANY

GERMANY

■ Stutthof

U. S. S. R.

● Bialystok

TREBLINKA ⊠

CHELMNO ⊠

● Warsaw

Lodz ■

⊠ SOBIBOR

● Lublin

Kielce ■

MAJDANEK ⊠

BELZEC ⊠

● Krakow

Lvov ●

⊠ AUSCHWITZ-
BIRKENAU

N
↑

CZECHOSLOVAKIA

HUNGARY

ROMANIA

⊠ Death Camp

● Ghetto

– – – – – Partition between
Nazi Germany and
the Soviet Union

■ Concentration Camp

Poland before 1939 partition

MAP OF THE DEATH CAMPS IN NAZI-OCCUPIED TERRITORIES

Source: Yitzhak Arad, ed., *The Pictorial History of the Holocaust* (New York: Macmillan, 1990.)

in the United States, were opened reluctantly, if at all, for Jewish refugees from Hitler's Germany.

World War II began with Germany's invasion of Poland on September 1, 1939. With the notable exception of its failure to subdue England by air power, the German war machine had things its own way until it experienced reversals at El Alamein and Stalingrad in 1942. By the end of that year, 4 million Jews had already been murdered.

As Hitler's forces had advanced on all fronts, huge numbers of Jews, far exceeding the 600,000 who lived in Germany when Hitler took control, came under Nazi domination. For a year after the war began, Nazi planning had still aimed to enforce massive Jewish resettlement, but there were no satisfactory ways to fulfill that intention. Other tactics had to be found. The Holocaust did not result from a detailed master plan that timed and controlled every move in advance. When one step reached an impasse, however, the next was always more drastic, because the Nazis did not deviate from their basic commitment: Somehow the Jews had to be eliminated.

In the spring of 1941, as plans were laid for the invasion of the Soviet Union, Hitler decided that special mobile killing units—*Einsatzgruppen*—would follow the German army, round up Jews, and kill them. In the fateful months that followed, a second prong of attack in Germany's war against the Jews became operational as well. Instead of moving killers toward their victims, it would bring victims to their killers.

Utilizing a former Austrian military barracks near the Polish town of Oświęcim, the Germans made their concentration camp of Auschwitz operational in June, 1940, when 728 Polish prisoners were transferred there. By the summer of 1941, the original camp (Auschwitz I) had been supplemented by a much larger camp at nearby Birkenau (Auschwitz II). Within the next year—along with five other sites in occupied Poland (Chelmno, Belzec, Sobibor, Treblinka, and Majdanek)—Auschwitz-Birkenau became a full-fledged killing center. Auschwitz "improved" killing by employing fast-working hydrogen cyanide gas, which suppliers offered in the form of a deodorized pesticide known as Zyklon B. Efficiency at Auschwitz-Birkenau was further improved in 1943 when new crematoria became available for corpse disposal. Optimum "production" in this death factory meant that thousands of Jews could be killed per day. When *Schutzstaffel* (SS) leader Heinrich Himmler ordered an end to the systematic killing at Auschwitz in late 1944, his reasoning was not based entirely on the fact that Russian troops were nearby. For all practical purposes, he could argue, the Final Solution had eliminated Europe's "Jewish problem."

With Hitler's suicide on April 30, 1945, and the subsequent surrender of Germany on May 7, a chapter ended, but the history and the legacy of the Final Solution continue. Everyone who lives after Auschwitz is affected by the Holocaust. Everyone, moreover, ought to be affected particularly by the ethical problems and moral challenges left in its wake.

Ethical Problems and Moral Challenges. Ethics clarifies what people should and should not do. It explores differences between what is right, just, and good and what is wrong, unjust, and evil. What Nazi Germany did to the European Jews belongs in the latter categories or nothing can. Thus, the most crucial moral problem posed by the Holocaust is that no moral, social, religious, or political constraints were sufficient to stop Nazi Germany from unleashing the Final Solution. Only when military force crushed the Third Reich did the genocide end.

David Rousset, a French writer who endured German concentration camps, understated the case, but he was surely correct when he said simply, "The existence of the camps is a warning." Two aspects of that warning are especially challenging.

First, the Holocaust warns about the depth of racism's evil. It shows that racism's destructive "logic" ultimately entails genocide. If one takes seriously the idea that one race endangers the well-being of another, the only way to remove that menace completely is to do away, once and for all, with everyone and everything that embodies it. If most forms of racism shy away from such extreme measures, Nazi Germany's anti-Semitism did not. The Nazis saw what they took to be a practical problem: the need to eliminate "racially inferior" people. Then they moved to solve it.

Consequently, the Holocaust did not result from unplanned, random violence. It was instead a state-sponsored program of population elimination made possible by modern technology and political organization. As Nazi Germany became a genocidal state, its anti-Semitic racism required a destruction process that needed and got the cooperation of every sector of German society. The killers and those who aided and abetted them directly—or indirectly as bystanders—were civilized people from a society that was scientifically advanced, technologically competent, culturally sophisticated, and efficiently organized. These people were, as Holocaust scholar Michael Berenbaum has noted, "both ordinary and extraordinary, a cross section of the men and women of Germany, its allies, and their collaborators as well as the best and the brightest."

Teachers and writers helped to till the soil in which Hitler's virulent anti-Semitism took root; their students and readers reaped the wasteful harvest. Lawyers drafted and judges enforced the laws that isolated Jews and set them up for the kill. Government and church personnel provided birth records to document who was Jewish and who was not. Other workers entered such information into state-of-the-art data processing machines. University administrators curtailed admissions for Jewish students and dismissed Jewish faculty members. Bureaucrats in the Finance Ministry confiscated Jewish wealth and property. Postal officials delivered mail about definition and expropriation, denaturalization and deportation. Driven by their biomedical visions, physicians were among the first to experiment with the gassing of *lebensunwertes Leben* (lives unworthy of life). Scientists performed research and tested their racial theories on

Jewish victims of the Holocaust. (National Archives)

those branded subhuman or nonhuman by German science. Business executives found that Nazi concentration camps could provide cheap labor; they worked people to death, turning the Nazi motto, *Arbeit macht frei* (work makes one free), into a mocking truth. Stockholders made profits from firms that supplied Zyklon B to gas people and from companies that built crematoria to burn the corpses. Radio performers were joined by artists such as the gifted film director Leni Riefenstahl to broadcast and screen the polished propaganda that made Hitler's policies persuasive to so many. Engineers drove the trains that transported Jews to death, while other officials took charge of the billing arrangements for this service. Factory workers modified trucks so that they became deadly gas vans; city policemen became members of squadrons that made the murder of Jews their specialty. As the list went on and on, so did the racially motivated destruction of the European Jews.

Short of Germany's military defeat by the Allies, no other constraints—moral, social, religious, or political—were sufficient to stop the Final Solution. Accordingly, a second Holocaust warning is the challenge that no one should take human rights for granted. To make that warning more personal, consider Hans Maier. Born on October 31, 1912, the only child of a Catholic mother and Jewish father, he considered himself an Austrian, not least because his father's family had lived in Austria since the seventeenth century. Hans Maier, however, lived in the twentieth century, and so it was that in the autumn of 1935 he studied a newspaper in a Viennese coffeehouse. The Nuremberg Laws had just been passed in Nazi Germany. Maier's reading made him see that, even if he did not think of himself as Jewish, the Nazis' definitions meant that in their view he was Jewish. By identifying him as a Jew, Maier would write later on, Nazi power made him "a dead man on leave, someone to be murdered, who only by chance was not yet where he properly belonged."

When Nazi Germany occupied Austria in March, 1938, Maier drew his conclusions. He fled his native land for Belgium and joined the Resistance after Belgium was swept into the Third Reich in 1940. Arrested by Nazi police in 1943, Maier was sent to Auschwitz and then to Bergen-Belsen, where he was liberated in 1945. Eventually taking the name Jean Améry, by which he is remembered, this philosopher waited twenty years before breaking his silence about the Holocaust. When Améry did decide to write, the result was a series of remarkable essays about his experience. In English, they appear in a volume entitled *At the Mind's Limits: Contemplations by a Survivor on Auschwitz and Its Realities.* "Every morning when I get up," he tells his reader, "I can read the Auschwitz number on my forearm. . . . Every day anew I lose my trust in the world. . . . Declarations of human rights, democratic constitutions, the free world and the free press, nothing," he went on to say, "can lull me into the slumber of security from which I awoke in 1935."

In *The Cunning of History: The Holocaust and the American Future,* Richard L. Rubenstein echoes Améry's under-

standing. "Does not the Holocaust demonstrate," he suggests, "that there are absolutely no limits to the degradation and assault the managers and technicians of violence can inflict upon men and women who lack the power of effective resistance?" Rubenstein's outlook may be debatable, but he believes that "the dreadful history of Europe's Jews had demonstrated that *rights do not belong to men by nature.*" If Rubenstein is correct, then, practically speaking, people can expect to enjoy basic rights such as those proclaimed by the Declaration of Independence—life, liberty, and the pursuit of happiness—only within a political community that honors and defends those rights successfully.

The Holocaust is forgotten at humanity's peril. Remembering it provides warnings that perhaps can make a shield for the future.   —*John K. Roth*

See also Anti-Semitism; Ethnic cleansing; Eugenics; Fascism; Genocide; Genocide, cultural; Genocide, frustration-aggression theory of; Hitler, Adolf; Human rights; Milgram experiment; Natural rights; Nazi science; Nazism; Pogrom; Racial prejudice; Racism; Segregation; U.N. Covenant on Civil and Political Rights; War crimes; Wiesel, Elie.

BIBLIOGRAPHY

Améry, Jean. *At the Mind's Limits: Contemplations by a Survivor on Auschwitz and Its Realities.* Translated by Sidney Rosenfeld and Stella P. Rosenfeld. Bloomington: Indiana University Press, 1980. These reflections by a survivor of the Holocaust consider the status of human rights and responsibility after Auschwitz.

Berenbaum, Michael. *The World Must Know: The History of the Holocaust as Told in the United States Holocaust Memorial Museum.* Boston: Little, Brown, 1993. Well written and helpfully illustrated, this book provides an excellent overview of Holocaust history and highlights effectively American responses to the destruction of the European Jews.

Browning, Christopher R. *Ordinary Men: Reserve Police Battalion 101 and the Final Solution in Poland.* New York: HarperCollins, 1992. One of the most important case studies to emerge from Holocaust scholarship, Browning's book examines how a unit of ordinary German men became a killing squadron that produced extraordinary inhumanity.

Gutman, Israel, et al., eds. *Encyclopedia of the Holocaust.* 4 vols. New York: Macmillan, 1990. This encyclopedia's substantial articles—each written by a highly qualified scholar—concentrate on major figures, places, and particular events that are central to the ethical dilemmas posed by the Holocaust.

Haas, Peter J. *Morality After Auschwitz: The Radical Challenge of the Nazi Ethic.* Philadelphia: Fortress Press, 1988. Arguing that the Nazis had their own understanding of morality, Haas analyzes how their "idealism" led many people to accept genocide as tolerable and even routine.

Hallie, Philip P. *Lest Innocent Blood Be Shed: The Story of the Village of Le Chambon and How Goodness Happened There.* New York: Harper & Row, 1979. Written by an important moral philosopher, this book investigates how and why the people in the French village of Le Chambon risked their lives to rescue some 5,000 Jews.

Hilberg, Raul. *The Destruction of the European Jews.* Rev. ed. 3 vols. New York: Holmes & Meier, 1985. Hilberg's book is an unrivaled study of the bureaucratic process of destruction that the Nazis directed toward the Jews of Europe. The author's reflections on the Holocaust's consequences contain important ethical content.

Lifton, Robert Jay. *The Nazi Doctors: Medical Killing and the Psychology of Genocide.* New York: Basic Books, 1986. Raising profound moral questions, Lifton shows how the Holocaust emerged from the Nazis' "biomedical vision" and documents how German physicians became deeply implicated in mass murder.

Rittner, Carol, and John K. Roth, eds. *Different Voices: Women and the Holocaust.* New York: Paragon House, 1993. Drawing on the memoirs of Holocaust victims, historical studies, and philosophical and religious reflections, this volume discusses moral dilemmas created by the Holocaust's impact on women.

Rubenstein, Richard L. *The Cunning of History: The Holocaust and the American Future.* New York: Harper & Row, 1987. In this succinct, hard-hitting account, Rubenstein discusses how the Holocaust calls traditional moral outlooks into question, particularly the idea that human beings possess natural rights.

Rubenstein, Richard L., and John K. Roth. *Approaches to Auschwitz: The Holocaust and Its Legacy.* Atlanta: John Knox Press, 1987. The authors show how religious conflict and racism intensified the anti-Semitism that led to Auschwitz. This study also focuses on the roles played by the churches, industry, and the professions during the Nazi era.

Sereny, Gitta. *Into That Darkness: An Examination of Conscience.* New York: Vintage Books, 1983. Emphasizing what she calls "the fatal interdependence of all human actions," Sereny maps the circumstances that led Franz Stangl, an Austrian policeman, to become the commandant of Nazi death camps at Sobibor and Treblinka.

Wiesel, Elie. *Night.* Translated by Stella Rodway. New York: Bantam Books, 1982. The winner of the 1986 Nobel Peace Prize describes his experiences in Auschwitz and Buchenwald. In this classic, one of the most famous Holocaust memoirs, Wiesel repeatedly asks disturbing moral and religious questions.

Holy war

TYPE OF ETHICS: Religious ethics
DATE: From antiquity
DEFINITION: The presence, in a situation of war, of a "sanctifying" principle that transfers religious righteousness to the acts of participants in violence
SIGNIFICANCE: Going beyond the broader secular ethical question of justifying "morally just" wars fought to defeat evil and injustice, the concept of holy war relies on God as the highest authority justifying war against a religious enemy

Wars involving intense religious animosity have been fought in almost every period of recorded history. When it comes to the ethical implications of the specific term "holy war," however, important distinctions must be made. Political wars involving enemies of different religions do not necessarily involve levels of institutionalization of individual "holy warriors'" commitment to religiously motivated warfare.

Although examples of holy war have occurred in other civilizations, the most commonly cited phenomena come from the experiences of Islam and Christianity. In both cases, one can find, according to the specific juncture of otherwise political warring action, a form of religiously institutionalized "sanctification" bestowed on holy warriors. The ethical content of such institutionalization, however, varies between the two prototypes.

Medieval Christianity and the Crusades. Saint Augustine (in his *City of God*, written c. 400) and other fathers of the Christian Church held that God stood behind certain wars, if their cause could be considered morally just and aimed at destroying evil. Defense of what can be seen as morally "right," however, did not necessarily mean service to a higher religious cause. These earliest searches for a possible "ethical" justification for some wars, therefore, fell short in a number of ways of the technical phenomenon of holy war.

As far as very early Western European concepts are concerned, the origins of "sanctified struggle" may have predated Christianity. Elements of the ancient Germanic heroic tradition, particularly ceremonies consecrating warriors and their weapons, would reappear in the tenth century, when the Church performed similar ceremonies to "ordain" knights. In roughly the same period, wars against pagans carried out by the successors of the Frankish emperor Charlemagne received active support from bishops, some of whom proclaimed forced conversion to be a "spiritually meritorious" act.

The Christian prototype of "sanctification" of warfare in the name of religion dates from the eleventh century, when Pope Gregory VII (1073-1085), adding to the less specific suggestions of Pope Leo IV (in 853) and Pope Leo IX (in 1053), assured that death in war against a religious enemy freed the holy warrior from the consequences of his sins. From the beginning in 1095 of the Crusades to regain the Holy Land of Palestine from Islam, there was a linkage between the existing institution of knighthood and formal military orders whose fighting members were devoted to the Crusades as a spiritual calling. Historically, various orders (such as the Knights Templars and the Knights Hospitaliers, actively organized until Napoleon's time) would continue even after the formal period of Crusades to the Holy Land.

Holy War Against Christian Heretics. Another aspect of Church "sanctification" of violence in the name of religion that did not disappear with the passing of a particular historical era was the "holy war" against Christian heretics proclaimed by the Third Lateran Council (1179). Fighters in what was to be known as the Albigensian Crusade, launched by Pope Innocent III in 1208, would receive the same papal indulgences that were granted to those who had served in the Crusades against the Muslims of the Near East.

Holy War in Islamic Law. The Islamic religion, in its "classical" theological origins, identifies two domains: the *Dar al Islam* (Domain of Islam) and the *Dar al Harb* (Domain of War). This is a concept that has often been interpreted as a necessarily continuous state of war between Islam and any representative of non-Islamic belief. Along with this general concept of the hostile separation of the world between Islamic believers and non-believers, a more specific term emerged that would be rife with presumptions of ethical obligations falling on individual Muslim believers: *jihad*. *Jihad* is not one of the five formal "Pillars of the Faith," but an individual conscience-binding obligation on believers (*fard*).

Although it is not uncommon to see *jihad* translated as "holy war," one comes closer to the ethical core of this concept through examination of Islamic legal discussions of the term. The first striking observation is that—in contrast to Christian equivalents to holy war—*jihad* is taken to be a society-wide ethical obligation. Its legal meaning—although clearly extending into the realm of physical struggle to extend the "borders" of the *Dar al Islam*—includes a sense of effort, in a variety of forms, to strengthen the bases of the Islamic faith. Indeed, the broadest possible legal and ethical sense of individual effort—*ijtihad*, deductive effort to reach balanced decisions—suggests not religious war per se but "individual application" to protect the essential principles of the faith.

This observation notwithstanding, there is considerable evidence suggesting that, at almost every stage of military conflict associated with Islamic expansionism, believers were exhorted to consider their physical struggle to be service in "holy war." Although an oft-quoted speech attributed (in the *Sira* of Ibn Hisham) to the first Caliph, Abû Bakr (632-634), probably refers to the spirit of later ages, this meaning predominates: "If any people holds back from fighting the holy war for God, God strikes them with degradation."

Unlike what is found in Christian concepts of holy war, it is difficult to say what periods of Islamic "warring for the faith" should be characterized as specifically embodying the ethical "code" of *jihad*. On the Islamic as well as the Christian side, it was during the period of the Crusades that this individual ethical dedication to holy war took on its most notable attributes. Much more modern, and even late-twentieth century phenomena in both cultures, however, contain elements of dedication to holy war in varying degrees.

Modern "Mixtures" of Political and Religious Ethics. Although too numerous to list here, there are a number of twentieth century cases in which individual dedication to what is essentially a political cause has brought about levels of religious ethical devotion that are very close to what has been defined as holy war. Among Asian religions, for example, the concept of *kamikaze* (Japanese for "divine wind") pushed Japanese fliers to undertake suicidal missions to serve the Emperor-God in World War II.

HOLY WARS THROUGHOUT HISTORY	
Selected Models of Political-Religious Wars Approved by Religious Authority	
1618-1648	Thirty Years' War in Europe
1690	Protestant William II of Orange defeats Catholic King James at the River Boyne in Ireland
1880-1900	Mahdiyyah Movement in the Sudan
1947-1948	Muslim-Hindu strife in the wake of Indian and Pakistani independence
Selected Models of Holy Wars Sanctified by Religious Authority	
800-1000	Frankish Knights' war to convert pagans east of former Roman imperial borders
1095-1099	First Crusade to the Holy Lands
1147-1149	Second Crusade
1189-1192	Third Crusade, following Muslim crusader Saladin's 1187 recapture of Jerusalem
1202-1204	Fourth Crusade
1208	Albigensian Crusade by Pope Innocent II against Christian heretics
1212	Children's Crusade
1217-1221	Fifth Crusade (in Egypt)
1228-1229	Sixth Crusade (a truce makes possible partial Christian control in Jerusalem)
1248-1254	Seventh Crusade (Saint Louis—King Louis IX— travels to Egypt)
1270	Eighth Crusade (Saint Louis dies in Tunisia)
1271-1272	Ninth Crusade
1291	Fall of Acre, last Christian stronghold in the Holy Lands

Other manifestations of the "mixed" application of religious fervor and essentially political violence approach, but do not fully correspond to, holy war in the ethical sense of the term. While Irish Catholic underground forces opposing Protestant domination of Northern Ireland include (as do Protestant "fighting brotherhoods") a form of spiritual bonding in their secret army organization (the IRA), they, like Islamic radial organizations declaring "war"—either against the state of Israel or, increasingly, against the effects of what they consider to be corrupt secular governments in several Islamic countries—have aimed more at the establishment of alternative political regimes. Nevertheless, in some cases, the religious "sanctification" of such struggles (including Muslim-Hindu strife in certain regions of India in the 1990's) brings them close to the category of holy wars.

—Byron D. Cannon

See also Bushido; Military ethics; War and peace.

BIBLIOGRAPHY

Abraham, Antoine J. *The Warriors of God.* Bristol, Ind.: Wyndam Hall Press, 1989.

Armstrong, Karen. *Holy War: The Crusades and Their*

Impact on Today's World. New York: Doubleday, 1991.

Brundage, James A., ed. *The Crusades, Holy War and Canon Law.* Aldershot, England: Variorum, 1991.

Khadduri, Majid. *War and Peace in the Law of Islam.* Baltimore: The Johns Hopkins University Press, 1955.

Lyons, Malcolm C. *Saladin: The Politics of the Holy War.* Cambridge, England: Cambridge University Press, 1982.

Homicide

TYPE OF ETHICS: Personal and social ethics
DATE: The action is as old as humanity, but as a legal concept it dates to approximately 2000 B.C.E.
DEFINITION: The unlawful killing of one human by another
SIGNIFICANCE: No matter how immoral or harmful an act may be, it is not a crime unless it is covered by a law that prohibits it and prescribes punishment for it

All contemporary societies regard the premeditated murder of another human as a crime; the research of various ethologists working amongst a large number of species suggests, however, that it is not uncommon for an animal to play an active role in taking the life of another member of its own species. For example, black widow spiders are named for killing their mates and chimpanzees have been reported to kill members of their own troops. Such observations may suggest that members of the species *Homo sapiens* have from time to time killed one another for as long as humans have existed. Furthermore, no matter how antisocial or repulsive such behavior may seem, it would be inappropriate to label such action as criminal or homicidal, since such labels introduce the notion of legality. Additionally, while the origin of such actions may prompt ethical and moral concerns, various social and natural scientists have discussed the evolutionary advantage of such behavior while addressing kin selection and the origin of altruism. A review of anthropological literature suggests that various human societies have sanctioned the killing of humans in certain specific situations, including suicide, infanticide, war, and euthanasia. Although both activities are legally acceptable, some in the United States have called abortion murder, while others have said the same thing about capital punishment.

Regarding human behavior and the origin and evolution of society, an action did not become criminal until it was covered by a law prohibiting it that prescribed a punishment for it. Crime is generally considered to be an assault against the state or government because it disrupts public order and disturbs social tranquillity. According to fragments of a clay tablet recovered from what was Sumer, the earliest legal prohibitions were prepared by approximately 2000 B.C.E. The Code of Lipit-

Ishtar was established during the eighteenth century B.C.E. and represents the first documented attempt to codify the laws governing human behavior. Specifically, the code outlined the rights and privileges of all members of Sumerian society. Similar codified laws representing a Babylonian dynasty of 1200-1700 B.C.E. are referred to as Hammurabi's code, and like those that preceded them, they outline the legal and social contract between members of society and society. These codes established courts, fines, and penalties, as well as the rights and obligations of each member of society. As is true of present laws, the early laws reflected the values of their time and incorporated the notion of an "eye for an eye." For example, a portion of Hammurabi's code states, "If a man destroys the eye of another man, he shall have his destroyed." Elsewhere it states, "If a man breaks the bone of another man, he shall have his like bone broken." Certainly a notable homicide for some was that of Abel by his brother Cain, which is discussed in the book of Genesis in the Bible.

Throughout the Western world, criminal violations are classified as those perpetrated against a person (such as kidnapping and rape), those against property (such as robbery), and those against the state (such as treason). Furthermore, they are classified as felonies and misdemeanors based upon society's perception of the severity of each crime and thus

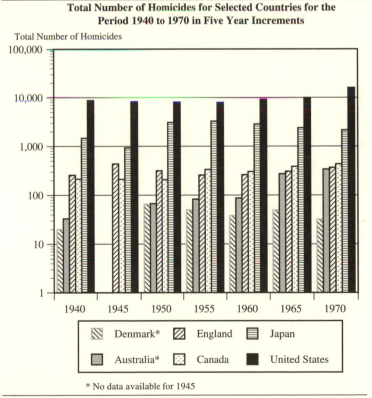

Total Number of Homicides for Selected Countries for the Period 1940 to 1970 in Five Year Increments

Total Number of Homicides

Denmark* □ England ▤ Japan
Australia* ▨ Canada ■ United States

* No data available for 1945

Source: Archer, Dane, and Rosemary Gartnes. *Violence and Crime in Cross-National Perspective.* New Haven, Conn.: Yale University Press, 1984.

the penalty associated with it. In the United States, felonies carry a sentence of at least one year in prison, while misdemeanors are punishable by jail terms of less than a year or by a fine, or both. In the West, traditionally, the three major felonies are murder, arson, and sexual assault, although other crimes such as kidnapping and bank robbery have been added in some countries.

In the United States, murder is practically the only capital felony, or one that authorizes the death penalty for its perpetration. Under special circumstances, however, a homicide may not be considered a crime. Specifically, in cases involving self-defense, or when a homicide is carried out to prevent the commission of a further serious felony, the perpetrator may not be prosecuted. Homicides are classified as those that are premeditated, those involving manslaughter, and those caused by negligence. The most serious type is that which is planned in advance or is premeditated. The least serious homicide is one caused by carelessness or resulting from a negligent act. Manslaughter is defined as a homicide resulting from recklessness or a violent emotional outburst. By convention, homicide rates are reported as the number per 100,000 population, although not all countries distinguish among murder, manslaughter, and negligent homicide. The homicide rate for various countries from 1940 to 1970 are shown in the accompanying table in five-year increments. Because of the effect of population size, the number of such deaths is also reported. For example, for Australia, the rate jumps from 0.46 to 0.90 between 1940 and 1955, while the increase in the number of deaths is only 50. This is because of the relatively small population of Australia. This should be kept in mind while noting the smallest five-year difference in the number of deaths in the United States (147 between 1950 and 1955), which is nearly three times the difference in number for Australia between 1940 and 1955.

It is clearly demonstrated by the table that the homicide rate for each country has remained relatively stable (Australia's shows the greatest rate of change—from 0.46 in 1940 to 2.38 in 1970), while there is a notable difference between countries (the lowest thirty-year average is that of England, at 0.70, while the highest is that of the United States, at 5.79). Such intercountry differences may be attributed to cultural differences and a society's attitudes toward the value of human life, the availability of weapons, and accepted techniques for resolving interpersonal conflict.

—*Turhon A. Murad*

See also Abortion; Death and dying; Ethnic cleansing; Euthanasia; Kevorkian, Jack; Life and death; Lynching.

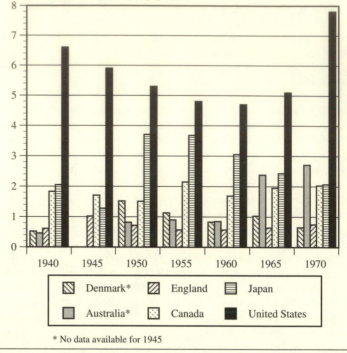

The Homicide Rate for Selected Countries for the Period 1940 to 1970 in Five Year Increments

Number of homicides per 100,000 population

Denmark* England Japan
Australia* Canada United States

* No data available for 1945

Source: Archer, Dane, and Rosemary Gartnes. *Violence and Crime in Cross-National Perspective.* New Haven, Conn.: Yale University Press, 1984.

BIBLIOGRAPHY

Archer, Dane, and Rosemary Gartner. *Violence and Crime in Cross-National Perspective.* New Haven, Conn.: Yale University Press, 1984.

Daly, Martin, and Margo Wilson. *Homicide.* New York: Aldine de Gruyter, 1988.

Geberth, Vernon J. *Practical Homicide Investigation.* 2d ed. New York: Elsevier, 1990.

Robbins, Sara, ed. *Law: A Treasury of Art and Literature.* New York: Hugh Lauter Levin, 1990.

Samaha, Joel. *Criminal Law.* St. Paul, Minn.: West, 1983.

Homophobia

TYPE OF ETHICS: Civil rights

DATE: Coined 1972

ASSOCIATED WITH: The struggle for gay, lesbian, bisexual, and transgender equality and liberation

DEFINITION: Homophobia, the fear and hatred of those who love and sexually desire those of the same sex, includes prejudice and acts of discrimination resulting from that fear and hatred

SIGNIFICANCE: The relatively modern construction of sexual identities has forced a basic reevaluation of conventional religious, medical, and societal notions of homosexuality and bisexuality—as well as basic relations between males and females—with an attendant backlash by those attempting to preserve conventions

Derived from the Greek *homos*, meaning "same," and *phobikos*, meaning "having a fear of and/or aversion for," the term "homophobia" was coined by George Weinberg in 1972 in his book *Society and the Healthy Homosexual*. Other terms that have been used include: "homophilephobia," "homoerotophobia," "homosexphobia," "homosexophobia," "homosexism," "homonegativism," "lesbian-" and "gay-hatred" or "-hating," and "sexual orientationalism" (giving a parallel structure with "racism," "sexism," and "classism"). "Biphobia" is the fear and hatred of those who love and sexually desire both males and females, and it can include prejudice and acts of discrimination against bisexual people.

"Heterosexism" (a close ally to homophobia) is the system of advantages bestowed on heterosexuals. It is the institutional response to homophobia that assumes that all people are or should be heterosexual and therefore excludes the needs, concerns, and life experiences of lesbians, gay males, and bisexuals. At times subtle, heterosexism is a form of oppression by neglect, omission, and/or distortion, whereas its more active ally—homophobia—is oppression by intent and design.

Heterosexism forces lesbians, gay males, and bisexuals to struggle constantly against their own invisibility, and makes it much more difficult for them to integrate a positive identity. This is not unlike the situation of a Jew or a Muslim in a predominantly Christian country, a wheelchair user in a town with only stepped entrances to buildings, or a Spanish-speaking visitor in a country in which Spanish is not spoken.

Homophobia and heterosexism (like all forms of oppression) operate on four distinct but interrelated levels: the personal, the interpersonal, the institutional, and the societal (or cultural).

The personal level refers to an individual's belief system (bias or prejudice). Forms of personal homophobia include the beliefs that sexual minorities (gay males, lesbians, and bisexuals) either deserve to be pitied as unfortunate beings who are powerless to control their desires or should be hated; that they are psychologically disturbed or genetically defective; that their existence contradicts the "laws" of nature; that they are spiritually immoral, infected pariahs who are disgusting—in short, that they are generally inferior to heterosexuals.

Personal heterosexism, the belief that everyone is or should be heterosexual, is in operation, for example, when parents automatically assume that their children are heterosexual and will eventually marry a person of the other sex.

The interpersonal level is manifested when a personal bias affects relations among individuals, transforming prejudice into its active component—discrimination.

Interpersonal homophobia includes name calling or joke telling intended to demean or defame sexual minorities; verbal and physical harassment and intimidation as well as more extreme forms of violence; the withholding of support; rejection; abandonment by friends and other peers, cowork-

ers, and family members; and the refusal of landlords to rent apartments, shop owners to provide services, insurance companies to extend coverage, and employers to hire on the basis of actual or perceived sexual identity.

Interpersonal heterosexism occurs, for example, when teachers assume that all their students are heterosexual and teach only the contributions of heterosexuals. This leaves sexual minorities without a legacy and sense of history.

The institutional level refers to the ways in which governmental agencies, businesses, and educational, religious, and professional organizations systematically discriminate on the basis of sexual orientation. Sometimes laws, codes, or policies actually enforce such discrimination.

Institutional homophobia includes "sodomy laws" that remain on the books in many states to punish people engaging in same-sex sexual activity; "anti-gay rights laws," such as the prototype Colorado Constitution Ballot Amendment 2 (approved by 53 percent of the voters on November 3, 1992) *prohibiting* equal protection under the law on the basis of sexual orientation; state and municipal policies restricting gay, lesbian, and bisexual people from serving as foster and adoptive parents and making it more difficult for them to win custody of their own children in the courts; military policy excluding gays, lesbians, and bisexuals; the doctrines of some religious denominations that oppose homosexuality; the classification of homosexuality as a "disordered condition" according to the American Psychiatric Association until 1973 and the American Psychological Association until 1975; and school policies clearly stipulating that same-sex couples may not attend proms and other social functions.

Institutional heterosexism includes religious and governmental sanction of the marriages of only heterosexual couples; companies providing employee benefits only to "legally" married spouses and children; the heterosexual bias on government, business, and community groups' printed forms when listing only the categories "single," "married," and "divorced" in reference to relationship status; municipal, state, and national governments giving special tax benefits to heterosexually married couples; medical policy permitting only "blood relatives" or spouses certain hospital visitation rights; and school dances designed specifically to encourage the socialization of males with females, and vice versa.

The societal (or cultural) level refers to the social norms or codes of behavior that, although not expressly written into law or policy, nevertheless work within a society to legitimize oppression. Societal homophobia includes the stereotypes of sexual minorities that are taught in the culture, ranging from their alleged predatory appetites, to their physical appearance, to the possible "causes" of their desires. It also includes active attempts to falsify historical accounts of same-sex love—through censorship, deletion, half-truths, and the altering of pronouns signifying gender—making accurate reconstruction extremely difficult.

An example of societal heterosexism is evident whenever the only positive and satisfying relationships portrayed in the media are heterosexual. This is not unlike media portrayals of white people, especially in the United States during the 1950's and 1960's, which excluded positive images of people of color.

Gay, lesbian, and bisexual people are not immune to the destructive effects of homophobia, biphobia, and heterosexism. Internalized homophobia and biphobia occur when gay, lesbian, and bisexual people incorporate or "internalize" society's negative notions of homosexuality and/or bisexuality and of gay, lesbian, and bisexual people, thus inhibiting their ability to establish a positive self-identity or to form close and intimate relationships. This internalization may result in the denial of one's sexual and emotional attractions on the conscious and/or unconscious level to oneself and others; overachievement as a bid for acceptance; contempt for the more open and "obvious" members of the lesbian, gay, or bisexual community; attempts to alter or change one's sexual orientation; projection of prejudice onto another minority group (reinforced by society's already existing prejudices); delayed or retarded emotional and/or cognitive development; attempts to "pass" as heterosexual, sometimes marrying someone of the other sex to gain social approval; increased fear and withdrawal from friends and relatives; conflicts with the law; unsafe sexual practices and other destructive risk-taking behaviors, including substance abuse; and suicidal ideation, attempts, and completion.

—*Warren J. Blumenfeld*

See also Gay rights; Homosexuality; Oppression; Sexism; Stonewall Inn Riots.

BIBLIOGRAPHY

Blumenfeld, Warren J., ed. *Homophobia: How We All Pay the Price*. Boston: Beacon Press, 1992.

Blumenfeld, Warren J., and Diane Raymond. *Looking at Gay and Lesbian Life*. Boston: Beacon Press, 1993.

Comstock, Gary David. *Violence against Lesbians and Gay Men*. New York: Columbia University Press, 1991.

DeCecco, John P., ed. *Bashers, Baiters, and Bigots: Homophobia in American Society*. New York: Harrington Park Press, 1985.

Hutchins, Loraine, and Lani Kaahumanu, eds. *Bi Any Other Name: Bisexual People Speak Out*. Boston: Alyson, 1991.

Pharr, Suzanne. *Homophobia: A Weapon of Sexism*. Inverness, Calif.: Chardon Press, 1988.

Homosexuality

TYPE OF ETHICS: Sex and gender issues

DATE: From antiquity

DEFINITION: The disposition to seek feelings of romantic love and to have sexual relations with persons of one's own sex in preference to the opposite sex

SIGNIFICANCE: Necessitates an understanding of the human nervous system in its need for and processing of sexual relationships as a basis for sexual decisions

The human body, like the bodies of many animal species, cannot perpetuate itself by itself. Human reproduction requires the union of sperm and egg cells. When this union is initiated within the body of the female of the species, the involvement of the nervous system, especially the brain, results in an awareness of sensory pleasure. Social behavior is enhanced as a result of sexual sensory input into the central nervous system, especially if there is emotional input of care, gentleness, esteem, trust, and increased well-being associated with the outward physical actions. Some people perform heterosexual activities with their own sex; this is the case with homosexuals. Various disciplines such as psychology, psychiatry, theology, philosophy, sociology, anthropology, and the biological and medical sciences have attempted to gather information in order to understand homosexuality better.

History. The early legal codes of Mesopotamia do not mention homosexual acts, except for the provision in the Code of Hammurabi (1726 B.C.E.) that concerns sons adopted by palace eunuchs. David Greenberg, in *The Construction of Homosexuality* (1988), comments that while some scholars have claimed that the second millennium B.C.E. Hittite law provided for male homosexual marriages, this concept is now found only in the writings of the nonspecialist. At about the same time in Babylon, there was an *Almanac of Incantations*, which contains prayers that bless the love of a man for a man as well as that of a man for a woman and a woman for a man. It is not easy to be sure about homosexuality in very ancient papyri from Egypt. Greenberg was unable to find any basis for a claim that new pharaohs were masturbated and sodomized by a high priest. It was believed, however, that homosexual intercourse with a god would be a great blessing. Two fragmented manuscripts from the Sixth Dynasty, about 2272-2178 B.C.E., describe a conspiracy to obstruct a court hearing involving a homosexual relationship between a top royal administrator and his military general. In the Eighteenth Dynasty, a set of religious and mortuary spells called the *Book of the Dead* has the deceased proclaiming the absence of homosexual activity in his life, and a copy of the book prepared for women indicates the existence of lesbianism. The Hebrews address homosexuality, but there is much controversy over dating and interpretation. Homosexuality within Sodom and Gomorrah seems to be implied, and the suggestion of inhospitality as the chief sin of Sodom and Gomorrah could easily include homosexual rape.

Overt homosexuality seems to have been a part of life among the Greeks by the early part of the sixth century B.C.E. Kenneth James Dover, in *Greek Homosexuality* (1989), refers to homosexual expressions that were included in graffiti on the rocks of a Spartan colony, Thera; these graffiti may even be from the seventh century B.C.E. There seem to be no elements of homosexuality in the poetry from the seventh century B.C.E., even though there are explicit heterosexual references. By the sixth century B.C.E., lesbian poetry from Sparta did exist, as did many indications of male homosexuality. Images on many vases depict every level of intimacy between males, including the touching of genitals. The time between 570 and 470 B.C.E. seems to be the great age of erotic vase painting. Plays that date from 425 to 388 B.C.E. used homosexuality as material for humor, but this use seemed to decline after the mid-fourth century B.C.E. in Greece. Plato's philosophical writings extol homosexuality. There exists, however, a copy of a trial that dates to 346 B.C.E. in which a citizen of Athens, a politician, was prosecuted for prostituting himself to another male.

In the Middle Ages, King Charles V promulgated the *Constitutio Criminalis Carolina* (1532) which punished homosexuality with death by fire. Jonathan Katz, in *Gay American History* (1976), reports that approximately one percent of the erotic Peruvian pottery that dates from 100-1200 C.E. depicts lesbianism. The writings of a Franciscan friar in 1565 refer to sodomy and lesbianism in Mexico. In writing between 1742 and 1750, missionaries of the Moravian church, a German Protestant denomination, describe the Native Americans of Pennsylvania, New York, and North Carolina as decent in public, yet committing unnatural sins in private. The term "berdache" was used for the homosexual male in some Native American tribes.

As early as 1924, prohomosexual organizations existed in the United States. The Chicago Society for Human Rights received its charter as a nonprofit organization on December 10 of that year. This group published two issues of "Friendship and Freedom" and, later, the monthly homosexual emancipation magazine *One*. Various novels and plays appeared that depicted homosexuals as a misjudged and misunderstood minority. In England, Radclyffe Hall wrote *The Well of Loneliness* (1928), which was published in New York after it was banned in England. In California in 1948, Henry Hay founded the Mattachine Society, a homosexual emancipation organization for males. Two years after attending a meeting of the one-year-old lesbian organization the Daughters of Bilitis in San Francisco in 1956, Barbara Gittings founded the first East Coast chapter. She was the first editor of its periodical, *The Ladder*, which began publication in 1963. In 1961, Illinois led the way for a number of states to decriminalize homosexual activity in private between two consenting adults. In the summer of 1969, customers at the Stonewall Inn, a homosexual bar on Christopher Street in New York, rebelled against a police raid. This event is considered to mark the beginning of group rebellion, the beginning of the "Gay Rights" movement.

Ethical Principles. It is basic that every person be free to make decisions regarding sexual activity within the realm of others' rights. To make a free decision requires that the person has attained maturity and an appropriate level of knowledge. The acquisition of pertinent facts regarding homosexual behavior and reasoned reflection on its outcomes should precede one's decision at all levels of sexual intimacy. One's actions should also, at all times, respect the dignity of life.

Two women enjoying the festivities at a 1989 Lesbian and Gay Pride Weekend in New York City's Central Park. (AP/Wide World Photos)

Ethical Issues. Ethical issues in the area of homosexuality fall into one of two categories. They are either microcosmic, related to the concerns and care of the individual or a small unit of society, or they are macrocosmic, related to society on a large scale.

Allowing a person the freedom to make personal choices is one of the highest forms of respect. Some say that this microcosmic approach is the only sensible one. Each person may have programmed limits of freedom that are the result of genes, early family relationships, and cultural relationships. The uniqueness of the human nervous system makes possible an unusual awareness that seems to transcend the physical.

At the macrocosmic level, sexuality touches not only the whole personality of the individual but also the personalities of others and even society in general. If there is a gene for homosexuality, or alcoholism, or a score of mental diseases, how should all these be allowed to affect society? Should those who possess such genes be considered mutants? These questions continue to be debated.

Health Care Allocation. In Europe and the United States, late-nineteenth century physicians began to say that homosexuality was a problem for them to treat rather than something for judges, lawyers, and legislators to address. Karl Heinrich Ulrichs, impressed with the discovery that the early human embryo contained both male and female organs, then lost one set as development continued in the uterus, began using the term "third sex." Psychiatry, especially, began treating people who wanted to be helped. Some states in the United States adopted compulsory sterilization for homosexuals. Some homosexuals in the early 1900's sought castration to stem unwanted homosexual desires.

The rise of the acquired immunodeficiency syndrome (AIDS) in the 1980's put the homosexual issue firmly into the health care realm. The medical world had not only the problem of dealing with the human immunodeficiency virus (HIV) but also that of treating the many health problems related to a suppressed immune system in the human: pneumonia, AIDS-related cancers such as Kaposi's sarcoma, and various types of brain involvement. Homosexual men are at particularly great risk of contracting AIDS.

Research. Psychological studies show that environmental influences, especially parental relationships before age two, may irreversibly determine a person's sexual identity. Sigmund Freud suggested that people who react negatively to homosexuals are exhibiting "reaction formation"; there is a desire but the superego forbids its expression. The transmission of this prohibition happened at an early age, but this does not explain the origin of the primary prohibition. Even though research into homosexuality continues, in 1975 the American Psychiatric Association deleted the word "homosexuality" from its *Diagnostic and Statistical Manual of Mental Disorders.*

Many religions attest the perversity of homosexual activities. To Jews, moral law and natural law are products of the one God, and nature clearly seems to intend that human males and females should engage in sexual relations only with each other. Not only Judaism and Christianity but also Islam and Zoroastrianism condemn homosexual actions. In the Hindu civilization, the Laws of Manu impose only a mild penance for homosexual conduct.

Sociological inquiry into homosexuality has attempted to find out how the homosexual stigma has produced dramatic consequences for these individuals. A landmark paper by Mary McIntosh, "The Homosexual Role," which was published in *Social Problems* in 1968, states that only when the homosexual person sees himself or herself in terms of a social category does that person start to act in terms of that role. The homosexual role is not universal, even though homosexual experiences are. In 1978, Barry Adam presented the results of his study in *The Survival of Domination: Inferiorization and Daily Life.* He shows that gays have restricted opportunities, their lives are dominated by unacceptance, and their mental lives are devalued. Not all sociologists, however, consider homosexuality an issue of social concern that is worth their research time and effort.

Anthropological studies on homosexuality are sparse and do not give a clear picture. In most societies, however, sexual activity takes place in private. In 1976, Gwen Broude and Sarah Greene, in their article "Cross-Cultural Codes on Twenty Sexual Attitudes and Practices," published in Ethnology, suggested that little homosexuality is reported because it is not customary to do so. Information on the frequency of homosexuality is given for only 70 of 186 societies in the Human Relations Area File's Standard Sample, and there are only 42 reports on attitudes toward homosexuality. Native reluctance to share such information with Western, white anthropologists has been reported. Many anthropologists have been men, so questions on lesbian activities have been prevented by norms of propriety. If sex is a part of religious ritual, that can be a further reason for secrecy.

Science has shown that hormones, chemicals circulating in the blood, have a profound effect upon sexuality, but human sexual activity is not totally controlled by hormones and cycles, as it is in many animals. In 1982, Christine de LaCoste-Utamsing and Ralph Holloway reported, in *Science,* the presence of sexual dimorphism in the part of the brain called the corpus callosum. In 1985, a sexually dimorphic nucleus, or area that consists of a collection of nerve cell bodies (gray matter) surrounded by the white matter of the brain, was reported in the hypothalamus, a primitive part of the brain that functions in eating as well as in reproductive activities. In 1991, Simon LeVay published in *Science* the results of his study of forty-one human brains. Six were from heterosexual women, sixteen were from heterosexual men, one was from a bisexual man, and eighteen were from homosexual men. Four nuclei in the anterior part of the hypothalamus (interstitial nuclei 1, 2, 3, and 4) were studied. Differences were found only in the interstitial nuclei 3 in these postmortem brains. Nucleus 3 was twice the size in the homosexual men compared to its size in the heterosexual men. The size of this nucleus in the homosexual men was about equal to that found in the heterosexual women. The sample size used in this study is small. Also, it is not known whether nucleus 3 was larger at birth, became larger in early childhood, or became larger as the result of homosexual activity. The last possibility is important to consider, because the projections, or dendrites, from pyramidal cells in the cortex of young mammals increase with sensory input.

Some studies of the sexual preferences of twins have shown a high correlation between them. In one study, 52 percent of identical twins were homosexual, compared with 22 percent of fraternal twins and 11 percent of adopted brothers. Again, the sample size is small (only 161 sets of twins).

Nature of Homosexuality. Science has not shed definitive light on the physical basis of homosexuality, although biologists tend to look to genetics for an answer. History seems to indicate that homosexuality was a part of ancient civilizations, but it was especially banned by the Hebrew religious code, which separated homosexuals from others who were called pagans. The Hebrew evaluation of homosexuality was adopted by the Christian community, and especially, by the Roman Catholic church, which holds that each person can be respected even though the actions of the homosexual person are difficult to judge and are not approved. There have always been those who have been both heterosexual and homosexual in their activities. The members of the "gay movement" want homosexuality to be a way of life that is accepted and considered equal to heterosexuality in every way.

Ethical Decision Making. This activity involves both content and process. For the individual, there needs to be a clear understanding of the preference to seek sexual pleasure with the same sex and the performance of the action at whatever level of intimacy it may be. One needs to reflect upon the effect of sexual sensory input into the central nervous system, and especially the human brain, with its ability to remember, imagine, and affect the entire person. The process might also include answering some of the following questions. How do my actions relate to the dignity of my personhood? Do my actions show responsible stewardship of the human species? Does this pleasure ensure my future health and well-being? Do my actions promote the common good?

Public Policy. Greenberg relates governmental laws regarding homosexual activity to the rise of capitalism. The development of the political power of the working class resulted in the state's assuming a greater role in civil society. As the industrial revolution continued, educational requirements for jobs increased. The public education of both male and female children caused children to be considered asexual. By 1885, the law put English children into a category that was out of the sexual reach of adults. In the United States, statutory penalties for homosexual activity were enacted. For example, the 1881 *Revised Statutes for the State of Indiana*, section 100 of chapter 32, states, "Whoever commits the abominable and detestable crime against nature, by having carnal knowledge of a man or a beast, or who, being a male, carnally knows any man or any woman through the anus, and whoever entices, allures, instigates or aids any person under the age of twenty-one years to commit masturbation or self-pollution, is guilty of sodomy, and, upon conviction thereof, shall be imprisoned in the State prison not more than fourteen years nor less than two years." Between 1880 and 1890 the number of people in prison in the United States for homosexual activity increased 350 percent compared to a 25 percent increase in population.

In the 1970's, attempts were made to change public policies on this matter in the United States. On June 7, 1977, in Dade County, Florida, a referendum to ban discrimination regarding housing, employment, and public accommodations based on a person's public statements regarding affectual or sexual preference failed to pass. A similar bill in

New York City had been defeated in the city council by a vote of twenty-two to nineteen on May 23, 1974. Many laws that favor professed homosexuals did pass, however, especially in Washington, D.C., and San Francisco, California. In many situations, no questions are asked regarding one's sexual preference. —*Rose Ann Bast*

See also Ethics/morality distinction; National Gay and Lesbian Task Force.

BIBLIOGRAPHY

Dover, K. J. *Greek Homosexuality*. Cambridge, Mass.: Harvard University Press, 1989. This well-researched book contains a section of analyzed photographs of art objects to support the statements made.

Greenberg, David F. *The Construction of Homosexuality*. Chicago: University of Chicago Press, 1988. An extensive treatment of ancient and modern homosexuality. There are 113 pages of references at the end of the book.

Horgan, John. "Eugenics Revisited." *Scientific American* 268 (June, 1993): 122-131. Twin studies are reported to have found about 50 percent predisposition to male or female homosexuality, but these findings are disputed.

Katz, Jonathan. *Gay American History*. New York: Thomas Y. Crowell, 1976. This is an unique documentary—a collection of passages organized under the topics of trouble, treatment, women, Native/gay Americans, and resistance, with an introduction to each section.

LeVay, Simon. "A Difference in Hypothalamic Structure Between Heterosexual and Homosexual Men." *Science* 253 (August 30, 1991): 1034-1037. This report is very technical. It is the original report of a difference between an area of the brain in heterosexual men and homosexual men.

Mirkes, Renée. "Science, Homosexuality, and the Church." *Ethics and Medics* 17 (June, 1992): 1-3. This article gives a current view of the Catholic church's approach to homosexuality.

Plummer, Kenneth, ed. *The Making of the Modern Homosexual*. Totowa, N.J.: Barnes & Noble, 1981. This collection of eight articles by different authors ends with an appendix that suggests a research format for doing one's own research and a listing of research sources.

Honesty

TYPE OF ETHICS: Personal and social ethics

DATE: From antiquity

DEFINITION: Fair and truthful conduct, free from deception and fraud

SIGNIFICANCE: Like truth, honesty is one of the traits that produce a sure foundation of ethical theory; its opposites, dishonesty and untruthfulness, would destroy all ethical systems

As a virtue, honesty belongs to the ethical *genus* of justice. Other concepts relative to honesty are dignity, uprightness, fidelity to the truth, and chastity in words and actions. Because they harm other people, the opposites of honesty are generally condemned; among those opposites are lying, dishonesty, sham, covetousness, unscrupulousness, inaccuracy, treachery, and infidelity in words and actions.

Dishonesty, Society, and Individuals. All groups, including the family, the clan, and the larger society as a whole, must practice honesty, for to do otherwise would undermine the group by destroying mutual confidence. Subsequently, the group would disintegrate. Treachery of any kind can flourish between hostile groups but never within a group, for it scatters people and breaks down groups.

Dishonesty is a type of war in disguise. Unless honesty and truth are observed and practiced by people, no one can trust anyone else and no one can know what to expect from others. Society would then fragment and—as Thomas Hobbes mentioned long ago—revert to a "state of nature," a war of one against all and all against all. Life, Hobbes said, would become "solitary, poor, nasty, brutish, and short." Another philosopher held that falsehood was the worst of "evils" because its negative consequences—including the end of society—would be so great.

Many types of dishonesty exist. One type involves lying in an attempt to deceive, and prevarication is probably the most effective form of lying. Prevarication is the attempt to leave a false impression by using words that in some other sense might be true. The best example of prevarication is the case of the two diplomats who promise that their two countries will remain at peace so long as they stand upon "this earth." Immediately after such agreement, both diplomats go to a private place to remove their shoes and pour the sand out of them. Thus can a lie be told with words that are technically "true" but are false in context.

A lie can be told without words—by means of gestures or silence. A forger lies with the pen, a medical quack with fraudulent prescriptions, a smuggler by "expert" packing, and the pickpocket with his hands. Robbers and thieves are also, in a sense, liars, for they are dishonest when they take money or goods that rightfully belong to someone else. Such lies and dishonesty in effect break the implied promise that civilized people make to one another to be truthful and to cause no harm.

In addition to harming others, the dishonest one also hurts himself or herself. The liar's attacks on society wear it down, and as society "loses," so, too, do its individuals. Furthermore, dishonesty tears away at the character of the offender. Once the dishonest one is caught in a crime or even a simple lie, society damns him, and no one will ever believe him again, not even when he speaks the truth. Additionally, many dishonest people eventually start to believe their own lies or justify their crimes, whatever those crimes may be. Someone, for example, might steal goods and "justify" it by saying, "The rich owe me this much" or "Society owes me at least this much." When such thinking occurs, internal honesty is replaced by internal dishonesty and self-deceit. Since inner truthfulness is a key to moral growth and personal vigor, the dishonest person throws away his or her chances to achieve that growth and vigor.

Developing a Philosophy of Honesty. First, the question of relativism must be resolved, and one type of relativism involves recognition that different cultures have differing customs and mores. Different cultures may also have different moral values. One need look no further than Eskimo society. The men not only practice polygamy but also share their wives with male guests, for such behavior is considered the proper sign of hospitality. Furthermore, a dominant male might also have access to all other men's wives. Eskimos also practice infanticide, with female newborns being most likely to be killed. Eskimo society also approves of leaving old people, who have ceased to be productive, out in the snow to die. While American laypersons might be shocked by such practices, relativists are not. They argue that there is no standard "right" and "wrong" and that moral rules vary from society to society. In other words, cultural relativists challenge the view that there are universal moral truths.

Despite the arguments described above, many thinkers remain critical of relativism. First, critics contend that relativists confuse what people simply believe or want with objective truth. For example, if nations make war to enslave other people, is that war justified simply because the aggressive nation believes that it is? In the World War II era, Nazi Germans had elaborate reasons to justify the murder of millions of Jews. Were such exterminations justified simply because the Nazis thought that they were? Similarly, in some societies of the past, people believed that the world was flat, but does that mean that there is no objective truth in geography? No. Similarly, there are objective truths in moral philosophy, and honesty is one of them.

Cultural relativism's "big brother" is relativism in general. Some thinkers hold that there should be no fixed principles to guide human words and actions. According to them, everything is relative and ethical decisions must be rendered on a case-by-case basis. The idea that all is relative is, however, a fixed principle. Everything is not relative, and certain ethics *should* be obeyed by all. An ethical philosophy of honesty, for example, allows but few examples wherein it is "right" to be dishonest and/or to lie.

The case of the "inquiring murderer," however, does bedevil a thinker: Jane Doe sees a man running down the street on a dark, rainy night. As the man turns a corner and disappears, a second man rushes up. Jane notices that the second man is carrying a gun at just the moment when he asks Jane, "Which way did he go?" Should Jane tell the truth? That course might lead to the murder of another human being. Here, one must conclude that no, in this case Jane *should* lie because saving a human life outweighs Jane's responsibility to tell the truth to an armed man. Said another way, one duty that Jane owes humanity is greater than another. Thus, there are times when honesty and dishonesty are relative, but those cases are few and far between. Only a person's strongest powers of reason can discern the rare occasions when it is correct to be dishonest.

Exceptions aside, honesty in most avenues of life is still

the best policy. One really needs to look no further than the philosophy of Immanuel Kant to justify that policy. Kant held that there were certain absolute rules—called "categorical imperatives"—that were not relative and that did not change no matter what the circumstances. Basically, his imperatives called for people to think, speak, and act only in ways that would be acceptable if they were mandated as universal laws to be followed by all people everywhere; that is, people should ask, before they decide on an action, should my behavior become a universal law? Thus, is it permissible for one to steal the money or goods of another? No, because if everyone became a thief, civilized society would crumble. Is it permissible to lie (except in a life-threatening emergency such as that of the aforementioned Jane Doe)? No, because if lying became a universal law, the war of all against all would start. Kant's imperatives would also ban such acts as armed robbery, murder, adultery, incest, and so on. Except for certain moral dilemmas, Kant's system seems to work well as a general guide for determining honesty: Tell the truth, do not rob or steal, do not kill others, do not physically or mentally assault others, and so on.

Kant's lines of reasoning are as follows: You should take only those actions that conform to rules that you are willing to adopt as universal laws. If you are dishonest, you are announcing that universal dishonesty is permissible. The last point is absurd, however, because it is a self-defeating proposition. If all people were liars, cheats, and thieves, people would stop trying to believe one another, and it would do no good to be a dishonest liar, because one would not be believed. Therefore, it is best not to lie, cheat, or steal.

Kant's categorical imperatives seem even more correct if one considers other philosophical doctrines. For example, some thinkers still hold that religion is the key to truthfulness, honesty, and right action: Simply do what God commands. Such a view does little, however, to guide atheists or agnostics. Kant's imperatives do.

The utilitarian philosophy is also unacceptable as a replacement for Kant's imperatives. The three founders of utilitarian thought—David Hume, Jeremy Bentham, and John Stuart Mill—and their followers held that people should be guided by the principle of happiness and the greatest good for the greatest number. To make people happy was the greatest good, and questions about honesty and dishonesty would become the servants of the greatest good; that is, dishonesty could be practiced if it made people happier. To give Hume, Bentham, and Mill their due, all three were reformers who were trying to make English law and society more just, but their philosophy falters on the issue of dishonesty. For example, consider the person who breaks into a home and steals most of the family's treasures, including jewelry, televisions, personal computers, microwave oven, and money. The thief next distributes the goods to his many friends. If one were a strict, no-exceptions-allowed utilitarian, one would have to conclude that the theft was acceptable because the thief made more people happy than unhappy.

Utilitarianism in its extreme form is hedonism, a philosophy that justifies behavior based on how people "feel." If what one "feels" is the criterion for action, then all is allowed—even dishonesty. Additionally, other virtues might well disappear if they conflict with hedonism, virtues including, but not limited to, justice, the rights of other human beings, and truthfulness.

Honesty and Dishonesty in Modern American Society. Although many millions of Americans are most likely honest in all their endeavors, if one looks at public life, one must conclude that it is a rare public official who tells the truth. Scandal has been the order of the day for decades. In the Cold War era, for example, some individuals in the state department, the military, and the Central Intelligence Agency (CIA) were dishonest with the American people in striving to make them terrified of the Soviet Union, which was only a regional power at best. During the Vietnam War, the same agencies were regularly dishonest in what they told the people. Then, when the Gulf War was being fought in the 1990's, generals "managed" the news about the war, leaving an impression that the American victory was greater than it really was. It was only later that investigators discovered, for example, that "friendly fire" killed many soldiers and that American missiles had not been as accurate as the generals had said. As the turn of a new century neared, many Americans became so jaded that they took it for granted that the government would be dishonest and would lie about most military matters.

Dishonesty is also rampant in American internal affairs and has been for decades. By 1952, despite his own best efforts, President Harry Truman's administration became hopelessly corrupt; that fact helped the Republicans retake the Oval Office, but the Eisenhower administration had its scandals, too. President John F. Kennedy contributed to the trend of dishonesty among public figures. He received the Pulitzer Prize for *Profiles in Courage*. The problem? He did not write it. His staff, headed by Theodore Sorensen, did. Next, President Lyndon B. Johnson did his best with the internal "War on Poverty," but he lied about the shooting war in Vietnam. One need say little about the Nixon administration except one word—Watergate. On and on the trend goes. In the 1992 political campaign, president-to-be Bill Clinton was less than candid about certain matters in his private life. His immediate predecessors, Ronald Reagan and George Bush, were no better; both became mired in the "Irangate" arms-for-hostages scandal.

Dishonesty also flourished in Congress, especially in the 1980's, as one scandal after another occurred. For example, in their bank, members of Congress regularly engaged in the practice of check "kiting." In their post office, other irregularities occurred. In their restaurant, members of Congress charged but refused to pay their bills—this while voting themselves such massive pay raises that they could disengage themselves altogether from the concerns of the lower and middle classes. Even though some dishonest Congresspersons were "retired" after the scandals, many of the guilty returned to Washington to continue their corrupt careers. Sex scandals, racism, gender discrimination—all these ills can also be laid at the feet of Congress, and all such ills have an aspect of dishonesty about them.

In the modern United States, it is not only politicians who are dishonest. Before he left office in 1961, President Dwight D. Eisenhower warned about the development of the "military-industrial" complex. Indeed, the alliance between the military and big business grew by leaps and bounds, and dishonesty flourished as many defense contractors defrauded the government. Worse, many businesspersons seemed to lose whatever honesty they might have had. In the 1980's and 1990's, for example, Americans had to watch the spectacle of the savings and loans scandals. For decades, taxpayers will pay billions of dollars and therefore be punished for the criminal acts of a handful of dishonest bankers.

Religionists are also numerous among the dishonest. In front of a television audience that numbered millions of people, Protestant fundamentalist Jimmy Swaggert thundered against sin and actually laughed heartily about all the awful tortures that sinners would receive when they all went to hell. He said that shortly before he was caught more than once being unfaithful to his wife by frequenting prostitutes. Jim Bakker was a "man of God" who built a ministry of millions of both people and dollars, only to be convicted later of fraud and sent to prison. Yet Protestants were not the only guilty religionists. Newspapers reported one case after another of Catholic priests who molested children or adults, while Jewish rabbis heading schools that received federal and state money enrolled imaginary students to receive more money.

In almost any field that one surveys, dishonesty exists, and society is in danger of decline as trust is increasingly lost. Worse, when the young see the dishonest behavior of preachers, lawyers, physicians, politicians, and so on, they come to believe that dishonesty is acceptable. When those children grow into young adults, they may become corrupted by tempting situations wherein they must choose between honesty and dishonesty.

Conclusions. All people who wish to live ethically must understand the consequences of dishonesty. First, it threatens all of society. If dishonesty becomes widespread enough, civilization itself will decline. Second, dishonesty also threatens the dishonest person by slowly working to destroy that person's character, integrity, and honor. It may well be time to reembrace Kant and to declare that of his categorical imperatives, the imperative that demands honesty is one with the greatest reason on its side. Dishonesty can never become universal or "natural" law, because it is self-defeating in the end. —*James Smallwood*

See also Cheating; Corruption; Lying; Relativism; Truth; Utilitarianism, Watergate break-in.

BIBLIOGRAPHY

Cabot, Richard C. *Honesty*. New York: Macmillan, 1938. After providing several chapters on the nature of honesty, this study focuses on honesty and dishonesty in various career fields, including education, science, industry, and government.

_____. *The Meaning of Right and Wrong*. Rev. ed. New York: Macmillan, 1936. Like Cabot's *Honesty*, this volume discusses similar themes, including dishonesty and its harmful consequences to all.

Greider, William. *Who Will Tell the People: The Betrayal of American Democracy*. New York: Simon & Schuster, 1992. A journalist rather than a trained philosopher, Greider nevertheless subjected Americans to an honesty "test" and found that fraud, deception, and dishonor were rife in American life—including a less-than-ethical national government, giant corporations driven by greed, and bankers who stole money from their own depositors.

Payne, Robert. *The Corrupt Society: From Ancient Greece to Present-day America*. New York: Praeger, 1975. Although he wrote almost twenty years ago, Payne focused on dishonesty through history while emphasizing frauds and falsehoods in modern American life. Payne dedicated this book to President Richard Nixon, who headed the most scandal-ridden political administration in U.S. history.

Rachels, James. *The Elements of Moral Philosophy*. Philadelphia: Temple University Press, 1986. This author surveys topics such as morality, honesty, and relativism in ethical philosophy. He also examines religion, utilitarianism, and the social contract and discusses them in relation to ethics.

Riley, Sue Spayth. *How to Generate Values in Young Children: Integrity, Honesty, Individuality, Self-Confidence, and Wisdom*. Washington, D.C.: National Association for the Education of Young Children, 1984. Although this volume targets the parents and teachers of young children, all would benefit from examining it. Spayth's subtitle expresses the most important themes that the book discusses.

Taylor, A. E. *The Problem of Conduct*. New York: Macmillan, 1901. Dishonesty and "the liar" are Taylor's topics. He points out, among other things, the absurdity of the liar, who must assume that everyone else is honest and truthful.

Honor

TYPE OF ETHICS: Personal and social ethics

DATE: From antiquity

ASSOCIATED WITH: Aristocracies and patrician elites

DEFINITION: A consciousness of self-worth and corresponding code of behavior thought particularly appropriate to individuals whose self-esteem is grounded in their ancestry and breeding

SIGNIFICANCE: A worldly and exclusive ethic, honor was particularly compatible with traditional, hierarchical societies in which allegiance was directed to individuals rather than to an impersonal state governed by abstract law

Honor is an elusive term whose meaning has undergone considerable change from antiquity to the present. It refers to a personal sense of worth and dignity as well as to a corresponding code of behavior or standard of conduct expected by one's peers. Honors are marks of approbation or recognition bestowed by virtue of one's actions in accordance with such codes and standards.

Some social scientists contend that honor is universal, found in virtually all societies. Some scholars refer to "primal honor," as evident in pagan and Indo-European societies, signifying a code of behavior that emphasized valor, the reputation of family and group with which the individual identified, male virility and ferocity, and loyalty. Primal honor, as the term suggests, was archetypal and universal, the moral property of the whole community and consequently neither class-based nor elite-based. Above all, it valued the opinion of others as a gauge of self-esteem and worth. It was, however, an exclusively masculine property. Presumably, the more traditional the society, the more visible would be the qualities of primal honor.

Literary scholars and historians are more inclined to confine honor to Western civilization, as an ethic first evident in antiquity, altered in the Middle Ages, and subsequently transformed during the Renaissance and later. Honor's primal qualities were transmuted by the medieval Church in the cult of chivalry that elevated the lady. When applied to the lady, honor referred to purity or chastity. Nevertheless, if a lady's honor was impugned, it remained a man's responsibility to defend it. Renaissance humanists joined learning, manners, and civility to the earlier code and produced, especially in the Anglo-Saxon tradition, a more reified code of honor. With its emphasis upon inner worth along with external expressions of respect and esteem, this more elevated variety of honor was exclusive, as opposed to primal honor's alleged universality. The historian Jacob Burckhardt referred to the Renaissance concept of honor as "an enigmatic mixture of conscience and egoism."

In medieval England, an honor was originally a large estate granted by the crown. It was a physical property that was the outward sign of a man's dignity and was heritable. While honor's meaning was subsequently translated from land to character, its heritability was retained, as was its elitist associations. Honor was a quality associated with the hereditary ruling elite and was to be emulated. Thomas Hobbes referred to honor as "the opinion of power." Edmund Burke considered honor a quality "to be found in the men the best born, and the best bred, and in those posses'ed of rank which raises them in their own esteem, and in the esteem of others, and posses'ed of hereditary settlement in the same place, which secures with an hereditary wealth, an hereditary inspection." Honor, then, was a peculiarly aristocratic quality.

While some critics of the Scottish Enlightenment professed that honor was universal, the examples they provided of its operation were invariably drawn from the world of privilege. Even such critics of honor as William Paley, who saw it as an instrument of social control, defined honor as an aristocratic code that "regulates the duties *betwixt equals.*"

Insofar as a man of honor sought the rewards of approbation, honor was a worldly ethic that was often at odds with the ascetic or other-worldly aspirations sometimes associated with a higher morality. The man of honor subscribed to a code distinct from and sometimes in conflict with the laws of God or the laws of his country. A sensitivity to personal reputation was foremost, and, especially in early modern European history, the "point of honor" became the duel, despite condemnation of the practice by both Church and state law.

Many theorists from the Renaissance to the Enlightenment sought to reconcile honor with public virtue, particularly in the form of benevolence. For such theorists as Adam Smith, Baron de Montesquieu, and David Hume, aristocratic honor was necessary for the preservation and transmission of liberty. Nevertheless, the association of honor with traditional societies that valued privilege and patronage resulted in its attenuation and further transformation once those traditional societies were replaced by the modern industrial state. The French Revolution's assault upon the old regime's world of privilege implied a rejection of the code of aristocratic honor that had been linked with monarchy, the king having been the "fount of honor." The quality that had once been personal, however, having been associated with serving the monarch, came to be associated with serving the impersonal nation. Hence, in the nineteenth and twentieth centuries, the concept of national honor became prominent. It was not an altogether new concept, since varieties of collective honor persisted when men of rank identified with their families or clans. Moreover, while honor as a personal ethic characteristic of elites was being weakened, the collective honor associated with those elites was strengthened.

When aristocracies controlled their nations, national honor was a projection of their personal honor. In the nineteenth and twentieth centuries, the concept of national honor acquired mass appeal, as the nation displaced the individual as the object of loyalty. Numerous statesmen appealed to national honor in the diplomacy of the countries they represented, and the phrase "peace with honor" was frequently used to justify a particular policy or arrangement. It has been invoked by such disparate figures as British prime ministers Benjamin Disraeli, after the Congress of Berlin in 1879, and Neville Chamberlain, when he returned from his meeting with Hitler at Munich in 1938. In seeking to conclude the Vietnam War, President Richard Nixon and Secretary of State Henry Kissinger claimed to bring peace with honor.

—*Abraham D. Kriegel*

See also Chivalry; Dignity; Elitism; Self-love; Self-respect.

BIBLIOGRAPHY

Best, Geoffrey. *Honour Among Men and Nations: Transformations of an Idea.* Toronto: University of Toronto Press, 1981.

Peristiany, J. G. *Honour and Shame: The Values of a Mediterranean Society.* Chicago: University of Chicago Press, 1966.

Pitt-Rivers, Julian. "Honor." In *The International Encyclopedia of the Social Sciences,* edited by David L. Sills. Vol. 6. New York: Macmillan, 1968-1991.

Watson, Curtis. *Shakespeare and the Renaissance Concept of Honor.* Princeton N.J.: Princeton University Press, 1960.

Wyatt-Brown, Bertram. *Southern Honor: Ethics and Behavior in the Old South.* New York: Oxford University Press, 1982.

Hsūn Tzu (c. 313 B.C.E., Chao Kingdom, China—after 238 B.C.E., Lan-ling, Ch'u Kingdom, China): Philosopher

Type of ethics: Religious ethics

Achievements: Author of the *Hsūn Tzu,* a book of essays whose principal concerns are culture and ethics

Significance: Hsūn Tzu superseded Mencius (371-289 B.C.E.) as the foremost interpreter of Confucius (551-479 B.C.E.); a logician, semanticist, and writer, he expanded on Confucius' thought rigorously and systematically, while differing significantly from the views of Mencius, who had held that people are born good, that they should project universal love, and that they should depend on transcendental power; Hsūn Tzu's humanistic philosophy was primarily concerned with self-cultivation based on education and character development based on moral training

Hsūn Tzu's philosophy was primarily humanistic and realistic, being focused on humanity and the investigation of things. He rejected human dependence on any transcendental power or spirit, such as heaven (*t'ien*). Instead, he recommended that people depend on their own proper actions as spelled out by the rules of right conduct (*li*), especially in the *Li chi* (*The Book of Rites*), and by justice (*i*), combined with their own experience. Although people are born evil—that is, "uncivilized"—and are moved by desire, like other animals, they have intelligence and sympathy, which are beyond the abilities of other animals, and can learn to act righteously through knowledge and wisdom acquired by education, self-cultivation, and moral training. They can thus control their animal drives by an act of will and sense of discipline. Hsūn Tzu thought that Mencius' idea of universal love (*chien ai*), which involved loving everyone in the world equally, was unrealistic and impractical. Instead, he held that knowledge gained by study (*hsüeh*) and wisdom (*chih*) would enable people to control their desires. He also realized that the basis of education was the proper understanding of language and a rational approach. Hence, he stressed the importance of linguistic analysis under the rubric of "the rectification of names."

See also Confucian ethics; Mencius; Taoist ethics.

Hui-neng (638, Hsin-chou, Kwangtung Province, China— 713, near Hsin-chou, Kwangtung Province, China): Buddhist monk

Type of ethics: Religious ethics

Achievements: Sixth patriarch of Chinese Ch'an (Japanese, Zen) Buddhism

Significance: Taught that liberation consisted not in overcoming desire but in not producing it

Both the life and thought of Hui-neng are recounted in records that are legendary and polemical, so certainty about either is impossible. It is likely, however, that Hui-neng came from an impoverished family and went to the East Mountain in 674 to study Ch'an with Hung-jen, quickly gaining enlightenment. Hui-neng succeeded his master at Hung-jen's death, becoming the sixth patriarch. He emphasized that enlightenment came all at once. Subsequent to enlightenment, one engaged in various exercises to develop what had been born or discovered. Hui-neng was monistic but did not care to elaborate that monism. Consequently, he believed that good and evil, while contradictory, are only temporal realities. Behind that dualism lay a unity out of which the enlightened person acted. The implication of this idea is that acts are not so much right or wrong as measured by some standard as they are in harmony or out of harmony with the unity of things. Differently put, since there is no difference between oneself and others, one harms oneself if one harms others. If one realizes that there is no self, one will produce no desire.

See also Bodhidharma; Dōgen; Zen.

Human Genome Project

Type of ethics: Bioethics

Date: Begun 1988

Place: United States

Associated with: National Institutes of Health

Definition: Scientific research project whose goal is to make a genetic map of the human chromosomes

Significance: The project furthers knowledge of human genetics and enhances the ability to locate new genetic variants; some people have expressed concern that genetic information about individuals may be used to discriminate against them

The Human Genome Project is an attempt on the part of scientists to make a genetic map, or catalog, of the known genetic variants of *Homo sapiens.* Human illnesses known for centuries were proved to have a basis in genetic variants as early as 1906. Many human genes were identified throughout the twentieth century, but the chromosomal locations of these genes were seldom known. The Human Genome Project was begun to map the chromosomal location of all human genes and to determine their DNA sequences.

The medical uses of genetic testing, marital counseling, and prenatal testing were already well established when the Human Genome Project was begun. Major ethical issues regarding the project include the furthering of medical knowledge about human genetic defects. Increased knowledge about these genetic traits will make it possible to discover new ways of treating these conditions, including the possibility of genetic surgery using recombinant DNA techniques in human cells.

See also Genetic counseling.

TABLE OF SELECTED HUMAN GENES

Chromosome	Gene	Description	Chromosome	Gene	Description
Chromosome 1	Rh	rhesus blood group	Chromosome 13	EsD	esterase D
	Fy	Duffy blood group		RB	retinoblastoma
	Amy-1	salivary amylase	Chromosome 14	NP	nucleoside phosphorylase
	Amy-2	pancreatic amylase	Chromosome 15	PK-3	pyruvate kinase-3
	PKU	phenylketonuria		Hex-A	hexosaminidase A (Tay-Sachs disease)
Chromosome 2	IDH-1	isocitrate dehydrogenase-1	Chromosome 16	APRT	adenine phosphoribosyltransferase
	MDH-1	malate dehydrogenase-1		LCAT	lecithin-cholesterol acyltransferase
Chromosome 3	GALT	galactose-1-phosphate uridyltransferase	Chromosome 18	PepA	peptidase A
Chromosome 4	PGM-2	phosphoglucomutase-2	Chromosome 19	PVS	polio virus sensitivity
	MN	MN blood group	Chromosome 20	ADA	adenosine deaminase
	HD	Huntington's disease	Chromosome 21	AVP	antiviral protein
Chromosome 5	Hex-B	hexosaminidase B		SOD-1	soluble superoxide dismutase-1
Chromosome 6	MHC	major histocompatibility complex		Alz	Alzheimer's disease
	SOD-2	superoxidase dismutase-2	Chromosome 22	ACO-1	acotinase-1
Chromosome 7	GUS	beta-glucuronidase	Chromosome 23 (X)	PGK	phosphoglycerate kinase
	MDH-M	malate dehydrogenase, mitochondrial		αGALA	alpha galactosidase (Fabry disease)
	CF	cystic fibrosis		G6PD	glucose-6-phosphate dehydrogenase (fava bean disease)
Chromosome 8	GSR	glutathione reductase		CB	color blindness (protan & deutan types)
Chromosome 9	ABO	ABO blood groups		HEM$_A$	hemophilia A (Classic type)
	NPa	nail-patella syndrome		DMD	dystrophin (Duchenne muscular dystrophy)
Chromosome 10	HK-1	hexokinase-1		BMD	Becker muscular dystrophy
	ADK	adenosine kinase		HGPRT	hypoxanthine-guanine phosphoribosyl transferase (Lesch-Nyhan syndrome)
Chromosome 11	LDH-A	lactate dehydrogenase A	Chromosome 23 (Y)	TDF	testis determining factor
	ACP-2	acid phosphatase-2		H-Y	histocompatibility Y antigen
Chromosome 12	GAPD	glyceraldehyde-3-phosphate dehydrogenase			
	LDH-B	lactate dehydrogenase-B			

Human nature

TYPE OF ETHICS: Theory of ethics

DEFINITION: The general inherent character or innate disposition of humankind

SIGNIFICANCE: Practical ethical theories are based on assumptions of human nature; to be effective and successful, ethics must conform with the reality of human behavior, experience, capacities, and goals

The question of "human nature" figures prominently in ethical theory. There is a broad consensus that, for all practical purposes, ethics must take into account the basic facts of human nature. Otherwise, it will be inefficient and ineffective.

Although moral philosophers agree on the centrality of human nature to ethics, they do not agree on the meaning of the term.

Definitions. Some definitions of human nature seek to identify the essential qualities and universal characteristics that all people have in common. Here it is necessary to distinguish between *human* nature and *animal* nature. While all people, by nature, have physical needs such as air, food, sleep, and an imperative to survive, these exigencies are by no means uniquely human. In addition, some distinctly human attributes or features, such as art, culture, creativity, cruelty, and historical consciousness, are by no means universal. Plenty of people lack a disposition toward creativity, a personality capable of torture, or a historical sense of themselves in relation to their ancestors and progeny. Further complicating the problem of definition is the fact that human nature is a subject of study in numerous academic disciplines, each of which has a different approach. Philosophers must consider the views of psychologists, anthropologists, economists, criminologists, theologians, and sociobiologists, and reconcile the ways in which they understand and use the term "human nature." Another problem is the challenge posed by skeptics, such as Hannah Arendt, Jean-Paul Sartre, and Richard Rorty, who deny, on various grounds, that there is such a thing as human nature. Skeptical claims rest on defining the term in a way that emphasizes its universal aspects (for which exceptions provide falsification) or emphasizing the importance of environmental influences (which serves to downplay the innate dimension of human personality). The varieties of usage and the many existing definitions create a problem of ambiguity.

For practical purposes, this article will use an operational definition of human nature as "the general inherent character or innate disposition of humankind." The remainder of this article offers a brief discussion of some of the major questions and theories and their implications for ethics, and concludes by arguing for an eclectic account of human nature.

Perennial Questions. Since ancient times, debates about human nature have revolved around the most basic questions of philosophy. Are humans essentially spiritual beings or primarily physical and rational beings? Are people basically good? Are human actions determined or does free will exist? To what extent are humans influenced by heredity and environment? Does human nature change? Are women significantly different from men? Although often posed as false dilemmas, these questions help define the parameters of the debate. Responses to these complex questions result in varying approaches to ethics.

Most controversial, perhaps, is the tension that exists between spiritualism and secularism. For those who regard humans as essentially spiritual creatures, it follows that ethics should help bring out humans' divine nature or promote their religious/spiritual welfare. Those who hold such a view believe that it is appropriate for ethical teachings to present people with the highest ideals. Religions call upon their adherents to master their natures. Moral responsibility implies that through knowledge, self-discipline, and will, people can control their desires, passions, and moods. Unfortunately, the variety of religious beliefs gives rise to conflicting prescriptions of right action. For those who embrace a secular view, religious ethical ideals lead to frustration and failure because they seem more appropriate for angels than for humans. Emphasizing spiritual values is illusory, often distracting people from the urgent problems of this world. For those who believe that humans embody souls, however, emphasizing the ephemeral, materialistic aspects of life neglects that which is truly important.

A belief in the basic goodness of people generates a moral outlook that is optimistic and trusts people to behave ethically. David Hume observed that humans are distinguished by their capacity for benevolence. People have sympathetic feelings that stem from the consciousness that others experience pleasure and pain. Social theorists Jean-Jacques Rousseau and Karl Marx and humanistic psychologists Carl Rogers and Abraham Maslow all believed that humans are basically good, and they attributed human evil entirely to societal influences. Rousseau and Marx regarded people as communitarian, and they sought to re-create society in a way that would bring out moral goodness. The humanist psychologists held that to be human is to have virtually unlimited potential for growth, and they called for freedom to promote self-actualization. Thomas Hobbes and Jonathan Edwards, however, denied the inherent goodness of people. Hobbes regarded people as fundamentally selfish, and Edwards saw people as morally depraved—deserving of hellfire and damnation. To control evil human impulses, both thinkers called for restraint to prevent human negativity from manifesting immoral behavior.

The vast majority of ethicists believe in free will. If actions are determined, people cannot be held morally responsible. Nevertheless, many metaphysicians, theologians, psychologists, and scientists argue for determinism in ways that would have dramatic ramifications for ethics as well as for education, law, and criminal justice. Arguments for determinism come in many forms: divine foreknowledge or fate, Sigmund Freud's claim that early childhood experience determines the basis of adult personality, B. F. Skinner's claim that human behavior is explainable in terms of operant conditioning, and scientific claims that "biology is destiny" and that "genes hold culture on a leash." If one accepts any of these theories, then one must reexamine the ethical principles of human accountability, autonomy, and choice. Moreover, these determinist theories also have various implications for the ongoing nature/nurture controversy.

Gender also raises interesting questions. Influenced by Stoic philosophy, some early Christian theologians, such as Tertullian, Saint Augustine, and John Chrysostom, based a belief in women's moral inferiority on Eve's sin of tasting the forbidden fruit in the Garden of Eden. Many feminists, such as Betty Friedan, argue that aside from the obvious physiological distinctions, the differences between men and women are caused by cultural factors and that conceptions of femininity are essentially social constructs. Motivated by an activist agenda for political and social change, the feminist movement emphasizes the environmental factors in shaping sex roles. Attributing gender differences to human nature makes permanent change less likely, since it is far easier to change society than it is to alter nature. Carol Gilligan, showing that Lawrence Kohlberg's model of moral development has been misapplied to females, argues that the sexes conceptualize moral problems differently. She explains that the male-dominated culture idealizes the moral values of autonomy, independence, and impartial justice. Women, who tend to stress such communitarian values as caring, relationships, and responsibilities to others, are unfairly held to a male standard. Hence, they are judged to be less developed morally rather than appreciated for communicating "in a different voice." A parallel view in traditional Judaism carries this idea further in claiming that women are, by nature, more gentle, caring, and refined than men, and that therefore they require fewer laws to regulate their behavior.

Leading Theories. Perceptions of human nature lie at the heart of several important ethical theories. Ethical egoism asserts that only self-interest is intrinsically good and that a person ought to do that which is in his or her self-interest. This follows directly from psychological egoism, which claims that human beings are so constituted that they act only in ways that promote their (perceived) interest. The operative principle here is that "ought implies can." If one accepts this descriptive claim, then a viable moral system must appeal to a person's self-interest. An ethics based on altruism would be contrary to human nature and would therefore fail. Many cite the collapse of the Soviet Union to illustrate this point. The egoist view is shared by Thomas Hobbes and Ayn Rand and is supported by capitalist economic theory. Sophisticated versions of ethical egoism attempt to create a moral order by channeling the natural motivative force toward self-interest in a way that is beneficial for society as a whole. Those with an "enlightened self-interest" recognize their personal interest in the welfare of society. It is noteworthy that although religions preach altruism, they all appeal to self-interest by promising rewards and threatening punishments.

Hedonism is another moral theory that makes a normative claim based on a descriptive claim. Ethical hedonism asserts that happiness (that is, the presence of pleasure and the absence of pain) is the sole intrinsic good, and thus one always ought to do that which will promote the greatest happiness. This follows from the claim of psychological hedonism that humans are constituted in such a way that they always pursue pleasure and avoid pain. The fundamental tenet of Epicurus' moral teaching is that pleasure is the standard by which every good and every right action is evaluated. Similarly, the British utilitarians Jeremy Bentham and John Stuart Mill considered hedonism to be the primary law of human nature, and their ethical writings stress the need to maximize pleasure and minimize pain. In their theory, hedonism is distinguished from egoism by its commitment to the universalist value of taking everyone's happiness into account. Simply pursuing one's own happiness is selfish and unethical. Defending hedonism, Mill's version of utilitarianism emphasized the distinctly human capacity to develop and refine one's tastes and preferences, and he underlined the importance of pursuing the "higher pleasures."

Ethical theories that regard humans as basically rational creatures make appeals to reason to motivate people to right action. Some major theories, such as those of Aristotelian and Kantian ethics, objectivism, and natural law, rely on humans' power of reason to lead them to universal moral truth. Theories such as subjectivism and relativism, however, discount the power of reason. They are also based on the belief that humans are characterized by individuality and diversity. This belief leads to a denial of absolute, objective, and universal values and points instead to the importance of personal feelings, tolerance, and/or cultural influences. Many proponents of these beliefs deny that there is such a thing as universal human nature.

Hume, an outspoken subjectivist, believed that human reason is limited. He was a skeptic who recognized the unlikelihood of uncovering the ultimate qualities of human nature, yet he also thought that careful observation of human behavior could lead to some knowledge about human nature. His empirical approach led him to emphasize passions or feelings as the source of voluntary actions. In *A Treatise of Human Nature* he wrote: "Reason is and ought only to be the slave of the passions, and can never pretend to any other office than to serve and obey them." Hume argued that feelings of benevolence and sympathy are universal tendencies of human nature. People have a natural concern for the welfare of others, just as they care about themselves. He recognized self-love as a powerful principle of human nature, but he rejected Hobbes's sweeping claims for psychological egoism. Hume also incorporated hedonism into his theory. He identified good with pleasure and evil with pain, establishing happiness as the moral standard for judging behavior. Moreover, he gave a central role to utility (defined as "usefulness" or the "tendency to ulterior good") in assessing right and wrong. By combining a number of motivating factors into his theory, Hume avoided the trappings of reducing human nature to a single, dominant drive.

Another nonreductionist theory was developed by the American philosopher John Dewey, who sought to base morality on a scientific understanding of the human being. For Dewey, morality involves the relationship between human nature and the social environment. He describes human nature as an unorganized mass of reflexes and impulses that are shaped by the social forces of habit, custom, and institutions. Because human nature is a part of nature, morality is linked with the natural sciences. Likewise, because people interact with others in social settings, morality is linked with the social sciences. Dewey held that people live in a social world characterized by change and that people have the ability to restructure their social environment and change human nature. Ethics entails making choices, and Dewey advocated conscious, reflective conduct that would lead to growth and improve the world. Through education, it is possible to encourage those habits that foster creative problem solving and intelligence.

An important, ambitious theory of human nature that presents a challenge to moral philosophy is E. O. Wilson's sociobiology, which he defines as "the systematic study of the biological basis of all forms of social behavior in all kinds of organisms, including man." Drawing upon genetics, population biology, ethology, and entomology and interpreting them all in terms of Darwinian evolutionary theory, Wilson sees genetic survival as the overriding aim of life. Morality is subordinated to this goal, because the cultural development of higher ethical values will not overcome the power of genetic evolution. Wilson reduces such phenomena as love, altruism, aggression, and religion to his theory and insists that a viable system of ethics must conform to that theory. For example, he considers altruism to be "disguised genetic selfishness." Sociobiology remains highly controversial. It rocks the premises of both religious and secular ethics by questioning the view that humans are the only rational animal as well as the claim that humans have a morally distinct status. Moreover, sociobiology can be construed to justify the status quo or to offer a rationale for Social Darwinism. Wilson's own interpretation argues for tolerance, cooperation, diversity, peace, and environmentalism, but these lofty (and voguish) values do not necessarily follow from his descriptive claims.

Conclusion. The many theories touched upon here have something to teach. While most of them identify some aspect or truth about human nature, sweeping reductionist claims to validity generate exceptions or contradictions that are not easily resolved. For example, a stubborn proponent of egoism or sociobiology must really stretch to redefine all acts of altruism as ultimately selfish. The many competing theories, and the different approaches to ethics that follow from them, underscore the difficulty of reducing human nature to a single factor or tracing it to some given set of causes. This is because reality does not easily conform to theory or handy

categorizations. People are not uniform, and their priorities, interests, and values are legitimately diverse. The numerous perceptions in circulation lend credence to the conclusion that there may be a variety of human natures, just as there are a variety of personality types. While it may contradict the claims of hedonism, not everyone pursues a life of happiness. Some people shun physical comfort or emotional and intellectual pleasures and instead choose to endure suffering and hardship. A soldier, artist, or religious devotee may rationally pursue a lifestyle characterized by sacrifice and pain, without any desire or hope for happiness. Similarly, while many people live according to the principles of sociobiology, many do not. It is hardly unusual to encounter people who have no interest in having children; or who are kinder to strangers than they are to their own relatives; or who consider cats, whales, or jewelry more important than people.

The existence of diverse human natures is not only evident among people or groups of people on a macro level, it is also observable on a micro level. Individuals, over time, demonstrate a combination of drives that support several theories in a limited way rather than inclusively. For example, a man may be motivated by self-interest as a consumer; by aggression, self-sacrifice, and selfless devotion to strangers as a soldier; by altruism and generosity as a father; by piety when performing religious rituals; and by some combination of these characteristics in his professional career. Moreover, the same man may act with reckless disregard for his health, family, religious beliefs, and career while intoxicated or angry. Human diversity and intricacy on both the individual level and the group level make the task of articulating universal generalizations about human nature extremely problematic. Thus far, the complexity of the human experience lends itself neither to a clear and convincing theory of human nature nor to a moral philosophy upon which most people agree. The questions surrounding human nature remain unresolved. For this reason, the study of human nature continues to be a fascinating and open field for speculation and research. —*Don A. Habibi*

See also Altruism; Anthropological ethics; Communitarianism; Egoism; Hedonism; *Human Nature and Conduct*; Social Darwinism; Utilitarianism.

BIBLIOGRAPHY

Berry, Christopher J. *Human Nature*. Atlantic Highlands, N.J.: Humanities Press International, 1986. An informative survey of how the concept of human nature shapes political theory and how all moral and social doctrines make claims about human nature.

Carruthers, Peter. *Human Knowledge and Human Nature*. New York: Oxford University Press, 1992. Examines human nature as it pertains to epistemology. Carruthers defends empiricism in conjunction with innate knowledge and realism by examining the historical roots of contemporary debates on the nature of knowledge.

Dewey, John. *Human Nature and Conduct*. New York: Henry Holt, 1922. Analyzing the interaction between psychology and ethics, Dewey focuses on the social power of habit. Individual human nature is an unorganized mass of impulses that comes to be shaped by the social environment. By reconstructing society, people can change human nature. Social institutions such as education can promote habits that constitute intelligence and growth.

Hume, David. *A Treatise of Human Nature*. London: John Noon, 1739. 3 vols. Reprint. Oxford: Clarendon Press, 1958. Hume's masterpiece follows his conception of philosophy as the inductive science of human nature. His observations of human thinking and behavior led him to a nonreductionist ethical theory that combines benevolence, sympathy, self-love, hedonism, custom, and justice.

Wilson, Edward O. *On Human Nature*. Cambridge, Mass.: Harvard University Press, 1978. A readable and thought-provoking synthesis based on Wilson's theory of sociobiology. His consideration of evidence is somewhat uneven, since he gleans information from academic studies ranging from anthropology to zoology.

Human Nature and Conduct: Book

TYPE OF ETHICS: Modern history
DATE: Published 1922
AUTHOR: John Dewey (1859-1952)
SIGNIFICANCE: Fostered a positive, liberal view of human nature, proposed that philosophy should provide practical service to humanity, and reemphasized the role of creative intelligence in controlling events

The American philosopher John Dewey bared many of his seminal ideas in *Human Nature and Conduct*. Drawing on themes found in Charles Darwin's *On the Origin of Species* (1859), one of the modern world's most influential studies, Dewey defined human beings as creatures within the natural order who, like members of other species, were obliged to adapt continually to one another and to their environments in order to survive. In this context, Dewey argued that past philosophies had been too abstract and too concerned with constructing intellectual systems to serve humanity's practical needs. Much like his fellow American philosopher William James, Dewey also believed that truth was what happened to an idea and therefore, that truth changed over a period of time. For Dewey, life began and ended in human experience; in other words, humans who used appropriate methods could successfully negotiate life's confusing, obscure, and indeterminate situations. The key to coping with such problems, Dewey insisted, was using insight to define problems, establishing a set of possible solutions, determining the likely consequences of each possibility, and then evaluating the best possibility through observation and experiment. These flexible steps, which produced what Dewey called "warranted assertibilities," were, he believed, as relevant to social reform as they were to laboratory science. The purpose of warranted assertibilities and the inquiries of which they were a part was changing specific situations. Ideas, in short, were instruments. Humankind, like other species, had no fixed natural end;

therefore, events could be shaped by open-ended, democratized inquiry and the freeing of human intelligence. The greater the number of human alternatives, the freer humans could become. In *Human Nature and Conduct*, Dewey championed both naturalism and instrumentalism, upon which he elaborated later in his many writings. As a reformer, he earned international esteem for the fresh directions that he advocated in education and in the democratization of social and political institutions—a democratization that he regarded as essential to human adaptability and the problem-solving play of the human intellect.

See also Bradley, Francis Herbert; Darwin, Charles; James, William; Peirce, Charles Sanders; Pragmatism; Relativism.

Human rights

TYPE OF ETHICS: Human rights
DATE: Seventeenth century to present
DEFINITION: A body of claimed rights inhering in the individual person that are recognized and protected by governments through domestic legislation and international agreements
SIGNIFICANCE: Provides a body of recognized standards by which governments agree to respect and protect the lives, liberties, property, and well-being of individuals—whether citizens or aliens—who fall under their jurisdiction

Human rights as a field of study and as a body of legal rights and obligations is a relatively recent phenomenon that has grown out of ancient roots and faces two timeless problems. The fundamental problems facing the enterprise are, first, what to recognize as a human right, and, second, and even more troublesome, how to guarantee the protection of such rights once they have been recognized. These problems have been part of the political and social life of human beings for all time. How does one protect people from the unjust and sometimes brutal treatment of their fellows? Many governments throughout the ages have devised legal systems to reduce, mitigate, and relieve injustices committed by citizens or subjects against one another, but how does one protect the citizens or subjects of a country from their own government? These timeless and fundamental problems continue to face governments in both their domestic and their foreign affairs.

From the standpoint of ethics, human rights serve as a statement of the aspirations of peoples and governments toward ideals that are not always attained in practice and that at times lead to contradiction and conflict. Human rights represent an effort by governments, international agencies, and nongovernmental (NGO) advocacy groups to overcome the harsher aspects of political life within and between countries. Although considerable progress has been made in recognizing human rights during the twentieth century, the fact that they are referred to as human rights rather than legal rights reminds one how far modern practices are from stated ideals and aspirations. Moreover, the pursuit of human rights objectives involves hard choices about whether members of the international community may, how they should, and even whether they can punish the most egregious offenders of human rights, which are often governments that can claim and defend traditional rights of sovereignty against external scrutiny and encroachment.

History. The notion of human rights is a relatively recent innovation in the history of political thought, tracing its roots to the social contract thinkers, such as Thomas Hobbes and John Locke, who insisted during the seventeenth and eighteenth centuries that individuals possess certain natural rights that serve as the very foundation of political order and that may not be legitimately revoked by governments. This revolutionary concept served as the foundation upon which the great statements of individual rights and liberties—the American Declaration of Independence and the French Declaration on the Rights of Man—were based.

If the concept of natural rights is relatively new, the notions that individuals deserved dignity and respect, and that particular citizens of particular cities were invested with certain rights were ancient. The ancient Greek polis, for example, recognized that its citizens had certain rights and privileges that were denied to aliens, while also recognizing that the polis and its individual members might have obligations to aliens, but whatever rights or privileges a citizen or subject enjoyed by custom, tradition, or statute were potentially subject to revision. The rights, in other words, were conventional in nature. They could be granted or taken away. They did not inhere in individual persons. Indeed, whatever rights citizens or even aliens might have were ultimately overshadowed by their duties to the state and to their fellow citizens or subjects. So it was later in Rome. A Roman citizen might have a right to suffrage and a means of political participation through the tribunes in republican Rome, but the empire's constitutional shift to monarchy saw these rights substantially altered. Rights came and went with the vagaries of politics and constitutions.

In the ancient world, the emergence of the Stoic and the Christian conceptions of human equality and dignity foreshadowed a more universal and abiding conception of rights. Both the Stoics and the Christians believed in the divine origin of creation. Both believed that human beings were endowed by that creator with a basic equality and that virtue rather than vice, mercy rather than severity, and charity rather than cruelty were the standards of upright living, whether for the ruler or the ruled. Yet still the concept of rights rested on convention and was rooted in the tumultuous, changing, and unreliable world of politics, where brutality was often respected as greatly as clemency was admired.

In Europe, after the eclipse of Roman domination, Christianity gradually gained ascendancy. The rulers as well as the ruled operated within a system of duties and responsibilities defined by Christianity itself. Customary and canonical restraints helped to prevent outrages against humanity, but the rough and tumble of political competition was never really fully tamed, and centuries of contention over the proper roles of the church and state in moral and temporal affairs culminated in the brutal wars of religion during the sixteenth and seventeenth centuries, following the Protestant Reformation. Catholic and Protestant monarchs and princes gradually recognized that a new order resting on the sovereignty of states would be necessary to quell the sectarian violence. States would create their own rules and regulations without outside interference. They would treat their citizens as they pleased, without regard to any "higher law" that a church might assert. They would be the ultimate sovereigns.

It was at this time, then, that Hobbes and Locke asserted the conception of natural rights, offering to ground the newfound virility of the independent and sovereign state on a principle that would recognize the rights of its people. Their notion did not find wide support among the monarchs of their own time, who were just then enjoying the unlimited powers associated with the rule of an absolute sovereign, but in time the conception of natural rights took root. Modern experiments with democratic regimes founded on the principle emerged, and with them came regimes that were committed to a universal conception of human rights.

Realization of this broader conception of human rights was hampered, however, by the very international system that made it possible for certain governments to develop constitutions that were rooted in conceptions of natural and human rights. Democratic regimes resting on such principles found themselves in contention with authoritarian regimes that either did not recognize such principles or only paid them lip service. Even the democratic regimes often failed to live up to their own standards. Nevertheless, democratic states in the late nineteenth and early twentieth centuries made the first international efforts to protect human rights by pursuing the gradual abolition of slavery and beginning to enforce anti-slave trading measures. Similarly, in the early part of the twentieth century, governments in Europe took interest in protecting minority populations and promoting the development of humanitarian law, especially to protect vulnerable groups in time of war.

Human rights today, as in the past, can only be effectively guaranteed by individual governments that agree to respect them. The international system is still composed, even as the twenty-first century approaches, of sovereign states that have exclusive legal control over their own territories and citizens. There is no world government or authority higher than the governments of states that can impose human rights obligations, although some regional systems for protection of human rights have developed, particularly in Europe. Rather, governments, at their sole discretion, may agree voluntarily to develop domestic legislation guaranteeing human rights or to sign international agreements promising to respect them.

Nevertheless, the twentieth century has witnessed a veritable explosion of human rights activity, much of which was given impetus by the horrible atrocities witnessed during two global wars. First, after World War I, the League of Nations, gingerly and without great success, and then, after World War II, the United Nations (U.N.), with greater effectiveness, addressed the problems of collective insecurity, war, and abuse of human rights. Governments determined the pace of progress in these endeavors, since the League and the U.N. lacked sovereignty and possessed only those authorities and mandates that had been granted to them by their member states. Nevertheless, especially since World War II, the world has witnessed a proliferation of U.N.-related human rights agreements by which governments sought to recognize, promote, and guarantee the development of human rights. Most of the guarantees, however, are very fragile, and continue to call upon governments as the principal mechanisms through which human rights are protected.

U.N. Activity in Human Rights. Article 1(3) of the U.N. Charter stipulates that one of the purposes of the U.N. is "to achieve international cooperation . . . in promoting and encouraging respect for human rights and for fundamental freedoms for all without distinction as to race, sex, language, or religion." Numerous additional references to human rights are made in the Charter. The Charter also stipulates in Article 2(1), however, that "the Organization is based on the principle of the sovereign equality of all its Members," and in Article 2(&) that "Nothing contained in the present Charter shall authorize the United Nations to intervene in matters which are essentially within the domestic jurisdiction of any state." Protection of human rights may be a fundamental purpose of the U.N., but state sovereignty serves as a fundamental organizing principle. States, not the U.N., would do the determining about how human rights would be encouraged and protected, although they agreed to pursue these ends jointly and separately. To this end, U.N. member states created a Human Rights Commission that would report to the Economic and Social Council (ECOSOC). In short, the U.N. Charter reflected the still rather ambiguous status of human rights. They became a priority for governmental attention, but governments preferred to protect their sovereign prerogatives. Hence, governments paradoxically remained, as they had for centuries, the chief guarantors, as well as the chief violators, of human rights.

Still, much progress in recognizing, if not in fully protecting, human rights has been made. The U.N. General Assembly, on the recommendation of the Human Rights Commission, adopted the Universal Declaration of Human Rights in 1948. This Declaration, though not legally binding, did articulate the full range of human rights that states proclaimed should be respected, including the rights to life, liberty, security of person, nationality, and equal protection under and nondiscrimination before the law, and freedom from slavery and torture, freedom of religion, of political preference, and of movement, to name only a few of the most important provisions. Subsequent human rights treaties sought to provide legally binding protections, while many governments incorporated the Declaration in whole or in

part into their constitutions. Unfortunately, not all governments that have taken these steps are known for their scrupulous adherence to human rights principles, while many others have not signed the most important conventions—the Covenant on Civil and Political Rights and the Covenant on Economic and Social Rights—which were adopted by the U.N. General Assembly in 1966 and entered into force for the signatories in 1976. Numerous treaties dealing with more specific issues have also been promulgated, including international agreements on refugees, stateless persons, elimination of racial discrimination, the political rights of women, the rights of children, and the rights of migrant workers. Added to this are numerous regional treaties, the most important and effective of which is the European Convention on Human Rights.

Like all past efforts at protecting individual rights and liberties, U.N. activity has faced the question of how to enforce human rights standards given the prevailing standard of state sovereignty. In general, formal international enforcement mechanisms remain rather weak, with states taking the leading role through their domestic systems in protecting human rights standards through domestic legal institutions. Informal pressure through private diplomatic channels, NGO advocacy groups, and the public media does, however, often lead to better state compliance with human rights standards.

Ethical Considerations. To a very large extent, human rights standards remain guidelines for how governments *should* behave, rather than legal descriptions about how they actually *do* behave. Moreover, human rights often posit potentially contradictory standards. Human rights obligations may require states to ensure that their people receive adequate nutrition, security of person, and a rudimentary education while at the same time calling for popular political participation, free elections, and freedom of speech. In a very poor country plagued by civil war, however, achieving stability may be incompatible with modern democratic norms. Governments are concerned primarily with survival, and only secondarily with reform. Human rights are most regularly and routinely violated in countries where meeting the most basic needs of people is most difficult. These governments may well subscribe to international human rights treaties, but if domestic political circumstances are not favorable, compliance with them is doubtful. Some human rights treaties bow to this reality, granting states the right to derogate from certain human rights obligations once due notice and explanations are provided. The U.N. Covenant on Civil and Political Rights, for example, allows governments, during times of national emergency, to revoke or curtail rights to privacy, liberty, security of person, peaceable assembly, and political activities. Other rights, however, such as freedoms of religion, thought, and conscience, as well as prohibitions against slavery and torture, remain obligatory at all times.

What should be done with those governments that routinely shock the conscience of humanity by brutalizing their own citizens? An ethical dilemma is created here, since the principle of sovereignty imposes a duty of nonintervention in the affairs of states. A state may have a legal right to intervene to protect its own citizens from human rights abuses at the hands of other governments, but what right does it have to do this on behalf of another state's citizens? Under current international mechanisms, such an intervention would have to be conducted under U.N. auspices and justified, not by recourse to human rights, as such, but as a matter constituting a threat to international peace and security.

These questions have been faced in several recent civil war situations, including Iraq's treatment of Kurds and Shiites, Serbian treatment of Moslems in Bosnia, and in Somalia. In cases in which a country's population is facing genocide or disaster threatens large numbers of people, strong and quick action is required to save life. In all such situations, the problem that emerges is whether and how force should be used to achieve human rights objectives. One factor that must be taken into account is the circumstances surrounding the threat to life. Does the threat exist because of the deliberate policy of the government or because of the government's inability to cope with disaster? In Somalia, the situation involved anarchy produced by the lack of any effective government. Humanitarian intervention in that case was relatively easy to justify and to accomplish. The issue is considerably more complicated and dangerous when governments undertake deliberate genocidal or persecutory policies. How much killing should the international community resort to in order to prevent killing? What severity of economic pressure should be imposed to prevent persecution or ensure nondiscrimination? What degree of force will be effective? Is any degree of potential force or pressure likely to succeed? Enforcement of international law and human rights in conflict situations sometimes presents very painful ethical and prudential choices. This explains in part the international indecision about how to deal with ethnic cleansing in Bosnia, where the use of force to achieve human rights objectives raises a series of thorny questions. In the case of Iraq, a more determined U.N. response to Iraqi government persecution of its own people was made possible by its clearly illegal invasion of neighboring sovereign, Kuwait, and by the cease-fire obligations it agreed to in the aftermath of its expulsion from Kuwait by coalition forces.

Fortunately, there are relatively few cases in which the courses of action open to governments, international agencies, and private groups are so stark. In most instances, the ethical questions for international human rights policy turn on how to apply the right amounts of persuasion, diplomacy, and publicity to realize humanitarian objectives. The humane treatment of prisoners, for example, is constantly monitored by the International Committee for the Red Cross and Amnesty International. By pursuing quiet modes of diplomacy or by publicizing human rights violations, such groups can bring pressure to bear on governments to comply with more acceptable human rights practices. These informal efforts,

together with ongoing attempts to convince governments to ratify and comply with international human rights agreements, hold out hope that human rights will in fact one day become legal rights widely protected by governments.

—*Robert F. Gorman*

See also Amnesty International; Bill of Rights, U.S.; Ethnic cleansing; International justice; International law; Universal Declaration of Human Rights.

BIBLIOGRAPHY

Brownlie, Ian, ed. *Basic Documents on Human Rights.* 2d ed. Oxford, England: Clarendon Press, 1981. This valuable resource includes the texts of the most important international and regional human rights agreements.

Buergenthal, Thomas. *International Human Rights in a Nutshell.* St. Paul, Minn.: West, 1988. This user-friendly reference book describes the essential contents of regional and international human rights agreements, ranging from the U.N. Charter and U.N. Declaration and Covenants to European, inter-American, and African documents on human rights.

Donnelly, Jack. *Universal Human Rights in Theory and Practice.* Ithaca, N.Y.: Cornell University Press, 1989. This philosophical inquiry into the meaning of human rights and the policy contexts in which human rights operate is both thoughtful and realistic, especially in distinguishing between human rights and legal rights.

Ellis, Anthony, ed. *Ethics and International Relations.* Manchester, England: Manchester University Press, 1986. This compilation of papers and essays addresses a range of ethical issues in international relations, including questions of citizenship, asylum, intervention, human rights, and humanitarian aid.

Falk, Richard. *Human Rights and State Sovereignty.* New York: Holmes & Meier, 1981. In this provocative work, a prominent and innovative proponent of human rights takes on the issue of sovereignty as the most critical issue in effective enforcement of human rights agreements.

Forsythe, David. *Human Rights and World Politics.* Lincoln: University of Nebraska Press, 1983. A readable, generally realistic treatment of the international and domestic contexts of human rights protection. It distinguishes between formal and informal efforts to protect human rights.

Gibney, Mark, ed. *Open Borders? Closed Societies? The Ethical and Political Issues.* New York: Greenwood, 1988. This collection of articles addresses questions concerning rights and duties surrounding asylum, refugee resettlement, and assistance. The contributions explore the ethical and political obligations that arise between peoples and states in international relations.

Hannum, Hurst, ed. *Guide to International Human Rights Practice.* 2d ed. Philadelphia: University of Pennsylvania Press, 1992. This volume contains numerous articles exploring the actual means by which NGOs and advocacy groups can lobby effectively for the advancement of human rights.

Henkin, Louis. *The Rights of Man Today.* Boulder, Colo.: Westview, 1978. A well-written and reasonably compact treatment of the historical development and current significance of human rights.

Robertson, A. H. *Human Rights in the World.* Manchester, England: University of Manchester Press, 1972. This somewhat dated book contains a brief but useful treatment of the modern antecedents of human rights and an inside look at the evolution of U.N. treaties and regional institutions for the protection of human rights.

Humane Society of the United States

TYPE OF ETHICS: Animal rights
DATE: Founded 1954
ASSOCIATED WITH: World Society for the Protection of Animals
DEFINITION: The goals of the HSUS are the alleviation of animal suffering and public education
SIGNIFICANCE: The HSUS was founded to counteract the conservatism then inhibiting the effectiveness of other

The Humane Society of the United States promotes the idea that people should treat animals with respect and compassion. (Elaine Query)

animal welfare societies, such as the American Humane Association (AHA) and the Society for the Prevention of Cruelty to Animals

In the 1940's, legislation was passed requiring the provision of animals for research laboratories by federally supported humane societies. Initially, the AHA, led by president Robert Sellar, vigorously opposed these "pound seizure laws." With Sellar's death, however, a new conservative leadership was elected to the AHA. Frustrated by the ineffectiveness of their organization, three key AHA personnel, all appointees of Sellar, formed a new association, the Humane Society of the United States (HSUS). Dedicated to the alleviation of suffering in domestic and wild animals, the HSUS polices animal research centers, zoos, and the entertainment industry. Furthermore, the HSUS opposes all hunting sports and calls for a drastic reduction in the use of animals in biomedical experiments. The Society also lobbies for the strengthening and extension of protectionist legislation. Public education related to the inherent rights of animals and human responsibility in securing those rights is furthered through a division within the Society, the National Association for the Advancement of Humane Education.

See also Animal research; Animal rights; Cruelty to animals; Moral status of animals.

Humanism

TYPE OF ETHICS: Personal and social ethics
DATE: Nineteenth and twentieth centuries
ASSOCIATED WITH: John Dewey, Erich Fromm, Karl Marx, Jean-Paul Sartre, American Ethical Union, American Humanist Association, Fellowship of Religious Humanists, North American Committee For Humanism, Society for Humanistic Judaism, Unitarian-Universalist Association, and the International Humanist and Ethical Union
DEFINITION: A naturalistic philosophy of living (*lebensphilosophie*) based on the freedom, responsibility, and rationality of human beings; a celebration of human creativity lived in awareness of human finitude
SIGNIFICANCE: Offers a naturalistic, democratic, and this-worldly approach to moral judgment and action

Although it has classical and Renaissance roots, modern Humanism is a child of the European Enlightenment. Elsewhere—for example, in India, Japan, and China—it appears in some forms of Buddhism (Theravāda Buddhism, Zen) and Confucianism. Among Humanism's modern antecedents were "natural religion," deism, "free thought" and "the religion of humanity" (proposed by the nineteenth century French sociologist Auguste Comte). The development of natural science, of liberal democracy, and of secular society marked the institutional context of Humanism. Nineteenth century social reform in the United States and democratic socialism in England and Europe reinforced the move toward a human-centered philosophy. Critical studies—for example, the "higher criticism" of scripture, archeology, and comparative religious scholarship—encouraged a skeptical view of transcendent and supernatural bases for ethics and politics. With the advent of Darwinism and the development of modern biology, sociology, and psychology, the stage was set. Thus, in the early decades of the twentieth century, modern Humanism appeared as both a secular philosophy of living and a religious movement.

The term "Humanism" was not always used. For example, American pragmatism and instrumentalism were both naturalistic and humanistic. Explicit use of the term in its modern form appeared with the emergence of a "religion without god" in the thought of three twentieth century Unitarian ministers: John H. Dietrich, Curtis Reese, and Charles Francis Potter. While they and a few of their colleagues in Unitarianism and the Ethical Culture Societies were moving toward a "religious" Humanism, a secular expression of the same notion was appearing in the work of naturalistic philosophers such as Roy Wood Sellars and John Dewey. Both threads came together with the publication of *The Humanist Manifesto* (1933). A second *Manifesto* (1973) and *A Secular Humanist Declaration* (1981) expanded but did not alter the meaning of the 1933 document. Signed by some thirty-five philosophers and religious leaders, *The Humanist Manifesto* marked the entry of an independent explicit Humanism into the Western world. Before that, Humanism had been attached to existing movements, such as Christian Humanism and Socialist Humanism, or had other names, such as Ethical Culture and Free Religion. With the founding of The American Humanist Association (1941) and The North American Committee For Humanism (1982), Humanism as a philosophy of living was formally established. After World War II, similar developments in Great Britain, The Netherlands, Belgium, France, Germany, and India led, in 1952, to the organization of The International Humanist and Ethical Union, which had its headquarters in Utrecht, The Netherlands.

Humanism rests, philosophically, on two classical notions: the sophist Protagoras' belief that "man is the measure of all things" and the poet Lucretius' naturalistic interpretation of life and world. In these two root ideas, the career of modern Humanism was foreshadowed. The human-centered feature of Humanism appears in its commitment to human responsibility and freedom. Denying the mistaken view that Humanism is merely the arrogant replacement of God by the human person, freedom and responsibility require human beings to acknowledge their obligation to judge, choose, and act and their opportunity to make a difference to themselves and the world around them. Human beings, thus, are autonomous moral agents (for example, see the ethics of Immanuel Kant). From this view flows the commitment to democracy as the social and political expression of agency, to education as the method of developing competence as an agent, and to science as the outcome of organized intelligence. From this view, too, flows Humanism's skepticism about God and the gods, a skepticism rooted in a rejection of authoritarianism at least as much as in a theological argument about the existence or nonexistence of an all-powerful and all-knowing Being.

From classical Humanism comes modern Humanism's acknowledgment of the interdependence of all beings as well as an appreciation of the beauties and harmonies of the world. At the same time, a tragic note is heard, since Humanists are sensitive to the fact that the world is as precarious as it is dependable and that experience is as surprising (for good or ill) as it is predictable. Thus, Humanist agency is admittedly finite as human insight, and human existence itself is finite. A stoic quality, therefore, attaches to Humanism, a sense of acceptance of the givenness of the world and of the uncontrollable in nature and the individual. Admittedly, the Enlightenment notion of "progress" interpreted the direction of history as ultimately positive, and early twentieth century Humanism interpreted "evolution" as confirming that direction. Post-World War II Humanist thought, particularly because of its Existentialist inspiration, is likely to acknowledge the darker sides of both the individual and the world.

Finally, agency and creativity evolve on the basis of human rationality—the ability to make and understand distinctions, to grasp connections and consequences, and to draw sensible conclusions. Institutionally, this appears as Humanism's commitment to science. It also appears in the celebration of human powers, which it owes to Renaissance Humanism, the move from naturalistic appreciation to Humanist aesthetic sensibility. Overall, then, Humanism is a philosophy of living that views the human person as a rational agent living in a world that both supports and limits him or her. Instead of bemoaning fate or escaping to another and more secure world—a supernatural or transnatural world—the Humanist accepts, enjoys, and works within the constraints that he or she acknowledges as given with the givenness of being.   —*Howard B. Radest*

See also Atheism; Enlightenment ethics; Existentialism; Kantian ethics; Pragmatism; Progressivism; Secular ethics.

BIBLIOGRAPHY

Blackham, Harold J. *Humanism.* Harmondsworth, England: Penguin Books, 1968.

Bullock, Alan. *The Humanist Tradition in the West.* New York. W. W. Norton, 1985.

Dewey, John. *A Common Faith.* New Haven, Conn.: Yale University Press, 1934.

Ericson, Edward L. *The Humanist Way.* New York: Continuum, 1988.

Fromm, Erich. *Marx's Concept of Man.* New York: Ungar, 1961.

Huxley, Julian. *Religion Without Revelation.* New York: Mentor, 1957.

Kurtz, Paul. *Eupraxophy: Living Without Religion.* Buffalo, N.Y.: Prometheus, 1989.

Lamont, Corlis. *The Philosophy of Humanism.* 6th ed. New York: Ungar, 1982.

Olds, Mason. *Religious Humanism in America.* Washington, D.C.: University Press of America, 1978.

Radest, Howard B. *The Devil and Secular Humanism.* New York: Praeger, 1990.

Sartre, Jean-Paul. "Existentialism Is a Humanism." In *Existentialism From Dostoevsky To Sartre,* edited and translated by Walter Kaufmann. New York: Meridian Books, 1956.

Storer, Morris B., ed. *Humanist Ethics.* Buffalo, N.Y.: Prometheus, 1980.

Hume, David (May 7, 1711, Edinburgh, Scotland—Aug. 25, 1776, Edinburgh, Scotland): Philosopher

TYPE OF ETHICS: Enlightenment history

ACHIEVEMENTS: Author of *A Treatise of Human Nature* (1739-1740), *An Enquiry Concerning Human Understanding* (1748), *An Enquiry Concerning the Principles of Morals* (1751), and *Dialogues Concerning Natural Religion* (1779)

SIGNIFICANCE: Hume worked to free ethics or morals from a metaphysical basis rooted either in religion or in natural law

In his philosophy and in his theory of ethics—or morals, the term he preferred—David Hume was the complete empiricist. That is, he denied the validity of any knowledge that existed outside the realm of sensory experience. His ideas and writings were diametrically opposed to the teachings of the established church which maintained that a vast body of metaphysical knowledge existed that could be revealed to humankind only by the grace of God. This was the basis for the formulation of Christian ethics, which were considered eternal.

The philosophers of the Enlightenment had in many ways created a similar metaphysical world of science or nature and had charged humankind with the task of discovering its secrets. For Hume, no knowledge for which there was no antecedent sense impression could claim any validity.

A Treatise of Human Nature. This seminal work has had a profound effect on the development of Western philosophy in many areas: on the evolution of human institutions, on the limitations of knowledge, and on changing moral values. The book is, in a sense, Hume's only work, since all of his subsequent writings were either related to or were reworkings of parts of the original work. Divided into three parts, "Of the Understanding," "Of the Passions," and "Of Morals," the book consists essentially of two parts: one examining how knowledge comes into being and another focusing on the relationship of knowledge to the development of ethics or morals.

An Enquiry Concerning Human Understanding. The basic theme of the *Enquiry,* a reworking of the first part of *A Treatise of Human Nature,* is that all opinions, all theories, all knowledge, in order to be validated, must be submitted to the test of experience. The idea of unknowable substance has no empirical justification in either the spiritual or the material sense. Hume posited the validity of causality. A given cause has always been followed by a given effect. Only custom, repeated experience, and familiarity, however, make it possible to ascertain the development of the effect. Were the knowledge or theory not in the mind, it would not exist. Hume anticipates the relativity of the nineteenth century when he asserts that the opposite of every fact remains possible and that no amount of deductive reasoning from first principles can determine in advance what course nature actually will follow.

An Enquiry Concerning the Principles of Morals. To free ethics or morals of their religious bases, Hume first had to attack the religious establishment, which he did in a subtle but devastating manner. So fearful were his supporters of the reaction to his work that the *Enquiry* was published posthumously. In his *Essay on Miracles,* published in 1748, Hume stated that a miracle in the sense of a supernatural event as a sign of the divinity cannot possibly be established. Rather than constituting evidence of moral and spiritual value, such events are characteristic of sorcery or wizardry.

Once he had stripped away the religious connection, Hume developed his theory of ethics or morals on the basis of pleasure, pain, and utility. It was useless to reason that virtue was "natural" and vice was "unnatural," since both were "natural." Reason is equally useless. Perfectly inert, it can never be the source of so active a principle as conscience or a sense of morality. The solution devolves on the individual. Inherent in all humans are basic feelings or instincts toward family, neighbors, and society. Turning inward, one tends to project oneself into another's situation and to imagine how one would feel under certain circumstances. Happiness in others creates joy, while misery generates sorrow. In other words, conduct is good in proportion to its capacity for producing happiness; conversely, conduct is evil in proportion to its capacity to produce pain. The result of the first is virtue; the result of the second is vice. The greater the pleasure or joy, the greater its utility. It is left to the cognitive and reasoning facilities of humankind to create from these myriad pleasure-pain-utility experiences a coherent ethical code.

Limiting the hedonistic application of this system of ethics and morals based on pain and pleasure was Hume's concept of justice. This was not arrived at by nature but by human conventions. Of all the animals, humans alone suffer a great disparity between their wants and their means of satisfying them. Stability of possession, transference by consent, and the performance of promise are the three fundamental laws of nature. Society is necessary for human existence, and society in the name of justice doles out the rewards that may on the surface seem capricious but upon which ultimately the peace and security of human society depend.

Implications for Ethical Conduct. The implications of Hume's thought are threefold. First, Hume broke the individual's tie with God and transferred it to society. Punishment and rewards were immediate, not confined to the hereafter. Second, Hume invited human society to create its own system of ethics. Third, rather than being static, based on values created by other societies in other times, ethics and morality are organic and ever-changing. Since ethics are subjective, it is society that determines their applicability.

—Nis Petersen

See also Christian ethics; Hobbes, Thomas; Skepticism; Smith, Adam; State of nature; Utilitarianism; Voltaire.

BIBLIOGRAPHY

Flage, Daniel. *David Hume's Theory of Mind.* New York: Routledge, 1990.

Hume, David. *Dialogues Concerning Natural Religion.* Edited by Norman K. Smith. Indianapolis: Bobbs-Merrill, 1981.

_____. *Enquiries Concerning Human Understanding and Concerning the Principles of Morals.* Edited by L. A. Selby-Bigge. 2d ed. Oxford, England: Clarendon Press, 1966.

_____. *An Enquiry Concerning the Principles of Morals.* Edited by J. B. Scheewind. Indianapolis: Hackett, 1983.

_____. *A Treatise of Human Nature.* Edited by Ernest Mossner. New York: Penguin Books, 1984.

Merrill, Kenneth R., and Robert W. Shahan, eds. *David Hume: Many-Sided Genius.* Norman: University of Oklahoma Press, 1976.

Passmore, John Arthur. *Hume's Intentions.* 3d ed. London: Duckworth Press, 1980.

Russell, Bertrand. "David Hume." In *A History of Western Philosophy.* New York: Simon & Schuster, 1945.

Humility

TYPE OF ETHICS: Personal and social ethics
ASSOCIATED WITH: The Judeo-Christian tradition
DEFINITION: Humility is an attitude of self-deprecation that expresses itself through modest and submissive behavior toward others who are deemed superior
SIGNIFICANCE: Whether one regards humility as a virtue or a vice will have a powerful influence on one's view of the good life

Humility is a disposition of character that is usually acquired through training. It consists of an inner attitude of low self-esteem that motivates an outward pattern of deferential behavior. Humble persons are not self-assertive, since they do not pridefully suppose that they possess much merit of their own. Their sense of inferiority leads them to defer respectfully to the wishes of those whom they regard as superior.

To be sure, the term "humility" sometimes is used in other ways. For example, the feminist Sara Ruddick (in her *Maternal Thinking*), after saying that humility is an important virtue for mothers to have, then reveals that she thinks it consists in recognizing that one cannot control everything. Her usage is potentially misleading because she is equating humility with the mere absence of something contrary to it.

Every society regards at least some degree of humility as desirable in at least some of its members. Parents often want their children to be humble toward them, and many customers prefer to be served by humble salespersons. Societies differ greatly, however, in the degree to which they think this trait of character ought to pervade life. Some prize humility highly and advocate it for everyone; others think that inferior members of

the community should be humble but that superior ones should recognize their own merits proudly.

In the Judeo-Christian tradition, humility is assigned a prominent place among the qualities that all human beings ought to cultivate in themselves. Although Christianity does not classify humility as one of the cardinal virtues, it nevertheless continually commends humility, and Saint Thomas Aquinas describes humility as the foundation of all other human virtues.

This stress on humility comes about because one of the most distinctive features of the Judeo-Christian tradition is the vast moral difference it sees between God and human beings. God is described not only as all-powerful and all-knowing but also as supremely good. He is the one faultless being. Moreover, He is quick to become angry at those who fail to show Him respect. To heighten the contrast between the human and the divine, human beings are regarded as utterly contemptible in their sinful weakness and moral corruption. They are seen as deserving no credit for any good qualities that they may possess, since these come entirely as gifts from God. Pride is considered to be the fundamental vice, because it involves a declaration of self-worth apart from God. Thus, the Judeo-Christian view is that human beings should recognize their lack of any independent worth and should seek to walk humbly before God, desiring that in all things His will, not theirs, be done.

The ancient Greek outlook is substantially different. Although believing that their gods were powerful and that it was dangerous to fail to show them respect, the Greeks did not consider their gods to be morally superior. Indeed, according to the Greek myths, every type of misbehavior of which mortals are capable was engaged in by the gods. Far from regarding human beings all as corrupt and contemptible, the Greeks thought that only some of them (especially the non-Greeks) were so. They believed that humans of the better type sometimes can manage on their own to be temperate, courageous, and wise, and are entitled to be proud of such great deeds as they occasionally succeed in performing.

In his *Nicomachean Ethics*, Aristotle lists many moral virtues, each of which he interprets as an intermediate (or "golden mean") between two vices, one of excess and the other of deficiency. With regard to self-appraisal, he sees one extreme as overweening pride, or boastfulness (the vice of having an excessively favorable opinion of oneself), and at the other extreme he places humility (the vice of being deficient in favorable opinion of oneself). For him, the balanced, correct attitude is proper pride. Thus, he sees constant groveling before the gods as a sign of faulty character; people show excellence, he thinks, who have merits of their own and do not hide this from themselves or anyone else.

Aristotle seems to have supposed that the habit of appraising one's own merits accurately should always be cultivated. Some Judeo-Christian thinkers might agree with this recommendation, but they embrace a view of human nature that is different from Aristotle's, and so they think that accuracy dictates an abysmally low appraisal of all merely human qualities. Yet surely accuracy is not quite what one should be seeking here.

Consider someone whose humility is admirable; someone, for example, who displays extraordinary courage in a good cause or unusually energetic devotion to helping the unfortunate, and who then brushes aside praise, sincerely denying that what has been done was in any way remarkable. In such a person, this self-deprecation is inaccurate, since what was done really was outstanding. Yet here this self-deprecation makes the individual's character more admirable, for courage or devotion combined with such humility is even better than courage or devotion without it. An element of self-deception is thus to be welcomed; it is admirable to have trained oneself to underrate one's own merits to some extent.

Why is it deemed to be admirable that people should cultivate an inaccurate humility, rather than strict accuracy in self-appraisal? Surely it is because inflated self-estimates are so widespread and troublesome that society needs to fight against them very forcefully. To set up accuracy in self-appraisal as one's goal would not be sufficiently forceful. Stronger than that as a defense against the pressing dangers of overweening pride is the requirement that one should underrate oneself. Inaccurate humility, because of its social utility, thus rightly comes to be valued above accurate self-appraisal.

—*Stephen F. Barker*

See also Aristotelian ethics; Christian ethics; Jewish ethics; *Nicomachean Ethics*; Pride.

BIBLIOGRAPHY

Aristotle. *Nicomachean Ethics.* 2d ed. London: George Routledge, 1910.

Bowra, C. M. *The Greek Experience.* Cleveland: World, 1957.

Driver, Julia. "The Virtues of Ignorance." *Journal of Philosophy* 86. (July, 1989): 373-384.

"The Gospel According to Matthew." In *New American Standard Bible.* La Habra, Calif.: Foundation Press, 1971.

Häring, Bernard. *The Law of Christ.* Translated by Edwin G. Kaiser. Vol. 1. Westminster, Md.: The Newman Press, 1961.

Hunger

TYPE OF ETHICS: Human rights

DEFINITION: A strong desire or craving for food; in extreme cases, hunger is associated with famine, which causes widespread death by starvation

SIGNIFICANCE: Thomas Hobbes argued that it is in people's self-interest to feed those who are hungry because to do so will reduce competition for food sources and decrease the number of crimes that are committed because of hunger

Hunger is as old as history. More than 15 percent of the world's people are malnourished in even the best of years, and this situation has existed throughout recorded history. In bad years, up to 67 percent of the world's people may suffer from malnutrition. Hunger is an ordinary part of life for many people, even in developed nations such as the United States. Millions of people do not get either enough food or enough nourishing food, and the results are disease and death. Globally, 50 percent of malnourished children in poor countries die before reaching the age of five. Countless others become physically or mentally handicapped for life because of malnutrition.

Hunger is deadly during famines. Throughout history, famines have afflicted one area or another every few years. The principal causes of famine are drought, floods, plant disease, and war. Of these causes, drought is the most frequent.

Drought. In 3500 B.C.E., the Egyptians documented the first famine to be recorded, which was caused by drought and a plague of locusts. The death rate was extremely high, but no accurate estimates of the number of lives lost are available. The Romans documented the second known drought in 436 B.C.E. Thousands of Roman citizens threw themselves into the Tiber River so that they would not have to face starvation. Many early civilizations believed that famines were punishments sent by God.

Mohandas Gandhi once said, "If God should appear to

FAMINE TIME LINE		
3500 B.C.E.	Egypt	Earliest recorded famine
1700 B.C.E.	India	Indus Valley civilization collapses because of drought
436 B.C.E.	Rome	Romans throw themselves into the Tiber River to avoid death by starvation
450 C.E.	Italy (Dufresnoy)	Parents eat children to survive
1300	Southwestern U.S.A.	Cliff Dwellers vanish after drought
1769-1770	India	Drought kills 3-10 million
1790-1792	India	Doji Bara, or skull famine; given this name because the human skulls were too numerous to count
1846-1851	Ireland	Potato famine kills more than 1 million
1876-1878	India	5 million die
1876-1879	China	9-13 million die
1921-1922	Russia	5 million die
1932-1934	Russia	5 million die
1943-1944	India	More than 1.5 million die
1960-1980	Sahel (West Africa)	More than 1 million die
1967-1970	Biafra (Nigeria)	More than 1 million die
1984-1992	Ethiopia/ Somalia	Famines kill more than 1 million

an Indian villager it would be as a loaf of bread." Five of the ten deadliest known famines have occurred in India. Most were caused by the failure of the monsoon rains, which caused drought and crop failure. One of the worst famines in Indian history occurred in 1865, when the monsoons failed to arrive. India was a British colony at the time, but Britain decided to export the extra food that was produced in India rather than send it to the areas that were affected by the famine. The reason that the British gave was that the people in the affected areas could not pay for the food, whereas hungry people in other countries could. Ten million people ultimately died. The monsoon rains failed again between 1876 and 1878, killing 5 million people. A three-year drought that occurred in China between 1876 and 1879 killed more than 13 million people. Tragedy struck again in the Calcutta region of India in 1943 and 1944, killing 1.5 million people.

In the early 1970's and again in 1984, drought plagued many African nations. The Sahel nations lost more than a million people in the 1970's, and eastern and southern Africa lost more than 1.5 million people throughout the 1980's because of drought.

Archaeologists believe that droughts have caused the collapse of whole civilizations. About 4,500 years ago, a great civilization arose in the Indus River valley. Drought caused this civilization, whose major cities were Harappa and Mohenjo-daro, to vanish by 1700 B.C.E. In the southwestern United States, the civilization of the Cliff Dwellers may have ended as a result of drought in approximately 1300.

Floods. Although the lack of rainfall is the major cause of famine, too much rain can also be disastrous. China has suffered hundreds of famines because of floods of the Yellow River. These disasters are so common that the Chinese have nicknamed the river "China's Sorrow." In 1889, as many as 2 million people died in floods, and between 1929 and 1930 the river claimed another 2 million lives. People died in such large numbers that they were buried in mass graves called "ten-thousand-man holes." Women and children were sold to obtain food, and cannibalism spread rapidly. Hurricanes also cause floods that cause famines in many nations.

Plant Disease. Plants suffer from diseases just as humans do. Plant diseases can wipe out crops, causing famine and starvation. Perhaps the most famous example of such a famine occurred in Ireland in the 1840's, when a fungus wiped out most of the potato crop, which was the staple food of the Irish. The resulting famine claimed more than a million lives. Ireland was an English colony at the time, but the English expended little effort to help Ireland. In fact, Irish peasants who could not pay their rent were thrown out into the cold and left to starve in ditches. Many perished, and others tried to escape by migrating. The emigrants were so weak when they boarded ships leaving the country that these ships became known as "coffin ships," because so many people died on board of sickness and starvation before reaching America, England, or Australia. More than a million Irish emigrated because of the "Great Hunger."

A breadline in New York City during the Great Depression. (Library of Congress)

War. Drought, flood, and plant diseases have caused tremendous suffering, but the hunger and famine caused by war are even more horrifying, because they are avoidable.

The people of Russia, the largest country in the world, have suffered often because of famines caused by humankind. One of the worst such famines occurred between 1921 and 1922. World War I was the cause of this tragedy. When many Russians went off to war, beginning in 1914, agricultural production dropped sharply, and by 1920, food was scarce. A drought hit the Volga River valley in 1920 when the rains failed. By 1921, much farmland looked like desert land, and 30 million Russians went hungry. People made bread out of tree leaves, dirt, and water, and they ate cooked grass. Civil war made it difficult to send donated food to the affected areas, and ultimately 5 million people died from hunger. More Russians were killed by the famine than were killed in World War I.

During the Biafran Civil War in Nigeria between 1967 and 1970, more than a million people, mostly women and children, died of starvation when federal forces withheld food from rebels to force them to stop trying to secede from Nigeria. It is not uncommon for governments to use famine as a weapon of war. The Ethiopian government used such tactics in its war against Eritrea, and they have also been used in Mozambique and Angola. The results were that thousands of people died.

Effects of Hunger. People who lack food lose weight and grow weak. Many become so weak that they die of diarrhea or other simple ailments. This weakened condition is called marasmus. Children who have some food but not enough suffer from kwashiorkor, or malnutrition. One symptom of kwashiorkor is edema, which manifests as a swollen stomach, puffy face, and swollen arms and ankles. Hair and skin often take on an orange or white color. Victims who survive kwashiorkor often suffer lifelong mental and physical handicaps. In addition, when it is weakened by hunger, the human body cannot fight off disease. To make matters worse, during most famines, survivors crowd together into relief centers to wait for food, creating the potential for epidemics of diseases such as influenza, measles, cholera, dysentery, typhus, pneumonia, and tuberculosis.

Worse yet are the effects of skyrocketing crimes during droughts, floods, wars, and famines. Desperate people loot, steal, and kill to secure goods that are not otherwise available to them. They may sell stolen goods to purchase food. Women may prostitute themselves for food or sell their children for a meal. Children may band together to obtain food by looting. Violence may break out near food distribution centers, creating panic and anarchy, as occurred in Somalia in 1992. Adaptation to hunger can lead to desperate responses such as cannibalistic murder, which would not be practiced under other circumstances.

Crops are not the only things to be destroyed; livestock often die in record numbers during prolonged famines. Those that do not die may be killed for food. In addition, seed reserved for planting may be eaten to avoid starvation. This lowers agricultural production levels and makes returning to a normal way of life extremely difficult.

Conclusions. Thomas Hobbes noted that people are inherently selfish, mean, and aggressive. History demonstrates that, when they are hungry, parents will take food from the mouths of their own children. The Chinese have argued that if a child dies, it is easy to make another, but an older person who dies is more difficult to replace. During the Italian famine of 450, known as "Dufresnoy," parents allegedly ate their children. Well-fed people are likely to be content; are less likely than hungry people to be angry, hostile, and aggressive; and are less inclined to engage in desperate behavior that may cause harm to others. Therefore, it is in the interest of humankind to reduce or eliminate hunger. A world without hunger would be a safer place for humankind.

—*Dallas L. Browne*

See also Charity; Duty; Generosity; Morality.

BIBLIOGRAPHY

Byron, William, ed. *The Causes of World Hunger*. New York: Paulist Press, 1982.

Lappe, Frances Moore, and Joseph Collins. *World Hunger: Twelve Myths*. New York: Grove Press, 1986.

Lucas, George R., Jr., and Thomas Ogletree, eds. *Lifeboat Ethics: The Moral Dilemmas of World Hunger*. New York: Harper & Row, 1976.

McCuen, Gary E. *World Hunger and Social Justice*. Hudson, Wis.: G. E. McCuen, 1986.

Schwartz-Nobel, Loretta. *Starving in the Shadow of Plenty*. New York: Putnam, 1981.

Toton, Suzanne C. *World Hunger: The Responsibility of Christian Education*. Maryknoll, N.Y.: Orbis Books, 1982.

Ḥusayn ibn ʿAlî

Ḥusayn ibn ʿAlî (c. 626, Medina, Arabia—October 10 [10th of Muharram], 680, Karbala, Iraq): Grandson of the Prophet Muhammad

TYPE OF ETHICS: Religious ethics

ACHIEVEMENTS: His death was one of the formative events in Shîʿa Islam

SIGNIFICANCE: The annual remembrance of the death of Ḥusayn is the most important event in Shîʿa communal life

Ḥusayn and Ḥasan were the sons of ʿAlî ibn Abî Ṭâlib (the cousin of Muhammad) and Fâtima (Muhammad's daughter). Following Muhammad's death, leadership of the Islamic community passed to, in order, Abû Bakr, ʿUmar, ʿUthmân, and ʿAlî. This succession was not without controversy: the "party of ʿAlî" (*shîʿat ʿAlî*; later, simply the Shîʿa) had always held that ʿAlî should be *khalîf*, or leader, of the community. The assassination of ʿAlî in 661 led to a convulsive dispute. ʿAlî was succeeded by Muʿâwiyya, of the Umayya family (whom many mistrusted as outwardly converting to Islam only for selfish gain). Although Ḥasan relinquished his claims to the khalifate (and died c. 670, some claim of poisoning), his younger brother Ḥusayn gathered the *shîʿat ʿAlî* to challenge

Mu'âwiyya. Ḥusayn and most of his party were killed by Mu'âwiyya's troops at Karbala. Shî'a Muslims recognize that as the martyrdom of Ḥusayn, and their annual public remembrance serves as a visceral reminder that human lives belong only to God and are to be surrendered to His service.

See also 'Alî ibn Abî Ṭâlib; Fâṭima; Muḥammad al-Muṣṭafâ; Shî'a.

Hypnosis

TYPE OF ETHICS: Psychological ethics

DATE: Eighteenth century to present

ASSOCIATED WITH: Franz Anton Mesmer, James Braid, John Elliotson, James Esdaile, Sigmund Freud, Clark L. Hull, and Ernest R. Hilgard

DEFINITION: A state of consciousness, achieved through techniques of induction, in which a person may have an increased ability to perform a chosen behavior or acquire a chosen state of mind

SIGNIFICANCE: Because hypnosis gives the appearance of yielding control of one's behavior and mind and conforming to the wishes of the hypnotist, a potential for abuse is perceived

History. Although the eighteenth century Viennese physician Franz Anton Mesmer (1734-1815) no doubt hypnotized some of his patients ("mesmerism"), the concept of hypnosis was unknown before the work of the English physician James Braid (1795-1860). Braid invented the term "hypnosis" and conducted the first scientific studies of hypnotism. Braid devised numerous techniques for inducing the hypnotic state and extensively studied the psychological factors involved. Braid and the British physicians John Elliotson (1791-1868) and James Esdaile (1805-1859) made extensive use of hypnosis in their medical practices as an adjunct to surgery. Esdaile, for example, reported more than three hundred cases in which he performed major operations on unanesthetized but hypnotized patients who apparently experienced no pain.

The psychoanalyst Sigmund Freud (1856-1939) found that hypnosis could be used to relieve symptoms of neurotic and abnormal behavior. Freud repudiated hypnosis as a therapeutic tool, however, because it could only relieve symptoms; it revealed nothing about the causes of the behavior.

Contemporary interest in hypnosis has passed from the physician and psychoanalyst to the experimental psychologist. Psychology's concern with hypnotism involves understanding its nature and mechanisms. Clark L. Hull's (1884-1952) 1933 book *Hypnosis and Suggestibility* was the first systematic attempt to apply modern psychological methods to hypnosis, and Ernest R. Hilgard (b. 1904) and others added significantly to the understanding of this phenomenon.

Characteristics of the Hypnotized State. In *Introduction to Psychology* (1993) Rita L. Atkinson et al. have summarized seven characteristics of the hypnotic state as follows:

1. Planfulness ceases. Hypnotized subjects do not wish to initiate activities; instead, they prefer to be given suggestions by the hypnotist.

2. Attention becomes more than usually selective. The person attends to what the hypnotist commands and ignores other events.

3. Enriched fantasy is readily produced. Unreal events, not unlike dreams, can be experienced easily.

4. Reality testing is reduced and reality distortion is accepted. Altered perceptions of the real world can be produced and believed; for example, talking with an imagined person believed to be sitting in a chair.

5. Suggestibility is increased. The person willingly agrees to cooperate with the induction technique in order to be hypnotized. Some increase in suggestibility—but less than is commonly assumed—also appears to follow.

6. Posthypnotic amnesia is often present. Some hypnotized persons, if instructed to do so, will forget most of what has occurred during the hypnotic suggestion. When a prearranged signal is given, the memories are restored. Also, a signal introduced during hypnotic suggestion, when given posthypnotically, may cause the previously hypnotized person to carry out a prearranged action even though the person will have no memory of having been given the instruction.

7. Responsiveness to hypnotic induction varies. About 5 to 10 percent of people cannot be hypnotized at all, about an equal percentage are very easily hypnotized, and most people fall in between the two extremes. What appears to be the best predictor of susceptibility to being hypnotized is the degree to which the person enjoys daydreaming, can produce vivid mental images, and has a rich imagination.

Ethical Issues of Hypnosis. The above characteristics of the hypnotic state raise the question of whether the hypnotized person becomes unduly dependent upon, controlled by, or influenced by the hypnotist. While in the hypnotic state, could the person be persuaded by an unethical hypnotist to engage in behaviors that he or she otherwise would not perform? Is it possible to induce, for example, irrational, antisocial, criminal, unethical, immoral, or self-destructive behaviors such as impulsively buying a new car, robbing a bank, committing murder, injuring oneself, committing suicide, or having sex with one's hypnotherapist?

The consensus very firmly states that hypnosis *cannot* induce or persuade a person to do anything that he or she would not otherwise do. The belief otherwise undoubtedly arises from the misconception that hypnosis is a condition induced in the person by the hypnotist.

In fact, the hypnotist acts simply as a facilitator, guiding and teaching the person how to think and what to do to produce a particular behavior within the person's capabilities. The person is responsible for and decides whether to perform that behavior. Before a behavior can occur, the person must be willing and able to produce it.

Therefore, the question of ethics is really a pseudoethical issue. The hypnotist is not doing anything to which the person does not consent and cannot compel a person to commit an act that is repugnant to that person or beyond his or her capabilities. As Roy Udolf (1981) cogently observed, antisocial and self-destructive behavior can and have been obtained from hypnotized persons, but the hypnotist cannot induce the hypnotized person to commit those acts. The person had decided to do so already. An unethical hypnotist could, however, facilitate the performance of that act. For example, a hypnotist could make a criminal less nervous and more self-assured during the commission of a crime.

—Laurence Miller

See also Behavior therapy.

BIBLIOGRAPHY

Atkinson, Rita L., et al. *Introduction to Psychology.* 11th ed. New York: Harcourt Brace Jovanovich, 1993.

Gregory, Richard L., ed. *The Oxford Companion to the Mind.* New York: Oxford University Press, 1987.

Hilgard, Ernest R. *The Experience of Hypnosis.* New York: Harcourt, Brace & World, 1968.

Hilgard, Josephine R. *Personality and Hypnosis: A Study of Imaginative Involvement.* 2d ed. Chicago: University of Chicago Press, 1979.

Moss, C. Scott. *Hypnosis in Perspective.* New York: Macmillan, 1965.

Udolf, Roy. *Handbook of Hypnosis for Professionals.* New York: Van Nostrand Reinhold, 1981.

Hypocrisy

TYPE OF ETHICS: Personal and social ethics
DATE: From antiquity
DEFINITION: Feigning to be what one is not, assuming a false appearance of virtue or religion, "posturing"
SIGNIFICANCE: Hypocrisy is the enemy of goodness and honesty; it must be identified and exposed by those whose motives and actions are sincere or "authentic"

Hypocrisy (the act of pretending to have more virtue than one actually possesses) is, in one manner of speaking, the exact opposite of a moral and ethical philosophy, for its practitioners are liars, deceivers, and manipulators. People living according to a just ethical standard must exercise care, for hypocrites can copy the attitudes and behaviors of "good" people and will try to control the good for their own self-centered gain.

Characteristics of Hypocrites. The words "hypocrite" and "hypocrisy" connote the very dispositions and characters of people who are immoral or amoral but who hide their relative immorality with the appearance of morality. The hypocrite "undervalues" noble ideals and is ruled by inferior passions; he or she is inclined to do "bad" things rather than "good" things. He or she is totally corrupt and is a willful liar yet always presents the image of a virtuous person.

Hypocritical behavior. In their worship, religious people worldwide pray, lament, and make promises to their God. Too often, they promptly forget those promises as they scurry to make money, showing little love, little mercy, little

trust, little kindness, no brotherhood, and no forgiveness. Many people who call themselves Christians, Muslims, Jews, and so forth are curiously unmoved by the suffering of others.

To find religious hypocrites, one need not look beyond religious leaders. In the United States alone, the 1980's and 1990's witnessed many religious scandals. One Christian televangelist (a married parent), in preaching to his flock, often condemned sinners and showed much glee as he sadistically described their suffering in the "pits" of hell for all eternity. Later, he was photographed patronizing a prostitute who later averred that he was a "pervert." The televangelist then tearfully repented on his television show. Later, he was caught again patronizing a prostitute, but he continued his television show, the main purpose of which seemed to be begging for money; the same man had earlier ruined another preacher by making references to the other's bad character.

Yet another televangelist, famed for the development of a religious theme park, was eventually imprisoned because he misappropriated contributions from the faithful. Although several pentecostal leaders appeared to have attracted the largest news headlines, Catholic priests have not been immune to criticism. In recent years, many priests have helped women commit adultery and have engaged in various sex crimes, including the molestation of children. Recently, another televangelist staged an unsuccessful campaign for high political office; he was noted for his sincere religious beliefs and his no-nonsense view of morality. Frequently, he thundered about sinners, especially fornicators. Before his political campaign was over, however, his detractors found evidence proving that he had married his wife only after she became pregnant.

Of course, the world's hypocrites come not only from the realm of religion but from all "walks" of life. In the 1970's, as the United States faced the Watergate scandal, President Richard Nixon, in a nationwide television broadcast, righteously proclaimed that he was not a "crook"; this event occurred shortly before he resigned rather than face impeachment proceedings. Later, in the 1980's and 1990's, bankers all across the land lied to cover up their part in the savings and loan scandals, with many still lying just before authorities indicted, convicted, and sentenced them to very light terms in white collar prisons. Additionally, in the 1990's, many members of Congress showed "self-righteous indignation" upon learning that their "bank" was under investigation; shortly thereafter, it was proved that many of them were overdrawn and in arrears (check "kiting" is a crime, and common folk most likely would have been prosecuted).

Even the world of sports has its own kind of hypocrisy. A former football star of the University of Oklahoma's "Sooners" lent his name to and made television appearances on behalf of the "Just Say No" campaign against drugs. Additionally, he spoke on many occasions to youth groups—all this shortly before he was found guilty and sent to prison for the illegal use of drugs.

Conclusion. The dangers that the hypocrite poses are largely self-evident. The hypocritical politician "looks out for number one." While bespeaking the public interest, he or she may "sell out" to special interest groups, and if found out will likely scream about assaults on his or her good character. The hypocritical religious leader will use—for selfish purposes—the very foundations of religious faith. Even the action of the aforementioned hypocritical football star had the negative effect of affecting young people's views of the adult world, in which leaders and "stars" to often are consummate liars—to the detriment of society.

—*James Smallwood*

See also Cheating; Lying.

BIBLIOGRAPHY

Eck, Marcel. *Lies and Truth*. Translated by Bernard Murchland. New York: Macmillan, 1970.

Evans, Donald. *Faith, Authenticity, and Morality*. Toronto: University of Toronto Press, 1980.

——————. *Struggle and Fulfillment: The Inner Dynamics of Religion and Morality*. London: Collins, 1979.

Fingarette, Herbert. *Self-Deception*. New York: Humanities Press, 1969.

Goleman, Daniel. *Vital Lies, Simple Truths: The Psychology of Self-Deception*. New York: Simon & Schuster, 1985.

Martin, Mike W. *Self-Deception and Morality*. Lawrence: University Press of Kansas, 1986.

Newman, Jay. *Fanatics and Hypocrites*. Buffalo, N.Y.: Prometheus Books, 1986.

Scott, John Finley. *Internalization of Norms: A Sociological Theory of Moral Commitment*. Englewood Cliffs, N.J.: Prentice-Hall, 1971.

Trilling, Lionel. *Sincerity and Authenticity*. Cambridge, Mass.: Harvard University Press, 1971.

Wittgenstein, Ludwig. *Culture and Value*. Translated by Peter Winch. New York: Basil Blackwell, 1984.

I and Thou: Book

TYPE OF ETHICS: Modern history
DATE: Published 1922 as *Ich und du*
AUTHOR: Martin Buber
SIGNIFICANCE: Buber's work views reality as fundamentally social, consisting of interpersonal relationships among persons, relationships that are defined in moral action and are expressed in the symbiotic kinship of humankind and nature

Buber's central question of the meaning of humanness is expressed in his recurring word *Wesen* (essence, being, nature), as understood in terms of two primary word-pairs: "I-You" and "I-It." The I-You relationship is total involvement of self and other in intimacy, sharing, empathy, caring, openness, and trust. The I-It relationship consists of self viewing other in abstract terms, resulting in possession, exploitation, and distrust. The I-It pair permits the self to objectify the other, creating a state of manipulative dependency, and the I-You pair encourages an atmosphere of interdependence, permitting growth and respect. Only through genuine I-You encounters do people discover their humanity and, by mutually affirming and confirming one another, come face to face with the Eternal Thou. Realistically, Buber recognized that every I-You can become an encounter, and in his poetic *Sprachdenken* ("thinking in terms of language"), he counseled that one's essential humanity is lost if one treats every You (animate and inanimate) as an It (acts of hate, killing, vandalism). "Without It man cannot live; but he who lives with It alone, is not a man." In the area of religion, Buber insisted that any religious form that is not in the category of I-You is illicit or at least nonreligious. Thus, he was critical of Jewish Halachah (religious orthopraxy) and Christian sacraments; he believed that the nature and essence of God are not restricted to doctrines and dogmas. Buber's classic statement on essentials is essentially existential.

See also Buber, Martin.

Ibn al-ʿArabî, Muhyî al-Dîn Muhammad (July 28, 1165, Murcia, Spain—Nov. 16, 1240, Damascus, Syria): Philosopher

TYPE OF ETHICS: Religious ethics
ACHIEVEMENTS: Author of *al-Futûhât al-Makkiyat* (*Meccan Revelations*), *Fusûs al-Hikam* (1229; *Gems of Wisdom*), and other influential philosophical treatises on mysticism
SIGNIFICANCE: Ibn al-ʿArabî presented Sufism in systematic philosophical form; his work is often seen as the creative zenith of Sufism and is still widely influential

Ibn al-ʿArabî's work captured the devotional spirit of earlier Sufism, gave it sophisticated and original philosophical expression, and, in so doing, both gave it new force and made it more acceptable to more conservative Muslims. His singular obsession was with *wahdat al-wujûd* (perhaps, "the unity of Being"). He argued that God is the only true reality (*al-haqq*) and the inner nature of all things; the phenomenal world is a manifestation or mirror of that reality. God, considered as manifestation, is creation (*al-khalq*)—a claim that has led to controversies about whether Ibn al-ʿArabî was a pantheist. Annihilation or immersion of the soul (*fanâ'*) in the real unity of Being is, he argued, the ultimate human good. Humans occupy a special position in the cosmos because they are able to know God both in His phenomenal nature through sense perception and in His inner nature by achieving *fanâ'*. One who has perfected all the potentials of the soul is the Perfect Man, who, in Ibn al-ʿArabî's thought, is exemplified by Muhammad.

See also Islamic ethics; Muhammad al Mustafâ; Sufism.

Ibn Gabirol, Solomon ben Yehuda (c. 1020, probably Málaga, Spain—c. 1057, Valencia, Spain): Philosopher and poet

TYPE OF ETHICS: Religious ethics
ACHIEVEMENTS: Author of *Fons vitae* (*The Source of Life*, 1963), which was originally written in Arabic but is known only in its Latin translation; introduced Neoplatonism into Europe and strongly influenced the Christian scholasticism of the Middle Ages
SIGNIFICANCE: Considered one of the greatest poets of the "Golden Age" of Spanish Jewry (ninth century through twelfth century), Ibn Gabirol utilized philosophy and poetry in an attempt to penetrate the ultimate truth of life

Orphaned early in life and raised in Saragossa, Ibn Gabirol devoted much of his life to the pursuit of wisdom (philosophy), in which he found solace from his serious physical ailments and his squabbles with wealthy patrons and town elders, which caused him great mental anguish. His *Fons vitae* is more Neoplatonic than Aristotelian, more religious than theological. It holds that the purpose of human life is for the soul to commune with the upper world, and it emphasizes knowledge and contemplation rather than action. The subjects of the *Fons vitae* are three: God, or pure spiritual substance; divine will, which is separate from the essence of God; and universal matter and universal form, which, in combination, produce universal reason. The universe is a gradual series of emanations of substances, and the farther a substance is from the source of all, the more material and corporeal it becomes. The gradation of substances is unified by the divine will, which permeates the whole series of gradations. In this point, Ibn Gabirol departs from classical Neoplatonism, which teaches the system of emanations in a mechanical way that is totally alien to the Jewish idea of creation. The human soul, an emanation of the world-soul, is eternal, but, in uniting with the body in the corporeal world, it is lowered from its pristine purity. The soul retains its desire to return to its source, however, and this is accomplished in two ways: through knowledge of the divine will as it extends into matter and form, and apart from matter and form; and by reason, by means of which the soul unites with world reason and ultimately attaches to the "source of life." Ibn Gabirol's long philosophical poem *Keter Malkhut* (*The Kingly Crown*, 1911) is addressed to the human intellectual aspiration to discover God ("I flee from You, to You") and praises figuratively the attributes of God. This classic poem is included in the High Holiday services of Ashkenazic and Sephardic Jews.

See also Jewish ethics; Kabbala.

Ibn Rushd. *See* Averroës.

Ibn Sînâ. *See* Avicenna.

Ibn Khaldûn (May 27, 1332, Tunis—Mar. 16, 1406, Cairo, Egypt): Philosopher

TYPE OF ETHICS: Religious ethics

ACHIEVEMENTS: Author of *Kitâb al-'ibar* (1382), the first history of Muslim North Africa, and *Muqaddimah* (1375-1379; *The Muqaddimah*)

SIGNIFICANCE: A founder of historicism, or history as philosophy, Ibn Khaldûn developed a system of political ethics that he hoped would benefit society and aid in the development of civilizations

Born into a family of scholars and government officials, Ibn Khaldûn lost his family in 1349 to the Black Death. After the completion of his formal studies, he became a roving ambassador, serving a series of rulers in North Africa and Moorish Spain. At the same time, he began collecting material for his *Kitâb al-'ibar*, or universal history, which he completed in 1382. The most important part of this work was its "Prolegomena," or introduction, which made an attempt to establish a purpose for history. Disturbed by the decline of the Muslim states and Muslim civilization, Ibn Khaldûn sought to find reasons for it, after which he set forth a series of ethical principles that he believed must be followed to reverse the decline. Although he was a good Muslim, Ibn Khaldûn introduced the concept of natural causality. He believed that society was the creation and the responsibility of human beings. Ibn Khaldûn believed that social organization, and especially the state, was the key to improved individual welfare and the refinement of civilization. He held that rulers should develop ethical political principles such as placing the welfare of society before individual aggrandizement, ameliorating taxes, infusing the state with a sense of purpose, and avoiding unnecessary wars. Ibn Khaldûn spent the final years of his life in Cairo, where he was a Muslim judge and a professor.

See also Islamic ethics.

Ideal observer

TYPE OF ETHICS: Theory of ethics

DATE: Eighteenth century

ASSOCIATED WITH: Francis Hutcheson, David Hume, and Adam Smith

DEFINITION: A person or being who has an ideal degree of nonmoral knowledge and intellectual abilities, and who, according to some theories, lacks certain kinds of bias or prior value commitments

SIGNIFICANCE: Can be used to define what is right, good, or virtuous without making controversial moral assumptions, and in accordance with naturalism

The idea of an ideal observer emerged in the eighteenth century in the work of British moralists such as Francis Hutcheson, David Hume, and Adam Smith. These writers emphasized the importance of full information and impartiality in moral judgment, and they considered the approval of an observer with such characteristics to define moral truth. For the British moralists, such approval depended on the existence of certain moral sentiments, such as benevolence and sympathy. In the twentieth century, the ideal observer, which has been thought of as mainly self-interested, has been used to provide naturalistic theories of moral judgment and moral truth. For example, Richard Brandt has defined a person's own good as what that person would want if he or she had full information and had reflected on it in the appropriate way. Some philosophers, such as John Rawls, have also defined moral rightness in terms of the idea of self-interested, impartial observers.

See also Smith, Adam.

Idealist ethics

TYPE OF ETHICS: Theory of ethics

DATE: Fourth century B.C.E. to present

ASSOCIATED WITH: Plato

DEFINITION: A view of moral decisions that accents first principles, rather than the consequences of actions, in affirming appropriate behavior

SIGNIFICANCE: Based on the application of universal moral laws to human behavior, idealist ethics catalyzed relativistic views of ethics, principally pragmatism and utilitarianism, during the nineteenth century; provides a logic for evaluating moral conduct deontologically, according to formal rules of ethical behavior

Proponents of idealist ethics view values as unchanging, timeless realities. Values are real existents. The efficacy of values is situated in an ongoing, vital interrelationship between the uniqueness of a person's value experiences, on the one hand, and the harmonious totality of life, often termed the "Universal Self" or "Absolute," on the other hand. The ethics of human behavior are governed by immutable universal moral laws that are binding on all persons. These laws are known through the exercise of human reason.

History. The originator of idealist ethics, Plato (c. 428 B.C.E.—348/347 B.C.E.) established a world of absolutes consisting of eternal Ideas or Forms such as "goodness," "justice," and "virtue," which were discussed respectively in his *Protagoras, Republic,* and *Meno,* on the basis of which to formulate ethical concepts. Plato's assumption that the ethical quality of human life is governed by the person's obligation to form a rational moral personality, succinctly stated in the maxim "All virtue is knowledge," is present in the views of his disciples regarding ethical behavior.

The Christian Platonist Augustine of Hippo (354-430 C.E.) viewed human behavior as governed by a priori (existing prior to the event) absolutes—the right direction of love, for example. In the post-Renaissance and post-Enlightenment interpretations of Platonic idealism and its accent on centering ethics in a spiritual or intelligible universe, major variations of idealistic ethics occurred: Among them were German Idealism, exemplified in the writings of Immanuel Kant (1724-1804) and Georg W. F. Hegel (1770-1831), and American Transcendentalism, present in the philosophy of Ralph Waldo Emerson (1803-1882). Each philosopher defined ethics within an idealized world of abstract reality, influential on yet divorced from a world of sensory experience. More contemporary idealists, such as Josiah Royce (1855-1916) and Alfred North Whitehead (1861-1947), continued the idealist tradition of founding ethical considerations on absolute, presumed permanent ideals. Royce's student Herman Harrell Horne (1874-1946) applied idealist ethics to education in his *This New Education* (1931), which was reminiscent of an earlier American idealist's work: that of William T. Harris (1835-1909), editor of *The Journal of Speculative Philosophy* and post-Civil War spokesperson for the neo-Hegelians of the St. Louis, Missouri, Philosophical Society. Of Plato's impact on the subsequent development of Western philosophy, Alfred North Whitehead wrote: "The safest general characterization of the European philosophical tradition is that it consists of a series of footnotes to Plato."

Principles of Idealist Ethics. Idealist ethics originates in human comprehension of and adherence to the Platonic ideational forms of the "good": justice, knowledge, and virtue. Enunciated in *Republic* by Plato's allegory of the metals, the just society is an idealized one in which rulers, guardians (those who enforce rulers' decisions), farmers, and craftspeople harmoniously coexist by internalizing the four cardinal virtues of wisdom, courage, temperance, and justice, defined as a state of human affairs in which each contributes to society according to the predetermined limits of his function. Kant's ethical treatise *Critique of Practical Reason* (1788) accented conformity of ethical behavior to a priori principles of the mind. According to the Kantian categorical imperative, every person possesses an innate imperative to do good and is ethically bound by a duty to obey universal moral laws predicated on an idealized state based on the maxim Kant announced in *The Fundamental Principles of the Metaphysics of Ethics* (1785): "Act so that . . . you are treating mankind also as an end, never merely as a means." Kant's famous categorical imperative assumes that human behavior should conform to idealized moral law, not human self-interest: "Act only according to a maxim by which you can at the same time will that it shall become a general law."

Nineteenth century neo-Kantians adhered to the Platonic principle that human actions must conform to the dictate of absolute value—"the good"—as revealed, through the exercise of reason, by "the *Geist* or absolute spirit" (Georg W. F. Hegel) or the "God-reliance" of Ralph Waldo Emerson. This principle is clearly enunciated in Hegel's *Encyclopedia of the Philosophical Sciences in Outline* (1817) and Emerson's *The Conduct of Life* (1860).

Idealist ethics accents the principle that human self-realization occurs within a societal context providing development and nurture; morality or ethical behavior is, however, essentially ideational in nature. Hence, the ethics through which human lives are lived results not from sensory experience but from cognitive deliberation.

Idealist Ethics: An Appraisal. In the late nineteenth century and throughout the twentieth century, principles of idealist ethics were on the defensive. Realist Bertrand Russell (1872-1970) saw in idealist ethics a failure to distinguish between a person's perceptual act and the separately existing content, or "sense datum," of that act, a weakness attributed to the British empiricist George Berkeley's (1685-1753) statement *esse est percipi* ("to be is to be perceived"). In *Religion and Science* (1936), Russell viewed ethical values as totally subjective and hence unknowable: "What science cannot discover, mankind cannot know." Positivists and pragmatists have disagreed with the idealist accent on the pivotal place of the ideal or the spiritual in determining the criteria for ethical behavior. Linguistic philosophy finds ambiguities in the technical terms of idealist ethics; existentialists and phenomenologists take exception to the Platonist assumption that there exists in the universe a normative, prescriptive, intelligible or spiritual reality, independent of the sensory world, as the source of ethics.

While idealist ethics are on the wane in Western culture, support for the principles of idealist ethics—indeed, advocacy of those principles—has not diminished. Claiming Plato's *Republic* as "*the* book on education," Allan Bloom argues for a return to the "essential being" of idealist ethics through a "common concern for the good" in *The Closing of the American Mind* (1987). It is difficult to view idealist ethical concerns and their underlying rich tradition as totally absent in the contemporary world. —*Malcolm B. Campbell*

See also Emerson, Ralph Waldo; Hegel, Georg Wilhelm Friedrich; Kant, Immanuel; Plato; Platonic ethics; *Republic*; Russell, Bertrand.

BIBLIOGRAPHY

Bloom, Allan. *The Closing of the American Mind.* New York: Simon & Schuster, 1987.

Butler, J. Donald. *Four Philosophies and their Practice in Education and Religion.* New York: Harper & Row, 1957.

Foster, John. *The Case for Idealism.* Boston: Routledge & Kegan Paul, 1982.

Hoernle, R. F. A. *Idealism as a Philosophy.* New York: George H. Doran, 1927.

Inwood, Michael. *A Hegel Dictionary.* Cambridge, Mass.: Blackwell, 1992.

Kant, Immanuel. *Lectures on Ethics.* Translated by Louis Infield. Indianapolis, Ind.: Hackett, 1980.

Kuntz, Paul Grimley. *Bertrand Russell.* Boston: Twayne, 1986.

Lucas, George R., Jr. *The Rehabilitation of Whitehead: An Analytic and Historical Assessment of Process Philosophy.* Albany: State University of New York Press, 1989.

Plato. *The Republic*. Translated by Allan Bloom. New York: Basic Books, 1968.

Sainsbury, R. M. *Russell*. Boston: Routledge & Kegan Paul, 1979.

Sprigge, T. L. S. *The Vindication of Absolute Idealism*. Edinburgh, Scotland: University of Edinburgh Press, 1983.

Urban, W. M. *The Intelligible World*. New York: Macmillan, 1929.

Vesey, Godfrey, ed. *Idealism, Past and Present*. New York: Cambridge University Press, 1982.

Walhout, Donald. *The Good: And the Realm of Values*. Notre Dame, Ind.: University of Notre Dame Press, 1978.

Ideology

TYPE OF ETHICS: Theory of ethics

DATE: Coined 1795

ASSOCIATED WITH: Marxism and the sociology of knowledge

DEFINITION: Ideology may refer to any set of beliefs and values or it may refer to a set of false ideas used to conceal reality

SIGNIFICANCE: The difference between ideology and ethics may determine whether ethics and moral norms are just instruments used by the ruling class to sanction their power and authority

The French savant Antoine Destutt de Tracy can be credited for coining the term "ideology" in 1795. For Destutt de Tracy, ideology had a neutral value signifying only ideas and ideals. In the history of its development, ideology has acquired two distinct senses. In a general sense, it applies to any set or system of ideas, whether they are philosophical, political, theological, or ethical. In a more critical sense, ideology refers to any false set of ideas used by the dominant classes to control the subordinate classes.

Approaching ethics from an ideological point of view means to inquire into the relationship between ethics and social classes. Ideological critique presupposes a conflictual model of society in which dominant social classes and subordinate or oppressed social classes struggle for power and autonomy.

The Marxist tradition has given more prominence to ideology in its social and ethical analysis than to any other theory. Karl Marx partly derived his concept of ideology from his intellectual mentor, the German philosopher Georg Wilhelm Friedrich Hegel, who, in his philosophy of history, set forth the claim that human history moves forward by the "Cunning of Reason," independent of any individual human awareness. From Ludwig Feuerbach, a critic of Hegel, Marx appropriated the idea that theological, moral, and metaphysical beliefs stem from the wishful projections of human psychology. Marx, however, deepened Feuerbach's position and asserted the sociological roots of ideology.

In the 1859 "Preface" to a *Contribution to a Critique of Political Economy*, Marx summarized his historical method. He utilized a structural approach that divided society into "structure" and "superstructure." By structure, he meant the economic and social relations generated by the productive sphere. By superstructure, Marx referred to the state, its juridical-legal system, and the cultural realm of morality, religion, art, and philosophy—in short, ideology. Marx believed that the form of the economic foundation of the state determined the form and content of the state's ideological superstructure. For example, in a capitalist society, the laws protect private property and moral norms justify the disparity between the rich and poor. In an earlier work called the *German Ideology*, Marx criticized the ideological nature of German philosophy for its justification of the Prussian state. There also appears the metaphysical claim that the material conditions of life determine forms of social consciousness. In *Das Kapital*, Marx claims that capitalism generates a form of illusory consciousness that Marx names "commodity-fetishism." By commodity-fetishism, Marx means the false belief that commodities exchange on the basis of intrinsic value. In reality, values are extrinsic to the commodities and are based on ratios of social labor. In the *Critique of the Gotha Programme*, Marx refers to morality as ideological nonsense and calls the modern liberal ideas of equality and justice "bourgeois" and "ideological." Nevertheless, Marx was not beyond inveighing moral dictums against the exploitative and alienating features of capitalism like a Hebrew prophet.

Later Marxists followed the lines of thought opened up by Marx. Antonio Gramsci, founder of the Italian Communist Party, formulated the concept of hegemony to express the ideological forces of the modern bourgeois state. Hegemony refers to the power and authority attained and maintained by the ruling classes through the coercive apparatus of the state and through the consent gained by the cultural institutions of civil society. Louis Althusser, a French communist philosopher, developed the idea of ideological state apparatus. Briefly put, in order for society to maintain the status quo, it must also reproduce the fundamental economic social relations; that is, reproduce workers who submit to the bourgeois social control. This submission is made possible by ideological state apparatuses such as schools and churches, which express the ideas of the ruling classes. Jürgen Habermas stressed the notion of legitimation as the acceptance of a social system by the members of that society.

In the sociology of knowledge tradition, intellectuals sensitive to the crisis of relativism and skeptical of human rationality developed similar notions of ideology critique parallel to those of the Marxists. Max Weber linked up certain religious tendencies to affinities with different social classes. He also set forth the idea of a theodicy of legitimation for the privileged and a theodicy of compensation for the oppressed. For Weber, ideology meant the consciousness of an epoch. Thus, ideology entailed ethical relativism. Karl Mannheim showed how Christianity provided an ideology for the dominant classes and utopias for the oppressed. He also believed that there was a need for a class of individuals freed from any social class loyalty. These he found among academic intellectuals, the so-called free-floating intelligent-sia. Sociology in general studies how social structures coerce individual human behavior and morality.

Several questions are raised by an ideological approach. How do social classes develop forms of consciousness containing particular ideologies? What role do ideologies play in social change? Does not the claim that ethics is ideological lead to ethical skepticism and ethical relativism?

—*Michael R. Candelaria*

See also Capitalism; Communism; Marxism; Weber, Max.

BIBLIOGRAPHY

Althusser, Louis. *Lenin and Philosophy and Other Essays.* Translated by Ben Brewster. New York: Monthly Review Press, 1971.

Gramsci, Antonio. *Selections from the Prison Notebooks.* Edited and translated by Quintin Hoare and Geoffrey Nowell Smith. New York: International, 1971.

Lukacs, Georg. *History and Class Consciousness: Studies in Marxist Dialectics.* Translated by Rodney Livingstone. Cambridge, Mass.: MIT Press, 1983.

Marx, Karl. *The Marx-Engels Reader.* Edited by Robert C. Tucker. 2d ed. New York: W. W. Norton, 1978.

Weber, Max. *The Protestant Ethic and the Spirit of Capitalism.* Translated by Talcott Parsons. New York: Charles Scribner's Sons, 1976.

Illness

TYPE OF ETHICS: Bioethics
DEFINITION: Lack of health; presence of disease
SIGNIFICANCE: An accepted definition of illness provides guidelines for responsibilities of medical professionals, patients, and society in the treatment of both healthy and ill people

In the twentieth century, particularly since World War II, advances in medicine have taken place so rapidly that the health care profession has ballooned. With this expansion has come consistently increasing, often unattainable, expectations about what can and should be treated by the medical profession.

Health. It is impossible to focus on a particular definition or viewpoint of illness without looking at its counterpart, health. Some people hold that illness is simply lack of health, but any definition of health is controversial. The World Health Organization (WHO) in 1946 offered this definition: "Health is a state of complete physical, mental and social well-being." It is easy to see why this is controversial. This definition places such states as grief in opposition to health, as well as such social problems as racial oppression and poverty. Simultaneously, by classifying these things as health problems, it obligates the health care profession to broaden its scope to include them. Many people have taken issue with the WHO definition of health, but no one has yet been able to formulate one that is any more widely accepted.

Views of Health and Illness. There are three predominant views of the concepts of health and illness. The first, the empirical view, proposes that the health of any organism is determined by whether that organism functions the way it was designed by nature to function. Illness, then, is any situation or entity that hinders the ability of the organism to function in the way in which nature intended. Proponents of this view point out that this definition is equally applicable to plants, animals, and humans. An organism is determined to be ill or healthy without reference to symptoms subject to interpretation by either the patient or the evaluator.

Another view of health and illness holds that health is that which is statistically normal, and illness is that which is statistically deviant. The problem with this view is that it ends up classifying many things society sees as positive traits, such as extreme intelligence or strength, as illness. Proponents, however, point out that what nature intended for a specific organism is often determined by statistical evidence.

The third view is that of normativism. Normativists believe that the concepts of health and illness incorporate cultural and societal values, because what is viewed as illness depends on what the particular culture considers desirable or undesirable. For example, in seventeenth century America, there was a "disease" called drapetomania, which caused otherwise content slaves in the South to have the uncontrollable urge to escape. The designation of illness also depends on the ability or willingness of a society to recognize a situation as undesirable. A society without any written component would not be likely to consider dyslexia an impairment.

The normative view is especially prevalent (and compelling) in the field of mental health. The designation of what is a disease is a product of the culture of the time. For example, in the nineteenth century, women who enjoyed sexual intercourse were considered mentally dysfunctional, while in the twentieth century, the opposite is true. Certain factions, such as advocates for alcoholics, have fought long and hard to have their particular problems labeled as disease. Others, such as homosexuals, have fought equally hard to keep themselves from being so labeled.

Implications of Definitions. Why is the label of illness so desirable or undesirable? When a particular set of symptoms or problems is labeled as an illness, its presence carries with it certain properties of the "sick role." Behaviors that would otherwise be seen as unacceptable or immoral are excused. Responsibility is diminished, both for actions and for inaction. The label of illness also carries with it, however, a certain stigma; that of the necessity to strive for a cure. This is why groups such as homosexuals have fought it so strenuously.

On a more general level, definitions of health and illness define the boundaries and obligations of the medical profession. It is reasonably clear that ideas about health care needs follow the line of ideas about health. The current conception of health care in Western society, the medical model, tends to support the paternalism of health care professionals as interventionists who relieve patients of their responsibility to care for themselves. A nonmedical model, however, tends to emphasize individual responsibility for health.

European immigrants traveling to the United States during the late 1800's. (Library of Congress)

Disease Versus Illness. Most people consider the terms "disease" and "illness" to be synonymous. Some, however, separate illness into a subcategory of disease. This separation bridges the gap between the empirical and the normative definitions of health. Disease is seen as simply the impairment of natural function, as in the empirical view. Illnesses are diseases that incorporate normative aspects in their evaluations. An illness is a disease whose diagnosis confers upon its owner the special treatment of the sick role. Not all diseases are illnesses. Diseases such as sickle-cell anemia may not impair the health of the individual, and thus do not incur the sick role.

Generally accepted definitions of health, illness, and disease are becoming more necessary as the health care profession grows. Until society clarifies these concepts, health care will be called upon to mitigate every problem society has, not only the enormous number it is traditionally expected to solve. —*Margaret Hawthorne*

See also Mental illness.

BIBLIOGRAPHY

Beauchamp, Tom L., and LeRoy Walters, eds. *Contemporary Issues in Bioethics.* 3d ed. Belmont, Calif.: Wadsworth, 1989.

Boorse, Christopher. "On the Distinction Between Disease and Illness." *Philosophy and Public Affairs* 5 (Fall, 1975): 49-68.

Callahan, Daniel. "The WHO Definition of 'Health.'" *The Hastings Center Studies* 1, no. 3 (1973): 77-88.

Caplan, Arthur L. "The Concepts of Health and Disease." *Medical Ethics.* Edited by Robert M. Veatch. Boston: Jones & Bartlett, 1989.

Engelhardt, H. Tristam, Jr. "Health and Disease: Philosophical Perspectives." In *Encyclopedia of Bioethics.* Edited by Warren T. Reich. New York: Free Press, 1978.

Macklin, Ruth. "Mental Health and Mental Illness: Some Problems of Definition and Concept Formation." *Philosophy of Science* 39 (September, 1972): 341-364.

Immigration Reform and Control Act

TYPE OF ETHICS: Politico-economic ethics

DATE: Passed 1986

ASSOCIATED WITH: Senator Alan Simpson; Immigration and Naturalization Services

DEFINITION: The IRCA was designed to ease social and economic problems caused by illegal immigration

SIGNIFICANCE: With the IRCA, the United States attempted for the first time to punish the employers of illegal immigrants, not only the illegals themselves, recognizing both as lawbreakers

The Immigration Reform and Control Act was passed after emotional debate in Congress. Nearly everyone recognized that immigration policy needed to be overhauled, but many opponents felt that the proposed law was designed specifically to keep out Hispanics and other people of color. The act had three main goals. Illegal immigrants already in the United States lived in fear of being found and deported; therefore, they were easily exploited by unscrupulous employers who paid unfair wages. Under the terms of the act, illegal aliens who came forward to register were granted amnesty and could eventually apply for citizenship. The act further increased funding for Immigration and Naturalization Services (INS) to turn back illegals at the borders. Later years showed this attempt to be very successful. Finally, the act made it more difficult for illegals to be hired for work in the United States; it was hoped that this would discourage them from attempting to come in the first place. Employers were now required to document that new employees were legally eligible for work in the United States.

See also Citizenship.

Immortality

TYPE OF ETHICS: Theory of ethics

DATE: Believed in by the ancient Egyptians by around 3500 B.C.E.

ASSOCIATED WITH: Major world religions such as Christianity and Islam; the German philosopher Immanuel Kant

DEFINITION: Belief in eternal life

SIGNIFICANCE: Many people believe that ethical grounds such as the demand for moral perfection, the justice of the universe, the value of the individual, and the goodness of God support belief in personal immortality

Immanuel Kant, in his *Critique of Practical Reason* (1788), argued for the immortality of the soul along the following lines. "We are morally obligated to achieve moral perfection, a complete correspondence between our intentions and the moral law. Anything we are obligated to do is something we can do. But we cannot achieve moral perfection in this life. So given that moral perfection is obligatory, an infinite life during which moral perfection can be attained must be postulated." In effect, Kant claims that the moral law requires as a corollary the immortality of the soul.

Kant's argument has several questionable aspects. Some people, claiming that morality is solely a matter of societal opinion or individual feeling, will reject outright the idea of a moral law and therefore will not be moved by Kant's argument. Even objectivists in ethics may claim that Kant's argument does not prove the existence of immortality, since it does not prove an objective moral law. Optimists about human nature may say that if people can control themselves in any given case, they may also be able to control themselves in every case, and therefore moral perfection in this life is possible even though it is difficult. Others may question whether people are obligated to be morally perfect. Does the moral law require people to be perfect as well as to do their duty? If people are not obligated to achieve moral perfection but only to strive to achieve it, there is no need to postulate immortality. Those who think that they have independent grounds against the belief in immortality may say that no one is obligated to be morally perfect, since it is not possible to achieve such perfection in a single lifetime. Finally, it may be asked why achieving moral perfection requires postulating immortality rather than an extremely long afterlife.

Other moral arguments for immortality clearly rest on religious assumptions. Some appeal to a divine recompense, as follows: "In this life, the virtuous are not always rewarded, and the vicious are not always punished. Since God is just and powerful, however, there is an eternal life in which each receives his or her just recompense." No doubt, many people are motivated by a desire to avoid hell and reach heaven. Others worry that raising questions about immortality will undermine the motivation to act morally. They think that if there is no ultimate recompense, it is irrational for people to do what is right when it conflicts with their self-interest.

It is a mistake, however, to assume that moral behavior cannot be rational unless it promotes one's own welfare. If rational behavior instead only promotes one's ends, then since one can have altruistic ends, one can behave rationally without promoting one's own welfare. Thus, moral behavior that is not rewarded in this life can be rational even if it is not rewarded in a future life. A major motive for moral behavior is concern for other people, respect for their value. This kind of motivation does not depend on immortality, and this kind of concern is an important part of a fully human life; therefore, it is not irrational.

The recompense argument is based on the assumption that God exists. To accept God's existence on faith is to accept immortality on faith. To the extent that God's existence is not proved, the future life based on it is not proved. Granting God's existence, would divine recompense take an eternity? Even if it would, would God balance the scales of justice? Some people maintain that God's goodness would require this, but that conclusion does not follow. Even if a just God regards human mortality as bad, that does not mean that God should or would end it. To do so may require God to sacrifice something He regards as more important. God's overall best plan for the universe may include this evil as well as others. The evil of human mortality may be a necessary part of a greater good.

Some claim that a good and powerful God would guarantee our immortality because people are such valuable beings, full of infinite potentialities, or because God would not disappoint those in whom He has instilled a desire for immortality. These reasons are not convincing.

It is a mistake to think that humans cannot be valuable if they are not permanent. Many things, such as good health, are valuable even though they cannot last forever. It also seems clear that Socrates and Gandhi were valuable individuals even though they did not last forever. From the claim that humans are worthy of being immortal, it does not follow that humans are immortal.

The idea that a good God would not disappoint those in whom He has inspired a natural desire for immortality also does not stand scrutiny. Does this desire come from God or from society? Many Hindus and Buddhists do not desire immortality. They strive to avoid being reborn, because they believe that blessedness involves a complete extinction of the individual. Even assuming that the desire for personal immortality were universal, it is clear that a good God would not necessarily satisfy every human desire.

—*Gregory P. Rich*

See also God; Religion.

BIBLIOGRAPHY

Ducasse, C. J. *A Critical Examination of the Belief in a Life After Death.* Springfield, Ill.: Charles C Thomas, 1961.

Flew, Antony. "Immortality." In *The Encyclopedia of Philosophy,* edited by Paul Edwards. Vol. 4. New York: Macmillan, 1972.

Hick, John. *Death and Eternal Life.* San Francisco: Harper & Row, 1980.

Lamont, Corliss. *The Illusion of Immortality.* 4th ed. New York: Frederick Ungar, 1965.

Wainwright, William J. *Philosophy of Religion.* Belmont, Calif.: Wadsworth, 1988.

Impartiality

TYPE OF ETHICS: Theory of ethics
DATE: First used in the early 1600's
ASSOCIATED WITH: David Hume, Immanuel Kant, John Stuart Mill, Kurt Baier, and John Rawls
DEFINITION: Freedom from prejudice or bias; fairness
SIGNIFICANCE: A central concept in ethical theories that otherwise differ significantly; many theorists assert that an ethics without impartiality is impossible

The concept of impartiality is suggested by various early writings and is implied by the golden rule of Jesus, which states that you should do unto others as you would have others do unto you. The idea of freedom from prejudice, even from prejudice toward oneself, however, occurs most often in ethical writing after 1700. David Hume claims that impartiality prevails when making moral judgments. Socially useful acts are approved. In "The Standard of Taste" (1757), Hume asserts

that people accept as their own "the judgments of an impartial observer." Immanuel Kant, putting forward a very different theory from that of Hume, also stresses impartiality. He claims that duty is the same for all people. John Stuart Mill, developing a utilitarian ethical theory, asserts that utilitarianism requires one to be strictly impartial.

This concept of impartiality also occurs in writings of the twentieth century. In *The Moral Point of View* (1958), Kurt Baier states that the same rules should pertain to all. He asserts that we must adopt an impartial viewpoint. John Rawls, in *A Theory of Justice* (1971), urges a "veil of ignorance" where the rules of society are established by individuals who do not know what their own position will be in the society. In this approach, the rules that are developed will be impartial and fair to all.

See also Hume, David; Kant, Immanuel; Mill, John Stuart; Rawls, John.

In re Gault

TYPE OF ETHICS: Children's rights
DATE: 1967
ASSOCIATED WITH: U.S. Supreme Court
DEFINITION: The Court held that states must provide many elements of due process of law in criminal proceedings against juvenile defendants
SIGNIFICANCE: The decision stands for the proposition that juveniles are as entitled as adults to many of the basic procedural guarantees and evidentiary rules

In re Gault was the result of the arrest of Gerald Gault in 1965 for making a lewd telephone call to a neighbor. Gault, who was then fifteen years old, was on probation for an earlier minor offense. On the basis of police rumor about Gault as well as statements elicited from him in the absence of his parents or his lawyer, and without evidence or hearing, the juvenile judge found Gault to be delinquent. He was committed to a state industrial school until his eighteenth birthday. Gault's appeal to the Arizona Supreme Court was unsuccessful, and he brought the case to the U.S. Supreme Court. The Court decided by a vote of 7-2 that juveniles are entitled to notice of charges, right to counsel, right to confrontation and cross-examination of witnesses, privilege against self-incrimination, a transcript of the proceedings, and appellate review. The majority argued that these minimal guarantees assure fairness without unduly interfering with any of the benefits of less formal procedures for juveniles.

See also Bill of Rights, U.S.; Due process; *Goss v. Lopez.*

In vitro fertilization

TYPE OF ETHICS: Bioethics
DATE: First performed 1959
ASSOCIATED WITH: American Fertility Society, Patrick C. Steptoe and Robert G. Edwards, and RESOLVE, Incorporated
DEFINITION: The physiological union of sperm and ovum outside the female's body

Significance: Permitted both the separation of the genetic from the gestational role of motherhood and the embryo's early development away from the mother's body

The term's origins are unknown, since the terms *in vitro* ("in glass") and "fertilization" have long been used in science. Attempts at in vitro fertilization (IVF) had been reported since 1878 but had not been confirmed until M. C. Chang reported successful pregnancies from rabbit ova that had been fertilized externally and placed in foster wombs. After scientists mastered the preliminary steps to human IVF, Patrick C. Steptoe and Robert G. Edwards reported a tubal pregnancy in 1976. Articles decrying the new reproductive technique and its potential monstrosities ran beside articles heralding the advent of a cure for infertility. The birth of Louise Joy Brown in 1978 was among the most publicly covered events of the century, and her birth turned the tide of public sentiment. About one in six couples experiences infertility; IVF and related technologies show promise for 10 to 15 percent of those who do not respond to other treatments. The government reported about five thousand births from IVF worldwide by 1988.

Noncoital Parenthood. The Catholic Church and some non-Catholic theologians oppose all noncoital reproductive techniques, including artificial insemination, because they separate the marital and the reproductive functions of love. Others see nothing problematic about achieving human parenthood "artificially," since control over the environment intrinsically defines human nature. A middle position admits that IVF's artificiality may harm marriage but holds that the overall benefits provided by parenthood outweigh those harms for some couples.

Similar secular objections are that IVF's artificiality will affect society's conception of humanness and will lead to the objectification of all embryos and of women. Others worry about its psychological effects on the parents and children. Most consider the reproductive technologies to be no more of an "interference with nature" than is any other medical procedure.

Many IVF programs do not accept unmarried or lesbian women. Although many would argue that children should be raised in traditional families, this screening singles out IVF and makes physicians the moral arbiters for society. Some allege that IVF reinforces, without examination, societal views that women must provide husbands with a genetically related child in order to achieve full womanhood.

The Embryo's Status. When a single embryo is implanted to produce a live birth, IVF closely resembles coital conception. For those who believe that human life and personhood begin at implantation or later, the embryo's status presents few problems. For those who believe that human life and personhood begin at conception, however, IVF can be problematic, especially when it is used to study embryonic development or contraception. Does using embryos in research to provide a cure for diabetes or Parkinson's disease constitute unauthorized experimentation on unborn children? Even as a substitute for normal conception, IVF results in

greater "wastage" of embryos because of more failures to implant and more miscarriages. Because "harvesting" ova is expensive and invasive, women are often hormonally induced to produce several ova. Often, physicians implant multiple embryos to increase the chances of live births; this procedure increases the possibility of multiple births or selective abortion if too many embryos are implanted. Alternatively, because cryogenic preservation is possible after fertilization, some physicians implant embryos one at a time. Should excess frozen embryos be allowed to "die" or be donated to other infertile couples? A wealthy couple's 1983 death raised the issue of whether their frozen embryos should become their heirs. What happens if a couple divorces? A judge facing the issue awarded "custody" to the mother who wanted the embryos implanted. In 1992, the Tennessee Supreme Court reversed that decision, declaring that the embryos were neither property nor persons but an interim category entitled to respect because of their potential for human life; it held that both parents had rights to decide the embryos' fate prior to implantation but that the father's right not to be a genetic parent outweighed the mother's desire to donate the embryos. All the government commissions examining the embryo's status adopted this interim category, recommending that experimentation be allowed until the fourteenth day of development and that the embryo be "treated with respect" but not accorded full rights of personhood.

Experimental Technique. As soon as IVF live births demonstrated success, "infertility centers" sprouted around the country. Since humans were only the fourth species that demonstrated success with IVF, some people accused scientists of rushing to experiment on women before properly studying IVF in animals. In the 1980's, many infertility "specialists" were inadequately trained and promised overgenerous results. Although there are no apparent problems, negative effects on the children of IVF cannot, as the DES tragedy demonstrated, be ruled out until the test group is larger and reaches reproductive age. Moreover, the long-term effects of superovulating women are unknown. A de facto federal moratorium on funding IVF has resulted in no regulatory research to demonstrate the efficacy or safety of IVF and no development of guidelines; most research is connected with commercial interests. Moreover, IVF is expensive and has a low rate of successful pregnancies (an average rate of 10 to 15 percent per procedure); some question making these expenditures to overcome infertility when resources are needed to care for or adopt living children and for research into avoiding the causes of infertility. Distributive justice concerns are also raised; even if covered by health insurance, which often declares IVF too experimental, IVF will not be affordable for most couples.

Possible Uses of IVF. As with artificial insemination, IVF makes the donation of gametes possible; this possibility raises questions of the advisability of separating the genetic from the other roles of parenthood, including the possibility of detrimental effects on the children's identities. In fact, through surrogacy, the gestational mother need be neither the biological mother nor the intended mother. IVF is used to treat both male and female infertility. Some people question the reliance on using surgery on the woman to overcome the husband's low sperm count, particularly in the light of the dearth of research on the causes of and cures for male infertility. Preimplantation genetic testing of the embryo can be accomplished harmlessly, thus raising the advisability of genetic screening, including sex selection.

—Ileana Dominguez-Urban

See also Brown, Louise; Life and death; Medical ethics; Right to life; Surrogate motherhood.

BIBLIOGRAPHY

Bonnicksen, Andrea L. *In Vitro Fertilization: Building Policy From Laboratories to Legislatures*. New York: Columbia University Press, 1989.

Elias, Sherman, and George J. Annas. *Reproductive Genetics and the Law*. Chicago: Year Book Medical, 1987.

McCartan, M. Karen. "A Survey of the Legal, Ethical, and Public Policy Considerations of In Vitro Fertilization." *Journal of Law, Ethics, and Public Policy* 2 (1986): 695-731.

Robertson, John A. "In the Beginning: The Legal Status of Early Embryos." *Virginia Law Review* 76, no. 3 (April 1, 1990): 437-517.

Sherwin, Susan. *No Longer Patient: Feminist Ethics and Health Care*. Philadelphia, Pa.: Temple University Press, 1992.

Smith, George P. "Assisted Noncoital Reproduction: A Comparative Analysis." *Boston University International Law Journal* 8, no. 1 (Spring, 1990): 21-52.

U.S. Congress. Office of Technology Assessment. *Infertility: Medical and Social Choices*. OTA-BA-358. Washington, D.C.: Government Printing Office, 1988.

Incest

TYPE OF ETHICS: Sex and gender issues
DATE: From antiquity
ASSOCIATED WITH: Societal sexual taboos
DEFINITION: Sexual intercourse or sexual activity leading to arousal that occurs between certain categories of relatives, such as father and daughter, mother and son, and so forth
SIGNIFICANCE: An incest taboo exists in most societies, although societies differ in the ways in which they define incest; the incest taboo is particularly powerful; incest is not only illegal in most societies but is also considered heinous

The Problem. Incest seems to be a growing problem. In the United States, at least, reported cases of incest are on the rise. Prior to the 1970's, incest seemed to be kept hidden. Increasingly, however, victims and their protectors began speaking out, and the public and legal authorities became more aware of the problem than ever before.

The "typical" offender in incest cases is the father (in approximately 90 percent of the reported cases), and the victim is usually his daughter. Fully 97 percent of all reported cases of parent-offspring incest involve father-daughter couplings or arousing sex "play." Only 3 percent of the perpetrators are female. When incest involves the father and the son, as it does in approximately 7 percent of reported cases, the young male has a second issue to grapple with—that of the father's bisexuality or homosexuality. Men who take sexual advantage of young relatives typically suffer from low self-esteem brought on by physical, mental, and, sometimes, sexual abuse that they suffered as children.

Many reasons for forbidding incest have been offered. Society has been "told," for example, that incestuous relations are likely to produce mentally and/or physically defective offspring. Although modern geneticists have learned that that fear is unfounded, laypersons still fear incest for this reason. Another reason to forbid incest involves family stability: Incest could create chaos in the family by causing jealousies and the exchanging of, or confusion about, roles, which could cause the family to become "organizationally dysfunctional." Such a family would not survive as a unit, and if enough families engaged in the practice, society itself would break down. Hence, a ban or taboo on the practice becomes a "functional prerequisite" for society.

Another reason to avoid incest exists. Many authorities emphasize the psychological harm done to victims. The "crime" is so heinous that victims are often sworn to secrecy, becoming in a sense "responsible" not only for the act but also for keeping the family together by not talking. Fighting such strains, victims emerge with poor self-esteem and related psychological problems. As time passes, most victims cannot engage in "age-appropriate" play, and they tend to develop few outside interests. Some create discipline problems at home and at school. Furthermore, incest teaches some victims that if they like someone, they should act out their feelings sexually.

Apparent Exceptions. Recently, some scholars have begun to question the "negative only" view of incest. William Arens, for example, cited an investigator who studied twenty brother-sister marriages that occurred in one state. The investigator reported that the couples, all of whom were living in middle-class suburbia, led fruitful lives and were happily raising their offspring as normal human beings. Another case involved a twenty-eight-year-old married middle-class woman who regularly visited her elderly widowed father to clean his house and cook for him. The two regularly had sex because the woman had promised her mother that she would "take care of Dad."

Another case involved a nineteen-year-old college coed. When she was preparing a research paper for a class in abnormal psychology, she had a severe anxiety attack that required hospitalization. She had just read that incest was a taboo, a heinous crime; in apparent innocence, she had been having sex with her father and three brothers since she was thirteen. Her analyst reported that she had had to take over the domestic duties of the family upon the death of her mother and that she had "assumed" that sex was part of her "responsibility" because men "needed it." Furthermore, the analyst reported that the coed seemed well adjusted, happy, and guilt-free—until she went to the college library and read about the "horrors" of incest.

Such cases led some experts to talk of "functional" incest, which makes possible a shift in traditional family "roles" that enables the family to continue as a unit rather than to disintegrate. One scholar analyzed 425 published case studies of incest from America and Europe and identified ninety-three as "nonpathological" cases in which incest was a "functional" response that allowed the families to stay together.

One researcher recounted the story of a family in South America whose members had been shunned by their community because some family members engaged in prostitution and others engaged in bootlegging. The ostracism eventually resulted in incestuous relations among as many as forty family members and created a monstrous problem for those exploring the family genealogy. One man had relations with his mother, who bore his daughter. Years later, he had relations with his daughter, who then had a daughter. He thus became father, brother, and mate to his first daughter and grandfather, father, brother, and mate to his second daughter. In this case, however, incest did not mean disintegration of the family; in fact, the family members handled the cross-generational and sibling incest quite well. The family stayed together, and the individual members seemed well adjusted and happy.

Such cases should be regarded as exceptions. In most cases of incest, tragedy and suffering result; incest usually tears a family asunder, partly because of the behavior itself and partly because of the learned aversion to incest.

—James Smallwood

See also Child abuse; Rape; Sexual abuse and harassment; Sexuality and sexual ethics.

BIBLIOGRAPHY

Herman, Judith Lewis, with Lisa Hirschman. *Father-Daughter Incest.* Cambridge, Mass.: Harvard University Press, 1981.

Maisch, Herbert. *Incest.* Translated by Colin Bearne. New York: Stein & Day, 1972.

Renshaw, Domeena C. *Incest.* Boston: Little, Brown, 1982.

Rush, Florence. *The Best-Kept Secret.* Englewood Cliffs, N.J.: Prentice-Hall, 1980.

Starcke, Carl Nicolai. *The Primitive Family in Its Origin and Development.* Chicago: University of Chicago Press, 1976.

Stern, Curt. *Principles of Human Genetics.* San Francisco: W. H. Freeman, 1973.

Storr, Anthony. *Human Destructiveness.* 2d ed. London: Routledge, 1991.

Wilson, Edward O. *On Human Nature.* Cambridge, Mass.: Harvard University Press, 1978.

Index librorum prohibitorum

TYPE OF ETHICS: Arts and censorship
DATES: 1557-1966
DEFINITION: For the Roman Catholic church, the *Index librorum prohibitorum,* or list of forbidden books, served as a catalog of books determined to be against the faith or morals of Roman Catholicism and, accordingly, censored by the church; members of the Roman Catholic

INDEX LIBRORUM PROHIBITORUM TIME LINE	
1557	The first *Index librorum prohibitorum* is drawn up by the Congregation of the Inquisition, under Pope Paul IV but never published.
1559	The first version of the *Index* is published, in a larger and more extensive format than that compiled in 1557.
1571	Pope Pius V establishes a special "Congregation of the Index" to oversee the list and revise it as necessary.
1664	The *Index* begins to list books and authors alphabetically.
1753	Pope Benedict XIV develops new, detailed rules to be followed in future compilations of the *Index.*
1757	Under Benedict, the *Index* is revised extensively and cleared of previous errors.
1897	In the *Officiorum ac munerum,* Leo XII outlines censorship duties for diocesan bishops, which include control of literature judged contrary to faith or morals. The *Index* begins to occupy a less prominent place in hierarchical Church affairs.
1917	Pope Benedict XV transfers the charge of the *Index* to the Holy Office.
1948	The final edition of the *Index,* containing 4,100 entries, is published.
1966	The *Index librorum prohibitorum* is abolished after the Vatican Council II and becomes a historic document for Roman Catholicism. Church officials do, however, retain the authority to prohibit future books that constitute a threat to the faith or morals of Catholics.

church were forbidden, except in special circumstances, to read or possess books included in the catalog

SIGNIFICANCE: Example of church censorship

The *Index librorum prohibitorum* was never intended to be an exhaustive catalog of forbidden literature. Rather, it represented those works condemned by the church in response to specific requests from people around the world. The majority of works included in the *Index* were theological in nature. During the first century (1559 to 1649) of its four centuries of existence, 469 texts appeared in the *Index*; in its second century, 1,585 were added; in its third, 1,039 were added; and in its final century, 1,585 were added. By the time the status of the *Index* became that of a historical document, 4,126 writings were listed. Some entries denoted specific titles, whereas others designated authors with Latin notations such as *omnia opera dramatica* ("all dramatic works" [forbidden]) or, the most severe censure, *opera omnia* ("all works" [forbidden]). Among those whose writings were forbidden were such notables as Émile Zola (all works), Stendhal (all love stories forbidden), Samuel Richardson (*Pamela: or Virtue Rewarded*, 1740), Lawrence Sterne (*A Sentimental Journey through France and Italy*,1768), Edward Gibbon (*The History of the Decline and Fall of the Roman Empire*, 1776-1788), and the complete works of British philosophers Thomas Hobbes and David Hume. Only four American authors (whose writings were theological in nature) have ever been listed on the *Index*.

See also Art; Art and public policy; Book banning; Censorship.

Individualism

TYPE OF ETHICS: Personal and social ethics
DATE: Seventeenth century to present
ASSOCIATED WITH: Egoism, free enterprise, and political liberty
DEFINITION: The theory that individual human beings are the fundamental units of reality and value
SIGNIFICANCE: Places the value of the individual at the foundation of all ethical and social principles; opposes collectivism

At the core of most debates about human nature, ethics, and politics is the debate about the power and value of the individual. In analyzing human nature, individualists emphasize that individuals have the power to control their own thoughts and actions and therefore to form their own characters by their choices. In ethics, individualists emphasize the value and potential of each individual, and so they encourage self-reliance, independence, and the quest for each person to realize his or her own unique self. In politics, individualists encourage laissez-faire—that is, leaving individuals free to pursue their own ends—and therefore they encourage free enterprise and limited government. In each area, individualists oppose the collectivist idea that individuals are molded by or subordinate to larger social groups.

History. Individualist ideas predate the use of the term "individualism." Early in the modern era, Thomas Hobbes (1588-1679) and John Locke (1632-1704) argued that political power begins with individuals and is consequently transferred to governments. They opposed the traditional idea that power naturally resides with an aristocracy or monarchy and is imposed on individuals. Government exists to serve its citizens, not vice versa. A gradual decentralization of power followed the rise of individualist ideas, giving rise to more democratic political institutions and free market economic institutions. A highlight year for individualism was 1776, for in that year the United States of America was founded explicitly on individualist political ideas and Adam Smith published *The Wealth of Nations,* an influential description and defense of the free market system of economic individualism.

Alexis de Tocqueville is usually credited with the first use of the term "individualism," in his *Democracy in America* (1835-1839). He used "individualism" to describe the American character to which he had had mixed reactions; while he admired the energy and vitality of American individualism, he also feared that it would eventually degenerate into atomic selfishness.

F. A. Hayek has noted that the Saint-Simonians (named for Claude Saint-Simon, 1760-1825), the founders of modern socialism, used "individualism" to describe the free market, competitive society they opposed.

Ethics. Individualism in ethics is associated with egoism, the theory that each individual's life is his or her highest value. Individuals are ends in themselves, not servants or slaves to the needs or interests of others. Since in order to survive and prosper individuals need to think and act independently, self-reliance, initiative, pride, and courage in the face of disapproval are encouraged as virtues. Individualism thus is opposed to collectivism in ethics, the theory that larger social groupings are more important than the individuals that make them up and that individuals have a duty to sacrifice for the benefit of the group, whether the group be class, race, tribe, family, or nation. Individuals recognize the great value of cooperation but emphasize that cooperative social groups exist solely for the benefit of the individuals that participate in them; individuals do not exist to serve the group.

Politics. Individualism has important implications for economics and politics. Economically, valuing independence of thought and action translates into encouraging economic independence. Independence does not mean that individuals live as hermits. Rather, in a society based on the division of labor, it means providing for one's needs by producing the value-equivalent of what one needs and trading with others for mutual benefit.

Politically, valuing independence translates into recognizing and protecting individual spheres of autonomy. Individual autonomy can be violated in three broad ways: killing, assault (including slavery and kidnapping), and theft. Therefore, protecting individual autonomy means protecting individuals' lives, liberties, and property. The social institution established for this purpose is government, and to prevent abuses, political power will be decentralized as much as possible and limited to protective functions.

Thus, individualism encourages the decentralization of both political and economic power. The foundation of political authority resides in the individual citizens, and the power of government is limited to serving individuals' need for autonomy. Along with political decentralization goes economic decentralization: Economic power resides in individual ownership of property, and investment and consumption decisions remain in individual hands. Individualism is thus associated with limited government and free enterprise.

Human Nature. All the above depends on an analysis of human nature. To support individualism in ethics and politics individuals must be both capable and worthy of autonomy. This leads us to the three most fundamental debates about human nature between individualists and collectivists:

1. Whether only individuals exist and groups are only aggregates of individuals, or social groups are organic wholes of which individuals are only dependent fragments.

2. Whether individuals are born cognitively and morally *tabula rasa* ("blank slate") or are born with the inherently destructive elements (for example, with Christian Original Sin or a Freudian id) and therefore require strict social constraints.

3. Supposing that individuals are born *tabula rasa,* either they have the capacity to create their own characters and destinies by controlling their own thoughts and actions or they are formed and controlled by the social groups to which they belong.

Issues 2 and 3 raise the complex of nature versus nurture versus free will issues, and it is in the resolution of these issues of human nature that the fate of individuals lies.

—*Stephen R. C. Hicks*

See also Self-interest.

BIBLIOGRAPHY

Bellah, Robert N., et al. Habits of the Heart: Individualism and Commitment in American Life. New York: Harper & Row, 1986.

Hayek, Friedrich A. "Individualism: True and False." In Individualism and Economic Order. Chicago: University of Chicago Press, 1948.

Macpherson, C. B. The Political Theory of Possessive Individualism. Oxford: Oxford University Press, 1988.

Rand, Ayn. *The Virtue of Selfishness.* New York: New American Library, 1964.

Tocqueville, Alexis de. *Democracy in America.* Edited by J. P. Mayer. Translated by George Lawrence. New York: Harper & Row, 1988. See especially part 2: chapters 1 and 2 of book 1, and chapters 2 and 4 of book 2.

Infidelity. *See* **Adultery.**

Information, access to

TYPE OF ETHICS: Media ethics
DATE: 1950's to present
ASSOCIATED WITH: Computer technology, privacy
DEFINITION: The access and exchange of personal information stored on computers
SIGNIFICANCE: As computers are used to gather, store and exchange more information about individuals, access to that information comes into conflict with the right to privacy

Ethical Issues. The ability to store and exchange computerized information about individuals raises ethical questions about access to that information. Who should have access to personal information? Does the right of the government to know take precedence over an individual's right to privacy? What kind of information should not be kept or shared? Complicating these issues is the tendency to accept information obtained from a computer as totally accurate. Given authorized access, how can the information be verified as accurate? Do people have a right to examine information pertaining to them?

The Rise of Information Technology. Since World War II, computer and communications technology have combined to produce a major influence on Western society.

The first generation of computers had thousands of vacuum tubes, required huge amounts of electricity for power and cooling, and cost so much that only governments and very large corporations could afford them. The development of the transistor, the integrated circuit, and the microprocessor led to generations of ever-more-affordable computers. By the 1970's, computer technology had reached virtually every level of the economic infrastructure. Computers became repositories for criminal and tax records, health and employment records, and credit and financial information. The communications revolution parallels the computer revolution. Satellites and fiber optic lines have made possible the almost instant transmission of data between geographically distant computers.

Federal Legislation. The first two decades of computer technology progressed without much discussion of ethical issues. By 1965, the Federal Bureau of Investigation (FBI) began to develop the National Crime Information Center as a central repository of criminal arrest records. That same year, the proposed idea of centralizing government records of individual citizens in a National Data Center was met with strong opposition in Congress. Debate over the National Data Center focused national attention for the first time on the issue of invasion of privacy as people began to fear the prospect of an Orwellian all-seeing, all-knowing government becoming reality.

In *Menard v. Mitchell,* a landmark 1971 federal case, the court ruled that a "compelling public necessity" had to be proved before an individual's arrest record could be widely disseminated. Legislation by Congress followed. The Privacy Act of 1975 regulated the use of criminal justice information, and the Freedom of Information Act of 1977 gave individuals the right to access nonclassified government records.

The Private Sector. The first attempt to regulate the retail credit industry's use of personal credit information had come with the Fair Credit Reporting Act of 1969. By the 1980's and 1990's, however, personal information had become a lucrative commodity driving a huge industry. The two largest credit bureaus maintained separate databases of more than 150 million files, which they made available to banks, credit card companies, and virtually any other business willing to pay for the service. Many people believed that the protection of the Fair Credit Reporting Act was no longer adequate. Reports by the news media and consumer advocates documented cases of individuals being victimized by false and ruinous credit information. A 1991 Consumer Union study found inaccuracies in nearly half the records it sampled.

Smaller companies specialized in providing demographic and consumer information to direct marketing firms. For a small monthly fee, customers had access to detailed information on millions of households, including address, telephone number, property ownership, and legal records. Manufacturers often routinely sold information taken from cards returned by consumers for product warranty registration to direct marketers, who used it to target potential customers more accurately.

Prospects for Regulation. Because access to personal information has reached virtually every level of modern society, regulation by a single law or agency is impossible. Federal and state governments struggle to sort out the questions of access versus privacy and enact appropriate legislation, while some critics question the government's ability to regulate itself. By 1982, U.S. government computers contained more than 3.5 billion personal files. The FBI continues to build a database of the arrest records of 25 million people, whether or not their arrests resulted in convictions.

In the 1970's, the National Security Agency (NSA) and International Business Machines (IBM) developed the Data Encryption Standard (DES) to ensure secure transmission of classified information over telephone and data lines. Data or conversations that are transmitted between two points are encrypted with a mathematical key. In 1993, the introduction of a DES integrated circuit chip, to be made available in commercial products, led the Clinton administration to support its widespread use. Privacy advocates hailed the advent of the DES chip but worried that a new standard with government control of the keys could trigger abuses of wiretapping and that computer hackers might be able to duplicate the new standard's classified algorithm.

Meanwhile, groups such as the Consumer Union and the American Civil Liberties Union, as well as individual citizens, continued to press for protection against abuses by both the government and the private sector.

Summary. The ethics of information access began with the issue of privacy versus the government's right to acquire knowledge for the public good but expanded as businesses began to perceive their access to personal information as part of their right to do business in a free-market economy.

Some social analysts claim that the Information Age has brought a change in values to modern society, where the benefits and convenience of free access to information outweigh the individual's right to privacy. It has even been proposed that since an individual's personal information is a commodity with commercial value, that person should be compensated with a royalty whenever the information is sold.

The Industrial Revolution was welcomed as an unmixed blessing to humankind for many years before society began to consider such ethical issues as child labor and pollution. The Information Age has brought sweeping changes to society at a much faster pace. Sorting out the ethics of information access and creating systems for control is a slow process, with much opportunity for abuse in the meantime, because the very concepts of information and privacy are being redefined by this rapidly developing technology.

—Charles E. Sutphen

See also American Civil Liberties Union (ACLU); Computer technology; Confidentiality; Freedom of Information Act; Privacy.

BIBLIOGRAPHY

Allen, Dennis. "Ethics of Electronic Information." *Byte* 17 (August, 1992): 10.

Begley, Sharon, et al. "Technology: The Code of the Future." *Newsweek* 121 (June 7, 1993): 70.

Hoerr, John, et al. "Privacy." *Business Week*, March 28, 1988, 61-68.

Lacayo, Richard. "Nowhere to Hide." *Time* 138 (November 11, 1991): 34-40.

Marchand, Donald A. *The Politics of Privacy, Computers, and Criminal Justice Records.* Arlington, Va.: Information Resources Press, 1980.

Roszak, Theodore. *The Cult of Information.* New York: Pantheon Books, 1986.

Wayner, Peter. "Clipped Wings? Encryption Chip Draws Fire." *Byte* 18 (July, 1993): 36.

Inside information

TYPE OF ETHICS: Media ethics

DATE: First prosecuted 1961

ASSOCIATED WITH: Stock market trading; property rights of information

DEFINITION: Knowledge obtained from someone in a position of power or from someone who has access to confidential information or who is in a position to influence the decisions of a company

SIGNIFICANCE: Allows for the violation of employment and civic contracts by using information obtained through professional performance for personal gain or other unintended purposes

Confidential information that derives from the fulfillment of professional or civic duties is a valuable commodity. Misappropriation of such knowledge is a common occurrence in the banking and securities industry, where frequent opportunity exists to convert one's knowledge into a monetary profit through the buying and selling of stocks about which one has secret information. The Securities and Exchange Commission explicitly prohibits such practices and vigorously prosecutes violators. Media professionals, too, have access to information that is proprietary in nature and that has the potential for misuse. The wide scope of the First Amendment and the privileges guaranteed to the press therein, however, preclude the existence of both a regulatory body and legal restrictions designed to control the use of information. Therefore, the press, as with other questions of conduct, is obliged to address the ethical issues on a situational basis, weighing circumstances along with values, loyalties, and journalistic principles.

Two central issues exist regarding the issue of inside information: how the information is obtained and how it is used. In regard to the securing of information, journalists are morally obligated to remain objective and uncompromised and to respect the boundaries of legal as well as ethical codes. Because a journalist's primary obligation is to distribute information, however, even these simple tenets must be weighed in the light of a situation's defining circumstances. *The New York Times*, for example, in the publication of the Pentagon Papers, knowingly accepted stolen materials in the light of what the editors reasoned was a greater moral good—the exposition of a governmental effort to misrepresent the realities of the Vietnam War.

The second question concerns how inside information can be ethically used by media professionals. The code of ethics of the Society of Professional Journalists states that journalists who use their professional status as representatives of the public for selfish or other unworthy motives violate a high trust. A vigorous and effective press relies on the public trust, so it is incumbent upon journalists to use information humanely, intelligently, and ethically. This process involves questioning the motives of both the reporter and the source of the information, any obligation that may be created on the part of the journalist in exchange for the information, and the nature of the relationship in which the information became known.

That the public interest is best served by making known everything that is knowable is a journalistic standard that justifies much of what is presented as news. When journalists become the recipients of confidential information, however, an ethical dilemma arises that challenges this utilitarian philosophy and the accompanying assertion that an action is just as long as it achieves the greatest good for the greatest number. The debate lies in an opposing belief that people are not to be treated as a means to a journalistic end. A corollary to this principle is that the journalist should not allow himself or herself to be so treated, which may well be the case when publishing information "leaked" from confidential sources. Journalists, therefore, are morally obligated to seek out competing perspectives and confirming

information and to question whether they are being used by someone whose interest is counter to the public interest, such as a campaign worker who might provide information about an opponent's sexual history. Journalists must also inquire about their own motives for pursuing confidential information. Bob Woodward and Carl Bernstein of *The Washington Post* were guilty of unethical conduct when they sought to lure information from grand jurors sworn to secrecy. Even though a corrupt administration was eventually wrestled from power partly as a result of their investigation of the Watergate break-in, they did not foresee this event at the time, and the immoral means they employed to obtain information violated ethical codes.

A second ethical question raised by the use of inside information relates to the obligation it establishes on the part of the reporter. Does the journalist incur responsibility toward the informant when he or she has taken risks to provide the information? If he or she has broken the law to do so, does the reporter assume culpability as well? Such concerns refer again to the principle that people are to be treated with respect and not as a means to an end, and also begin to encroach into other ethical problems for journalists, those of source-reporter confidentiality and the use of anonymous sources.

Finally, the issue of respecting the nature of the relationship in which confidential information is learned presents yet another ethical challenge. Reporters, as representatives of the public trust, frequently find themselves privy to sensitive information that they are obligated to preserve in respect to their roles as journalists. Even seemingly insignificant violations of the public trust, such as providing friends with advance notice of an upcoming sale to be advertised in the local paper, is unethical by intention regardless of the consequences.

The press, by nature, is not governed by a concise, explicit code of professional conduct. The ethics codes that do exist offer guidelines for performance and not absolute standards of behavior. Journalists and other media professionals, therefore, are encouraged to weigh situational factors along with their principles of duty in a thoughtful, critical effort to determine the ethical use of inside information.

—*Regina Howard Yaroch*

See also Insider trading; Journalistic ethics; Pentagon Papers; Sources of information.

BIBLIOGRAPHY

Bain, George. "The Subtleties of Inside Information." *Mclean's* 102 (May, 1989): 48.

Black, Jay, Bob Steele, and Ralph Barney. *Doing Ethics in Journalism: A Handbook with Case Studies.* Greencastle, Ind.: The Sigma Delta Chi Foundation and The Society of Professional Journalists, 1993.

Christians, Clifford G., Kim B. Rotzoll, and Mark Fackler. *Media Ethics: Cases and Moral Reasoning.* 3d ed. New York: Longman, 1991.

Day, Louis A. *Ethics in Media Communications: Cases and Controversies.* Belmont, Calif.: Wadsworth, 1991.

Donaldson, Thomas, and Patricia Werhane. "Introduction to Ethical Reasoning." In *Case Studies in Business Ethics*, edited by Thomas Donaldson and A. R. Gini. Englewood Cliffs, N.J.: Prentice-Hall, 1990.

Insider trading

TYPE OF ETHICS: Business and labor ethics
DATE: Prohibited by Section 10(b) of the Securities Exchange Act of 1934
ASSOCIATED WITH: U.S. Securities and Exchange Commission (SEC)
DEFINITION: Occurs when a corporate "insider" acquires "material nonpublic information" and subsequently trades securities upon the basis of that confidential information
SIGNIFICANCE: Insider trading laws attempt to regulate the ethical behavior of corporate "insiders"

The securities regulations of the United States are designed to prevent corporate executives, directors, attorneys, accountants, investment bankers, and other "insiders" from using their positions to gain unfair advantage in the market trading of the corporation's securities. To buy or sell securities on the basis of confidential information or to recommend trading to others on that basis constitutes a violation of federal securities regulations, potentially subjecting the insider to criminal prosecution by the SEC and civil lawsuits by injured investors. While no formal definition of insider trading has been enacted by the U.S. Congress, the SEC and the courts have developed a detailed description of insider trading in numerous individual cases, most notably in the U.S. Supreme Court's decisions in *U.S. v. Chiarella* (1980) and *Dirks v. SEC* (1983). Insider trading became widely publicized in the 1980's when two prominent financiers, Ivan Boesky and Michael Milken, were convicted of numerous securities violations, sentenced to prison, and fined more than $700 million.

See also White-collar crime.

Institutionalization of patients

TYPE OF ETHICS: Psychological ethics
DATE: c. 1820 to the present
DEFINITION: The involuntary confinement in mental health facilities of mentally ill individuals by mental health professionals and court orders
SIGNIFICANCE: This issue is characterized by a conflict between the ethics of autonomy (mainly championed by legal professionals) and the ethics of beneficence (mainly championed by mental health professionals)

Religions teach that the "least of these" deserve aid and comfort. To apply this rule to the mentally ill often requires some degree of forced institutionalization. To fulfill the ethical rule not to restrict liberty without good cause means to allow people to live on the streets and to conduct costly court hearings. Many solutions to the problem of the seriously mentally ill have been tried, but all are flawed.

A History of Institutionalization. Various societies at various times have attempted to find humane solutions to the problem of mentally ill persons. Many homeless mentally ill persons wandered the towns and roads of the American colonies. In 1752, Benjamin Franklin influenced the Pennsylvania colony legislature to open the first mental hospital in the thirteen colonies. In the mid-1800's, many people hailed Dorothea Dix as a great reformer because her efforts on the behalf of the homeless mentally ill resulted in the creation of thirty mental hospitals that soon were filled with patients. Placing people in mental hospitals deprived them of liberty. Common law principles allowed the taking of a person's liberty only if that person was dangerous to himself or herself or the community, required due process, and maintained that a defendant was innocent until proved guilty. Application of the common law rules could have stopped physicians from attempting to treat the mentally ill.

In 1849, the Association of Medical Superintendents of American Institutions for the Insane (now the American Psychiatric Association) appointed a well-known expert, Isaac Ray, to draft a model law for involuntary confinements. He proposed that the involuntary confinement of the deranged for treatment be treated as a medical decision without legal formalities. After several years most states accepted Ray's idea. During the 1800's and the first half of the twentieth century, the states constructed many large mental asylums. In the United States in 1963, 679,000 persons were confined in mental hospitals, whereas only 250,000 were confined in state and federal prisons. From the medical viewpoint, confinement in mental institutions represented an opportunity to "help" those suffering from a disease.

The Deinstitutionalization Movement. "In the past, men created witches: now they create mental patients"—*Thomas Szasz*

By the 1950's many critics, including the well-known psychiatrist Thomas Szasz, attacked the involuntary confinement of the mentally ill unless the patients were dangerous to themselves or others. For Szasz, mental illness was a myth, a name for problems in living rather than a medical condition correctable by medical action. He proposed the deinstitutionalization of mental patients and the dismantling of community mental health centers. Szasz pointed to misuses of psychiatry in the former Soviet Union to institutionalize and "treat" political prisoners.

Patients' rights advocates who sued hospitals to release patients and improve conditions joined forces with fiscal conservatives who recommended the release of patients to more cost-effective community care. Judges forced mental hospitals to use more stringent criteria for involuntary admissions, to grant extensive rights to patients, to stop exploiting patients economically, and to improve conditions. The "need for treatment" criterion was rejected, and only the mentally ill who were a danger to themselves or others or were gravely disabled could be confined involuntarily, and then only by means of a judicial decision. By 1984, the mental hospital population had dropped to roughly 125,000.

The courts also granted mental patients basic rights. Mental patients were to be treated as normal human beings, they were not to be embarrassed by disclosure of their patient status, and they were to be paid for work done in the institutions. They had a right to refuse most extreme treatments, such as shock therapy. Their rights included absolute access to an attorney and qualified rights for free communication. The restrictions on commitment and the new rights for mental patients made it more expensive and difficult to commit patients and more expensive to keep them. Mental hospitals had partially supported themselves by the unpaid labor of the patients, but this was now forbidden.

The theory behind deinstitutionalization was that community mental health facilities such as halfway houses would replace the large asylums, but legislatures did not fund adequate numbers of the new centers and communities resisted having the facilities in their midst. Outpatient care using chemotherapy was initiated, but most patients did not use such services. Deinstitutionalization freed patients but did not improve their overall welfare. Many freed patients moved to the streets and endured terrible conditions. Some had children on the streets. Citizens complained about the activities of mental patients in their neighborhoods. The argument that the mentally ill should have the same legal protection as criminals is flawed. The consequences of confinement and freedom for each group of persons and for society are different.

Today, state laws specify the procedures for involuntary confinement of the mentally ill. The normal grounds for such confinement are that the patient is a danger to self or others or is gravely disabled. As patients' loss of liberty increases through longer confinements, the courts play a larger role and patients have more due process rights. The state must provide an appointed attorney if one is requested and must allow jury trials.

Treatment and a Clash of Values. A second factor that acted together with court rulings to promote the deinstitutionalization of the mentally ill was the discovery of powerful antipsychotic drugs in the 1950's. Chemotherapy treated symptoms but did not cure the mentally ill, and it often produced very unpleasant side effects. Because most patients could function as long as they took their medication, it made it possible to release many of them. Many patients improved during confinement because of therapy and drugs, won release, stopped taking their medication, and then relapsed.

Ironically, once the patients' rights advocates won the deinstitutionalization battle, they then attacked forced chemotherapy. Psychotherapists argued that chemotherapy liberated the mind from delusions. A majority of state courts granted patients rights to refuse chemotherapy, while the federal courts applied a "need-for-treatment" analysis and left the decisions in the hands of psychiatrists. As chemotherapy declined, hospital stays became longer and the use of physical restraints increased.

The basic institutionalization issue involves deciding which profession and which set of ethical values will control the treatment and confinement of the mentally ill. The patients' rights attorneys see themselves as being in conflict with arrogant physicians who deprive patients of civil rights. In fact, most therapists do tend to overdiagnose mental illness. The idea that judging a sick person to be well is more to be avoided than judging a well person to be sick is built into the medical model. Therapists are wary of public criticism and of lawsuits triggered by the violent acts of a few dangerous released mental patients, and they view involuntary confinement and treatment as being ethically required to protect patients and the public.

—Leland C. Swenson

See also Psychology; Therapist-patient relationship.

BIBLIOGRAPHY
Appelbaum, Paul S. "The Right to Refuse Treatment with Antipsychotic Medications: Retrospect and Prospect." *American Journal of Psychiatry* 145 (April, 1988): 413-419.

Bartol, Curt R., and Anne M. Bartol. *Psychology and American Law*. Belmont, Calif.: Wadsworth, 1983.

Brooks, Alexander D. *Law, Psychiatry, and the Mental Health System*. Boston: Little, Brown, 1974.

Lickey, Marvin E., and Barbara Gordon. *Medicine and Mental Illness: The Use of Drugs in Psychiatry*. New York: W. H. Freeman, 1991.

Schwitzgebel, Robert L., and R. Kirkland Schwitzgebel. *Law and Psychological Practice*. New York: Wiley, 1980.

Swenson, Leland C. *Psychology and Law for the Helping Professions*. Pacific Grove, Calif.: Brooks/Cole, 1993.

Insurance, medical

TYPE OF ETHICS: Bioethics
DATE: 1883 to present
DEFINITION: Provision of or payment of costs incurred by health care services, given to a particular group whose membership is limited by factors such as payment of premiums, employment, income, or citizenship
SIGNIFICANCE: Inequalities in health insurance coverage are both indicative of and result in unjust policies and practices with regard to the poor

Health insurance is possibly the greatest cause of the rapidly escalating cost of medical care in the United States. The lack of regulation, the control of the industry by those who profit from it rather than those who purchase services, and the openness to abuse by both the insured and the providers of care combine to charge the insurance industry with helping to cause one of the most unfair aspects of modern American society: lack of access to needed care by a large portion of the population.

Health insurance is a relatively recent development in the medical field. Only within the last century has access to health care been of general concern, primarily because earlier health care was for the most part ineffectual. The care of the sick was the responsibility of families and churches, and the costs mainly consisted of lost wages, not payment to outside providers.

History. In 1883, Germany enacted laws providing compulsory national health insurance to all workers. This was done to produce a more productive labor force and to enhance national defense rather than out of concern for the individual. Other countries in Western Europe quickly followed suit. In the United States, commercially provided insurance policies were available from the turn of the century, but it was not until the Depression that health insurance became a major industry. At this time, since few people had money to spend on anything but necessities, all but the most crucial medical treatments were foregone. Hospitals found themselves in increasing financial straits; therefore, they banded together to form Blue Cross, an organization designed to elicit prepayment of hospital costs to insure against future need. Soon after, a similar organization was formed by local and state medical associations in order to collect funds to reimburse physicians for expenses incurred in service. This was known as Blue Shield.

The commercial insurance industry (as opposed to the "nonprofit" nature of Blue Cross and Blue Shield) expanded after World War II, with the increasing demands of labor unions to provide health insurance for all workers. The federal government got involved in 1965, when the plans for Medicare, which provides coverage for people over 65, and Medicaid, designed to give access to health care to the poor, were enacted as amendments to the Social Security Act.

Current Status. Today, almost 90 percent of U.S. citizens are covered by some form of health insurance. The United States is the only industrialized nation to provide total health care protection for less than 25 percent of its population. Only two other industrialized nations, Libya and Cyprus, provide for less than 90 percent of their populations. The majority of completely uninsured people in the United States are young people working at low-income jobs. Most are employed but work at jobs that do not provide group health coverage. In most states, Medicaid does not provide care for employed persons, and the cutoff income for coverage is lower than the national poverty level; therefore, many people who are living in poverty do not have any form of medical insurance.

Benefits of Insurance. The greatest benefit derived from health insurance is security from financial risk in case of illness, security that health care will be available if needed. The other, more global benefit, is ethical. Health insurance provides some equity by spreading the costs of undeserved illness between the sick and the healthy. While this does not compensate the ill for the loss of health, it does allay some of the financial burden. Insurance also allows people the immediate gratification of providing for the possibility of bad times by spending a little less during the good.

Costs of Insurance. Aside from the actual premiums for insurance, there are several hidden costs. There are the administrative costs and risk of liability to the insurer. More ethically significant are the consequences of insurance. The amount of money spent for care increases when people are insured. This, in turn, raises costs for all. Physicians, who are usually the decision makers regarding what services are used, are more willing to order marginally useful services when the patient is insured. Hospitals are quicker to buy unproved or rarely used equipment when they know the cost will be borne by insurance companies. Furthermore, people have less incentive to keep themselves well when they know there will be little financial consequence if they do not.

In response to this decreased incentive, insurers have instituted cost-sharing plans including deductibles, coinsurance (in which the patient pays a certain percentage), and copayment (in which a flat fee is paid at the time of service). These cost-sharing means are much harder on the poor, because they take a larger portion of their income.

Medical insurance can be said to be an inherently unfair means of providing health care. If health care is considered to be a right, it cannot depend on individual ability to pay.

—*Margaret Hawthorne*

See also Health care allocation.

BIBLIOGRAPHY

Bodenheimer, Thomas, Steven Cummings, and Elizabeth Harding. "Capitalizing on Illness: The Health Insurance Industry." In *Health and Medical Care in the U.S.: A Critical Analysis,* edited by Vicente Navarro. Farmingdale, N.Y.: Baywood, 1977.

Menzel, Paul T. *Medical Costs, Moral Choices.* New Haven, Conn.: Yale University Press, 1983.

Phelps, Charles E. *Health Economics.* New York: HarperCollins, 1992.

Riesenfeld, Stefan A. "Health Insurance." In *Encyclopedia of Bioethics,* edited by Warren T. Reich. New York: Free Press, 1978.

Roemer, Milton I. *National Health Systems of the World.* New York: Oxford University Press, 1991.

U.S. President's Commission for the Study of Ethical Problems in Medicine and Biomedical and Behavioral Research. *Securing Access to Health Care: A Report on the Ethical Implication of Differences in the Availability of Health Services.* Washington, D.C.: Government Printing Office, 1983.

Integration

TYPE OF ETHICS: Race and ethnicity

DATE: 1954-1968

ASSOCIATED WITH: The Supreme Court, the civil rights movement, and Martin Luther King, Jr.

DEFINITION: The goal of the complete participation of a previously disadvantaged minority group in the social, political, and economic opportunities offered by society

SIGNIFICANCE: Integration, as government policy, supplanted and stigmatized as unfair the pre-1940 government policy of enforcing or condoning the compulsory segregation of African Americans from whites

A racially integrated society would be one in which African Americans can participate in all aspects of national life without being handicapped by their color. In such a society, there should be no neighborhood where an African American could not reside simply because of being black; no hotel, restaurant, or other public facility that an African American could not use on equal terms with whites; no school that an African American child could not attend because of being black; no kind of vocational training, university education, or line of work from which an African American would be barred because of being black; and no public office for which an African American could not contend. In an integrated society, whites would see African Americans not as pariahs but as fellow Americans, fellow veterans, coworkers, and neighbors. By 1990, the goal of a racially integrated society, despite much progress, was only half achieved; the role that public policy should play in creating a more racially integrated society was still a matter of lively debate.

James Meredith, the first African American to enroll at the previously all-white University of Mississippi. (Library of Congress)

Ethical and Legal Principles. Those who discuss the ethics of integration are dealing with the ethics of public policy rather than (as is the case, to some extent, with prejudice and racism) the morality of private behavior. The promotion of racial integration has been seen by its proponents as essential to the realization of an important value in public policy ethics: that of equality under the law regardless of race or color. This principle had first been publicly recognized in the United States by the Fourteenth Amendment to the Constitution (ratified in 1868), which mandated that every state guarantee its citizens the equal protection of the laws. Liberals tend to be more optimistic about the possibilities for achieving greater racial equality through government-sponsored integration; conservatives tend to perceive a conflict between achieving integration and preserving other cherished American values.

Milestones of Progress Toward an Integrated Society: 1945 to 1968. Signposts of progress during these years (which witnessed the flowering of the civil rights movement) included the gradual desegregation of the American military, which began with President Harry S Truman's executive order in 1948; the Supreme Court decision of 1954, that struck down the constitutionality of segregated schools; the admission of African Americans into southern state universities; the Civil Rights Act of 1964, which established the right of equal access to public accommodations and banned discrimination in employment; the Voting Rights Act of 1965; the Supreme Court decision of 1967 that overturned state laws against black-white intermarriage; and the federal fair housing law of 1968. By 1990, many of these changes had achieved general acceptance; efforts to integrate employment, schools, and housing, however, continued to arouse controversy.

The Affirmative Action Controversy. By the late 1970's, affirmative action, in which the presence or absence of a fixed percentage of African Americans in a business, government department, or university is used to determine whether that institution discriminates, had become the chief tool by which the federal government tried to open up opportunities for African Americans. In 1975, in the book *Affirmative Discrimination*, the white sociologist Nathan Glazer condemned the application of this policy in both private businesses and government employment. Glazer argued that affirmative action undermines respect for merit and encourages ethnic and racial divisiveness; unlike many liberals, he denied that the underrepresentation of African Americans in a particular job or profession is necessarily evidence of discrimination. Some African American conservatives believe that affirmative action stigmatizes as inferior those African Americans who do gain entrance to prestigious universities or get good jobs. Yet other thinkers—white as well as African American—argue that many employers would hire no African Americans at all if they were not prodded to do so by the existence of a numerical goal.

Racial Integration of Elementary and Secondary Schools: Supreme Court Decisions. In *Brown v. Board of Education*, in 1954, the Supreme Court declared that officially enforced school segregation by race (then found mostly in the southern states) violated the Fourteenth Amendment to the Constitution. In a 1968 decision, the Supreme Court exerted pressure on southern school boards to end segregation more quickly; in a 1971 decision, *Swann v. Board of Education*, the Court held that school busing—the transportation of children out of their neighborhoods for schooling—might be an appropriate tool for achieving desegregation.

In the 1960's, the question arose of what to do about the de facto racial segregation of the schools, based on neighborhood racial patterns rather than on the law, found in many northern cities. In 1973, the Supreme Court ordered, for the first time, a northern school district (Denver, Colorado) to institute a desegregation plan. In 1974, however, the Court, in a sudden shift, banned (in the decision *Milliken v. Bradley*) busing for integration purposes across city-suburban boundaries. In general, the Court has ordered steps toward ending de facto segregation only when evidence exists that local authorities have deliberately rigged school district boundaries to keep the races apart.

Integration of Elementary and Secondary Schools: How Necessary and How Achievable? Ever since 1954, people have argued about how necessary integration of the races in the classroom is to providing equal educational opportunities for African American children. In the 1980's, even some maverick conservative African American thinkers, such as Thomas Sowell and Robert Woodson had their doubts. Woodson argued that a neighborhood school, even if it is exclusively African American, can become a valuable focus of neighborhood pride for low-income city dwellers; Sowell pointed nostalgically to a high-quality African American secondary school of the pre-1954 era of segregation, Dunbar High School in Washington, D.C. (Critics stress how atypical Dunbar was.)

Integrationist scholars, however, argue that forcible exclusion from the company of white schoolchildren stigmatizes and psychically wounds African American children; the African American journalist Carl Rowan thinks that such exclusion is psychically wounding even if it results from white flight to the suburbs rather than government edict. White liberal political scientist Gary Orfield suggests that racial integration of the schools is necessary if African American children are to have greater access to information about jobs and other opportunities; white liberal education writer Jonathan Kozol contends, like many African American thinkers, that all African American public schools are more likely than integrated ones to be starved of money by legislatures that are beholden to white-majority electorates.

The Tension Between Integration and Parental Rights: How to Resolve It? Although the compulsory busing of children into schools predominantly of the other race may be necessary to achieve racial integration in some cases, it does severely limit the rights of parents, thereby causing some resentment. The Supreme Court's 1974 ban on busing across city-suburban boundaries means that the most bitter white foes of school integration could often shield their children from it by moving to the suburbs; even if this decision were overturned, achieving complete racial integration of the schools in defiance of segregated neighborhood patterns would be both a herculean task and a politically controversial one.

The rights of parents over their children are, as the African American philosopher Bernard R. Boxill points out, by no means absolute. There is a societal interest in promoting interracial harmony, Boxill suggests, that perhaps should be allowed to prevail over the wish of bigoted white parents to preserve their children from all contact with African American children. Rejecting the notion (found in the writ-

ings of African American conservative Glenn Loury) of an unresolvable tension between integrationist goals and individual rights, Boxill also argues that government can use inducements as well as penalties to promote integration, in education and in other areas.

To promote integration of the schools while keeping busing to a minimum, some local school authorities have instituted so-called magnet schools. By placing elementary and secondary schools with above-average endowment in facilities and curricula in the middle of African American neighborhoods, authorities hope to persuade, rather than force, white parents to accept racial integration of the schools. Yet because funds are limited, the number of magnet schools that can be established is also limited; inevitably, some African American schoolchildren remain in all-African American schools, and some white parents cannot get their children into magnet schools. The magnet school solution is not perfect.

Housing Integration: Is It Achievable? By 1990, neither the federal Fair Housing Act of 1968 nor the many state and local laws banning discrimination in the sale or rental of housing had solved the problem of racially segregated neighborhoods. One troublesome issue that arises with respect to housing integration is the tension between individual rights and the goal of keeping a neighborhood integrated over time. Many whites are reluctant to live in a neighborhood or an apartment complex when the percentage of African American residents exceeds a certain number. To prevent wholesale evacuation by whites, so-called benign quotas have been introduced limiting the African American influx in the interest of stable integration. Benign quotas have been used by realtors in the Chicago suburb of Oak Park and by the management of the Starrett City apartment complex in New York City; in the latter case, the constitutionality of benign quotas was challenged in the 1980's.

Another difficult question is whether poor as well as middle- or upper-income African Americans should be given the chance to live in the prosperous and mostly white suburbs. White suburbanites who might tolerate the occasional prosperous African American homeowner as a neighbor would almost certainly oppose the building of public housing projects in suburbia; yet it is the poorer African American who might benefit most from the greater employment opportunities found in the suburbs. In Chicago, the Gautreaux program attempted to circumvent the problem by settling small numbers of carefully selected poor African American families in prosperous white suburbs.

Nathan Glazer, in a 1993 magazine essay, argued that only an extremely intrusive government could make racially integrated neighborhoods remain racially integrated over time. Bernard Boxill contends, however, that not every action that is beyond the penalties of law is necessarily moral, and that government, if it cannot force whites to stay in integrated neighborhoods, can at least offer inducements for them to do so.

—Paul D. Mageli

See also Affirmative action; *Brown v. Board of Education*; Civil Rights Act of 1964; Civil rights movement; King, Martin Luther, Jr.; Racism; Segregation.

BIBLIOGRAPHY

Boxill, Bernard R. *Blacks and Social Justice*. Totowa, N.J.: Rowman & Allanheld, 1984.

Conti, Joseph G., and Brad Stetson. *Challenging the Civil Rights Establishment: Profiles of a New Black Vanguard*. Westport, Conn.: Praeger, 1993.

Ezorsky, Gertrude. *Racism and Justice: The Case for Affirmative Action*. Ithaca, N.Y.: Cornell University Press, 1991.

Glazer, Nathan. *Affirmative Discrimination: Ethnic Inequality and Public Policy*. New York: Basic Books, 1975.

Graglia, Lino A. *Disaster by Decree: The Supreme Court Decisions on Race and the Schools*. Ithaca, N.Y.: Cornell University Press, 1976.

Hacker, Andrew. *Two Nations: Black and White, Separate, Hostile, Unequal*. New York: Charles Scribner's Sons, 1992.

Hughes, Graham. "Compensating the Disadvantaged." In *The Conscience of the Courts: Law and Morals in American Life*. Garden City, N.Y.: Anchor Press, 1975.

Kozol, Jonathan. *Savage Inequalities: Children in America's Schools*. New York: Crown, 1991.

Loury, Glenn C. "Matters of Color—Blacks and the Constitutional Order." In *Slavery and Its Consequences: The Constitution, Equality, and Race*, edited by Robert A. Goldwin and Art Kaufman. Washington, D.C.: American Enterprise Institute Press, 1988.

Massey, Douglas S., and Nancy A. Denton. *American Apartheid: Segregation and the Making of the Underclass*. Cambridge, Mass.: Harvard University Press, 1993.

Molotch, Harvey. *Managed Integration: Dilemmas of Doing Good in the City*. Berkeley: University of California Press, 1972.

Rowan, Carl T. *Dream Makers, Dream Breakers: The World of Justice Thurgood Marshall*. Boston: Little, Brown, 1993.

Integrity

TYPE OF ETHICS: Personal and social ethics
DATE: Fourth century B.C.E. to present
ASSOCIATED WITH: Virtue ethics, moral psychology, and anti-utilitarianism
DEFINITION: Consistent adherence to moral, intellectual, professional, or artistic principles despite temptation to abandon them
SIGNIFICANCE: Integrity is an important personal characteristic in ethical systems based on virtue and moral character

The etymology of the word "integrity" reveals its relationship to the Latin *integritas*, meaning "soundness, health, unimpaired condition," and to the English "integral," meaning "necessary for completeness" and "made up of parts forming a whole." On the assumption that this etymological relationship is relevant within a moral context, integrity as a moral virtue may be identified as early as the fourth century B.C.E. in Plato's ethical theory. The Platonic soul is tripartite, consisting of reason (intellect), spirit (feelings), and passion (desire). The harmonious interaction of these three parts, with reason dominant over the other two, is central to human virtue. The virtues corresponding to the correct exercise of each of these three parts are, respectively, wisdom, courage, and self-control, which together constitute the virtue of justice. A person in whom either spirit or passion is out of control is both morally and psychologically impaired, existing in a state of moral fragmentation. In such a case, the tripartite soul is splintered, making the person less than morally whole or complete. If justice is the harmonious interaction of the three parts of the soul, then Platonic justice is Platonic integrity, and Plato's understanding of integrity simultaneously serves as the benchmark for subsequent Western ethical theory and presages the development of modern moral psychology.

If integrity is defined as the willingness to abide by and defend one's principles, whether they are artistic, intellectual, professional, or moral, it is evident that the first three kinds of integrity are rooted in a more fundamental moral integrity, since without the latter, one cannot be relied on to retain and to act on whatever other principles one holds. The definition of integrity entails that, because of deeply held beliefs and commitments, there are some things that one is unwilling to do, an unwillingness that may persist even under extreme circumstances. The artist whose artistic identity and principles are rooted in her originality might refuse to produce tasteless but lucrative popular art, even if this refusal means a life of relative poverty. A scholar, to preserve his intellectual integrity, may refuse to publish anything that will not make a genuine, worthwhile contribution to his discipline, even if he might advance professionally with more frequent but less qualitative publication. The business person, faced with the temptation to compromise important professional principles, declines to do so in the interest of both personal and corporate integrity. Moral integrity, which is at once more fundamental and more comprehensive, requires that an individual refuse to abandon important moral principles even when it is advantageous to do so, and that the content of these principles be such that reasonable people would recognize them as moral. Moral steadfastness on behalf of manifestly sound moral principles entitles one to the esteem of others as an honorable person who maintains a high degree of consistency between principle and behavior when faced with the temptation to do otherwise.

In modern ethical theory, the discussion of integrity has centered more on its importance than on its definition. Emphasis on moral traits such as integrity is a defining feature of ethical systems based on personal virtue, in which individual moral character assumes primary importance and moral evaluation focuses on persons rather than (or in addition to) actions. For consequentialist ethical systems such as utilitarianism, however, actions and consequences rather than persons are the primary object of moral evaluation. The latter system is more typical of modern ethical theory, while the former is more traditional, dating back to the Greeks and Romans, and especially to stoicism, in which personal character assumes a centrally important place. This difference reflects the modern tendency to distinguish between an individual's personal character and that individual's actions, and to regard actions as being morally more important than character, since they have direct or indirect consequences for the well-being or harm of others.

Bernard Williams, in *Utilitarianism: For and Against*, underscores the traditional importance of integrity by making it a focal point in his criticism of utilitarianism, according to which an action that increases the totality of human well-being is moral, regardless of the motives or character of the agent. Williams argues that one of the chief flaws in utilitarianism is that it constitutes an attack upon personal integrity by dismissing as unimportant the deeply held commitments from which emanate a person's most significant actions. Utilitarianism, which by its nature mandates taking into account only the consequences of actions, requires that one disregard personal convictions in favor of doing what ensures, on balance, an acceptable utilitarian outcome of greater good than harm. How one feels about one's action is irrelevant. Integrity is a strong component of moral conviction, however, and conviction is an important source of action. Williams argues that alienating a person from strongly held convictions by requiring that they be disregarded is unreasonable and unfair, amounting to the destruction of much of what constitutes the agent's identity.

Alasdair MacIntyre, in *After Virtue: A Study in Moral Theory*, argues for a reintegration of character and action, contending that since personal virtue is an important determinant of actions, character is therefore an essential component of any complete moral context. To separate character and action is to displace virtues such as integrity from this context, making comprehensive moral judgments impossible. Such a separation destroys the "unity" or wholeness—integrity in the Platonic sense—of an individual life. A person's life, to be of genuine moral significance, must be one in which a set of virtues, firmly held and consistently acted upon, unifies the various roles that the individual occupies, and confers upon that individual a corresponding set of obligations. Such a life requires integrity (in both the ancient and modern senses), which is intelligible only in relation to a more universal good.

Finally, integrity is a characteristic for which one bears special individual responsibility, as enunciated by Aleksandr Solzhenitsyn upon receiving the Nobel Prize in Literature: "And the simple step of a simple courageous man is not to take part in the lie, not to support deceit. Let the lie come into the world, even dominate the world, but not through me."
—Barbara Forrest

See also Character; Consequentialism; Honor; Stoic ethics; Utilitarianism; Virtue ethics.

BIBLIOGRAPHY

Blustein, Jeffrey. *Care and Commitment: Taking the Personal Point of View*. New York: Oxford University Press, 1991.

McFall, Lynne. "Integrity." In *Ethics and Personality: Essays in Moral Psychology*, edited by John Deigh. Chicago: University of Chicago Press, 1992.

MacIntyre, Alasdair. *After Virtue: A Study in Moral Theory*. 2d ed. Notre Dame, Ind.: University of Notre Dame Press, 1984.

Plato. "Phaedrus." In *The Dialogues of Plato*. Translated by R. E. Allen. New Haven, Conn.: Yale University Press, 1984.

Solzhenitsyn, Alexander. *One Word of Truth*. Nobel Speech on Literature, 1970. London: Bodley Head, 1972.

Williams, Bernard. "A Critique of Utilitarianism." In *Utilitarianism: For and Against*, edited by Bernard Williams and J. J. C. Smart. Cambridge, England: Cambridge University Press, 1987.

Intellectual property

TYPE OF ETHICS: Legal and judicial ethics
DATE: 1623 to present
ASSOCIATED WITH: English Statute of Monopolies, U.S. Constitution, and concepts of copyrights and trademarks
DEFINITION: The right of inventors, authors, and other creative people to control the use of their ideas or creations
SIGNIFICANCE: Recognizes that both creative individuals and the society within which they live have an interest in the products of creative activity

Society has a vested interest in encouraging useful inventions and artistic creations. Modern legal theory treats the ideas, designs, texts, images, or musical compositions of such persons as their private intangible property and allows them to restrict the use of this intellectual property for a set time or until certain events occur. Intellectual property law generally recognizes four forms of intellectual property: trade secrets, patents, copyrights, and trademarks. Inventors are considered to have the right to keep their invention *trade secrets* if it is practicable for them to do so but are encouraged to disclose fully their inventions in return for the exclusive rights provided by the issuance of a *patent* to practice their inventions for a fixed period of time. Authors, artists, and composers generally can claim a *copyright* for their work, which will prevent others from using their ideas or reproducing or performing their creative work without permission, for which they may then receive a fee or royalty. A *trademark* is a word or symbol that a manufacturer can use to distinguish its products from those of its competitors. In effect, a trademark allows a firm to profit from its (intangible) reputation for quality or reliability. The owner of intellectual property is free to sell it to another or to grant a license for its use. Unauthorized use of intellectual property is called *infringement. Plagiarism,* the intentional misrepresentation of an idea or creation as one's own, is considered a serious breach of ethical behavior in almost every area of creative endeavor.

History. In ancient times, no formal protection was given to inventors, who had to resort to secrecy to prevent others from using their inventions. In the absence of printing presses and high-speed communication, there was little point in forbidding others to copy a work. In the Middle Ages, ideals of personal modesty encouraged anonymous authorship. It is only with the rise of capitalism and economic competition that the notion of intellectual property entered into legal and ethical thinking.

A monopoly is an individual or group that has been awarded an exclusive right to conduct a business or practice a profession. Since monopolies can demand a higher price for goods and services than can businesses that have competition, the existence of monopolies is generally considered undesirable unless required in a given area for the public good. The development of patent and copyright law is usually considered to begin with the English Statute of Monopolies of 1623, which in general was an attempt to eliminate monopolies but excepted patents on inventions and methods as necessary means of encouraging the development of industry. The Constitution of the United States expressly grants to the federal government the right to issue patents and copyrights "to promote the progress of science and the useful arts."

Ethical Principles. Underlying the general concept of intellectual property is the notion that an individual is entitled to compensation for the products of his or her labor. In the case of inventions, there is the additional question of the inventor's right to privacy. In most legal systems, someone who develops a new process or recipe for, say, a long-lasting paint, is under no obligation to share the process with the public. He and his heirs may treat it as a trade secret forever. If anyone else, however, were to discover the process by any legitimate means, such as chemically analyzing a can of paint that had been purchased, he or she would be free to manufacture and sell the identical product at a lower price. In applying for a patent on this process, the inventor, in effect, enters into a contract with society in which secrecy is abandoned in return for the exclusive right to control the use of the process for a fixed number of years. Very few individuals could afford to be authors, composers, or filmmakers if anyone who wished to could make multiple copies of their works and sell them freely.

Ethical Problems. The question of where to draw the line between individuals' rights to their intellectual property and the welfare of the public has not been fully resolved. Some countries, including the United Kingdom, refuse on humanitarian grounds to issue patents for medicines. Many countries permit the suppliers of military hardware to infringe the patent rights of inventors, possibly with a provision for compensation but without advance permission, when such an act is justified by the requirements of national security. Even the existence of public libraries in effect deprives authors of the revenue they might otherwise gain from the readers of their books. The development of computer networks allows, in effect, many persons to use the same copy of a copyrighted program.

There are also possible conflicts between the rights of authors, artists, and composers and the rights of subsequent owners of a copyright. Many governments recognize as moral rights of creative individuals the rights of *attribution,* or recognition as being the creator of one's own work, and of *integrity,* or having one's work presented as a whole or in an acceptable abridgment, even though the work may have been purchased or performed for pay. It can also, of course, be argued that allowing the owners of intellectual property greater control over the form in which it is disseminated could increase their profits and thus ultimately benefit the creators. —*Donald R. Franceschetti*

See also Business ethics; Freedom of expression; Property.

BIBLIOGRAPHY

Alderson, Wroe, Vern Terpstra, and S. J. Shapiro, eds. *Patents and Progress.* Homewood Ill.: Richard D. Irwin, 1965.

Dratler, Jay, Jr. *Intellectual Property Law: Commercial, Creative, and Industrial Property.* New York: Law Journal Seminars-Press, 1991.

Miller, Arthur R., and Michael H. Davis. *Intellectual Property.* 2d ed. St. Paul, Minn.: West, 1990.

Rosenberg, Peter D. *Patent Law Basics.* New York: Clark Boardman Callaghan, 1992.

Strong, William S. *The Copyright Book: A Practical Guide.* Cambridge, Mass.: MIT Press, 1981.

Intelligence testing

TYPE OF ETHICS: Bioethics
DATE: Since the 1890's
ASSOCIATED WITH: Alfred Binet
DEFINITION: Attempts to measure human intelligence
SIGNIFICANCE: Intelligence testing may involve problems related to test bias and the misuse of results in eugenics

Alfred Binet (1857-1911) and his colleagues first devised tests to assess the mental abilities of French children in the 1890's. A child's "mental age," divided by chronological age, gave an "intelligence quotient" (IQ). Binet thought that IQ scores could be improved through education, but many British psychologists insisted that intelligence was hereditary. Data on this issue were gathered by Cyril Burt, but some of his data were later shown to have been fabricated. American psychologists modernized Binet's tests but applied them, with considerable bias, against African Americans and immigrants. Despite early claims that the tests measure "innate intelligence," careful studies show that educational influences are strong and that most early studies were flawed. In particular, a fifteen-point average difference between unselected whites and African Americans disappears when comparison is made between samples matched by social status, family income, and similar factors. African Americans who have attended good schools and have had similar advantages achieve higher scores than do students from disadvantaged backgrounds regardless of race.

Test bias occurs because the test is given in a particular language and because it assumes a middle-class cultural environment; the results are therefore biased against the poor and against those who speak a different language. More subtle bias includes questions about activities that are common to middle-class white males, thus discriminating against females and blacks. Bias-free exams are difficult to write.

Proponents of eugenics have advocated favorable treatment of high-IQ individuals and unfavorable treatment (including sterilization) of low-IQ subjects. Since test results can be modified by education and are subject to bias, such proposals have lost much favor since about 1940.

See also Eugenics.

Intention

TYPE OF ETHICS: Theory of ethics
DATE: Fourth century B.C.E. to present
ASSOCIATED WITH: Ancient Greek philosopher Aristotle, medieval philosophy, the nineteenth century German philosopher Franz Brentano, and contemporary intentionalist philosophy
DEFINITION: The abstract relationship of "aboutness," reference, or directedness of thought to an object or state of affairs; also (especially in the plural) that which is intended—intended objects or states of affairs
SIGNIFICANCE: Agents typically must intend to do something or be directed toward a certain intended state of affairs as a purpose or end in order to be morally responsible for their actions

The idea that action is intentional and that an agent must intend to do something in order to be morally responsible for it is represented in everyday moral reasoning and legal theory. Intention is an abstract semantic relationship. To intend an object means to be directed in thought toward it or for the thought to be about or refer to the intended object. By extension, language and art intend objects derivatively as expressions of thought. Intended objects can include the things or states of affairs as goals or ends toward which actions are directed.

History. The idea of the intentionality of action is commonly atrributed to Aristotle's *On the Soul*. Aristotle's theory was transmitted through late medieval to modern and contemporary philosophy primarily by Thomas Aquinas and William of Ockham. In the nineteenth and early twentieth centuries, intentionalism was associated with Franz Brentano's 1874 work *Psychology from an Empirical Standpoint* and his 1889 *The Origin of Our Knowledge of Right and Wrong*. Contemporary moral philosophy in the intentionalist tradition includes the work of, among others, G. E. M. Anscombe, Robert Audi, Roderick M. Chisholm, Donald Davidson, Joseph Margolis, and Richard Taylor.

Intended Objects. There are several kinds of intentional attitudes that can be taken toward intended objects. Objects of the appropriate sorts can be believed, doubted, feared, loved, hated, desired, loathed, and so on. Desire or wanting is the intentional attitude that is relevant to most actions for which agents are thought to be morally responsible. Intended objects need not exist, as, for example, when someone thinks about an unrealized state of affairs in projecting a desire and trying to achieve a purpose through action. The intended objects of desire can be things in the ordinary sense, as when an agent desires an apple, or states of affairs, such as that achieved by donating money to a charity. It may be possible to reduce one of these categories to the other, leaving a single category of intended objects. To reduce desired things to states of affairs is the most commonly proposed reduction, in which instead of saying that an agent desires an apple, the agent is said instead to desire the state of affairs in which the agent possesses or eats the apple.

Primacy of the Intentional. Intentional relations are often said to be primitive or undefinable. This means that they cannot be theoretically reduced to any more basic concepts or analyzed in terms of simpler ideas. The reason for this classification is partly that attempts to reduce intentional connections have either failed to capture the sense of intentionality or appear to do so only by unknowingly or surreptitiously incorporating into the definition other intentional concepts. Treating intentional relations as primitive has the advantage of offering a more satisfactory explanation of certain phenomena about the reference of thought and its expression to intended objects. This includes the fact that in referring to an object there are no special psychological occurrences and nothing else one need do in order to intend the object other than simply to intend it. The primacy of the intentional has the unfortunate effect of suggesting to some critics that there is something mysterious about intentionality, on the grounds that intentional relations cannot be reduced or further explained in terms of more basic concepts. The objection is avoided by considering that every conceptual scheme must include some undefined concepts in order to avoid an infinite regress or circularity of definitions, and there are good reasons for regarding intentionality in particular as primitive or undefined.

Intention in Moral Theory. An agent's intention is what the agent intends to do. It is the possibly nonexistent state of affairs that the agent assumes as the purpose or goal of action, toward which the action is directed. Some examples of intentions are to help another person, to perfect one's abilities, to achieve a career objective, and to move a finger.

It is standardly agreed that agents are not morally responsible for their actions unless they intend to do them. Behavior performed entirely without intention is not action or doing in the philosophically correct sense of the word, but something that a person suffers or undergoes. Doing something unintentionally, when there is no negligence or overriding obligation to determine the likely effects of an action, is often considered to render a person morally blameless for bad consequences. Agents are sometimes praised or blamed even for their unrealized or failed intentions, as a reflection of their moral attitudes and inclinations.

The main division in moral philosophy between deontological and consequentialist ethics can be drawn in terms of the role that intention is thought to play in moral evaluation. For the deontologist, having a good or morally approved intention, usually one that intends an action because it is prescribed by duty, is the most important factor in ethical conduct, regardless of the consequences. Consequentialists are unconcerned with the state of mind with which an action is undertaken, except insofar as it leads to good consequences, which are often understood as whatever maximizes happiness. Although the concept of intentionality does not resolve the dispute between these two types of moral philosophy, the fact that their disagreement can be characterized in terms of intentions indicates the importance of the concept of intentions to moral theory. —*Dale Jacquette*

See also Aristotle; Consequentialism; Deontological ethics; Desire; Responsibility; Thomas Aquinas.

BIBLIOGRAPHY

Anscombe, G. E. M. *Intention.* 2d ed. Oxford, England: Blackwell, 1963.

Bratman, Michael. *Intention, Plans, and Practical Reason.* Cambridge, Mass.: Harvard University Press, 1987.

Gustafson, Donald F. *Intention and Agency.* Dordrecht, The Netherlands: D. Reidel, 1986.

Meiland, Jack W. *The Nature of Intention.* London: Methuen, 1970.

Mohanty, Jitendranath. *The Concept of Intentionality.* St. Louis: W. H. Green, 1972.

Ryan, Thomas Arthur. *Intentional Behavior: An Approach to Human Motivation.* New York: Ronald Press, 1970.

International justice

TYPE OF ETHIC: Legal and judicial ethics
DATE: Seventeenth century to present
DEFINITION: The system established by governments to resolve disputes and punish offenders of international law
SIGNIFICANCE: Serves as a counterweight to the anarchical tendencies of international relations by encouraging orderly resolution of disputes

The term "international justice" has three connotations. First, it refers to the mechanisms by which governments seek to fairly and legally resolve disputes among themselves. Second, it refers to the formal and informal systems by which governments are punished for wrongdoing. Finally, and more broadly, it has in recent years been used to call for a more fair allocation of global resources among nations.

Ethical considerations surrounding all these connotations are conditioned by the lack of centralized and completely effective mechanisms by means of which international justice can be effected. The international system is built on the principle of national sovereignty, which requires coordination of state policies to attain justice, rather than a system of subordination under which countries submit to a global authority exercising ultimate and binding jurisdiction over them. As sovereigns, nation-states are the highest authorities and are beholden to no higher authority unless they voluntarily concede by treaty to limit their sovereignty. Conflict in such a system is an ever-present threat. The achievement of order and justice, then, is accomplished by mutual accommodation, negotiation, political maneuvering, and sometimes through the use of collective force. Ethical constraints are not irrelevant in this system, but they are typically subordinated to political interest.

Legal Resolution of Disputes. Assuming that governments prefer to resolve disputes peacefully, rather than through conflict or force, numerous options are available to them, including political mechanisms such as direct bilateral negotiation, third-party mediation and conciliation, and legal mechanisms such as arbitration and adjudication. Political solutions are very common means of resolving international disputes. Arbitration and adjudication are less common at the international level. Disputes between citizens or business interests of two countries are quite common, however, and these are often resolved by the domestic courts of the involved countries or by mixed claims commissions that have been established by treaty. When a legal dispute arises between two governments, they may choose to seek arbitration and adjudication to avoid conflict. When seeking arbitration, governments agree to submit the legal issue to an ad hoc panel of experts composed of members proposed by each of the countries involved and whose final judgment is accepted in advance as binding both parties to the dispute. Arbitration has been practiced for centuries by nations, and its roots go back at least as far as the ancient Greeks in the fifth century B.C.E. In modern times, states created the Permanent Court of Arbitration, which was established by the Hague Peace Conference of 1899 but has been resorted to only infrequently since World War I.

In addition to arbitration, states may seek to adjudicate disputes through standing courts, such as the International Court of Justice (ICJ) at the international level, or through various regional courts, such as the European Court of Justice. The sole international court, the ICJ, lacks compulsory jurisdiction over states, which means that no state is required, unless it consents to do so, to bring cases before the court or to appear in court to defend itself from suits brought against it by other states. Fewer than a third of the members of the United Nations recognize the ICJ's jurisdiction as compulsory. Once governments agree to the ICJ's jurisdiction, however, they are bound to abide by its decisions. Enforcement of court decisions, however, has not been completely satisfactory or effective. The ICJ operates, then, in a less than perfect environment in which states are not required to submit disputes to it and, even in those rare cases

General Colin Powell (right) was ultimately responsible for U.S. Operation Desert Storm, which was part of the U.N. effort to remove Iraqi troops from Kuwait. (AP/Wide World Photos)

when they do, there is no guarantee that its judgments will be honored.

Punishing Wrongdoers. Given its weak legal structures, international justice is often conducted either through collective punishment of offending states or by the self-help of individual governments. Members of the United Nations are required by the UN Charter to resolve disputes peacefully. Aggressor states that violate this obligation may be punished by the United Nations through the collective application of economic sanctions and even force. If the UN cannot agree to punish an aggressor, however, the injured state is left to defend itself. It may do so by recourse to the traditional laws of retaliation. Ultimately, the success of all such collective and individual efforts depends on the cooperation of powerful states. When powerful states are on the side of justice, justice can be done. If they are not, or if powerful states actively flout international law, the only prevailing justice is that of the strongest.

International Economic Justice. Apart from the legal resolution of disputes and the use of force to punish aggressor states, international justice is increasingly used to refer to the fair distribution of global resources. Significant inequities currently prevail among nations. This leads many poorer countries to call for a fairer international economic order. In many of the poorest countries, however, wealth is equally badly distributed. The ethical claim of the elite in such a country to an entitlement to greater access to international wealth for their nation rests on shaky ground. There exists no current legal principle by which wealthy states must transfer wealth to poorer ones, and even where ethical considerations demand it, as in the case of famine or disaster, the claim of a wealthy elite in a poor country to have absolute control over the internal allocation of foreign aid lacks justification.

Conclusion. The achievement of international justice depends to a very large extent on the voluntary cooperation of governments and peoples. Governments often do cooperate to mutual advantage. They often resolve disputes peacefully and help each other in time of need, but there is no world government to ensure that they do so. They do so out of a sense of either political interest or legal or ethical obligation. A government's first obligation is to its own people's security and prosperity. At the international level, its obligation to the security and prosperity of other nations is governed by traditional friendships and ties, by voluntarily accepted treaty and legal norms, and by prudence and expediency. —*Robert F. Gorman*

See also Arbitration; Human rights; International law; Intervention; Power; Sanctions; Sovereignty; War and peace.

BIBLIOGRAPHY

Bennett, A. LeRoy. *International Organizations.* 4th ed. Englewood Cliffs, N.J.: Prentice-Hall, 1988.

Henkin, Louis, et al. *Right v. Might: International Law and the Use of Force.* New York: Council on Foreign Relations Press, 1989.

Jessup, Philip. *The Price of International Justice.* New York: Columbia University Press, 1971.

Kaplan, Morton, and Nicholas Katzenbach. *The Political Foundation of International Law.* New York: Wiley, 1961.

Tucker, Robert. *The Inequality of Nations.* New York: Basic Books, 1977.

International Labour Organisation

TYPE OF ETHICS: Business and labor ethics

DATE: Founded 1919

DEFINITION: The ILO was established to facilitate the improvement of working conditions and standards of living

SIGNIFICANCE: Formation of the ILO legitimized goals of international labor groups

As a result of lobbying by international labor unions and the governments of several countries, the Treaty of Versailles, which ended World War I, recognized the International Labour Organisation (ILO). Its declarations and resolutions were not, however, made enforceable.

During the Great Depression, the ILO encouraged governments to plan for the reemployment of workers and to develop relief and unemployment insurance schemes. The United States joined the ILO in 1934. Other countries had delayed joining; some also dropped their membership.

The ILO was the first specialized agency to be affiliated with the United Nations, which was created in 1946. It took on a more proscribed role, with some of its concerns delegated to other agencies. Its membership also changed, including many more developing rather than industrialized countries. The ILO became more of a statistical and information center that also provided technical assistance to developing countries. It turned its attention more to problems of poverty and social conditions rather than narrow labor issues. The agency is concerned with international disparities in the treatment of workers, and it attempts to prevent exploitation. As part of that program, it promotes relatively free immigration and emigration of workers. The ILO is unique among intergovernmental agencies in that member states send representatives not only from their governments but also from worker and employer groups.

See also American Federation of Labor (AFL); Employees, safety and treatment of; Knights of Labor; League of Nations; Universal Declaration of Human Rights.

International law

TYPE OF ETHICS: International relations

DATE: Fifth century B.C.E. to present

DEFINITION: The body of obligatory customs, conventions, rules, and principles by which governments of nation-states order their interrelations

SIGNIFICANCE: Seeks to minimize international conflict and promote cooperation among nations

Unlike domestic systems of law, in which supreme legislative, executive, and judicial organs make, enforce, and interpret law, international law has developed between and among rather than above states in international relations. Possessing sovereignty, these states alone can make international law, and when they do so it is of their voluntary accord rather than under the compulsion of any higher authority. This lack of a higher authority above states leads potentially to a system of anarchy in which evils of unspeakable proportions can be committed. Governments have, since the earliest dawn of civilizations, attempted to limit their sovereign prerogatives in an effort to avoid anarchy, preserve harmony in their interrelations, and promote the welfare of their respective populations. Even when cooperation broke down and war occurred, governments recognized a need to limit their behavior, protect innocent life, and curb the excessive brutality associated with violent war. They did so by devising systems of international law.

History. The roots of international law can be traced back at least to the times of the ancient Greeks and Romans, who developed principles of interstate law to govern diplomatic exchanges, treaties, the legal status of aliens, usages in war, and principles of citizenship and asylum. These ancient states saw the benefits of reciprocity—that is, of treating citizens and representatives of other nations with decorum and respect so that similar treatment would be accorded their own citizens and representatives by other states. Much of this law was based in custom, but some was established by statute and treaty. The Roman conceptions of *jus civile*, *jus gentium*, and *jus naturalae* established the foundation on which international law is today based. The *jus civile*, or law of cities, concerned the rules distinct to each city of the Empire based on its own customs and traditions. The *jus gentium*, or law among nations, was the law that applied to citizens of all states in their relations to one another. The *jus naturalae*, or the natural law, comprised those overarching principles in nature that human reason could discern regardless of national affiliation. The closer the *jus civile* and *jus gentium* approximated the *jus naturalae*, the more perfect they became.

During the Middle Ages in Europe, Christian moral principles served as a means of inhibiting the excesses of governments against their subjects and against other governments. Rules of war called for the protection of civilians and noncombatants, humane and fair treatment of prisoners, and even proscribed conflict during certain seasons and on certain days. Laws of diplomatic immunity persisted and developed. Rules for acquiring and disposing of territory gradually developed.

With the onset of the Protestant Reformation and the resulting religious wars in Europe, however, the princes and monarchs of Europe ultimately found it necessary to establish clear rules regarding state rights and duties. At the Peace of Westphalia in 1648, they determined that states were sovereign, equal, and independent; the sovereign within a particular territory had exclusive control over it and the right to determine its laws and its religion. No sovereign was obliged to abide by any treaty or rule that he or she did not explicitly and voluntarily accept or recognize. These principles continue to serve as the basis of modern international law, although governments in the intervening centuries have shed themselves of monarchs and in many instances adopted republican government.

As the Industrial Revolution, commercial expansion, and colonial competition grew, governments found the need to recognize both customary and treaty principles in order to promote a degree of cooperation and to curb excessive conflict. In the twentieth century, states agreed that force should not be used to settle international disputes, unless used in self-defense or under the aegis of a collective authority such as the United Nations. In addition, governments increasingly developed rules to protect aliens living, traveling, and working in foreign lands. States undertook the responsibility to protect aliens at a level commensurate to that enjoyed by their own citizens. Should the host state fail in this responsibility, an injured alien could, after exhausting available local remedies, appeal to his or her country of nationality to file a claim against the host government to obtain redress for the injury.

Current Ethical Principles and Issues. As noted earlier, most international law is made and observed by states out of reciprocal self-interest. Once states make promises to one another in treaties, they are obliged to honor them, and in the vast majority of cases they do. If states should fail to honor their treaty or customary legal obligations, however, the injured parties may seek judicial remedies, or, failing this, they may seek to punish offending states through sanctions or other retaliatory measures. When engaging in such retaliation, governments are obliged to observed the principle of proportionality, which means that they can take actions of roughly similar kind and degree against a state committing a prior wrong. Excessive retaliation is itself considered wrong.

During the twentieth century, with the emergence of guerrilla wars, total wars, and nuclear weaponry, the old distinction between civilian and combatant has been blurred in practice. The customary laws of war, in turn, have often been disregarded, and many innocent lives have been lost. The Geneva Red Cross Conventions and Protocols have been promulgated to reassert the distinction between combatants and noncombatants and to preserve the rights of prisoners of war. In addition, since World War II, governments have increasingly adopted a wide range of human rights declarations and treaties in order to define more clearly the respective rights and responsibilities of individuals and states under international law. Such agreements include the Universal Declaration of Human Rights, the Genocide Convention, and the Conventions on Civil and Political and Economic and Social Rights. Thus, although states remain the principal subjects of international law, they increasingly recognize the need to protect, usually through domestic legal mechanisms, the human rights of their respective citizens. In turn, individuals can be held directly accountable for a variety of international crimes, including war crimes, piracy, genocide, counterfeiting, and slave trading.

International law represents one of the means by which governments have countered the anarchic tendencies of international relations and thereby remained conscious of their legal and ethical obligations to one another and to their own citizens as well as to aliens. —*Robert F. Gorman*

See also Arbitration; Deterrence; Genocide; Human rights; International justice; Intervention; Natural law; Power; Sanctions; Sovereignty; U.N. Covenant on Civil and Political Rights; War and peace.

BIBLIOGRAPHY

Akehurst, Michael. *A Modern Introduction to International Law*. 4th ed. London: George Allen & Unwin, 1982.

Brierly, James. *The Law of Nations*. 6th ed. New York: Oxford University Press, 1963.

Corbett, Percy. *The Growth of World Law*. Princeton, N.J.: Princeton University Press, 1971.

Jessup, Philip C. *A Modern Law of Nations*. New York: Macmillan, 1948.

Kaplan, Morton, and Nicholas Katzenbach. *The Political Foundations of International Law*. New York: John Wiley & Sons, 1961.

Von Glahn, Gerhard. *Law Among Nations*. 6th rev. ed. New York: Macmillan, 1992.

International Organization of Consumers Unions

TYPE OF ETHICS: Business and labor ethics

DATE: Founded 1960

ASSOCIATED WITH: The United Nations and the consumer protection movement

DEFINITION: The IOCU works with government agencies and consumer organizations to further the interests of the consumer

SIGNIFICANCE: The IOCU is the main vehicle through which national and regional consumers' groups share information with one another

Headquartered in The Hague, The Netherlands, the International Organization of Consumers Unions (IOCU) is affiliated with 175 national and local consumer organizations in sixty-eight countries. Its purpose is to bring together the efforts and results of these smaller organizations to increase the power of consumers worldwide. Specifically, the IOCU has worked on such issues as the safety and effectiveness of infant formulas, and the safe distribution and use of pesticides. The IOCU gathers and shares published information from its affiliates; provides a forum for further sharing of information and problems; encourages nations to cooperate with one another in testing product safety and in sharing the results of these tests; and studies and interprets local, national, and international laws relating to consumers. Because it works closely with the United Nations and other international bodies but not with any individual national governments, the IOCU can be an important advocate for consumers in developing nations. These consumers have sometimes been deceived or coerced into buying products that have been judged too dangerous or ineffective for sale in the developed nations where they were manufactured. Working with the United Nations, the IOCU offers consumer education and protection programs in developing nations.

See also Consumerism; Public interest.

Internment of Japanese Americans

TYPE OF ETHICS: Modern history
DATE: 1942-1946
ASSOCIATED WITH: The War Relocation Authority's sending of Japanese Americans to relocation centers throughout the western United States during World War II
DEFINITION: Japanese Americans, both United States citizens and Japanese citizens, were ordered from their homes and sent to internment camps because they were thought to be a threat to the United States after the Japanese surprise attack on Pearl Harbor
SIGNIFICANCE: Japanese Americans were interned in concentration camp-style relocation centers, based strictly on their national origin without due process of law

On December 7, 1941, the Japanese made a surprise attack on the United States naval base at Pearl Harbor in Hawaii. This action led to a declaration of war by the United States against Japan the next day.

Before 1941, an anti-Orientalist movement existed on the West Coast of the United States. The attack on Pearl Harbor intensified this regional animosity and provided an opportunity to rid the region of this unwanted race. Suspicion ran high against the Japanese living in the United States. Many leaders were arrested and many others endured personal attacks and violence. Both American-born (Nisei) and Japanese-born (Issei) people of Japanese descent were considered a threat simply because of their national origin.

The California Joint Immigration Committee; the U.S. Army, represented by General John L. DeWitt; the Pacific congressional delegation; and other anti-Japanese organizations recommended that President Franklin D. Roosevelt evacuate the Japanese population. On February 19, 1942, Roosevelt responded with Executive Order 9066, which authorized the secretary of war, or any military commander designated by him, to establish military areas and exclude therefrom any and all persons. DeWitt, Commander of the Western Defense Command, became the person responsible for the evacuation under the executive order. This was unfortunate because he was extremely prejudiced against the Japanese.

On March 2, 1942, DeWitt issued Public Proclamation Number One, which defined the West Coast exclusion zone. The western halves of Washington, Oregon, and California became Military Area Number One. All persons of Japanese ancestry living in that area would be relocated in the interest of military necessity. This left opponents of mass evacuation defenseless and brought no opposition from public or civilian leaders, who were forced to accept military authority. It also afforded those of Japanese ancestry a brief period of voluntary relocation. Only a few thousand took this opportunity to move, and they were faced with anti-Japanese feelings wherever they went.

The Wartime Civilian Control Authority (WCCA), a military organization, and the War Relocation Authority (WRA), a civilian agency created by executive order on March 18, 1942, were established to aid in the movement of the evacuees. The WRA had the authority to provide for the relocation of evacuees in appropriate places and to provide for their needs and activities. Milton S. Eisenhower was the WRA's director for the first three months. Both he and his successor, Dillon S. Myer, attempted to find a just way to relocate the Japanese Americans, which won them gratitude from that community. Millions of dollars in property and belongings were lost, however, by the Japanese Americans who were forced to relocate.

After the failure of the voluntary relocation, Eisenhower realized that some form of detention on federally managed, army-guarded land was necessary. In making the decision on internment, the WRA faced the constitutional question of whether it had the legal authority to detain American citizens without bringing charges against them. The Fifth Amendment to the Constitution guaranteed every citizen the right of life, liberty, and property with due process of law. The WRA thought, however, that it was justified in forgoing this amendment during wartime as a necessity for national security. The court system supported the relocation argument by virtue of the words "war necessity." Although the United States was at war with Italy and Germany, only a few people of these nationalities were detained.

By late May, 1942, almost 112,000 Japanese Americans were in assembly centers. They were forced from their homes with only what they could carry with them. Assembly centers were hastily set up at fair grounds, race tracks, and stadiums with barbed wire placed around them. The evacuees spent between six weeks and six months at these temporary centers, until the relocation camps were completed.

A total of 117,116 people were evacuated to assembly or relocation centers or came under some phase of the evacuation program between March 2 and October 31 of 1942. This included 151 persons transferred from the Territory of Alaska to the custody of the WCCA and 504 babies who were born to mothers in assembly areas. Another 1,875 persons were sent from the Territory of Hawaii—1,118 to relocation centers and 757 to Justice Department internment camps. More than 70,000 were American citizens.

INTERNMENT CAMPS FOR U.S. RESIDENTS OF JAPANESE DESCENT			
Name	Location	Population	Dates
Central Utah	Delta, Utah	8,130	9/11/42-10/31/45
Colorado River	Poston, Arizona	17,814	5/08/42-11/28/45
Gila River	Rivers, Arizona	13,348	7/20/42-11/10/45
Granada	Lamar, Colorado	7,318	8/27/42-10/15/45
Heart Mountain	Heart Mountain, Wyoming	10,767	8/12/42-11/10/45
Jerome	Jerome, Arkansas	8,497	10/06/42-06/30/44
Manzanar	Manzanar, California	10,046	06/01/42-11/21/45
Minidoka	Hunt, Idaho	9,397	08/10/42-10/28/45
Rohwer	McGehee, Arkansas	8,475	09/18/42-11/30/45
Tule Lake	Newell, California	18,789	5/27/42-03/20/46

Life in the relocation centers was very difficult at first. Many families were crowded into hastily erected barracks and living conditions were poor. Supplies were short. After the relocation authorities finally had the logistics worked out, conditions gradually improved. During 1943 and 1944, violence broke out and demonstrations were conducted in the camps to protest the treatment of the internees.

Early in 1943, the situation regarding the Japanese Americans lightened somewhat. Secretary of War Henry L. Stimson announced plans to form a Japanese American combat team made up of Nisei volunteers from the mainland and Hawaii. This unit served with distinction throughout the war. Director Myer wrote a letter to Stimson asking for an immediate relaxation in the West Coast Exclusion Zone, but Stimson rejected it. On March 20, 1943, Myer took the first step in decentralizing the relocation program by authorizing project directors to issue leave permits in cases in which leave clearance had previously been granted by the Washington office.

Finally, on December 17, 1944, the War Department announced the revocation of the West Coast mass exclusion orders of 1942, and the next day Myer announced that all relocation centers would be closed by June 30, 1946. On March 20, 1946, Tule Lake Segregation Center, the last of the WRA centers, was officially closed.

After the war, the government permitted the internees to file claims for losses during internment. The ceilings were low in relationship to the property losses and certainly did not cover the personal humiliation and suffering endured by the internees. In October 1990, after many years of debate, U.S. Attorney General Dick Thornburgh presented the first reparation checks of $20,000 to those interned during World War II. The government finally admitted that it had been wrong.
                                                    —Larry N. Sypolt

See also Bigotry; Military ethics.

BIBLIOGRAPHY

Collins, Donald E. *Native American Aliens, Disloyalty and the Renunciation of Citizenship by Japanese Americans During World War II*. Contributions in Legal Studies 32. Westport, Conn.: Greenwood Press, 1985.

Hosokawa, Bill. *Nisei, The Quiet Americans*. New York: William Morrow, 1969.

Irons, Peter. *Justice at War*. New York: Oxford University Press, 1983.

Myer, Dillon S. *Uprooted Americans: The Japanese Americans and the War Relocation Authority During World War II*. Tucson: University of Arizona Press, 1971.

U.S. Army. Western Defense Command and Fourth Army. *Final Report: Japanese Evacuation from the West Coast 1942*. Washington, D.C.: Government Printing Office, 1943.

Intersubjectivity

TYPE OF ETHICS: Theory of ethics; Beliefs and practices
DATE: Nineteenth and twentieth centuries
ASSOCIATED WITH: Charles Sanders Peirce, Jürgen Habermas, and Karl-Otto Apel
DEFINITION: Communicative interaction and agreement among subjects or at least between an ego and an alter ego
SIGNIFICANCE: The presupposition for the possibility and validity of ethics may be found in the ethical community of moral actors who jointly agree on ethical judgments

Whereas subjectivism makes truth and knowledge dependent upon an individual knower, and objectivism holds that truth exists independently from any subjective state of mind, intersubjectivity makes the objective validity of truth depend upon the consensus of a community of subjects. In so doing, intersubjectivity avoids the relativism of subjectivism without granting to truth a status independent of the human mind.

Intersubjectivity has been used as a heuristic concept to aid in the formulation of solutions for two thorny issues. First, how is meaning determined? Second, what is the foundation for the possibility and validity of ethics?

The Problem of Meaning. Charles Sanders Peirce (1839-1914) established pragmatism as a philosophical method for determining meaning and truth. Two elements stand out in his pragmatic theory. First, the conception of an object consists of the conception of its effects. Second, truth is indefinite. Truth is that upon which the ultimate community of investigators would agree. The ultimate community of investigators constitutes the intersubjective preconditon for the possibility of meaning and of science.

In addition to pragmatism, Peirce also developed a theory of semiotics, the science of the interpretation of signs. He rejected the traditional philosophy of consciousness that interpreted knowledge in terms of a two-place relationship—the object in the world and its mental representation. Semiotic theory introduces a third element; that is, a sign not only stands for something in the world but is also addressed to an interpreter. The three-place relationship is essentially intersubjective. Signs have meaning only within the intersubjective framework of an interpretation community. The traditional role of the subject of knowledge is replaced by the interpretative community. Subjectivity is replaced by intersubjectivity. Signs can represent only if they are related to the intersubjective world of interpreters, and only those assertions are true that would be reaffirmed by an indefinite community.

Jürgen Habermas, influenced by the pragmatism of Peirce and his semiotic theory, formulated discourse ethics. Discourse ethics emphasizes the use theory of meaning. Meaning consists of a threefold relationship—what is meant, what is said, and the way it is used. Use theory builds on the third element and focuses on the interactive contexts of communication in which expressions function. These contexts were called "language games" by Ludwig Wittgenstein. Language games include the totality of linguistic expressions and nonlinguistic activities. The analysis of language games discloses the intersubjectively shared backgrounds of the forms of life and lifeworlds that influence the meaning and function of language.

Meanings of symbols, therefore, are never subjective but always intersubjective. Symbolic meaning does not derive validity from private interpretation but from intersubjective agreement.

Because of the interconnectedness of language and lifeworld, intersubjectivity is fixed in ordinary language. Interactive communication and agreement between human beings make social life possible.

Habermas also rejects the traditional concept of the subject understood as an ego. The subject is a community of investigators. For Habermas, the moral subject, as a subject of action, cannot even be conceived apart from communicative interaction with other human beings.

Karl-Otto Apel, a German philosopher, insisted that language and intersubjective agreement make meaningful ethical judgments possible. Apel held that the intersubjective community of investigators is the precondition for the possibility and validity of objectively valid ethics. Apel maintained, along with Kant, the necessity for universal preconditions for the possibility and validity of ethics. Unlike Kant, however, he did not find these "transcendental" conditions in the consciousness of the solitary individual; following Peirce, Apel located them in the discursive ethical community.

Apel conceptualized this idea by utilizing a synthesis between transcendental idealism and historical materialism. From idealism, he postulated the normative and ideal presupposition of the "ideal communication community." The ideal communication community functions as an imaginary hypothetical community free from inequality and unjust constraints. From materialism, he derived the "real communication community" as a given historical society in which real conflict and inequality exist. The dialectical relationship existing between the ideal communication community and the real communication community is characterized as an antagonism between the ideal and the factual. Notwithstanding its antagonistic character, this dialectical relationship results in the conceptualization of the discursive community as the precondition for both the ethical community as a moral subject and, at the same time, the discursive community as the object of ethical action. In this manner, Apel avoids the extremes of subjectivism and objectivism. In Apel's thought, ethics is made possible because of the search for mutual understanding that occurs intersubjectively between persons in conversation.

The heuristic model of the communication community functions in the same way as Wittgenstein's concept of the language game. In either case, consensus functions as a regulative principle. Truth and knowledge arise from communicative action under rule-governed institutions. It is this communicative interaction that makes the objective validity of ethics possible. —*Michael R. Candelaria*

See also Kantian ethics; Peirce, Charles Sanders; Wittgenstein, Ludwig.

BIBLIOGRAPHY

Apel, Karl-Otto. *Towards a Transformation of Philosophy.* Translated by Glyn Adey and David Frisby. London: Routledge & Kegan Paul, 1980.

Habermas, Jürgen. *Communication and the Evolution of Society.* Translated by Thomas McCarthy. Boston: Beacon Press, 1979.

Hohler, T. P. *Imagination and Reflection. Intersubjectivity. Fichte's Grundlage of 1794.* The Hague: Martinus Nijhoff, 1982.

Husserl, Edmund. *Cartesian Meditations: An Introduction to Phenomenology.* Translated by Dorion Cairns. The Hague: Martinus Nijhoff, 1988.

Peirce, Charles. *Philosophical Writings of Peirce.* Edited by Justus Buchler. New York: Dover, 1955.

These American Marines were part of the American intervention in Vietnam that escalated and became the Vietnam War. (U.S. Marine Corps photo, courtesy DAVA)

Intervention

TYPE OF ETHICS: International relations
DATE: Coined c. twelfth century
DEFINITION: Action taken to "proscribe" the actions of others; activity undertaken by a state that coercively interferes in the domestic affairs of another
SIGNIFICANCE: Barring humanitarian intervention, in most, if not all cases, intervention jeopardizes the public internal realm of another sovereign state

Theoretically, no state has the right to interfere in the domestic affairs of another sovereign state. Such an act is a contradiction of the principles of sovereignty and therefore an attack on the very system on which the freedom of nations rests. Intervention comes in many forms: propaganda; espionage; discriminatory economic policies; and support or denial of support to governments or subversive movements in domestic crises, especially where such foreign support might prove to be decisive. The most notorious form, however, is military intervention. It is not always easy to determine the morality of intervention, and where interventionist activities are concerned, morality may not always be the highest value. Instead, what matters most is the relationship of morality, power, and knowledge, which, when gainfully exploited, in its contemplative stage may be called wisdom and in its active phase may be called justice. Unfortunately, more often than not, this is not the case. During most of the Cold War, for example, intervention was undertaken on behalf of issues of national power far more often than because of poverty, tyranny, or exploitation. During that period, any action against the communist or imperialist threat, especially if it was successful, was considered by the interventionist power to be moral by definition, or else merely a problem of techniques.

See also Covert action; Espionage.

Intrinsic good

TYPE OF ETHICS: Theory of ethics
DATE: Fourth century B.C.E.
ASSOCIATED WITH: Aristotle, G. E. Moore, and utilitarianism
DEFINITION: The value that something has in itself, rather than its value based on its usefulness or what it can bring about

SIGNIFICANCE: Identifies the basis of all value

The concept of intrinsic good goes back to Aristotle's notion of "the good" as that for the sake of which one chooses all other things. The contrast is with extrinsic good, which is understood as something that is good only because it brings about something else that is intrinsically good. Standard candidates for intrinsic goods are pleasure and happiness; pluralist theories include such things as friendship and virtue. G. E. Moore introduced a useful test for intrinsic goodness and a theory about its nature. For example, to see whether music is intrinsically good, Moore would have one imagine a universe with only music in it—and therefore with no listeners to enjoy the music—and consider whether the universe seems a better one than a universe without any music. If the universe with music in it does seem better, music is intrinsically valuable; if not, music is valuable only because of its effects, such as its effects on listeners. Moore also argued that intrinsic goodness is an objective, nonnatural property and that rightness can be defined in terms of it.

See also Intuitionist ethics; Moore, G. E.

Intuitionist ethics

TYPE OF ETHICS: Theory of ethics

DATE: Developed in fourth century B.C.E. Greece

ASSOCIATED WITH: The Greek philosopher Plato and the British philosophers Francis Hutcheson, Richard Price, H. A. Prichard, W. D. Ross, G. E. Moore, and A. C. Ewing

DEFINITION: Intuitionist ethics ground ethics on intuition, which is either rational understanding, perception, or considered judgment; intuitionist ethics also include the view that there is not one single guiding moral principle but several

SIGNIFICANCE: Intuitionist ethics provide an answer to the important question, "What justifies our moral beliefs?"; in some versions of this approach to ethics, moral qualities cannot be defined in terms of empirical qualities, and in that case ethics are autonomous—that is, cannot be explained in terms of other disciplines, such as sociology, psychology, or biology

According to one version of intuitionist ethics, normal people can simply see the truth about at least some moral matters. In this view, the intuition that something is right or good is not just a hunch or a feeling. Instead, it is an immediate awareness, something like the awareness that three-sided plane figures have three angles. Thinking carefully about a particular act leads one simply to see that the act would be right. In this view, the judgment that this act would be right is self-evident—that is, knowable without reliance on further evidence. In a similar way, some intuitionists claim that some general moral principles are self-evident in the same way that mathematical axioms are self-evident.

The analogy with geometry and mathematics is, however, problematic. "Any three-sided plane figure has three angles" is self-evident, but "Always tell the truth" is not self-evident.

General moral principles, unlike geometric principles, have exceptions, and therefore they cannot be self-evident in the same way. In the case of particular moral judgments, one cannot be sure that there is no hidden aspect of the situation that will make the judgment incorrect. Thus, such particular moral judgments also lack the self-evidence of geometric principles.

Some intuitionists think of "seeing" as *looking* instead of as *understanding*. For them, moral intuitions are like perceptions of colors as opposed to apprehensions of axioms. One objection to this approach is that perceiving requires a sense organ, and it does not seem that people have a moral sense organ. It seems clear, however, that seeing moral qualities only requires some means, not necessarily anything like "a moral eye or a moral nose."

Moral disagreement within societies, between societies, and across time periods presents a more serious problem for intuitionist ethics. How can one be sure that one is perceiving right and wrong if there is so much disagreement about them? Disagreement about what is red would raise serious questions about one's power to detect color qualities, and the same seems true about the power to detect moral qualities.

Intuitionists may respond that some people have a faulty moral faculty. Such people may be biased or lack relevant experiences, such as knowing what it is like to be without enough food to eat. The idea is that, just as some people suffer from color blindness, some people suffer from moral blindness. Unlike the case of color blindness, there is no agreed-upon test for determining moral blindness. Intuitionists may emphasize the "intuitions" of "normal moral observers" or "moral experts" and discount the "intuitions" of everyone else. Then, however, the difficulty is to say what a moral expert is, without making a moral judgment that rests on intuition.

Also responding to the problem of moral disagreement, other intuitionists claim that there is not really that much disagreement. For example, one culture may leave the elderly to die in the cold while another culture cares for the elderly. Yet both cultures may be trying to do what they think is good for the elderly and merely have different factual beliefs about what that is. All the same, it seems that people may agree on all "the facts" of abortion and still disagree about whether the fetus has a right to life.

Some intuitionists may try to lessen moral disagreement by talking about *prima facie* obligations. A *prima facie* obligation to keep promises, for example, is an obligation to keep promises unless there is an overriding moral reason not to keep them. This approach does away with some disagreement, but disagreement remains, since different intuitionists have different lists of *prima facie* obligations.

If having an intuition is supposed to guarantee that one has determined the truth, then what are the criteria for determining that one has actually had an intuition? Disagreeing parties may be equally certain that they are right. If intuition is a "seeming to see," something like a conviction, then how can it provide a solid foundation for moral judgments?

This appeal to intuition is not an appeal to one's general beliefs, but instead an appeal to one's *considered* beliefs, beliefs that one has arrived at after a process of rationally considering alternatives. These beliefs are not supposed to be self-evident; one checks them against one's other beliefs and against the considered beliefs of others. Beliefs that pass this test become part of the basis for testing other beliefs.

This approach makes justification largely a matter of "coherence" among beliefs. If this approach can avoid a vitiating circularity, can it avoid a built-in bias in favor of traditional beliefs? Might not traditional prejudices survive the process of testing beliefs? In any case, the problem of disagreement remains, since two incompatible sets of beliefs may be equally coherent. —*Gregory P. Rich*

See also Epistemological ethics; Moral-sense theories; Naturalistic fallacy.

BIBLIOGRAPHY

Donagan, Alan. *The Theory of Morality*. Chicago: University of Chicago Press, 1977.

Garner, Richard T., and Bernard Rosen. *Moral Philosophy: A Systematic Introduction to Normative Ethics and Meta-ethics*. New York: Macmillan, 1967.

Hudson, W. D. *Ethical Intuitionism*. New York: St. Martin's Press, 1967.

Ross, W. D. *The Right and the Good*. Indianapolis: Hackett, 1988.

Shaw, William H. "Intuition and Moral Philosophy." *American Philosophical Quarterly* 17, no. 2 (April, 1980): 127-34.

Is/ought distinction

TYPE OF ETHICS: Theory of ethics
DATE: Eighteenth century to present
ASSOCIATED WITH: David Hume
DEFINITION: Asserts that prescriptive (value) statements differ from descriptive (empirical) statements in neither being verifiable nor representing a definable body of knowledge
SIGNIFICANCE: Seeks to understand the nature of ethical reasoning as it relates to the concrete world of sense experience

One of the oldest continuing debates in moral philosophy concerns the relationship of "prescriptive" statements (about what one *ought* to do) to "descriptive" statements (about what one *is* doing) Descriptive statements are defined as statements of fact that refer to events or properties that are obtained through the experiences of the senses and therefore are verifiable—that is, they can be categorized as true or false. Since descriptive statements are empirical in nature, they are thought collectively to form a body of "scientific" knowledge. An example of such

a statement is "The water is hot." Both the subject and the predicate in this sentence can be verified; the liquid in question can be tested as to its composition, while its temperature can be measured and compared to accepted conventions of heat and cold. Once the sentence is analyzed, its truthfulness will either be affirmed or denied, but in either case, a concrete "fact" will have been established.

Prescriptive statements, however, do not always seem to proceed from the same empirical foundations, and it is not always possible to verify their truth or falsehood as one would verify that of a descriptive statement. Again, consider an example: "One ought never to cheat." Here, no actual event is necessarily referred to; thus, there is nothing concrete to verify as either true or false. Instead, the statement seems to express an attitude about a possible course of action—in this case, to assert disapproval. The debate in moral philosophy, however, is whether such statements have any relation at all to empirical facts and thus form a body of "knowledge" similar to that of descriptive statements. About this there remains much disagreement.

The Distinction's Origins. The origin of the modern philosophical debate about the nature of prescriptive statements is traditionally ascribed to the eighteenth century British philosopher David Hume. In his *Treatise of Human Nature* (1740), Hume criticized previous philosophers who attempted to draw prescriptive conclusions from descriptive premises. Since for Hume the two types of statements have fundamentally different natures, he considered it impossible to derive the former from the latter. Statements of value, in other words, were not reducible to statements of fact.

Hume's critique was challenged later in the eighteenth century by Immanuel Kant, who, in his *Fundamental Principles of the Metaphysics of Morals* (1785), attempted to avoid the trap of moral relativism that seemed to ensue from Hume's position. While Kant agreed that statements of value could not be derived from statements of fact, prescriptive statements could nevertheless be verified if they were derived from a universal moral principle that could be shown to be self-evidently true. Kant's categorical imperative ("I am never to act otherwise than so that I could also will that my maxim should become a universal law") represented one attempt to frame such a universal moral principle and thus allow prescriptive statements in general to form a body of knowledge.

Modern Debate. More recent attempts to either affirm or resolve the is/ought distinction have led to the formation of a number of schools of thought. In the main, those who make such attempts fall into two major groups: the cognitivists, who claim that prescriptive statements do form a recognizable body of knowledge, and the noncognitivists, who deny such a possibility. Cognitivists further subdivide into two separate schools: naturalists (such as Jeremy Bentham and R. B. Perry) believe that prescriptive statements are simply different forms of factual statements that are, like any scientific fact, empirically verifiable. Such verification may occur through analyzing those acts that happen in accord with particular prescriptive principles (Are such acts consistent with established ethical norms?) or by observing the consequences of those acts (Have they led to desirable results?). In either case, the naturalist asserts that such observation takes place on the level of the senses and thus value statements themselves are considered to be facts.

The nonnaturalist (such as David Ross and G. E. Moore) differs, seeing prescriptive statements as unique forms in themselves, which cannot be reduced to the level of scientific fact. Values may be considered to be true or false, but they must be verified not according to the observations of sense experience, but instead by direct appeal to moral intuition, to a universal value-principle, or to a set of properties that define intrinsic moral value. This appeal to universals has led to the nonnaturalist position's also being defined as intuitionism. In addition, G. E. Moore, in his monumental work *Principia Ethica* (1903), framed a critique of the naturalist position based on what he termed the naturalistic fallacy. Moore claimed that naturalistic statements attempt to equate value properties with empirical properties as if statements about each conveyed the same kind of meaning. ("Gandhi is a good man" as being no different from "The ball is green"). Since it can be shown, said Moore, that such statements are not the same, naturalistic statements are inherently fallacious.

Noncognitivists (such as Charles Stevenson and A. J. Ayer) continued Moore's critique of naturalism but extended it to include all cognitivist theories in general. Both naturalism and nonnaturalism are thought by this group to be incorrect in claiming that prescriptive statements can in any way be proved to be true or false. Rather, prescriptive statements communicate a person's attitudes about a particular event, property, or course of action and attempt to convince others to agree. Since attitudes are not verifiable, they cannot be considered true or false, and, since attitudes are not intrinsic value-properties (as nonnaturalism asserts), there can be no such thing as a body of moral knowledge.

More recently, noncognitivism itself has come into question from a variety of directions. Philippa Foote has claimed that when one examines how one actually uses prescriptive statements, no "logical gap" exists between one's observation of facts and one's moral evaluation of them. Also, Mortimer Adler has proposed his own form of cognitivism by distinguishing between "natural desires" (which he calls "needs") and "acquired desires" (called "wants"). Since what one needs is by definition good for one, and since one cannot do the opposite and not desire what one needs, one may thus construct an imperative that is self-evidently true. Having done this, one may then observe specific actions and measure them empirically according to one's established norm—a process that allows prescriptive statements to be verifiable and to form a body of knowledge after all.

—*Robert C. Davis*

See also Cognitivism and noncognitivism; Hume, David; Intuitionist ethics; Kantian ethics; Moore, G. E.; Naturalistic fallacy; Prescriptivism.

BIBLIOGRAPHY

Adler, Mortimer. *Ten Philosophical Mistakes*. New York: Macmillan, 1985.

Edwards, Paul, ed. *The Encyclopedia of Philosophy*. New York: Macmillan, 1967.

Ferm, Vergilius, ed. *Encyclopedia of Morals*. New York: Philosophical Library, 1956.

Jones, W. T. *A History of Western Philosophy*. 2d ed. New York: Harcourt, Brace & World, 1969.

Taylor, Paul, ed. *Problems of Moral Philosophy: An Introduction to Ethics*. 3d ed. Belmont, Calif.: Wadsworth, 1978.

Islamic ethics

TYPE OF ETHICS: Religious ethics

DATE: Beginning with the first revelations to Muḥammad, c. 609

ASSOCIATED WITH: Islam, the Qur'ân, Muḥammad, and the traditions that developed from and in association with them

DEFINITION: Any of the several ethical traditions associated with Islam

SIGNIFICANCE: The traditions of Islamic ethics provide guidance in the daily, religious, and political life for approximately one-quarter of the world's population

A multitude of ethical traditions have evolved in association with Islam. Islamic ethics includes the revealed text and exegesis of the Qur'ân, and the *ḥadîth*; several traditions of *sharî'a* (Islamic law); philosophical schools, only some of which take the Qur'ân as their point of departure; and a vibrant and diverse mystical tradition. Before examining that diversity further, this article will begin by examining the fundamentals of Islam.

Al-Islâm literally means "submission," or "surrender," to the Will of God. The Qur'ân explains that earlier revelations of the Divine Word were given to humankind through earlier prophets, such as Abraham and Jesus, but that humans had not developed sufficiently to hear the perfect revelation of that Word until the time of Muḥammad, to whom the Qur'ân, the final and perfect revelation, was given. The Just and Merciful God desires that humans should actualize their potentialities as much as finite beings are able, and He has provided guidance toward that end.

A distinctive feature of Islam is its power to unify otherwise diverse facets of life. Submission to the Will of God requires proper religious observance and behavior, as well as adherence to the moral strictures given in the Qur'ân. The five pillars of Islam (the professions that there is no god but God and that Muḥammad is His messenger, prescribed prayer and fasting, and the pilgrimage to Mecca) are obligatory, although dispensation of the last two may be granted in special circumstances, and the Qur'ân also provides specific prescriptions and proscriptions for behavior.

Islam also requires, though, training and habituation in

Muslims at the Grand Mosque in Mecca. (AP/Wide World Photos)

virtues of character and intellect so that Muslims will have the proper comportment toward this world and toward God. The Qur'ân frequently provides practical guidance for the development of good character, the traditions of the life of the Prophet are looked to frequently as a model, and such philosophers as al-Ghazâlî have devoted additional major efforts toward understanding and encouraging the virtues.

Islam requires, further, that the life of the faithful be communal. Except in some philosophical and mystical traditions, Islam places great emphasis on the cohesion of the community of the faithful, and there are numerous Qur'ânic prescriptions toward that end. The Friday noon prayers, for example, must always be in public congregation of the whole community so that the faithful are reinforced in their identity as a Muslim community. The community is also bound together by *zakât* (alms).

Zakât is required by the Qur'ân (for example, in *sûra* 9:103). God has granted material success to individuals not merely for their own gain but also for the return of some of that gain to promote the success of the whole community: There is no justification of individual property unless a part of that property is given over to the good of the whole community. The Qur'ân thus enjoins Muslims to be prudent in managing their material wealth, because prudence is a virtue leading to wisdom and so that communal wealth will be conserved (Qur'ân 17: 26-30). Social responsibilities in the distribution of wealth remain a major component of Islamic social and political ethics today.

The ability of Islam to unify religion, personal ethics, and social/political responsibility gives it the character not merely of a body of religious doctrines but also of a *Weltanschauung* and a way of life. All aspects of life—worship, private and public behavior, political and economic organization—are submitted to and are reminders of Divine Will.

Sources of Islamic Ethics. The primary source of Islamic ethics is the Qur'ân and its exegesis, and most traditions follow the example of the life of Muḥammad in areas that are not specifically addressed by the Qur'ân. Which additional sources are acceptable depends on the school of *sharî'a* (Islamic law, whose domain includes areas that many European thinkers would assign to ethics or political theory) that is consulted. Sunnî traditions usually accept the consensus of the *ulamâ* (orthodox specialists expert in *sharî'a*), Shî'a traditions usually accept the guidance of an *imâm* who leads the community of the faithful, and some philosophical traditions rely on reason alone or even on direct apprehension of God.

Sufism. An extraordinarily rich variety of mystical traditions have developed in association with Islam, and these traditions and their central figures often play an important role in guidance of popular ethical behavior. Furthermore, Sufi literature (which is often written in vernacular languages) and instrumental religion surrounding the spiritual power often believed to reside at the tombs of Sufi saints have served to assimilate local populations into Islam.

Sufism thus has a dual role in Islamic ethics: It provides a personal, mystical path for its adepts, who might not have been assimilable to more exoteric Islam; and it provides means for dissemination of Islam to the general population.

Philosophical Developments. The Islamicate world always has been philosophically vigorous (and sometimes eclectic or even heterodox), and Greek, Iranian, Indian, and other influences have found their way into Islamic ethical philosophy. The need—brought on by the yoke of European imperialism and emergence from it, and by the crises of modernity that have challenged all cultures—for a renewed sense of Islamic identity has made the twentieth century an especially vigorous period in Islamic social, political, and ethical philosophy. There has been renewed interest in classical philosophers (such as Avicenna and al-Ghazâlî) and the traditions of *sharî'a*, with a special concern to move forward by applying these traditional resources to the pressing problems of nationalism, economic development, socialism, and the existential predicament of modernity. —*Thomas Gaskill*

See also al-Ghazâlî, Abû Ḥâmid; *Ḥadîth*; Muḥammad al-Muṣṭafâ; Qur'ân; *Sharî'a*; Sufism.

BIBLIOGRAPHY

Cragg, Kenneth. *The House of Islam*. 2d ed. Encino, Calif.: Dickenson, 1975.

Fakhry, Majid. *Ethical Theories in Islam*. Leiden: E. J. Brill, 1991.

Hovannisian, Richard G., ed. *Ethics in Islam*. Malibu, Calif.: Undena, 1985.

Isolationism

TYPE OF ETHICS: International relations

DATE: 1796

ASSOCIATED WITH: Nineteenth and early twentieth century American foreign policy

DEFINITION: A limitation upon the action of the U.S. government in foreign affairs

SIGNIFICANCE: Isolationism required the avoidance of permanent alliances and of involvement in the diplomatic affairs of other continents; it provided a positive and realistic course for the young and weak nation

Taken together with such major concepts as neutrality and the Monroe Doctrine and such lesser ones as nonintervention, recognition of de facto governments, and equality of trade opportunity, isolationism was one element of a larger policy of U.S. independence on the international stage. George Washington's declaration of as "little political connections as possible" and Thomas Jefferson's admonition of "no entangling alliances" did not preclude a different course from being adopted when the United States reached maturity. George Washington's Farewell Address constituted a foreign policy of independence, not one of isolationism. His primary concern was to keep the operations of the government immune from foreign intrigue and the decisions of the people free from alien domination.

See also Sovereignty.

Israel

TYPE OF ETHICS: Religious ethics

DATE: Fourteenth century B.C.E. to present

DEFINITION: Since 1948, Israel has been the homeland of those members of the international Jewish community who wish to live there

SIGNIFICANCE: The existence of Israel is crucial to Jews, and the ethical questions related to its existence must be resolved to the satisfaction of Jews, Arabs, and the world community if there is to be peace in the Middle East

No religious or ethnic group has faced continuing persecution for longer than has the international Jewish community. Millions of Jews were abused, degraded, and killed in Asia, Europe, Africa, and elsewhere from the sixth century B.C.E. to the middle of the nineteenth century. So strong is antipathy toward Jewish people that dictionaries define it as "anti-Semitism" (no comparable term for antipathy toward any religious or ethnic group is found in any dictionary). In 1948, Israel (a country of not quite 8,000 square miles)—which was claimed by virtue of historical roots, worldwide persecution, and Nazi genocide—was mandated as a Jewish homeland by the United Nations. During the next thirty-nine years, its inhabitants faced four wars and numerous terrorist acts, and the violence continues. Sensible, ethical solutions to the problem of the coexistence of Israel and its Arab neighbors are essential to the world community.

Facts About Israel. The State of Israel is 250 miles long from north to south, and its greatest east-west width is approximately 74 miles. Bordering tiny Israel, whose population was approximately 5 million in 1991, are Egypt, Jordan, Lebanon, and Syria (total population approximately 50 million). About 80 percent of Israelis are Jews; most of the remainder are Muslim Arabs.

The nation's economy includes varied, strong agricultural and industrial components. Most agriculture is concentrated in the northern third of Israel. Much of the land is irrigated, because much of Israel is arid semidesert or desert. Among the country's meager natural resources are copper, a little petroleum, and some natural gas. The economy has a vigorous industrial base that includes the manufacture of electronics components, all kinds of machinery, chemicals, weapons, and a wide variety of precision instruments. Contrary to popular belief, the Israeli per capita gross national product is at the lower end of the range for developed countries.

With this information in mind, one wonders why Israelis tenaciously hold on to this arid land. The answer lies in the history of the Hebrews, today's Jews, which brought about an insatiable hunger in Jews to return to Israel (Zion) that existed for many generations.

History. The Hebrews came out of an Aramean tribe that arose in southern Mesopotamia. Led by the patriarch Abraham, they migrated to Phoenicia, or, as it was known to them, Canaan ("the purple land"), in the fourteenth century B.C.E. At that time, Canaan was a very fertile land "of milk and honey" that had seen many invaders.

Historians agree that Abraham's tribe settled there, blending with the Philistines, until drought forced their migration to Egypt, where they became a semi-enslaved social class called Habiri (or Hebrews). It is there that Moses' actions in leading the Hebrews out of Egypt and codifying the Levitical laws (for example, The Ten Commandments) are believed to have led to the emergence of the Jewish religion and the nation of Israel, named for the grandson of Abraham.

The Israelites reentered a Canaan filled with warring city-states c. 1100 B.C.E. They fought for decades and conquered all of the land west of the Jordan River. A golden age developed for the Israelites that lasted until several consecutive waves of Assyrian and Babylonian conquest (c. 730 B.C.E. to 587 B.C.E.) led to the Jewish depopulation of Israel. Waves of return, self rule, and depopulation continued as conqueror after conqueror strove to rule the area between 550 B.C.E. and 150 C.E. Consequently, the Jews became spread out throughout Africa, Asia, and Europe. Jewish depopulation and dispersal peaked after Rome conquered Israel. The Romans, by 150 C.E., had reduced the Jewish population to a tiny fraction of its original number and had destroyed the Jewish state.

Thus, the Jews, now dispersed and without a homeland, were at the mercy of their adopted countries. For the next 1800 years, the segregation, abuse, degradation, and murder of Jews occurred everywhere. The Christian clergy, European and Asiatic rulers, and the man on the street preached anti-Semitism for various self-serving, often ridiculous reasons. Jews were robbed, stoned, and flayed alive in many places. Where tolerated, they were made to live in ghettos, to dress so that all would know that they were despised Jews, limited in their rights to own land, and restricted as to professions they could enter. To top things off, six million Jews were murdered by Adolf Hitler's Third Reich. During this period, most nations of the world ignored the plight of the Jews.

Throughout 1800 years of worldwide persecution, which reached a horrific peak when the Nazis were in power in Europe, the never-ending refrain in Jewish homes and synagogues was the fervid desire to return to Israel (Zion). In the 1860's, a formal Zionist movement arose and sought to accomplish this return. By fits and starts, the goal was realized, and in May, 1948, the modern State of Israel was established. Then began a series of Arab-Israeli wars and acts of terrorism.

Conclusions. A number of ethical issues have arisen regarding the existence of Israel. The first is whether Jews deserve a homeland in Israel by virtue of their historical roots and because of the unspeakable acts that have been perpetrated against them during their centuries of exile. Believers in both answers to the question are very vocal. Many people who propose that Israel be disestablished have great sympathy for the displaced Palestinian Arabs who have suffered self-imposed exile for about half a century. Supporters of Israel believe that such persons lack sympathy for Jews who suffered—too often, much more horribly—for nearly two thousand years. They also point out that the opponents of Israel give no credence to the fact that one-sixth of Israel's people are Arabs who enjoy a much higher standard of living than do Arabs who live in surrounding countries.

Clearly, however, it is important to recognize the plight of the Palestinians and to resolve the Arab-Israeli conflict peaceably. Therefore, it is essential to identify sound ethical solutions to these dilemmas that address the problems of both Arabs and Israelis. The answers that most people hope will ultimately be found may help in formulating an approach to the problems associated with other minorities, including American Indians and Kurds. Furthermore, such answers could help in the fight against anti-Semitism, which still flourishes throughout the world.   —*Sanford S. Singer*

See also Anti-Semitism; Holocaust; Jewish ethics; Moses; Nazism; Talmud; Torah.

BIBLIOGRAPHY

Arnold, Caroline, and Herma Silverstein. *Anti-Semitism. A Modern Perspective*. New York: Julian Messner, 1985.

Gilbert, Martin. *Exile and Return: The Struggle for a Jewish Homeland*. Philadelphia, Pa.: Lippincott, 1978.

Goldston, Robert C. *Next Year in Jerusalem: A Short History of Zionism*. Boston: Little, Brown, 1978.

Levine, Etan, ed. *Diaspora: Exile and the Contemporary Jewish Condition*. New York: Steimatzky/Shapolsky Press, 1986.

Viorst, Milton. *Sands of Sorrow: Israel's Journey from Independence*. New York: Harper & Row, 1987.

Jain ethics

TYPE OF ETHICS: Religious ethics

DATE: Sixth century B.C.E. to present

DEFINITION: A religious tradition indigenous to India focusing on mystical insight leading to spiritual and total nonviolence

SIGNIFICANCE: The central Jain principle of *ahimsā*, or nonviolence, became important to a number of later philosophies, among them Gandhi's philosophy of nonviolent political action

The Jains constitute less than 1 percent of the population of contemporary India, but their importance today and historically far exceeds their numbers. The founder of the Jain faith, Vardhamāna Mahāvīra (called the *Jina*, or "conqueror") lived in what is now Bihar in north central India. He was roughly contemporaneous with the Buddha (both lived in the sixth century B.C.E.), and Jainism and Buddhism have many similarities. Central to Jainism is the principle of *ahimsā*, or nonviolence, which might be considered its primary contribution to ethics.

The History and Character of Jainism. It is probable that Jainism was a continuation of ancient aboriginal traditions of north central India rather than a radical innovation of its "founder," Mahāvīra. The Jina himself is known as the twenty-fourth *tīrthaṅkara*, or "ford-maker" (that is, builder of a bridge between the mundane world and the world of the spirit). He was, however, responsible for organizing the Jaina *saṅgha* (community), which was notable for its inclusion of both men and women and its refusal to accept caste distinctions. Although Jainism was never a missionary religion per se, it spread from its homeland in Bihar along the trade routes and eventually acquired powerful converts such as the emperor Chandragupta Maurya.

Like Buddhism, Jainism was in some measure a populist response to the elite character of Vedic religion. It was preached not in Sanskrit, which few could understand, but in *prakrits*, or local dialects. Education, which was restricted to the few in Vedicism, was encouraged as a key antidote to the suffering caused by ignorance. Jains were therefore from the beginning a highly literate community, which they remain today.

In 79 C.E., the Jaina community split into two main sects, the *Digambara* ("sky-clad," or naked) and the *Śvetāmbara* ("white-clad"). As well as differing in dress, the two groups differ in their definition of the Jaina canon, which is, given this tradition's emphasis on literacy, an extensive one. They also differ in the disciplines and austerities that they recommend; the Digambara is the more rigorous sect.

The Jaina conception of the universe basically emphasizes change rather than stasis and rejects the personified dieties of Vedicism (the system of faith ancestral to today's Hinduism). The central theological component of the Jaina system is the *jīva*, which can be roughly translated as "soul." *Jīvas* are immortal, but they become entangled in worldly attachments that must be shed in order for them to escape the cycle of rebirth and attain *mokṣa* ("liberation").

The attainment of liberation is a difficult task that is pursued most diligently by Jaina monks and nuns, who strive to be *nirgrantha*, or "free from bonds." Abandonment of all property is the first prerequisite, accompanied by the taking of vows. During parts of the year, monks wander from place to place, begging for their food, meditating, and studying. Along with abstaining from causing injury to any life form, monks and nuns commit to a life of chastity, honesty, and service. These are also the ideals to which laypersons of the Jaina community aspire.

Jainism as a Way of Life. All Jains try to cultivate the "three jewels" of "right faith," "right knowledge," and "right conduct." Among the elements of Jainism most characteristic of the Jaina lifestyle is the principle of *ahimsā* (nonviolence). This is translated in everyday life into total vegetarianism, a dietary habit shared by other communities in India such as those of the high-caste Hindus and Buddhists. In addition to vegetarianism, however, the Jains' characteristic concern for the protection of all life forms is expressed in their support for veterinary hospitals, animal shelters, and means of livelihood that do not injure life. The Jaina community in India, which is unequivocally pacifistic in terms of military matters, influenced Mohandas K. Gandhi to develop his famous methods of nonviolent noncooperation.

Ahimsā as a principle stems from the notion that all life forms contain *jīvas*, or souls, which are striving for liberation in their own unique ways. The path of an ant or a cow, for example, is different from the path of a human but equally valuable. This basically relativistic stance is expressed in such Jaina traditions as the use of brooms to sweep the path as one walks (to avoid stepping on small life forms) and covering one's mouth with a cloth (to avoid inhaling insects). Because of *ahimsā*, agricultural occupations are essentially closed to Jains, involving as they do turning the earth, which may kill worms and other creatures dwelling in the soil. The ultimate aim of the Jains is to live lightly on the earth, doing as little harm as possible.

Jain communities are generally quite well to do and support temples that are among the finest monuments of the subcontinent. Their iconography concerns key figures from the history of the Jaina tradition and various mystic symbols and designs. There are no deities in the Hindu sense, but ritual offerings are made at various Jaina sites.

Today, the Jains are found primarily in the states of Gujarat and Rajasthan in western India, where they tend to live in urban environments. Despite their small numbers, they are prominent in education, the media, business, and the professions. —*Cynthia Keppley Mahmood*

See also Ahimsā; Buddhist ethics; Hindu ethics; Vardhamāna.

BIBLIOGRAPHY

Chatterjee, A. K. *A Comprehensive History of Jainism.* Vols. 1 and 2. Calcutta: Firma KLM, 1984.

Dundas, Paul. *The Jains*. New York: Routledge, 1992.

Jaini, Padmanabh S. *The Jaina Path of Purification*. Berkeley: University of California Press, 1979.

Matilal, Bimal Krishna. *The Central Philosophy of Jainism*. Ahmedabad: L. D. Insititute of Indology, 1981.

James, William (Jan. 11, 1842, New York, N.Y.—Aug. 26, 1910, Chocorua, N.H.): Philosopher

TYPE OF ETHICS: Religious ethics

ACHIEVEMENTS: Author of *The Principles of Psychology* (1890), *The Varieties of Religious Experience: A Study in Human Nature* (1902), *Pragmatism: A New Name for Some Old Ways of Thinking* (1907), and *A Pluralistic Universe* (1909)

SIGNIFICANCE: Interpreted ethics as an expression of humanity's freedom of choice, since the dilemma of determinism versus indeterminism is a metaphysical problem whose solution depends on untestable speculation

William James (Library of Congress)

From 1873 to 1907, James taught anatomy and physiology, psychology, and then philosophy at Harvard University. The first distinguished American psychologist, he won international recognition for his philosophy of "pragmatism" and "pluralism." James believed that ethics rests on the free choice to be moral; that is, to see life as better lived within a moral framework. That conviction, of course, can never be proved or refuted by factual evidence. Even so, the choice empowers a person to make specific ethical decisions, in defense of which a person may gather reasons. Since each person is free to make choices, a moral philosophy must be constructed from the study of widespread ethical choices. James thought that over the course of time, certain ethical principles had taken precedence over others. These principles could be used to construct a unified moral system. Though not appealing directly to Christian (or, more broadly, religious) teachings, James nevertheless made room for explicitly religious systems. On an individual level, James thought that ethics consisted of adjudicating the conflict between duty and inclination. His solution was that individuals should perform the duties that led to a more becoming life or made life worth living.

See also Determinism and freedom; Duty; Morality.

Jealousy

TYPE OF ETHICS: Personal and social ethics

DEFINITION: Intolerant rivalry or hostility toward a rival or one believed to enjoy an advantage, or apprehension about the loss of another's exclusive devotion

SIGNIFICANCE: Jealousy can influence a person's actions or perceptions

Jealousy begins at about the age of two and develops rapidly during the preschool years. An early form of jealousy is sibling rivalry, which consists of feelings of resentment toward a brother or sister. Sibling rivalry is typical between brothers and sisters in a family.

Sibling rivalry is typically higher in cases of same-sex siblings than in cases of opposite-sex siblings. It is also typically higher in cases of smaller age differences; that is, sibling rivalry occurs more between siblings that are less than two years apart than it does between siblings that are more than three years apart. In the latter case, the closeness in age probably heightens competition; siblings may prefer the same friends, the same toys, and the same activities. Sibling rivalry is also higher when the siblings have the same interests, and lower when they have different interests. In other words, sibling rivalry may be greater when two sisters are strongly inclined toward mathematics than when one is inclined toward mathematics and the other toward literature. Some sibling rivalry is typical in families, and it often is the first time the child experiences jealousy.

Jealous feelings are typically caused by insecurity, such as when parents decrease the amount of warmth and attention they give the child and increase the number of prohibitions imposed on the child. Toddlers may show evidence of jealousy by doing such things as wedging themselves between mother and father as they are hugging, hitting a brother whom the mother just kissed, or asking "When are we taking the new baby back to the hospital?" These actions and comments reflect the small child's jealousy.

Parents can minimize the sting of jealousy and sibling

rivalry by taking some specific steps. First, they can introduce firstborns early to their new role as "big sister" or "big
brother." Telling the child beforehand that a new brother or
sister is coming and involving the child in the pregnancy
will lessen the impact of sibling rivalry. Second, parents can
encourage and reward firstborns for helping in the care of
the new baby. Though close supervision is necessary, even
young children can be involved in the care of an infant.
Third, parents can diminish jealousy and sibling rivalry by
discussing the new baby as a person. Examples of helpful
comments to a first child are, "She likes her bath, doesn't
she?" and, "Look, he's calling you." Fourth, parents can
diminish sibling rivalry and jealousy, and foster better relationships between siblings, by refraining from comparing
children and, instead, recognizing and valuing each child as
an individual. Thus, though some sibling rivalry may be
inevitable, it can be increased or decreased by how parents
handle the situation.

A later form of jealousy is sexual jealousy, which can
occur in a marriage or a sexual relationship, chipping away
at the foundations of trust and love that hold the two people
together. In relationships in which jealousy occurs, it is
sometimes extremely difficult to resolve the problem, because explanations are turned away as untrue and even exacerbate the jealousy.

In the United States, the single greatest reason for sexual
jealousy is the commonly held standard of sexual exclusivity
in monogamous relationships. Most jealousy centers on the
belief that the other person is sexually interested in or involved with another person. Typically, one partner plays the
role of the jealous one and the other plays the role of the
accused.

Other forms of jealousy are nonsexual. Generally, when anything threatens to weaken the relationship bond, jealousy can
occur. The result is often possessiveness, which can be either
reassuring or suffocating. Feelings of jealousy make a relationship less rewarding and lower the individual's self-esteem.

Jealousy in a relationship can result in several different
scenarios. In some cases, the jealousy becomes pervasive,
and adults wind up fighting in all related and tangential areas. In other cases, the jealousy represents a more deeply
imbedded conflict: The partners are in effect denying the
deeper conflict by emphasizing the jealousy. In still other
cases, the jealousy may play a positive role in the relationship, serving to bring the partners closer together. The beneficial effects, however, are often short-lived.

Adults sometimes act to maximize jealousy in a relationship. They may play intentional games that are aimed at
increasing their partners' jealousy. Their hidden agenda in
this situation may be to increase their own feelings of security by causing their partners to feel less secure.

When surveyed, about 54 percent of adults describe themselves as jealous. Highly jealous people are frequently dependent. They may also harbor feelings of inadequacy and
be concerned about sexual exclusiveness.

Jealousy has been successfully treated with systematic de-
sensitization, a technique that involves encouraging the person to relax deeply and then introducing scenarios that are
slightly jealousy-provoking. Then, as the person becomes
adept at relaxing in these situations, additional scenarios are
introduced that are slightly more jealousy-provoking. This
process continues until the person has no more feelings of
jealousy. This counter-conditioning process is based on the
fact that it is impossible to be jealous and highly relaxed at
the same time; the two feelings are mutually exclusive.

—Lillian M. Range

See also Passions and emotions; Psychology; Sexuality
and sexual ethics.

BIBLIOGRAPHY

Clanton, Gordon, and Lynn G. Smith, eds. Jealousy.
Englewood Cliffs, N.J.: Prentice-Hall, 1977.

Mathes, E. W., H. E. Adams, and R. M. Davies. "Jealousy:
Loss of Relationship Rewards, Loss of Self-Esteem, Depres-
sion, Anxiety, and Anger." Journal of Personality and Social
Psychology 48 (June, 1985): 1552-1561.

Minnet, A. M., D. L. Vandell, and J. W. Santrock. "The
Effects of Sibling Status on Sibling Interaction: Influence
of Birth Order, Age Spacing, Sex of Child, and Sex of Sibling." Child Development 54 (August, 1983): 1064-1072.

Turner, Samuel M., Karen S. Calhoun, and Henry E.
Adams, eds. Handbook of Clinical Behavior Therapy. New
York: Wiley, 1981.

Jefferson, Thomas (Apr. 13, 1743, Shadwell, Gooch-
land [later Albemarle] County, Va.—July 4, 1826, Mon-
ticello, Va.): Philosopher, politician

TYPE OF ETHICS: Enlightenment history

ACHIEVEMENTS: Was third president of the United States,
author of the Declaration of Independence, and father of
the University of Virginia

SIGNIFICANCE: Advocated civil rights, public education, religious liberty, and democratic government

The oldest son of Peter Jefferson and Jane Randolph, Thomas
Jefferson was born on the frontier of Virginia. He studied at
the College of William and Mary and was admitted to the
Virginia Bar, but he chose not to practice law. He inherited
approximately 10,000 acres of land, which freed him from
having to earn a living. Jefferson served as a Virginia legislator,
delegate to the Continental Congress, author of the Declaration
of Independence, governor of Virginia, and Commissioner to
France. While governor, Jefferson championed freedom of
religion and conscience, state- supported public education, and
gradual emancipation. He suggested the principles, including
the subsidization of public education and the prohibition of
slavery, for the Northwest Ordinance, which organized the
Northwest Territory. Upon Jefferson's return from France in
1789, George Washington appointed him secretary of state.
Jefferson left the Washington administration and formed the
opposition Democratic Republican Party during the administration of John Adams. Jefferson was elected president in 1800

and 1804. In 1803 he purchased the Louisiana Territory. A principal problem of his administrations was the defense of neutral rights on the seas during the Napoleonic Wars. He used the policy of economic coercion in that struggle.

See also Civil rights; Human rights.

Jesus (c. 6 B.C.E., Bethlehem, Judaea—C.E. 30, Jerusalem): Religious teacher

TYPE OF ETHICS: Religious ethics

ACHIEVEMENTS: Originator of Christianity, which regards Jesus as prophet, messiah, and savior

SIGNIFICANCE: Taught the supreme value of love for God and others, clarified the spirit of morality, and condemned legalism, hollow observance of ceremony, and hypocrisy

Jesus taught ethics in the context of first century Judaism, which had both the (Old Testament) Scriptures and a long tradition of interpretation. He based his teaching on Scripture and sometimes used basic principles of reason to refute opposing interpretations.

His method and message often clashed with those of other Jewish scholars, as when he violated the detailed commandments of their venerated tradition of scriptural interpretation in order to keep the spirit of the original scriptural commandment. For this he was condemned by many Pharisees, who were teacher-scholars. In one incident, Jesus taught that eliminating human suffering on the Sabbath did not violate the spirit of the command that Israel rest on that day (Matt. 12:10-13). He condemned those who scrupulously donated one-tenth of their property to the point of counting grains of spice yet overlooked the "weightier" matters of the law, such as justice, mercy, and faithfulness (Matt. 23:22). He also condemned as hypocritical teachers who allowed religious duty to cover violations of the spirit of the law, such as those who taught that property "dedicated" to God need not be used to care for one's parents (Mark 7:11-13).

Jesus focused on attitudes as the sources of action: From the heart come sins such as theft, murder, and envy (Mark 7:21-22). Thus, murder is wrong, but so are anger and contempt. Adultery is wrong, but so is lust (Matt. 5:22, 28).

He taught that love should dominate one's inward attitudes. Insofar as all morality can be summed up, it can be reduced to the command to love God and others. To Jesus, love was a commitment to the good of another regardless of that person's attitudes or actions toward one. It should extend even to one's enemies, since God loves even those who are evil. Doing to others what one would want them to do to one (Matt. 7:12), the "golden rule," requires service to others and excludes apathy and self-centeredness. The conviction that God actively loves people in this way can give believers courage and dispel anxiety (Matt. 8:26; 6:26, 30).

Jesus showed that a leader should exemplify this loving attitude by seeking to serve, not by trying to dominate or to gain wealth or fame. More than once he reproved the apostles who sought exalted positions, and he himself washed his disciples' feet as an example of humble service (John 13:5). He regarded his very life as a sacrifice for human sin that would allow righteousness to be graciously attributed to those who sought forgiveness from God. Humble confession and faith in God's gracious forgiveness provide access to divine mercy for moral failure.

A person who loves others and believes that God is loving can be free from concern about personal rights. The response to a slap on the cheek, a lawsuit, or the compulsion to carry another's load can be turning the other cheek, giving up more than the plaintiff asked for, and voluntarily carrying a load an extra distance (Matt. 5:38-42). After all, life is short, and someday everyone will be confronted with the absolute rule of God.

The rule of God creates paradoxes that defy conventional moral wisdom. The meek, not the assertive, will inherit the earth (Matt. 5:5). Those who try to exalt themselves will be humbled, whereas those who humble themselves will be exalted. Those who sacrifice for the good of others will find happiness themselves.

Jesus motivated people with rewards, but not always the sort that would appeal to a selfish person. Those who do such things as love their enemies and lend expecting nothing in return will receive a "great reward" and will be true "sons of the Most High" (Luke 6:35). Jesus also said that people will generally give back what one gives them and more; "shaken down, pressed together, and running over" (Luke 6:38).

Although this should motivate people to do good, they should be willing to "take up the cross," a symbol of complete renunciation of personal or worldly gain. The mature person acts out of pure love for others and a desire to emulate a morally pure and altruistic God.

Jesus voluntarily lived in poverty, but he did not condemn ownership. He advocated the compassionate use of private wealth: Those with means should be quick to share with those in need. Herein lies a profound difference between Jesus' teaching and various types of communism, which seek to eliminate private ownership as the solution to society's fundamental problems.

Jesus rejected insurrection as a means to effect change and was a disappointment to those who sought political or military deliverance for Israel. He did not confront the Roman methods of taxation or slavery, but in the ancient world he was radical regarding the treatment of women, as Paul Jewett shows in *Man as Male and Female* (1975). In a society that treated women little better than animals, he treated them with seriousness and dignity. He allowed them to follow his itinerant band and to serve tables, a function previously reserved for men. Domestic chores provided material for a number of parables. He confronted the double standard that allowed men but not women to divorce on a pretense; furthermore, he affirmed marriage as a lifelong commitment, breakable only in the case of serious sexual sin.

Jesus' ethics were moderate in that he advocated neither asceticism nor indulgence, neither legalism nor license. Yet he was passionate about righteousness and even chased officially sanctioned profiteers out of the Jerusalem Temple with a hastily improvised scourge (John 2:15). He lived and taught devotion to God as expressed in a life of self-sacrificing love.   —*Brian K. Morley*

See also Christian ethics; Divine command theory; God; Moses; Ten Commandments.

Bibliography
Briggs, Charles Augustus. *The Ethical Teaching of Jesus.* New York: Charles Scribner's Sons, 1904.
Bruce, A. B. *The Training of the Twelve.* 4th ed. New Canaan, Conn.: Keats, 1979.
New American Standard Bible. Anaheim, Calif.: J. B. McCabe, 1977.
Scott, Ernest F. *Ethical Teaching of Jesus.* New York: Macmillan, 1924.
Stalker, James. *The Ethic of Jesus According to the Synoptic Gospels.* New York: Hodder & Stoughton, 1909.

Jewish ethics

Type of ethics: Religious ethics
Date: First century to present
Associated with: Western religious thought, Islamic ethics, and Christian ethics
Definition: The ideals and norms that characterize ethical decision making and moral speculation within Rabbinic Judaism from approximately the first century to the present
Significance: Represents the ongoing attempt of a Western monotheistic religion to define the good life and the ideal community on the basis of the biblical text and the historical experience of the Jewish people

Jewish ethics is based on the premise that the Jewish people are in a covenant relationship with God. This covenant demands that society be organized and personal lives be conducted in accordance with God's revelation. As a result, Jewish ethics has generally been understood to be a matter of *imitatio Dei* and to have as its characteristic form legal discourse. Thus, Jewish ethical literature moves between two poles. On the one hand, it stresses adherence to a certain life-regimen as spelled out in Jewish law (*halachah*), while on the other, it calls for the cultivation through this lifestyle of character traits, attitudes, and intentions that help the individual to be more God-like.

Although the earliest literature of Rabbinic Judaism (from the first century through the seventh century) is devoted almost exclusively to developing Jewish law, the importance of proper attitude and intention is not ignored. The late Mishnaic book *Pirqe Avot* ("Chapters of the Fathers"), edited in the third century, is a collection of moral aphorisms stressing the importance of honesty and selflessness in dealing with others and the need to act responsibly in the world.

These attitudes are given more formal recognition in the Talmuds (from the fifth century through the seventh century). Made up largely of real and hypothetical case law, the Talmudic literature not only illustrates how the letter of the law is to be understood and applied but also recognizes that there is a moral duty that goes beyond what the law requires. This extra-legal duty is referred to as *lifnim mishurat hadin* ("beyond the edge of the law"). In some instances (*Baba Metzia* 30b, for example), the Babylonian Talmud seems to regard such going beyond the call of duty to be not merely supererogation but an expectation that rests on all Jews.

In the Middle Ages, Jewish ethics took three different forms: the further development of Jewish law, philosophical speculation on the nature of the moral life, and the cultivation of humility and other beneficial character traits. The first was largely a result of the practical application of received Jewish law to new situations. In this connection, rabbis from the eighth century on created a large literature devoted to identifying and understanding the principles and values that were to guide them in their legal deliberations. Despite the diversity of situations, certain common principles seem to emerge from the practical application of Rabbinic law: the overriding imperative to protect human life; the importance of avoiding even the appearance of idolatry; and the values of sexual modesty, education, and childrearing.

Philosophical speculation on the nature of morality began in earnest among Jewish scholars with the rise of philosophical schools in the Islamic world. For the most part, Jewish philosophers from the ninth century on adopted the major philosophical principles and conclusions of Islamic scholars and applied them more or less directly to Judaism. Early writers such as Saadia Gaon in his *Book of Beliefs and Opinions* stressed that God's word as given in the Hebrew Scripture and interpreted by the rabbis is the only reliable source of truth. Since God's law is fully known and since people have free will, Saadia argues, each individual bears full responsibility for acting in accord with God's word. Subsequent Judeo-Arabic philosophers, influenced by Arabic Neoplatonism, claimed that the true reward of the soul lay in contemplating the divine. Adherence to Jewish law was the necessary first step in directing the soul toward a fuller apprehension of the divine. This line of thought reached its culmination in the Jewish neo-Aristotelians such as Moses ben Maimon (also known as Maimonides). In his *Eight Chapters*, Maimonides argues that actualizing the potential of the rational soul depends on proper discipline of the body and that such a discipline is precisely what is spelled out in the *halachah*.

Finally, pietistic writings attempted to instill in the readers moral sensitivity beyond mere obedience to the *halachah* and the contemplation of its principles. In some cases, these writings take the form of ethical wills, testimonies bequeathed to children by dying parents or relatives. These wills usually stress the importance of study, humility, and charity. In other cases, whole sects appeared that encouraged members to practice a life that was holier than that lived by the majority of the Jewish population. The Hasidai Ashkenaz of thirteenth century northern Germany is such a group. Its view of the moral life is spelled out in *Sefer HaHasidim*. Similar ideas seemed to have influenced the Hasidic movement that sprang up in Eastern Europe in the mid-eighteenth century. Many early Hasidic stories presume that true virtue stems from the intention of the soul and at times may even run counter to the formal demands of *halachah*. The ethical writings of Hasidism have influenced such modern Jewish moral philosophers as Martin Buber, Abraham Joshua Heschel, and Elie Wiesel.

In modern times, Jewish ethical speculation has again drawn heavily on the philosophical currents of the day. Modern Jewish movements (Orthodoxy, Conservative Judaism, and Reform Judaism), which have their roots in nineteenth century Germany, have been heavily influenced by the writings of Immanuel Kant. Modern Jewish thought has argued that simply following the letter of Jewish law out of habit is not sufficient. Instead, one must choose to abide by the *halachah* purely for its own sake or because it is one's duty to conform to God's will. More recently, Reform and Conservative rabbis in particular have struggled to identify the rational and universal ideals behind the *halachah* as a basis for approaching ethical dilemmas posed by new technologies. —*Peter J. Haas*

See also Buber, Martin; *I and Thou*; Maimonides; Moses; Spinoza, Baruch; Ten Commandments; Wiesel, Elie; Zionism.

BIBLIOGRAPHY

Dorff, Elliot, and Arthur Rosett. *A Living Tree: The Roots and Growth of Jewish Law*. Albany, N.Y.: SUNY Press, 1988.

Kellner, Menahem Marc, ed. *Contemporary Jewish Ethics*. New York: Sanhedrin Press, 1978.

Novak, David. *Jewish Social Ethics*. New York: Oxford University Press, 1992.

Samuelson, Norbert M. *An Introduction to Modern Jewish Philosophy*. Albany, N.Y.: SUNY Press, 1989.

Siegel, Seymour, ed. *Conservative Judaism and Jewish Law*. New York: Rabbinical Assembly, 1977.

Spero, Shubert. *Morality, Halakha and the Jewish Tradition*. New York: KTAV, 1983.

Jihâd. *See* Holy war.

Journalistic ethics

TYPE OF ETHICS: Media ethics
DATE: Codified by Sigma Delta Chi in 1926
DEFINITION: Guidelines that attempt to balance journalists' efforts to serve the public's right to know with their responsibility to observe certain moral and occupational restraints
SIGNIFICANCE: The First Amendment guarantees a free press, but journalists cannot function free of obligations to society such as truthfulness, objectivity, and fair play

Unlike doctors and lawyers, journalists do not control who may practice in their field or police their own ranks; neither do they prescribe a body of knowledge with which those entering the field must be familiar. In this sense, journalists do not fit within the traditional definition of a "profession." Nevertheless, responsible journalists—like members of these other professions—do adhere to a set of occupational principles, many of which are addressed in the ethical code (the "Code") of Sigma Delta Chi, the Society of Professional journalists.

Responsibility and Freedom of the Press. The first three sections of the Code concern what many journalists regard as their occupational imperative: to observe a constitutional mandate to serve the public's right to know. Such a right is not, in fact, explicitly stated in the Constitution and has been discounted by such eminent legal authorities as former Chief Justice Warren Burger. Other media critics point to abuses—such as invasion of privacy and interference with the right to a fair trial—stemming from overzealous pursuit of the journalistic mission. Still, courts have consistently upheld the media's First Amendment rights, which are regarded as so central to the nation's democratic principles that they can overcome—as they did in the 1971 "Pentagon Papers" case, *U.S. v. New York Times Company*—a countervailing concern as compelling as national security.

The "Pentagon Papers" case illustrates the Code's precept that "[journalists] will make constant effort to assure that the public's business is conducted in public and that public records are open to public inspection." Other, less august, journalistic exercises—such as traffic reports and celebrity gossip—illustrate not so much the public's right to know as its need or desire to know. In such contexts, there is perhaps less justification for the kind of aggressive, sometimes invasive techniques employed by investigative journalists.

Accuracy, Fairness and Objectivity. It would seem fundamental—and the Code takes it for granted—that one of a journalist's primary duties is to report truth rather than falsehoods. Yet the news business has always been plagued with so-called "yellow journalism," which distorts or exaggerates facts in order to create sensationalism and attract consumers. In this sense, the blatant jingoism of the Hearst papers in the 1890's is not unrelated to more recent attempts on the part of television broadcasters to dramatize news through fictionalized "reenactments" of espionage exchanges and enhancements of automobile collision explosions.

Another method by which journalists can take liberties with the truth is through misattribution or misquotation. Although the plaintiff in *Westmoreland v. CBS* (1984), General William C. Westmoreland, commander of United States troops in Vietnam during the late 1960's, ultimately lost his libel action against CBS, the defendant clearly played fast and loose with the truth by deliberately misrepresenting a damaging cable regarding the deadly Tet offensive as Westmoreland's. In 1990, however, the Supreme Court permitted psychoanalyst Jeffrey Masson to proceed with his lawsuit against *New Yorker* magazine writer Janet Malcolm because her allegedly purposeful misquotation of him (for example, that he intended to turn the Freud Archives into "a place of sex, women, fun") could amount to libel.

Ironically, it was Malcolm herself, in her book about the relationship between convicted murderer Jeffrey MacDonald and his journalist/chronicler Joe McGinniss, who pinpointed one of the primary reasons that journalists sometimes violate the ethical imperative of fairness emphasized in the Code: "The moral ambiguity of journalism lies not in its texts but in the relationships out of which they arise—relationships that are invariably and inescapably lopsided." Malcolm's contention is that McGinniss insinuated himself into Mac-Donald's confidence in order to obtain exclusive information and then betrayed him by writing a damning portrait of him. Seen in this light, MacDonald is just as culpable as the reporter who fails to protect the confidentiality of his sources. If this evaluation is accurate—and if Jeffrey Masson's allegations about Malcolm are accurate—then clearly both McGinniss and Malcolm have violated the Code's tenet that "Journalists at all times will show respect for the dignity, privacy, rights and well-being of people encountered in the course of gathering and presenting the news."

Just as MacDonald and Malcolm could be accused of not playing fair, they could also stand accused of bias, of failing to observe the journalistic objectivity that the Code requires. They could, alternatively, be seen to be overcompensating for the intimate access they had to their respective subjects. The Code states that "Journalists must be free of obligation to any interest other than the public's right to know." The most obvious interpretation of this precept is that journalists should not compromise their integrity by accepting payoffs. It can also be seen, however, to apply to situations such as McGinness' and Malcolm's and to journalist-celebrities, who can themselves influence and even become the stories they cover.

Most of the ethical principles espoused in the Code are simply restatements of common sense and courtesy. Because of the media's ability to influence and shape society, however, it is of particular importance that purveyors of news take seriously not only their First Amendment rights but also their moral obligations. —*Carl Rollyson*

See also Libel; Pentagon papers; Privacy; Sources of information.

Bibliography

Adams, Julian. *Freedom and Ethics in the Press*. New York: R. Rosen Press, 1983.

Elliott, Deni, ed. *Responsible Journalism*. Beverly Hills, Calif.: Sage Publications, 1986.

Fink, Conrad C. *Media Ethics: In the Newsroom and Beyond*. New York: McGraw-Hill, 1988.

Merrill, John C., and Ralph D. Barney, eds. *Ethics and the Press: Readings in Mass Media Morality*. New York: Hastings House, 1975.

Olen, Jeffrey. *Ethics in Journalism*. Englewood Cliffs, N.J.: Prentice-Hall, 1988.

Jung, Carl Gustav (July 26, 1875, Kesswil, Switzerland—June 6, 1961, Küssnacht, Switzerland): Psychologist

Type of ethics: Modern history

Achievements: Founded analytical psychology

Significance: Jung approached ethical questions as medical problems concerning the mind; mental health, he believed, could be cultivated by bringing disturbing elements of the unconscious self to consciousness

Jung studied medicine in Basel and psychiatry in Zurich. He collaborated for a time with Sigmund Freud but founded his own school of *analytical psychology* in 1914.

Jung's theory of the conscious personality, or *ego*, differentiates between the *extroverted*, or outgoing, personality, and the *introverted*, or inward-turning type. Both types of conscious personality are influenced by the unconscious *self*, which has two levels: the *personal* and the *collective*.

The *personal* unconscious includes knowledge that is too obvious to become conscious, together with repressed ideas and emotions that are too painful for conscious thought. The personal unconscious grows through individual experience, but the way it grows, Jung believed, is conditioned by the collective unconscious, which is common to all people.

The personal unconscious is found to include elements such as the *old wise man* and the *earth mother*, which appear, with variations, in dreams and myths all over the world. Jung called these elements *archetypes* and considered them inherited structures of the *collective unconscious* that condition the ways in which experience enters consciousness.

See also Freud, Sigmund; Psychology.

Jurisprudence

Type of ethics: Legal and judicial ethics

Definition: Jurisprudence is the science of law

Significance: Jurisprudence is concerned with the nature of law and legal systems and their rules, which are derived from traditional concepts of ethics and morality

Jurisprudence is the science of law; namely, that science that seeks to ascertain the principles on which legal rules are based, in order to not only classify those rules in their proper order and to show their relationships, but also to settle the manner in which new or doubtful cases should be brought under the appropriate rules. When a new or doubtful case arises out of two or more equally applicable rules, it is the function of jurisprudence to consider the ultimate effect if each rule were to be applied to an indefinite number of similar cases and to choose the rule that, when so applied, would produce the greatest advantage to the community. Jurisprudence forms the basis for precedents, which provide the foundation for most judicial decision making, since most judges use the doctrine of *stare decisis* ("let the decision stand") to make future decisions based on precedents formed from past decisions. Jurisprudence, defined as the philosophy of law, deals with the legal reasoning behind the making of law and the decisions

Carl Gustav Jung (Library of Congress)

that judges make. Therefore, it has an overwhelming impact on society.

According to the nineteenth century English philosopher John Austin, there are two basic philosophies of jurisprudential reasoning, or patterns of jurisprudential thought. These philosophies of jurisprudential reasoning are analytical jurisprudence (known as positive law) and normative jurisprudence. Analytical jurisprudence studies the law as it actually is. It seeks to interpret, clarify, classify, and arrange in a legally systematic order actual legal concepts and doctrines. According to the analytical theory of jurisprudence, concepts of morality are totally distinct from one another. To legal positivists, such as John Austin, the law is a matter of what is simply laid down, or posited, by the legislature, regardless of its moral status. A speed limit is an example of a positive law. The other school, or pattern of jurisprudential thought, is normative jurisprudence, which concerns what the law should be. It subjects legal doctrines to moral evaluation and criticism in the name of social reform and justice. According to this theory, concepts of law and justice are equally related. For example, laws related to the constitutional principles that ban the use of cruel and unusual punishment, unreasonable searches and seizures, and denial of equal protection under the law, which cry out for moral interpretation, are more likely to be solved under the theory of normative jurisprudence than they are under the theory of analytical jurisprudence. One example of this can be found in *Brown v. Board of Education*, which overturned *Plessy v. Ferguson*. The doctrine of *stare decisis* and the theory of analytical jurisprudence would have upheld the decision that the separate-but-equal theory of segregation was constitutional. Upon much criticism and examination of the moral and ethical issues involved in segregation, however, the United States Supreme Court overturned precedent, declaring that the United States Constitution is color-blind and that all of its citizens are entitled to equal protection before the law, regardless of the color of their skin. Some legal philosophers will say that moral, societal, and ethical evolution cried out for the overturning of the anti-abortion laws of all fifty states, as was done in *Roe v. Wade*, an example of normative jurisprudence that gave women equal rights under the law. Normative jurisprudence is much more activist than is analytical jurisprudence, and judges who practice it create more law according to the needs of the particular case than do judges who adhere to the analytical philosophy of jurisprudence.

There are several other schools of jurisprudential thought that influence judges in their reasoning, from United States Supreme Court justices to county court judges. They are the natural law theory, the historical conception theory of law, the sociological conception school of jurisprudence, the realist conception theory of law, the economic conception theory of law, and the critical conception school of jurisprudence. The natural law theory states that law is ordained by nature. Higher principles exist independent of human experience. Natural law exists as an ideal condition that is either inherent in human nature or is derived from a divine source. Just as ethical standards transcend legal standards, natural law transcends human notions of what is right and just. The historical school of jurisprudence defines law as an embodiment of society's customs. Historical jurisprudence asserts that customs are the chief manifestation of the law and that law evolves with social development. Sociological conception jurisprudence defines law in terms of present human conduct. The law, according to sociological jurisprudence, is the sum of what the lawbooks permit and what human nature provides. A realist conception of justice is that the law is only what is actually enforced. For example, if a speed limit is 55 miles per hour, that is technically the law. If the police do not pull people over unless they are driving 65 miles per hour, however, then, to the legal realist, the law is not 55 miles per hour but 65 miles per hour. The economic conception of law is that the United States Constitution is merely an economic document that was written to ensure citizens economic freedom from the government. Therefore, every decision must be looked at in the light of how a law or statute or judicial decree will affect the economic freedom of the citizens. The critical conception of jurisprudence is involved with literary criticism, and is not as publicized or as frequently used in jurisprudential decision making as are the other types of jurisprudence.

All these forms of jurisprudential reasoning are used by every judge, but most judges have a particular pattern or philosophy that guides their decision making. The ethical dilemmas involved in jurisprudence involve determining which applications of which concepts or jurisprudence allow that judge to fulfill his or her moral and vocational responsibilities to society while defining the standards that the society's members must meet when interacting with one another.

—*Amy Bloom*

See also Law.

BIBLIOGRAPHY

Bodenheimer, Edgar. *Jurisprudence: The Philosophy and Method of the Law*. Rev ed. Cambridge, Mass.: Harvard University Press, 1974.

Dworkin, R. M. *A Matter of Principle*. Cambridge, Mass.: Harvard University Press, 1985.

Hart, H. L. *Essays in Jurisprudence and Philosophy*. Oxford, England: Oxford University Press, 1984.

Murphy, Jeffrie G. *Philosophy of Law: An Introduction to Jurisprudence*. Rev ed. Boulder, Colo.: Westview Press, 1990.

Jury system

TYPE OF ETHICS: Legal and judicial ethics

DATE: Established constitutionally in the United States in 1783; term coined 1188

DEFINITION: An institution consisting of groups of persons selected by law to decide specific questions based on the evidence presented

SIGNIFICANCE: The jury system is one of the most fundamental checks and balances in law, allowing a common-sense working of justice in a particular case that would not otherwise occur, because of the general nature of laws Some hard historical data show how important a well-functioning jury system is to the encouraging of ethical behavior. The verdict in the famous Los Angeles, California, police brutality case involving the videotaped beating of black motorist Rodney King sparked an explosion of riots that lasted five days and set new records in terms of the number of casualties and the amount of damage; there were 60 dead, 2,383 injured, at least $1 billion in damage to property, and at least 20,000 residents lost jobs as a result of the business closings that followed. Some people argue that the riots were a rebellion that was akin to the Boston Tea Party and that it was unethical neglect of the problems of the underclass in Los Angeles that provided the powder keg that was ignited by the spark of the jury's verdict. The tragic riots focused much more attention on these problems.

Law is often complex and abstract. The jury system serves to forestall the potential injustice of a large or remote government. A jury of one's peers, to which U.S. citizens are constitutionally entitled, often prevents the law from running roughshod over people in situations that could not have been foreseen by the legislators who, often decades earlier, created the law. At the point of application of law, the jury can work justice in the particular case. Jury nullification is the jury's refusal to apply an unethical law. A jury can see people in court and adjust its views based on the equities it observes.

A major ethical issue surrounding the jury system is how representative of the larger community a jury should be. Many people believe that the verdict leading to the riots in the King case was the result of the facts that no African Americans were on that jury and that King was African American. During the *voire dire*, lawyers for each side have a limited power to prevent some people from serving on the jury without even showing why they may not serve. Lawyers have the right to remove any juror by showing cause (for example, that a juror is related to the accused). Lawyers use many psychological profiles involving stereotypes to remove potential jurors without cause. This may be unethical, because some discriminatory stereotypes are used in this process.

Jurors are drawn from ordinary life. Therefore, the jury system is also a check and balance against unethical elitism in a democracy. This is why some states make jurors with extraordinary qualifications (such as a law degree) ineligible for jury duty. The jury system is used in both criminal prosecutions and civil suits. Usually, a unanimous verdict is needed to avoid a hung jury, but some states have allowed a nearly unanimous verdict to be decisive in some civil suits. The jury system is part of an adversary system in which two sides clash and thereby, according to theory, provide the best picture of the whole truth by presenting both sides

of the issue. Some countries use an inquisitorial system that uses judges or panels of authorities as investigators. The adversary system is often emotional and messy, but it provides a powerful incentive for each side to present its story. With this greater incentive comes a greater chance for the jury to hear the whole truth.

See also Jurisprudence; Law.

Justice

TYPE OF ETHICS: Theory of ethics

DATE: From antiquity

DEFINITION: There is no consensus regarding a standard definition of justice, but the concept of justice is often epitomized by the Latin phrase *suum cuique tribuere*, meaning "to each his own"

SIGNIFICANCE: All societies are based on some concept of justice; all concepts of justice connote a desire for order Such words as fairness, equality, honesty, equity, integrity, and lawfulness, which are sometimes used as synonyms for justice, indicate the social order that is connoted by the term. In common speech, justice indicates both right relationships among people and a correct social norm—that is, one that establishes a course of expected conduct.

The roots of the modern Western view of justice can be traced to the Hebrew Bible, on the one hand, and to Greek philosophy, on the other. Many social reformers, in particular, have been influenced by the Hebrew prophets. Thus, for example, the Martin Luther King, Jr., memorial in Montgomery, Alabama, is inscribed with the words of the eighth century B.C.E. prophet Amos: ". . . until justice rolls down like waters, and righteousness like a mighty stream" (Amos 5:24). In the Hebrew Bible, justice (*tsedaqah*) is a quality of God. God delights in it and wishes it for his people. The laws of God make clear his nature and his will. If the people do as he has commanded, then they too will be just. Thus, *tsedaqah* indicates a right relationship between the people and God. It indicates proper balance or right order. The fruits of justice are peace and abundance. The Hebrew prophets especially emphasized the social dimension of *tsedaqah* by claiming that a right relationship with God is possible only when people act justly toward one another. According to the prophet Amos, this meant that God would not revoke punishment from a society that allowed the righteous to be sold for silver and the poor to be trampled into the dust of the earth (Amos 2:6-7).

The oldest surviving Western writings that examine the nature of justice are those of the Greek philosopher Plato (c. 427-c. 347 B.C.E.). Although Plato raised questions concerning justice (*dikaiosyne*) in several dialogues, his fullest treatment of the subject is found in the *Republic*. In that work, one of the characters, Thrasymachus, defines justice as the interest of the stronger—namely the ruling class—as expressed in society's laws. As in the case of the Hebrew prophets, justice in this context indicates correct relationships among people. Since according to Thrasymachus the activity of rulers is governed by self-interest, however, and the obedience of the subjects is dictated by their weaker position, for him just subjects are those who obey the rulers of the state. Thus, Thrasymachus closely identifies justice with civil power, and since the rulers formulate the laws of the state, he also equates justice with civil lawfulness.

Socrates, the protagonist of the *Republic*, however, counters by claiming that justice is not only good for rulers but is also good "for its own sake." He does this, first, by arguing that rulers do not always act in their own self-interest. According to Socrates, states exist precisely because people are not self-sufficient. In an ideal state, the rulers would be those who would act always for the good of the state, putting at all times its interests ahead of their own. The good unites the state, while the bad divides it. A good state, like a good person, contains the four cardinal virtues of wisdom, bravery, temperance, and justice. Justice, for Socrates, means that each person in the state performs his or her proper function. Thus, justice provides the right balance or harmony among the parts. To Socrates, the unjust person is dominated by the appetites and emotions, whereas the just person is controlled by reason. The unjust state would be governed by a despot; the just state would be ruled by a philosopher-king.

The views of justice advocated by Thrasymachus and Socrates have been represented many times in the history of Western philosophy. The positive law theory of justice holds that justice depends on authority, agreement, or convention. For example, the social contract advocated by Thomas Hobbes in *Leviathan* closely connects justice with civil law. Hobbes imagined life without laws to be akin to a war in which each person seeks his or her own advantage, "a war as if of every man against every man." Out of their fear of anarchy and in order to preserve themselves, then, people agree in common to hand power over to the state, or Leviathan, which has coercive power and can enforce its laws. A just person, according to Hobbes, is one who follows the laws of the state.

Like Socrates, John Locke held to a natural rights theory of justice. In *Concerning the True Original Extent and End of Civil Government*, he wrote that the law of nature taught that all people were equal and independent, and that "no one ought to harm another in his life, health, liberty or possessions." It was the duty of the state to protect people's natural rights. While Locke agreed with Hobbes in thinking that people willfully entered into a compact and thus formed the state, sovereignty, he thought, ultimately remained with the people. The purpose of the laws and the duty of rulers should be to represent and execute the will of the people. If the legislative or executive powers should betray their trust, they then should be counted as unjust and should be deposed.

One of the characters of the *Republic*, Glaucon, hints at but does not elaborate on a third view of justice; namely, that it is a social convention. According to this view, as developed by advocates such as David Hume and John Stuart Mill, justice is what promotes the welfare of society. It depends upon society, and it is a social product rather than a natural right. Justice is the basis of rights and laws, which are either just or unjust insofar as they promote the social good. Thus, this view of justice is sometimes called the social good theory of justice, and its proponents are perhaps most concerned with questions of how to perceive and identify the common good. —*James M. Dawsey*

See also Fairness; Hobbes, Thomas; *Leviathan*; Locke, John; Platonic ethics; *Republic*; Socrates.

BIBLIOGRAPHY

Adamiak, Richard. *Justice and History in the Old Testament*. Cleveland, Ohio: J. T. Zubal, 1982.

Adler, Mortimer J. *Six Great Ideas: Truth, Goodness, Beauty, Liberty, Equality, Justice: Ideas We Judge By, Ideas We Act On*. New York: Macmillan, 1981.

Allen, Sir Carleton Kemp. *Aspects of Justice*. London: Stevens, 1958.

Feinberg, Joel. *Rights, Justice, and the Bounds of Liberty*. Princeton, N.J.: Princeton University Press, 1980.

Rawls, John. *A Theory of Justice*. Cambridge, Mass.: Belknap Press of Harvard University, 1971.

Tillich, Paul. *Love, Power, and Justice: Ontological Analyses and Ethical Applications*. New York: Oxford University Press, 1954.

Kabbala

Type of ethics: Religious ethics
Date: Believed to have originated between the third and sixth centuries
Associated with: Jewish mysticism
Definition: A Hebrew word meaning literally "receiving" or "tradition"; used both as a general term for Jewish mysticism and as a specific designation for its major medieval expression
Significance: The Kabbala, an occult formulation of the doctrines of the Jewish religion, is intended to supply a focus in contemplation, leading to a state of mystical awareness

The Kabbala, an occult body of mystical teachings in the Jewish religion, focuses primarily on the notions of creation, revelation, and redemption. These teachings were usually surrounded by secrecy, and they were transmitted orally or in a highly veiled literature that proceeds by hints rather than by explicit declarations. The secrecy surrounding the Kabbala stems from the belief that its ideas were too subtle for the average mind. The Kabbalists, moreover, believed that their doctrines endowed certain individuals with mystical powers by which they might control nature itself. Those who sought to study the Kabbala were, therefore, screened to be certain that they would not invoke their powers too casually or for dishonorable ends. Only a chosen few in each generation were worthy of being the recipients of the wisdom of the Kabbala.

Sources of the Kabbala have been traced not only to the doctrines and literature of Judaism but also to a wide variety of cultures with which the Jewish people had come into contact in their dispersion. These influences include Persian, Neoplatonic, and neo-Pythagorean elements entering Judaism during the Hellenistic period. Christian and Gnostic themes were introduced somewhat later, as were borrowings from Muslim sectarianism following the emergence of Islam. This mixture of elements explains the difficulty that scholars have found in elucidating the Kabbala's sources. The Kabbala itself became one of the spiritual sources of the popular mysticism known as Hasidism, which flourished in the eighteenth and nineteenth centuries, especially in eastern Europe.

The Doctrine of Creation. All Jewish mysticism has attempted to reinterpret the literal account of creation rendered in the book of Genesis. The mystics maintain that the account in Genesis does not sufficiently emphasize the transcendence of God. The reinterpretation has generally taken form as a demiurgic theory. In such a theory, God Himself, who is boundless, infinite and transcendent, did not perform the material act of creating the world. This was the work of a lesser spirit, or demiurge, who was brought into existence by God for this particular purpose. As the conception of God's transcendence developed, one demiurge seemed insufficient to express the sense of imposing distance between divinity and the material world. The remoteness of God from the world was intensified, therefore, by adding other intermediaries and thus forming a chain from God to matter in links of increasing materiality.

A second problem in the biblical account of creation, according to the Jewish mystics, concerns matter. If God is accepted as infinite, all must be contained within God. The question then arises, however, whether matter exists outside of God. This issue was finally resolved by a theory that God, prior to creation, was actually infinite. To a make room for creation, however, He voluntarily contracted or limited himself. Some excess of spiritual substance overflowed into the space from which God had removed Himself, and this excess, or emanation, provided both the demiurgic intermediaries and the matter out of which the world was created. Because all substance is thus ultimately an overflowing of God's substance, Kabbala is a pantheistic doctrine (the doctrine or belief that God is not a personality, but that all laws, forces, and manifestations of the self-existing universe are God). The completed series of emanations also served the purpose of providing the route by which the human ascending spirit might reach the heights of divinity.

The Doctrine of Revelation. After the first destruction of the Temple at Jerusalem, and particularly after its second destruction, the scriptures served as a focus for the religious devotion of the Jews. Their state no longer existed; their culture had been destroyed. All that remained was their belief in God and His word. If the Jewish religion were to endure, it seemed necessary that not only the content of revelation but also even its physical form should be considered inviolate and unchangeable. The level on which mystics interpreted revelation to serve their purpose was highly symbolical. To make this interpretation possible, the Kabbalists developed letter and number symbolism of great variety, complexity, and obscurity.

The Doctrine of Redemption. The Kabbalists maintained and even intensified the traditional Jewish view of redemption. In the Kabbalistic view, salvation of the individual was of little significance. It entered only as a means to the greater end of the salvation of humankind. This would come about through the agency of a messiah and the Davidic line, who would lead the Jews in triumph to the Holy Land and inaugurate a reign of truth, justice, and mercy. The ideal of salvation is thus the establishment of an earthly paradise of human life, raised to its highest humanity. Other elements clouded this doctrine at various times in the history of mystical messianism. In general, however, the Kabbalistic view of redemption was an extreme form of traditional messianism. Attempts to calculate the exact date of the coming of the messiah were widespread. The coincidence of various calculations in fixing on dates close to each other inspired a wave of messianic movements.

—*Genevieve Slomski*

See also Hasidism; Jewish ethics; Talmud; Torah.

Bibliography

Bokser, Ben Zion. *From the World of the Cabbalah.* New York: Philosophical Library, 1954.

Heschel, Abraham Joshua. *God in Search of Man: A Philosophy of Judaism.* New York: Farrar, Straus and Cudahy, 1955.

Idel, Moshe. *Kabbalah: New Perspectives.* New Haven, Conn.: Yale University Press, 1988.

Ruderman, David B. *Kabbalah, Magic, and Science.* Cambridge, Mass.: Harvard University Press, 1988.

Scholem, Gershom. *Origins of the Kabbalah.* Edited by R. J. Zwi Werblowsky. Translated by Allan Arkush. Philadelphia, Pa.: Jewish Publication Society, 1987.

Kant, Immanuel (Apr. 22, 1724, Königsberg, East Prussia—Feb. 12, 1804, Königsberg, East Prussia): Philosopher

TYPE OF ETHICS: Enlightenment history

ACHIEVEMENTS: Author of *Grundlegung zur Metaphysik der Sitten* (1785; *Foundations of the Metaphysics of Morals,* 1950) and *Die Metaphysik der Sitten* (1797; *The Metaphysics of Morals*)

SIGNIFICANCE: Viewed moral rules as self-imposed, binding on all humans, and derived from one supreme principle of morality: the categorical imperative

Autonomy. Late in his life, after his revolutionary work in epistemology, Kant first presented his mature moral philosophy in *Foundations of the Metaphysics of Morals.* Here, Kant developed his influential idea that human beings as rational agents are "autonomous," or have the capacity for moral self-government. For Kant, autonomy means that, as rational beings, people set the own standards of conduct, as distinct from the demands made by their desires, and are able to decide and act on these standards. On the basis of a complex argument, Kant concluded that autonomy is possible only if the will is guided by a supreme principle of morality that he called the "categorical imperative." Kant viewed this imperative as the product of reason and as the basis for determining moral duties. He expressed it in three basic formulations.

The Formula of Universal Law. "Act only according to that maxim by which you can at the same time will that it should become a universal law." Kant defined a maxim as a subjective principle on which a person intends to act, and a universal law as a principle that applies to everyone. Therefore, his formula of universal law demands that one act only on maxims that one can rationally will that everyone adopt. Kant provided the following example of how to use the formula: Suppose that a person must borrow money for a personal need and knows that he is unable to repay it. Is it morally permissible for him to act on the maxim of falsely promising to pay back a loan in order to get the loan? The formula tells that the person may act on the maxim if he can rationally will its universalization. The person cannot rationally will this because it would mean that people would no longer trust promises to repay loans, including his own. Kant added that the immorality of the maxim is clear in that the person really wants people to keep their promises so that he can be an exception to the rule for this one occasion.

The Formula of Humanity. "Act so that you treat humanity, whether in your own person or in that of another, always as an end and never as a means only." For Kant, "humanity" refers to people's uniquely human characteristics, their rational characteristics, including autonomy and the capacity to understand the world and to form and pursue life-plans. Thus, his formula of humanity demands that people always act so that they respect themselves and others as beings with a rational nature.

In *The Metaphysics of Morals,* Kant used the formula of humanity to argue for a variety of duties to oneself and others. According to Kant, respect for rational nature in oneself implies that one ought not to destroy or deny one's intellectual and moral capacities through suicide, drug abuse, lying, self-deception, or servility. It also implies that one must further one's own rational nature through developing one's natural talents and striving to become virtuous. Respect for rational nature in others involves that one ought not harm them and must uphold their individual liberty, but Kant discussed these duties as part of his legal and political philosophy. More exclusive ethical duties to others are that one must fulfill the duty of beneficence, contributing to the flourishing of rational nature in others, and that one must not deny people's humanity through arrogance, defamation, or ridicule.

The Formula of the Realm of Ends. "All maxims . . . ought to harmonize with a possible realm of ends." This formula shows that the two previous formulas are interconnected. (Kant held them all to be equivalent, but this has not been widely accepted.) Kant described the realm of ends as a harmony between human beings, resulting from each acting only on maxims that can become universal laws. It is a harmony of ends in that its members, by acting only on universalizable maxims, act only on maxims that can meet everyone's consent; thus, they respect one another as rational self-determining agents, or ends in themselves. It is also a harmony of ends in that people will seek to further one another's individual ends.

Moral Vision. Kant held that people must mirror the realm of ends in their moral choices and actions, and that it is humanity's duty to bring about this ideal. He viewed the French Revolution and the Enlightenment as steps in the right direction; argued for a worldwide league of democratic states as a further step toward the realm of ends; and claimed, moreover, that the religious institutions of his time must embrace the ideal, setting aside their historically evolved differences. Kant maintained that moral philosophy must not formulate new duties, but should only clarify the moral principle operative in "common moral reason" in order to help ordinary persons more adequately resist immoral desires. Kant's clarification went beyond these confines and ended with an inspiring moral vision of the realm of ends as the purpose of history, the kingdom of God on Earth, and the ultimate individual and collective vocation.

—*Harry van der Linden*

See also Autonomy; Consistency; Deontological ethics; *Foundations of the Metaphysics of Morals*; Kantian ethics; Universalizability.

BIBLIOGRAPHY

Aune, Bruce. *Kant's Theory of Morals*. Princeton, N.J.: Princeton University Press, 1979.

Hill, Thomas E., Jr. *Dignity and Practical Reason in Kant's Moral Theory*. Ithaca, N.Y.: Cornell University Press, 1992.

Kant, Immanuel. *Foundations of the Metaphysics of Morals and What Is Enlightenment?* Translated by Lewis White Beck. New York: Liberal Arts Press, 1959.

——————. *The Metaphysics of Morals*. Translated by Mary Gregor. Cambridge, England: Cambridge University Press, 1991.

Paton, H. J. *The Categorical Imperative: A Study in Kant's Moral Philosophy*. 6th ed. London: Hutchinson, 1967.

Sullivan, Roger J. *Immanuel Kant's Moral Theory*. Cambridge, England: Cambridge University Press, 1989.

Yovel, Yirmiahu. *Kant and the Philosophy of History*. Princeton, N.J.: Princeton University Press, 1980.

Kantian ethics

TYPE OF ETHICS: Enlightenment history

DATE: 1780's to present

ASSOCIATED WITH: Immanuel Kant, Hermann Cohen, John Rawles, and Jürgen Habermas

DEFINITION: The moral theory of Immanuel Kant and later moral theories based on his ethics

SIGNIFICANCE: A main current in philosophical ethics, emphasizing that moral rules must be so constructed that their general observance creates harmony among self-determining agents with different individual ends

The term "Kantian ethics" is commonly used to refer to the ethics of Kant, as set forth in his *Foundations of the Metaphysics of Morals* and other moral writings of the 1780's and 1790's. The term is also frequently used to refer to later moral theories that are similar to Kant's ethics but contain modifications in response to its perceived shortcomings. Three important examples are the moral theories of Hermann Cohen, John Rawls, and Jürgen Habermas.

Kant. The ultimate purpose of moral rules, Kant argued, is to make possible his ideal society, the "realm of ends," which has two main aspects: All its members respect one another as self-determining agents who pursue different individual ends, and they seek to promote one another's ends. Kant believed that this moral ideal would evolve if everyone followed the fundamental principle of his ethics: the "categorical imperative." This imperative demands that one act only on those personal policies of conduct ("maxims") that one can rationally will to become universal laws or principles that guide everyone's conduct. According to Kant, obedience to the categorical imperative implies respect for others as self-determining beings with different individual ends; in acting only on maxims that can become universal laws,

one acts only on principles to which others can rationally consent, and thus one upholds their right to legislate their own moral rules and pursue their own individual ends. Moreover, Kant argued that general obedience to the categorical imperative would bring about universal mutual promotion of individual ends (as the other aspect of the realm of ends) because the imperative prohibits refusing to assist others. The reason for this prohibition is that one cannot rationally will that everyone adopt a maxim of not assisting others in the pursuit of their individual ends, for in such a world one would lack the assistance of others as a means for realizing one's own happiness.

Attempts to overcome the shortcomings of Kant's ethics, while preserving its strengths, have led to such influential examples of Kantian ethics as the moral theories of Hermann Cohen, John Rawls, and Jürgen Habermas. The most significant shortcomings are the following: The categorical imperative, does not offer a sufficient criterion for determining universal laws, Kant failed to provide an adequate justification of the categorical imperative, he described moral agents as isolated legislators of universal laws, and he failed to address satisfactorily how the realm of ends can be institutionalized.

Cohen. During the later part of the nineteenth century, Kant's philosophy regained in Germany the great influence it had had during his own lifetime. This resurgence is known as neo-Kantianism, and one of its most important representatives is Hermann Cohen, who transformed Kant's ideal of the realm of ends into a democratic socialist ideal. Cohen held that human agents can only arrive at universal laws, or approximations thereof, if all people become decision makers or colegislators in their institutions. Thus, Cohen argued that the realm of ends requires for its realization not only political democracy, as Kant himself claimed, but also democracy in the workplace. Moreover, Cohen held that workplace democracy, in order to be effective, requires workers' ownership of productive property. Cohen also maintained that these democratic socialist proposals were necessary for realizing the aspect of the realm of ends that all of its members promote one another's individual ends.

Rawls. A second main philosophical movement of renewed interest in Kant's ethics and corresponding attempts to improve his ethics occurred in the 1970's and 1980's. The American philosopher John Rawls and the German philosopher Jürgen Habermas are the two major figures of this movement. Rawls's primary concern is to argue for principles of justice that create a political society in accord with the realm of ends. More specifically, he argues for an extensive liberal welfare state based on the principles of justice that all persons must have equal political and civil liberties and that social and economic inequalities must be corrected to the greatest benefit of the least advantaged. Rawls holds that rational agents will opt for these principles of justice once their situation of choice, the "original position," is made impartial by a "veil of ignorance" that makes them temporarily forget about all the specific facts concerning themselves and their society. Whether this innovative transformation of the categorical imperative—the veil forces one to opt for principles that are acceptable to all—justifies Rawls's two principles of justice, and whether it can more generally be used to justify and explicate Kantian moral rules, are questions that have generated much debate.

Habermas. The basic principle of the "discourse ethics" of Jürgen Habermas is a clear modification of the categorical imperative. The principle is that for a norm to be valid it must be accepted in a practical discussion by all those who are affected by the norm. The participants in the practical discourse must then also foresee the consequences of the general observance of the norm for the realization of the particular interests of each of them. This view that moral norms must be constructed by communities engaged in free practical discourse implies that the good society must be fundamentally democratic; unlike Cohen and Rawls, however, Habermas has been somewhat vague and hesitant about the specific institutional ramifications of his Kantian ethics.

—Harry van der Linden

See also Autonomy; Consistency; Deontological ethics; *Foundations of the Metaphysics of Morals*; Kant, Immanuel; Rawls, John; Universalizability.

BIBLIOGRAPHY

Habermas, Jürgen. *Moral Consciousness and Communicative Action.* Translated by Christian Lenhardt and Shierry Weber Nicholsen. Cambridge, Mass.: MIT Press, 1990.

Kant, Immanuel. *Foundations of the Metaphysics of Morals.* Translated by Lewis White Beck. New York: Liberal Arts Press, 1959.

Rawls, John. *Political Liberalism.* New York: Columbia University Press, 1993.

_____. *A Theory of Justice.* Cambridge, Mass.: Harvard University Press, 1971.

Van der Linden, Harry. *Kantian Ethics and Socialism.* Indianapolis: Hackett, 1988.

Willey, Thomas E. *Back to Kant: The Revival of Kantianism in German Social and Historical Thought, 1860-1914.* Detroit, Mich.: Wayne State University Press, 1978.

Karma

TYPE OF ETHICS: Religious ethics
DATE: Early first millennium B.C.E. to present
ASSOCIATED WITH: Hinduism, Buddhism, and Jainism
DEFINITION: Action; specifically, a person's deeds and the effects of those deeds
SIGNIFICANCE: The ethical law of cause and effect according to which one reaps what one sows

The word *karma* is a Sanskrit term meaning "action," "deed," or "work." By extension, it also came to mean the results of one's deeds and the law of retribution according to which one reaps what one sows.

In Hindu Ethics. The term *karma* does not appear in its extended sense in the oldest hymns of the Hindu scriptures.

Nevertheless, the idea does appear that evil deeds have consequences that one would want to avoid. Furthermore, a person could obtain forgiveness from the god Varuṇa. The early hymns also taught continued personal existence beyond death, sometimes in an undifferentiated state, but sometimes with good men going to heaven and others to a sort of hell.

In the Upaniṣads (composed roughly between the eighth and fifth centuries B.C.E.), Hindu speculation arrived at the conclusion that if one did not reap all that one had sown in this lifetime, one would inherit those uncompensated after-effects in a future life. The cycle of rebirths came to be understood as the condition from which salvation was necessary. Furthermore, the law of karma was held to operate automatically; it was independent of the efforts of any god.

In its fully developed form, the law of karma is held to explain such phenomena as premature death (the result of misdeeds committed earlier in one's life or in a previous life), child prodigies (the child continues to develop skills already learned in a previous life), and differences in socioeconomic status (karma determines the caste into which one is born). In a moral universe, everything that happens to a person is earned; nothing is accidental or in any other way undeserved. In short, one determines one's own fate, in this and future lives.

Over time, Hindus developed several paths by which to escape the cycle of rebirth. The most important were enlightenment, work, love and devotion, and meditation, which also could be a method employed in other paths. The Bhagavad Gītā (variously dated between the fifth and first centuries B.C.E.) dealt with the relationship between karma and one's caste duty. Simply put, it was the duty of each person to fulfill his or her role, even if the person found that role distasteful. Failure to do so would entangle one more tightly in the cycle of rebirth. Actions undertaken out of a desire for reward would also lead to rebirth. Hence, the ideal was to perform one's duties to society without desiring to reap the benefits of one's actions. Such detached behavior would build up no karma, particularly if it were combined with other methods of salvation. Thus, one could escape from the cycle of rebirth.

In Buddhist Ethics. Buddhism retained from Hinduism the ideas of karma and reincarnation but denied the existence of a permanent soul that could be reincarnated. Instead, Theravāda Buddhists argued that everything in the phenomenal world was temporary, passing in and out of existence every instant. Furthermore, nothing originated from itself; rather, everything originated from something that had existed previously. This transitoriness was not random, however; discrete streams of karma held one's flashes of existence together in a continuum and separate from other streams of karma. An analogy often used by Buddhists was the passing of a flame from one candle to another. In that process, the second flame is neither identical to nor completely different from the first. Thus, a "person" could commit good or bad deeds and experience the rewards or punishments appropriate to each. Furthermore, over time a person could "use up" all acquired karma and pass into nirvāṇa.

Buddhists were not oblivious to the logical difficulties implicit in this view. On the one hand, if things passed completely out of existence before being replaced by others, it would appear that anything could cause anything, a conclusion that Buddhists denied. On the other hand, if something connected the flashes of existence, that something would at least resemble a permanent soul. Various Buddhist schools debated the nature of that resemblance, with several Mahāyānist thinkers returning to monistic thinking.

Buddhists generally hold that three factors regulate the acquiring of karma: (1) the intention of the person committing an act; (2) physical actions, including speech; and (3) the abiding effects of the action. A person's karma may be changed by subsequent good deeds performed by the person or (in popular Buddhism) by someone else (for example, a monk or a Buddha) acting on that person's behalf.

In Jain Ethics. Jainism held that the life force, or *jīva*, within a person is pure and intelligent but can be clouded by karma, which Jains (like some Hindu schools) understood as a subtle form of matter that attaches itself to the *jīva*.

Virtuous acts color the *jīva* only slightly, while vices darken and weigh it down. Even the unintentional harming of a lower form of life results in the accumulation of karma. Hence, Jains are strict vegetarians and make every effort to avoid stepping on or breathing in even the tiniest insects. Release from rebirth is possible only if one ceases to acquire new karma and removes the karma already present by means of physical austerity and meditative concentration.

—Paul L. Redditt

See also Buddhist ethics; Hindu ethics; Jain ethics.

BIBLIOGRAPHY

Glasenapp, Helmuth von. *The Doctrine of Karman in Jain Philosophy.* Edited by Hiralal R. Kapadia. Translated by G. Barry Gifford. Bombay: Trustees, Bai Vijibai Jivanlal Panalal Charity Fund, 1942.

Herman, A. L. *An Introduction to Indian Thought.* Englewood Cliffs, N.J.: Prentice-Hall, 1976.

Hume, Robert Ernest. *The Thirteen Principal Upanishads.* 2d rev. ed. London: Oxford University Press, 1931.

King, Winston L. *In the Hope of Nibbana.* LaSalle, Ill.: Open Court, 1964.

Saddhatissa, H. *Buddhist Ethics.* London: Allen & Unwin, 1970.

Zimmer, Heinrich. *Philosophies of India.* Edited by Joseph Campbell. New York: Pantheon Books, 1951.

Helen Keller (Library of Congress)

Keller, Helen (June 27, 1880, Tuscumbia, Ala.—June 1, 1968, Westport, Conn.): Activist

TYPE OF ETHICS: Disability rights

ACHIEVEMENTS: Author of *The Story of My Life* (1903) and many other works

SIGNIFICANCE: One of the most influential disabled women of the twentieth century, Keller published many books and devoted her life to helping blind and deaf people

At the age of eighteen months, Helen Keller suffered a severe illness that left her blind and deaf. She could not communicate with other people. When Helen was eight years old, her parents hired a teacher, Anne Sullivan, from the Perkins Institution for the Blind. Ms. Sullivan taught Helen a manual alphabet and finger-spelled the names of various objects. Within two years, Helen learned to read and write in Braille. At age ten, Helen learned to speak by feeling the vibrations of Ms. Sullivan's vocal cords. In 1990, Anne Sullivan accompanied Helen Keller to Radcliffe College. Four years later, Helen graduated cum laude and began writing essays on the rights of the handicapped. Her published articles caused people to become more aware of handicapped people. She lectured worldwide and gained the support of famous people on improving the rights of the disabled. Her publications include *The World I Live In* (1908), *Out of the Dark* (1913), *Helen Keller's Journal* (1938), and *Teacher: Anne Sullivan Macy* (1955). Helen Keller was an activist for the rights of the disabled until her death in 1968.

See also Americans with Disabilities Act; Disability rights.

Kevorkian, Jack (b. May 26, 1928, Pontiac, Mich.): Pathologist

TYPE OF ETHICS: Bioethics

ACHIEVEMENTS: Author of *Prescription: Medicide* (1991), which advocates a medical specialty ("obitiatry") for suicide assistance, organ harvesting, and experimentation on the moribund

SIGNIFICANCE: Galvanized public debate on the issue of physician-assisted suicide

On June 4, 1990, Jack Kevorkian assisted a woman who was suffering from Alzheimer's to commit suicide. His career-long focus on death—from trying to ascertain its onset in patients' eyes to trying to salvage some benefit from it—has alienated him from the medical establishment. Kevorkian advocated cadaver blood transfusions and lobbied along with death-row inmates for execution by lethal injection because it would be more merciful and would permit organ donation and experimentation under irreversible anesthesia. Kevorkian wrote various journal articles promoting his controversial ideas, but his objectives were repeatedly frustrated, and he turned his attention to patients who desired euthanasia. In 1989, he developed a saline drip by means of which a severely disabled person could activate a lethal drug, and he marketed this machine on talk shows. Kevorkian later developed another "suicide machine" that used carbon monoxide. By August of 1993, he had used his machines in sixteen more suicides. The resulting media attention and controversy made Kevorkian's name a household word. Besides questioning the propriety of assisted suicide, critics condemn Kevorkian's lack of medical experience with living patients; his brief relationships with the suicides; and the fact that many of the suicides were not terminally ill but merely in pain or afraid of advancing physical or mental disability, and possibly depressed. The number of people contacting him for assistance or openly endorsing his actions, however, demonstrates substantial dissatisfaction with available options for the terminally and chronically ill.

See also Bioethics; Euthanasia; Right to die.

Kierkegaard, Søren Aabye (May 5, 1813, Copenhagen, Denmark—Nov. 11, 1855, Copenhagen, Denmark): Philosopher and theologian

TYPE OF ETHICS: Religious ethics

ACHIEVEMENTS: Author of numerous books, notably *Enten-Eller: Et Livs Fragment* (1843; *Either/Or: A Fragment of Life*, 1844); *Frygt og Baevan* (1843; *Fear and Trembling*; and *Afsluttende uvidenskabelig Efterskrift til de Philosophiske Smuler: Mimisk-pathetisk-dialektisk Sammenskrift, existentielt Indloeg* (1846; *Concluding Unscientific Postscript*, 1941)

SIGNIFICANCE: Widely regarded as "the father of existentialism," Kierkegaard focused throughout his writings on the situation of the concrete individual who must freely choose how to live without the benefit of objectively known criteria with which to make choices

In a span of just thirteen years, from 1842 to 1855, Kierkegaard authored a richly varied, challenging, and copious body of works. These include philosophical and theological treatises, novels, literary criticism, psychological investigations, social analysis, devotional literature, polemical pamphlets, and a literary autobiography. Despite the diverse character of his writings, many of the same themes and concerns run through all of them. In particular, Kierkegaard was concerned by what he saw as the growing tendency to discount the significance of the individual person's existence and to focus instead on large-scale social and historical phenomena. He regarded this trend as closely related to the tendency to overvalue knowledge and undervalue ethical endeavor.

The Pseudonymous Authorship. Most of the best-known of Kierkegaard's writings were published not under his own name but under those of fictional creations of Kierkegaard. These were not mere pen names to keep secret Kierkegaard's role as author. Instead, Kierkegaard presented the main options for human existence by creating ideally consistent representatives of the "stages on life's way" and then letting them speak for themselves. That way, the reader does not simply learn about the various forms of existence as a removed observer. Rather, the reader imaginatively enters into the worlds of the various pseudonyms and gets a feel for what it is to exist as they exist.

Kierkegaard identifies three main forms, or stages, of existence: the aesthetic, the ethical, and the religious. His classic presentation of the aesthetic and ethical stages is his first major work, *Either/Or*. The first volume of this monumental book contains a variety of essays by an unknown aesthete who lives for pleasure, amusement, stimulation, and, above all, the avoidance of boredom. The volume ends on a dark note, with the copied pages of another aesthete describing the cynical seduction and abandonment of a young woman. The second volume, depicting ethical existence, consists of two very lengthy letters from a lower-court judge and family man, Judge William, to the aesthete of volume 1 encouraging the aesthete to change his ways and adopt an ethical form of existence. By placing these two volumes before his readers, Kierkegaard sought to force a choice: either choose to live for pleasure, amusement, success, and so forth, or choose to devote yourself to doing the right thing and fulfilling your duties. The point is not simply to learn about these forms of existence but to choose which to live. By using pseudonyms and disappearing from the scene, Kierkegaard refuses to tell the reader which way he or she should choose.

Kierkegaard considerably complicates the issue of existential choice in subsequent pseudonymous works. In *Fear and Trembling*, the pseudonymous author, John of Silence, intensely examines the story of Abraham and Isaac from the book of Genesis. Abraham's readiness to sacrifice his son at the command of God shows the difference between ethical and religious existence, a difference that Judge William had effectively denied. Subsequent pseudonymous works, notably *Philosophical Fragments* and *Concluding Unscientific*

Postscript by Johannes Climacus, distinguish between two types of religious existence: the immanent, in which the divine is believed to be within each person; and the transcendent, which views fallen humans as radically alienated from the divine and in need of divine assistance to gain salvation. Climacus identifies this latter form of religion as the Christian. While Climacus denies that he himself is a Christian, he is fascinated by Christianity and stresses the paradoxical nature of its central claims. He sharply criticizes contemporary philosophical and theological attempts to diminish that paradoxicality so as to assimilate Christianity to comfortable ways of thinking and being.

Kierkegaard's Non-Pseudonymous Writings. At the last moment before its publication, Kierkegaard added a brief statement to the end of *Concluding Unscientific Postscript* admitting responsibility for the whole pseudonymous authorship and explaining his unusual form of writing. He expected at this point to stop writing and become a pastor, a position for which he was already fully trained. Instead, he commenced a second and distinctive career as an author. Most of the works in this "second authorship" were written under his own name and from an explicitly Christian point of view. In *Works of Love*, he develops a Christian ethic that is grounded in Jesus' command to love one's neighbor.

By showing how radical this ethical demand is, Kierkegaard set the stage for an increasingly acrimonious confrontation with the Danish Lutheran Church. In the writings from the last years of his life, Kierkegaard asserted that the Danish church systematically diluted Christianity as part of an implicit deal with the social status quo: In return for good pay and high social status for pastors, "official Christianity" (which Kierkegaard referred to as "Christendom") legitimates the social order and avoids causing the sorts of disturbances occasioned by the radical demands of genuine Christianity. While Kierkegaard first stated these charges in books such as *Practice in Christianity*, he eventually addressed a broader audience by writing letters to the editor of a major Copenhagen newspaper and then producing a publication of his own, *The Instant*. Shortly after publishing the ninth issue of *The Instant* and at the height of his battle with the Danish Lutheran church, Kierkegaard fell ill and was taken to a hospital, where he died some weeks later.

—*George Connell*

See also *Either/Or.*

BIBLIOGRAPHY

Kirmmse, Bruce. *Kierkegaard in Golden Age Denmark.* Bloomington: Indiana University Press, 1990.

Lowrie, Walter. *A Short Life of Kierkegaard.* Princeton, N.J.: Princeton University Press, 1942.

Mackey, Louis. *Kierkegaard: A Kind of Poet.* Philadelphia: University of Pennsylvania Press, 1971.

Malantschuk, Gregor. *Kierkegaard's Thought.* Translated by Edna Hong and Howard Hong. Princeton, N.J.: Princeton University Press, 1971.

Taylor, Mark. *Kierkegaard's Pseudonymous Authorship.* Princeton, N.J.: Princeton University Press, 1975.

al-Kindî, Abû Yûsuf Yaʿqûb ibn Isḥâq (c. 800, Kufa, south of Karbala, Iraq—866, Baghdad, Iraq): Philosopher

TYPE OF ETHICS: Religious ethics

ACHIEVEMENTS: A prolific author who wrote on many subjects; al-Kindî was the first major Arab philosopher

SIGNIFICANCE: Al-Kindî provided the first systematic philosophical expression of ethics and moral psychology in Arabic, and he was influential in Islamic and medieval European philosophy

Al-Kindî, "the philosopher of the Arabs," argued that the soul is immaterial and is analogous to divine substance. The appetites and passions have their source in the material body and can lead a person into excessive love of physical pleasures. To avoid that development, the soul must be purified through the quest for truth and the rigorous study of philosophy. As the soul is thus further actualized, it can come to rule rationally over the lower faculties. If the virtuous soul has not been sufficiently purified here in the lower world, it will require further purification in the sphere of the moon and in those spheres beyond the moon before it is sufficiently cleansed to be able to partake in the intellectual apprehension of God (the bliss toward which all people should aim). Al-Kindî drew upon the work of Neoplatonic and Pythagorean predecessors and, as is common for later Islamicate thinkers such as al-Fârâbî, intermingled the metaphysics and moral psychology of both Plato and Aristotle. His work was important in medieval European attempts to understand Aristotle's *De Anima*.

See also al-Fârâbî, Muḥammad ibn Muḥammad ibn Ṭarkhân; Islamic ethics.

King, Martin Luther, Jr. (Jan. 15, 1929, Atlanta, Ga.—Apr. 4, 1968, Memphis, Tenn.): Civil rights reform leader

TYPE OF ETHICS: Race and ethnicity

ACHIEVEMENTS: Won the 1964 Nobel Peace Prize; was founding president of the Southern Christian Leadership Conference (SCLC)

SIGNIFICANCE: As president of the SCLC from 1957 to 1968, King was the major American spokesman for nonviolent social change intended to end racial oppression

Influenced chiefly by the Indian liberator Mohandas K. Gandhi and the southern black evangelical tradition, King combined nonviolent activism and Christian theology in his ethic of social change. He maintained throughout his public career that he was not seeking to change only laws but also attitudes, so that people of all races and classes could live in the Beloved Community, a concept borrowed from Social Gospel advocate Walter Rauschenbusch. Central to King's philosophy was an ethic of love drawn largely from traditional Christian morality and combined with a strong reformist mission. King openly challenged the acquiescence of both blacks and whites. It was time for change, he believed, because the status quo was perpetuating wrong behavior that was harming all races, but meaningful change would come only by ethical means. "Returning hate for hate," he affirmed, "multiplies hate, adding deeper darkness to a night already devoid of stars. Darkness cannot drive out darkness; only love can do that."

The Love Ethic. By love, King meant more than a positive feeling. Drawing upon the rich linguistic heritage of the Greeks, he defined love not in terms of *eros* (romantic love) or even *philos* (brotherly love), but *agape*, a word used in the New Testament to mean unselfish, redemptive love. Like Gandhi, King believed that love is a potent force in human relations, capable of effecting reform without crushing the opponent. The real "enemy" in this view is not a group of people but a system that exploits both the oppressor and the oppressed. People should love their enemies, he said, because "love is the only force capable of transforming an enemy into a friend."

The Higher Law. After years of studying the ideas of Rauschenbusch, Reinhold Niebuhr, Karl Marx, Gandhi, Jean-Paul Sartre, and others, King developed a synthesis of Christianity and Gandhian nonviolence that satisfied his longing for a method "that would eliminate social evil." He found in Gandhi's thought what he could not find elsewhere, and the result was a synthesis: "Christ furnished the spirit and the motivation and Gandhi furnished the method."

Ambiguities had to be resolved in real situations. One that King often faced was the question of breaking segregationist laws without appearing to oppose rule under law, a particularly frustrating issue in the Birmingham campaign of 1963. Jailed for defying a federal injunction, he was criticized by several local clergymen who characterized him as an outside agitator. Although he rarely responded to criticism, this time he felt compelled to answer in what is called his "Letter from a Birmingham Jail." Of all people, he felt, clergymen should most readily understand that his actions were consistent with the prophetic tradition of leaving one's home to carry God's message. He could not be an outsider, because "injustice anywhere is a threat to justice everywhere"; he was violating the injunction on the same grounds used in the thirteenth century by Saint Thomas Aquinas to denounce laws that were contrary to God's higher law. "A just law is a man-made code that squares with the moral law or the law of God." Ethics and the legal codes that enforce public morality were thus linked to the moral order of creation.

Martin Luther King, Jr. (Library of Congress)

The Elements of Nonviolent Ethics. The higher moral law was one of the four main components of King's social ethics. The second, the principle of reconciliation, went beyond law to the level of community. To damage society permanently was contradictory, in his view. Just as God in Christian theology is a reconciler, so the social reformer must seek reconciliation. All sides in the confrontation must emerge with dignity and confidence that their interests will be protected in the new society.

Third, King believed that resistance by public officials or private citizens to social justice was only the surface manifestation of deeper evil. Reforms could not in themselves destroy that evil. For every pharaoh lying dead on the seashore—in a popular analogy to the Old Testament Exodus from Egypt—others will arise. The final victory over evil lies in the eschatological future. In that sense, King's social ethic combined a vision of the final victory of good with the necessity of confronting specific societal flaws with confidence that even partial victories are important.

No ethical principle was more basic to King's nonviolent ethics than was the concept of redemptive suffering. He knew that even the most limited gains in the civil rights movement would come with difficulty. Freedom would never be granted voluntarily. It had to be taken, and suffering would often result. Making frequent allusions in sermons and speeches to Christ's suffering on the cross, King compared the nonviolent struggle against racism to the redemptive suffering of the Judeo-Christian tradition. Suffering in a righteous cause would expose evil to public consciousness, as Gandhi had done with British oppression in India, and offer an alternative model of behavior. "Recognizing the necessity for suffering," wrote King, "I have tried to make of it a virtue." This did not mean that King invited martyrdom, but it did suggest an approach to morality that recognized the persistence of evil despite dedicated opposition.

Implications for Ethical Conduct. King's ethics demanded adherence to nonviolence based on the prophetic tradition. Although he was not primarily an original thinker, King infused nonviolent theory with a new intellectual integrity and created an effective grassroots movement to apply and test its viability in social reform efforts, international relations, and personal living. The nonviolent social ethics he articulated required discipline and the willingness to suffer for a good higher than that of one's personal safety or comfort.
—*Thomas R. Peake*

See also Apartheid; Bigotry; Christian ethics; Civil rights; Civil rights movement; Gandhi, Mohandas Karamchand; Mandela, Nelson; Racism.

BIBLIOGRAPHY

Ansbro, John J. *Martin Luther King, Jr.: The Making of a Mind.* Maryknoll, N.Y.: Orbis Books, 1982.

Colaiaco, James A. *Martin Luther King, Jr.; Apostle of Militant Nonviolence.* New York: St. Martin's Press, 1988.

Hanigan, James P. *Martin Luther King, Jr., and the Foundations of Nonviolence.* Lanham, Md.: University Press of America, 1984.

Morris, Aldon D. *The Origins of the Civil Rights Movement: Black Communities Organizing for Change.* New York: Free Press, 1984.

Peake, Thomas R. *Keeping the Dream Alive; a History of the Southern Christian Leadership Conference from King to the Nineteen-Eighties.* New York: P. Lang, 1987.

Watley, William D. *Roots of Resistance; the Nonviolent Ethic of Martin Luther King, Jr.* Valley Forge: Judson Press, 1985.

Knights of Labor

TYPE OF ETHICS: Business and labor ethics
DATE: Founded December 28, 1869
ASSOCIATED WITH: Uriah S. Stevens, Garment Cutters (Philadelphia), and Terence V. Powderly
DEFINITION: A national union organizing all labor regardless of skill, sex, race, creed, or nationality to promote social reform through worker cooperatives and government legislation
SIGNIFICANCE: The Knights was the first national union to seek economic justice for unskilled labor by promoting a classless society in which each worker would also be an entrepreneur

Established originally as a secret league, the Knights experienced tremendous growth when it became an open organization in the 1880's through the efforts of Terence Powderly, its grand master workman from 1879 to 1893. With the exception of professional workers, the Knights melded all labor into a single disciplined army to check the power of concentrated wealth that, according to the Knights, was degrading labor. The Knights believed that labor could regain its moral worth if it received a proper share of the wealth that it created and adequate leisure time to enjoy the blessings of a civilized society. The Knights sought to check the power of corporations through legislation to secure safe working conditions, equal pay for the sexes, an eight-hour day, a national banking system, public lands for settlers, weekly pay in full, the substitution of arbitration for strikes, and the abolition of contract labor and child labor. The Knights declined after 1886 when many skilled workers who desired less-utopian reform joined the newly organized American Federation of Labor.

See also American Federation of Labor; National Labor Union.

Kohlberg, Lawrence (Oct. 25, 1927, Bronxville, N.Y.—c. Jan. 17, 1987, Boston, Mass.): Psychologist

TYPE OF ETHICS: Modern history
ACHIEVEMENTS: Author of *Essays on Moral Development* (1981)
SIGNIFICANCE: Developed a widely accepted theory of moral development based on the premise that morality is a form of reasoning that develops in structural stages parallel to Jean Piaget's cognitive stages of growth

While serving as professor of education and social psychology at Harvard University, Kohlberg refined his theory of moral development. He forced a rethinking of traditional ideas on moral development by asserting that one's maturity in moral decisions develops as one thinks about moral issues and decisions. With cognitive growth, moral reasoning appears, and moral reasoning allows children to gain control over their moral decision-making process. From approximately four years of age through adulthood, a person experiences six stages of development that are divided into three levels. Because it is a cognitive developmental process, moral reasoning is taught using scenarios of moral dilemmas, causing students to justify the morality of their choices. Upon reaching cognitive maturity, a person will use reason to fashion an ethic of justice that is consistent with universal principles of justice and use it to satisfy the moral dilemma. For Kohlberg, moral judgment is the key ingredient in morality, taking precedence over other noncognitive factors. Some critics have challenged the universal application of the theory by claiming that the path of moral development is different for women.

See also Dilemmas, moral; Is/ought distinction.

Ku Klux Klan

TYPE OF ETHICS: Race and ethnicity
DATE: Founded 1866
DEFINITION: A white supremacist organization dedicated to racial segregation and the subjugation of people of color and other minorities
SIGNIFICANCE: Conflicts over the Ku Klux Klan highlight the tensions between freedom of speech and other social values (such as racial tolerance)

Few ethicists celebrate or condone the activities of the Ku Klux Klan; there is, however, a legal debate about how best to control these activities without unduly infringing on individual freedom.

The First Klan (c. 1865-1900). The Klan initially appeared toward the end of 1865 as a social club for former Confederate soldiers, who adopted the hooded sheet as their uniform. Members of the Klan wore masks to disguise their identity. The Klan gained notoriety during the Reconstruction period (1865-1877) for harassing newly freed African Americans who tried to exercise their newly won privilege of voting. Cross-burning on the property of the African Americans and their white Republican political allies was one form of harassment that the Klan practiced; whipping was another. By 1877, when conservative white Democrats had wrested control of southern state governments from the coalition of African Americans and white Republicans, Klan activity had subsided. By 1900, when African Americans had been effectively deprived of the right to vote in most southern states, the Klan had effectively disappeared as an organization; it had lost its reason for being.

The Second Klan (1915 to c. 1930). In 1915, a new national organization was formed, which took the name and the distinctive costume of the old Ku Klux Klan. The leadership of this new organization viewed Jews, Catholics, and immigrants as posing a danger to America that was equal to, if not greater than, that presented by African Americans. Although the Klan in the South did take part in outrages against African Americans in the immediate post-World War I years, the principal targets of the Klan in the North and the Midwest were the Roman Catholic church, Jews, and all immigrants from southern and eastern Europe. It also claimed to enforce the traditional small-town virtues of alcoholic abstinence and Victorian sexual morality against all deviants. During this time, the

Klan received much backing from Protestant ministers. It spread rapidly for a while throughout the Midwest and the Northwest but went into a sharp decline after the leader of the Indiana Klan was convicted, in 1926, of the rape of a young white woman. During the Great Depression (1929-1941), what remained of the Klan was eclipsed in importance by various other hate groups.

The Third Klan (1954 onward) and the Hate Speech Versus Free Speech Debate. There was a revival of the Ku Klux Klan in the 1950's and 1960's in the South. This revival was sparked by the 1954 Supreme Court decision *Brown v. Board of Education*, which mandated racial integration of the schools, and by the African American drive for voting rights in Mississippi and Alabama in the early 1960's. Many police officials condoned or cooperated with the Klan. The Klan was implicated in the deaths of three civil rights workers in Mississippi in 1964, military officer Lemuel Penn in 1964, and white civil rights worker Viola Liuzzo in 1965. After 1954, three main Klan organizations were formed: the Knights of the Ku Klux Klan; the United Klans of America; and the Invisible Empire, Knights of the Ku Klux Klan.

Toward the end of the 1960's, Klan influence in the South began to wane. Vigorous prosecution of Klan crimes by the Federal Bureau of Investigation, under federal civil rights statutes, reduced its power. As African Americans, protected by federal registrars after the passage of the Voting Rights Act of 1965, more and more came to exercise their right to vote, the once-common collusion between the Klan and local police became somewhat less frequent.

The Ku Klux Klan spread to the North in the 1970's and 1980's, as racial tensions spread across the country. The possibility that white males might lose jobs or promotions as a result of affirmative action policies was one Klan selling point. Klansmen practiced violence and intimidation, not only against African Americans but also, for a while, against post-1975 Indochinese refugee fishermen who had settled in the Gulf Coast states. Many Klansmen also opposed Mexican immigration; hostility to the Roman Catholic church, however, was no longer emphasized.

Unpopularity of the Klan in the 1980's Among Opinion Leaders. In the 1980's, the reputation of the Ku Klux Klan was probably worse than it had ever been. The association of the Klan with acts of violence was one mark against it. Other elements that limited the spread of Klan ideas were the adoption by the Klan of anti-Semitism and the organization's close association with the neo-Nazi movement. Condemnation of the Klan appeared even in the pages of the conservative religious magazine *Christianity Today*; the author of the article was appalled not only by the Klan's hatred of African Americans but also by its insistence that Jesus Christ was not a Jew. The Klan and its rituals seemed more and more limited to the South, although hate groups with similar ideas did arise in the North. When ex-Klansman David Duke ran for the offices of Louisiana state legislator,

An 1869 depiction of Ku Klux Klan members ambushing an African American family. (Smithsonian Institution)

senator from Louisiana, and governor of Louisiana, in 1989, 1990, and 1991, respectively, he soft-pedaled his past activity in the Klan; he won only the first election.

The Klan and the Issue of Free Speech. In June, 1990, two white youths in St. Paul, Minnesota, burned a cross on the home of an African American family that had moved into a previously all-white neighborhood; the city of St. Paul immediately passed a law banning cross-burning. In June, 1992, this law was overturned by the U.S. Supreme Court. In Georgia, a law banning the wearing of masks—a traditional practice among Klansmen—was struck down by the courts in May, 1990, as a violation of the Klan's right to free speech.

At that time, controversy erupted in the racially tense town of Kansas City, Missouri, when the Missouri Knights of the Ku Klux Klan tried to broadcast a program on local cable television. Mayor Emmanuel Cleaver, an African American man, opposed this idea as likely to cause trouble; so did many other people in Kansas City. In June, 1988, the city passed a law that would have kept the Klan off cable television. In May, 1989, however, a federal district court ruled against the city. Despairing of a Supreme Court victory, the city eventually allowed the Klan the right to broadcast in Kansas City; the first episode of the Klan cable program was broadcast on April 3, 1990.

Among white liberals, the issue of whether the Klan should be allowed free speech proved to be divisive in the 1980's. Some urged that the white-sheeted hate group's right to propagate its views be curbed. Other liberals, such as Nat Hentoff, while by no means accepting Klan viewpoints, insisted that the First Amendment to the Constitution guaranteed the right to propagate even views that most people consider to be evil. By the early 1990's, this debate was still unresolved.

Limits to the Klan's Rights. When Klan activity led to violence and intimidation, the courts in the 1980's sometimes assessed penalties against it. In Alabama, when an African American woman's young son was killed by Klansmen in the early 1980's, a white civil rights lawyer, Morris Dees, successfully sued the Alabama branch of the United Klans of America. The courts, by holding the organization responsible for the murder, effectively bankrupted the organization. In 1983, a court decision ordered the Klan to cease its harassment of Vietnamese refugee fishermen who plied their trade off the Gulf Coast of Texas.

—Paul D. Mageli

See also Bigotry; First Amendment; Lynching; Racism; Segregation.

BIBLIOGRAPHY

Alderman, Ellen, and Caroline Kennedy. "Freedom of Speech: Missouri Knights of the Ku Klux Klan v. Kansas City." In *In Our Defense: The Bill of Rights in Action.* New York: Morrow, 1991.

Becker, Verne. "The Counterfeit Christianity of the Ku Klux Klan." *Christianity Today* 28 (April 20, 1984): 30-35.

Dees, Morris, with Steve Fiffer. *A Season for Justice: The Life and Times of Civil Rights Lawyer Morris Dees.* New York: Maxwell Macmillan International, 1991.

Downs, Donald A. "Racial Incitement Law and Policy in the United States." In *Under the Shadow of Weimar: Democracy, Law, and Racial Incitement in Six Countries*, edited by Louis Greenspan and Cyril Levitt. Westport, Conn.: Praeger, 1993.

George, John, and Laird Wilcox. *Nazis, Communists, Klansmen, and Others on the Fringe: Political Extremism in America.* Buffalo, N.Y.: Prometheus Books, 1992.

Hentoff, Nat. *Free Speech for Me—But Not for Thee: How the Right and the Left Relentlessly Censor Each Other.* New York: HarperCollins, 1992.

Kronenwetter, Michael. *United They Hate: White Supremacist Groups in America.* New York: Walker, 1992.

Levin, Jack, and Jack McDevitt. *Hate Crimes: The Rising Tide of Bigotry and Bloodshed.* New York: Plenum Press, 1993.

Pascoe, Elaine. *Freedom of Expression: The Right to Speak Out in America.* Brookfield, Conn.: Millbrook Press, 1992.

Stanton, Bill. *Klanwatch: Bringing the Ku Klux Klan to Justice.* New York: Weidenfeld, 1991.

Kūkai (Kōbō Daishi; July 27, 774, Byōbugaura, Sanuki Province, Japan—Apr. 22, 835, Mt. Kōya, Japan): Buddhist monk

TYPE OF ETHICS: Religious ethics

ACHIEVEMENTS: Founded the Shingon school of Japanese Buddhism

SIGNIFICANCE: Taught that conformity to social and moral rules constituted the second of the ten rungs on the ladder that leads to true Buddhahood

Kūkai entered university studies in Confucian classics at age eighteen, but converted to Buddhism and soon (in 804) made a two-year trip to China to learn about esoteric Buddhism. Its "secrets," which were transmitted from master to pupil, were available to anyone dedicated enough to master them. Kūkai subsumed all types of Buddhism under a ladder of ten spiritual rungs: (1) the physical rung of food and sex, (2) morality typical of lay Buddhism, (3) deliverance from underworlds, (4) realization that there is no soul, (5) attainment of Theravādist disinterest, (6) sharing the secret of liberation with others, (7) meditation on the emptiness of things, (8) seeing the true way of salvation, (9) perceiving the Buddhahood of everything, and (10) enlightenment. Philosophically, Kūkai's system was monistic, with the ultimate Buddha manifesting in the form of Mahāvairochana (Japanese, Dainichi), the Great Sun. Other Buddhas and bodhisattvas were emanations. A person uncovers his or her innate Buddhahood through meditating, repeating formulas, and performing hand gestures. Despite the esoteric nature of his rituals, Kūkai's Buddhism appealed to the laity. Some Shingon adherents believe that he exists in the Heaven of the Satisfied, from which he will return with Maitreya, the future Buddha, and many people make pilgrimages to his tomb. After Kūkai's death, the Japanese bestowed on him the title Kōbō Daishi (Great Teacher of Karma).

See also Buddha; Buddhist ethics; Four noble truths.

Labor-Management Relations Act

TYPE OF ETHICS: Business and labor ethics

DATE: August 22, 1947

DEFINITION: A labor law that attempted to check the power given to labor unions under the National Labor Relations Act of 1935 by listing a series of unfair union labor practices

SIGNIFICANCE: Fearing the growth of communism both internationally and among union officials, Congress desired to curb significantly the power of unions and preserve traditional American capitalism

After the passage of the National Labor Relations Act (Wagner Act) in 1935, manufacturers began a decade-long media blitz to educate the public and Congress on the evils of the new state of industrial relations. Manufacturers extolled the virtues of the free enterprise system and blamed the Wagner Act for allowing an unregulated growth of organized labor and producing the social and industrial unrest of post-World War II America. Probusiness Republicans turned the Democrats out of office in 1946 and promptly amended the Wagner Act, detailing six unfair labor practices and monitoring officials of labor organizations. Changes in the law included outlawing the closed shop, prohibiting unions from participating in secondary strikes, allowing for an eighty-day injunction for emergency disputes, and requiring union officials to renounce any Communist Party affiliation or belief. This legislation provided a necessary balance between the interests of business and labor and proved the viability of the American system of government to keep her traditional economic institutions intact while meeting the current needs of all of her people.

See also National Labor Relations Act.

Language

TYPE OF ETHICS: Theory of ethics

DATE: The nature of ethical language has been an important concern in moral philosophy since the teaching of Socrates in fifth century B.C.E. Athens

ASSOCIATED WITH: Value theory

DEFINITION: The interrelationship of ethics and the terminology that that study employs

SIGNIFICANCE: Language is central to the meaning and meaningfulness of ethics, and competing and conflicting theories of ethical language dominate the concerns of ethical philosophers today

Since the modern division of ethics into normative ethics and metaethics, the latter study has concentrated almost exclusively on the meaning of ethical terminology, its nature, and the rules of its interrelationships.

The concern of ethics with language is scarcely a modern phenomenon, and even in the dialogues of Plato, Socrates challenges his interlocutors with demands for precision in their use of terms such as good, just, right, piety, and virtue.

As modern metaethics analyzes language today, there are vital divisions in ethical thought that depend entirely on particular approaches to ethical language. Moral (or ethical) realism maintains that ethical statements make truth claims and that ethical terms signify real properties and relationships. In addition, ethical information is seen as enjoying an objectivity that transcends culture, class, gender, and other categories.

Realism has suffered, however, under the criteria utilized by the school of logical positivism for verifiability, confirmation, and so forth in the twentieth century. In the wake of the decline of positivism, a renewed interest in moral realism has appeared, but serious problems remain regarding the relation of the moral to the nonmoral and regarding the explanatory role that moral propositions have in understanding the world. In regard to the latter, it is clearly the case that one can understand certain events and individuals in history better by understanding their morality, but it is not certain that one need know more than the empirical fact that those individuals simply believed in a particular moral code and acted upon it.

Noncognitivism has arisen as a way around imputing facticity and truth-value to moral statements. The three forms of noncognitivistic ethics are emotivism, imperativism, and emoto-imperativism.

Emotivism constitutes a grouping of theories that are metaevaluative in nature. Throughout the full range of axiology (the study of values), those theories deny that moral, aesthetic, economic, or other sorts of evaluations convey information or are susceptible of truth-value analysis.

Emotivism portrays ethical statements as mere emotional utterances, in line with the attempt of logical positivism to eliminate truth claims from all nonempirical statements. Early emotivists included philosophers such as Sir A. J. Ayer, C. L. Stevenson, J. L. Austin, and, later, Paul Edwards and Margaret MacDonald.

R. M. Hare's theory of prescriptivism has been claimed by many thinkers, including C. L. Stevenson, to be a form of near-emotivism, although this analysis is in dispute.

Imperativism espouses the position that all ethical language is imperative in character. Obviously, much ethical language is overtly and undeniably imperative—for example, "Thou shalt not kill" or "Remember thou keep holy the Lord's Day." In imperativist theory, however, even ethical statements that have the outward form of factual claims are only disguised commands: "Murder is evil" equates to "Do not commit murder," and "Theft is blameworthy" amounts to "Don't steal." Furthermore, because they are commands, they have no informational import and are not susceptible of any truth-claims, since a command can never be true or false.

Since there was no inherent contradiction between the emotivistic and the imperativistic interpretations, a third school evolved that combined both theories into a single supertheory. Emoto-imperativism maintains that any ethical utterance is actually an emotional response, a command, or both simultaneously. Thus, "murder is immoral" can be rendered as "Murder—ugh!" "Do not murder," or "Murder—ugh!—do not commit it."

On the cognitive side of the debate, ethical naturalism interpreted ethical language in terms of nonmoral empirical meanings. A clear example of ethical naturalism is Thomas Hobbes's assertion that to say that a thing is good has the simple meaning that the speaker likes that thing. As one of several alternative theories, one might hold "good" to mean that which would be desired for its own sake by any normal person with knowledge and experience of it, as Jeremy Bentham asserted.

G. E. Moore's discovery of the naturalistic fallacy has been seen by many as fatally undermining ethical naturalism, and that is certainly the case if there is any attempt in the particular ethical theory to imply a conjunction of the specific empirical content of the good and the notion that the good is "that which one ought to do." Without this prescriptive linkage, however, the naturalistic fallacy leaves ethical naturalism unscathed.

Intuitionism has a long history in ethics, dating back at least to the moral philosophy of Lord Shaftesbury (1671-1713), but in modern ethical thought, it has especially been viewed as a possible solution to the metaethical enigmas surrounding ethical language.

The heart of intuitionism holds that ethical statements can be justified without being derived from other types of statements. This noninferential justification of moral judgments has often led intuitionists to call them "self-evident," but in any case, the clear import of modern intuitionism has been to avoid many of the epistemological pitfalls that have beset other theories of ethical language. Some intuitionists have gone so far as to assert a faculty of moral intuition as a source for all ethical judgments.

Despite the concern of ancient and medieval ethical philosophy with precision of language, it is modern philosophy that has made language one of the central concerns of ethics. Undoubtedly, David Hume's is/ought problem has been the source of much of this concern.

"Hume's Law"—the rule that one cannot deduce a prescriptive conclusion from descriptive premises—had the necessary effect of radically cleaving the empirical sphere of facts from the sphere of values. This radical divorcement of is and ought forced a search for new meanings in ethical language, together with the search for an epistemology of ethics that confines ethical terminology within the parameters of general philosophy of language, logic, and truth theory.   —Patrick M. O'Neil

See also Fact/value distinction; Goodness; Is/ought distinction; Moral principles, rules, and imperatives; Moral realism; Morality; Naturalistic fallacy; Right and wrong; Values.

BIBLIOGRAPHY
Ayer, Alfred J. Language, Truth, and Logic. London: V. Gollancz, 1936.

Belfrage, Bertil. "Berkeley's Theory of Emotive Meaning." History of European Ideas 7 (1986): 643-649.

Carnap, Rudolph. Philosophy and Logical Syntax. 1935. Reprint. New York: AMS Press, 1979.

Edwards, Paul. The Logic of Moral Discourse. Glencoe, Ill.: Free Press, 1955.

Stevenson, Charles L. Ethics and Language. New Haven, Conn.: Yale University Press, 1944.

_____. Facts and Values. New Haven, Conn.: Yale University Press, 1963.

Stroll, Avrum. The Emotive Theory of Ethics. Berkeley: University of California Press, 1954.

Lao Tzu (traditionally, 604 B.C.E., Ch'ü-jen, Ch'u, China—sixth century B.C.E., place unknown): Philosopher

TYPE OF ETHICS: Classical history

ACHIEVEMENTS: Founder of Taoism and supposed author of the Tao Te Ching

SIGNIFICANCE: One of the three principal teachers of what later became known as Taoism, Lao Tzu ("Old Master Lao") is commonly considered to be the founder of that religion; Taoism calls on its adherents to withdraw from society, to cease striving, and to seek contentment without worldly fame in order to achieve order in society and harmony in personal life

Basic facts about the life of Lao Tzu are difficult to verify. Although he is traditionally believed to have lived in the sixth century B.C.E., the earliest information regarding his life and work is found in the works of a Chinese historian of the second century B.C.E. According to this source, Lao Tzu was a native of a small village in the south of China in a state then called Ch'u, which corresponds roughly to the modern-day region of eastern Honan Province. It is said that he served as an official historian to the royal house of Chou and became well known for his versatile learning. He has been associated with the Li clan, a family whose existence is historical fact, but it seems that this connection was created during the Han dynasty, several centuries after Lao Tzu supposedly lived. At this time, the Li clan decided to adopt him as their ancestor, a practice that was common among noble families who wished to relate themselves to heroes of China's past. Some scholars contend that Lao Tzu is a wholly fictitious person, posited by later generations of his followers who wished to ascribe various writings of Taoism to a single source.

Tao Te Ching. The document attributed to Lao Tzu, the *Tao Te Ching*, or the *Way and Its Power*, is the oldest text of the Chinese mystical tradition. Known also as the *Lao Tzu* after its alleged author, it is a short text of about five thousand Chinese characters. The work is probably not as old as tradition holds it to be. It was most likely compiled from various aphorisms that emerged during China's Warring States period, around 250 B.C.E. Scholars dispute whether it is the product of a single mind or simply a collection of adages drawn from several ancient sources. The *Tao Te Ching* can be read in various ways: as a philosophical handbook on how to live prudently in the world, as a discourse on the ways of politics, as a treatise on military strategy, and as a religious tract. Chinese scholars have written hundreds of commentaries on it. A body of popular belief and religious ritual emerged from it that continues to be practiced as one of the major religions of China today.

Lao Tzu believed that genuine knowledge of and insight into the nature of things could be obtained only through mystic intuition. He maintained that all things were composed of two opposite aspects, a kind of unity of contradiction, and much of his teaching inverted the generally assumed order of things. He said, for example, that "the softest thing in the universe overcomes the hardest" and that "seeing the small is insight, yielding to force is strength."

Popular Taoism. The debate about Lao Tzu's life derives from the context in which Taoist thinking gained popularity. The fourth and third centuries B.C.E., a period of anxiety caused by social disturbance and upheaval in China, fostered conditions that were particularly favorable to the development of philosophical and religious reflection. Some people saw Confucianism as the answer to the chaos. This school of thought maintained that social harmony derived from the fulfillment of mutual responsibilities in a clearly defined hierarchical system. Others believed that Legalism, which promoted meticulously enforced and stringent laws, was the solution for disorder. Both of these philosophies were rejected by the Taoists. They argued that the salvation of both individuals and society could not be attained by rigorous loyalty to social codes or laws, but rather by pursuing retirement from the world as a means of mastering it. The aim, they taught, was to preserve and increase one's vital energy by recourse to various disciplines, including contemplation of the Way (Tao) as well as proper diet, breathing, and exercise. This did not exclude work, for the *Tao Te Ching* assumes that work is necessary. Rather, work was to be done without rivalry, so that desire, competition, and those motivations that produce conflict would be avoided.

Legacy of Lao Tzu. Later Taoists ascribed a religious connotation to the mystical aspects of the original doctrine of Taoism. The impersonal and infinite force beneath nature became transformed into individual finite human souls, which, after death, became powerful spirits. Many important Chinese gods (of rain, fire, medicine, agriculture, and the kitchen) arose in the Taoist school. The popular Taoism of later times increasingly emphasized magical aspects that typically became attractive when daily life seemed hopelessly difficult. Particularly drawn to this form of Taoist thinking were Chinese peasants who lived on a narrow economic margin where hard work and skill were not always sufficient to guarantee even survival. As a consequence, the average person began to associate Taoism with the world of spirits who had to be placated and appeased. Increasingly, Taoists were expected to select lucky days for such important events as funerals and weddings. A fear of death emerged. This debasement of Taoism in its popular form departs significantly from the teachings of such early philosophical Taoists as Lao Tzu. —*Margaret B. Denning*

See also Chuang Chou; Confucian ethics; Confucius; Taoist ethics.

BIBLIOGRAPHY

Fung Yu-lan. *A History of Chinese Philosophy.* Vol. 1. Translated by Derk Bodde. Princeton, N.J.: Princeton University Press, 1953.

Lao Tze. *Treatise on Response and Retribution.* Translated by D. T. Suzuki and Paul Carus. Edited by Paul Carus. LaSalle, Ill.: Open Court, 1973.

Lao Tzu. *Tao Te Ching.* Translated by Gia-fu Feng and Jane English. New York: Vintage Books, 1972.

The Texts of Taoism. Part 1: The Tao Te Ching of Lao Tzu, The Writings of Chuang Tzu (books 1-17). Translated by James Legge. New York: Julian Press, 1959.

Wang Pi. *Commentary on the Lao tzu.* Translated by Ariane Rump and Wing-tsit Chan. Honolulu: University of Hawaii Press, 1979.

Law

TYPE OF ETHICS: Legal and judicial ethics
DEFINITION: Rules of conduct determined by a controlling legal authority and having binding legal force
SIGNIFICANCE: The laws and how they are ruled upon by the courts determine the nature of society and the values and morals that are enforced by the courts and the judicial system

The Nature of Law. Law is that which is laid down, ordained, or established. It is a body of rules of action prescribed by controlling legal authority and having binding legal force. It is a written code of rules that must be obeyed by citizens or those citizens will be subject to sanctions or legal consequences. Law is a solemn expression of the will of the supreme power of the state. Law is different from ethics. Ethics have been defined by former Supreme Court Justice Potter Stewart as "knowing the difference between what you have a right to do and what is the right thing to do." Ethics involve following not only the letter of the law but also its spirit. Ethics are not codified in books. They are that which is moral. Ethics deal not only with conduct but also with motives and character. Ethics constitute a higher standard than that of law; law dictates the minimum standards of behavior required of a person by society, whereas ethics go beyond what is required. Law comes from principles of morality; morality does not descend from law. Morality is that which pertains to character; it governs conduct not by legislative action or by force but by conscience and a desire to adhere to general principles of right conduct. Morality is a strict belief or conviction in the mind that is independent of legal proof or positive law. Law is essential to preserve society; ethics and morality are essential to sustain it at a higher level.

Ethics, Law, and Morality. Ethics are concerned with human values. Often, these values are reflected in jurisprudence and in laws. Legal theory has always concerned itself with morality. Two legal philosophers who wrote a great deal concerning the relationship between law and ethics were Saint Thomas Aquinas, who founded the natural law theory of jurisprudence, and John Austin, who helped establish legal positivism. Theirs are two very different views of law, but both men stressed that law is subject to criticism from a moral point of view, and both believed that there are standards by which it may be properly judged.

Thomas Aquinas, in his *Treatise on Law*, says that "Law is nothing else than an ordinance of reason for the common good, promulgated by him who has the care of the community." He views law as something that is established for the good of all. Austin, however, sees the law as a social element that can be used for good or bad, which can be exploited as a power tool by those in authority. Austin appears to be more realistic in his assessment of the possibility of the use of law by some to suppress others, since history has demonstrated that law is capable of doing good but has great capacity for evil. It can settle disputes and provide security, and it can lead to and enforce slavery. Law does not necessarily serve the common good and is not necessarily designed to do so. Austin recognizes that law can be good, if it is just and is derived from the laws of nature, as opposed to the laws that are framed by humankind. He says, "unjust human laws are a perversion of the ideal of law, which is given by right reason and the law of nature." Aquinas taught that human laws are just when they serve the common good. Laws that distribute burdens fairly, show no disrespect for God, and do not exceed the lawmaker's authority are good laws. When laws fail to satisfy these conditions, however, they are unjust. Then, according to Aquinas, they do not "bind in conscience." One is morally bound to obey just laws but not unjust laws. Unjust laws should be obeyed only when circumstances warrant it or "in order to avoid scandal or disturbance." Human law does not automatically merit respect, and its legitimate claim to obedience depends on moral and ethical considerations that are independent of human law.

The Moral Basis of Law. The role of law in enforcing morality is another ethical dilemma in the relationship between law and ethics. Conduct, the immorality of which involves serious rights violations (such as rape and murder), is obviously a proper object of state regulation and laws. The real conflict between law and ethics, however, involves state regulation of conduct that is not unjust or harmful in the sense of committing serious rights violations, but instead is regarded as immoral by the public, such as laws that prohibit sodomy between private consenting adults or laws criminalizing cohabitation. Should the mere fact that the majority of society's members and their elected representatives view such conduct as immoral serve as sufficient ground for making such conduct against the law? Democratic societies such as the United States are, of course, supposed to allow the majority to have its way. Sometimes, however, liberty-maximizing societies will not be pure democracies and will place severe limits on the will of the majority in

order to protect the rights of the individual, as does the Bill of Rights of the U.S. Constitution. Thus, a full moral discussion of the legitimacy of using the law to regulate private behavior that is judged to be immoral by a majority of citizens will mandate, at the very least, a moral theory of justified state coercion, and a moral theory of basic rights will be accorded to citizens in a just society. John Stuart Mill, in his treatise *On Liberty*, claims that the only purpose that justifies a society in coercing any of its members is to prevent harm to others.

Law has an interaction with moral opinion. Laws governing sexual conduct and drug usage confront the ethical issues head-on. What are the rights of the individual in relationship to society? What rights may the collective social body claim to the individual? When people form a society, how are the respective rights of both the individual and society at large to be structured? The general consensus is that both the individual and the society at large have rights that each must recognize, yet what those rights are and what boundaries restrict their invocation are matters of continuing struggle.

The struggle expresses itself in a number of ways, the most significant of which is the conflict between the individual conscience and the law. Should morality be legislated and enforced by law? When law and conscience conflict, which one should be obeyed? Laws seem to originate from moral convictions. Since it is morally wrong to take someone else's life without justification, murder is illegal. It is by no means clear, however, that all moral convictions of a society, even those of a majority in a democracy, should be enforced by judicial sanctions. Should moral opposition to prostitution and abortion, for example, result in laws prohibiting such activity? Which moral convictions should be incorporated into the legal code? Who decides which moral convictions are allowed to be incorporated into law: judges, the people, or both? Should the law concern itself with traditionally private immorality (such as homosexual acts) unless the behavior is offensive to public order and decency or exposes to the ordinary citizen something that is offensive or injurious? Is an established code of morality essential to preserving social order, even at the expense of private acts? Should individual liberty and personal choice be limited simply by the moral feelings and convictions of others?

Principles of Law and Ethics. There have been many great legal philosophers who have debated these ideas. H. L. A. Hart, professor of jurisprudence at Oxford University in 1959, published a detailed view of his theory of the relationship of law and morality in his treatise *Law, Liberty, and Morality*, in which he concluded that there was almost no legitimacy in making certain conduct illegal or criminal unless the conduct was harmful to others. The immorality of an action was not sufficient to make it illegal. Hart believed that "there must be a realm of private morality and immorality which is not the law's business."

There are several principles that are often used in the legal enforcement of morality as justification for limiting the freedom of individuals. There are the "harm" principles, which state, as did John Stuart Mill, that behavior should be prohibited only if it harms someone. There is the "offense" principle, which states that behavior should be coercively prohibitive if it is publicly offensive to others, and there is the "principle of legal moralism," which holds that behavior should be punished simply because it is immoral. This perception that it is the responsibility of the law to enforce morality is used to justify the regulation of sexual and reproductive conduct, such as homosexuality and abortion. Joel Feinberg, in his essay *Hard Cases for the Harm Principle*, holds that in order to characterize the kind of behavior that society is justified in controlling, the harm principle must be supplemented with a carefully drafted version of the offense principle.

There is a conflict between the individual conscience and the law. If one person believes that abortions are always morally wrong, but the law permits abortions under any circumstance, should that person attempt to prohibit women from obtaining legally permissible abortions? When the conscience and the law conflict, which takes priority? Conscience is an individual's convictions regarding what actions are right and wrong, morally good or bad. When a person's moral convictions lead him or her to object to abortion, or to a particular military position taken by the country, that person is also opposed to legal sanctions of abortion or that military position. A law is a rule of conduct prescribed by a properly constituted governing authority, enforced by sanctions, and justified by a mandate to legislate for the public benefit. A law is a rule of conduct that is "on the books."

Given these principles of conscience and law, a fundamental question arises. When a person is morally convinced that he or she ought to do one thing, yet a legally constituted authority directs otherwise, what is that person to do when the two courses of action are at odds with each other?

People faced with these choices can obey the law; follow their consciences and suffer the legal consequences because it conflicts with the law; or follow neither of the previous choices, thus choosing to obey the law or follow personal conscience as the particular circumstances require. The third alternative seems to require specifying principles in terms of which the decision is made in any given instance to obey the law or follow one's conscience.

Another set of moral questions about the law is derived from the realization that law is not only a set of rules used to govern society but also a profession. Lawyers, people trained in the law who give legal advice and assistance in legal matters, have certain responsibilities as advocates that may at least appear to conflict with larger responsibilities as a whole. For example, if a defense lawyer makes the best defense for his client and obtains freedom for him, even when he is both guilty and a danger to society, the ethical question is whether this is morally justifiable. As the defendant's advocate, the lawyer must work for the client's best interests. As a citizen, however, does the lawyer not owe the best interests of society concern and attention as well? Some people would argue that it is the job of the adversary system to aim at justice and the common good, and that the lawyer's job is to merely play a part in the system, aiming not at justice but rather at vigorous advocacy of the side to which the lawyer has been assigned. Is this a valid moral defense or simply a retreat from social responsibility?

Concepts of Jurisprudence. There are several different philosophies that guide the rule of law as interpreted by the judiciary system, as opposed to the laws that are created by legislatures and elected officials. These are the patterns of jurisprudence, or legal reasoning, which create legal standards of behavior that are as important as the statutes themselves, because they set precedents for others to follow in the enforcement of the law. There are those legal philosophers who are deeply skeptical of both doctrinal analysis and moral evaluation of the law, who see those approaches to law as so infected by prejudices in the status quo as to make them little more than covert political activity. These writers often follow the lead of "legal realism," which can be defined as the idea that law is simply a prediction of what the courts will decide, and suggest bringing such advocacy into the open and accepting an overtly political conception of the courts and the law, law being simply the exercise of power. The jurisprudential movement known as the "economic analysis of law," which encourages judges to decide cases in such a way as to ensure that economic freedom and wealth are protected and expanded, is a free-market version of the realist philosophy. "Critical legal study," which advocates interpreting the law in ways that will assist the disadvantaged and exploited, is a socialist version of the same perspective. None of these versions, however, can exist without moral values and moral theory, because it is impossible to justify the importance of caring about whether a person has been exploited or oppressed unless moral values and moral theory have been imposed. After all, exploitation is simply a kind of unjust treatment. Thus, it appears that normative jurisprudence, the moral evaluation of law and the legal profession, will have important tasks to perform as long as human beings seek to regulate their conduct through the use of law. Normative jurisprudence deals with the appraisal of law and the moral issues that law generates. Human law can be made and changed by deliberate decisions. What direction should those decisions take? Law claims the authority to lay down rules and enforce them. Are its claims warranted? Can people legitimately refuse to comply? Things are done in the name of the law that are not normally justifiable; people interfere in other people's lives, depriving them of goods, liberty, even life itself. How, if at all, can these practices be defended?

"Analytical jurisprudence" is the form of jurisprudence that questions the fundamental nature of law. What is law? How is it part of a system? How can a decision be made according to the law when the law is unclear? How is the law like or unlike moral standards? Analytical and normative questions concerning law are closely related. The law speaks of rights and responsibility, duties and obligations, fairness, justice and justification: Does this mean that the law inevitably contains or satisfies moral standards? Ideas about the essential nature of law have emphasized either its connections with or its separation from morality: Which view is right? Law is a social fact. Laws are commands. By its very nature, however, law is connected with morality. There are legal obligations that are moral obligations, but not all moral obligations are legal obligations, and the constant ethical struggle and changes in the law represent attempts to determine which obligations should be legal obligations and should be sanctioned by law enforcement and the courts. Are there proper limits to the reach of the law? Are there areas of human conduct that are, in principle, properly beyond legal sanction? Is there a point at which it is correct to say that, notwithstanding the morality and the social preferences and spiritual values and the sensibilities of the public, the suppression of certain actions by law is not the business of the government and must be left up to each individual to determine what is moral and ethical conduct?

From time to time, the facts of a particular legal case will raise an issue that forces people to go beyond precedent, beyond statute, and even beyond the task of constitutional interpretation. The facts of a case may take one to that area where law and philosophy intersect, where one finds lawyers thinking like philosophers and philosophers reasoning like lawyers. As the ethical issues and underlying principles that form American law and jurisprudence evolve, it becomes ever clearer that these cases play a very important role in what American society is to be and what values and standards of conduct it will set for its citizens. In trying to answer such difficult questions, the profession of law and the discipline of philosophy have much to offer each other as they combine to form and reflect the ethical, legal, and economic standards of American society.   —*Amy E. Bloom*

See also Conscience; Jurisprudence; Morality.

BIBLIOGRAPHY

Baird, Robert M., and Stuart E. Rosenbaum, eds. *Morality and the Law*. Buffalo, N.Y.: Prometheus Books, 1988. A textbook containing the writings of the legal philosophers H. L. A. Hart, Patrick Devlin, Joel Feinberg, and Erich Fromm, among others. Highly informative in referring to the different varieties of legal philosophy.

Davis, Philip, ed. *Moral Duty and Legal Responsibility*. New York: Appleton-Century-Crofts, 1966. An excellent book that compares the actual legal responsibilities of citizens under law with moral duties. Usually, the legal duties are less binding on human behavior than are the moral duties, since moral duties are held to a higher standard.

Kipnis, Kenneth, ed. *Philosophical Issues in Law*. Englewood Cliffs, N.J.: Prentice-Hall, 1977. A book containing Supreme Court cases and writings from legal philosophers that comments on not only judicial decisions but also the philosophy applied to the decisions.

Lyons, David. *Ethics and the Rule of Law*. New York: Cambridge University Press, 1984. A treatise on the relationship between morality and the law. It details how moral judgment affects the law and how it applies to the rule of law by judges as well as legislatures.

Wasserstrom, Richard A., ed. *Morality and the Law*. Belmont, Calif.: Wadsworth, 1971. Part of the *Basic Problems in Philosophy* series, this volume contains the writings of legal scholars (such as John Stuart Mill's *On Liberty*) as well as treatises that discuss other applications of morality and law, such as morality in criminal law, treason, and the Model Penal Code.

Lawyer for the situation

TYPE OF ETHICS: Legal and judicial ethics
DATE: Invented 1907
ASSOCIATED WITH: Supreme Court Justice Louis Dembitz Brandeis
DEFINITION: A lawyer representing parties engaged in a joint endeavor or seeking an amicable settlement who is not partisan for any of those parties
SIGNIFICANCE: Represents one view in the ongoing debate about the proper role of a lawyer who represents multiple parties simultaneously

During the 1916 confirmation hearings on Louis D. Brandeis' nomination to the Supreme Court, opponents alleged that Brandeis was an unscrupulous lawyer who was unfit for the high court. Another Boston lawyer, Sherman Whipple, testified about his 1907 conversation with Brandeis on a bankruptcy matter in which the bankrupt party believed that Brandeis had favored his creditors. Brandeis informed Whipple that he had not represented the bankrupt party personally but had agreed to act fairly and equitably in everyone's interests. Asked whom he represented, Brandeis had replied that he "was counsel for the situation."

In contrast, the prevailing ethical model of a partisan advocate acting zealously and with absolute loyalty to a single client frowns upon a lawyer with divided loyalties, since no one "may serve two masters." Proponents, such as Yale law professor Geoffrey C. Hazard, Jr., argue that a lawyer for the situation can often act more efficiently, with less acrimony, and with a greater insight than is possible with separate representation. Lawyers often represent family members and business associates with largely harmonious interests when relations among them are cooperative rather than adversarial. Though tensions remain, the concept's official recognition has increased since it was publicized in 1916. The 1983 Model Rules of Professional Conduct recognize that a lawyer may "act as intermediary between clients" under strict limitations.

See also Adversary System; Brandeis, Louis Dembitz; Law.

Laziness

TYPE OF ETHICS: Personal and social ethics

DATE: Twelfth century

ASSOCIATED WITH: Medieval concept of the seven deadly sins

DEFINITION: Laziness is a disinclination toward physical or mental exertion; the medieval concept of sloth (*acedia*) denotes specifically disinclination in a person's relationship with God

SIGNIFICANCE: The way in which a society views laziness is a key to the ethical structure and morality of that society

Acedia ("sloth") was one of the seven deadly sins of medieval ethical tracts, which were termed deadly not because they were necessarily mortal, or unforgivable, but because they were deemed singularly attractive. Acedia is a lack of diligence in the love of God, which may in turn lead to a lack of diligence in performing good works and an inclination toward inactivity.

The idea that idleness is inherently sinful is a post-Reformation one that is tied to the notion that economic prosperity is a sign that a person is one of God's elect. The popular moral literature of the eighteenth and nineteenth centuries is exemplified by William Hogarth's industrious apprentice, who marries the boss's daughter, and the idle apprentice, who is hanged at Tyburn.

The concept of laziness as a character defect is almost absent from late twentieth century ethical thought; lazy behavior is viewed as the product of physical or mental illness. Disinclination toward exertion frequently accompanies depression, a complex of physiological and mental symptoms triggered by the perception that the situation is hopeless and effort will not change it. To the extent that it avoids futile effort, such inactivity is biologically adaptive.

Attitudes toward inactivity vary widely from culture to culture. The Western attitude that effort expended toward accumulating goods in excess of what is needed for survival is virtuous is far from universal, and the contempt of nineteenth century Europeans for "lazy, shiftless natives" reflects a narrow moral outlook. Avoidance of effort within a social context is damaging in a cooperative enterprise (such as marriage), however, because it deprives others of the fruits of their labors, and is generally censured.

See also Anger; Envy; Gluttony; Greed; Lust; Pride; Sin; Thomas Aquinas.

League of Nations

TYPE OF ETHICS: International relations

DATES: Established January 10, 1920; dissolved April 19, 1946

ASSOCIATED WITH: Woodrow Wilson proposed the establishment of a league of nations in his Fourteen Points and promoted it at the Paris Peace Conference

DEFINITION: The League of Nations was the first general international organization whose purpose was the promotion of international cooperation and the achievement of international peace and security

SIGNIFICANCE: The League effort to prevent war failed, but the experience of the League in the interwar period provided important lessons for the great powers in creating the United Nations as a successor organization

The idea of a league of nations gained currency during World War I in large part because of the enormous human losses caused by the war and the belief of many leaders that only an international organization could prevent the recurrence of such a terrible cataclysm. Woodrow Wilson is credited with promoting the idea of the League, because of the call in his Fourteen Points for the creation of "a general association of nations." There were others, however, whose influence generated support for an international association of peace-loving states; notably, President William H. Taft in the United States, Sir Edward Grey and Lord Robert Cecil in Great Britain, and Field Marshall J. C. Smuts in South Africa. In several allied and neutral countries during World War I, organizations were formed to enlist support for a postwar world organization. Nevertheless, special credit does belong to Wilson because of his leadership at the Paris Peace Conference in 1919 in drafting the Covenant of the League of Nations. The League Covenant was incorporated into the Treaty of Versailles, which was adopted at Paris in 1919.

The central purpose of the League was to promote international peace and security. It sought to achieve this end by means of a variety of techniques, of which the most notable was a system for the peaceful settlement of disputes between states and for taking collective action against those nations that committed aggressive war. Other important objectives of the League were economic and social cooperation, disarmament, and national self-determination.

There were three principal organs of the League: an Assembly in which each member was represented; a Council that was to be composed of representatives of the United States, Great Britain, France, Italy, and Japan as permanent members plus four others elected by the Assembly; and a permanent Secretariat headed by a Secretary General. The Assembly met annually beginning in September. Assembly decisions required a unanimous vote, thus giving every member a veto. In practice, members who disagreed with the majority often abstained, permitting many decisions to be taken by consensus. During the life of the League, sixty-three states were members, seventeen members withdrew from the Assembly, and one, the Soviet Union, was expelled.

Since the United States declined to join the League, it never joined the Council. The number of elected members was increased first to six and later to nine. The Council generally met four times a year. While the scope of discussion in the Assembly encompassed any issue of international affairs, the Council confined its discussion to political problems. Decisions in the Council required a unanimous vote, though if the subject was a dispute that was likely to lead to conflict, the parties in contention could not participate in the vote.

The principal purpose of the League was to resolve disputes between states and keep the peace. This responsibility was spelled out in Articles 10 to 17 of the Covenant, which embodied what has become known as the idea of collective security. According to Article 10, each member undertook "to respect and preserve as against external aggression the territorial integrity and existing political independence of all Members of the League." Members were to settle their disputes peacefully, and under the provision of Article 16, League members were committed to join in common action against any state that went to war without observing the procedures for peaceful settlement specified in the Covenant. Economic sanctions were to be the principal, though not necessarily exclusive, form of sanctions used to bring an aggressor state to heel.

Though the League is remembered primarily for its political activities, it also made major contributions of a social, scientific, economic, and humanitarian nature. These include work in controlling drug trafficking, protection of women, child welfare, abolition of slavery, and support for refugees. In the political realm, the League is considered to have been a failure, as indicated by the outbreak of World War II less than two decades after World War I. In fact, the political contributions of the League were significant. Some of its major successes came in the 1920's: settlement of the Swedish-Finnish dispute over the Aland Islands; settlement of the Polish-German frontier dispute in Upper Silesia; and prevention of war between Greece and Bulgaria in 1925. Germany's entrance into the League in 1926 was an important step in the reconstruction of Europe. That step was linked to the signing of treaties known as the Locarno Pact, which guaranteed the inviolability of the Franco-German frontier and the demilitarization of the Rhineland.

The League's political accomplishments were, however, outweighed by its failures, particularly in the 1930's. A major blow to the League's prestige resulted from its inability to act against Japan when that country invaded Manchuria in September, 1931. The Lytton Commission, created by the League Council, determined that Japan was guilty of aggression. The only consequence of the League's investigation was Japan's withdrawal from the organization. The League's first major test of collective security was a failure.

Even more fateful for the League were the half-hearted economic sanctions imposed upon Italy to stop Mussolini's invasion of Ethiopia in 1935. Because oil was not included in the embargo, the sanctions failed to stop the Italian dictator, and in July the Assembly abandoned the sanctions. This blow to League prestige proved to be fatal. Within the next three years, Nazi Germany embarked upon a campaign of aggression that the League was powerless to stop. The Rhineland was remilitarized in violation of the Versailles Treaty (1936), Austria was annexed (1938), Czechoslovakia was occupied (1938-1939), and Poland was invaded (1939). The expulsion of the Soviet Union for its war against Finland was the League's last action, but that action reflected the organization's impotence rather than its efficacy.

Several explanations have been advanced to account for the political failure of the League of Nations. The first was the absence of the United States as a member. Without American involvement, economic and military sanctions were very difficult to institute. Second, the decision-making rules of the League made it difficult for the organization to take strong and decisive measures. Third, there were legal loopholes in the Covenant that permitted members to evade their responsibilities. Fourth, the League lacked teeth; that is, it did not have military forces at its disposal to use against an aggressor. Fifth, the great powers that dominated the League were unwilling to subordinate their national interests to their commitments under the Covenant.

Students of international organization are still divided in their general evaluation of the League: Did it fail because it was too weak or did it attempt to accomplish more than was possible in a world of sovereign states? Whatever the answer, there was enough faith in the principles of the League to make a second effort. The United Nations was organized in such a way as to overcome what many believed to be the flaws of the League. The Security Council of the United Nations has enforcement power that the League of Nations never possessed. —*Joseph L. Nogee*

See also International justice; International law.

Bibliography

Cecil, Robert, Viscount. *A Great Experiment*. New York: Oxford University Press, 1941.

Riches, Cromwell A. *The Unanimity Rule and the League of Nations*. Baltimore: The Johns Hopkins University Press, 1933.

Schiffer, Walter. *The Legal Community of Mankind: A Critical Analysis of the Modern Concept of World Organization*. New York: Columbia University Press, 1954.

Walters, Francis P. *History of the League of Nations*. New York: Oxford University Press, 1969.

Zimmern, Alfred E. *The League of Nations and the Rule of Law*. London: Macmillan, 1936.

League of Women Voters

Type of ethics: Sex and gender issues
Date: Founded 1920
Associated with: Women's suffrage; voter education
Definition: Founded in the first year in which women were eligible to vote in federal elections, the League attempts to encourage its members and the public at large to obtain and study political information, to take positions on political issues, and to participate actively in the political system
Significance: The League of Women Voters was founded on the principle that democratic government requires political responsibility on the part of the citizenry

The League of Women Voters is a direct descendant of the women's suffrage movement. At its jubilee convention in 1919, the National American Women's Suffrage Association, which was the leading women's suffrage organization, voted to dissolve itself because of the final ratification of the Nineteenth Amendment and to form a new body to be known as the League of Women Voters. The amendment enfranchised women in all federal elections. Ratification was completed in 1920, and the League was formally launched at a convention in Chicago. Although many of its organizational principles and bylaws

tions. By 1992, it had some 125,000 members in 1,350 chapters all over the United States.

The major thrust of the League's activities continues to be voter education. At the local level, League chapters study issues, distribute information, and sponsor "candidates' nights" at which local political candidates appear and discuss the issues and their candidacies. At the national level, the League of Women Voters has been very active in ar-

Members of the League of Women Voters with a list of recommendations for the Democratic Platform Committee. (Library of Congress)

were not clear at that point, the new organization was based on several principles that have been maintained throughout its history. The purpose of the League was to educate the public in general and women in particular regarding public issues by preparing and distributing information and encouraging political participation. Until 1946, the center of the League's internal organization lay in relatively autonomous state associations similar to those that had been so successful during the struggle for women's suffrage. There was considerable disunity. In 1946, the League reorganized itself into a membership association of individuals rather than a federation of state associa-

ranging presidential campaign debates and in attempting to establish debating rules that enhance the quality and educational value of the discussion. The League, although nonpartisan, has never shied away from taking positions on national issues; for example, the League supported American foreign aid during the 1940's and 1950's, and the recognition of China in the 1960's. The League continues to be a force for the rational study of public issues and for moderation in politics.

See also Civil rights; Equal Rights Amendment; Suffrage; Women's ethics.

Gottfried Leibniz (Library of Congress)

Leibniz, Gottfried (July 1, 1646, Leipzig, Saxony—Nov. 14, 1716, Hanover): Philosopher

TYPE OF ETHICS: Enlightenment history

ACHIEVEMENTS: Author of *Essais de théodicée sur la bonté de Dieu, la liberté de l'homme, et l'origine du mal* (1710; *Theodicy*, 1951) and *Nouveaux Essais sur l'entendement humain* (1765; *New Essays Concerning Human Understanding*, 1896), among other works

SIGNIFICANCE: A leading Protestant philosopher of the Enlightenment, Leibniz attempted to reconcile faith and reason, resulting in a rational, optimistic, spiritual worldview

A "universal genius"—mathematician, scientist, diplomat, historian, ecumenist, and philosopher—Leibniz was "the pathfinder of the German Enlightenment." For the last forty years of his life, he worked for the House of Hanover, principally as the royal librarian. A devout Lutheran, Leibniz, in an age of increasing determinism and materialism, strove to envision a worldview that was rational, hopeful, and spiritual. Reality for Leibniz was composed of an infinite number of individual spiritual substances ("monads," from the Greek word meaning "one"), arranged in an ascending order of consciousness from nearly nothing to God ("the Supreme Monad"). Created by God, this is "the best of all possible worlds," since in it an infinite being chose to honor the limitations of finitude. So-called evils (material, mental, or moral) contribute to the ultimate good of the universe. This intelligent and benevolent world is rational, and all things in it exhibit a pre-established harmony, or "unity." Such a universe invites ethical action that is both personal and social, both thoughtful and charitable.

See also Enlightenment ethics; Idealist ethics; Religion.

Lenin (Vladimir Ilich Ulyanov; Apr. 22, 1870, Simbirsk, Russia—Jan. 21, 1924, Gorki, U.S.S.R.): Political leader

TYPE OF ETHICS: Modern history

ACHIEVEMENTS: Founder of the Union of Soviet Socialist Republics (U.S.S.R.)

SIGNIFICANCE: By founding the Soviet Union on the basis of Marxist theories, Lenin paved the way for other countries to follow suit, thereby altering the history of the twentieth century

Vladimir Ilich Ulyanov Lenin was one of the most influential individuals of the twentieth century. His significance was both theoretical and practical. His two more significant theoretical contributions revolved around his theory of imperialism and his conception of the Communist Party. His practical contribution was as the maker and sustainer of one of the great revolutions of modern history.

Leninism in Theory. Lenin's theory of "imperialism, the highest stage of capitalism," attempted to address the principal problem confronting Marxism during the last years of the nineteenth century and the early years of the twentieth century. Simply put, the advanced industrial powers appeared to have avoided many of the debilitating contradictions that Marx had predicted would cause the final crisis in the fourth stage in his theory of the historical process—capitalism. Marx believed that the anticipated crisis of capitalism would inevitably trigger a worker revolution, thereby advancing history to its fifth and culminating stage of history—socialism. Conversely, however, without the crisis of capitalism, there could be no revolution. Drawing upon the thought of several other European Marxist and English Liberal theorists, Lenin posited that the advanced industrial economies had temporarily avoided the contradictions central to Marxist theory by expanding their economies to engulf the entire globe. In doing so, the capitalists had been able to secure cheap labor and raw materials, as well as markets for products and outlets for surplus capital. This process had allowed the capitalists to derive "superprofits," which had, in turn, been partly used to bribe the workers in the advanced industrial countries and thereby postpone the inevitable crisis and revolution. Lenin referred to this expansion of the industrial economies to a global scale as "imperialism."

Lenin went on to maintain, however, that imperialism could not last in perpetuity but would inevitably be overcome by its own contradictions and give way to socialism as Marx had originally predicted. In the broadest sense, Lenin argued that once the industrial economies had expanded to engulf the entire world, the contradictions that Marx had anticipated would eventually be activated. Monopolies and states would violently compete for global domination, with weaker competitors being driven from the field. Lenin further theorized that the imperial states would fight wars for the distribution of colonies and semicolonies, conflicts that would devastate both winners and losers. Ultimately, the decline in superprofits and the costly international conflicts would force the capitalists to withdraw first some, and eventually all, of the material and political concessions made earlier to the workers in the advanced industrial countries. This, combined with the suffering caused by the imperialist wars, would yield a dramatic increase in societal tension. Thus, the final crisis of capitalism would emerge, resulting in the eventual but inevitable overthrow of capitalism by the workers of the industrial states and the entry into history's culminating stage of socialism.

Lenin's other principal theoretical contribution to the Marxist movement was his conception of the Communist Party and its role as an agent to advance the historical process. Marx had expressed optimism that the workers of the advanced industrial countries would acquire both the impetus and organizational skills necessary to make the Proletariat Revolution merely by experiencing the deteriorating socio-economic conditions within mature capitalist systems. Lenin, however, disagreed. He acknowledged that the workers would be aware of their increasingly miserable conditions and would, periodically and spontaneously, rise in revolt against their oppressors. Lenin maintained, however, that this nonrational impulse to revolt was not, in itself, motivated or guided by any understanding of the historical significance of the action. For Lenin, only the "conscious" individuals in society, those who had studied the flow of history as interpreted by Marx and his successors, could understand where their particular society had been and currently was in the flow of history. Only these conscious people were capable of understanding where society was inevitably going and, perhaps most important, assessing the current revolutionary tasks confronting their society as it traversed the road of history. On this basis Lenin defined

the Communist Party as composed of those individuals who had gained "consciousness" and were prepared to dedicate their lives on a full-time basis to promoting the revolution and advancing the historical process.

Lenin charged the Party with the task of preparing for the moment when the impulse for a spontaneous outburst by the masses against local conditions fully ripened. When that outburst finally occurred, the Party would seize the leadership of the revolt and channel it into action that would meaningfully advance the historical process. In short, the Party alone was incapable of successfully making a revolution, while the masses alone, without guidance from the Party, would similarly be incapable of taking historically meaningful action. Together, however, the masses, led by the Party, would be the agents of history.

Based upon these considerations, Lenin posited two missions for the Party. The long-range mission was to educate the masses so that they might eventually acquire consciousness. Until that long-term goal was achieved, the immediate task of the Party was to lead the masses. Since only the Party knew what was appropriate policy and proper action for the unconscious masses, the Party had a responsibility to guide or, if necessary, coerce the masses into proper action. Thus, although the means to move the masses along lines determined to be appropriate by the Party might be manipulative, ruthless, or cruel, in Lenin's eyes, the Party knew what was ultimately in the best interests of society. In short, for Lenin, the goal of future societal fulfillment via entry into the stage of socialism justified whatever means were deemed necessary to advance society in that direction.

Finally, since Lenin conceived of the Party as being critical to historically significant action, he felt that the Party's decision-making process must not be paralyzed by internal division and indecisiveness. To avoid that danger, Lenin argued that the Party must employ the decision-making principle of "democratic-centralism." Lenin believed that all Party members shared a common commitment to advancing the historical process under the leadership of the Party. Thus, Lenin maintained that, with respect to specific policy questions confronting the Party, the members of the Party should be free to exchange opinions frankly prior to a decision having been taken. Once a final decision was taken by the Party leadership, however, Lenin required all Party members to defer to their common commitment to the Party as the instrument of history, unreservedly accept that decision, and enthusiastically work toward its implementation. Any further dissent regarding the announced decision would constitute a breach of Party discipline. Henceforth, discussion could only center on the manner in which the decision would be implemented.

While Lenin hoped that the principle of democratic-centralism would unite diversity of opinion and freedom of expression with resolute, united action, in fact, the principle was fraught with difficulties. In reality, any decision and its manner of implementation are much more closely inter-

Vladimir Ilich Lenin (National Archives)

twined than the principle of democratic-centralism allowed. Moreover, while in principle the Party rules provided for the democratic election of its leadership, in reality leadership recruitment into the Party hierarchy soon came to be based upon cooption by the incumbents. Overall, in practice, the democratic element of democratic-centralism yielded to the centralizing component.

Finally, connecting his conception of the Party with his theory of imperialism, Lenin came to believe that it would be easier to start a revolution in the less industrially developed countries than in the advanced capitalist states, although he believed that the revolutionary momentum would be more difficult to sustain in these countries. This conclusion would shape Lenin's views regarding the nature and timing of the revolutionary process in Russia.

Leninism in Practice. Armed with these theoretical concepts, Lenin made his practical contribution to history—as the maker of the Bolshevik Revolution and the founder of the Soviet Union. In Lenin's eyes, World War I, the first of the anticipated imperialist wars, offered a unique opportunity to advance the historical process internationally. He believed that if the Russian proletariat could seize power, that act would have profound consequences for the entire international system. He argued that Russia was a semicolony, exploited by the advanced industrial powers. Thus, a successful Russian proletariat takeover would disrupt the entire global economy upon which imperialism was based. Moreover, a successful revolution in Russia would signal the overthrow of what many in Europe regarded as the system's most reactionary state. Finally, in the largest sense, a successful takeover by Russian workers would provide a heroic example for the workers of the advanced industrial economies to emulate. In short, a revolution in Russia, even a democratic one, would serve as the "spark" that would ignite the pyres of revolution in the advanced industrial countries and yield a quantum leap in the historical process. Based upon these considerations, Lenin moved decisively to capitalize upon the revolutionary situation in Russia in 1917; in the autumn, he employed the Party to seize power on behalf of the Russian workers.

It soon became obvious that the proletariat of the developed industrial countries would fail to advance history by following the Russian example, overthrowing the existing capitalist order, and resolutely moving toward the final Marxist stage of socialism. Prior to taking power, Lenin had suggested that under these circumstances the Russian workers should launch a revolutionary war designed to liberate the European workers from their capitalist overlords. After taking power, however, Lenin realistically recognized that the new Soviet state lacked the resources to launch such a war of liberation. Moreover, to do so would jeopardize the revolutionary gains that had already been made. Therefore, Lenin decided that the foremost priority for the new Soviet regime would be to protect the revolutionary gains already made in Russia; only insofar as those gains would not be jeopardized would the Soviet Union attempt to spread revolution abroad.

Within Russia itself, however, retaining power was far from certain. The new Soviet regime was immediately confronted by a series of challenges emanating from both within and outside Soviet-controlled territory. Externally, the Soviets were threatened by counterrevolutionaries, national separatists, and the troops of foreign powers. Internally, a variety of non-Communist elements challenged the authority of the Communist Party of the Soviet Union (CPSU). To defeat these challenges, Lenin launched what became known as the period of War Communism. Between 1918 and 1921, Lenin orchestrated a series of campaigns at various levels that were designed to suppress ruthlessly all internal challenges to the monopoly rule of the CPSU, while simultaneously increasingly centralizing the Party itself at the expense of interparty democracy. Similarly, Lenin aggressively mobilized Russia's economic resources, although at the expense of such early policies as worker control over industry. Finally, Lenin oversaw the formation of the Red Army and, under his overall leadership, that instrument was used to crush the counterrevolutionaries and national separatists. In the eyes of many Party members, however, many of the measures taken during the period of War Communism constituted an abandonment of the ideals of the Revolution and were justifiable only as temporary expedients necessary to retain Communist control in Russia. Finally, by late 1920, it appeared that the enemies of the Soviet regime had been routed and that the CPSU had successfully retained power.

Organized elements within the Party now began to emerge, calling themselves by such names as the Workers Opposition and the Democratic Centralists, arguing that with the passage of the initial period of threat to the Revolution, the Party could now turn its attention to realizing the ideals of the Revolution, ideals that had been compromised during the period of War Communism. Indeed, the issue of the future of the Party and the Revolution came to a head at the Tenth CPSU Congress in 1921. Here, Lenin not only successfully defeated the platforms presented by the Party dissenters but also resolutely moved to drive them from the Party hierarchy and permanently ban factionalism from the Party. Fatefully for the future of the CPSU, Lenin opted to sustain and intensify the bureaucratic, centralized, and authoritarian character that the Party had increasingly assumed during the period of War Communism. Moreover, he intensified the campaign to crush any opposition to the CPSU monopoly rule over the Soviet Union. Finally, under Lenin's leadership, the Party continued its relentless campaign to penetrate and exercise control over all elements of Soviet society. Thus, although with the inauguration of the New Economic Policy in 1921 the regime retreated from some of the extreme economic measures taken during the period of War Communism, the foundations and character of the Soviet sociopolitical, totalitarian system were firmly established by V. I. Lenin and his lieutenants.

Although, in his final months of life, Lenin may have had some regrets concerning the direction that the Soviet Union and the CPSU had taken under his leadership, everything that Lenin did during these formative years was consistent with the theoretical approach that he had formulated prior to the takeover in 1917. The ends—the advancement of the historical process—justified any means utilized in pursuit of that goal. Lenin's goal had been to make and consolidate a revolution in Russia led exclusively by the Communist Party. With enormous determination and ruthlessness, Lenin had succeeded in attaining his objective.

—Howard M. Hensel

See also Communism; Marx, Karl; Marxism; Socialism; Stalin, Joseph.

BIBLIOGRAPHY

Chamberlin, William H. *The Russian Revolution 1917-1921.* 2 vols. New York: Grosset & Dunlap, 1965.

Daniels, Robert V. *The Conscience of the Revolution.* New York: Simon & Schuster, 1969.

Fischer, Louis. *The Life of Lenin.* New York: Harper & Row, 1964.

Lenin, Vladimir Il'ich. *Lenin on Politics and Revolution.* Edited by James E. Connor. New York: Pegasus, 1968.

Meyer, Alfred G. *Leninism.* New York: Praeger, 1962.

Schapiro, Leonard. *The Origin of the Communist Autocracy.* 2d ed. Cambridge, Mass.: Harvard University Press, 1977.

Leopold, Aldo (Jan. 11, 1887, Burlington, Iowa—Apr. 21, 1948, near Baraboo, Wis.): Scientist, writer

TYPE OF ETHICS: Environmental ethics

ACHIEVEMENTS: Caused first U.S. Wilderness Area to be established; wrote *A Sand County Almanac* (1949)

SIGNIFICANCE: Formally stated the "Land Ethic," which placed humanity within, rather than in charge of, the ecosystem

Aldo Leopold's boyhood was dominated by sports and natural history. After completing one year of postgraduate work in forestry at Yale, Leopold spent fifteen years with the U.S. Forest Service in Arizona and New Mexico. There, he developed the idea of preserving large, ecologically undisturbed areas for ecological preservation; in 1924, he precipitated the establishment of the first U.S. forest Wilderness Area in the Gila National Forest of New Mexico. In 1933, he became professor of wildlife management at the University of Wisconsin. He was a founder of the Wilderness Society in 1935, and in 1934 he became a member of the federal Special Committee on Wildlife Restoration. Leopold made a family project of restoring the ecosystem to its original condition on an abandoned farm he had purchased near Baraboo, Wisconsin. His posthumous publication relating to this experience, *A Sand County Almanac,* has become an environmentalist classic, and the farm has become a research center, the Leopold Reserve. Four of Leopold's five children became prominent, environ-

mentally oriented scientists. Three of them, Starker, Luna, and Estella, became members of the National Academy of Sciences. His son Carl became an established research scientist, and his daughter Nina became director of the Leopold Reserve.

See also Ecology; Environmental movement; Wilderness Act of 1964.

Leviathan: Book

TYPE OF ETHICS: Enlightenment history

DATE: Published 1651 as *Leviathan: Or, the Matter, Form, and Power of a Commonwealth, Ecclesiastical and Civil*

AUTHOR: Thomas Hobbes

SIGNIFICANCE: This political philosophical work incorporated a rational, systematic study and justification of natural rights, sovereignty, and state absolutism, and logically deduced an ethical political theory from a scientific and mathematical investigation of human nature

The moral language utilized by Hobbes in his *Leviathan* was expressed by the precise vocabulary of geometry, empirical science, and physics. The mathematical and scientific study of politics adopted by Hobbes did not incorporate a value-free or ethically neutral perspective. Hobbes's political ethical theory was grounded in a causal-mechanical and materialistic metaphysical theory. Hobbes's mechanistic scientific model was explanatory of all existence, since the universe consisted of interconnected matter in motion. This complex political theory and set of ethical arguments were deduced from Hobbes's pessimistic interpretation of human nature in the context of an original, or primitive, condition. It was in this highly unstable, anarchic, and violent state of nature that individuals competitively pursued their self-interests. Hobbes depicted with bleak realism "the life of man solitary, poor, nasty, brutish, and short." The political ethics in *Leviathan* were justified primarily by the natural human egoistic motivation of fear of violent death, and secondarily by the passions for power and material possessions. Therefore, self-preservation was the most fundamental natural right and was the central reason for individuals to leave the state of nature and enter into commonwealths. Hobbes's articulation of the normative egalitarian principle of universal natural rights was expressed in conjunction with his radical rejection of the principle of the divine right of kings. Hobbes's rejection of moral objectivism was articulated in conjunction with his moral relativism, which claimed that the diverse corporeal natures of individuals were explanatory of the multiplicity of value judgments. Moral judgments were identified by a particular individual's appetites and aversions, or mechanical movements toward or away from material objects. There was no *summum bonum,* or universal absolute common good, although the common evil to be avoided was violent death.

Hobbes expressed a political theory of authority that was justified by means of scientific, rational, and logical arguments, in lieu of traditional theories of political legitimacy based upon convention, theology, or the divine right of kings. Citizens of Hobbes's prescribed commonwealth were bound by a social contract or by the superior power of the sovereign to obey all the government's commands, regardless of the moral content of such commands or the intention of the sovereign. Hobbes's core assumption of the natural insecurity of human life was linked to his prescription of an absolute monarchy or a highly centralized parliamentary body as the most desirable form of government.

See also Hobbes, Thomas; Locke, John; Machiavelli, Niccolò; Machiavellian ethics; Social contract; *Two Treatises of Government.*

Libel

TYPE OF ETHICS: Media ethics
DATE: Coined 1631
DEFINITION: The defamation of a person or group by means of writing or visual images
SIGNIFICANCE: Libel is a rare exception to the legal protection of freedom of speech in the United States, a freedom that many ethicists consider essential for democracy and ethical government

Libel is often confused with slander, which is oral defamation rather than written or visual defamation. One's good reputation is usually among one's most valuable possessions. Since libel, by definition, damages the reputation of another, it does serious harm and thus is clearly unethical. Criminal libel is the malicious publishing of durable defamation. In common law and under most modern criminal statutes, criminal libel is a misdemeanor (an infraction usually punishable by a year or less in prison) rather than a felony (a more serious infraction punishable by more than a year in prison). Libel is also a tort, a noncontractual and noncriminal wrongdoing. Libel is thus grounds for a civil lawsuit in which one may seek to recover money to compensate for the damage that the libel has caused to one's reputation. Truth, however, is a defense against libel, and even if the damage is caused by a false claim, if the damaged person is a public figure, then one must show malice (intent to harm) or a reckless disregard for the truth in order to prove libel. Honest mistakes do not constitute libel against public figures. (Civil lawsuits against libel and punishment for criminal libel are both limited by the First Amendment of the Constitution.) This was the upshot of the landmark Supreme Court case *New York Times Co. v. Sullivan* (1964) and its progeny. This landmark case was designed to preserve the vigor and variety of public debate in a democracy, balancing democracy against serious harms to reputations in order to avoid a chilling effect on the exercise of the constitutional right of free speech.

See also Lying.

Liberalism

TYPE OF ETHICS: Modern history
DATE: Coined early nineteenth century
ASSOCIATED WITH: Anglo-American and continental European social theorists and organized political parties, or factions thereof, in Britain, the United States, and Western Europe
DEFINITION: While not a systematic ideology, liberalism is a progressive attitude toward social change that has historically been characterized by the gradual abolition of privilege and the extension of liberty for individuals and, subsequently, for groups
SIGNIFICANCE: Liberalism implies a generosity of spirit, liberality of sentiment, and attitude of tolerance that value individual differences and human dignity. It places primacy on the individual as opposed to the state

The combination of ideas about humankind and society that is associated with modern liberalism evolved over time. Some characteristics associated with the concept may be traced as far back as ancient Greece. Among these are an emphasis on human dignity and a confidence in reason as a mechanism to improve the human condition. Other qualities subsequently associated with liberalism first appeared in the Middle Ages. Such is the case with the central component of liberalism, the concept of liberty. Contrary to current usage, a liberty originally signified a privilege or distinction provided those belonging to a defined group. The thirteenth century English document Magna Carta, for example, refers to the liberties of the barons, the liberties of the church, and the liberties of the City of London. These feudal liberties were exclusive privileges restricted to specific social orders. Liberty, then, was associated with a corporate order of society. The emergence of modern liberalism involved the transformation of plural, exclusive liberties into an all-embracing liberty that was applied equally to all individuals, a process generally considered to have commenced in seventeenth century England.

While the word derived from the Spanish *Liberales,* an early-nineteenth-century constitutionalist party that opposed royal absolutism, liberalism is associated in a broader sense with a school of thought initiated by John Locke that incorporated a complex of attitudes toward humanity and society. Just as late-seventeenth-century scientists thought the universe to be composed of interconnected atoms, Locke and his successors had an atomistic conception of society in which the fundamental unit was the individual. These individuals were assumed to be rational creatures, their decision to establish government and society being the result of their enlightened self-interest, as represented in Locke's *Second Treatise of Government* (1690). Therefore, the public interest or the interest of society was identical with the private interests of the individuals who composed it. The individual came first in time and importance, society and government deriving from the agreement of individuals. This view of society was also ahistorical, and liberalism in its formative stages placed little value on history or on the organic development of social institutions.

The basic tenets of liberalism as developed in the eighteenth century found expression in the American Declaration of Independence and the French Declaration of the Rights of Man and the Citizen.

The atomistic and ahistorical conception of society was subscribed to by those eighteenth and early nineteenth-century figures who are generally included in the liberal school of thought. Adam Smith applied this conception of society to economic relations. He argued that the wealth of the nation was the sum total of the wealth of the individuals constituting it. Since these individuals were rational creatures and knew which lines of business to follow, Smith and his disciples argued that government should refrain from the regulation of business activity. This emphasis on laissez-faire, the absence of governmental regulation, became a principal component of liberalism in its classical form, as was its corollary, free trade.

strictly associated with constitutional government and established procedures of due process. Liberalism, moreover, was compatible with elitism. Hence there was a liberal element among the English aristocracy, principally in the Whig party. Many of those leaders valued the extension of liberty within a traditional hierarchical order. Such aristocrats emphasized a generosity of spirit and liberality of sentiment while maintaining aristocratic ascendancy, as is evident in their arguments for the abolition of the slave trade and slavery, a moderate extension of suffrage, and the abolition of restrictions

President Franklin Delano Roosevelt was known for his liberal New Deal policies. (Courtesy of FDR Library)

Classical liberalism of the early nineteenth century, then, emphasized limited government. So long as the individual, fundamentally free and rational, was unhampered by governmental regulation, he could fulfill his potential. This attitude accorded with an older assumption that arbitrary government constituted the principal danger to liberty. In England, arbitrary government had been associated historically with the prerogative powers of the crown, and in both England and the United States, limits placed on executive power were for a time considered essential to the preservation of liberty. Although liberalism was compatible with emerging democracy, it long preceded it and was more

on the press and of infringements on religious liberty.

Utilitarianism, a variety of liberalism associated with Jeremy Bentham and his followers, characteristically conceived of society as simply the sum total of the individuals in it. The utilitarian principle of the greatest happiness for the greatest number was at first construed as requiring the abolition of governmental regulations. As society was vastly transformed by the process of industrialization, however, the greatest happiness for the greatest number appeared to many people to require governmental intervention.

Liberalism was gradually transformed from the mid-nineteenth century. Such figures as John Stuart Mill recognized the organic nature of society. Moreover, the liberal school of thought from Mill through L. T. Hobhouse in the early twentieth century gradually recognized the need for the abandonment of laissez-faire and increased state intervention to redress the inequities of an increasingly industrialized society. While still valuing the individual, modern liberalism had an increasingly collectivist element. Liberals began to advocate, along with civil, religious, and political liberty, measures of social justice. The legislation of England's Liberal government before World War I was no longer confined to removing infringements on individual liberty or even regulating the conditions of labor. It involved financial support through taxation of a national insurance or social security program that after World War II led to the emergence of the welfare state. A corresponding, if less extensive, development occurred in the United States, beginning in the Progressive Era and culminating in the New Deal, which established a program of active governmental involvement to fund programs designed to provide a modicum of security and opportunity to the disadvantaged. In the late twentieth century, American liberalism experienced tension between the principle of individualism and a newer inclination to empower traditionally deprived social groups.

—Abraham D. Kriegel

See also Bentham, Jeremy; Due process; Elitism; Freedom and liberty; Individualism; Libertarianism; Mill, John Stuart; *On Liberty*; Political liberty; Social justice and responsibility; *Two Treatises of Government*; Utilitarianism.

BIBLIOGRAPHY

Bullock, Alan, and Maurice Schock, eds. *The Liberal Tradition: From Fox to Keynes.* London: A & C Black, 1956.

De Ruggiero, Guido. *The History of European Liberalism.* Translated by R. G. Collingwood. Boston: Beacon Press, 1959.

Gray, John. *Liberalism.* Minneapolis: University of Minnesota Press, 1986.

Hartz, Louis. *The Liberal Tradition in America: An Interpretation of American Political Thought Since the Revolution.* New York: Harcourt Brace, 1955.

Hobhouse, L. T. *Liberalism.* New York: Henry Holt, 1911.

Libertarianism

TYPE OF ETHICS: Theory of ethics
DATE: Twentieth century
ASSOCIATED WITH: Free enterprise, individualism, and anarchism
DEFINITION: A political movement based on the idea that the defense of liberty requires either a severely limited government or no government
SIGNIFICANCE: Holds that individual autonomy is the fundamental social principle

The libertarian movement consists of a diverse group of individuals who are united in the view that any social or political institution is wrong if it interferes with individuals' control over their own lives. Libertarians defend property rights, the free-market economy, and the full range of civil freedoms, including the rights to abortion, freedom of speech and the press, sexual freedom, and the use of drugs and alcohol.

Libertarianism should be placed on the political spectrum in contrast to conservatism, modern liberalism, and totalitarianism. Conservatives are generally in favor of more economic freedoms but fewer civil freedoms; conservatives typically favor antiabortion, antidrug, antisodomy, and some censorship laws. Modern liberals are generally in favor of more civil freedoms but fewer economic freedoms; modern liberals typically favor compulsory wealth-redistribution schemes and increased regulation of business. Totalitarians eject liberty in the economic and civil realms. In contrast to these three major political movements, libertarians claim to advocate both civil and economic liberty consistently.

History. Libertarian theory has roots in the history of modern political and economic thought. It draws on elements of the classical liberal tradition in politics, as exemplified in such thinkers as John Locke (1632-1704). Some libertarians emphasize classical liberalism's contractarian tradition, while others emphasize its natural rights tradition. Contemporary philosophers Robert Nozick and John Hospers are representative of these positions. Libertarianism also draws upon the anarchist tradition of the nineteenth century. Murray Rothbard, usually acknowledged as the founder of contemporary libertarianism, is a major representative of this tradition. In economics, libertarianism has drawn inspiration from the "Austrian" school of economics, most notably from the work of Ludwig von Mises (1881-1973) and Nobel laureate F. A. Hayek, and from the "Chicago" school of economics, most notably from the work of Nobel laureates Milton Friedman and James Buchanan.

Justifications of Liberty. Libertarians disagree among themselves about how to justify the claim that liberty is the fundamental social value. Some believe that political liberty is an axiom: The value of liberty is self-evident and therefore not in need of justification. Most libertarians, however, offer arguments for liberty.

The most common argument starts with the premise that values are subjective. No individual's values are more right than any other's. The only universal points that can be made about values is that individuals have them, and in order to pursue their values, individuals need to be free of coercion by other individuals. Consequently, the only universal social principle is that the initiation of the use of force by one individual against another is wrong.

Other libertarians justify liberty via social contract arguments. Supposing a Hobbesian or Lockean state of nature, contractarians argue that rational individuals with conflicting interests would agree upon a set of legal constraints that would limit each individual's liberties only to the extent necessary to leave all other individuals at liberty. Therefore, rational individuals would voluntarily contract to institutionalize in their society the broad principle that the initiation of force is wrong.

A third group of libertarians justifies liberty by first arguing for universal and objective moral principles. Appealing to Aristotelian self-realization teleology, Lockean natural rights, or Kantian duties to treat others as ends in themselves, such libertarians derive the conclusions that using force against individuals is immoral and, accordingly, that only political liberty is compatible with their broader moral framework.

As much as these proposed justifications of liberty differ, all libertarians reach the same conclusion: Individuals must be left free to do what they wish with their own lives and property.

Role of the State. Libertarians also disagree among themselves about the extent of the role of the state in promoting liberty. The state is a coercive institution, and states have regularly used their coercive power to violate individuals' liberties through arbitrary laws, the sanctioning of various forms of slavery, compulsory taxation, compulsory military drafts, and so on. Reacting to these facts, libertarians fall into two major groups. One group, the anarchists, argues that the state is an inherently evil institution that should be abolished. The other major group, the "minarchists," allows that the state can play a limited role in promoting liberty. Minarchist libertarians are divided into two subgroups. Some minarchists agree with the anarchists that the state is an evil, but unlike the anarchists they believe it to be a necessary evil: The state can be valuable in protecting the liberties of some individuals, but this value must be balanced against the inevitable abuses of the state's coercive power to violate individuals' liberties.

Other minarchists argue that the state is an inherently good institution, as long as its coercive power is constitutionally limited to defensive purposes and these limits are enforced strictly. In either case, minarchist libertarians agree that the state's functions should not extend beyond basic police, military, and judicial functions, and that these functions should be funded through voluntary mechanisms, not compulsory taxation. Anarchist libertarians reject any role for the state and argue that even the minarchist state functions can and should be supplied by private, voluntary protection agencies.

In the political realm, however, libertarians agree that they can set aside foundational disputes about the justification of liberty and the scope of the state in order to work together for a goal on which they do agree: the reduction of the current scope of the state.   —*Stephen R. C. Hicks*

See also Conservatism; Liberalism; Social contract.

BIBLIOGRAPHY

Lomasky, Loren. *Persons, Rights, and the Moral Community*. New York: Oxford University Press, 1987.

Machan, Tibor, ed. *The Libertarian Reader*. Totowa, N.J.: Rowman & Littlefield, 1982.

Nozick, Robert. *Anarchy, State, and Utopia*. New York: Basic Books, 1974.

Rasmussen, Douglas, and Douglas den Uyl. *Liberty and Nature: An Aristotelian Defense of Natural Order*. LaSalle, Ill.: Open Court, 1991.

Rothbard, Murray. *For a New Liberty: The Libertarian Manifesto*. Rev. ed. New York: Collier, 1978.

Von Mises, Ludwig. *Liberalism: A Socio-Economic Exposition*. Edited by Arthur Goddard. Translated by Ralph Raico. Mission, Kans.: Sheed Andrews & McMeel, 1978.

Library Bill of Rights

TYPE OF ETHICS: Arts and censorship

DATE: Adopted June 18, 1948

ASSOCIATED WITH: The American Library Association (ALA) and the ALA Committee on Intellectual Freedom

DEFINITION: A document that outlines six basic policies that all United States libraries should use to guide the acquisition and availability of materials, and to guard against censorship

SIGNIFICANCE: Serves to prevent attempts at censorship in libraries; protects the rights of all citizens in the use of library materials

The original text of the Library Bill of Rights was drawn up by Forrest Spaulding. It was adopted for the American Library Association at the ALA Council in San Francisco in 1939. Subsequently, the ALA Committee on Intellectual Freedom was established to recommend any steps necessary to protect the rights of library users in accordance with the Bill of Rights of the United States and the Library Bill of Rights. Through discussion and approved emendation by members of the ALA Committee on Intellectual Freedom and by the membership of the ALA, the document was adopted on June 18, 1948, and amended in 1961, 1967, and 1980. The six basic policies that make up the Library Bill of Rights are summarized as follows: (1) library materials should be chosen for the interest and enlightenment of all people in the community; (2) libraries should provide materials that represent all points of view on issues and concerns; (3) censorship should be challenged; (4) libraries should cooperate with those concerned with resisting freedom of expression and free access to ideas; (5) rights of individuals to use libraries are not dependent on "race, religion, national origins, or political views"; and (6) meeting rooms of libraries should be available to community groups regardless of the beliefs and affiliations of their members, provided that the meetings are open to the public.

See also Book banning; Censorship.

Life, meaning of

TYPE OF ETHICS: Personal and social ethics

DATE: Fifth century B.C.E. to present

DEFINITION: Attempts to find a purpose for or to place an ultimate value on an individual human life

SIGNIFICANCE: Questions about the meaning of life are fundamental and pervasive concerns in our society; consequently, they are used to categorize and differentiate ethical views

Albert Camus' *The Myth of Sisyphus* (1942) opens with this claim: "There is but one truly serious philosophical problem, and that is suicide." According to Camus, judging whether life is worth living represents the most basic of all philosophical problems. Questions about the meaning of one's life are by no means confined to philosophers. Indeed, wondering why one is here and whether anything will come from what one is doing are familiar and pervasive activities. Ethicists offer a variety of responses ranging from the religious ("God provides a meaning for life and everything else"), to the existentialist ("I can give my life meaning"), to the nihilist ("There is no ultimate meaning to life or anything").

The Meaning of the Question. As with many philosophical inquiries, it is worthwhile to clarify the meaning of the question being asked: "What is the meaning of life?" It is easy to imagine such a question being asked by a severely depressed individual seeking psychological counseling or guidance, but this is not the context for the philosopher's concern.

The philosopher (or any reflective individual) comes to inquire about the meaning of life as a natural consequence of being self-conscious and rational. As people mature, they learn to make observations, generalize, offer explanations and predictions, and so on. Being rational means looking for explanations in terms of rules, principles, and theories, which are established by reason and by empirical methodologies. Being self-conscious involves awareness of one's rationality. Once one becomes aware of one's own rational nature and outlook, it is tempting to turn that rational outlook inward and seek an answer to the question "Why am I here?" in much the same way that one seeks an answer to the question "Why is that mountain here?" Another way of expressing the philosopher's question, then, is as follows: "Why am I self-conscious? What is the purpose of my self-awareness?"

This interpretation of the question about the meaning of life can be represented as "What is the meaning of my life?" Other questions about the meaning of life could focus on all life, or all animal life, or selected groups of human life, or all intelligent life, and so on. The philosophical question about the meaning of life, however, focuses on the meaning of an individual human life.

The reflective inquirer recognizes this principle: When one is wondering about the meaning of life, the most one can legitimately wonder about is the meaning of one's own life. One is not in a position to know the meaning of another person's life or to place a value on another's life.

Transcendental Responses. There are two sorts of responses to the question about the meaning of an individual's life. One sort of response seeks an answer in something transcendental, or beyond this world. By far the most prevalent views of this sort are religious, and they are too numerous and varied to review here. Some nonreligious, mystical views about the meaning of life also invoke a transcendental and nonrational reality.

Transcendental explanations are not satisfying to skeptics, who ask for direct and obvious evidence of nonevident re-

alities. The transcendental view that the meaning of an individual life (along with the sense of the whole universe) must lie outside the universe is subject to Ludwig Wittgenstein's criticism in *Tractatus Logico-Philosophicus* (1921) that things that are claimed by their very nature to be beyond the experiences of this world are among the things about which we are incapable of clear and meaningful discourse: "What we cannot speak about we must pass over in silence."

Nontranscendental Responses. There are responses to the question about the meaning of life that do not ultimately rely on appeals to transcendental realities. In addition, there are a variety of types of nontranscendental responses. For example, positivists argue that the meaning of life is a question without an answer, because potential answers are not subject to independent verification or refutation; as a consequence, the meaning of life must remain a permanent mystery. Hedonists argue that the meaning of life is determined by the pleasures enjoyed in this life. Nihilists argue that there are no enduring values of any kind, no sense to anything, including one's own life; they often cite the prevalence of natural disasters, wars, and pettiness as evidence supporting their own view. While these responses differ widely, they share a common emphasis on the evidence of this world as that which determines what, if any, meaning attaches to life.

The most prevalent philosophical view of this type traces its history from Socrates in ancient Greece to Jean-Paul Sartre and other modern existentialists. What existentialists have in common is an emphasis on the actions of an individual in this world as the primary determinant of the meaning of that individual's life. Existentialists generally believe that how one lives one's life shows what one thinks of oneself. Because existentialists emphasize individual choices and human actions, their views are categorized as generally nontranscendental, although many existentialists accept the existence of transcendental realities.

The Example of Socrates. The life of Socrates is often cited as an early example of existentialism. Most of what is commonly believed about the life and death of Socrates can be traced to four Platonic dialogues: *Euthyphro*, *Apology*, *Crito*, and *Phaedo* (for example, see Romano Guardini's *The Death of Socrates*, 1970). In the *Euthyphro*, Socrates is shown inquiring into the nature of piety. The situation is that the elder Socrates meets the youth Euthyphro at the city courthouse. Socrates is there to respond to charges of impiety and corruption of youth. Euthyphro, who is there to file questionable murder charges against his father, claims to understand the true nature of piety. Socrates' subsequent examination of Euthyphro's exaggerated claim is filled with irony and can be viewed as illustrating the character of Socrates as well as the general nature of Socratic inquiry. Socrates shows each of Euthyphro's definitions of piety to be deficient or confused, yet Euthyphro persists in his naïve belief that whatever is pleasing to the gods is holy and presumably proceeds to press charges against his father.

The *Apology* recounts the trial of Socrates. More of Socrates' irony and sharp wit are revealed, as Socrates mocks his politically powerful accusers while offering carefully reasoned defenses against each of the charges. Socrates is found guilty by a narrow majority of the 500 judges and is offered the opportunity to suggest an alternative to the death penalty proposed by the accusers. Socrates facetiously considers a series of alternative penalties, ranging from public support for his inquiries to a very minor fine, taking the opportunity once again to ridicule accusers and judges. Socrates is sentenced to death and takes the opportunity to make a final speech in which he repeats his faith in the divine voice that warns him of exaggerations and other wrongs, imagines an afterlife filled with interrogations of ancient heroes, and asks his friends to punish his sons if they claim to know things that they do not know.

The *Crito* depicts Socrates' brief stay in jail awaiting execution. Socrates refuses opportunities to escape as inconsistent with his beliefs and continues to make philosophical inquiries about the nature of justice and other issues. The death scene is depicted in the *Phaedo*. On the day that Socrates is given the poison hemlock, he is visited by a group of friends, and they discuss the meaning of life and death. Socrates' dying words to his friend Crito were: "I owe a debt to Asclepius [the Greek god of healing]; do not forget to pay it."

The Socrates that emerges from these dialogues is an individual entirely dedicated to a search for truth (especially with regard to ethical matters), determined to expose popular views as exaggerated and confused, capable of great irony and insight, and subject to the divine guidance of an inner voice. Socrates clearly reflects the basic existentialist outlook in the *Crito*: What one does shows what kind of person one is. Socrates is not the kind of person who acts against his beliefs and breaks the laws. The existentialist credo found in Socrates can be stated as follows: One's life shows what one thinks of oneself. Socrates urges everyone to think highly of themselves.

The Problem of Socrates. Socrates presents challenges to traditional views about justice, piety, and goodness but offers no positive account of his own about these ethical concerns other than the example of his own life. Yet Socrates' life is essentially unique—Socrates hears and obeys a divine inner voice. Socrates cannot say, "Be like me; get an inner voice." Socrates can give no account of his divine voice, and even he regards the fact that he hears this voice as mysterious.

In Friedrich Nietzsche's *Twilight of the Idols* (1889), another problem with Socrates is elaborated. On most ethical matters Socrates remained an inquiring skeptic, yet with regard to the value of life, Socrates became dogmatic, as best reflected in his dying judgment that life is worthless: "To live—that means to be sick a long time; I owe a debt to Asclepius, the savior." Nietzsche argues that the value of life can be estimated or judged neither by the living, for

they constitute an interested and biased party, nor by the dead, because they are not talking. Therefore, Nietzsche argues, the problem of determining the meaning of life is a problem of will, not one of reason.

The Existentialist View. The existentialist view is that each individual is responsible for beliefs held and actions selected, including whether to regard Socrates as a heroic seeker of truth, an eccentric teacher, or a corrupter of youth. Jean-Paul Sartre's *Existentialism* (1946) presents a clear explication of the fundamental tenets of existentialism, including the following: human existence precedes essence; subjectivity must be the starting point of any inquiry; some freedom of action exists; and in choosing who one becomes as an individual, one is choosing how to regard humanity. Part of the human condition is the predicament of choice—choosing one's emerging character. Sartre's existentialism carries a two-sided message: One has *freedom* and a *burden* of choice with regard to the kind of person one chooses to become. Sartre's advice is not unlike that of Socrates: Think highly of yourself. Of course, the existentialist leaves the specific interpretation of the word "highly" in the phrase "think highly" to the individual.

A recurrent theme in existentialist writings is that individuals can give meaning to their lives. While it is not possible to state precisely the particular meaning of an individual's life, it is possible to suggest what meaning an individual gave to life by an elaborate tale or story, as found in novels, for example. Indeed, the novels of Jean-Paul Sartre and Albert Camus are often cited as examples of existentialist literature, as are the works of Fyodor Dostoevski and Leo Tolstoy.

This existentialist notion that certain things (such as how one values life) show themselves or make themselves manifest is consistent with the positivist critique of ethical language as meaningless. Ludwig Wittgenstein's *Tractatus Logico-Philosophicus* makes this distinction explicit: there are things that cannot be put into words, these things make themselves manifest, and an example of something that makes itself manifest is "There are laws of nature" [ironically put in words].

The results of positivist attacks on ethical language include an eruption of all kinds of artistic endeavors meant to illustrate existentialist notions about enduring the human condition, choosing in the face of an absurd existence, accepting the responsibilities of choice, and so on. As a consequence, there now exists a substantial body of existentialist literature, philosophy, and art, which makes this area of philosophical inquiry unique in its multidisciplinary approach to the question of what it means to be a person. The appeal of an existentialist outlook is partly the focus on one's entire life rather than on a specific aspect of life such as one's physical attributes or intellectual abilities.

Existentialists typically place great emphasis on human choice and action, shifting the focus of the question about the meaning of life from reason to will. Existentialists would accept the usefulness of high-sounding ethical pronouncements (such as "The unexamined life is not worth living" or "To thine own self be true") but would argue that how one chooses to live in accordance with those and other maxims is the crucial issue—not the maxims themselves.

An existentialist ethical view might be encapsulated in words such as these: Become a voice that comforts and encourages, a hand that guides and assists, an eye that sees and reflects, a face that does not turn away, a person whose life shows what a person can become. Ultimately, however, it is not the words that matter. What matters is the comforting, encouraging, guiding, assisting, and so on.

In summary, there are two basic ways to understand questions about the meaning of life. One can think of the meaning of life in terms of what God can make it or in terms of what one can make it oneself.   —*J. Michael Spector*

See also Camus, Albert; Character; Existentialism; Platonic ethics; Sartre, Jean-Paul; Socrates; Will.

BIBLIOGRAPHY

Camus, Albert. *The Myth of Sisyphus and Other Essays*. Translated by Justin O'Brien. New York: Knopf, 1955. A persuasively written argument against suicide and nihilism, and a powerful expression of the existentialist belief that individuals can give their lives meaning.

Fabry, Joseph B. *The Pursuit of Meaning*. Boston: Beacon Press, 1968. A clear explication of logotherapy, a psychological theory that takes philosophical questions about the meaning of life seriously by conceiving of individual answers as a form of therapy.

Guardini, Romano. *The Death of Socrates: An Interpretation of the Platonic Dialogues: Euthyphro, Apology, Crito and Phaedo*. Translated by Basil Wrighton. Cleveland: World Publishing, 1967. This volume presents a translation of the four Platonic dialogues that deal with the death of Socrates, along with a running commentary and interpretation.

James, William. *The Varieties of Religious Experience*. London: Collins, 1968. This classic by one of America's most noted pragmatists represents the rich variety of religious practices and contains insightful discussions about religious views of the meaning of life.

Nietzsche, Friedrich. *Twilight of the Idols*. Translated by R. J. Hollingdale. Harmondsworth: Penguin Books, 1968. A critical analysis of the lives of Socrates and Christ as well as an attack on dogmatic attitudes about causality and free will.

Sartre, Jean-Paul. *Existentialism*. Translated by Bernard Frechtman. New York: Philosophical Library, 1947. A clear and concise statement of the primary tenets of existentialism.

Wittgenstein, Ludwig. *Tractatus Logico-Philosophicus*. Translated by D. F. Pears & B. F. McGuinness. London: Routledge & Kegan Paul, 1974. A carefully reasoned explanation of the limits of language, with implications for the inexpressibility of major ethical concerns including the meaning of life.

Life and death

TYPE OF ETHICS: Bioethics

DEFINITION: Life is what enables an entity to sustain a connection with its past and present while developing a future; death is the cessation of life; there is no universally acceptable definition of either life or death

SIGNIFICANCE: All ethical decisions are ultimately concerned with life and death. Decisions in business ethics result in sustaining human life through food, clothing, and housing. Definitions of life in bioethics determine the cost of health care as well as when and if to transplant organs. Definitions of life and death determine the beginning and the end of legal, ethical, economic, and personal obligations.

Since humans do the defining, all life is defined from the standpoint of human life. Definitions of life reflect the complexity of human life and the various cultural contexts within which the definitions are sought. Definitions of life and death therefore symbolize the concerns of the individuals seeking a definition as well as the culture that supports their search.

Definitions of life and death not only manifest the values and concerns of individuals and society but also determine who lives in that society. If a definition of death, for example, focuses on the irreversible loss of consciousness, then those who have irreversibly lost consciousness are no longer part of that human society because they are no longer considered human. If a definition of human life makes the possession of human DNA equal to being human, then every organism with human DNA is part of that human society.

Definitions also focus on one aspect of our existence rather than another. The word "death," for example, may refer to dying, the death event, or the time after the moment of death. A person who says "I am afraid of death" usually means that he or she fears dying. Others, who say they look forward to death, usually mean an afterlife. Today, many people use "death" as it is used in this entry to refer to the point at which a living entity changes from a living to a nonliving state.

The focus of modern Western society is on the biological nature of life and death; therefore, its ethical concern is with the biological aspects of life and death. This concern will be the focus of this article.

Society Must Define and Redefine Life and Death. No society can exist without explicit or implicit definitions of life and death. People must know when someone is dead. Without such knowledge, wills could not be probated, burial could not take place, leadership positions in business and politics could not be clearly defined, and life-support systems could not be removed. Without clear definitions of human life and death, one would consider a thing (a cadaver) to be a human person. To treat things as human is not only an intellectual error but also an ethical one.

Western society has had, and still does in many situations, both implicit and explicit definitions of life and death. A person who steps off a curb and is run over by a truck is alive when he or she steps off the curb and dead afterward.

One can point to a living person before the event and a corpse after the event. One "knows" both life and death in this situation. Since people need official recognition of what they know intuitively, common law developed a definition of death. In common law, death as the cessation of life is determined by "a total stoppage of the circulation of the blood." People's intuitive judgment and society's legal definition were adequate until modern technologies altered the ability to extend life. In modern industrial societies, acute death, such as occurs in a truck accident, does not happen often. Most people die slowly, die old, and balance on the edge of death for a long time. The end of life today more properly may be described as "living-dying," because it is an extensive period of time during which individuals know that they will die and usually act differently in the light of this knowledge. This "living-dying" phase of life results in experiences and relationships that never have been dealt with in cultures that do not possess the technological ability to produce such a phase of life. This phase is not present when one is run over by a truck: one moment one is alive, the next one is dead.

Things are different today not only for those in the "living-dying" phase of their life but also for those who are "patients"—those who are ill but will probably get better. A significant number of patients will recover only if they receive a living human organ to replace one of their dead ones. The ability to transplant organs such as the heart, liver, and lungs leads modern society to deal with life and death in a different way. This ability produces a culture whose new definitions of death challenge the human view of life and ultimately determine who is human and who is not.

Redefining Life and Death. Since death is basically the cessation of life, a definition of death is also a definition of life. If one examines the corpse of an individual run over by a truck, one might notice that, although the person is dead, some parts of her or him are still alive. The heart may be beating and thus may be alive. The hair, fingernails, and many cells are also alive. If someone who was unaware of the person's death examined these human parts, that person would not know whether they came from a live human or a dead human. It could be said, therefore, that human death is a process in which it takes a long time for everything human to die. Yet society treats human death as an event. The laws and customs surrounding dying and death seek to mark a point before which the person is alive and after which the person is dead. Obviously, something more than cellular death is needed to indicate when a person is dead.

A medical doctor declares a person dead based on certain criteria. Contemporary criteria are the result of centuries of experience. A doctor who declares someone dead is saying that experience has shown that when certain criteria are fulfilled, this dead human will never again be a living human.

Commonsense observations that the person was dead in the truck accident are officially confirmed by someone who has the authority to do so, and after that confirmation has been made, people begin to then treat the corpse in a different way.

For most of human history, commonsense observation was the only way to tell the difference between life and death. Part of that observation involved determining whether the person was breathing or not and whether his or her blood was flowing. The breath and the flow of blood were considered the criteria for life and death. Blood and breath, or spirit, are still central to many cultures' views of life. Commonsense observation told people that when their breath was gone, their life was gone. Common sense also demonstrated that if one lost a large quantity of blood, one's breathing stopped and one was dead. Certainly, human life was not only blood and breath, but without blood and breath one was not human.

The history of science has also been the history of challenging commonsense observations. The discovery of the human circulatory system and the invention of the stethoscope were challenges to commonsense observation. The discovery of the way in which the blood circulates demonstrated that when the heart stops pumping, there is effectively no blood; when the lungs stop functioning, there is no more breath. Commonsense observations were augmented by new scientific discoveries and inventions that showed that the previous criteria were ways of knowing that certain essential organs were dead. These criteria now were linked with certain places of death, such as the heart and/or lungs. People now believed that once these organs were dead, a corpse would never again be human.

Commonsense observation might lead one to believe that the lungs and the heart are not moving, whereas a stethoscope might indicate that they are. One no longer had to use a mirror held to a person's nose to know whether breathing had stopped; one did not have to see the loss of blood to know that the heart had stopped. The heart could stop for other reasons and still be dead. One could hear whether it was making noise and was alive. One could listen to the lungs to hear whether there was breath; if not, the person was considered dead. With the advent of the stethoscope, technology began to augment, and sometimes contradict, commonsense observations.

Modern technologies continue to augment and to defy commonsense observations, but the sequence of determining a death is the same: Certain criteria indicate that part of the human is dead; experience has shown that once these criteria are fulfilled, that person will never be alive again.

Because humans developed the ability to keep the heart and lungs alive, former commonsense observations about death were challenged. Many investigators were led to conclude that if the brain were dead, the human would never again be alive. Since for most of human history the life of the organs was identical with the life of the human organism, the challenge of developing new criteria included determining new definitions of death, such as those that focused on the brain.

The meaning and definition of life was always a concern for philosophers and theologians. Scientists usually viewed these definitions as too abstract for scientific investigation because they could not be quantified and subjected to experimentation. To many biologists, it made no difference whether they were operating on a human heart or a pig's heart. A muscle was a muscle. A primary model for many scientists working with human anatomy is that of the machine. They speak of human parts in the same way that a mechanic would speak of automobile parts. The realization that these parts form a conscious, willing, and loving machine is of little consequence to scientists using this model. This model's implicit definition of life seems to be that human life is equal to the efficient operation of the parts, which is indicated by the flow of blood and breath. Death occurs when there is an irreversible stopping of blood and breath; that is, when one of the parts no longer functions, the machine is dead.

When one views the human being from a perspective other than that of the machine model, one arrives at different definitions. Robert Veatch, in *Death, Dying, and the Biological Revolution,* provides an excellent summary of two contemporary definitions.

One definition is that death is the irreversible loss of the capacity for bodily integration and social interaction. Death occurs when the entire brain is dead. The criteria for determining that the brain is dead are that there are no spontaneous movements, breathing, or reflexes and that such unreceptivity and lack of response are confirmed by a flat electroencephalogram. These same criteria might be met by someone who was suffering from hypothermia or who was taking a central nervous system depressant, so these possibilities must be ruled out before death is determined. It could be that a person whose heart and lungs were functioning with the aid of machines would be declared dead using this definition. For those accustomed to linking death with the circulation of vital body fluids, to remove the person from the machine would necessitate the ethical decisions associated with euthanasia. For those who accept this definition of death, however, to continue to treat the person as if he or she were alive would be unethical.

Another definition of death is that death is the irreversible loss of consciousness or the capacity for social interaction. Notice that the capacity for bodily integration does not have to be irreversible according to this definition. If one's neocortex is dead, one has lost consciousness and cannot communicate with others. The easiest way to determine whether this is the case is with an electroencephalogram. Common sense is certainly challenged here, because a person in the living-dying phase of life could be breathing without a machine and still be considered dead.

In both of these definitions, human life is understood to be more than mere biological functions. The first definition assumes that both the biological function of spontaneous blood and breath circulation are necessary to be human, as is an ability to interact with others. If these are not present, then human life is absent. The second definition goes further; it says that consciousness and social function are uniquely human. If both are absent, then human life is absent.

The initial commonsense definition led to legal definitions of death. The new definitions also led to legal definitions. The common law definition was gradually redefined with the advent of the new technologies and discoveries. The most famous definition for legal purposes was that of the President's Commission for the Study of Ethical Problems in Medicine and Biomedical and Behavioral Research. The commission rejected the vague general definitions mentioned above for a more specific and biological definition, suggesting that the following definition be used in laws throughout the country: "An individual who has sustained either (1) irreversible cessation of circulatory and respiratory functions, or (2) irreversible cessation of all functions of the entire brain, including the brain's stem, is dead."

What Is Life? What Is Death? Definitions reflect the questions of persons and societies. These contemporary definitions reflect the concerns of the modern age: rational analysis and reductionism for the purpose of technological control. Other cultures have defined human life and death in terms of other concerns. Many times, the human life known and analyzed by the five senses was seen as limited in the face of something that transcended ordinary life. The sensual reality might be the spirit, or breath, but this sensual reality was a manifestation of a deeper reality that connected human beings with their past, present, and future. It has been called soul and *atman.* Many terms from many cultures attempt to define life and death. Contemporary arguments about definitions of life and death in Western culture are arguments about who human beings are and what they will become. Old views of life and death are no longer valid. Commonsense observation is insufficient. New views are still to be discovered. Contemporary definitions do not match human experience. Inevitably, there will be confusion as people search for definitions that reflect their experience and improve the quality of life in the face of its inevitable end.

Confusion as a Hopeful Sign. Contemporary popular literature uses four phrases that reflect definitional confusion: brain death, heart death, right to life, and right to death. The first two phrases reflect the difficulty experienced by many people who attempt to understand definitions of life and death. The last two phrases reflect attempts to argue for definitions within the political arena. Most people understand life and death not with the formal definitions stated here but within the parameters of "television-speak"; many decisions concerning social policy are made not by professionals but by the political process. These two phrases reflect the two major social constraints to definitions of life and death: the demand for simplicity in a very complex affair, and the unwillingness to change ideas about a very personal reality.

Modern Western society communicates through the media. The media need short and simple phrases to describe something. Such phrases show how one must think in using this technology.

To use the phrases "brain death" and "heart death" as many reporters do is to suggest that there are two different kinds of death. This is inaccurate. A person is either dead or alive. To say that someone is "heart dead" is to refer to common, primitive definitions of death. To say that a person is "brain dead" indicates that the brain comes into the judgment about death—nothing more. The use of "heart death" and "brain death" to refer to the death of the person also gives the impression that a human being is identified with the heart and/or brain. Such an identification implicitly supports a materialistic view of the person that is not accepted by many philosophers.

The supporters of the "right to life" and those of the "right to die" use modern "rights" language to argue about life and death. They know what they do not want society to do. Right-to-life supporters do not want human life maximized in such a way that large groups of people who are defective, or perhaps lack full consciousness, will find themselves defined out of the human race. Right-to-die supporters do not want human life minimized in such a way that if any of a person's organs is alive, society would be obliged to sustain that person's life. Rights mean obligations. Right-to-life supporters say that society is obliged to sustain human life under any circumstances. Right-to-die supporters say that society is obliged to allow an individual to choose a particular mode of death rather than experience a slow death of various organs. Most arguments about rights to life and death deal with the issue of euthanasia rather than the issue of definitions of death. The euthanasia issue concerns whether one may ethically hasten the death of someone in the living-dying phase of life. Definitions of death seek to determine whether a person is dead. These are two different issues.

Confusion and argument about definitions of life and death indicate that Western culture is undergoing significant change. They indicate that people are aware of the change that is taking place, thinking about it, and offering arguments for one side or the other. Being aware of these definitions means being aware of what arguments are offered and taking one's place in the conversation, not the confusion.

—*Nathan R. Kollar*

See also Bioethics; Right to die; Right to life; Suicide.

BIBLIOGRAPHY

Chidester, David. *Patterns of Transcendence.* Belmont, Calif.: Wadsworth, 1990. A review of the concepts of death and life in various world cultures and religions.

Gervais, Karen Grandstrand. *Redefining Death.* New Haven, Conn.: Yale University Press, 1986. A review and critique of all the major definitions of death according to their methodologies.

Goldberg, Steven. "The Changing Face of Death: Computers, Consciousness, and Nancy Cruzan." *Stanford Law Review* 43 (February, 1991): 659-684. An extension of the life-death debate into the area of artificial intelligence. The changes in the legal definition of death are shown to occur as science progresses.

Searle, John. *The Rediscovery of the Mind.* Cambridge, Mass.: MIT Press, 1992. A review of the arguments that identify the human person with the brain.

Veatch, Robert M. *Death, Dying, and the Biological Revolution.* Rev. ed. New Haven, Conn.: Yale University Press, 1989. An exploration of the philosophical, ethical, legal, and public policy consequences of the radical changes in the definitions of death and life.

Lifestyles

TYPE OF ETHICS: Beliefs and practices
DEFINITION: The external expressions of set patterns of values and beliefs
SIGNIFICANCE: What people believe to be valuable determines the choices they make and the ways in which they act

Everyone, either consciously or unconsciously, subscribes to some set of values and beliefs. A lifestyle is a person's active expression of his or her values and beliefs. People tend to inherit the lifestyles of those who are important to them and then individualize those lifestyles. Lifestyles are learned by experience.

Because it is impossible to deal with many lifestyles in a brief space, this article will focus on two sets of significant lifestyles. The first set consists of Eastern and Western lifestyles, which are based on the beliefs and values of two different parts of the world. The second set consists of the modern, conservative, liberal, and fundamentalist lifestyles, which are based on various ways in which people respond to modern life. An understanding of these lifestyles allows one to understand those values and beliefs that condition one's ethical choices. Many commentators would be quick to add that the world is moving into a postmodern age, which will generate significant change. Such significant change is always accompanied by an increase in the number of alternative lifestyles that are available in a given area. Alternative lifestyles offer people new ways of life and challenge the way of life of the majority in a given area. Alternative lifestyles should not be mistaken for fads, which last only for a short time, such as a year or two. Alternative lifestyles usually exist for at least a generation before they die out or become the lifestyle of the majority.

Eastern and Western Lifestyles. Eastern lifestyles are represented by the religions or philosophies of Hinduism, Buddhism, Taoism, Confucianism, and Shintoism. These lifestyles are very much oriented toward nature and tend to view time as a series of recurrent cycles. They also tend to de-emphasize the will of the individual and the role of choice. Western lifestyles are represented by the related religions of Judaism, Christianity, and Islam. Western lifestyles tend to emphasize history and time, believing that the world began at a specific point in time. Western thought is generally dualistic (right or wrong, yes or no), whereas Eastern thought is generally unified (right and wrong, yes and no). Western thought also tends to emphasize choice and the will of the individual.

Modern, Conservative, Liberal, and Fundamentalist Lifestyles. In the middle of the seventeenth century, new ideas initiated a new set of beliefs and values that can be called "the modern." In this case, modern does not mean contemporary. The modern lifestyle affirms most of the beliefs and values of the Western lifestyle. It adds to the Western lifestyle, however, the belief that the mind (reason) is the only instrument that should be used to examine and evaluate the nature of reality. This view constitutes a rejection of the roles of the supernatural and of religious traditions in providing models for behavior and belief. In the modern view, one should analyze how other people act and determine what nature requires. Only if actions are consistent with natural requirements should they become behavioral norms. As the sciences that grew out of modern thought developed, the importance of universal objective norms was minimized; more emphasis was placed on the pluralism of norms and, therefore, ways of living.

The liberal lifestyle accommodated itself to pluralism. The ideas of progress and rationality were central to this lifestyle. Life was viewed as an adventure that, because of the sciences, would continually improve. It was thought that the discoveries of the sciences should be used to improve the quality of life and to develop new behavioral norms.

The conservative lifestyle, however, did not wish to operate on the basis of the ideas of progress, pluralism, and scientific rationality. Instead, conservatism reflected a lifestyle that emphasized hierarchy, order, tradition, and religion. The old was held to be more important than the new. The most important values and beliefs were those that had been inherited from religion.

The fundamentalist lifestyle is based upon the religion (Eastern or Western) within which it is practiced. The Christian fundamentalist lifestyle generally reflects many of the beliefs of the modern in its belief in the literal truth of the Bible and the conviction that the end of the world will come soon. Christian fundamentalism rejects the modern's view of the supernatural by holding to the belief that God regularly intervenes in the world. Some other forms of fundamentalism—Islamic fundamentalism, for example—can be thought of more accurately as reflecting a conservative lifestyle. Although many people view fundamentalism in general as a violent lifestyle that rejects democracy and seeks to reorganize society on the basis of religion, that is not always the case. Each form of fundamentalism must be examined in its own religious, cultural, and national context.

Alternative Lifestyles. Alternative lifestyles are united in that they respond to the lifestyles that dominate the cultures in which they occur. Each alternative lifestyle rejects all or part of these dominant lifestyles and promotes a different set of beliefs and behavioral norms.   —*Nathan R. Kollar*

See also Conservatism; Liberalism; Religion.

BIBLIOGRAPHY
Lande, Nathaniel. *Mindstyles, Lifestyles.* Los Angeles: Price/Stern/Sloan, 1976.
Mitchell, Arnold. *The Nine American Lifestyles.* New York: Macmillan, 1983.
Postman, Neil. *Technopoly: The Surrender of Culture to Technology.* New York: Alfred Knopf, 1992.
Smart, Ninian. *Worldviews: Crosscultural Explorations of Human Beliefs.* New York: Scribner's, 1983.

Limited war

TYPE OF ETHICS: Military ethics
ACHIEVEMENTS: In the post-1945 nuclear age characterized by the menace of mutual destruction among the great powers, limited warfare made it possible to resolve disputes and tests of political will without precipitating total, suicidal conflict
SIGNIFICANCE: Limited war represented a return to recognition of the economic and social costs of total war and the acceptance of reciprocities and immunities among hostile powers

In the nuclear age, the likelihood that small-scale wars would escalate into total, suicidal conflicts encouraged hostile powers to accept limitations on the scope of their wars. World War I (1914-1918) and World War II (1939-1945) were highly technologized conflicts fueled by ideology or nationalism, in which belligerents on both sides sought the destruction of enemy societies. These total wars were accompanied by demands for the complete or unlimited surrender of the defeated nations. These conflicts aside, however, most warfare historically has been of a limited nature, although such wars have differed widely in their causes and character. The limitations typically invoked by belligerent states have taken several forms. Hostile powers have sometimes confined their military operations to specific geographical areas. On occasion, they have ignored the involvement of states that were important parties to the conflict. They have also resisted using weapons such as nuclear bombs and artillery, and chemical agents. Belligerents, likewise, have granted immunity from attack to civilian populations and to cultural centers: so-called "open cities." United Nations and American experience in Korea from 1950 to 1953 exemplified the warring powers' acknowledgment of these limitations, since the violation of any of them increased the risk of full-scale conflict between the superpowers. The geographical range of battle, therefore, was restricted—except for a controversial U.N. offensive—to the vicinity of the thirty-eighth parallel. Japan and Taiwan, which served as U.N. sanctuaries, and mainland China and the Soviet Far East, which served the same purpose for Chinese volunteers and Soviet airmen who fought in Korea, were not considered acceptable targets by the belligerents. Furthermore, in the effort to defend South Korea, the United States resisted the use of atomic weaponry. Roughly similar mutually recognized restrictions—always with some violations by both sides—have applied since 1945 in French Indochina (before independence), then in Vietnam, in Cambodia, in Iran and Iraq, in Kashmir, in Lebanon, and, among several other scenes of warfare, in Afghanistan.

See also *Art of War, The*; Deterrence; Mutually Assured Destruction (MAD); *On War*.

Lobotomy

TYPE OF ETHICS: Bioethics
DATE: Originated 1935
ASSOCIATED WITH: António Egas Moniz, Carlyle Jacobsen, Walter Freeman, James Watts, Ernest Spiegel, and Henry Wycis
DEFINITION: A medical procedure for treating certain mental disorders by performing a surgical operation on the brain and destroying brain tissue in specific areas
SIGNIFICANCE: Raises questions about whether the irreversible destruction of brain tissue is justified in treating mental disorders, the adequacy of the supporting evidence, and the effectiveness of psychosurgery

History. The lobotomy is based on the biomedical model of mental illness, which posits that mental disorders are caused by abnormalities in brain structure. If this is the case, surgically treating the brain should cure the disorder. The field that does so is called psychosurgery.

The antecedent of the lobotomy was the prefrontal leukotomy, which was invented by the Portuguese neurosurgeon António Egas Moniz (1874-1955) in 1935. In this procedure, a surgical device called a leukotome was inserted through a hole into the frontal lobe and rotated, destroying whatever nerve tissue it contacted. The prefrontal leukotomy was replaced by the prefrontal lobotomy, which was developed by the American neurosurgeons Walter Freeman and James Watts in 1937. The limitation of the prefrontal leukotomy was that it did not permit precise determination of the area to be cut. In the prefrontal lobotomy, larger holes were drilled into both sides of the skull, after which a leukotome was inserted and precisely moved in a sweeping motion through the frontal lobe. The prefrontal lobotomy was in turn replaced by the transorbital lobotomy, which was developed by Freeman in 1948. An ice pick-like knife was inserted through the top of the eye socket into the brain and then swung back and forth. This procedure was quick and efficient and could be performed as an office procedure.

The inspiration for these surgical procedures came from data presented by Carlyle Jacobsen that showed a marked change in the level of emotionality of a chimpanzee following destruction of a large part of the frontal lobe of the cerebral cortex. Formerly, the chimpanzee was highly emotional and obstinate. After the operation, the animal appeared calm and cooperative. Egas Moniz believed that this technique could be used on humans to relieve anxiety and other hyperemotional states. Egas Moniz claimed great success in alleviating extreme states of emotionality, and his work aroused worldwide interest, excitement, and practice. Psychosurgical techniques were seen as quick and effective methods for alleviating certain common mental disorders that could not be treated effectively and rapidly by other means, and as providing a partial solution to the problem of overcrowding in mental hospitals.

From 1936 to 1978, about 35,000 psychosurgical operations were performed in America, with perhaps double that number worldwide. Egas Moniz was awarded the Nobel Prize for Physiology or Medicine in 1949 in recognition of his work. The Nobel citation states: "Frontal leukotomy, despite certain limitations of the operative method, must be considered one of the most important discoveries ever made in psychiatric therapy, because through its use a great number of suffering people and total invalids have been socially rehabilitated."

Ethical Issues. Contrast Egas Moniz's Nobel citation, however, with David L. Rosenhan and Martin E. P. Seligman's assessment of the lobotomy in their 1989 textbook *Abnormal Psychology*: "Moreover, there is the danger that physicians and patients may become overzealous in their search for a quick neurological cure . . . the disastrous history of frontal lobotomies . . . should serve as a warning" (p. 596).

In fact, Rosenhan and Seligman were correct and the Nobel Prize citation was wrong. The leukotomy and lobotomies were a disaster. Their sorry history is rife with ethical violations, because of their rationale and because of the evidence that was used to justify their use on humans.

Within three months of hearing Jacobsen's account, Egas Moniz performed leukotomies. He did so despite the lack of clear evidence from animal experimentation to justify the procedure. Egas Moniz conducted no animal experimentation himself; in addition, his reading of the scientific literature to support his beliefs was spotty and selective, and he ignored contradictory evidence. Furthermore, there was a large animal and human literature that clearly demonstrated a range of serious side effects and deficits produced by lesions to the frontal lobe, such as apathy, retarded movement, loss of initiative, and mutism. With no supporting evidence, Egas Moniz insisted that these side effects were only temporary, when in fact they could be permanent. Egas Moniz's initial report on twenty patients claimed a cure for seven, lessening of symptoms in six, and no effect in six. An impartial review of these cases concluded, however, that only one of the twenty cases provided enough information to make a judgment.

There is also the question of whether it is ethical to destroy brain tissue as a means of treating cognition and action. Proponents of psychosurgery argue that newer techniques avoid the frontal lobes, the procedure is based upon a good understanding of how the nervous system functions, side effects are minimal, its use is much more strictly monitored and regulated, and it is undertaken only as a treatment of last resort.

Opponents of psychosurgery, however, argue that it is an ethically and morally unacceptable procedure of dubious value for several reasons. First, there are surprisingly few ethical or legal guidelines regulating psychosurgery. Second, psychosurgery has been used to treat a wide variety of disorders, such as schizophrenia, depression, obsessive-compulsive disorder, acute anxiety, anorexia nervosa, attention deficit disorder, uncontrollable rage or aggression, substance abuse and addictions, homosexual pedophilia, and intractable pain. Psychosurgery is performed with the belief that the specific locations in the nervous system that are associated with the above disorders are known and that surgically altering them will in turn alter the particular behavior. Opponents of psychosurgery argue that such knowledge does not in fact exist, and that the assumption that these behaviors are tied to specific locations in the brain has not been proved. Additionally, opponents argue, careful examination of the literature reveals psychosurgery to be an unpredictable, hit-or-miss procedure. Third, the destruction of brain tissue cannot be reversed, and undesirable side effects, which also cannot be reversed, are unavoidable.

—Laurence Miller

See also Bioethics; Institutionalization of patients; Psychology.

BIBLIOGRAPHY

Kleinig, John. *Ethical Issues in Psychosurgery*. London: George Allan & Univin, 1985.

Marsh, F. H., and Janet Katz, eds. *Biology, Crime and Ethics*. Cincinnati: Anderson, 1985.

Rodgers, Joann E. *Psychosurgery: Damaging the Brain to Save the Mind*. New York: HarperCollins, 1992.

Valenstein, E. S. *Great and Desperate Cures*. New York: Basic Books, 1986.

_____, ed. *The Psychosurgery Debate*. San Francisco: W. H. Freeman, 1980.

Locke, John (Aug. 29, 1632, Wrington, Somerset, England—Oct. 28, 1704, Oates, Essex, England): Philosopher

TYPE OF ETHICS: Enlightenment history

ACHIEVEMENTS: Author of *An Essay Concerning Human Understanding* (1690) and *Two Treatises of Government* (1690)

SIGNIFICANCE: Offered an almost unique mix of empiricism and theism that, despite its inconsistencies, proved to have enduring attractiveness

Locke is known for his political writings (the *Two Treatises of Government* are the basis for the principles used in the American and British constitutions) and for his epistemology, which is the central focus of *An Essay Concerning Human Understanding*. He never wrote a work devoted specifically to ethics, but he did develop a fairly clear stand on the nature of ethics. His *An Essay Concerning Human Understanding* is the most important of his works in terms of his ethical views, but *Two Treatises, Some Thoughts Concerning Education* (1693), and

The Reasonableness of Christianity (1695) also contain some of his ideas on the subject.

Biographical Background. Locke came from the non-Anglican Protestant community in England, learning as a child the virtues of Calvinist simplicity but little of the harsh, judgmental aspect of that sect. He was educated at Oxford University, but he moved away from the then-fashionable scholasticism and, under the influence of Robert Boyle, began to study practical science. He chose medicine as his specialty and worked with the famous Thomas Sydenham. He never took his degree or practiced medicine (the former was not required for the latter at that time), but the influence of his training would remain with him.

After completing a diplomatic mission in 1665, Locke returned to Oxford and immersed himself in the writings of René Descartes. Two years later, the Earl of Shaftesbury, a school friend, invited Locke to become his personal physician and live with him. Locke proved to be as much secretary as doctor, helping his patron with such projects as the Constitution for the Carolinas. He was also elected a fellow of the Royal Society.

In 1675, Locke began a long visit to France both for his health and to expand his study of Descartes. He returned home in 1679 only to face political problems when his patron, Shaftesbury, was accused of treason. Although he was acquitted, Shaftesbury fled to Holland in 1681, and Locke, who had held some minor government posts under Shaftesbury's influence, found it best to follow his example. After Monmouth's Rebellion (1685), Locke was branded a traitor, and the English government demanded his extradition. The Dutch paid little attention, and Locke lived quietly, continuing work on what was to be *An Essay Concerning Human Understanding*. He returned home after the Revolution of 1688 and increasingly divided his time between London, where he served as a commissioner of appeals, and Oates, the Essex home of his friends Sir Francis and Lady Masham. It was in this comfortable, supportive home that Locke, in the 1690's, was at his most prolific, though his *Essay* and *Two Treatises* had been in development for years.

Ethical Views. Like Thomas Hobbes and some other philosophers, Locke defined good as that which gives, or is conducive to, pleasure. His is a very individualistic view, for it allows no room for altruistic pleasure. He also asserted that there were no inborn attitudes, including ethical principles. As an empiricist, Locke, whom most students know for his assertion that the mind is at birth a *tabula rasa*, or blank slate, on which experience writes, logically concluded that ethical principles must be learned. He also asserted that such ethical principles were as logical and scientific as mathematics, but he was never able to prove his case.

Unlike most strict empiricists, however, Locke was also a theist. The natural laws of ethics, he asserted, could be learned deductively and hence applied to all human beings. They also came to people as revelation. Thus, natural law and divine law were the same. The importance of the former was that it was accessible to all, not only to mystics and those who believed in their pronouncements of God's messages.

Theism also influenced Locke's ethics in another way. When he had to consider why an individual would follow ethical principles, especially when another course of action might seem more conducive to his pleasure, Locke fell back on the fear of ultimate punishment. Whatever the potential for short-term pleasure, failure to observe the laws of ethics would result in long-term suffering.

Implications for Ethical Conduct. Despite the inconsistencies that other philosophers have pointed out in his ethical views, Locke's ideas have been consistently popular. This seems to be because, for most people, inconsistent beliefs are common, and Locke's positions are much like those of a typical modern Western person. Modernism has produced liberal Christianity, in which the believer is encouraged to select those principles that seem to fit his or her observations of life and produce happiness. While not exactly Locke's view, the view of liberal Christianity is close enough to encourage a continuing interest in his writings. Students are more likely to start reading his work because of his importance in political philosophy and epistemology than because of his ethics, but as they discover his ethical views and find them congenial, they will keep them in the public view.

—*Fred R. van Hartesveldt*

See also Behaviorism; Epistemological ethics; Hedonism; Intuitionist ethics.

BIBLIOGRAPHY

Cranston, Maurice. *John Locke: A Biography*. London: Longmans, 1957.

Seliger, Martin. *The Liberal Politics of John Locke*. London: Allen & Unwin, 1968.

Stephen, Leslie. *History of English Thought in the Eighteenth Century*. 3d ed. 2 vols. London: John Murray, 1927.

Swabey, William Curtis. *Ethical Theory: From Hobbes to Kant*. New York: Philosophical Library, 1961.

Yolton, John W. *John Locke: Problems and Perspectives*. London: Cambridge University Press, 1969.

_____. *John Locke and the Way of Ideas*. London: Oxford University Press, 1956.

Love

TYPE OF ETHICS: Theory of ethics
DATE: Fifth century B.C.E. to present
ASSOCIATED WITH: Philosophers from Plato in the fifth century B.C.E. to feminists in the twentieth century
DEFINITION: A variety of conceptions of love have been proposed
SIGNIFICANCE: Analysis of the nature of love; understanding human nature; being loving

Philosophers have treated a number of issues connected with love; the nature and value of romantic love, the distinction between agape and eros, the motivation of those who love, self-love, friendship, the possibility of altruistic love, and the nature of caring, compassion, benevolence, and sympathy.

Romantic Love. Most philosophers have been critical of romantic love. Stendhal claims that in passion-love, lovers "find" perfections in their beloved that are not really there. José Ortega y Gasset believes that in love the lover's attention becomes fixed solely on the beloved. All else that formerly absorbed the lover is eliminated from consciousness; therefore, the rest of the world does not exist for the lover. Ernest Becker, in *The Denial of Death* (1974), claims that romantic love is but another example of the basic human drive for heroism. Each person in a love relation endows the other with godlike qualities so that each can feel cosmically justified. In *The Second Sex* (1952), Simone de Beauvoir criticizes "orthodox patriarchal romantic ideology," in which a woman is to find her identity and value solely in her beloved's superiority and independence. Romantic love, she writes, makes a woman servile and devoid of self-respect; the woman is "pitiful, insecure, dependent, and powerless through her loving."

Not all philosophers, however, have been so negative about romantic love. Robert Solomon states that love is an ordinary but spectacular emotion. Ethel Spector Person argues that though romantic love can be harmful, it can also be enriching. It can liberate people from old habits, give them hope, move them to enlarge their possibilities, and incite them to transcend their self-centered concerns.

Agape and Eros. The classic description of eros-love is contained in Plato's dialogue *Symposium*. Plato characterizes love as a desire for pure beauty. One does not love others because of their beautiful qualities but because they are instances of, and point to, "the Beautiful itself." Moreover, those who love pure beauty do so in order to satisfy a self-directed desire—the desire to know beauty, not just for the moment, but forever. The receiving character of this love, which it has in common with sexual love, has been contrasted with the giving character of agape-love. Agape-love is said to bestow worth on its object instead of being derived from its object's worth, and it is said to exclude self-love, unlike eros, which is essentially self-love. From this it is inferred by some that only divine love is agapic, because only it is nonacquisitive and entirely other-directed; others, however, assert that some human love is agapic.

A number of questions arise about these descriptions of agape and eros. Are the two as mutually exclusive as they are sometimes claimed to be? Is all human love erotic? Is agape always a better love than eros? Is the element of self-sacrifice in agape-love appropriate to women's experience, which is said by some twentieth century feminists to contain too little self-regard, too much self-surrender, especially toward men, and insufficient concern for self-development?

Duty and Emotion. Should people love because they desire to be loving or because they believe that it is their duty to do so? Immanuel Kant and Søren Kierkegaard side with the latter alternative on the grounds that desire and emotion are capricious—they change easily, and people have little control over them. Moreover, Kant said, for any action to have moral worth, including a loving one, it must be motivated by a sense of duty. Other philosophers, including many twentieth century feminists, side with the first alternative. Desire and emotion are not so capricious as Kant and Kierkegaard thought, and the feature of love that gives it moral worth is its emotion—the acceptance felt by a beloved or the sympathy felt by a sufferer. Some writers characterize the duty approach as masculine because it conceives love as rational and impersonal, and the emotion approach as feminine because of its appeal to feeling and connectedness.

Caring. There is a rich philosophical literature that describes the nature of caring and similar phenomena. Caring is said to involve receptivity, which is depicted as "feeling with" the one who is cared for. The carer is attentive to the other, absorbed in the other, and aware of the other's thoughts, feelings, and facial expressions. Sensitivity to the cared for's situation is present; so also is a sense of "we-ness." For some, the essence of caring is the attitude of wanting to help the cared-for grow. For others, the essence of caring is the sense of being present with the other. Distinctions are drawn between caring and other states with which it is sometimes confused, such as being submerged in the other without the awareness that the other is a separate person.

The Possibility of Altruistic Love. For psychological, social, and religious reasons, some people have wondered whether other-directed love is possible. Imagination may make one think one loves when in fact one does not; emotionally distant parents may produce children who are unable to connect; competitive capitalism may make people feel alienated from one another; an emphasis on sexuality may make people strive for nothing but sexual satisfaction; sin may make people irremediably self-centered. In *Being and Nothingness* (1943), French philosopher Jean-Paul Sartre asserts that separateness and opposition are at the core of human relations, including love. Love is impossible, he says, because both the one who loves and the one who is loved are trying to get something from the other, and neither is able to do so. Sartre graphically portrays these ideas in his well-known play *No Exit*. Others believe that separateness can be overcome by certain sorts of "interpersonal oneness," such as Martin Buber's I-Thou relation, and that the obstacles to love can be met with a social or religious transformation.
                                                                    —*Clifford Williams*

See also Benevolence; Compassion; Friendship; Passions and emotions; *Second Sex, The*; Self-love.

BIBLIOGRAPHY

Kierkegaard, Søren. *Works of Love*. Translated by Howard and Edna Hong. New York: Harper, 1962.

Mayeroff, Milton. *On Caring*. New York: Harper & Row, 1971.

Noddings, Nel. *Caring: A Feminine Approach to Ethics and Moral Education*. Berkeley: University of California Press, 1984.

Nygren, Anders. *Agape and Eros*. Translated by Philip S. Watson. New York: Harper & Row, 1969.

Ortega y Gasset, José. *On Love: Aspects of a Single Theme*. Translated by Toby Talbot. New York: Meridian Books, 1957.

Person, Ethel Spector. *Dreams of Love and Fateful Encounters: The Power of Romantic Passion*. New York: W. W. Norton, 1988.

Singer, Irving. *The Nature of Love*. Vol. I: Plato to Luther. Vol. II: Courtly and Romantic. Vol. III: The Modern World. Chicago: University of Chicago Press, 1984-1987.

Solomon, Robert. *Love: Emotion, Myth, and Metaphor*. Garden City, N.Y.: Anchor Press, 1981.

Stendhal. *On Love*. Translated by H. B. V. under the direction of C. K. Scott-Moncrieff. New York: Da Capo Press, 1983.

Loyalty

Type of ethics: Personal and social ethics
Date: From antiquity
Associated with: Judaism, Christianity, Greek philosophy, Stoicism, and Josiah Royce
Definition: Commitment to a person, cause, country, or ideal, stemming from natural kinship, personal attachment, collective purpose, or common identity
Significance: Constitutes the foundation of other virtues by fostering an unwavering attitudinal commitment to those virtues

In the Old Testament, God's first commandment to Moses on Mt. Sinai requires the uncompromising loyalty of the Israelites: "I am the Lord thy God, which have brought thee out of the land of Egypt, out of the house of bondage. Thou shalt have no other gods before me." Thus, loyalty to God becomes the paramount duty of Judaism and, subsequently, Christianity, in which it is reaffirmed by Jesus: "Thou shalt love the Lord thy God with all thy heart, and with all thy soul, and with all thy mind." Jesus also acknowledges earthly loyalties, however, requiring one to "render therefore unto Caesar the things which are Caesar's" and to "love thy neighbor as thyself."

Loyalty was the essence of the ancient Greek *eusebia*, or "piety," meaning devotion to the gods but encompassing devotion to parents, friends, country, and anything else worthy of respect and veneration. Loyalty as such is specifically discussed by neither Plato nor Aristotle, even though both philosophers devote much attention to other virtues, defining them and subjecting them to exacting philosophical scrutiny. Yet *eusebia* was important not only to them but to all Greeks, constituting the heart of Greek citizenship. The greatest example of Greek loyalty was Socrates, who refused to repudiate his beloved Athens even when its laws punished him unjustly, just as he refused to repudiate philosophy, which he believed was the only means of leading Athenians to the moral truth that would restore the city's integrity. Choosing death at the hands of the state for refusing to give up philosophy, he preserved his loyalty to both.

Aristotle likewise attests the importance of loyalty in the *Nicomachean Ethics*: "It is also true that the virtuous man's conduct is often guided by the interests of his friends and of his country, and that he will if necessary lay down his life in their behalf." He also considers the problem of conflicting loyalties:

> A . . . problem is set by such questions as, whether one should in all things give the preference to one's father and obey him . . . and similarly whether one should . . . show gratitude to a benefactor or oblige a friend, if one cannot do both. . . . That we should not make the same return to everyone, nor give a father the preference in everything . . . is plain enough; but since we ought to render different things to parents, brothers, comrades, and benefactors, we ought to render to each class what is appropriate and becoming.

For Aristotle, specific loyalties are rooted in one's relationships with others, and the obligations attendant upon these loyalties are determined by the nature of these relationships.

Loyalty as piety is preserved in the Roman *pietas*, encompassing reverence for the gods and those to whom natural relationships bind one—family, countrymen, and all of humankind. "Natural" loyalties, springing from kinship to fellow humans, entail "natural duties" that are consonant with these loyalties. Since such kinships are part of the natural order, any violation of these duties transgresses natural moral law. *Pietas* reflects the Stoic belief in a cosmopolitan loyalty to all people by virtue of natural human kinship and obligation to God.

In the Middle Ages, loyalty was exemplified in the "fealty" owed by a vassal to his lord and by the lord to his king. Also included in the concept of fealty was the reciprocal obligation of the king to his subjects. The desire to depose rulers who violated this obligation led to the distinction between loyalty to the *office* of the king and loyalty to the *person* of the king. The Magna Carta constituted a statement that loyalty to the office did not require loyalty to the person; conversely, disloyalty to the person did not signify disloyalty to the office.

The transition to the modern world, which engendered a new political entity, the "nation state," resulted in loyalty's becoming a predominantly political virtue, from which sprang both the fanatical, nationalistic loyalty of fascism and communism and the pluralistic loyalties of democracy. Despite attempts to transcend national loyalties through organizations such as the United Nations, loyalty in the modern sense is associated with both benign patriotism and radical nationalism, in which loyalty is often interpreted as a call to military aggression. Even in democratic countries, national loyalty is often considered the highest political virtue. The Alien and Sedition Laws of 1798 and the Sedition Act of 1918 were attempts by the U.S. Congress to mandate loyalty by outlawing all publications that were considered defamatory or seditious. Uncertainty about the national loyalty of some Americans led to the internment of Japanese Americans during World War II and to the "blacklisting" of people suspected of subversive activities during the McCarthy era, from 1950 to 1954.

Among philosophers, only Josiah Royce has given loyalty sustained critical scrutiny. Royce's dismay at "that ancient and disastrous association" between loyalty and war prompted him to write *The Philosophy of Loyalty*, in which he defines loyalty as "the willing and practical and thoroughgoing devotion of a person to a cause." The cause to which one declares loyalty becomes the plan for one's life, which, combined with the personal gratification of serving this cause, makes life meaningful. Lest loyalty be construed as being consistent with devotion to an evil cause, Royce stipulates that genuine loyalty respects the loyalties of others and forbids actions that destroy them or prevent their being acted upon. Royce refers to respect for the loyalties of others as "loyalty to loyalty." *—Barbara Forrest*

See also Friendship; Military ethics; Nationalism; Royce, Josiah; Sedition; Sedition Act of 1798; Treason.

BIBLIOGRAPHY

Aristotle. "Nicomachean Ethics." In *Introduction to Aristotle*, edited by Richard McKeon. 2d rev. ed. Chicago: University of Chicago Press, 1973.

Konvitz, Milton R. "Loyalty." In *Dictionary of the History of Ideas: Studies of Selected Pivotal Ideas*, edited by Philip P. Wiener. Vol. 3. New York: Charles Scribner's Sons, 1973.

Ladd, John. "Loyalty." In *The Encyclopedia of Philosophy*, edited by Paul Edwards. Vol. 5. New York: Macmillan, 1967.

Plato. "Apology." In *The Collected Dialogues of Plato*, edited by Edith Hamilton and Huntington Cairns. 1961. Reprint. Princeton, N.J.: Princeton University Press, 1984.

Royce, Josiah. *The Philosophy of Loyalty*. New York: Macmillan, 1908.

Lust

TYPE OF ETHICS: Personal and social ethics
DATE: Middle Ages to present
ASSOCIATED WITH: Judeo-Christian theology
DEFINITION: Sexual behavior that is in conflict with societal or religious standards
SIGNIFICANCE: Indicates potential conflict between the biological limits of a natural function and the good of the individual and society; raises crucial questions about the conduct and the nature of interpersonal relationships

Injunctions against lust, in the sense of sexual activity outside of marriage (also called "lechery" in the Middle Ages), figure prominently in the Old and New Testaments of the Bible. The Jewish tradition emphasized the harmfulness of lust in its disruption of a family-centered social structure. It presented marriage as being handed down to humankind from the time of Adam and Eve, and being further reinforced by the Ten Commandments of Moses and other divine revelation. The

New Testament, while suggesting that more individual freedom of choice and forgiveness of repentant transgressors is permitted, assumes that the sexual behavioral norms of Jewish tradition are still very much in effect. The Letters of the Apostle Paul set the stage for a Christian tradition that makes sexual abstinence a good in itself. This finds parallels in the monastic movements of many of the world's religions.

From a societal standpoint, "lust" is a term of opprobrium for sexual activity that disrupts the social structure—above all, extramarital sex. For the individual, however, sexual behavior may be perceived as "lust" if it is performed without love and respect, even within the confines of marriage. All such loveless sex is designated as a form of "lust"—hence, one of the seven deadly sins—from the early Middle Ages onward. In a modern context, "lust" in this sense is replaced by such terms as "using" one's sexual partner and "sexual harassment."

See also Desire; Promiscuity; Sexuality and sexual ethics; Sin; Vice.

Luther, Martin (Nov. 10, 1483, Eisleben, Saxony—Feb. 18, 1546, Eisleben, Saxony): Protestant reformer

TYPE OF ETHICS: Religious ethics

ACHIEVEMENTS: Initiated the Protestant Reformation

SIGNIFICANCE: Gave a new place to "works" in relation to Christian salvation, while maintaining a conservative view of the nature of secular authority in the face of popular unrest

Only in modern Christian ethics is an artificial line drawn between religious doctrine and its practical application—Luther himself recognized no such boundary. His career as a reformer was imbued with the notion of ethics as an outgrowth of Christian faith, as it was with the faith that made ethics both possible and valid. Indeed, one could say that Luther's reforming activity was first occasioned by ethical concerns, since it was corrupt practice on the part of the Roman church that first led him to consider the possibility of corrupt doctrine. The preaching of indulgences in German churches in order to raise funds for papal building projects and for the purchasing of German bishoprics, along with traffic in relics and hastily recited masses for the dead, seemed to Luther to be symptoms of a larger spiritual decay—a decay that he was convinced would swiftly be reversed if those in authority knew of its existence. It was only when the authorities refused to alter these practices that Luther began to realize that a more fundamental change was needed, after which his career as a reformer started to take shape.

Justification by Faith. At the same time, Luther was undergoing a spiritual crisis of his own that would have a profound effect on his ethical thought. The medieval Church taught that, while salvation was to be obtained through Christ, the individual Christian could assist his or her own cause through participation in the sacraments of the church. Luther's time as an Augustinian monk was largely spent in such acts, but with no sense of spiritual relief. It was only

when he began a study of the scriptures—in particular, the Epistles to the Romans and the Galatians—in preparation for his teaching at the University of Wittenberg that he came upon the doctrine that would free him from his spiritual trials and start a theological revolution: "The just shall live by faith" (Rom. 1:17). It became Luther's contention that salvation could not be gained by any human effort but was solely a gift of God. All that was required to be "justified" was faith, which was itself a gift of God. Nothing else mattered, since nothing else was effective.

At the same time, Luther was not willing to give up good works, but it was clear that his ethics would have to occupy a new place in his system. This problem was worked out in several of his early works, including "Treatise on Good Works" and "On Christian Liberty," both written in 1520. The gist of Luther's maturing ethic is best summarized in a sentence from "On Christian Liberty": "Good works do not make a man good, but a good man does good works." Following the biblical writings of Paul and James, Luther asserted that Christian faith had to be enacted, both out of gratitude for what God had done for the believer and so that God could continue His perfecting work. It was Luther, anticipating John Wesley, who first suggested a doctrine of "sanctification." Furthermore, Luther's doctrine of the "priesthood of all believers" declared that all Christians were responsible for doing good works, not only the members of the clergy and the cloister, who were called to lives of "higher righteousness."

Living for Others. What works should the justified Christian do? Luther's definition of ethical behavior was, like his doctrine, taken directly from biblical models. The redeemed believer was to give no thought to his or her own needs, which had already been fulfilled through faith, but was to give himself or herself up wholly for the benefit of others, in the same way that Christ himself took no thought of his own interests, giving himself wholly for humankind. Though Luther's ethic contained practical elements—he recommended marriage and the public education of youth—at bottom it was primarily existential: "I will give myself as a Christ to my neighbor, just as Christ offered himself to me." The nature of ethical behavior was to be seen in self-sacrifice, through which Christ would be revealed in acts of service, as he had been revealed in the ultimate service of the cross.

Secular Authority. Luther did make specific ethical prescriptions that had to do with the nature of secular authority. As with everything else, Luther's politics were based on his doctrine: God has ordained two spheres of authority, or two "kingdoms"—one internal and moral, over which the Church was to have authority; and the other external, to be ruled by the "sword." Both were divinely ordained, the latter on the basis of Paul's dictum that everyone was to be subject to secular authority (Rom. 13:1).

With this belief as his starting point, Luther remonstrated with both rulers and their subjects. Rulers, he said, were not to stray outside their ordained boundaries into religious and moral legislation but were to concentrate on restraining, convicting, and punishing sinful behavior in their own sphere. That this was necessary was occasioned, Luther believed, by the fact that, although truly justified Christians had no need of such authority, most Christians were not yet in so spiritual a state but were still enslaved by sin, and thus were prone to disobedience and chaos. Rulers were needed to maintain order.

Subjects were to obey their rulers in all things (Luther included in this injunction justified Christians, who ought to remain obedient for the sake of their weaker neighbors). The difficulty arose when rulers became corrupt: Was there any point at which despotic rulers could be legally resisted? Luther's answer was a cautious and provisional yes, since the ultimate authority over both "kingdoms" was God, and no ruler could compel his subjects to disobey God in their obedience to the ruler. Again, Luther's foundation was biblical: "We must obey God rather than men" (Acts 5:29). Luther's insistence on the divine foundation of secular rule, however, led him to counsel obedience even to corrupt rulers so long as there was any doubt about the proper response. It was on this basis that Luther opposed the Peasants' Revolt of 1525, even though he affirmed the legitimacy of the peasants' grievances. Such opposition, while consistent with his overall ethic, cost him much support among his early followers.

One reason why Luther consistently opposed the overthrow of secular authority by oppressed subjects was that he was convinced that God Himself would end the rule of any authority that was mired in corruption, as He had in biblical times. Thus, Luther's political ethic, like the rest of his thought, was grounded in his personal confidence that God would ultimately set all things right, since nothing lay outside His power. —*Robert C. Davis*

See also Christian ethics; Politics; Religion; Revelation.

BIBLIOGRAPHY

Bainton, Roland. *Here I Stand: A Life of Martin Luther.* New York: Abingdon-Cokesbury Press, 1950.

Dillenberger, John, ed. *Martin Luther: Selections From His Writings.* New York: Anchor Books, 1962.

Luther, Martin. *A Compend of Luther's Theology.* Edited by Hugh T. Kerr. Philadelphia: Westminster Press, 1966.

_____. *Luther's Works.* Edited by Jaroslav Pelikan. Saint Louis: Concordia, 1955-1986.

Todd, John. *Luther: A Life.* New York: Crossroad, 1982.

Lying

TYPE OF ETHICS: Personal and social ethics

ASSOCIATED WITH: In philosophy, lying gradually came to be considered the opposite of truth; in religion, lying is associated with the eighth of the Ten Commandments: "Thou shalt not bear false witness"

DEFINITION: Making a false statement to another person with the intention of misleading that person (Sissela Bok's definition)

SIGNIFICANCE: In terms of ethics, lying is permissible in some cases; in general, however, it erodes the self-respect and the viability of both the liar and societal institutions

Although there is little sustained philosophical or religious discussion of the issue of lying and its consequences for society, there is some embryonic discussion of the ethics of lying, particularly in connection with the issues of truth and sin.

Saint Augustine (354-430). Influenced by Manichaean beliefs that pitted good against evil and truth against lies, Saint Augustine provided Catholic orthodoxy with the judgment that lying jeopardizes one's relationship with God, because God is truth and all lying is a form of blasphemy. Although Augustine holds that the teaching of false doctrine is the worst type of lying, he is opposed to lying in all its forms.

Hugo Grotius (1583-1645). A great scholar in the fields of law, the classics, theology, and history, Grotius was arrested for his anti-Calvinist views on tolerance and politics. Sentenced to life in prison, he arranged a clever escape and fled to France and Sweden, where he proceeded to write his most famous legal work, *The Laws of War.* His confrontation with Dutch Protestant internecine battles and the ruse he used in making his escape from jail may have led him to modify his theological opinions about lying. He argued eruditely that lying was permissible when directed toward children, the insane, thieves, and unrighteous persons, as well as when it was done for the public good.

Immanuel Kant (1724-1804). Kant's reliance on pure reason obviated any appeal to emotional or pragmatic reasons to excuse lying. Kant argued that a lie always harms humankind because it "vitiates the source of law itself." This deontological view does not excuse any form of lie even in a life-threatening situation.

Contemporary Views of Lying: Sissela Bok. The 1979 work *Lying: Moral Choice in Public and Private Life* by Sissela Bok is the first major, systematic philosophical study of the ethics of lying. Bok's contribution to the debate is her superb, detailed intellectual discussion of the taxonomy of lying. She analyzes "white lies," false excuses, inauthentic justifications, lies in a crisis, lies to liars, lies to enemies, lies for the public good, lies to protect peers and clients, deceptive social science research, lies to the sick and dying, and the effects of lying on both the liar and the person who is deceived.

Reflecting the contemporary lack of any single authority, Bok marshals up new categories of lying and analyzes them with an eclectic set of criticisms. She defines lying not as a sin or as an untruth but as "a false statement made to another person with the intention to mislead." Bok emphasizes the consequences of lying: The deceived person becomes distrustful of the liar and, by extension, the society that allows lies to be disseminated without any barriers. The liar loses both self-respect and a sense of reality as he or she continues to become absorbed in a system of transmitting lies to retain power or authority. From this point of view, lying harms not only the individual but also the community.

Bok partially shifts the responsibility for exposing and correcting the problems of lying from the individual to society. After all, she argues, how can an individual change the whole structure of a medical, legal, or business system that values sales, bottom-line income, and success more than it does honesty? How can an individual change misleading advertising, deceptive social science research, deceitful pharmaceutical claims, and fallacious government reports and regulations? These fraudulent activities contribute to the destruction of moral values, the loss of respect for authority, and the proliferation of individual despair in the pursuit of justice.

Bok is not an absolutist. She finds that there may be a need for certain types of lying. Like Grotius, she believes that one may lie to a terrorist or a criminal, or lie in other life-threatening circumstances. Lying to protect the innocent is not Bok's only exemption. She also allows provisionally for certain white lies. Lying to protect someone's feelings or to avoid a painful situation can be justified, but only as a last resort. One must always look at the overall context. Will one white lie lead to many more, cumulatively creating more distrust in and harm for the one who is deceived?

Sissela Bok has extended the significance of lying to all personal relations. She has also warned of the danger of the pressure to lie that derives from such institutions as the government and from such professions as the law, medicine, and business. She has called for the discussion of ethical standards in all institutions, and especially in the field of medicine. To see the act of lying as an authentic issue—separate from its relationship to sin or the individual's responsibility—is a major accomplishment. Bok concludes that without the active support of society and its institutions to correct the problem of lying, the individual will not be able to overcome the need and the temptation to lie.   —*Richard Kagan*

See also Honesty; Trustworthiness; Truth.

BIBLIOGRAPHY

Bailey, F. G. *The Prevalence of Deceit*. Ithaca, N.Y.: Cornell University Press, 1991.

Bok, Sissela. *Lying: Moral Choice in Public and Private Life*. New York: Vintage Books, 1979.

Goldberg, M. Hirsh. *The Book of Lies: Schemes, Scams, Fakes, and Frauds that Have Changed the Course of History and Affect Our Daily Lives*. New York: Morrow, 1990.

Kincher, Jonni. *The First Honest Book About Lies*. Minneapolis, Minn.: Free Spirit, 1992.

Nyberg, David. *The Varnished Truth: Truth Telling and Deceiving in Ordinary Life*. Chicago: University of Chicago Press, 1993.

Lynching

TYPE OF ETHICS: Race and ethnicity
DATE: 1865 to present
ASSOCIATED WITH: The southern United States
DEFINITION: The unlawful killing of a person by a mob, usually by hanging
SIGNIFICANCE: Defenders said that lynching was used to protect the virtue of white women; in reality, however, it was used to keep African Americans in fear for their lives

History. The term "lynching" comes from Captain William Lynch (1742-1820), a captain in the Virginia militia during the American Revolution. Lynch and his men sought to rid Pittsylvania County of Loyalists, Americans who supported the British during the war, and subjected them to trials before a hastily assembled court. Lynch said that the tribunal was justified because no other legal authority existed in the county, so citizens had the right to create their own system of justice and carry out its punishments. The court was said to practice "lynch law," and by the 1830's, that term was applied to instances in which mobs took the law into their own hands without waiting for legal authorization.

Lynching was common on America's western frontier in the 1800's, but no statistics are available concerning how many people were killed by this form of mob action. After the end of the Civil War and the abolition of slavery in 1865, lynching was most common in the southern United States, where it became a frequent occurrence, especially between 1882 and 1930. During that period, a total of 4,761 lynchings took place in the United States, 90 percent of them in the states of the Old Confederacy. Of the victims, 3,386 (71 percent) were African American and 1,375 (29 percent) were white. Half of these killings were carried out with the help of local police, and in 90 percent of the other cases, local legal and judicial authorities gave their approval. No member of any lynch mob was ever arrested or punished for participating in these crimes.

Ethical Issues. Defenders of lynching, and these included most Southern white political, business, and community leaders, argued that fear of such deadly violence alone prevented African American men from raping white women. Ben Tillman (1847-1918) defended lynching and announced that, although he was governor of South Carolina, he would still "lead a mob to lynch a man who had ravished a white woman. I justify lynching for rape, and before almighty God, I am not ashamed of it." Lynching from this perspective was ethically justified because it protected the purity and honor of a physically weak population, white women, from the violent attacks of sex-crazed fiends, African American men.

In only 23 percent of lynchings, however, was the victim accused of rape. More lynchings, 28 percent, happened because of some minor infraction of social customs, such as simply talking to a white girl or whistling at her from across the street, than because of violent sexual crimes attributed to the victim. Therefore, it appears that lynch law was used more as a way of maintaining white supremacy than as a way of punishing criminals. As the African American writer Richard Wright observed, a lynch mob could strike anywhere, anytime, and for any reason. Lynching was part of a reign of terror imposed by the white majority to keep African Americans subjugated. "The things that influenced my conduct as a Negro," Wright wrote about violence against his people, "did not have to happen to me directly. I needed but to hear of them to feel their full effects in the deepest layers of my consciousness." The real purpose of lynching was to maintain white supremacy by making all African Americans aware of the terrible penalty that could be imposed upon them for breaking the Southern code of racial ethics.

A campaign to end lynching by declaring it a federal crime instead of a state crime began in 1930. Two groups, both composed of white Southerners—the Association of Southern White Women for the Prevention of Lynching and the Atlanta-based Commission on Interracial Cooperation—called upon the Congress of the United States to pass an anti-lynching bill. Both organizations believed that through education and public pressure, a majority could be found to give the Federal Bureau of Investigation jurisdiction over cases in which local authorities had failed to protect victims of mob violence. Thirty people had been lynched that year, and a particularly brutal incident in Sherman, Texas, in which a retarded African American youth was slowly burned to death changed the hearts of enough Congressmen and Senators for the bill to win passage. Yet it was not to be. Though the House of Representatives approved the measure, the Senate did not. Instead, Senator Thomas Heflin of Alabama led a successful filibuster against the bill. Heflin made his position quite clear: "Whenever a Negro crosses this dead line between the white and Negro races and lays his black hand on a white woman he deserves to die."

Southern white leaders raised the constitutional issue of states' rights. States had always been responsible for enforcing criminal laws, and these leaders believed that that power should not be reduced. Raising any crime to a federal level would only lead to the creation of an all-powerful national police force that could threaten the freedoms of Americans everywhere. Arguments favoring local control helped to defeat later attempts to outlaw lynching through federal law, while masking the racially motivated intentions of its defenders.

That race and not constitutional issues lay behind opposition to anti-lynching legislation was demonstrated by events that occurred during the debate on lynching legislation in Congress in 1935. The horrible lynching of Claude Neal in Florida, in which a white mob cut off the victim's fingers and toes and forced him to eat his own flesh before mutilating his body with a hot poker and hanging it from a tree, received national attention. Still, the Senate did not act; Southerners killed the bill with a six-day filibuster. One op-ponent denounced the legislation for promoting federal interference in local affairs, while another defended the lynchers because Neal had allegedly raped his white girlfriend, though she denied it, and "the virtue of white women must be defended, at any cost." Not even a separate bill

An anti-lynching poster produced by the NAACP. (Associated Publishers, Inc.)

calling for a national committee to research the problem of lynching survived the Senate debate.

Lynchings were significantly reduced by the late 1930's to an average of fifteen per year, and by the 1940's, such mob-inspired murders had almost disappeared. Yet in the 1950's, two black men were killed in Mississippi for violating the Southern racial code. Fourteen-year-old Emmett Till was brutally killed apparently simply because he had talked to a white woman. The last officially recognized lynching happened in Mississippi in 1959, when Mack Charles Parker was hanged by a mob for allegedly raping a white girl. Apparently, no lynchings have taken place since then, though a young African American, chosen at random, was mutilated and murdered by the Ku Klux Klan in Mobile, Alabama, in 1981. The decline in lynching is attributed to increased press coverage and public awareness of the crime, plus progress in federal protection of civil rights.

Ethical Principles. The ethics of lynching was summarized in a long speech by Senator Allan J. Ellender of Louisiana in January of 1938. Again a horrible incident—a case in which two African Americans had been blowtorched to death by a Texas mob—had led to the introduction of an anti-lynching bill in Washington. Ellender led the fight against the bill and celebrated the South's long battle to subjugate blacks in which "lynch law" played a prominent part. "It was costly: it was bitter, but oh, how sweet the victory."

—*Leslie V. Tischauser*

See also Bigotry; Homicide; Racial prejudice; Racism.

BIBLIOGRAPHY

Hall, Jacquelyn Dowd. *Revolt Against Chivalry: Jessie Daniel Ames and the Women's Campaign Against Lynching.* New York: Columbia University Press, 1979.

Kluger, Richard. *Simple Justice.* New York: Alfred A. Knopf, 1976.

McGovern, James R. *Anatomy of a Lynching: The Killing of Claude Neal.* Baton Rouge: Louisiana State University Press, 1982.

Raper, Arthur. *The Tragedy of Lynching.* New York: Arno Press, 1969.

Smead, Howard. *Blood Justice: The Lynching of Mack Charles Parker.* New York: Oxford University Press, 1986.

Machiavelli, Niccolò (May 3, 1469, Florence—June 21, 1527, Florence): Political theorist

TYPE OF ETHICS: Renaissance and Restoration history

ACHIEVEMENTS: Author of *Discorsi sulla prima deca di Tito Livio* (1531; *Discourses on the First Ten Books of Titus Livius*, 1636), *Istorie fiorentine* (1525; *The Florentine History*, 1595), *Libro della arte guerra* (1521; *The Art of War*, 1560), *La Mandragola* (c. 1519; *The Mandrake*, 1911), and *Il principe* (1532; *The Prince*, 1640)

SIGNIFICANCE: One of the first early modern thinkers to distinguish between private and public morality, Machiavelli sought to provide rulers with guidelines for attaining and maintaining authority; "Machiavellianism" came to represent the unscrupulous use of any available means to manipulate power

Machiavelli grew up in the Florence of Lorenzo de Medici. He was disheartened by his city's decline following the French invasion of 1494. During the period of the Republic (1494-1512), Machiavelli, as second chancellor, was intimately involved with diplomatic relations involving France, Germany, the papacy, and other Italian states. When the Medici returned, he unsuccessfully sought employment in the government. He spent his time reflecting and writing about history and politics. His works reveal him to be a Florence patriot who held republican values. Machiavelli's most influential book, *The Prince*, dedicated to the new Medici, stresses the need for rulers to develop clear objectives and pursue them vigorously and boldly. They must be willing to resort to illicit behavior in the interest of self-survival. Although Machiavelli does affirm certain principles (for example, avoid dependence on others, establish a citizen militia), he advises princes to be flexible in carrying out their policies. Machiavelli believed that governments were sustained by their own morality, which might not always coincide with acceptable Christian standards.

See also Christian ethics; Machiavellian ethics.

Machiavellian ethics

TYPE OF ETHICS: Renaissance and Restoration history

DATE: Fifteenth century to present

ASSOCIATED WITH: Italian Renaissance writer and diplomat Niccolò Machiavelli

DEFINITION: Associated with the notion of political amorality, in that the goal of obtaining and holding political power justifies any policy

SIGNIFICANCE: Machiavelli argued that, in order to preserve the state and personal power, the wise leader must be above morality or moral considerations and capable of using both guile and force as needed.

The ideas of Niccolò Machiavelli have been associated with the darker side of politics. To be Machiavellian has for centuries meant to be willing to do anything in the quest for power. Machiavelli has been viewed as a political devil, advising leaders to embrace the arts of treachery, force, and cruelty in order to be successful. These notions derive almost wholly from his work *The Prince* (1513), and although they have persisted, they are exaggera-

tions of the substance of Machiavelli's ideas. Machiavelli also wrote plays, poetry, and histories. His most expansive work was *Discourses on the First Ten Books of Titus Livius* (1636). In it, the breadth of Machiavelli's political thinking may be seen, and especially his high regard for republican government.

History. For good or ill, it was *The Prince* that, as Count Carlo Sforza said, "made Machiavelli famous and infamous." Although it is unfair to say that Machiavelli was a preacher of treachery and evil, there is some truth in these perceptions of Machiavellian ethics. Moreover, there is an inheritance from Machiavelli's ideas that has deeply influenced political thinking into the modern era. Because of this influence of *The Prince*, it must be the focus of any discussion of Machiavellian ethics.

Excerpt from *The Prince*

From this circumstance, an argument arises: whether it is better to be loved rather than feared, or the opposite. The answer is that one would like to be both one and the other; but since they are difficult to combine, it is more secure to be feared than loved, when one of the two must be surrendered. For it may be said of men in general that they are ingrates, fickle, deceivers, evaders of danger, desirous of gain. So long as you are doing good for any of them they are all yours, offering you their blood, goods, lives, children, when any real necessity for doing so is remote, but turning away when such need draws near, as I have remarked. The prince who relies wholly on their words, and takes no other precautions, will come to ruin. Friendships gained at a price and not founded on greatness and nobility of soul, are indeed purchased but never possessed; and in times of need cannot be drawn upon.

Source: Machiavelli, Niccolò. *The Prince*. Translated by A. Robert Caponigri. Chicago: Henry Regnery, 1963.

Machiavelli was a citizen of the city of Florence in Renaissance Italy and a diplomat in the Florentine Republic from 1498 to 1512. In 1512, the Republic fell to the dynastic family of the Medici. Machiavelli was tried for treason and exiled to San Casciano. In exile, he devoted his life to writing, yet he sought a return to public life. Around 1513, Machiavelli wrote *The Prince* and dedicated it to Lorenzo di Medici. Although they had been enemies in the past, Machiavelli hoped that Lorenzo would be impressed by the work and employ his skilled advice. Machiavelli's work went unnoticed in his lifetime, but the succinct power of *The Prince*, a condensation of Machiavelli's thought regarding rulership, outlasted both its purpose and the Medici.

The Prince. If it has been unfair to say that *The Prince* and its interpretations accurately portray the depth of Machiavelli's thinking, it is equally fair to say that he meant every word of what he wrote. In *The Prince*, Machiavelli states that he will not speak of republics, for here he has a single purpose. *The Prince* discusses how principalities are won, held, and lost. It is a primer that tells how a single ruler may gain and maintain power. Machiavelli emphasized how power is garnered in a corrupt and dangerous political environment such as the one that existed in Renaissance Italy. In such treacherous times, a prince required special skills to control the state. This, the purpose of *The Prince*, accounts for the work's narrow focus and tone.

Machiavelli's Ideas. Machiavelli's attention to the mechanics of government in *The Prince* made political and military affairs paramount. He separated these from religious, moral, or social considerations, except as these might be politically expedient. The purpose of the state is to preserve power, and the one criterion of evaluation is success. Machiavelli was indifferent regarding whether a policy was brutal or treacherous, but he was aware that such qualities might affect the success of policy. Hence, Machiavelli preferred that policy be perceived as honorable and fair, but he emphasized that one should never risk failure for moral considerations.

In *The Prince*, Machiavelli openly discussed the advantages of skillful immorality. He was not immoral; instead, he advised princes to embrace political amorality, which encouraged virtuous behavior among subjects but accepted a rulership that transcended morality. This double standard for rulers and subjects is a hallmark of Machiavellian ethics. Machiavelli never advised cruelty for its own sake, but attempted political objectivity. This unabashed objectivity did not make him a devil, but he did exaggerate the quest for power and confuse the objectives of politics with the game itself.

Principles. Machiavelli's ideas were precursors to many modern political attitudes. He addressed human nature, rulership, the character of the state, and the role of popular government. His observations about skillful policy were based on the assumption that the primary human motivations are selfish and egoistic. Machiavelli assumed that government derives from human weakness and the need to control the conflict that grows out of human self-interest. People are naturally aggressive, and the role of the state is to provide security.

This perspective on human nature led Machiavelli to emphasize the role of lawgiver and ruler. He argued that moral and civic virtues grow out of law and government; they are not inherent in human nature. The ruler represents the law and implements morals but is above morality. For this reason, the ruler must be both a "lion and a fox." When necessary, a ruler must disguise the real intent of policy by controlling outward appearances. At other times, a ruler will have no recourse but to use brute force. Force must be used discreetly and effectively, but the ruler cannot flinch when the preservation of the state is at stake. Machiavelli argued that a ruler should be both loved and feared but stated that it is difficult to have it both ways. Thus, if one cannot be both loved and feared, it is better to be feared that to be loved. The ruler must have the virtues of strength and vision, and the flexibility to adapt to the whims of fortune.

Machiavelli was a national patriot, and he defined the state in terms of a personal identification of the citizens with the state. This idea accounts for Machiavelli's preference for popular government, whenever practical. He disliked noble classes because they were divisive and because noble class interests often clashed with those of the state. Machiavelli disdained the use of mercenary armies and encouraged a standing army of citizens who were willing to die for their country. Machiavelli believed that the goal of the state was to preserve national integrity and property, and he suggested that no state can survive without popular support.

Machiavelli was a realist, a skeptic, a patriot, a populist, and an adviser to tyrants, and his vision profoundly influenced political thinking. Even the meaning of the state as a sovereign institution appears to have originated with him. Unfortunately, Machiavellian ethics makes power the primary goal of politics, while moral, economic, and social forces are only factors to be controlled in the power game.

—*Anthony R. Brunello*

See also Power; Machiavelli, Niccolò.

BIBLIOGRAPHY

Berlin, Isaiah. "The Question of Machiavelli." *New York Review of Books* 17 (November 4, 1971): 20-37.

Cassirer, Ernst. *The Myth of the State*. New Haven, Conn.: Yale University Press, 1973.

Gilbert, Felix. *Machiavelli and Guicciardini*. Princeton, N.J.: Princeton University Press, 1965.

Machiavelli, Niccolò. *The Discourses*. New Haven, Conn.: Yale University Press, 1952.

_____. *The Prince*. Edited and translated by Thomas G. Bergin. Arlington Heights, Ill.: AHM, 1947.

MacIntyre, Alasdair (b. Jan. 12, 1929, Glasgow, Scotland): Moral philosopher

TYPE OF ETHICS: Modern history

ACHIEVEMENTS: Author of *After Virtue* (1981), *A Short History of Ethics* (1966), and *Whose Justice? Which Rationality?* (1988)

SIGNIFICANCE: MacIntyre's discussions of virtue and the relationship between the individual and the community have addressed questions of moral relativity and the role of religion

In his book *After Virtue*, Alasdair MacIntyre analyzes theories of morality with regard to culture and states that virtue is found within the community, in its *ethos*, or character, and not in the individual alone. He argues that the Enlightenment abandoned the belief in a divine origin of morality and overemphasized the individual. This leads, says MacIntyre, to a breakdown of the triad of ethics: "man-as-he-happens-to-be," "man-as-he-would-be-if-he-realized-himself," and a divine system of rules to be followed. Such grounding of morality in human nature can produce moral relativism. MacIntyre is looking for a balance between the utilitarian concept of morality as usefulness and the relativism of different social norms. This question of the individual and the society is addressed in MacIntyre's book *A Short History of Ethics*, in which he asserts that morality emerges out of human history rather than out of human nature. This conception places ethical decisions beyond the limits of individuals. MacIntyre believes that valid moral principles reflect what rational people would accept collectively as good for the individual, regardless of the individual's place in society.

See also Communitarianism; Comparative ethics; Relativism.

Mādhyamaka

TYPE OF ETHICS: Religious ethics

DATE: 250 to present

DEFINITION: School of thought in Buddhism based on moderation

SIGNIFICANCE: Established the idea of different levels on which various kinds of knowledge and action are appropriate

Mādhyamaka is a school of thought within Buddhism that derives from the notion of "one who follows the middle way." It was begun by the scholar and theologian Nāgārjuna, who lived from about 150 to 250 in India, and it is one of four central Buddhist schools. Mādhyamaka Buddhism spread throughout eastern Asia and is known by various other names, including *sanronshu* in Japan, *san-lun-tsung* in China, and *dbu-ma-pa* in Tibet.

History. Nāgārjuna, born in South India in the second century, was the author of several philosophical treatises. His central contribution was the idea of *śūnyatā*, or "emptiness," meaning the recognition that everything in this world, including human beings, is devoid of reality. His argument contradicted other contemporary philosophies of India, which looked on things as having substance in and of themselves. Nāgārjuna proposed that everything is defined or given meaning in terms of everything else. He called this contextualization of reality *pratītya-samutpāda*, or "interdependent co-arising." Recognition of the illusoriness of human perceptions of reality and the mutual dependency of things in the world is a first step toward true understanding, wrote Nāgārjuna and his major disciple Āryadeva (170-270).

In the so-called Middle Period of Mādhyamaka, eight Indian scholars wrote commentaries on the work of Nāgārjuna. During this period, Mādhyamaka split into two schools, the Prāsaṅgika and the Svātantrika. This distinction was primarily based on different logical and rhetorical methods for establishing the truths of Mādhyamaka Buddhism.

In the Later Period, scholars integrated aspects of other schools of thought in Indian Buddhism into Mādhyamaka. Mādhyamaka thought also spread to Tibet, China, and Japan, and more commentaries and treatises were written by scholars in those areas.

Philosophy. Though there are many complexities in the arguments presented by various thinkers within Mādhyamaka

Buddhism, some general trends stand out. Primary among these is the recognition that reality is one and whole, and the human perception of separable "things" in the world is based on artificially cutting up that single reality through rationality and language. Nothing actually exists in and of itself, and attachment to the notion of the reality of self and world is a basic source of human suffering. Nonattachment to the illusory notions of self and world is liberation, or *nirvāṇa*.

The meditative techniques emphasized in the Ch'an (Zen) tradition in China and Japan are focused on releasing the individual from the suffering that comes from attachment to atomized, hence false, conceptions of self and world. They seek to bring perception beyond the constraining rationalism of language, which is delusory in its fragmentation of reality.

Ethics. One might suppose that rejecting the reality of perceived things and selves in the world and declaring everything "empty" of meaning could lead to a moral nihilism in which no action is any more meaningful or better than any other action. This was not, however, the interpretation of at least some of the key thinkers in Mādhyamaka Buddhism. Nāgārjuna recognized that although everything was devoid of reality on an ultimate or philosophical level, on a pragmatic level people have no choice but to live fully in the world, however faultily defined it may be. Nāgārjuna believed the ideal to be that of the *bodhisattva*, or "enlightened being," who lives in the world and pursues a moral path but is aware of the ultimate insubstantiality of mundane reality.

The "Middle Way" of Mādhyamaka is a path of moderation between rejecting the world as illusion and accepting the world as fully real and substantive. One tentatively accepts reality as it is, creating meaning through moral action, while realizing all the time that there is no ultimate grounding behind the reality in which one lives. The Japanese sage Dōgen, founder of the Sōtō school of Zen Buddhism, said, "Before Enlightenment, carrying firewood. After Enlightenment, carrying firewood." The point is that one pursues daily activities in the world, but one's perception of them, one's mind, has changed. Though Dōgen is not properly considered part of Mādhyamaka Buddhism, this popular insight identifies clearly the position of the Mādhyamaka Buddhist with regard to action and philosophy.

—*Cynthia K. Mahmood*

See also Bodhisattva ideal; Buddha; Buddhist ethics; Dōgen; Five precepts; Four noble truths; Nirvana.

BIBLIOGRAPHY

Huntington, C. W. *The Emptiness of Emptiness: An Introduction to Early Indian Mādhyamika*. Honolulu: University of Hawaii Press, 1989.

Nagao, Gajin. *The Foundational Standpoint of Madhyamika Philosophy*. Translated by John P. Keenan. Albany: State University of New York Press, 1989.

Nāgārjuna. *The Philosophy of the Middle Way*. Translated by David J. Kalupahana. Albany: State University of New York Press, 1986.

Nishitani, Keiji. *Religion and Nothingness*. Translated by Jan Van Bragt. Berkeley: University of California Press, 1982.

Streng, Frederick J. *Emptiness: A Study in Religious Meaning*. Nashville, Tenn.: Abingdon Press, 1967.

Tuck, Andrew P. *Comparative Philosophy and the Philosophy of Scholarship: On the Western Interpretation of Nagarjuna*. New York: Oxford University Press, 1990.

Magna Carta

TYPE OF ETHICS: Legal and judicial ethics

DATE: Enacted June 15, 1215

DEFINITION: A grant of privileges conceded by King John to English barons concerning the well-being of individuals

SIGNIFICANCE: The Magna Carta dealt with the grievances of the feudal age, but succeeding ages have used its language as a guarantee of freedom under the law and judgment by peers

The Magna Carta, or Great Charter, is an English document that granted privileges and liberties that were to become the cornerstones of English constitutional government. It became a symbol of resistance to oppression, and many future generations looked upon it to formulate protection against their own threatened liberties.

Earlier kings of England had issued charters and granted concessions to their barons. The difference between those charters and the Magna Carta was that the former were granted by the kings whereas the Magna Carta was demanded by the barons under threat of civil war.

The English kings before John were Norman and Angevin rulers who centralized the government, demanded increased taxation, and expanded feudal and judicial systems as a means of political control. Consequently, when John succeeded his brother Richard I in 1199, he was able to exploit his subjects. John was unskilled in waging war, and when he lost all of his continental possessions except Aquitaine to Philip II of France, his barons sought redress of their wrongs.

John had demanded military service or large amounts of money in lieu of it, sold offices, favored friends, arbitrarily increased taxes, and shown little respect for feudal law, breaking it when it suited him. King John also took the Church's possessions and was excommunicated by Pope Innocent III in 1209. It was 1213 when John finally sought peace with the Church. In 1214, John returned from France in total defeat. His barons met with him and refused to serve him or pay for not serving in the military. The barons began to prepare for war against John, if he did not confirm their liberties.

In May of 1215, the barons formally renounced their allegiance to the King. John made concessions to the Church and granted London the freedom to elect its own mayor, hoping to gain support. John offered arbitration, but the barons refused. John finally agreed to grant the laws and liberties that the barons had demanded. They agreed to meet on June 15, at a place called Runnymede.

The barons came with a prepared list of demands, the Articles of the Barons. After the King had agreed to the terms, they were reduced to the form of a charter. King John finally affixed his royal seal to them on June 19, 1215. It was the custom to affix a seal instead of signature to royal documents.

The original charter was not carefully organized. It was later divided into sixty-three parts. These clauses can be divided into several groups, each dealing with specific issues.

The first of these groups concerns the church, stating that it is to be free. The King must not interfere in the matters and offices of the Church. Two more groups deal with feudal law pertaining to those holding land directly from the crown, tariff reliefs, and those who are subtenants. A particularly large group deals with law and justice. No man was to be imprisoned without lawful judgment of his peers or by the law of the land.

Another group of clauses relates to towns, trade, and free movement for merchants. The conduct of royal officials is the subject of other issues, while still others deal with the administration of the royal forest. Immediate issues were also mentioned, such as the recalling of foreign mercenaries, the returning of lands that had been seized unlawfully, and King John's compliance with the Charter. If he failed to live up to his agreement, the council of twenty-five barons had the power to wage war against him.

Although King John swore an oath to abide by the terms of the Magna Carta, he had Pope Innocent III annul it on August 24, 1215, on the ground that it had been enacted by force. Civil war followed. King John died in November, 1216, and was succeeded by his nine-year-old son Henry III.

The advisers of young Henry accepted the reforms of the Magna Carta in good faith. Reissues of the Charter were granted in 1216, 1217, and 1225. The Charter had been accepted by the government, to be used for guidance. Certain provisions, however, were omitted from the reissues. In 1216, the restraints and demands made against King John did not need to be retained. John's granting of freedom of elections in the Church was ignored, even though the declaration that the Church "should be free" remained. Also absent was the provision for a review of the king's performance by the twenty-five barons.

The 1217 Charter added provisions for suppressing the anarchy that was still prevalent in several districts, amended a few details of the original Charter that had proved to be defective or objectionable, and addressed new problems that had surfaced since the first charter. The final revision of the Magna Carta, which was made in 1225, contained only slight variations from the 1217 version.

The reissue of the Magna Carta in 1225 took the place that it still retains among the fundamental laws of England. It is this version that is always cited in editions of the statutes, courts of law, Parliament, and classical law books.

The Magna Carta is viewed as the cornerstone of the English Constitution. Before the close of the Middle Ages, it had been confirmed thirty-eight times. Edward I, with his confirmation in 1297, placed the Magna Carta on the statute books, and it remains there today. The declaration that statutes that are contrary to the Magna Carta are null and void carries a similarity to the language of the United States Constitution. The principle that no person shall be deprived of life, liberty, or property, without due process of law, was not merely a bargain between a king and barons. It was meant for free people in every age.   —*Larry N. Sypolt*

See also Civil rights; Freedom and liberty; Tyranny.

BIBLIOGRAPHY

Holt, James C., ed. *Magna Carta and the Idea of Liberty.* New York: John Wiley & Sons, 1972.

_____. *The Making of Magna Carta.* Charlottesville: University Press of Virginia, 1965.

Howard, A. E. Dick. *Magna Carta, Text and Commentary.* Charlottesville: University Press of Virginia, 1964.

McKechnie, William Sharp. *Magna Carta: A Commentary on the Great Charter of King John.* Glasgow: James Maclehose & Sons, 1905.

Thorne, Samuel E., et al. *The Great Charter.* New York: Pantheon Books, 1965.

Mahvra. *See* Vardhamāna.

Maimonides (Moses ben Maimon; March 30, 1135, Córdoba, Spain—Dec. 13, 1204, Cairo, Egypt): Philosopher

TYPE OF ETHICS: Medieval history

ACHIEVEMENTS: Author of *Mishneh Torah* (1180; *The Code of Maimonides*, 1927-1965; and *Dâlalat al-ḥâʾirîn* (1190; *Guide of the Perplexed*, 1881).

SIGNIFICANCE: The most influential Jewish thinker of the Middle Ages, Maimonides wrote extensively on philosophy, science, and medicine; although he wrote no works on ethics per se, ethical issues permeate all of his philosophical writings

Maimonides, who was certainly the greatest intellectual figure to arise from the Sephardic (Iberian) Jewish tradition, was one of the most respected and influential Jewish thinkers in all of history. He is known chiefly for his commentaries on Jewish law and the origins of ethical behavior, but he also wrote works on general philosophy, medicine, and astronomy. His writings sparked controversy, but he came to be regarded as preeminent among Jewish philosophers and (by some) as the spiritual descendant of the biblical lawgiver Moses.

His Life. Maimonides was born in 1135 in Córdoba, in Islamic Spain. His family was wealthy, his father a notable intellectual and judge in a rabbinical court. Recognizing his son's brilliance, Maimonides' father personally tutored him in Jewish law. Maimonides was born at the end of the "golden age" of Jewish Spain, a time of relative religious tolerance when the richness of Islamic thought intersected with Jewish and Christian traditions, drawing also on newly rediscovered Greek and Latin texts.

Unfortunately, when Maimonides was about thirteen, the relative peace and tolerance in Spain ended abruptly with the ascendancy of the Almohad Islamic sect, whose fanaticism included the forced conversion of Jews to Islam. Maimonides' family was forced to flee Córdoba, settling in 1160 in the Moroccan city of Fez (which was the center of the Almohad movement and therefore an odd choice).

In 1165, Fez became intolerable; the family moved first to Palestine and finally to Egypt. There, Maimonides' father died and Moses joined his brother David in the jewelry trade. When his brother died in a shipwreck, Maimonides supported himself as a physician, quickly rising to prominence as physician to the sultan, Saladin, and his vizier, al-Afdal. Thereafter, he practiced medicine, lectured to medical colleagues at a Cairo hospital, served as spiritual adviser to the local Jewish community, and wrote extensively on medicine, astronomy, and philosophy. He married late in life, fathered a son, Abraham (who also became a notable scholar), and died in 1204. It is likely that his varied life of surviving religious persecution, engaging in international commerce, and practicing medicine added a dimension of common sense and practicality to Maimonides' philosophical writings, enhancing his ability to communicate with a wide audience.

Mishneh Torah. Maimonides did not write books on ethics, as such, but wrote extensively on Jewish law, in which the distinction between law and ethics is unimportant. Probably his most significant legal work was the *Mishneh Torah*, which was completed in 1178 in Egypt and was written in Hebrew, unlike his other important writings, which were in Arabic. It consists of fourteen books and is widely regarded as among the most splendid and significant works of Jewish literature. The book attempts a systematic compilation of all Jewish law; rather than dwelling on points of contention or scholarly refinements, however, it tries to go to the heart of the issues, presenting the law in a clear and practical fashion. Maimonides believed that the law was closely connected to logic, a prejudice that produced clarity in his presentation. The influence of Aristotle, which was very much a factor in Jewish intellectual activity at that time, was everywhere apparent. Perhaps it was the Greek influence that enabled Maimonides to go beyond the conservativism of contemporary Talmudic scholarship and to place his own distinctive imprint on his work.

The section of the work dealing with "character traits" deals explicitly with ethical matters and shows the clearest Aristotelian focus. It is based on the notion that right actions are congruent with good character and the idea of a God-like mean. Thus, in matters of ethics, the wise man emulates the deity in following the mean course: that course of action that avoids all extremes that might reflect humanity's natural inclinations. The nobility of character that makes such action possible also dictates a lack of interference with others and renders an orderly society possible. This general precept leads in a natural way to a number of secondary conclusions, including the importance of speaking kindly, of paying attention to

Maimonides (The New York Academy of Medicine)

one's own health, and even of suppressing truth to the extent that it may inflict injury on others.

Guide of the Perplexed. Unquestionably the best-known of Maimonides' writings, the Guide, completed in 1190, was also his last important work. Written in Arabic it was translated into Hebrew and Latin. It attempted a synthesis of Hebrew religion and classical philosophy, an attempt that evidently succeeded, judging from the work's enormous authority in subsequent Jewish (and Christian) religious thought, and from the fact that it was immediately assailed by some contemporaries as heretical. The perplexity in the title refers to inconsistencies or tensions between the rabbinical and the classical philosophical traditions. The intended audience was, presumably, urbane Jewish intellectuals (who were literate in Arabic). The purpose of the work is clearly theoretical, but, interestingly, the portions dealing with ethical matters can operate on a distinctly practical level. Thus, the purpose of the law is the health of both body and soul, the health of the soul is a question of character, and good character is associated with right actions. Right actions, as discussed earlier, proceed from adherence to the mean and from the exercise of kindness.

—*John L. Howland*

See also Islamic ethics; Jewish ethics.

BIBLIOGRAPHY

Fox, Marvin. *Interpreting Maimonides: Studies in Methodology, Metaphysics, and Moral Philosophy.* Chicago: University of Chicago Press, 1990.

Gerber, J. S. *The Jews of Spain: A History of the Sephardic Experience.* New York: Free Press, 1992.

Heschel, A. J. *Maimonides.* New York: Farrar, Straus & Giroux, 1982.

Maimonides, Moses. *Ethical Writings of Maimonides.* Translated by Raymond L. Weiss and Charles E. Butterworth. New York: New York University Press, 1975.

_____. *A Maimonides Reader.* Edited by Isadore Twersky. New York: Behrman House, 1972.

Malcolm X

Malcolm X (Malcolm Little, el-Hajj Malik el-Shabazz; May 19, 1925, Omaha, Neb.—Feb. 21, 1965, New York, N.Y.): Islamic preacher and activist

TYPE OF ETHICS: Modern history

ACHIEVEMENTS: Author of *The Autobiography of Malcolm X* (1965), founder of *Muhammad Speaks* (1957), founder of Organization of Afro-American Unity (OAAU, 1964), and founder of Muslim Mosque, Incorporated (1964)

SIGNIFICANCE: His unique vision of a world of human rights and universal brotherhood based on truth, equality, righteousness, peace, justice, and freedom, which should be brought about by "any means necessary," touched the conscience of America and that of the Nation of Islam

Appalled at the racial discrimination that was widely practiced in predominantly Christian America, Malcolm X chastised Christianity as unethically enslaving African Americans through its teaching that the oppressed should focus on Heaven, where they will reap rewards and their wrongs will be righted, instead of doing something about their deprivation here on Earth. He taught that Islam could bring about true brotherhood because of the "color-blindness" of Muslims. Distancing himself from the "turn-the-other-cheek" philosophy of Christianity, he advocated the "fair exchange" of an "eye for an eye, a tooth for a tooth, a head for a head, and a life for a life," if that was what it took to obtain human rights for African Americans and to create an egalitarian society of true human brotherhood. Just as love should be reciprocated, so should enmity. He believed that violent confrontation was necessary to defend the weak (women and children) against the strong (the Ku Klux Klan, or KKK) but saw it as ethically wrong to form an African American Ku Klux Klan, since it "threatens the brotherhood of man." He was convinced that confrontation based on moral tactics succeeds only when the system one is dealing with is moral. He formed Muslim Mosque, Incorporated, to give a spiritual basis to the correcting of the vices that destroy the moral fiber of society, and founded the OAAU, a nonreligious, nonsectarian group intended to unite African Americans in the goal of attaining human rights.

See also Civil rights movement; Discrimination; Human rights; Nation of Islam.

Malthus, Thomas

Malthus, Thomas (Feb. 13, 1766, the Rookery, near Dorking, Surrey, England—Dec. 23, 1834, Claverton, Bath, England): Economist

TYPE OF ETHICS: Enlightenment history

ACHIEVEMENTS: Author of *An Essay on the Principle of Population, as It Affects the Future Improvement of Society, with Remarks on the Speculations of Mr. Godwin, M. Condorcet, and Other Writers* (1798) and *Principles of Political Economy* (1820)

SIGNIFICANCE: Responding to the demand for revision of England's Poor Laws, Malthus advocated limitations on human reproduction; he also encouraged private and public spending as a palliative for a lagging economy, thereby anticipating the 1930's economic system of John Maynard Keynes

Contrary to the philosophers Jean-Jacques Rousseau and William Godwin, who professed the inherent goodness and perfectibility of humanity, Malthus argued that poverty could not be abolished, because of the inevitability of population growth consistently exceeding the food supply. While population grew geometrically, according to Malthus, resources grew arithmetically. Thus, population increases always would be checked by famine, disease, and war. Practical application of Malthusian theory occurred in the renovation of English Poor Laws. Believing that poverty was encouraged by the old system, which allowed people to live in their homes with community aid, thereby encouraging them to have many children, Malthus advocated work houses in which the poor would be forced to live and work in conditions sufficiently bad to keep out all but the most desperate. Because of steadily rising food production

Malcolm X (Library of Congress)

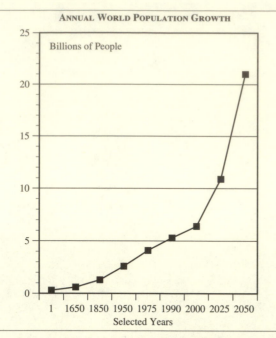

ANNUAL WORLD POPULATION GROWTH

Billions of People

Selected Years

rates brought about by increasingly sophisticated agricultural techniques, Malthusian predictions of food shortages—on an international scale—have failed to manifest. Yet mounting ecological devastation—frequently caused by exploitative agricultural practices—the poor distribution of food, and unprecedented, unchecked population growth in the twentieth

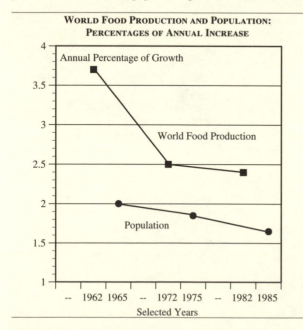

WORLD FOOD PRODUCTION AND POPULATION: PERCENTAGES OF ANNUAL INCREASE

Annual Percentage of Growth

World Food Production

Population

Selected Years

Although the food supply has so far grown faster than the population, its rate of growth in proportion to population has steadily decreased. Meanwhile, population growth continues in an alarmingly geometrical progression.

century, as well as predicted population growth in the twenty-first century, will undoubtedly result in a Malthusian ceiling.

See also Environmental ethics; Pollution; Population control.

Mandela, Nelson (b. July 18, 1918, Qunu, Transkei, South Africa): Lawyer and activist

TYPE OF ETHICS: Race and ethnicity

ACHIEVEMENTS: President of the Transvaal African National Congress (1952); recipient of the Nehru Award (1979); President of the African National Congress (1990)

SIGNIFICANCE: Preeminent leader of opposition to the system and structures of apartheid, Mandela was a political prisoner for twenty-seven years but remained a potent rallying symbol for oppressed South Africans

In 1948, South Africa's white domination and segregation became codified in the system of apartheid. Blacks, the majority, were voteless, needed passes to travel anywhere, held the lowest-paying jobs, and were confined either to rural areas called homelands or lived in shantytowns close to their work. Mandela challenged the system, calling for mass action (boycotts, strikes, and civil disobedience) to pressure the government into granting full rights to all South Africans.

Although he had joined the African National Congress (ANC) in 1944, Mandela became fully active in its anti-apartheid campaigns during the 1950's, being elected President of the Youth league in late 1950. He stressed nonviolent civil disobedience as the primary weapon against unjust laws. He inspired people to know their own worth and to demand their human rights while shunning hatred of and attacks on white people.

Elected President of the Transvaal ANC in 1952, Mandela increased his speaking tours, sharpening his political skills. The government banned him (that is, curtailed his speech and mobility), but he defied what he deemed unjust laws and, in 1954, helped found the Congress Alliance, a combination of groups cooperating in the antiapartheid struggle.

The 1960 Sharpeville massacre of black demonstrators by police brought worldwide attention to South Africa and renewed vigor to Mandela and his supporters. In 1961, Umkhonto we Sizewe (Spear of the Nation) was established, a unit independent of ANC, to pressure the government through sabotage. Mandela insisted that only property, not lives, would be Umkhonto's target. Several acts of sabotage destroyed government property and also caused deaths. Mandela accused the government of having taught force by using it brutally to maintain its own rule, but he reiterated his strong aversion to any loss of life.

Though banned several times, Mandela continued to write and speak for equal political and economic rights until his arrest on charges of treason. In 1962, Mandela was tried and imprisoned, and he was retried in 1963. At this second trial, he gave an impassioned speech, defending himself and the ANC. He pleaded for a democratic, free society in which all could live in harmony and with equal opportunities. Mandela argued that South Africa belonged to all the people and that, since lawful modes of opposition to white supremacy were foreclosed, opponents had to defy the government however they could.

In June, 1964, Mandela was found guilty of sabotage and sentenced to life imprisonment. The United Nations and the world press slowly began condemning South Africa's government. By the late 1980's, South Africa's government and economy were much weakened as a result of various sanctions imposed by many nations and organizations. In 1990, a desperate President F. W. De Klerk freed Mandela, calling upon him to help create a new South Africa, one with justice for all of its people. Mandela pledged his partnership in this cause as he took up the ANC presidency, acting as a revered spokesman for millions of South Africans.

—*S. Carol Berg*

See also Apartheid; Civil rights; Racial prejudice; Racism.

BIBLIOGRAPHY
Benson, Mary. *Nelson Mandela: The Man and the Movement*. New York: W. W. Norton, 1986.

Mathabane, Mark. *Kaffir Boy*. New York: Macmillan, 1986.

Meer, Fatima. *Higher than Hope*. New York: Harper & Row, 1990.

Naidoo, Indres. *Robben Island*. New York: Vintage Books, 1983.

Manhattan Project

TYPE OF ETHICS: Scientific ethics
DATE: Established August 13, 1942
ASSOCIATED WITH: The creation of the atomic bomb and the end of World War II
DEFINITION: An organization established by the U.S. War Department to create a superexplosive utilizing the process of nuclear fission
SIGNIFICANCE: Project workers developed a weapon of such destructive power that its use brought Word War II to a speedy conclusion, thus saving lives, but also causing its developers to reevaluate the morality of its use because it took so many lives instantly

In 1939, physicists in the United States learned of Nazi Germany's attempts to develop a fission bomb of unprecedented power and alerted President Franklin D. Roosevelt to the situation in a letter written by Albert Einstein. Given the brutality of the Nazis, the ramifications of such a weapon were frightening. In strict secrecy, on August 13, 1942, the Army Corps of Engineers established the Manhattan Engineer District and appointed General Leslie R. Groves to head up the entire effort (plan and organization), which was called simply the Manhattan Project. Physicist J. Robert Oppenheimer directed the scientific group that was responsible for actually designing the weapon. By 1944, the Project was spending $1 billion per year—a situation that some people believed was out of control. Project scientists detonated a prototype bomb on July 16, 1945, producing an energy yield that was beyond

their expectations. Two more bombs were readied and dropped in early August, and Japan surrendered soon after. At the time, only some contributing scientists protested the use of the atomic bomb against a live target. Qualms were dispelled by the thought that Germany and Japan would have used it if they had developed it. As the effects of the new weapon became more fully appreciated, however, many began to feel remorse.

See also Arms race; Atom bomb; Hiroshima and Nagasaki, bombing of; Research, weapons; Union of Concerned Scientists.

Manichaeanism

TYPE OF ETHICS: Religious ethics
DATES: Founded c. 240 C.E., Ctesiphon, Persia; flourished from 1300's in western Europe to 1400's in China
ASSOCIATED WITH: Persion religious leader Mani
DEFINITION: A proselytizing, gnostic, universal religion
SIGNIFICANCE: Manichaeanism expressed the human search for eternal life through discovering that inner light, or soul, a reflection of God, that freed people from the corruption of worldly matter

Manichaeanism was founded and organized by the Persian Mani, who was born on April 12, 216 C.E. in the province of Babylon (modern Iraq). Drawing on evidence such as the Turfan texts, discovered in Chinese Turkestan in 1904 and 1905, which contain portions of Mani's "bible," the Mani Codex, and on Manichaean literature, scholars accept the tradition that Mani's mother was a noble and that Mani was artistic, well-educated, and multilingual. His father was an Elkesaite, a member of a Jewish-Christian religious movement that practiced baptism, purifications, and food taboos, all of which the mature Mani rejected. At the ages of twelve and twenty-four, Mani reported visions of a heavenly twin that persuaded him to abandon the Elkesaites and to proclaim his own doctrine publicly.

The Spread of Manichaeanism. Expelled by the Elkesaites and persecuted by the Persian regime, Mani fled for a time to India. In either March, 242, or April, 243, however, the Persian Emperor Shapur I recalled Mani, sanctioned his religious views, and permitted him to preach throughout Persia. Having gathered a handful of converts, including his father, Mani thereafter rapidly won adherents within Shapur's realm before his rivals in cooperation with a new emperor, imprisoned and martyred him in 277.

Manichaean missionaries, even before Mani's death, had begun spreading their religion into Egypt and the Roman colonies of North Africa (where the young Augustine of Hippo was a convert), as well as across Central Asia. In Persia's eastern provinces, in fact, Manichaeans thrived until the tenth century, when their enemies drove them eastward into Samarkand, Turkestan. There, when the Uighur Turks conquered eastern Turkestan, Manichaeanism became the official religion until that area, in turn, was decimated by the Mongols in the thirteenth century. Meanwhile, during the fourth century, Manichaean influences in the West had reached their peak in Sicily, southern Gaul (France), and Spain. Manichaeans subsequently penetrated China in 696 and, despite persecutions during the ninth century, their doctrines persisted there, clandestinely, for another five hundred years. In medieval Europe, in large part because of the hostile fifth century writings of Augustine, "manichaean" was a pejorative term applied by Christian theologians to heretical sects such as the Paulicians, the Cathars, the Bogomils, and the Albigensians, whose dualism or gnosticism resembled Manichaeanism. In sum, for roughly a thousand years and across much of the Northern Hemisphere, Manichaean beliefs and ethical practices won innumerable converts and were exposed to the scrutiny of learned people and their governments.

Manichaean Beliefs and Ethics. Mani acknowledged that his religion was ecumenical, or all-encompassing, by design, and he openly drew upon a variety of philosophical and religious beliefs, including Judaism, Zoroastrianism, Greek philosophy, Chaldean astrology, Buddhism, Taoism, and Christianity. His primary objective was the salvation of men's souls (women were excluded as unredeemably corrupt) through personal acquisition of deeply experienced special knowledge, or *gnosis* (Greek for "wisdom"). For Manichees there were, at creation, two separate worlds. One world was paradisaical, suffused by the light of God, goodness, and beauty. In the present, however, humans lived in another world, a world of darkness, or evil, whose matter, although containing some mixtures of light, was corrupted almost totally. Human beings themselves were corrupt products of the mating of demons amid evil's partial triumph over light. That some of God's light remained mingled in the battle between light and evil and that it could still be discovered in man nevertheless offered Manichaeans hope of salvation. An elite—the elect or *perfecti*—therefore could be saved if they carefully, at times painfully, lived their lives in search of the light within them. Finding light, they also discerned the nature of reality and of the past, present, and future of the universe. Their souls were destined for the kingdom of light. Manichees whose vows were incomplete—hearers—were destined for reincarnation.

Manichaeanism demonstrated an attractive tolerance for other faiths. Jesus, Buddha, Zarathushtra, and Lao Tzu, for example, were important figures from whom Manichees believed Mani was descended or reincarnated. Their writings or sayings formed parts of Manichaean liturgies and literature. Strict and benevolent personal and social behavior were stressed, particularly among the five classes of Manichaean clergy. Prayer was expected four times a day. Taxes were levied to support temples and clergymen. Monogamy was prescribed. Violence, including suicide, was denounced. Fasting was expected once a week and for thirty days at the spring equinox. Believing that humans ate living entities, including plants and fruits, for whom tears were in order, Manichees were supposed to be strict vegetarians.

Ethical Implications. Manichaeanism, in a harsh world of savagely conflicting regimes and faiths, was a religion of hope and redemption, the key to which was gaining inner wisdom. With a well-ordered clergy, temple observances, rites, and strict rituals, it provided a culturally rich and secure framework for hopeful, benign, and tolerant living that deplored violence and avoided warfare.

—*Clifton K. Yearley*

See also Augustine, Saint; Buddha; Buddhist ethics; Christian ethics; Evil, problem of; Hindu ethics; Human nature; Lao Tzu; Muḥammad al-Muṣṭafâ; Taoist ethics; Vegetarianism; Zoroastrian ethics.

BIBLIOGRAPHY

Asmussen, Jes P. *Manichaean Literature.* Delmar, New York: Scholars' Facsimiles & Reprints, 1975.

Campbell, Joseph. *The Masks of God: Creative Mythology.* New York: Penguin Books, 1966.

_____. *The Masks of God: Occidental Mythology.* New York: Penguin Books, 1966.

Eliade, Mircea. *A History of Religious Ideas.* Translated by Willard R. Trask. Chicago: University of Chicago Press, 1985.

Noss, John. *Man's Religions.* 6th ed. New York: Macmillan, 1980.

Manifest destiny

TYPE OF ETHICS: International relations
DATE: Coined 1845
ASSOCIATED WITH: The nineteenth century expansion of the United States to its natural boundaries
DEFINITION: The belief of the people of the United States that the North American continent was destined to become U.S. territory
SIGNIFICANCE: Americans believed that their experiment in liberty and democracy was ordained by Providence to possess the whole North American continent.

The conviction that the United States was destined to possess North America became a reality during the nineteenth century. French claims to North America vanished with the Louisiana Purchase of 1803. Spanish claims received settlement in the Adams-Onis Transcontinental Treaty of 1819, after which Spain's lands contiguous to the United States came under the control of an independent Mexico. Russia's claim to Oregon Country was withdrawn as part of an 1824 Russian-American agreement. British claims to Oregon Country disappeared in a treaty signed in 1846. In addition, by 1848, Mexico's claims to Texas, New Mexico, and California were no more.

See also International law; Sovereignty.

Mapplethorpe, Robert (Nov. 4, 1946, New York, N.Y.— Mar. 9, 1989, Boston, Mass.): Photographer

TYPE OF ETHICS: Arts and censorship
ACHIEVEMENTS: Mapplethorpe's photographs have appeared in museums and galleries worldwide

SIGNIFICANCE: Upholding the U.S. Constitution's First Amendment, which prohibits laws that would restrict free speech, was the issue at stake in the criminal trial of the Cincinnati Contemporary Art Center and its director on obscenity charges for exhibiting Robert Mapplethorpe's photography

The work of the late photographer Robert Mapplethorpe, who frequently depicted homoerotic and sadomasochistic subjects, excited controversy throughout his career. With a slick and sophisticated style, Mapplethorpe often juxtaposed underground, subculture matter with classical composition. A 1989 exhibition of Mapplethorpe's photographs in Washington, D.C., which was partly funded by a grant from the National Endowment for the Arts, provoked a conservative campaign to halt government subsidies for what some considered to be "obscene" works. After an emotional debate, Congress enacted restrictions on National Endowment for the Arts grants that did not fully satisfy either side, although they were milder than many in the art world had feared they would be. Meanwhile, a Mapplethorpe exhibition at the Cincinnati Contemporary Art Center led to the first trial of an art museum and its director on obscenity charges. Against the odds, the defendants were acquitted by a jury that decided that Mapplethorpe's photographs were the work of a serious artist.

See also Art and public policy; Censorship; Freedom of expression.

Marcus Aurelius (Apr. 26, 121, Rome—Mar. 17, 180, Sirmium or Vindobona): Emperor

TYPE OF ETHICS: Classical history
ACHIEVEMENTS: Author of the *Tōn eis heavton* (c. 171-180; *Meditations*, 1634)
SIGNIFICANCE: As one of the greatest and best of the Roman emperors, Marcus Aurelius was able to articulate and implement his Stoic philosophy of ethics

While ruler of the Roman Empire during its greatest period, Marcus Aurelius practiced a simple, even austere personal lifestyle based on the sincere belief in Stoic philosophy, which emphasized the overwhelming importance of spiritual and intellectual values over physical or material pleasures. Noted publicly for his restraint, modesty, and nobility, Marcus Aurelius devoted many of his private hours to writing his *Meditations*, which contained the essence of his version of Stoic ethics. The core of his ethical beliefs may be summed up in a few basic rules: forgive others for their wrongs; be aware of the harm done to people by their own bad actions; avoid judging others; be conscious of your own faults; consider that you cannot know the inner thoughts of others; avoid anger, for life is brief; anger and grief can be worse than actual physical harm; and kindness and friendship are best for all. Although these rules are hardly revolutionary in theory, they assumed and retain importance because they were held by a Roman emperor.

See also Stoic ethics.

Marketing

TYPE OF ETHICS: Business and labor ethics
DEFINITION: The process of buying or selling in a marketplace
SIGNIFICANCE: Seeks to apply ethical practices of product pricing, promotion, distribution, and marketing research strategies to the marketing of products and services

Various personal, societal and environmental factors have led to an increased awareness of ethics in business practices. Frequently, this awareness is focused on marketing activities. Continual publicity about businesses involve with unethical marketing practices such as price fixing, unsafe products, and deceptive advertising has led many people to believe that marketing is the area of business in which most ethical misconduct takes place.

Marketing and Ethics. Broadly speaking, "ethics" implies the establishment of a system of conduct that is recognized as correct moral behavior; it concerns deciphering the parameters of right and wrong to assist in making a decision to do what is morally right. "Marketing ethics" is the application of ethical evaluation to marketing strategies and tactics. It involves making judgments about what is morally right and wrong for marketing organizations and their employees in their roles as marketers.

The American Marketing Association (AMA) is the major international association of marketers. It has developed a code of ethics that provides guidelines for ethical marketing practices. Marketers who violate the tenets of the AMA code risk losing their membership in this prestigious and influential association.

Marketing is involved with a variety of ethical areas. Although promotional matters are often in the limelight, other ethical areas deserving attention relate to marketing research, product development and management, distribution, and pricing.

Promotion. The area of marketing that seems to receive most scrutiny with respect to ethical issues is promotion. Because advertising, personal selling, and other promotional activities are the primary methods for communicating product and service information, promotion has the greatest visibility and generally has the reputation of being one of the most damaging areas of marketing. Misleading and deceptive advertising, false and questionable sales tactics, the bribing of purchase agents with "gifts" in return for purchase orders, and the creation of advertising messages that exploit children or other vulnerable groups are some examples of ethical abuses in promotional strategy.

Marketing Research. Marketing research can aid management in understanding customers, in competing, and in distribution and pricing activities. At times, however, it has been criticized on ethical grounds because of its questionable intelligence-gathering techniques; its alleged invasion of the personal privacy of consumers; and its use of deception, misrepresentation, and coercion in dealing with research participants and respondents.

Product Development and Management. Potential ethical problems in the product area that marketing professionals can face involve product quality, product design and safety, packaging, branding, environmental impact of product and packaging, and planned obsolescence. Some marketers have utilized misleading, deceptive, and unethical practices in their production or packaging practices by making unsubstantiated and misleading claims about their products or by packaging in a way that appeals to health-conscious or environmentally concerned shoppers. Ethical behavior involves using safe and ethical product development techniques, providing a product quality that meets customers' product specifications, using brand names that honestly communicate about the product, and using packaging that realistically portrays product sizes and contents.

Planned Obsolescence. Planned obsolescence represents an ongoing ethical question for marketers. Consumers are critical of it for contributing to material wear, style changes, and functional product changes. They believe that it increases resource shortages, waste, and environmental pollution. Marketers, on the other hand, say that planned obsolescence is responsive to consumer demand and is necessary to maintain sales and employment.

Distribution. Many of the potential ethical problems in distribution are covered by laws such as those contained in the Robinson-Patman Act. Nevertheless, distribution involves some ethical issues that merit scrutiny. Deciding the appropriate degree of control and exclusivity between manufacturers and franchised dealers, weighing the impact of serving unsatisfied market segments where the profit potential is slight (for example, opening retail stores in low-income areas), and establishing lower standards in export markets than are allowed in domestic markets are examples of some distribution cases that have significant ethical implications.

Pricing. Since pricing is probably the most regulated aspect of a firm's marketing strategy, virtually anything that is unethical in pricing is also illegal. Some of the primary ethical issues of pricing are price discrimination, horizontal/vertical price fixing, predatory pricing, price gouging, and various misleading price tactics such as "bait-and-switch" pricing, nonunit pricing, and inflating prices to allow for sale markdowns.

Marketing Ethics and Social Responsibility. It seems tenable to suggest that the areas of marketing ethics and social responsibility should be seen as concomitant. If marketing is authentically concerned with meeting consumer needs and concerns, it should also entail carefully evaluating how decisions impact and affect consumer expectations and quality of life.

Marketing activities can have significant societal and environmental ramifications. The rise of ecological consciousness among consumers gives social responsibility increasing stature. Consumers now are very concerned about whether the products or services they buy cause air or water pollution, landfill expansion, or depletion of natural resources.

Recognizing this increased ecological concern of consumers, many companies are reevaluating the ways in which they produce and package their products and are considering the alteration of other areas of their marketing mix.

—*John E. Richardson*

See also Business ethics; Sales, ethics of.

BIBLIOGRAPHY

Boone, Louis E., and David L. Kurtz. *Contemporary Marketing.* 7th ed. Fort Worth, Tex.: Dryden Press, 1992.

Bovée, Courtland L., and John V. Thill. *Marketing.* New York: McGraw-Hill, 1992.

Evans, Joel R., and Barry Berman. *Marketing.* 5th ed. New York: Macmillan, 1992.

Laczniak, Gene R., and Patrick E. Murphy. *Ethical Marketing Decisions; The Higher Road.* Boston: Allyn & Bacon, 1993.

Richardson, John E., ed. *Annual Editions: Business Ethics.* 5th ed. Guilford, Conn.: Dushkin, 1993.

_____. *Annual Editions: Marketing 93/94.* 15th ed. Guilford, Conn.: Dushkin, 1993.

Smith, N. Craig, and John A. Quelch. *Ethics in Marketing.* Homewood, Ill.: Irwin, 1993.

Marriage

TYPE OF ETHICS: Beliefs and practices
DATE: Marriage and the family concept are as ancient as history itself
ASSOCIATED WITH: All cultures
DEFINITION: The formalized union of members of the opposite sex governed by the customs of a specific society
SIGNIFICANCE: Myriad moral, religious, and legal sanctions relate to marriage and the family

Traditional Types of Marriage. In Western societies steeped in the Judeo-Christian tradition, marriages are monogamous, conjoining one member of each sex, but there are also polygamous cultures in which one male marries more than one wife (polygyny) or one female marries more than one husband (polyandry). Whatever its form, marriage provides a sanctioned context for mating and initializes the basic family unit.

Patriarchal Heritage. In Western societies, there is a strong patristic heritage that still influences marital laws and customs. Even in ancient cultures with no roots in Judaism there was a deeply ingrained, patriarchal bias. For example, in pre-Christian Rome, fathers had supreme authority, including the right to dispose of the property and even the lives of their wives and children.

In many ancient societies, including Rome, marriage involved tradition rather than law per se. Marriages were arranged by family patriarchs, particularly in cultures with stratified classes based on birthright and inheritance. Marriages of convenience were prevalent and often involved the endogamous union of close relatives to preserve social rank and family property. The emphasis in such marriages was on the bride's social rank, dowry, child-bearing potential,

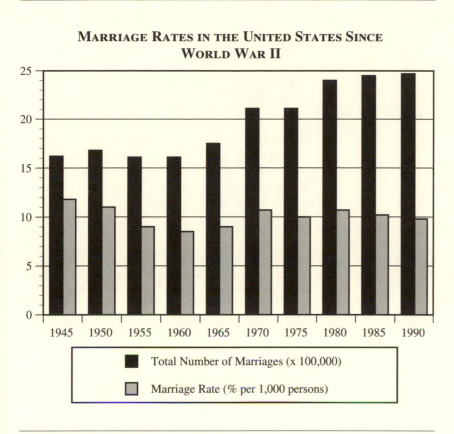

MARRIAGE RATES IN THE UNITED STATES SINCE WORLD WAR II

- ■ Total Number of Marriages (x 100,000)
- ▨ Marriage Rate (% per 1,000 persons)

Source: 1993 World Almanac

is legally binding but precludes any religious sanctions. Those who marry in a religious ceremony must obtain civil authorization, however, and the service itself must conform to law. In the United States, marriage is treated as a legal contract, but it differs from normal contractual agreements in that it cannot be dissolved without judicial arbitration. Although laws have gradually been liberalized to make divorce easier to obtain, the legal right to divorce may be inhibited by conflicting religious doctrines that, for many people, take precedence over legal rights.

Relationship to the Family. Because marriage was traditionally undertaken to provide generational continuity in name, blood, and property, it cannot be separated from the concept of family. Prior to the modern industrial and technological revolutions, in a more sparsely populated, less mobile world, many families took the form of extended families, in which the family patriarch held both dominion and roof over not only his children but also his grandchildren and even his great grandchildren. The nuclear family, consisting only of parents and their immediate children, eventually displaced the extended family as the norm in the more industrialized areas of the world.

The concept of marriage has also undergone modification. Beginning with the suffrage movement, women sought to achieve many rights and prerogatives that both tradition and law granted exclusively to men. Vigorously advanced was the idea of marriage as an equal partnership, with all rights equitably shared by husband and wife. Most laws governing such matters as property and the custody of children now reflect the principle of joint ownership and responsibility.

Modern Problems. The emancipation of women has raised new moral and legal issues that are yet to be resolved. An example is the notion of conjugal rape, an idea that is alien to much conventional thinking about marriage. Even legal redress in cases of spouse abuse has been difficult because law enforcement agencies still tend to view marriage problems as private matters. The battered wife, though not exclusively a twentieth century phenomenon, is relatively new to public awareness.

Closely linked to the concept of procreation, marriage has traditionally sanctioned only heterosexual unions, but even

and domestic management skills. As a result, male infidelity, even when officially condemned, was widely practiced; under an infamous double standard, however, no such sexual freedom was granted to wives. Moreover, vestiges of Roman law and custom geared to male primacy have remained in Western law, going unchallenged until the twentieth century.

Religious and Civil Sanctions. In the Middle Ages, the Catholic Church became the principal agent of change in those geographic areas formerly under Roman domination. Basing its arguments on scriptural prohibitions against sex outside marriage, the Church sought to modify the rules of courtship and marriage and vigorously condemned both fornication and adultery. The Church gave marriage a sacramental status and, technically, made it binding for life.

The Church also kept records of marriages, births, baptisms, and deaths until civil records were instituted, making all but baptismal and confirmation records redundant. Strongly influenced by the Church, criminal and civil law reflected both Christian ideology and its collateral Roman legacy. Civil codes made it extremely difficult to obtain divorces in secular courts, while criminal laws exacted harsh penalties for adultery.

In most Western countries, it is now possible to marry outside the purview of any church, in a civil ceremony that

that principle has been challenged by gays who wish to benefit from some of the legal guarantees extended to married couples and families. They have worked to redefine marriage legally to include the contractual mating of couples of the same sex with all the rights of heterosexual couples, including child adoption. Opposition to this goal, based on religious and moral grounds, remains strong.

—John W. Fiero

See also Abuse; Adultery; Divorce; Family; Gay rights; Lifestyles; Sexual revolution.

BIBLIOGRAPHY

Gies, Frances, and Joseph Gies. *Marriage and the Family in the Middle Ages.* New York: Harper & Row, 1987.

Harriss, John, ed. *The Family: A Social History of the Twentieth Century.* New York: Oxford University Press, 1991.

Henslin, James M., ed. *Marriage and Family in a Changing Society.* 3d Ed. New York: Free Press, 1989.

Macklin, Eleanor D., and Roger H. Rubin, eds. *Contemporary Families and Alternative Lifestyles.* Beverly Hills, Calif.: Sage, 1983.

Mintz, Steven, and Susan Kellog. *Domestic Revolutions: A Social History of American Family Life.* New York: Free Press, 1988.

Outhwaite, R. B., ed. *Marriage and Society: Studies in the Social History of Marriage.* New York: St. Martin's Press, 1982.

Marshall Plan

TYPE OF ETHICS: International relations
DATES: Proposed 1947; in effect 1948-1952
ASSOCIATED WITH: United States-European relations
DEFINITION: The Marshall Plan transferred economic resources from the United States to Europe in order to restore European economies to prosperity
SIGNIFICANCE: The best-known example of foreign aid, the Marshall Plan advanced the principle that relieving economic distress promotes a peaceful world order

The Marshall Plan, proposed in the spring of 1947 by General George C. Marshall, the American secretary of state, was intended to provide substantial economic aid to war-ravaged Europe. In order to prevent widespread economic collapse, the Plan proposed to restore European economies to their prewar levels of production. Enacted by the Congress under the Truman Administration, the Plan provided more than $12 billion in economic aid to eleven western European nations from 1948 to 1951. The amount equaled approximately 1.2 percent of the U.S. gross national product during each year of aid. Essentially designed as government-to-government aid, the Plan required each nation to formulate a list of needs and prescriptions for addressing them. Nations within the Soviet sphere of influence, unwilling to divulge their economic needs, quickly withdrew from consideration. After national programs had been approved, American aid, in the form of manufactured goods, machines, and raw materials, began to flow into the nations of Europe. American advisers supervised the program

throughout to assure that inflation did not destroy the gains. By 1951, the Plan had succeeded in its goal of raising levels of productivity to prewar levels. The Marshall Plan brought benefits to both Europe and America by improving the economies on both sides of the Atlantic. It also laid the groundwork for future international cooperation in both commercial and military affairs.

See also Truman Doctrine.

Marx, Karl (May 5, 1818, Trier, Prussian Rhineland— Mar. 14, 1883, London, England): Philosopher

TYPE OF ETHICS: Politico-economic ethics
ACHIEVEMENTS: Coauthor, with Friedrich Engels, of *Manifest der Kommunistischen Partei* (1848; *The Communist Manifesto,* 1850); author of *Das Kapital* (3 volumes, 1867, 1885, 1894. *Capital: A Critique of Political Economy,* 1886, 1907, 1909)
SIGNIFICANCE: Interpreted ethics as a manifestation of the "class struggle" in any society; believed that all moral principles were rooted in the economic self-interest of the contending classes and served as ideological justifications for their material demands

Karl Marx occupies a pivotal place in the history of the international socialist movement. A passionately committed revolutionary theorist and activist, he worked tirelessly to bring about the overthrow of capitalism and believed that he had discovered the historical laws that would inevitably produce its collapse. As an integral part of his philosophical system, he developed a materialistically based theory of ethics in which the prevailing moral principles of any historical period were seen as reflections of the underlying economic process and the interests and aspirations of the dominant social class. In presenting this view, he posed the question of capitalism's moral legitimacy more sharply than did any other philosopher of the nineteenth and twentieth centuries, and he offered a powerful alternative vision of a socialist society in which social classes would be abolished and all poverty and suffering would end.

Historical Materialism. At the center of Marx's system lies his philosophy of dialectical materialism. His views on historical evolution, economics, society, and theory of ethics all grow directly out of his materialist conception of the world. For Marx, it was not ideas that were the primary determinants of history, but material—particularly economic—facts. In the social world, in particular, the consciousness of human beings was determined by the conditions of their material existence and by the values and norms associated with the prevailing mode of economic production of the time.

All of history, Marx believed, moved through six distinct historical stages: primitive communism, the ancient slave state, feudalism, capitalism, socialism, and, ultimately, communism. At each stage in the process of historical development, the economic system created within it two antagonistic social classes, whose struggle for control of the productive property of the society was continuous and was reflected in their political and ethical ideas. In this struggle, the views

Karl Marx (AP/Wide World Photos)

of the dominant class—under feudalism, the landowning aristocracy, and under capitalism, the industrial bourgeoisie—tended to predominate. As Marx put it in *German Ideology* (1846): "The ideas of the ruling class are in every epoch the ruling ideas, i.e., the class which is the ruling *material* force of society is at the same time its ruling *intellectual* force."

Thus, for Marx, all ethical ideals—no matter how cleverly disguised—were class based and had their origin in the conflicts generated by the underlying social and economic system. They were, in a real sense, ideological weapons used by the dominant and contending classes in their struggle for political hegemony, and thus were an ineluctable part of the class struggle itself. That struggle, Marx believed, was always resolved by revolution, and it unfolded naturally according to historical laws that were independent of the individual's will.

Rejection of Moral Absolutism. The materialist foundations of Marx's philosophy led logically to a categorical rejection of abstract moral idealism. To Marx, universal ethical principles such as those proposed by Immanuel Kant or by the Christian church were pure historical fictions. All ethical perspectives, he contended, were influenced by material interests and rooted in the economic conditions of a specific time and place. Abstract moral concepts such as "liberty," "equality," and "justice" were, in his view, illusions. Each social class tended to define such concepts in terms of its own historical experience, seeking to shape them in order to satisfy its ongoing material needs.

During the capitalist stage of development, for example, the bourgeoisie, the primary purchaser of labor in the society, and the working class, the seller of labor, naturally came to see such concepts as "liberty" and "equality" differently. This difference in perspective was not based on abstract moral reasoning, but on contrasting positions of the classes in the productive process and the underlying economic relations of the age. In presenting their material demands, both classes made claims to absolute moral authority. No common moral ground in the class struggle existed, and the ultimate arbiter was always physical force.

Marx's belief that all morality was class morality took on a particular poignancy with regard to religion. The Church, he argued, like the state, was an institution that was dominated by the ruling class of any historical period. Therefore, it tended to espouse moral values that strengthened that class's political and social position. Specifically, the Church's promotion of the ideal of personal humility, scriptures against violence, and concentration on the afterlife were designed to teach the worker to be submissive to authority and to look to the next world for the ultimate reward. Religion, as Marx put it acidly, was "the opium of the people," and its destruction was an important step toward freeing the working class from the intellectual domination of the bourgeoisie.

Working-Class Morality. The vehemence with which Marx rejected the idea of universal ethical principles was accompanied by an equally disdainful attitude toward the more extreme forms of moral relativism. Since history, he argued, inevitably moved to materially "higher" and thus more potentially liberating stages, the ethical values of the ruling class of any historical period were inherently superior—in a developmental sense—to those of the ruling group that preceded it. Thus, the ethics of the bourgeoisie were "objectively" more progressive than those of the aristocracy and the slave-owning class before it, and those of the working class were the most liberating of all. Indeed, of all the classes that had appeared throughout history, the working class alone possessed a truly revolutionary morality. This was because its demands for human equality, an equitable distribution of property, and economic as well as political democracy grew directly out of its own material needs. It was this profoundly moral vision of the working class as a social carrier for a genuinely liberated society—even more than the purportedly scientific character of his historical analysis—that would account for much of Marx's influence after his death.   —*John Santore*

See also Class struggle; Communism; *Communist Manifesto*; Marxism; Socialism.

BIBLIOGRAPHY

Avineri, Shlomo. *The Social and Political Thought of Karl Marx.* Cambridge, England: Cambridge University Press, 1968.

Cohen, G. A. *Karl Marx's Theory of History: A Defence.* Princeton, N.J.: Princeton University Press, 1978.

Cohen, Marshall, Thomas Nagel, and Thomas Scanlon, eds. *Marx, Justice, and History.* Princeton, N.J.: Princeton University Press, 1980.

Elster, Jon. *Making Sense of Marx.* Cambridge, England: Cambridge University Press, 1985.

Nielsen, Kai, and Stephen Patten, eds. *Marx and Morality.* Supplementary vol. 7. *Canadian Journal of Philosophy,* 1981.

Marxism

TYPE OF ETHICS: Modern history

DATE: Mid- and late nineteenth century

ASSOCIATED WITH: Karl Marx and Friedrich Engels, the international communist movement, and derivative communist and socialist movements, especially in Europe

DEFINITION: A theory based on a materialistic interpretation of the world history, which posits that the course of history is determined by a series of class struggles that progress in a dialectical process

SIGNIFICANCE: Marxist theory challenged traditional Judeo-Christian ethics, posited that right and wrong in any era are a by-product of the class struggle, and implicitly defined a new ethics for the communist society of the future

Implicit in Marxism is a unique variety of ethics that combines traditional theories of "might makes right" with the belief that under communism the wrongs of past injustices will be righted. Marxism as a theory has two distinct parts: Marx's interpretation of society as he perceived it and his image of society in the future. Marx can also be understood on two levels: as an economic theorist and as a moral theorist. He is more widely regarded, however, as an economic theorist with little regard for anything but economic justice. In the twentieth century, some scholars have analyzed Marx as a moral theorist whose earlier writings in particular reflect values that are moral and perhaps even religious, although not in a traditional sense. These values were implicit in his theories of history and the revolutionary process.

Marx, in his early works, often spoke of the worker's alienation from society because of the division of labor and private property, which left the worker with little to show for his endeavors. Marx did not think that the situation could be corrected by invoking abstract theories of ethics and justice, since he believed that in every era ethics and values are imposed by the "ruling class." For example, Marx argued that in the Middle Ages, the feudal landowners who controlled the livelihood of others also set the norms of society. He believed that in the nineteenth century, capitalists (the bourgeoisie) controlled the means of production and therefore the political and social system. As part of their power, they set the standards of right and wrong. Although Marx criticized the ethical standards of his era, he accepted that the bourgeoisie had the right to set those standards.

Marx believed that it was important to understand the economic forces that propel the evolution of history. His theory of historical materialism rejected traditional idealism and substituted for it a materialist interpretation, which defined the progression of history as the history of class struggle. Marx also predicted a fundamental revolution that would end class struggle and alienation in society.

He described a class struggle between the capitalists (the ruling class) and the proletariat (the workers) in his own era. The former controlled the means of production and therefore dominated society. The proletariat worked for the bourgeoisie in conditions of exploitation and hardship and were alienated from the products of their labor. Marx was concerned about the long hours the proletariat worked and low wages they received, about child labor, and about other social problems that were prevalent in the early stages of European capitalism, but he did not believe that those problems could be remedied. Marx predicted that societal conditions would gradually worsen, as fewer and fewer people remained in the ruling class and more and more people joined the ranks of the proletariat. Eventually, Marx predicted, the proletariat would be so large and their conditions so terrible that they would rise up in spontaneous rebellion against the bourgeoisie. This revolution, born out of the dialectic and contradictions of history, would eventually provide the keys to ending exploitation. In the short run, the victorious proletariat would organize the dictatorship of the proletariat and begin to right the wrongs of history by removing privileges from the bourgeoisie—foremost among them, private property. In the transitional era, however, the

dictatorship of the proletariat, bourgeois values would still prevail. There would be a transitional period of undetermined length. Only in mature postcapitalist society, which Marx called "communism," would people embrace new values and ethics, shed traditional acquisitiveness, and work for the good of society. Eventually, classes would disappear and a classless society would emerge in which people would work according to their abilities and receive compensation according to their needs. In the new society, people would no longer be alienated from their work and from society.

Marx's theories of ethics were closely tied to his economic theories. He did not develop theories of ethics that were separate from his perception of economic reality. At the same time, the idea of transcending alienation and establishing new norms for society revealed an underlying idealism that was inconsistent with his conceptions of materialism.

Marx worked closely with Friedrich Engels from 1845 until his death. Their most famous publication, the *Communist Manifesto* (1848), contains guidelines for social norms and values that were to be followed after the proletarian revolution. Engels continued their work after Marx's death (1883). Engels' later writings on social issues, such as the family, and personal relations, contain ethical overtones. In particular, Engels' writings on the family give evidence of the applications of the division of labor and "class struggle" within the family itself.

Although Marx would have bristled at the suggestion that he was an ethical thinker, an ethical undertone to his theory of history can be seen in his prediction that the injustices of the class struggle would be corrected on Earth, not in a distant heaven, when the revolutionary process led to the eventual emergence of communism.

—Norma Corigliano Noonan

See also Alienation; Capitalism; Class struggle; Communism; *Communist Manifesto*; Dictatorship; Egalitarianism; Exploitation; Marx, Karl; Profit economy; Revolution; Socialism.

BIBLIOGRAPHY

Avineri, Shlomo. *The Social and Political Thought of Karl Marx.* London: Cambridge University Press, 1968.

Freedman, Robert. *The Marxist System: Economic, Political and Social Perspectives.* Chatham, N.J.: Chatham House, 1990.

Lichtheim, George. *Marxism: An Historical and Critical Study.* 2d rev. ed. New York: Praeger, 1970.

Marx, Karl, Friedrich Engels, and Vladimir Lenin. *On Communist Society: A Collection.* 3d rev. ed. Moscow: Progress, 1978.

Ozinga, James R. *Communism: The Story of the Idea and Its Implementation.* Englewood Cliffs, N.J.: Prentice-Hall, 1987.

Tucker, Robert C. *The Marx-Engels Reader.* 2d ed. New York: W. W. Norton, 1978.

_____. *Philosophy and Myth in Karl Marx.* 2d ed. Cambridge, England: Cambridge University Press, 1972.

Maximal vs. minimal ethics

TYPE OF ETHICS: Theory of ethics

DATE: From antiquity

ASSOCIATED WITH: Supererogation, utilitarianism, perfectionism, religious ethics, and Samaritanism

DEFINITION: Indicates the tension in ethics between minimum duties and saintly or heroic virtues

SIGNIFICANCE: Tests the maxim that "ought implies can" and wrestles with how far "can implies ought"

The tension between maximal and minimal ethics arises in the attempt to relate what people *can* do to what they *ought* to do. How far and in what way should what is possible govern what is required?

Who Is My Neighbor? When ethical theories examine duties to others, tensions quickly emerge between consideration of what is owed to others and consideration of the effect upon one's own interests or well-being. The Christian scriptures highlight these tensions in such stories as that of Jesus' telling the young man to sell everything and give it to the poor (Mark 10) or telling the lawyer to imitate the Samaritan who risked everything to help a man who fell among thieves (Luke 10).

In the field of medical ethics, Beauchamp and Childress argue in *Principles of Biomedical Ethics* (1989) that a physician is "not morally obligated to emulate the Good Samaritan but rather to be what Judith Thomson calls 'a minimally decent Samaritan.'" They characterize the tension between maximal and minimal ethics in their discussion of the distinction between the duty of nonmaleficence ("do no harm") and the duty of beneficence ("do good"). "[T]he importance of the distinction is evident. The obligation of nonmaleficence is more independent of roles and relations, allows less discretion, and, in general, requires a higher level of risk assumption than the obligation of beneficence, which requires positive actions."

Some ethical theories simply make "do no harm" the duty and leave "doing good" to individual decision making. Other theories attempt to determine how far a person might be required to venture into doing good. Philosophers usually appeal to what it is "reasonable" to require, but no satisfactory agreement has been reached concerning how to define responsibilities that go beyond the minimum. Peter Singer, for example, in discussing duties to victims of famine, has argued that "if it is in our power to prevent something bad from happening, without thereby sacrificing anything of comparable moral importance, we ought, morally, to do it." Many people, however, believe that his principle is unreasonably demanding. Michael Slote argues against Singer that it is not morally wrong to fail to prevent something bad from happening to someone else if preventing the evil "would seriously interfere with one's basic life style or with the fulfillment of one's basic life plans—as long as the life style or plans themselves involve no wrongs of commission."

In *Christian Faith, Health, and Medical Practice* (1989),

Hessel Bouma et al. have provided a survey, from a religious perspective, of reasons that attempt to locate the source and motivation of a whole range of duties from the minimal to the maximal: "[Picture ethical duties] on a spectrum, with minimal, legally enforceable ones at one end of the spectrum and, at the other end, those requiring heroic sacrifice for the sake of another's well-being. In the middle will be responsibilities such as truthfulness and civility that are morally mandated but not legally enforceable. . . . [A]t one end the state's sword power (its right and duty to use coercion, including its power to tax) provides added motivation, whereas at the other end the power of gratitude and the inspiring stories of good Samaritans and shepherds who lay down their lives for their sheep must be sufficient incentives."

Be All You Can Be. Maximal vs. minimal ethics concerns more than the tension between duties to others and care for one's own interests. The tension between the minimal and the maximal can arise in the attempt to delineate the excellences that characterize a well-lived life. Immanuel Kant, for example, argued that people have a duty to develop their talents. How far does that duty extend? Is a modest cultivation of a particular talent sufficient? How much is enough? In *Beyond Good and Evil*, Nietzsche urges a maximal standard of human development in the application of purifying discipline to the "creature" in humanity in order to bring the "creator" element to greater perfection: "The discipline of suffering, of *great* suffering—do you not know that only *this* discipline has created all enhancements of man so far?"

How Should We Classify the Maximal? Many ethical theories classify acts as forbidden, required, or simply permissible. In "Saints and Heroes" (1958), J. Urmson argued that a further class of acts should be identified and that the old Christian concept of *supererogation* should be employed for this classification. Supererogatory acts, according to Urmson, are those that are not required by duty but go beyond duty in a way that merely permissible acts do not.

Urmson's arguments have led many people to agree that ethical theories should have a place for maximal expectations that are recommended but not required. His critics, however, question whether ethical theories can or should try to define a point at which one says, "We have done enough; everything else is beyond duty." They worry that the attempt to make a precise definition of what is strictly required leads theories to be narrow and legalistic in their account of human duties. They prefer an approach in which a "reasonable" account of how maximal duties are required can be given.

—James V. Bachman

See also Altruism; Benevolence; Charity; Generosity; Perfectionism; Supererogation; Virtue.

BIBLIOGRAPHY

Beauchamp, Tom L., and James F. Childress. *Principles of Biomedical Ethics*. 3d ed. New York: Oxford University Press, 1989.

Bouma, Hessel, III, et al. *Christian Faith, Health, and Medical Practice*. Grand Rapids, Mich.: Eerdmans, 1989.

Goodin, Robert E. *Protecting the Vulnerable: A Reanalysis of our Social Responsibilities*. Chicago: University of Chicago Press, 1985.

Nagel, Thomas. *The Possibility of Altruism*. Oxford, England: Clarendon Press, 1970.

New, Christopher. "Saints, Heroes, and Utilitarians." *Philosophy* 49 (1974): 179-189.

Singer, Peter. "Famine, Affluence, and Morality." In *Social Ethics*, edited by Thomas A. Mappes and Jane S. Zembaty. New York: McGraw-Hill, 1977.

Slote, Michael. "The Morality of Wealth." In *World Hunger and Moral Obligation*, edited by William Aiken and Hugh LaFollette. Englewood Cliffs, N.J.: Prentice-Hall, 1977.

Urmson, J. O. "Saints and Heroes." In *Moral Concepts*, edited by Joel Feinberg. Oxford, England: Oxford University Press, 1969.

Mean/ends distinction

TYPE OF ETHICS: Theory of ethics

DATE: Late 1800's

ASSOCIATED WITH: The "end justifies the means"—a philosophy of consequential ethics

DEFINITION: An ethical prescription that emphasizes the outcome of an action and determines moral correctness by weighing the merits of that action against the merits of the outcome

SIGNIFICANCE: Provides a basis for analyzing and evaluating moral deliberations

Theories of ethics vary widely in their philosophical perspectives. Nowhere is this chasm more broad than between the strict legalistic rules set forth by Kantian ethicists and the subjective interpretations favored by situationists. Immanuel Kant, as the father of the categorical imperative, believed that moral actions must hold up universally and unconditionally. Situational ethics, however, as developed by the consequential school, maintains that circumstances alter cases. Actions have no meaning or value in and of themselves; they become meaningful only in the light of the purpose they serve. Situationists believe that any act—in fact, the same act—can be right or wrong, according to the situation. Such flexibility in moral reasoning lays the foundation for the popular maxim that the end justifies the means. Although unstated, the essential meaning of this philosophy is better represented by the clarification that a good end justifies a bad means. A good end achieved through good means needs no justification; a bad end, regardless of the quality of the means, deserves none.

The emphasis, then, is on the outcome, making the means/end distinction a favorite of consequential ethicists who argue that the moral act is the one that achieves the greatest good for the greatest number. With this reasoning, it is easy to extend the principle that an immoral act is justified if it is the vehicle by which a greater good is accomplished—telling a lie, for example, in order to save a life. Another school of thought,

however, that of the situationists, places the rationale for this maxim not on the relative merits of the means and the end, but on the circumstances that define each individual situation. Situationists believe that good and evil are not intrinsic properties belonging to a given act but are instead attributes that develop their character within the context in which the act occurs. The man who denies his financial problems as he provides comforting reassurance to his dying mother, for example, is acting in a compassionate and commendable way, not an immoral and deceitful one. The same subjectivity can be applied to other acts, too, including those conventionally considered good, such as self-sacrifice and philanthropy, and evil, such as thievery and murder. That the unscrupulous exploits of Robin Hood are hailed as heroic deeds by all but his villainous victims demonstrates the popularity of this notion. If acts are not intrinsically good or bad, then they must derive their merits from some other source. That source is the purpose that they serve or the intended outcome toward which they have been employed. Therefore, it is the end, and only the end, that justifies the means.

Although strict deontologists believe that such a subjective philosophy foreshadows nothing short of moral anarchy, the means/end distinction has long been employed. Indeed, even the Bible contains numerous instances in which valued outcomes are achieved through violent or destructive means, such as the flooding of the earth in order to restore goodness, an action that is inconsistent with modern Judeo-Christian moral prescriptions. Despite the fears of legalistic ethicists, however, the means/end argument, when properly applied, is a stiff and rigorous test of ethical principles, demanding a careful examination of four individual elements: the end, the motive for desiring this end, the means by which the end will be accomplished, and, in true consequential fashion, the foreseeable consequences. It is important to note that all consequences must be weighed, not only the intended ones. For example, the parent who successfully funds the family vacation by trimming household expenses must consider not only the financial effects of a debt-free summer sojourn but also the physical and psychological effects of lowered nutritional standards and clothing stretched beyond its normal wearability. In addition, responsible implementation of the means/end distinction recognizes that because means are seen not only as benign tools used to negotiate an outcome but also as ingredients that lend their attributes and characteristics to the creation of the outcome, they must be carefully selected, fitting, and appropriate to the hoped-for end. The following list offers specific questions to help address these issues.

1. Is the end really good? Does it simply appear to be good because of its desirability? Real good is commonly recognized as that which contributes to the achievement of full human potential.

2. Is it probable that the means will achieve the end? Utilitarian ethicists refer to this concept as maximizing expected utility.

3. Is the same good possible to achieve using other means? Is the bad means simply the easiest? Combined with the question above, the lower the expectation that the means will achieve the expected result, the greater is the obligation to seek alternative means.

4. Is the good end clearly and overwhelmingly greater than the bad means that will be used to attain it?

5. Will the use of a bad means in order to achieve a good end withstand the test of publicity? Will others agree with the decision reached in the question above?

Although the means/end distinction provides a useful tool as well as a popular philosophy for weighing ethical choices, it is not without its handicaps. A primary shortcoming, consistent with all consequential theories, is the lack of precision with which outcomes can be predicted. Therefore, the distinction is a more accurate measure of moral correctness in hindsight rather than in the development of situations. Despite this weakness, however, the means/end argument remains a strong and viable one. Its simple and obvious logic offers an understandable formula by which to weigh and resolve challenging ethical questions.

—Regina Howard Yaroch

See also Consequentialism; Deontological ethics; Kant, Immanuel; Kantian ethics; Situational ethics.

BIBLIOGRAPHY

Bovee, Warren G. "The End Can Justify the Means—But Rarely." *Journal of Mass Media Ethics* 6, no. 3 (1991): 135-145.

Fletcher, Joseph. *Situation Ethics: The New Morality.* Philadelphia: Westminster Press, 1966.

Smart, J. J. C. *Ethics, Persuasion, and Truth.* London: Routledge & Kegan Paul, 1984.

Medical ethics

TYPE OF ETHICS: Bioethics

DATE: Fifth century B.C.E. to present

DEFINITION: The discipline that analyzes the way in which moral decisions are made in the field of medicine

SIGNIFICANCE: Seeks appropriate patient care, humane biomedical research, equitable distribution of medical resources, and a just health care delivery system

Health care professionals are faced with many situations that have moral significance. These situations are characterized by such questions as whether or when to proceed with treatment, which therapy to administer, which patient to see first, how to conduct research using human subjects, where to assign resources that are in short supply, and how to establish an equitable health care system. The discipline of medical ethics seeks to engage in a systematic and objective examination of these questions.

History. An ethical code of behavior is central to the writings collected in the *Corpus Hippocraticum*, attributed to an ancient physician known as Hippocrates and other writers of the fifth through third centuries B.C.E. Medicine, according to these writings, should relieve suffering, reduce the severity of an illness, and abstain from treating that which is beyond the practice of medicine; the physician is defined as a good person, skilled at healing. The notion of a morally good dimension inherent in the medical practitioner has survived to this day. The Hippocratic texts were expanded upon by medieval physicians in the West so that, by the fifteenth century, rules of conduct had been established in the medical schools of the time.

Eighteenth century physicians such as Benjamin Rush, Samuel Bard, John Gregory, and Thomas Percival stressed the need for primary moral rules of medical practice and began to wrestle with questions of truth-telling in the physician-patient relationship. Percival's writings would become the basis for the first American Medical Association Code of Ethics, issued in 1847.

Nineteenth century physicians such as Worthington Hooker, Austin Flint, Sr., and Sir William Osler continued to refine a primarily beneficence-based understanding of medical ethics (that is, a code based on taking action only for the patient's good). Osler argued that physicians should be broadly educated in the liberal arts so as to be able to practice medicine properly.

The enormous growth of medical research in the twentieth century led to remarkable advances in health care but also raised troubling ethical questions. In 1949, the Nuremberg Code established the first basic ethical requirements for the conduct of medical research. This document was a direct result of the Nuremberg trials of Nazi war criminals who had engaged in human experimentation considered far outside the grounds of decency. The code was later expanded and revised to become the Declaration of Helsinki of the World Medical Association, originally issued in 1964.

In the 1950's, medical ethics began to move away from being primarily a set of internally generated rules of professional behavior. The writings of such nonphysicians as Joseph Fletcher and Paul Ramsey (both originally trained in theology) began to examine the impact of medicine and medical technology on the moral fabric of society.

The 1960's and 1970's brought an emphasis on patient autonomy to the consideration of biomedical ethics in the United States: Reverence for the wisdom of the medical doctor's decisions, which had been the rule during previous decades, was tempered by a growing respect for the patient's need to contribute to decisions affecting his or her future well-being. The ascendancy of autonomy parallels a rise in the technological capabilities of modern medicine, a time of unusually pronounced affluence in the West, and the appearance of what have since become paradigmatic legal challenges to the notion of the physician or medical institution as the sole participant in medical decision making. Concurrent with these developments was the appearance of new institutions dedicated to the study of biomedical ethics, such as the Kennedy Institute of Ethics at Georgetown University and the Hastings Center in New York. At the same time, ethical theories developed by nineteenth century philosophers such as John Stuart Mill and Immanuel Kant began to be applied to situations arising out of medical practice by a number of individuals whose primary training was in philosophy and theology rather than clinical medicine.

With the 1980's and 1990's, the prospect of scarcity came to dominate ethical discussion in the United States, raising concern about such questions as health care rationing and public access to medical care. An emphasis on distributive justice began to temper the preceding two decades' concern with obligations of social justice to the individual.

Ethical Principles. Ethical analysis consists of the application of primary principles to concrete clinical situations. It also employs comparative reasoning, whereby a particular problem is compared to other situations about which a moral consensus exists. Principled reasoning rests on four fundamental principles of biomedical ethics.

The principle of *respect for autonomy* requires that every person be free to take whatever autonomous action or make whatever autonomous decision he or she wishes, without constraint by other individuals. An example of respect for autonomy is the doctrine of informed consent, which requires that patients or research subjects be provided with adequate information that they clearly understand before voluntarily submitting to therapy or participating in a research trial.

The principle of *nonmaleficence* states that health care providers should not inflict evil or harm on a patient. Although straightforward in its enunciation, this principle may come into conflict with the principle of respect for autonomy in cases where a request for withdrawal of therapy is made. Similarly, the principle may come into conflict with obligations to promote the good of the patient, because many medical decisions involve the use of therapies or diagnostic procedures that have undesirable side effects. The principle of double effect in the Roman Catholic moral tradition has attempted to resolve this latter conflict by stating that if the intent of an action is to effect an overriding good, the action is defensible even if unintended but foreseen harmful consequences ensue. Some commentators suggest, however, that intent is an artificial distinction, because all the consequences, both good and bad, are foreseen. As a result, the potential for harm should be weighed against the potential for benefit in deciding the best course of action. A formal evaluation of this kind is commonly referred to as a risk-benefit analysis. Individual interpretation of the principle of nonmaleficence lies at the heart of debates over abortion, euthanasia, and treatment withdrawal.

The principle of *beneficence* expresses an obligation to promote the patient's good. This can be construed as any action that prevents harm, supplants harm, or does active good to a person. As such, this principle provides the basis for all medical practice, be it preventive, epidemiologic, acute care, or chronic care. Not all actions can be considered uniformly beneficial. Certain kinds of therapy which may prove to be life-saving can leave a patient with what he or she finds to be an unacceptable quality of life. An examination of the positive and negative consequences of successful medical treatment is commonly called a benefit-burden analysis. In this context, the principle of beneficence most frequently comes into conflict with the principle of respect for autonomy. In such situations, the physician's appeal to beneficence is often considered paternalistic.

The principle of *justice* applies primarily to the distribution of health care resources in what can be considered a just and fair fashion. Because there are many competing theories of justice, there is no single, clear statement of this principle capable of being succinctly applied to all situations. However, the principle does require careful consideration of the means by which health care is allocated under conditions of scarcity. Scarce resources in the United States, for example, include transplantable organs, intensive care beds, expensive medical technologies in general, and in some circumstances basic medical care itself. Under conditions of scarcity, one's understanding of justice can easily come into conflict with the obligations to each of the three preceding principles. In general, the scarcer the resource, the more concerns about distributive justice influence the deployment of that resource.

Ethical Issues. Questions of medical ethics generally fall into two categories: A *quandary* is a moral question about which detailed ethical analysis yields a single undisputed answer. A *dilemma*, on the other hand, is a moral question to which there are at least two ethically defensible responses, with neither one taking clear precedence over the other.

Ethical issues in medicine can also be divided into macrocosmic (large-scale, societal) and microcosmic (small-scale, often individual) concerns. Macrocosmic issues are those that apply to a broad social constituency and therefore often involve both statutory and common law. Microcosmic concerns, on the other hand, are those that arise in the day-to-day practice of medicine, the discussion and resolution of which generally have less impact on society as a whole.

Health Care Allocation. Primary among the macrocosmic ethical debates is the question of health care allocation, which centers largely on the development of health care delivery systems and health care financing. Proposals for reform of the U.S. health care system range from the creation of a single-payer national health insurance program, which would insure every citizen, to a series of proposals that would establish multiple requirements for private health insurance, often linking these requirements to employment. A problem common to all proposals for health care reform is the definition of what constitutes a basic minimum of health care to which each citizen is entitled. Even if consensus can be reached regarding a basic minimum, how and to whom scarce resources will be allocated remains to be determined. In both cases, solutions require an assessment of mechanisms for increasing supply and fairly distributing the resource in an ethically acceptable fashion.

Privacy. In medical ethics, respect for privacy stems both from the Hippocratic tradition and from the principle of respect for autonomy. Privacy also has been argued as a fundamental right of persons. All rights-based theories imply a correlative obligation on the part of others to respect these rights. Debate, therefore, centers on when an individual's unbridled right to privacy begins to abrogate the public good. For example, does an individual's right to choose privately to have an abortion or to request euthanasia place an unacceptable burden on society to comply with these requests? If a physician considers a patient to be a public menace, what levels of justification are required before confidentially obtained personal information is divulged? To whom is it appropriate to release this information? Concerns of this nature lie at the center of public discussions surrounding the rights of persons infected with the human immunodeficiency virus (HIV).

Research. Research ethics, as it applies to human subjects, deals primarily with two questions. First, does the proposed research appear to provide important information of substantial value to society at minimal risk to the research subject? Second, is the research subject completely aware of the personal risks and benefits of participation in the project so that consent is fully informed? In order to answer these questions, research involving human subjects must undergo ethical review at both the macrocosmic and the microcosmic level. Nationally, it is regulated by agencies such as the U.S. Food and Drug Administration (FDA). At the microcosmic level, the FDA mandates and supervises the administration of institutional review boards (IRBs), which are charged with the responsibility of assuring that human subjects are involved in creditable research, are treated in a humane manner, are not subjected to undue risks, and are fully cognizant both of the nature of the project in which they are participating and of any potential risks and benefits associated with it.

A third concern in biomedical research ethics, which does not directly apply to human subjects, is the question of what constitutes a conflict of interest on the part of the principal investigator or research institution. This becomes an increasing problem as more research is funded by private rather than public sources.

The Nature of Life. This is perhaps the thorniest of all issues in that it revolves around definitional questions about which no consensus exists. Is human life consistently of greater value than all other forms of life? Is the value of human life defined primarily by consciousness? Is human life defined by genetic information, and if so, is alteration of this information a moral enterprise? If genetic engineering is in principle morally acceptable, are there circumstances under which it becomes unacceptable? When precisely does life begin and end? Each of these questions has a profound effect on an individual's opinion of issues such as abortion, the appropriate circumstances for treatment withdrawal, brain death, organ transplantation, euthanasia, animal research, and allocation of health care.

Ethical Decision Making. Although some commentators tend to assign primacy to one of the four principles of medical ethics—autonomy, nonmaleficence, beneficence, or justice—relegating others to subordinate roles, the prevailing approach to principled reasoning interprets each principle as being *prima facie* binding; that is, each principle confers a binding obligation upon the medical professional to the extent that it does not conflict with another, equally binding principle. When two *prima facie* principles require actions that are diametrically opposed, there is an appeal to proportionality that allows the requirements of each principle to be evaluated in the light of circumstances at hand. On a case-by-case basis, one principle may be judged to be more binding than another, depending on the context of the problem.

An alternative form of ethical analysis employs the technique of *casuistry*, or case-based analysis. Using this method, the circumstances of a particular ethical quandary or dilemma (the "reference case") are compared to those of a case about which it is abundantly clear what the correct moral decision should be (the "paradigm case"). The degree to which the reference case resembles or differs from the paradigm case provides guidance as to what the ethically appropriate course of action might be. This method of analysis has the advantage of being similar to the way in which conclusions are reached both in common law and in clinical medicine. Clinical decisions are regularly made in medical practice by comparing the facts of a particular case about which the treatment may be in question with those of similar cases in which the correct treatment is known.

A problem for those who favor casuistic analysis is the *wedge argument*, sometimes known as the "slippery slope." Detractors suggest that the use of a particular logical argument, such as the defense for withholding or withdrawing certain kinds of therapy, will drive a wedge further and further into the fabric of society until an undesirable consequence (for example, active nonvoluntary euthanasia) ensues. Proponents of casuistry respond that the undesirable consequence is far enough removed from the paradigm case to no longer resemble it.

Most clinical ethicists combine principle-based analysis with case-based reasoning to answer the specific ethical questions that arise in the practice of medicine. In addition, clinical ethicists benefit from training in law, sociology, and psychology, as well as the primary studies of medical science and philosophy.

Public Policy. Macrocosmic, public issues are addressed publicly by a number of mechanisms. Blue-ribbon panels, such as the New York State Task Force on Life and the Law, can study a problem in depth, after which a consensus report with policy recommendations is issued. Such panels have the advantage of bringing together people who represent a wide range of opinion. Another avenue is the formation of grass-roots organizations, such as Oregon Health Decisions, that attempt to generate a public consensus on ethically sensitive issues.

In one fashion or another, issues of public concern often are argued on the floors of both federal and state legislatures. Numerous state laws regulate the withholding and withdrawing of therapy; federal legislation, such as the Patient Self-Determination Act, also governs the disclosure of patients' rights to determine the course of their care when they cannot make decisions.

Even with legislative guidance, individual institutions often find themselves beset by microcosmic ethical questions such as when to terminate life-sustaining therapy or who should be admitted to intensive care units. Other common microcosmic dilemmas involve maternal-fetal conflict, wherein the autonomous requests or medical best interests of the mother do not coincide with the presumed best interests of her unborn child. In such situations, health care facilities often solicit the assistance of institutional ethics committees. Such committees are characteristically composed of individuals representing a broad spectrum of professional disciplines as well as community members not directly employed by the facility. In situations that require an institutional response, these committees will often assist in policy development. Ethics committees also serve as primary educational resources for both the institutional staff and members of the surrounding community.

Many committees have established mechanisms for case consultation or case review for patients whose care raises ethical questions. Consultations of this type involve review of the patient's clinical condition as well as pertinent social, religious, psychological, and family circumstances. Consultants investigate the ethical arguments that support alternative courses of action before issuing a final recommendation. In most cases, the recommendations are not binding; however, certain models do require that consultative recommendations determine the outcome in specific settings.

Although intervention by an ethics committee often allows for the resolution of ethical disputes within the walls of an institution, sometimes irreconcilable differences require judicial review by a court of law. Under these circumstances, the court's decision becomes a matter of public record, providing precedent for similar cases in the future. Microcosmic cases can thereby generate a body of common law that has profound effects at the macrocosmic level.

—*John A. McClung*

See also Bioethics; Medical research; Physician-patient relationship; *Principles of Medical Ethics*.

BIBLIOGRAPHY

Beauchamp, Tom L., and James F. Childress. *Principles of Biomedical Ethics*. 3d ed. New York: Oxford University Press, 1989. A lucidly written textbook. Although some commentators are critical of a primarily principle-based approach to bioethics, this remains the major introductory resource.

Beauchamp, Tom L., and Laurence B. McCullough. *Medical Ethics: The Moral Responsibilities of Physicians*. Englewood Cliffs, N.J.: Prentice-Hall, 1984. An excellent introduction to common problems encountered in clinical ethics.

Each chapter opens with a case study that illustrates the focal topic. One of the best references for people completely new to the field.

Beauchamp, Tom L., and LeRoy Walters, eds. *Contemporary Issues in Bioethics*. 2d ed. Belmont, Calif.: Wadsworth, 1982. A composite of readings culled from legal decisions, seminal legislation, ethical codes of conduct, and the writings of well-known ethicists. Readings are organized by topic and are preceded by a summary of ethical theory.

Jonsen, Albert R., Mark Siegler, and William J. Winslade. *Clinical Ethics*. 3d ed. New York: McGraw-Hill, 1992. A handbook of medical ethics aimed primarily at the physician in training. The authors present a method for evaluating the ethical dimensions of clinical cases, after which the book is organized lexically so that commonly encountered problems can be easily located. A concise reference that concentrates on practical rather than theoretical priorities.

Jonsen, Albert R., and Stephen Toulmin. *The Abuse of Casuistry: A History of Moral Reasoning*. Berkeley: University of California Press, 1988. A well-constructed history of the technique of case-based analysis that concludes with a practical description of how this approach can be used as an alternative to principle-based analysis in clinical situations.

Reich, W., ed. *Encyclopedia of Bioethics*. 2d ed. New York: Free Press, 1992. A broad look at the entire field of bioethics and one of the most comprehensive collections of readings available under one title.

Veatch, Robert M. *Case Studies in Medical Ethics*. Cambridge, Mass.: Harvard University Press, 1977. A good survey of ethical issues, illustrated by 112 separate case presentations. Excellent for group discussions.

Medical research

TYPE OF ETHICS: Bioethics

DATE: Fifth century B.C.E. to present

ASSOCIATED WITH: Medical researchers performing animal experiments, clinical trials of drugs and procedures on humans, and epidemiological studies

DEFINITION: The application of bioethical principles to investigations whose goal is generalizable knowledge rather than individualized treatment

SIGNIFICANCE: Ethical medical research attempts to ensure that human subjects understand risks, to minimize harms to them, and to distribute the benefits of research equitably; also attempts to promote humane treatment of animals

Medical research, like other types of scientific inquiry, seeks to either discover patterns or test proposed solutions (hypotheses) to problems. Broadly, the research entails observation and experimentation in accordance with the scientific method. Observation may be entirely passive: for example, an epidemiological study that tracks the spread of a disease through a population. Experiments depend upon intervention, that is, introducing some variable, such as a new drug or surgical procedure, in order to define that variable's effect on a disease. Whether involving animal or human subjects, research poses complex ethical problems. In the case of human subjects, both the individual subject and the physician-researcher may face dilemmas if the social benefit of increased knowledge comes at the expense of the subject's health. The trend in contemporary medicine has been to limit or eliminate ethical conflicts through defined principles, governmental regulation, and oversight panels.

Every time physicians treat patients, some experimentation is involved, since however well tested a medicine or procedure may be, its use on the unique physiology of an individual amounts to a new test and carries some risk. In daily practice, however, physicians intend treatments to improve only the individual patient's health. By contrast, researchers hope to acquire generalized knowledge either to increase the basic understanding of the human psyche and soma or to treat all people who have a given disease. Accordingly, research has broader social and scientific implications than does treatment.

History. In Western medicine, the *Epidemics*, traditionally attributed to Hippocrates (approximately 460-377 B.C.E.), presented the first preserved general guidelines for physicians; its dictum to help patients or at least not harm them acquired pervasive moral authority. (Similar strictures appear in early Hindu and Chinese medical treatises.) The Hippocratic method stressed that physicians should observe the patient and his or her surroundings and assist nature in restoring the patient's health. The method was not innately experimental in the scientific sense.

Although Hippocrates' prestige was great, many early physicians approved of experimental procedures, and so the conflict between research and preserving patients from harm began early. The third century B.C.E. Alexandrian physicians Herophilus and Erasistratus believed that understanding anatomy must precede effective treatment of diseases; accordingly, they practiced vivisection on condemned prisoners, reasoning that the pain inflicted on them could lead to knowledge that would benefit humanity in general, which to them justified the vivisection. Later classical writers often disagreed. Celsus and the Christian philosopher Tertullian, for example, considered vivisection to be murder.

During the European Middle Ages, the teachings of the second century Greek physician Galen dominated medicine. Galen taught that nature does nothing without a purpose and that the physician simply must discover that purpose; medicine was primarily the application of the four-humors theory to specific cases, a method that was congenial to medieval Christian philosophy. Empirical experimentation was considered unnecessary and immoral.

When, after the Renaissance, physicians began to abandon the humors theory and investigated the pathology of disease, biochemistry, and anatomy, the impetus to experiment grew. Little research was rigorous, and most research involved experiments on patients, sometimes resulting in a public outcry. Such was the case in Boston during the smallpox epidemic of 1721-1722. Learning from England that small amounts of infected material stimulated immunity to the disease, Cotton Mather and Zebdeil Boylston inoculated 250 healthy Bostonians; 2 percent died, while 15 percent of plague victims died among the general population. Yet the immunization experiment was decried: not only did the procedure meddle with the workings of God, opponents claimed, but it killed that 2 percent who might not have contracted smallpox otherwise.

The debate over the welfare of patients and the need for validated medical knowledge began to assume its modern shape during the second half of the nineteenth century. In 1865 Claude Bernard, a French physician, published his *Introduction to Experimental Medicine*, a fundamentally influential treatise. In it he argued that researchers must force nature to reveal itself; since experimental trials and procedures, including vivisection, are the surest means to produce verifiable knowledge, the physician has a duty to employ them. He added, however, that all research must benefit the test subjects. Those experiments that do only harm must be forbidden.

Bernard's book appeared as an antivivisection movement was spreading, intent upon exposing the cruelty of medical experiments on both animals and humans. Antivivisectionists criticized researchers for looking upon research subjects as objects rather than living, individual beings and for using subjects for the researchers' own ambitions with careless disregard of the pain and injury they may inflict. Such attitudes, according to the argument, are immoral because they conflict with the Christian principle of benevolence and the physicians' Hippocratic oath.

Efforts to codify ethical principles increased following World War II, mainly in reaction to grisly experiments performed in concentration camps by Nazi doctors. The Nuremberg Code (1947-1948) sought to prohibit experiments upon humans against their will or when death is the likely outcome; most subsequent codes were modeled upon it. The World Medical Association's Declaration of Helsinki (1964, revised 1975) suggested methods of protecting human subjects and urged researchers to respect animals' welfare and be cautious about the effect of experiments on the environment. In the United States, various federal agencies published regulations for experiments financed by public funds, especially the Food and Drug Administration (1981) and the Department of Health and Human Services (1983), which required that institutional review boards (IRBs) approve research proposals before projects begin and monitor their execution.

In 1978, the National Commission for the Protection of Human Subjects of Biomedical and Behavioral Research released *The Belmont Report*, which proposed broad ethical principles to guide researchers in designing ethical studies. While widely influential, this brief document provided only a framework. Upon researchers and IRBs falls the task of interpreting and applying the principles to resolve ethical problems, sometimes in unprecedented contexts. For example, subsequent epidemics, such as acquired immunodeficiency syndrome (AIDS), and technology, such as recombinant deoxyribonucleic acid (DNA) technology, have challenged the ethics of clinical trials and research funding and raised concerns about public safety. Furthermore, although some government agencies regulate animal experiments, animal rights advocates condemn tests that harm animals for the benefit of humans.

Ethical Principles. *The Belmont Report* draws from assumptions about equity and autonomy that are common in modern cultures: Each human is to be treated as an individual, rather than as a component of a group; no individual is inherently superior, and no individual can be used primarily as the means to an end. The report's three *prima facie* principles—respect for persons, beneficence, and justice—assert these values' primacy when they conflict with the central value of scientific research, the acquisition of knowledge.

Respect for persons, also called autonomy, rests upon ensuring the self-determination of research subjects. Prospective subjects must not be enrolled in a study through coercion or deceit. Investigators must explain the nature of their study and its potential to harm subjects; then the subjects' formal consent must be obtained. For those subjects incapable of informed consent, such as children, the mentally impaired, and the brain dead, responsible guardians must consent to the enrollment. During the course of a study, researchers must protect the well-being and rights of subjects and permit them to end their participation at any time. In effect, researchers are to treat subjects as partners and collaborators, not as objects.

Beneficence obligates researchers to design a study protocol (the plans and rules for a study) so that the risk of harm to subjects is minimized and the potentiality for benefits is maximized. (Some ethicists divide this principle into beneficence, which assures the well-being of subjects, and nonmaleficence, which requires avoidance of harm. The division, they argue, reduces confusion and emphasizes the tenet in the Hippocratic oath against harming patients.) The Department of Health and Human Services has defined minimal risk as the risk one runs in daily life or during routine physical or psychological tests. Beneficence entails a dual perspective: Not only should each subject expect greater benefits to health than harms, but there should also be a reasonable expectation that the study's findings will benefit society.

Because research risks the health of a few subjects, even if voluntary, in order to improve medicine for everyone, an innate inequity exists. *Justice* seeks to moderate this inequity. No class of people, as defined by poverty, race, nationality, mentality, or condition of health, is to be exploited as research subjects so that they assume a disproportionate burden. The subjects are to be treated fairly; that is, their general human rights must be guarded. The benefits of research must be distributed equally among all groups in society.

Ethical Norms. Six norms, or standards, are widely used to verify that a study adheres to the principles of respect for persons, beneficence, and justice.

First, the design of the study should be rigorously defined and based upon the null hypothesis (also called equipoise). The null hypothesis assumes that, of the treatments involved in a study, none is known to be superior when the study begins; likewise, if a placebo (inert drug or harmless procedure) is used, there must be no persuasive evidence beforehand that the treatment is superior to the placebo. This norm protects subjects, especially those with disease, from receiving treatments known to be inferior, and it helps physician-researchers overcome their central dilemma in medical research: withholding the best available treatment in order to test new treatments. Thereby, good research design supports respect for persons and beneficence.

Second, researchers must be competent, possessing adequate scientific knowledge and skill to conduct the study and to give subjects proper medical care. This norm also supports respect for persons and beneficence.

Third, the study should either balance possible benefits with harms or expect more benefits. Furthermore, if in the course of the study one treatment proves to be superior to another or to the placebo, researchers must terminate or modify the study so that all subjects receive the better treatment. This norm incorporates all three ethical principles.

Fourth, researchers must obtain documented informed consent from each subject before a study begins, which assures respect for persons.

Fifth, to affirm the justice of a study, the selection of subjects must be equitable, drawing at random from the eligible population.

Sixth, again for the sake of justice, researchers should compensate subjects for any injuries incurred because of a study.

Ethical Issues. The most common form of medical research is the three-phase clinical trial, which usually tests new drugs. To eliminate possible biases toward the data and to provide equal treatment of subjects, researchers may incorporate one or more of the following four techniques. First, *randomization* assigns subjects by a lottery system, rather than on the basis of health, group affiliation, or economic condition. Second, one group of subjects receives the treatment under study, while a second, the control group, receives a *placebo*. When the first group reacts favorably to the treatment and there is no change to the control group, the researchers can conclude that the treatment causes the reaction, and it is not just an accident. Third, studies are *blinded*, which means that either the researchers, the subjects, or both (double-blinded) do not know which subjects are receiving treatment and which placebos. Fourth, the groups can exchange roles (*crossover*); that is, the first group changes from treatment to placebo and the second group from placebo to treatment. A study employing all these techniques is usually called a randomized, double-blinded, placebo-controlled clinical trial with crossover.

Ethical issues trouble every step of such studies. For example, government regulation requires that a new drug be tested on animals before humans try it, and animal rights advocates have long denounced this procedure as cruel and exploitative. A phase I study determines the toxicity, side effects, and safe dosage of a drug on a small group of people in good health. Since an experimental drug can confer no health benefit on these "normals," the study lacks beneficence; however, the trend has been to conduct phase I tests on subjects who have a disease for which a drug or procedure is a potential treatment, which obviates the ethical objection.

Phase II studies are controlled clinical trials on a small number of patients to determine whether a drug has a beneficial effect and is safe; Phase III trials, either controlled or uncontrolled, compare the effect of the new treatment with that of the standard treatment on a large group of subjects, while defining the former's medicinal properties and adverse effects as precisely as possible. When patients in a clinical trial are desperately ill, they may grasp at any new treatment with hope, so the use of randomization, blinded dispensation of treatment and placebos can seem a deprivation of well-being. Such was the case in the 1980's when azidothymidine (AZT) was tested on subjects carrying the human immunodeficiency virus (HIV) associated with AIDS; the phase I trial showed clinical improvements in some patients. Federal regulations called for a placebo-controlled phase II follow-up, yet scientists were sharply divided over the morality of withholding AZT from HIV-infected persons, since AIDS, once it developed fully, was thought to be universally fatal. A controlled study would be selective and would involve rationing of the drug, which they argued was unjust. Other scientists contended that only a thorough, controlled study could determine whether AZT had side effects more debilitating than the disease itself, and therefore the beneficence of the experimental treatment would remain in doubt.

When federal regulations made AZT the control drug for all further studies, concerns about confidentiality were raised. By selecting subjects for AIDS-related trials, researchers exposed the fact that these subjects were infected, and many subjects worried that they would face discrimination. Furthermore, the large amount of public funds devoted to AIDS research in the late 1980's brought complaints from scientists that other projects were left underfunded as a consequence. Some of these issues apply to studies of other widespread, deadly diseases, such as cancer and heart disease.

Ethical issues literally arise before subjects' birth and continue after their death. For example, some right to life advocates, whose religious convictions hold that all human life is sacred, object to the use of fetuses or fetal tissue in research. Use of the brain dead, even if a legal will affords permission, is potentially unethical if the subject's family objects.

Purely observational research may also be unethical when it withholds treatment and allows a disease to progress. For example, the Tuskegee Syphilis Study (1932 to 1972), designed to define the natural history of syphilis, illustrates harm by omission. The study followed four hundred black men with syphilis and about two hundred without it to determine the occurrence of untreated symptoms and mortality. The study continued even after penicillin, an effective treatment, appeared in the late 1940's.

Regulation. Scientists applying for public funding and pharmaceutical companies seeking FDA approval of a new drug must comply with federal regulations, many of which are designed to satisfy the ethical principles enunciated in *The Belmont Report*. The initial responsibility for compliance belongs to internal review boards (IRBs), which act on behalf of their parent institutions (mainly hospitals and universities), not as agents of the government. Composition of IRBs varies, but all must have doctors and scientists capable of reviewing the scientific merit of a proposed study; clergy, nurses, administrators, ethicists, and members of the public may also participate to safeguard the rights, well-being, and privacy of subjects. Even institutions that do not rely on public funds routinely convene IRBs to review research proposals.

Since federal agencies lack the resources to scrutinize every research project, medical research is largely self-regulated from a project's beginning, through IRBs, to its final product: publication. Medical journal standards call for editors to reject articles written by researchers who have not adhered to *The Belmont Report*'s principles, although some editors do publish such articles but follow them with editorials calling attention to ethical problems. —*Roger Smith*

See also Animal research; Bioethics; Experimentation, ethics of; Genetic engineering; Hippocrates; U.S. National Commission for the Protection of Human Subjects of Biomedical and Behavioral Research.

BIBLIOGRAPHY

Beauchamp, Tom L., and James F. Childress. *Principles of Biomedical Ethics*. 3d ed. New York: Oxford University Press, 1989. A general philosophical treatment of medical ethics, of which research ethics forms an appreciable part, and one of the most frequently cited analyses of the subject. Attempts to educe the ethical theory that best serves American health care.

Cohen, Carl. "The Case for the Use of Animals in Biomedical Research." *New England Journal of Medicine* 315 (Oct. 2, 1986): 865-870. Argues that animal experimentation reduces risks to human subjects while accumulating much knowledge that is beneficial to human and veterinary medicine; urges also that animals be used humanely. While sympathetic to research, Cohen provides a good introduction to the animal rights controversy.

Freedman, Benjamin. "Equipoise and the Ethics of Clinical Research." The New England Journal of Medicine 317 (July 16, 1987): 141-145. An excellent summary of conditions under which a physician's oath to provide the best treatment available may conflict with the investigator's goal of acquiring scientific evidence. Proposes ethical standards with which to resolve such conflict.

Levine, Robert J. *Ethics and Regulation of Clinical Research*. 2d ed. Baltimore: Urban & Schwarzenberg, 1986. Levine, a consultant to the National Commission for the Protection of Human Subjects in Biomedical and Behavioral Research, interprets and expands upon the principals enunciated in *The Belmont Report*, drawing also upon such documents as the Nuremberg Code and the Declaration of Helsinki. A valuable, thorough discussion of specific issues as well as theory.

Lo, Bernard, et al. "Addressing Ethical Issues." In *Designing Clinical Research*, edited by Stephen B. Hulley and Steven R. Cummings. Baltimore: Williams & Wilkins, 1988. A concise overview of ethical principles for researchers and of government review of experimentation involving human subjects.

The National Commission for the Protection of Human Subjects of Biomedical and Behavioral Research. *The Belmont Report*. Washington, D.C.: Government Printing Office, 1978. This brief document has widely influenced research ethics in the United States. Far from exhaustive, it nevertheless describes the basic principles that underlie most subsequent discussions.

Mencius (Meng K'o, Meng Tzu; c. 372 B.C.E., Tsou, state of Lu, modern Shangdong province, China—c. 289 B.C.E., China): Philosopher

TYPE OF ETHICS: Classical history

ACHIEVEMENTS: Author of the book of *Mencius* (*Meng Tzu* in Chinese)

SIGNIFICANCE: A Confucian sage second only to Confucius, Mencius articulated, defended, and developed Confucianism; he held that human nature is good and that the force of moral goodness is indefeatable

In China, "Confucianism" is often referred to as "the way of Confucius and Mencius." Mencius accepted Confucius' teachings without reservation, and his own teachings are largely elaborations of those of Confucius. He articulated Confucianism in an ingenious way; he defended Confucianism against rival ideologies such as Moism and Yangism; and he combined Confucianism with his own theory of human nature. The book of *Mencius* is therefore regarded as one of the four central Confucian classics (the other three are the *Great Learning*, the *Doctrine of the Mean*, and the *Analects of Confucius*). Mencius' moral courage and adherence to the practice of Confucianism exemplified the ideal personality of Confucianism.

***Jen* and *Yi*.** In Mencius' theory, as in that of Confucius, *jen* (benevolence, human-heartedness) and *yi* (righteousness) are central concepts. To be *jen* and to do whatever is in accordance with *yi* are essential to having a good life and a good society. According to Mencius, "*jen* is man's peaceful abode and *yi* his proper path." In other words, *jen* is the

standing position of a moral agent, and *yi* is the character of moral acts. *Jen* is moral perfection that results in wisdom, courage, honor, and *yi*. Though *jen* and *yi* do not derive their justification from beneficial consequences, the power of *jen* and *yi* is so great that nothing can stop it. The "kingly way" defined by *jen* and *yi* can render *pa tao* (hegemonic force, the way of a despot) totally ineffective.

Yangism and Mohism. To defend Confucianism against rival ideologies, Mencius focused his criticism on Yangism and Mohism. Yang Tzu advocated egoism. "He would not even pull out one hair to benefit the entire empire," because a hair is part of one's body, which is given by heaven. This attitude is in direct opposition to Confucius' teaching that one has moral obligations to society; it is also, as Mencius put it, "a denial of one's ruler." Mo Tzu, at the other extreme, advocated love without discrimination, which is not only unnatural but also amounts to a denial of one's father, for loving without discrimination will cause one's father to be treated in the same way as a stranger. "To deny one's ruler and one's father is to be no different from the beasts."

Theory of Human Nature. A fuller rejection of Yangism and Moism requires a theory of human nature, a theory that answers the question, What is the decree of heaven? According to Mencius, humans differ from other animals in that they have four hearts or incipient tendencies: The hearts of compassion (the germ of *jen*), of shame (of *yi*), of courtesy and modesty (of *li*, or rites), and of right and wrong (of wisdom). Their existence is indicated by the immediate impulses that one feels in certain situations. For example, when one suddenly sees a child on the verge of falling into a well, one would have an instantaneous feeling of compassion, although the feeling does not necessarily lead to an action. Since the feeling is spontaneous, it is the result of one's nature, which is given by heaven; since it is disinterested, it is purely good; and since everyone has the feeling, no matter how faint and momentary, it is universal. Evil is a result of human failure to care for those tendencies and guard them against bad external influences.

"Man has these four tendencies just as he has his four limbs. When, having these four tendencies, he says of himself that he is incapable (of developing them), he is injuring himself," Mencius wrote. "Everyone is capable of becoming a Yao or a Shun" (ancient sage-kings of China). Since human nature is initially good, the way to be moral is to "retain the heart of a new-born babe."

Hao Jan Chih Ch'i. One can nourish one's good nature by accumulating righteous deeds. As one does acts of righteousness, one will obtain and develop a *hao jen chih ch'i*, a floodlike, vital, and refined energy. "As power, it is exceedingly great and strong"; "nourish it with integrity and place no obstacle in its path and it will fill the space between heaven and earth." This *ch'i* is both ontological (it actually exists) and moral. One cannot have the *ch'i* without being morally right. "If on self-examination I find that I am not right, I would tremble before a common fellow coarsely clad. But if on self-examination I find that I am right, I can go forward even against men in the thousands."

Mencius' theory gives clear answers to the following important questions that any adequate theory of ethics needs to answer: Why be moral? Who decides what is moral? How can one be moral? One should be moral because it is one's nature to be so. One need only look deep inside one's heart to find the answer about what is moral. To protect one's good nature from bad influences and to develop it by doing good deeds is the way to become a morally good person.

—*Peimin Ni*

See also Confucian ethics; Confucius.

BIBLIOGRAPHY

Chan, Wing-tsit. *A Source Book in Chinese Philosophy.* Princeton, N.J.: Princeton University Press, 1963.

Chang, Carsun. "The Significance of Mencius." *Philosophy East and West* 8 (1958): 37-48.

Fung Yu-lan. *A History of Chinese Philosophy.* Vol. 7. Translated by Derk Bodde. Princeton, N.J.: Princeton University Press, 1953.

_____. *A Short History of Chinese Philosophy.* Edited by Derk Bodde. New York: Macmillan, 1958.

Graham, Angus C. *Disputers of the Tao.* La Salle, Ill.: Open Court, 1989.

Mencius. *Mencius.* Translated and with an introduction by D. C. Lau. Harmondsworth, England: Penguin Books, 1970.

Men's movement

TYPE OF ETHICS: Sex and gender issues

DATE: Late twentieth century

ASSOCIATED WITH: Feminism, gay rights, men's rights, and the recovery movement

DEFINITION: The men's movement is a multifaceted, generally decentralized response by men to the dissatisfaction with traditional gender arrangements; to a large degree, the men's movement was prompted by the second wave of feminism in the late 1960's and 1970's

SIGNIFICANCE: The men's movement is an extensive grassroots effort by men in the West to come to terms with the issues and problems of masculinity

There are actually several men's movements in North America, Europe, and other Westernized areas of the world. What is often taken to be a monolithic phenomenon is in fact composed of numerous groups that are sometimes in conflict with one another. Among these groups are profeminists, men's rights activists, spiritual revisionists, socialists, and African American and gay rights activists.

Profeminism, as the name implies, is a positive male response to feminism. In the United States, profeminism is institutionally centered in the National Organization of Men Against Sexism (NOMAS), formerly the National Organization of Changing Men (NOCM) and the National Organization of Men (NOM). Similar groups exist in Europe and Australia (in Great Britain, for example, Men Against Sexism). Profeminism developed in the late 1960's and early 1970's as groups of men began to take seriously the emerging body of feminist theory and began to consider ways to dismantle the male role in the maintenance of patriarchy, the institutionalization of male dominance. Drawing on the insights of feminist theory, profeminist men conducted critiques of male socialization and gender roles with an eye toward assisting women to gain political and economic parity with men; reducing male violence against women, children, and other men; and eliminating other expressions of

Poet Robert Bly, the most prominent figure in the men's movement of the early 1990's. (Jerry Bauer)

sexism against females. The theoretical and critical work of profeminists is embodied in political activism directed at ending specific manifestations of sexism such as rape, pornography, and homophobia.

The men's rights movements is also politically active, but the focus of its activism is decidedly different from that of profeminism. Men's rights groups are concerned that modern constructions of the male gender unfairly limit men legally, socially, emotionally, and psychologically. Activists in this sector of the men's movement have called attention to numerous legal and social realities that place the male at a disadvantage, such as gender-based military conscription, the tendency of courts to favor mothers in child custody suits, and the much higher rates of suicide and violent crime (both perpetration and victimization) among men. While not intrinsically antifeminist, men's rights groups have been often represented (and sometimes misrepresented) as such. To be sure, extremists within this group have reacted to what they regard as the excesses of feminism. In contrast to profeminists, some men's rights activists have argued that institutions and belief systems already overvalue the female. Principally, however, this movement is less a backlash against feminism than a utilization of feminist methods in the analysis of gender from the male point of view.

Spiritual revisionists share with men's rights activists a general dissatisfaction with traditional male roles, a ferment that may be rooted in countercultural tendencies of the 1950's, thus antedating the second wave of feminism. If this is true, the feminist movement that resurged in the late 1960's essentially provided a catalyst for the expression of a male discontent that was theretofore largely subterranean. Spiritual revisionism—or, as it is more commonly known, the mythopoetic men's movement—focuses primarily on the psychological and spiritual transformation of men. While there are certainly significant elements of political analysis and social activism in mythopoesis, spiritual revisionists usually focus attention on the individual self, maintaining that male malaise is fundamentally based on disorders of the soul. Proponents believe that males need to overcome alienation from their bodies, from their emotions, their work, other men, women, and the earth by recovering or creating myths and rituals, especially those that originate outside the industrialized Western world. This dimension of the men's movement has little or no organizational core; it is structured instead around small local support groups (akin to women's consciousness-raising groups), weekend retreats, and workshops. The mythopoetic movement has been influenced by the Jungian tradition in depth psychology and by recovery (Twelve Step) programs. Many credit poet Robert Bly and psychologist James Hillman with inspiring this movement.

Socialist, African American, and gay rights movements represent areas of overlap between the men's movement and other movements. Socialism has a broad political and philosophical perspective that involves more than gender analysis. Socialists in the men's movement view the construction of masculinities as part of larger economic conflicts, and hence they tend to be sensitive to the class differences between men. Profeminism, in particular, has ideological affinities with socialism.

The African American men's movement is especially concerned with the plight of the black male, who is faced both with the limitations and problems of the male sex role and with the injustices of racism. Many African American men have been comfortable in alliance with the spiritual revisionists, but others have criticized the men's movement for not making race a more prominent issue.

The gay rights movement intends to end social and political discrimination against homosexuals through political activity. Men who are involved in this movement are often allied with lesbians, profeminist men, and spiritual revisionists. Gay rights activists have called attention to the destructive effects of homophobia on all men, since the fear of homosexuality often leads to alienation between men and to insidious forms of self-hatred.

While the analyses and programs of these various groups differ considerably, they are all united in the conviction that traditional forms of masculinity require serious reevaluation and transformation for the greater well-being of both males and females. —*Mark William Muesse*

See also Feminism; Gay Rights; Homophobia; Pornography; Rape; Sexism; Sexuality and sexual ethics; Women's liberation movement.

BIBLIOGRAPHY

Brod, Harry, ed. *The Making of Masculinities: The New Men's Studies*. Boston: Allen & Unwin, 1987.

Clatterbaugh, Kenneth. *Contemporary Perspectives on Masculinity*. Boulder, Colo.: Westview Press, 1990.

Ehrenreich, Barbara. *The Hearts of Men*. Garden City, N.Y.: Anchor Press, 1983.

Seidler, Victor J. *Rediscovering Masculinity: Reason, Language, and Sexuality*. London: Routledge, 1989.

Stoltenberg, John. *Refusing to Be a Man: Essays on Sex and Justice*. Portland, Oreg.: Breitenbush Books, 1989.

Mental illness

TYPE OF ETHICS: Psychological ethics
DATE: From antiquity
ASSOCIATED WITH: Psychiatry, psychology, moral treatment revolution, community mental health movement, deinstitutionalization, competence, and insanity
DEFINITION: An abnormal mental or behavioral state that leads to personal discomfort, conflict with society, or impaired capacity to function
SIGNIFICANCE: Brings into focus issues related to paternalism, confidentiality, right to privacy, autonomy, informed consent, right to treatment, right to refuse treatment, and criminal responsibility

By conceptualizing mental disorders as illness, physicians are awarded primacy in regard to treatment decisions. Persons who suffer from mental illness may be viewed as requiring treatment, even when they do not desire such care. Under certain circumstances, persons who are mentally ill may be declared not responsible for their actions.

History. Historically, persons with mental disorders have been beaten, driven from their homes, subjected to inhumane treatments, and put to death. Early views of mental disorders were founded on a mixture of demonology and theories of organic causality. Demonology is founded on the idea that evil spirits or an angry god can dwell within or directly influence a person. Organic theories attribute the development of mental disorders to physical causes—injuries, imbalances in body fluids, or abnormal body structures.

Skulls dating back as far as 500,000 years show evidence

of trephining. In trephining, a stone instrument was used to scrape away a portion of the skull. It is assumed that these operations were performed to allow evil spirits to escape. A modified form of trephining was revived in Europe in the Middle Ages. As late as the 1500's, some patients were subjected to surgical procedures in which a physician would bore holes in a patient's skull and an attending priest would remove stones that were assumed to be a cause of insanity.

In 1811, Benjamin Rush invented the "tranquillizing chair," which was used to calm the mentally ill. (National Library of Medicine)

An Egyptian papyrus of 3000 B.C.E. describes recommended treatments for war wounds and shows that the Egyptians recognized the relationship between organic injury and subsequent mental dysfunction. Another papyrus, of the sixteenth century B.C.E., shows that in regard to diseases not caused by obvious physical injuries, the Egyptians were likely to rely on magic for their explanations and incantations for their cures. Still, superstition was tempered with humane care—dream interpretation, quiet walks, and barge rides down the Nile.

The Hebrews viewed insanity as resulting from God's wrath or the withdrawal of His protection. Without God's protection, a person was subject to invasion by evil spirits, which could cause madness. For the Hebrews, mental disease was a consequence of not living according to God's word.

Prior to the fifth century B.C.E. Greek beliefs concerning mental illness were founded on a mixture of religion and superstition. While the most typical responses to persons with mental abnormalities were banishment and stoning, some individuals received humane and supportive care. As did the Egyptians, the Greeks built temples devoted to healing and medicine. Baths, changes in diet, moderate exercise, and dream interpretation were aspects of the early Greek treatment regimen.

Subsequent to the fifth century B.C.E., Greek thought concerning diseases came under the influence of the physician Hippocrates. Hippocrates (460-377 B.C.E.) rejected the prevailing belief that attributed disease to possession. The writings of Hippocrates, nearly all of which were authored by his followers, are very clear in attributing diseases to natural processes. While many healthful remedies followed the Hippocratic idea that mental disorders could be traced to imbalances in body fluids, this same theory also led to many improper and inhumane interventions, such as bloodletting and the forced consumption of foul potions.

In addition to the deductions of Greek physicians, Greek philosophers also speculated concerning mental disturbances. The Greek philosopher Plato (429-347 B.C.E.) addressed the need to treat persons afflicted with mental disorders with compassion and argued that persons who commit a crime as a result of madness or disease should pay a fine but otherwise should be exempt from punishment.

The Early Romans expanded upon and refined Greek ideas in regard to mental diseases. After the death of the Greek physician Galen (130-200), however, who practiced in Rome for most his lifetime, Roman medicine stagnated.

While Europeans abandoned scientific explanations for mental disorders, Islamic countries continued the inquiries initiated by the Greeks. In 792, the first hospital devoted exclusively to the care of mentally ill persons was opened in Baghdad. Humane treatment and a concern for the dignity of disturbed persons were key aspects of treatments recommended by Islamic physicians.

In contrast to the Islamic tradition, Europeans routinely expelled, tortured, abused, and murdered the mentally disturbed. With the rise of Christianity, insanity was variously ascribed to demonic possession, hormonal imbalances, and folk superstitions. While some monasteries offered healing rituals based on incantations and prayer, it was far more common to view the mentally disturbed as abandoned by God or in league with Satan and in need of redemption rather than assistance.

In the mid-thirteenth century, the church focused on the need to search out and identify witches and warlocks. Mentally ill persons were perfect targets for the papal inquisitors, although it is believed that many more sane than insane persons died as a result of the Inquisition. Commonly, the accused were tortured until they confessed, after which they were burned to death.

The fifteenth century also saw a major movement that was directed toward the confinement of the mentally ill. The institutions for the mentally disturbed were administered by physicians, and as a result, doctors assumed primacy in the care of the mentally disturbed. While the care of persons with mental disorders was transferred from the clergy to physicians, the quality of the patients' lives showed little improvement. Bloodletting, emetic potions, straitjackets, chains, dunking chairs, spinning devices, and terror were the most frequently prescribed treatments.

It was not until the late eighteenth century that positive changes occurred in regard to the treatment of the mentally ill. In 1793 a French physician, Philippe Pinel, was put in charge of a Paris asylum. Dismayed by the treatment that was provided the inmates, Pinel initiated a series of reforms that became the foundation for what has subsequently been identified as the Moral Treatment Revolution. The Moral Treatment Revolution was founded on the principles that mental patients should be treated with compassion, provided with supportive counseling, housed in comfortable surroundings, and given purposeful work.

While a number of existent asylums adopted the Moral Treatment approach and new hospitals were dedicated to its principles, it did not take long for economics and neglect to make a mockery of the stated principles. Over time, mental hospitals became little more than warehouses where the mentally ill were admitted, diagnosed, and forgotten.

While the late nineteenth century saw the development of new theories and techniques for the treatment of mental disorders that were based on free association and catharsis, only a few affluent persons with mental disorders received these treatments. Still, by the early twentieth century, bloodletting, purging, terror, and treatments designed to cause disorientation were being abandoned. These treatments were replaced by somatic therapies and pharmacological interventions. Major problems existed, however, in that the somatic therapies caused brain damage, and the drugs that were available prior to the 1950's were sedatives that caused extreme lethargy and sometimes death.

By the early 1930's, psychiatrists began experimenting with various types of somatic therapy. Insulin coma therapy involved administrations of toxic doses of insulin to nondiabetic patients. Electroconvulsive therapy (ECT) involved passing an electric current through a patient's brain, causing a seizure. Between the late 1930's and the 1960's, several hundred thousand mental patients were involuntarily treated with ECT.

In the mid-1930's, the Portuguese physician António Egas Moniz introduced a surgical procedure that evolved into the prefrontal lobotomy. Between 1935 and 1955, more than 50,000 mental patients were subjected to lobotomies, in which healthy brain tissue was destroyed in a misdirected effort to treat mental illness.

By the mid-1950's, new pharmacological agents became available. The first of the drugs to be used was reserpine.

Although the effects of reserpine on the behavior of psychotic patients were profound, the drug had dangerous side effects. Reserpine was soon replaced by the drug Thorazine. Over the next several years, hundreds of thousands of patients, some voluntarily and many involuntarily, were given Thorazine and other major tranquilizers. One side effect of Thorazine and other drugs of its class is tardive dyskinesia, a disfiguring disturbance that manifests as facial grimacing, palsy, and a staggering gait. For most patients, the tardive dyskinesia disappears when the drug is discontinued, but for some the symptoms are irreversible.

Partially as a result of the availability of psychotropic medications and as a result of changes in social policy, the 1960's saw the beginnings of the community mental health movement. The community mental health movement promoted the concepts of deinstitutionalization, treatment in the least restrictive environment, and treatment as close to the person's home community as possible. Deinstitutionalization involved discharging as many patients as possible from state hospitals and discouraging new admissions. As a result of deinstitutionalization, state hospital populations went from a peak of more than 500,000 in the mid-1950's to fewer than 130,000 in the late 1980's.

Clarification of Terms. Throughout the preceding narrative the terms "mental illness," "mental disease," "insanity," "madness," "mental abnormality," "mental disturbance," "mental dysfunction," and "mental disorder" have been used interchangeably. While this is a common practice, it can lead to misunderstandings.

While medical practitioners, legal documents, and the general public, frequently refer to aberrant behavior and mental disorders as mental illness, this is a misuse of the term "illness." Illness implies that some underlying disease process exists. The American psychiatrist Thomas Szasz has argued that the complaints that are called symptoms of mental illness are simply communications concerning beliefs, discomfort, or desires that an individual experiences in regard to self or others. Labeling such communications as symptoms of mental illness is a sociopolitical process that vests authority in physicians to control and abuse persons whose communications make others uncomfortable or who are presumed to be dangerous.

While "insanity" is used interchangeably with "mental illness," it would be best if the term "insanity" were reserved to describe a mental state pertinent to legal proceedings. Most countries mitigate punishment if it is determined that a person was insane at the time of committing an illegal act. In fact, most states in the United States allow a finding of not guilty by reason of insanity. This means that a person who commits an illegal act while insane should be found not guilty of any criminal offense.

The terms "madness," "mental abnormality," "mental disturbance," and "mental dysfunction" are simply descriptive in nature. They have no particular standing in regard to the legal system or the medical establishment.

The term "mental disorder" is the official term adopted by the American Psychiatric Association and the American Psychological Association to describe abnormal behavioral or psychological states that cause personal distress, impaired functioning, or conflict with society. The Diagnostic and Statistical Manual of Mental Disorders (DSM-III-R) catalogs the symptoms and behaviors of the various types of mental disorders. Only a minority of the several hundred disorders listed fit the criteria for identification as diseases. That is, it is not possible to identify infectious processes, biochemical imbalances, organ malfunctions, or physical trauma as causes of most disorders. Therefore, it is questionable to refer to them as illnesses.

Ethical Issues. The treatment of persons with mental disorders brings into consideration a number of ethical issues. Among the ethical issues that are of importance in regard to the treatment of persons identified as mentally ill are the following: paternalism, confidentiality, right to privacy, autonomy, informed consent, right to treatment, right to refuse treatment, and criminal responsibility.

In the United States, persons may be involuntarily confined in mental hospitals if they are "mentally ill" and a danger to self or others. Additionally, many states allow the commitment of "mentally ill" persons who are likely to deteriorate mentally or physically if they do not receive care. While at one time simply having a mental disorder could serve as grounds for loss of freedom, states now require an additional finding of dangerousness or probability of deterioration. The right of the state to confine selected citizens involuntarily is based on the concepts of paternalism and police power. Paternalism, or *parens patriae*, allows the state to protect citizens from themselves.

Confidentiality is central to the practice of psychotherapy. Professional codes and legal procedures require that certain communications be held in confidence. Still, all states provide exceptions to confidentiality, which include the following: when criminal charges have been filed, in child custody cases, when a criminal offense is planned, when the client is a danger to self or others, and when the client has been informed that certain communications are not privileged.

While the right to privacy is a fundamental right that most citizens enjoy, it is frequently denied persons who have been diagnosed as mentally ill. If the mentally ill person does not cooperate with treatment, divulge personal secrets, and participate in routine hospital activities, he or she will be identified as an uncooperative patient and will find it very difficult to obtain his or her freedom.

Autonomy is the right to act in a manner that is consistent with one's personally held beliefs and to make decisions that affect one's fate and destiny. This is a right that is refused many mentally ill persons. Through involuntary commitment and forced treatment, persons deemed to be suffering from mental diseases are denied the right to make key decisions that affect their quality of life and their personal survival. Concerning personal survival, only two states have

laws making suicide illegal. Furthermore, all states allow a competent adult to make decisions regarding the continuation of life-support devices. Most states either allow or are mute on the right of a competent person to terminate his or her life. Still, all states allow the forced incarceration of a mentally ill person who attempts suicide.

Informed consent requires that persons understand the nature of the procedures they are to experience, that their participation be voluntary, and that possible consequences be explained. Involuntary commitment, forced treatment, and failure to discuss side effects of psychotropic medications are examples of violations of informed consent in regard to mentally ill persons.

Right to treatment refers to the concept that persons involuntarily confined in mental institutions have a right to humane care and therapeutic treatment. In the 1971 Alabama case *Wyatt v. Stickney*, Judge Frank Johnson stated, "to deprive any citizen of his or her liberty upon an altruistic theory that the confinement is for humane and therapeutic reasons and then fail to provide adequate treatment violates the very fundamentals of due process." In the 1975 case *O'Connor v. Donaldson*, the Supreme Court ruled that Donald Donaldson, who had been confined to a mental hospital in Florida for fourteen years, deserved a periodic review of his mental status and could not be indefinitely confined if he was capable of caring for himself and was not a danger to himself or others. While not directly ruling on the issue of right to treatment, the court let stand an earlier decision that if Donaldson was not provided treatment, he should have been discharged from the hospital.

Right to refuse treatment is an issue that causes a great deal of controversy. Prior to the 1960's, it was common practice to force patients to undergo dangerous and disabling treatments. Involuntary sterilizations, electroconvulsive therapy, and psychosurgery were frequently prescribed for recalcitrant or difficult patients. While patients now have specific rights in regard to certain invasive treatments, their right to refuse unwanted medications was undefined as late as the early 1990's. In the 1979 case *Rogers v. Okin*, a patient who had been committed to the Boston State Hospital complained that he should not be required to take psychotropic medications against his will. While the initial court finding was that Rogers should have had a right to refuse medication, as of 1991 this case was still under appeal, and express rights and procedures related to refusing medications were still unspecified.

The issue of criminal responsibility is bound up with the concept of insanity. If a person, because of mental defect or state of mind, is unable to distinguish right from wrong, then most states would find the person exempt from criminal punishment. Beginning in 1975, however, Michigan adopted an alternate verdict of "guilty but mentally ill." As of 1993, eleven states had followed the Michigan example. The option of finding a person guilty but mentally ill increases the probability that incarceration will follow a crime committed by a person who previously have been declared insane. Additionally, it allows for mitigation of the length of sentencing and provides for specialized treatment in a prison hospital.

—*Bruce E. Bailey*

See also Child psychology; Confidentiality; Electroshock therapy; Eugenics; Illness; Institutionalization of patients; Lobotomy; Psychology; Psychopharmacology; Soviet psychiatry; Suicide; Therapist-patient relationship.

BIBLIOGRAPHY

Bednar, Richard L., et al. *Psychotherapy with High-Risk Clients: Legal and Professional Standards*. Pacific Grove, Calif.: Brooks/Cole, 1991. Discusses legal and ethical issues related to the practice of psychotherapy. Topics related to client rights and therapist responsibilities are reviewed.

Goffman, Erving. *Asylums: Essays on the Social Situation of Mental Patients and Other Inmates*. Garden City, N.Y.: Anchor Books, 1961. Explores sociological and environmental influences within institutions that inappropriately shape and change behavior.

Medvedev, Zhores. *A Question of Madness*. Translated by Ellen de Kadt. New York: Knopf, 1971. Provides an account of the involuntary confinement and forced psychiatric treatment of the Russian biochemist Zhores Medvedev. Documents how Soviet psychiatrists collaborated with other agents of the state to silence his criticism of the government.

Szasz, Thomas S. *The Myth of Mental Illness: Foundations of a Theory of Personal Conduct*, rev. ed. New York: Harper & Row, 1974. Explores issues and ethics related to the diagnosis and treatment of mental disorders. Promotes the concept that individuals and members of the medical establishment must assume responsibility for their behavior.

Valenstein, Elliot S. *Great and Desperate Cures*. New York: Basic Books, 1986. Examines the historical, social, scientific, and ethical issues that led to the development and use of psychosurgery as a cure for mental illness.

Mercy

TYPE OF ETHICS: Personal and social ethics

ASSOCIATED WITH: All major religious traditions and most philosophical systems

DEFINITION: Compassion shown toward another

SIGNIFICANCE: Mercy is generally thought of as an ethically positive quality, since the merciful individual acts toward others in a way that indicates compassion and concern for them; Friedrich Nietzsche, however, believed that mercy and compassion typically arise out of guilt and therefore indicate weakness and evil

Mercy originated as a theological term. Although it came into the English through the French and Latin, its meaning goes back to an ancient Israelite concept of how God acted toward people and how he expected people to act toward one another. Mercy most often is used to translate the word *hesed* in the Hebrew Bible, a word that is also often translated as "kindness," "loving kindness," and "steadfast love." In Jewish scripture, *hesed* denotes God's attitude toward people as pledged in a covenant relationship. If the people of Israel would be loyal to their agreement with God, then God's attitude would be one of mercy.

Hesed more often describes an activity than it does a disposition. Thus, after crossing the Red Sea and escaping from Egypt, Moses and the Israelites sang a song in which they called God's saving act *hesed*: "In your steadfast love (*hesed*) you led the people whom you redeemed; you guided them by your strength to your holy abode" (Exodus 15:13). *Hesed* is not used in the Hebrew Bible only to describe God's activity. It also denotes the mutual, right attitude that God expects of people in a covenant relationship. Thus, the trust and faithfulness that should characterize relations between relatives, friends, and other societal groups is *hesed*, and without *hesed*, society would be characterized by disorder. For example, the prophet Hosea (Hosea 4:1-3) claims that since the Israelites are living without *hesed*,

> Swearing, lying, and murder, and stealing and adultery break out; bloodshed follows bloodshed.
> Therefore the land mourns, and all who live in it languish; together with the wild animals and the birds of the air, even the fish of the sea are perishing.

In the Septuagint, which is the oldest surviving Greek version of the Old Testament, *hesed* was most often translated as *eleos*. *Eleos* also carried the connotations of the Hebrew *hesed* into the Christian New Testament. For example, Matthew's Gospel twice cites the announcement in Hosea that God desires mercy (*eleos*) rather than sacrifice. (Hosea 6:6; Matt. 9:13, 12:7).

Eleos also carried with it other meanings, however, and it is from this Greek heritage that "mercy" received connotations of a sentiment. In prebiblical Greek literature, *eleos* denoted that feeling or emotion that occurs when witnessing suffering that is undeserved. Aristotle defined it "as a feeling of pain caused by the sight of some evil, destructive or painful, which befalls one who does not deserve it, and which we might expect to befall ourselves or some friend of ours, and moreover to befall us soon." The sentiment described here, resembles pity more than anything else.

In the Christian New Testament, mercy is sometimes an activity and sometimes a sentiment. As in later Judaism, the merciful activity of God in the Christian scripture is sometimes connected to God's judgment at the end of time. In fact, the old French *merces* signified a payment or reward, and thus indicated the heavenly reward awaiting the compassionate person. Also, Christianity reinterpreted *eleos* in light of Jesus' death on the cross. Thus, there is more of a tendency in Christian literature than in the Hebrew Bible to think of God's mercy as preceding people's mercy and to relate mercy to suffering activity. For example, in the very influential parable of the good Samaritan (Luke 10:29-37), the merciful Samaritan, following the model of Jesus, pays a price on behalf of the one who was assaulted. He is a good neighbor because he goes out of his way to care for another person who needs help.

In Jerome's *Vulgate*, the Hebrew *hesed* and the Greek *eleos* were often translated by *misericordia*, which combines the meanings of pity, compassion, kindness, and leniency. The Latin root emphasizes wretchedness and sorrow. Thomas Aquinas defines a merciful person as being sorrowful at heart (*miserum cor*); that is, as being affected with the sorrow or misery of another as if it were one's own. God's work of dispelling misery is the effect of his mercy. God's mercy, then, especially in medieval theology, connotes God's unmerited grace as he reaches down to wretched humans. Thus, Augustine can love and thank God "because Thou has forgiven me these so great and heinous deeds of mine. To thy grace I ascribe it, and to Thy mercy, that Thou hast melted away my sins as it were ice."

Although Shakespeare claimed in *Titus Andronicus* that "Sweet Mercy is nobility's true badge," and wrote in the *Merchant of Venice* that "It [mercy] blesseth him that gives, and him that takes," mercy has not always been thought of as something good. For example, it was not included among Plato's cardinal virtues (justice, temperance, prudence, and fortitude), and because the Stoic philosophers thought that mercy was an emotion that might sway reason and misdirect justice, they did not trust it. The nineteenth century philosopher Friedrich Nietzsche tended to associate compassion with guilt and thus to think of mercy as an evil. Likewise, the proponents of "lifeboat ethics" tend to think that the sentiment of mercy masks and makes it difficult for society to deal with the moral dilemma posed by a world population that is outstripping the available resources. Finally, from a different perspective, mercy's close association with power—for example, in the definition of mercy as "forbearance to injure others"—has led liberation theologians to associate human mercy with paternalism and imperialism. They call for solidarity with the poor rather than for mercy upon the poor.   —*James A. Dawsey*

See also Aristotle; Christian ethics; Compassion; Generosity; Jewish ethics; Nietzsche, Friedrich; Thomas Aquinas.

BIBLIOGRAPHY

Aristotle. "Rhetoric." In *The Works of Aristotle*, translated by W. R. Roberts. Vol. 2. Chicago: University of Chicago Press, 1952.

Buetow, Harold A. *The Scabbardless Sword: Criminal Justice and the Quality of Mercy*. Associated Faculty Press, 1982.

Callahan, Sidney. *With All Our Heart and Mind: The Spiritual Works of Mercy in a Psychological Age*. New York: Crossroad, 1988.

Erasmus, Desiderius. *The Immense Mercy of God*. San Francisco: California State Library, 1940.

Murphy, Jeffrie G., and Jean Hampton. *Forgiveness and Mercy*. New York: Cambridge University Press, 1988.

Wilson, Matthew. *Mercy and Truth*. Menston, England: Scholar Press, 1973.

Merit

TYPE OF ETHICS: Theory of ethics
DATE: Coined 1526
ASSOCIATED WITH: Egalitarianism, justice, fairness, and desert
DEFINITION: One has merit, the opposite of demerit, to the extent that one has earned qualifications, credentials, and expertise and to the extent that one is morally worthy
SIGNIFICANCE: Merit, the key concept of one of the main types of justice, might serve as the basis of one form of ethical government: meritocracy

As Goethe said, "It never occurs to fools that merit and good fortune are closely united." Thus, types of justice can clash. Two main types of justice are meritocratic justice and distributive justice. Meritocratic justice requires that only the most qualified and worthy person be chosen for any position in question. Distributive justice requires people to minimize serious inequalities in well-being; for example, those arising from good or bad fortune.

Robert K. Fullinwider (1980) gives an example that undermines the decisiveness of meritocratic justice. He says that meritocracy is "too rigid and specific" and would condemn acts that "seem unobjectionable."

> Suppose . . . an employer had two well-qualified applicants for a position, the slightly better qualified applicant already having a good, secure job, the other being unemployed. If the employer hired the unemployed applicant, would he have violated a . . . moral principle? To suggest [so] is . . . strongly counter-intuitive.

The distributive justice of hiring the unemployed seems to outweigh the problem with meritocratic justice.

Moreover, Norman Daniels (1978) tries to show that the argument from meritocracy is not an argument from justice. Daniels considers the following example:

> Jack and Jill both want jobs A and B and each much prefers A to B. Jill can do either A or B better than Jack. But the situation S in which Jill performs B and Jack A is more productive than Jack doing B and Jill A (S'), even when we include the effects on productivity of Jill's lesser satisfaction. [Meritocracy] selects S, not S', because it is attuned to macroproductivity, not microproductivity. . . . It says, "Select people for jobs so that *overall* job performance is maximized."

Daniels anticipates the objection that meritocracy would select S', not S, because meritocracy implies that "a person should get a job if he or she is the best available person for *that* job." He admits that this objection appears to be based on the point of justice "that it seems *unfair* to Jill that she gets the job she wants less even though she can do the job Jack gets better than he can." Daniels, however, thinks that the seeming unfairness derives from "inessential features of our economic system"; namely, that promoting microproductivity happens to be "the best rule of thumb" to follow to achieve macroproductivity. He says that favoring microproductivity (S') over macroproductivity (S) because S seems unfair is relying on an intuition that is "just a by-product of our existing institutions" rather than based on justice. The happenstance that there is a mere rule of thumb in existing institutions is too superficial and arbitrary to be a fundamental consideration of justice. Once it is realized that the basis of meritocracy is macroproductivity, meritocracy will not support the intuition that Jill, in justice, deserves her favorite job A or the claim that justice requires S'. That the "inessential features of our economic system" are irrelevant to justice undermines that standing of meritocracy—when conceived of as microproductivity—as a principle of justice. Meritocracy as macroproductivity survives.

Furthermore, Ronald Dworkin (1985) gives the following argument, which supports Daniels' claim that there is no merit abstracted from macroproductivity. Dworkin says,

> There is no combination of abilities and skill and traits that constitutes "merit" in the abstract; if quick hands count as "merit" in the case of a prospective surgeon, this is because quick hands will enable him to serve the public better and for no other reason. If a black skin will, as a matter of regrettable fact [e.g., the need for black role models], enable another doctor to do a different medical job better, then that black skin is by the same token "merit" as well. That argument may strike some as dangerous; but only because they confuse its conclusion—that black skin may be a socially useful trait in particular circumstances—with the very different and despicable idea that one race may be *inherently* more worthy than another.

One may object that black skin cannot count as merit, since pigmentation is an inherited accident of birth rather than a matter of choice and achievement. As Dworkin argues, however,

> it is also true that those who score low in aptitude or admissions tests do not choose their levels of intelligence. Nor do those denied admission because they are too old, or because they do not come from a part of the country underrepresented in the school, or because they cannot play basketball well, choose not to have the qualities that made the difference.

Tests allegedly measuring merit are often biased. Furthermore, a lower score under inferior conditions often indicates more ability than does a higher score under superior conditions. African Americans tend to take the tests under conditions (poverty, reduced parental supervision, reduced incentives, bleaker prospects caused by racism, and so forth) that are dramatically inferior to the conditions under which whites take such tests. For example, consider the dramatic differences between the best group and the worst group of American public high schools. The best group will generally give its students at least the following advantages over the students in the worst group: better teachers, better equipment, more programs (for example, extracurricular activities), better atmospheres in which to lean (atmospheres with less crime, noise, and disorder), better role models, and more peer pressure to achieve.

For example, Peter Singer notes, affirmative action programs "taking into account a student's race would merely be a way of correcting for the failure of standard tests to allow for the disadvantages that face blacks in competing with whites on such tests." Such disadvantages include less ability to afford preparation courses, which whites commonly take and which the free market has specifically designed to boost scores on standard tests (such as the SAT). Similarly, Richard Wasserstrom argues,

> Most of what are regarded as the decisive characteristics for higher education have a great deal to do with things over which the individual has neither control nor responsibility: such things as home environment, socioeconomic class of parents, and of course, the quality of the primary and secondary schools attended. Since individuals do not deserve having had any of these things vis-à-vis other individuals, they do not, for the most part, deserve their qualifications.

In contrast, George Sher argues that society's conventions establish merit. He takes his view to extremes when he says, "We could even flog or torture in direct proportion to merit. . . . If the convention existed, our suggestion would imply that the meritorious deserved their beatings and abuse." Sher seems to be mistaken, since recognizing merit for what it is (good) implies that merit should be rewarded. If the convention were to punish merit, then the society would make the mistake of failing to recognize the value of merit, since its actions (punishment) speak louder than words (calling something merit).   —*Sterling Harwood*

See also Affirmative action; Discrimination; Egalitarianism; Elitism; Equality; Excellence; Fairness; Justice.

BIBLIOGRAPHY

Adkins, Arthur W. H. *Merit and Responsibility: A Study in Greek Values*. Oxford, England: Clarendon Press, 1960.

Daniels, Norman. "Merit and Meritocracy." *Philosophy and Public Affairs* 7 (1978): 206-223.

Fullinwider, Robert K. *The Reverse Discrimination Controversy: A Moral and Legal Analysis*. Totowa, N.J.: Rowman & Littlefield, 1980.

Furer-Haimendorf, Christoph von. *Morals and Merit: A Study of Values and Social Controls in South Asian Societies*. Chicago: University of Chicago Press, 1967.

Gould, Stephen Jay. *The Mismeasure of Man*. New York: W. W. Norton, 1981.

Harwood, Sterling, ed. *Business as Ethical and Business as Usual*. Boston: Jones & Bartlett, 1994.

Lewis, Lionel S. *Scaling the Ivory Tower: Merit and Its Limits in Academic Careers*. Baltimore: The Johns Hopkins University Press, 1975.

Sandel, Michael J., ed. *Liberalism and Its Critics*. New York: New York University Press, 1984.

Sher, George. *Desert*. Princeton, N.J.: Princeton University Press, 1987.

Singer, Peter. "Is Racial Discrimination Arbitrary?" In *Moral Issues*, edited by Jan Narveson. New York: Oxford University Press, 1983.

Young, Michael Dunlop. *The Rise of the Meritocracy, 1870-2033*. New York: Random House, 1959.

Messianism

TYPE OF ETHICS: Religious ethics
DATE: First articulated eighth century B.C.E.
ASSOCIATED WITH: Judaism and Christianity
DEFINITION: Belief in a messiah; that is, one who will deliver followers from political and/or spiritual difficulties in a future messianic period
SIGNIFICANCE: Messianism may dictate the behavior of believers and offer criteria for judging any existing religious or political leader

Though the term "messiah" is rarely used in the Old Testament, the concept of an ideal ruler was expressed as early as the eighth century B.C.E. Isaiah 9 expressed hopes for a king who would give wonderful counsel (Isaiah 11 spoke of his wisdom), be godlike in battle, continuous in fatherly care, and establish peace. Jeremiah 33:14-22 and Ezekiel 34:23-24 spoke of a future David who would administer the future golden age that God would usher in. The idea of a permanent Davidic dynasty (2 Samuel 7) developed the royal ideology of ancient Israel (see Psalms 2, 72, and 110). Other passages (for example, Isaiah 24:23 and Zechariah 14:9) looked toward a messianic age with God ruling directly. The Dead Sea Scrolls, the Talmud, and subsequent Jewish sources reveal an ongoing, though not universal, hope among Jews for a Messiah. In debates with Jews, early Christians claimed that Jesus was the messiah; indeed, the title "christ" is the Greek translation of the Hebrew title "messiah." Christians modified Jewish belief by identifying the messiah with the suffering servant (see Isaiah 52:13-53:12), claiming that he was divine, and looking forward to his return at the end of time. Certain rules of behavior (see, for example, Matthew 5:19, 6:1-6, 10:42, 16:27) tied gaining rewards to following the teachings of Jesus.

See also Christian ethics; Jewish ethics.

Metaethics

TYPE OF ETHICS: Theory of ethics
DATE: Primarily twentieth century
DEFINITION: The specialization within moral philosophy that is concerned with fundamental conceptual and epistemological questions in ethics
SIGNIFICANCE: Asks questions that appear to be logically prior to questions about normative ethics

First and foremost, metaethics seeks to answer the question What is the subject matter of ethics? Moral philosophy may be divided into three sets of concerns: metaethical theory, normative ethical theory, and applied ethics. In applied ethics, philosophers reflect upon the significance of some general moral point of view for a particular problem of moral decision making. For example, a philosopher might consider whether, according to rule utilitarianism, the practice of euthanasia is morally permissible. Further distinctions (such as the distinction between active and passive euthanasia) might be made to help clarify the difficulty. In contrast to applied ethics, normative ethical theory focuses upon a comparative study of such general ethical theories as utilitarianism, egoism, Kantian formalism, virtue ethics, and so forth. The fundamental question in normative ethics is: What makes an action, any action whatsoever, right or wrong?

It can be seen from these brief descriptions of normative ethical theory and applied ethics that both are interested in deciding what is right and what is wrong. Normative ethical theory attempts to develop a completely general account of what is right and what is wrong. Applied ethics investigates the moral quality of agents and their actions in specific moral contexts, usually by appealing to some normative ethical theory.

Metaethics differs from both normative and applied ethics in that it explores conceptual and epistemological questions that arise for those who use moral discourse and who devise and apply normative theories of right and wrong. Conceptual questions are posed for moral terms and statements; epistemological questions are raised about the possibility and character of moral reasoning.

Conceptual Questions. Metaethics did not emerge as a major preoccupation in philosophy until early in the twentieth century, when the problems of metaethics became insulated from the rest of moral philosophy primarily through the influence of Anglo-American linguistic philosophy. The change in path that led to the emergence of contemporary analytic philosophy has been called "the linguistic turn." In ethics, this change meant refined analysis of the terms used in moral discourse and of the structure and meaning of moral utterances. Thus, terms such as "good," "evil," "right," or "wrong" (called moral predicates) are examined directly. This sort of analysis is supposed to clarify what it means to use a moral predicate within a sentence of the form "X is right" or "X is wrong."

Locutions of the form "X is right" or "X is wrong" have the grammatical appearance of being simple judgments of fact. Many contemporary ethicists have suggested, however, that their grammatical appearance may be misleading. It is not obvious what facts one could point to to determine the truth value of a statement such as "Unrestricted abortion is morally wrong." Perhaps, then, such forms of discourse have no truth value at all; that is, perhaps they are neither true nor false. Perhaps they have a very different sort of meaning. Metaethicists who reach this conclusion about the general significance of moral utterances are called noncognitivists. They hold that normative ethics is impossible.

The cognitivists, those who believe that moral utterances are genuine statements with truth values, differ as to what sort of fact a moral fact is. Many have tried to analyze the good in terms of some more basic natural fact (such as pleasure or personal survival). They are called naturalists. G. E. Moore objected that all such attempts to define "good" commit the naturalistic fallacy. One cannot define "good" in terms of some natural property, since one can always ask without redundancy whether that property itself is good. Instead, he argued, the good should be regarded as a basic, indefinable, nonnatural property.

Epistemological Questions. If one adopts the cognitivist view that moral expressions are genuine judgments with truth values, a further question arises: How does one go about determining which moral judgments are true and which are false? Clearly, the possibility of genuine moral disagreement presupposes that moral utterances of the form "X is right" are either true or false, but how does one know which statements of that form are true? What sorts of reasons are relevant for adjudicating between conflicting moral judgments and between systems of normative ethics?

A related but even more fundamental question intrudes as well: Why adopt the moral point of view at all? This question demands the presentation of nonmoral reasons why one ought to be moral. Some have suggested that no nonmoral reasons can be given and that it is therefore not rational to adopt the moral point of view. Others agree that there are no nonmoral reasons for being moral but that this is unimportant since the question itself is mistaken. For them, moral philosophy begins with the observation that people do care about being moral. Still others have attempted to provide nonmoral reasons to justify taking the moral point of view.

Significance of Metaethics. It is commonplace to assume that the questions of metaethics are logically prior to those of normative and applied ethics, and that there is no use proceeding with either normative or applied moral philosophy without coming to certain definite conclusions about matters of metaethical concern, but this assumption has also been disputed. For one may be right in regarding moral statements as cognitive and moral argument as possible without having any sort of elaborate metaethical theory to justify this view. —*R. Douglass Geivett*

See also Cognitivism and noncognitivism; Epistemological ethics; Fact/value distinction; Moore, G. E.; Naturalistic fallacy; Normative vs. descriptive ethics; Reason and rationality.

BIBLIOGRAPHY

Beauchamp, Tom L. *Philosphical Ethics: An Introduction to Moral Philosophy.* New York: McGraw-Hill, 1982.

Finnis, John. *Fundamentals of Ethics.* Washington, D.C.: Georgetown University Press, 1983.

Foot, Philippa. "Moral Arguments." *Mind* 67 (October, 1958): 502-513.

Hancock, Roger. *Twentieth Century Ethics.* New York: Columbia University Press, 1974.

Hare, R. M. *The Language of Morals.* Oxford, England: Clarendon Press, 1952.

Hudson, W. D. *Modern Moral Philosophy.* London: Macmillan, 1970

Moore, G. E. *Principia Ethica.* Cambridge, England: Cambridge University Press, 1903.

Nowell-Smith, P. H. *Ethics.* London: Penguin Books, 1954.

Pojman, Louis P. *Ethics: Discovering Right and Wrong.* Belmont, Calif.: Wadsworth, 1990.

Snare, Francis. *The Nautre of Moral Thinking.* London: Routledge, 1992.

Stevenson, Charles L. *Ethics and Language.* New Haven, Conn.: Yale University Press, 1944.

Taylor, Paul W., ed. *The Moral Judgement: Readings in Contemporary Meta-Ethics.* Englewood Cliffs, N.J.: Prentice-Hall, 1963.

Toulmin, Stephen. *The Place of Reason in Ethics.* Chicago: University of Chicago Press, 1986.

Warnock, Geoffrey James. *Contemporary Moral Philosophy.* London: Macmillan, 1967.

Warnock, Mary. *Ethics Since 1900.* London: Oxford University Press, 1960.

Milgram experiment

TYPE OF ETHICS: Scientific ethics

DATE: First published 1963

ASSOCIATED WITH: American social psychologist Stanley Milgram

DEFINITION: A series of studies designed to determine the degree to which subjects would be willing to obey an authority's instructions to harm another person

SIGNIFICANCE: The Milgram investigations addressed an important issue but created extreme stress for the participants, leading to a reconsideration of the ethical guidelines governing such research

Stanley Milgram, horrified by the atrocities that had been committed by the Nazis during the Holocaust, conducted a program of research designed to explore the process of obedience to authority. The disturbing nature of his results and the ethical issues raised by his methods make this some of the most controversial and widely discussed research in the history of social science.

Recruited through a newspaper advertisement, a diverse group of adult subjects reported (individually) to Milgram's laboratory at Yale University expecting to participate in a study of memory and learning. Each participant was greeted by an experimenter dressed in a lab coat. Also present was a middle-aged gentleman, an accomplice who was ostensibly another participant in the session. The experimenter then described the research, which would investigate the effect of punishment on learning. Then, through a rigged drawing, the accomplice was assigned the role of "learner," while the actual subject became the "teacher."

Next, the three went to an adjacent room, where the learner was strapped into an "electric chair" as the experimenter explained that shock would be used as punishment. The teacher was then escorted back to the first room and seated in front of a shock generator, the front panel of which consisted of a series of thirty switches that could be used to administer shock. Each was labeled with a voltage level, starting with 15 volts and increasing by 15-volt increments to 450 volts; several verbal labels below the switches also indicated the severity of the shock. After receiving instructions and a demonstration from the experimenter, the teacher presented a sequence of simple memory tests to the learner through an intercom. The learner made "errors" according to a script, and the teacher was instructed to respond to each error by pushing an switch, thus delivering a shock to the learner. The teacher started with 15 volts and was directed to use the next higher switch with each successive error.

The goal of this procedure was simply to determine how long the subject/teacher would continue to obey the order to administer shock. (The accomplice/learner never actually received any shock.) As the shocks grew stronger, the learner began protesting—eventually pleading to be let out, then screaming, and finally ceasing to respond at all. When the teacher balked, the experimenter provided one of several firm verbal "prods" to continue (for example, "you *must* go on"). The procedure was discontinued if the teacher refused to obey after four such prods for a given shock level.

Milgram and other experts felt that few if any participants would demonstrate obedience under these circumstances, particularly after the learner began protesting. Nearly two-thirds of them, however, obeyed the experimenter's orders all the way to the highest level of shock (450 volts). This result occurred with both men and women, even in a version of the study in which the learner was portrayed as having a heart condition.

The typical subject in these studies showed clear signs of distress over the plight of the learner. Subjects often perspired or trembled, and some exhibit nervous laughter or other indications of tension. Indeed, it is this aspect of the research that has been cited most frequently by those who consider the studies unethical. Critics argue that Milgram compromised the welfare of the participants in this research by subjecting them to inappropriately high levels of stress. Many of these same critics have also suggested that Milgram failed to provide his subjects with enough advance information to enable them to make a fully informed decision about whether to participate.

In his defense, Milgram points out that his procedure was not intended to cause stress for the participants. Furthermore, he and other experts did not anticipate the stress that did occur because they expected that subjects would be reluctant to obey these orders. It is also important to note that Milgram did take care to protect these subjects and their dignity, as indicated by the activities that followed the experimental sessions. These measures included a discussion of the experiment and its rationale, a meeting with the learner involving an explanation that he had not really been shocked, and reassurances that the subject's behavior (obedient or not) was entirely normal given the circumstances. Some three-fourths of all the participants indicated that they had learned something personally important as a result of being in the study, and additional follow-up by a psychiatrist a year later found no evidence of lasting psychological harm in any of those examined.

More generally, this research illustrates a basic ethical di-lemma faced frequently by experimental social psychologists. These researchers often need to create and manipulate powerful situations if they are to generate enough impact to observe something meaningful about social behavior, but doing so sometimes risks causing undue stress to subjects. This ethical issue is sometimes complicated still further by the need to deceive participants in order to preserve the authenticity of their behavior.

Few will deny that Milgram's research yielded significant insights into how obedience to an authority can prevent a subordinate from taking responsibility for inflicting harm on another person, but does the end justify the means employed to gain this knowledge? Ultimately, decisions of this sort must be made by carefully weighing the costs and benefits involved. Regardless of one's position on the ethics of the obedience studies, Milgram's work has done much to heighten sensitivity to ethical considerations in social research. Since Milgram's investigations were conducted, psychologists have adopted a more conservative set of principles governing research with people—guidelines that today would probably not allow the procedures he used.   —*Steve A. Nida*

See also *Ethical Principles of Psychologists*; Experimentation, ethics of; Obedience; Psychology; Science, ethics of.

Bibliography

American Psychological Association. "Ethical Principles of Psychologists." *American Psychologist* 45 (March, 1990): 390-395.

Baumrind, Diana. "Some Thoughts on Ethics of Research: After Reading Milgram's 'Behavioral Study of Obedience.'" *American Psychologist* 19, no. 6 (1964): 421-423.

Milgram, Stanley. *Obedience to Authority.* New York: Harper & Row, 1974.

Miller, Arthur G., ed. *The Social Psychology of Psychological Research.* New York: Free Press, 1972.

Myers, David G. *Social Psychology.* 4th ed. New York: McGraw-Hill, 1993.

Military ethics

Type of ethics: Military ethics
Date: Sixteenth century to present
Definition: Military ethics defines the appropriate actions of the military
Significance: As long as the world contains competing nation states, the military will be a necessity; hence, it is crucial that the military infrastructure act morally and ethically, in a fashion that ensures reasonable safety and the honorable treatment of all members of the armed forces and of the civilians who are affected by military decisions

Conflict over the appropriate actions of the military has faced humanity throughout history. By the early nineteenth century, military ethics was well defined. The soldier-officer was viewed as an honorable individual who voluntarily, and somewhat selflessly, entered a very demanding career in service of a given nation out of respect for that nation's ideals. Concepts of military ethics were not subject to major redefinition until the middle of the 1950's when advancing technology necessitated a more technologically modern military. In addition, social issues, the evolution of voluntary armies, and changing ideas about women's rights led to a need for conceptual change, and this need continues to evolve.

Basic Issues. The concept of the military officer has long been one of "an officer-gentlemen" imbued with honesty, integrity, almost selfless love of country and the military, and great physical courage. Many scholarly military writers describe such professionals as having priestlike vocations, and it is often believed that a combination of this vocation and the characteristics of officers both holds the military together and assures its ethical action within reasonable limits.

In recent years, a moral dilemma has developed within the military as a result of the evolution of some officers into minor corporate executive functionaries who enter the military only for what they can obtain financially. The presence of large numbers of such individuals disillusioned the main body of the military—its enlisted personnel. The resultant unfortunate consequences have ranged from military corruption to the murder of officers, to hard drug use and widespread cynicism.

Another aspect of the moral dilemma faced by the military in operating ethically is the widespread decline of respect for the military profession by many civilians. Whereas in the past, the military was held in awe, by the time of the Vietnam War, military personnel were reviled. They were insulted by individuals and the media, and the nation scorned them when they returned to civilian life. It is not surprising that the resultant damage to the professional self-image of military personnel has further aggravated the problems associated with ethical behavior.

History. Most military scholars believe that real philosophical discussion of military ethics began with the writings of Niccolò Machiavelli, in the sixteenth century. Concepts of military ethics developed after that time and were codified by the nineteenth century.

Some important ethical qualities of the "officer-gentleman" ethos that developed were morality, integrity, honor, selfless love of country, and physical courage. Officers were supposed to lead by example, and military ethics was expected to be imbued in the military rank and file. Morality, of course, depends upon the moral precepts of a given nation, and Western military ethics tends to emphasize sensible caring interactions with both subordinates and civilians.

Integrity is the quality of being morally sound, upright, honest, and sincere. This characteristic implies sensitivity to the wants, needs, and aspirations of others. Moreover, it indicates an awareness of the consequences of one's actions on others and on the world. Honor, of course, is a similar quality. Specifically, it encompasses honesty, loyalty to individuals in the professional milieu, service to one's country and to others, and personal sacrifice.

Physical courage is also deemed essential to military ethics, and it is viewed as a characteristic that is passed on to subordinates. Many military thinkers view physical courage as the glue that holds armies together in time of war and as a characteristic that shapes the military profession's actions in peace.

Beginning in the 1950's, technological advancements in society placed strains on the "officer-gentleman" concept. The first was the need for a military elite with greatly enhanced technical skills. The second was the later, widespread development of voluntary armies, which required the military elite to convince rank-and-file members to reenlist. Thus was born a need for officers who were much like civilian corporate managers.

This need, along with the erosion of the public's respect for the military, has led to the increased entry into the military of individuals who lack some of the characteristics that are essential for the maintenance of the military ethos. Their presence in the armed forces has weakened military ethics and the bonds that unite military professionals.

Conclusions. Three issues that cause military disharmony and weaken military ethics are the erosion of the public image of the military professional, stresses on military personnel caused by the need for more technical expertise, and the need for corporate managerial skills that make it possible to retain subordinate personnel via reenlistment. It is essential that top military leadership find ways to combat public dissatisfaction. In addition, the armed forces must continue to identify and attract, as officers, individuals who possess technical and managerial skills, as well as appropriate ethical views. It might be beneficial to increase the number of required ethics courses in military schools, ROTC programs, and throughout the military. In addition, the development of appropriate rewards for ethical behavior and reenforcement of such behavior would optimize such efforts.

—Sanford S. Singer

See also *Art of War, The*; Machiavellian ethics; *On War*; War and Peace.

BIBLIOGRAPHY

Axinn, Sidney. *A Moral Military*. Philadelphia: Temple University Press, 1989.

Brown, James, and Michael J. Collins. *Military Ethics and Professionalism: A Collection of Essays*. Washington, D.C.: National Defense University Press, 1981.

Hartle, Anthony E. *Moral Issues in Military Decision Making*. Lawrence: University Press of Kansas, 1989.

Nagle, William J. *Morality and Modern Warfare: The State of the Question*. Baltimore: Helicon Press, 1960.

Military Ethics: Reflections on Principles—The Profession of Arms, Military Leadership, Ethical Practices, War and Morality, Educating the Citizen-Soldier. Washington, D.C.: National Defense University Press, 1987.

Wakin, Malham M., ed. *War, Morality, and the Military Profession*. Boulder, Colo.: Westview Press, 1981.

Mill, John Stuart (May 20, 1806, London, England—May 8, 1873, Avignon, France): Philosopher and economist

TYPE OF ETHICS: Modern history

ACHIEVEMENTS: Author of *A System of Logic* (1843), *Principles of Political Economy* (1848), *On Liberty* (1859), *Considerations on Representative Government* (1861), *Utilitarianism* (1863), *The Subjection of Women* (1869), *Autobiography* (1873), and *Three Essays on Religion* (1874); advocate of revised English utilitarianism

SIGNIFICANCE: Mill revised and enhanced the English utilitarian approach to ethics through arguing the need for the development of the "spiritual" values of humanity; nevertheless, Mill sustained the fundamental utilitarian position that ethics was embedded in a comprehensive social contract

John Stuart Mill (Library of Congress)

Maintaining that a science of society was feasible, Mill focused his philosophic writings on four major issues: the methodology of the social sciences, the principle of utility, individual freedom, and the structure of government. While Mill supported Jeremy Bentham's corollary that moral problems could never be resolved through sentimental appeals to righteousness, he emphasized the importance of developing the spiritual aspects of humanity. Mill developed an "ethology" that consisted of the elements that were essential in the development of "character"—individual, societal, and national; he argued that secular society must define and expand its ethical base so that happiness—freedom from pain—may be attained. Unlike Bentham, Mill maintained that an educated elite was necessary to guide society; Mill agreed with Alexis De Tocqueville's concern that democratic sentiments may lead to the "tyranny of the majority." Mill's fullest statement on ethics was advanced in *Utilitarianism*.

See also Bentham, Jeremy; *On Liberty*; Utilitarianism.

Miranda v. Arizona

TYPE OF ETHICS: Civil rights

DATE: 1966

ASSOCIATED WITH: U.S. Supreme Court

DEFINITION: With this decision, the Court mandated that all prisoners be read their rights prior to any questioning, thereby profoundly changing police procedure

SIGNIFICANCE: This landmark decision has served to protect indigent or ignorant prisoners by extending to them at the time of arrest the constitutional right to silence

The manner in which Ernesto Miranda's rape confession was obtained—without coercion but without benefit of counsel—aroused the conscience of the nation. Despite the fact that he had not been informed of his right to an attorney prior to signing it, Miranda's written confession was admitted as evidence at his first trial, resulting in his conviction and imprisonment. His conviction was appealed to the Supreme Court, however, where Chief Justice Earl Warren, speaking for a divided Court, established guidelines for police interrogations: "Prior to any questioning, the person must be warned that he has a right to remain silent, that any statement he does make may be used as evidence against

---

MIRANDA WARNING

1. You have the right to remain silent.

2. Anything you say can and will be used against you in a court of law.

3. You have the right to talk to a lawyer and have him present with you while you are being questioned.

4. If you cannot afford to hire a lawyer, one will be appointed to represent you before any questioning, if you wish one.

Police officers read these statements to any person they arrest, to make sure that person knows his or her rights.

Source: Courtesy of Clinton, Iowa, Police Department.

him, and that he has a right to the presence of an attorney, either retained or appointed." This decision, denounced by presidents from Richard Nixon to Ronald Reagan, has served to protect the ignorant and the indigent, and has resulted in a profound change in police procedure popularized in the media as the so-called "Miranda Warning."

See also Civil rights; First Amendment.

Mo Tzu (c. 480—420 B.C.E., Kingdom of Sung, China): Philosopher.

TYPE OF ETHICS: Religious ethics

ACHIEVEMENTS: Founder of the Mohist school of philosophy and supposed author of the *Book of Mo Tzu*

SIGNIFICANCE: Mo Tzu maintained that wars, social disasters, and similar forms of chaos resulted because people did not love one another; he was alone among the Chinese philosophers of his day in not only condemning acts that were harmful to others but also calling on people to care for others as they cared for themselves and their own families

Mo Tzu lived during the fifth and fourth centuries B.C.E., an era of Chinese history known as the period of the "hundred philosophers" for its flowering of philosophical and religious thought. According to tradition, Mo Tzu came from a declined noble family, served as an official of the kingdom of Sung, and studied the Chinese classics, including the writings of Confucius. Confucian thought maintained that social order could only be achieved if mutual responsibilities were fulfilled in a clearly defined hierarchical system. Some sources say that although Mo Tzu was born into a clan of the kingdom of Sung, his family later emigrated to the kingdom of Lu, home of Confucius. It is said that here Mo Tzu grew increasingly hostile to the Confucian classism and political conflicts of his day and abandoned Confucian thinking to establish the Mohist school, a system of thought based on principles described in the *Book of Mo Tzu*. In this work, Mo Tzu calls for a new, egalitarian society based on a sense of mutual aid and commitment to the common good.

The Book of Mo Tzu. The collection of philosophical essays bearing Mo Tzu's name was probably compiled by his disciples in the generations after his death. In this document, Mo Tzu condemned the desires for profit, luxury, and wealth as the societal ills of his day. He also condemned the corresponding manifestations of these desires, including the practice of offensive warfare, the development of military power, the use of rituals, the pursuit of entertainment, and the cultivation of music. He considered offensive warfare to be mere thievery and supported strong defensive preparations only to prevent it. He deemed music, entertainment, and rituals to be costly activities of the wealthy that detracted from the material well-being of the poorer classes. As remedies for these desires and the conflicts they produced, Mo Tzu championed frugality, strict respect for laws, advancement of people based on performance instead of class, and fear of the gods and spirits. The coordinating mechanism for these was the principle of universal love, of loving all others equally.

The religious characteristic of Mo Tzu's thinking derived from his admonitions concerning the Will of Heaven and a belief in spirits. Mo Tzu maintained that heaven rewarded those who conducted themselves in a manner consistent with universal love—loving others as themselves and engaging in activities that benefited everyone. He believed that heaven punished the evildoers—especially those who had been charged with the job of ruling others. He opposed fatalism, insisting that through work and honorable hardship, order could be achieved.

Mo Tzu held that knowledge came through the experiences of the senses. In judging the validity of knowledge, he applied three criteria: the basis of the knowledge itself, its potential for verification, and its utility.

The Mohists. During the last two hundred years before the unification of China (221 B.C.E.) Mohism attracted numerous converts. Its philosophy of defensive warfare, coupled with the belief that promotion should be based on merit rather than social status, led to the growth of a sect whose behavior was characterized by a soldierly discipline. Probably recruited from among the knights for hire or petty aristocrats, Mohists sold their services as specialists in defensive warfare. When a leader planned to invade or annex another territory, Mohists argued eloquently and passionately against it. If the leader could not be dissuaded, they joined the opposite side, defending the attacked kingdom. Hence, Mohists became known as both noteworthy orators and skillful defensive soldiers. Their obedience to the law and unswerving loyalty were also legendary, for they would even kill their own sons if they had committed crimes requiring the death penalty.

Legacy of Mohism. The philosophy of Mo Tzu lost ground after the onset of China's imperial period in the third century B.C.E. Mohism maintained that wars were unjust because they interfered with the survival of the agricultural classes by interrupting planting and harvesting as well as by destroying fields. Although the assessment of the impact of war on farmers was accurate, the conclusion that war was to be avoided was incompatible with the objectives of early imperial Chinese leaders, who saw territorial expansion as a means of obtaining more power and resources. Mo Tzu's admonition against preferential treatment based on status was also distasteful to the increasingly hierarchical society that attended imperial rule. Consequently, the Mohist sect declined after the third century B.C.E. Its unique contribution to Chinese ethical thought lies in advocating universal love as the operative method for ordering society and avoiding chaos and harm.

—*Margaret B. Denning*

See also *Art of War, The*; Confucius; Egalitarianism; Military ethics.

BIBLIOGRAPHY

Chan, Wing Tsit. *A Source Book in Chinese Philosophy.* Princeton, N.J.: Princeton University Press, 1963.

Fung Yu-lan. *A History of Chinese Philosophy.* Vol. 1.

Translated by Derk Bodde. Princeton, N.J.: Princeton University Press, 1953.

Lowe, Scott. *Mo Tzu's Religious Blueprint for a Chinese Utopia: The Will and the Way.* Lewiston, N.Y.: E. Mellen Press, 1992.

Mo Ti. *Basic Writings.* Translated by Burton Watson. New York: Columbia University Press, 1963.

_____. *The Ethical Works of Motse.* Translated by Yi-pao Mei. Westport, Conn.: Hyperion Press, 1973.

Monopoly

TYPE OF ETHICS: Business and labor ethics
DATE: 1300's
ASSOCIATED WITH: Adam Smith, U.S. antitrust law, and English Common Law
DEFINITION: In English Common Law, monopoly is a technical term meaning that a person has acted to prevent others from engaging in fair competition with him or her; it is an economic concept based on gaining exclusionary control of a good or service in a particular market
SIGNIFICANCE: Excluding others by gaining a monopoly interferes with the autonomy of the individual to engage in mutually beneficial trades, which is the cornerstone of the moral justification for a competitive market economy

In 1340, an English listing of the "evils of trade" included such things as forestalling (the physical obstruction of goods coming to market, or cornering the supply of goods, which deprived the owner of the market stall his rental), regrating (buying most or all the available goods at a fair for resale at a higher price), and engrossing (contracting for control of goods while they are still being grown or produced). These are all attempts at monopolization of a market, and such actions have been thought wrong since they began. The United States has had laws against monopoly since its founding, based on these terms taken from English Common Law, and justified by reference to an abiding public interest in the maintenance of competition. Competition by ethical individuals results in the completion of mutually beneficial transactions, protects consumers from unreasonable price increases, and, according to Adam Smith (*An Inquiry Into the Nature and Causes of the Wealth of Nations*, 1776), leads to the greatest wealth for the nation.

See also Profit economy.

Monroe Doctrine

TYPE OF ETHICS: International relations
DATE: December, 1823
ASSOCIATED WITH: American president James Monroe
DEFINITION: American foreign policy conceived to confine American interests to the North American continent
SIGNIFICANCE: While the Monroe Doctrine warned non-American powers to refrain from expanding in the Western Hemisphere, it did not require the United States or other American powers to refrain from such expansion

After the defeat of Napoleon Bonaparte in 1815, the continental European leaders, led by Prince Klemens von Metternich of Austria, were concerned with keeping a lid on revolutionary disturbances. During the Napoleonic years, the New World colonies of Spain successfully gained their independence through revolution. Between 1815 and 1823, the European leaders discussed the idea of returning the colonies to Spain. These discussions inspired the Monroe Doctrine. In essence, the Doctrine declared that the United States would keep out of the territories, wars, alliances, spheres of influence, and politics of the world outside the Western Hemisphere, and in return non-American powers would be expected to stay out of the political affairs of the Americas. Non-American countries with colonies in the Western Hemisphere could keep them, but they were to acquire no more colonies.

See also Isolationism.

Montesquieu, Charles-Louis (Jan. 18, 1689, La Brède, near Bordeaux, France—Feb. 10, 1755, Paris, France): Political philosopher

TYPE OF ETHICS: Enlightenment history
ACHIEVEMENTS: Author of *The Persian Letters* (1721) and *The Spirit of the Laws* (1748)
SIGNIFICANCE: As the leading *philosophe* during the early French Enlightenment, Montesquieu stimulated discussion on the nature of government, laws, and society

Born Charles-Louis de Secondat, Montesquieu grew up in and around Bordeaux, where he studied law and sat in the *parlement*. He disliked the tyrannical and warlike tendencies of the governments of Louis XIV and the Regency. Montesquieu became the most popular critic of the French government, Church, and social customs with his satirical *Persian Letters*. After being admitted to the French Academy, he traveled throughout Europe. He idealized England as a model of liberty, independent judiciary, and commerce. His *Spirit of the Laws*, which influenced both the French and American revolutions, considers various types of constitutions and laws. He examined societies in terms of their customs and history, not as abstract types. The work's critical tone marks it as the foundation of modern political science. In addition to providing a detached analysis, the *Spirit* argues for personal freedom, toleration of opposing views, separation of church and state, intermediate bodies (particularly a hereditary aristocracy) to prevent royal despotism, sensible and equitable laws, a more rational and just criminal law system, and the separation of powers.

See also Democracy; Freedom and liberty; Justice.

Moore, G. E. (Nov. 4, 1873, London, England—Oct. 24, 1958, Cambridge, England): Philosopher

TYPE OF ETHICS: Modern history
ACHIEVEMENTS: Author of *Principia Ethica* (1903) and *Ethics* (1912); appointed to the Order of Merit (1951)
SIGNIFICANCE: Moore propounded the view that "goodness" is an unanalyzable (indefinable), nonnatural property discoverable by a special faculty of intuition or direct moral awareness

American president James Monroe, architect of the Monroe Doctrine. (Library of Congress)

Moore was professor of mental philosophy and logic at Cambridge (1925-1939) and editor of the philosophical journal *Mind* (1921-1947). In ethics, he thought it quite important to distinguish two questions: "What ought to be?" (or "What is good in itself?") and "What ought we to do?" The first question can be subdivided: "What is the nature of goodness?" and "What things possess the property of goodness?" Regarding the nature of goodness, Moore was a nonnaturalist. He maintained that the term "good" stands for a basic or ultimate property that could not be defined in terms of anything else. Every attempt to define the good in terms of something else commits what Moore called "the naturalistic fallacy." Indeed, even to assume that "good" "*must* denote some *real* property of things" is to make this same mistake. With regard to the question "What things are good?" Moore is an intuitionist. The answer to this question is self-evident, but only in some defeasible sense. Finally, the question of morally obligatory conduct "can only be answered by considering what effects our actions will have." Thus, Moore was a consequentialist, though not of the egoistic or hedonistic utilitarian variety. For him, an action is right if it is, among all alternative actions, most productive of the nonnatural property "goodness." Moore was a severe critic of all forms of ethical subjectivism, including emotivism.

See also Emotivist ethics; Goodness; Intuitionist ethics; Metaethics; Naturalistic fallacy.

Moral education

TYPE OF ETHICS: Beliefs and practices
DATE: From antiquity
ASSOCIATED WITH: John Wilson's morally educated person (MEP), Lawrence Kohlberg's cognitive-developmental theory, and Sidney Simon's values-clarification strategies
DEFINITION: Learning that results in an advancement in thought and emotions from a self-centered orientation to socially responsible behavior
SIGNIFICANCE: Communicates that guidance and instruction are necessary for persons to become ethically mature

Instruction in morality has traditionally been considered to be the province of the home or of the church. Parents are the child's first teachers and are obligated to communicate to their young what behaviors and attitudes are socially acceptable and what behaviors and attitudes will not be tolerated. "Listen, my son, to your father's instruction and do not forsake your mother's teaching" (Prov. 1:8), wrote King Solomon thousands of years ago. "Then you will understand what is right and just and fair—every good path" (Prov. 2:9). The approach used was didactic, unilateral, and passed down from generation to generation. Directly telling the child what is right and what is wrong has long been the most popular way of inculcating morality.

Indoctrination is also used by religious groups. The minister or rabbi or priest, being ordained of God, interprets the sacred writings of the faith in order to convey to the people what is good and what is evil. This interpretation is put in the context of what is pleasing to God. A moral person loves and fears the Lord, obeys God's commandments, and treats others in a way that makes for harmonious living. The question of whether a person can be morally educated without having religious faith has long been debated. The question "Why be moral?" has both philosophic and religious implications.

Provision must be made for those children who are not taught in the home or do not attend a place of worship where ethical instruction is given. The logical answer is the school. A few have argued that the school is even preferable because it introduces the child to a larger, more democratic community. Émile Durkheim, a French sociologist, maintained that the school frees the child from excessive dependency, from being a slavish copy of the family. Jean Piaget, a Swiss philosopher, believed that the morality of cooperation (autonomy) encouraged by the school was more mature than the morality of unilateral constraint (heteronomy) taught in the home. Durkheim and Piaget differed, however, on the method to be used. Durkheim favored the direct teaching of moral values as essential for the child to become a fully functioning social being. Piaget opted for the use of moral dilemma stories to encourage the child's natural propensity to understand the good as a consequent of a maturing intellect.

Within the last quarter of the twentieth century, moral education programs became part of the regular school day in many public and private institutions. This was done in one of two ways. Either the teacher would set aside a special period for a moral lesson or a discussion of an ethical problem would be incorporated into the regular academic curriculum. Which method is better has long been debated, and it is not expected that an agreement will be reached.

In England, the best-known program was designed by British philosopher of education John Wilson, who combined universally accepted principles with individual personal ideals. Wilson believed that the morally educated person has incorporated within the self the principles of a concern for others based on an understanding of the concept of "person," a sense of feeling for others as well as for oneself, basic knowledge and skill in knowing how to deal with moral situations, and acting upon that knowledge in real-life situations. There are sixteen subcategories within these four major areas, each one contributing to the formation of a rational, autonomous, morally educated person. Curricular materials have been developed but are not in a form that makes for ease in implementation in some educational settings. Wilson's desire to have in place a carefully developed philosophy of moral education before it was practiced in the classroom has contributed to the slow and deliberate pace with which it has been used.

In the United States, the two major programs are Lawrence Kohlberg's moral reasoning and Sidney Simon's values clarification. Both Kohlberg and Simon believe that indoctrination is unacceptable, that a person is not morally educated unless he or she has developed within the self an understanding of what is good and right. Morality by definition must come from within; it is never imposed by an outside source. This stance came in part from research that shows that only a minor portion of moral education occurs at the "facts" level. Simply knowing what society expects does not ensure that one will act in accordance with that knowledge. This idea of self-developed morality also came about because in a pluralistic society there is not always agreement among the groups that constitute a community regarding what is right and what is wrong.

Borrowing from Piaget, Kohlberg made use of the moral dilemma story. Each child in the classroom states a position on the dilemma. Responses fall into one of six stages of moral understanding with two stages at each of three levels. At the first level (preconventional), the child makes statements that show an egocentric orientation: "It is good if it's good for me." At the second (conventional) level, the young person is concerned with pleasing others and winning their approval. Obeying the law and doing one's duty are also important: "A good person does what society expects of its members." At the third level, the adult wants justice for everyone alike: "Do unto others as you would have them do unto you." As students discuss the stories, they advance in moral understanding by listening to the reasoning of others within the classroom who are one stage or one level higher than their own.

The values-clarification approach used by Simon begins by asking students questions about the way they look at such topics as money, friendship, religion, prejudice, or love. The student must be able to state a position freely, consider alternatives as given by other students, make a choice after considering the possible consequences of each alternative, be happy with the choice made, tell others about the choice, act upon it, and incorporate the choice into his or her lifestyle. Curricular materials abound and are available for use not only in the school but also in the home and the church. According to Simon, the morally educated person is one who is given the freedom to choose, to affirm, and to act upon those values that make him or her a fully functioning individual. —*Bonnidell Clouse*

See also Kohlberg, Lawrence; Values clarification.

BIBLIOGRAPHY

Chazan, Barry. *Contemporary Approaches to Moral Education: Analyzing Alternative Theories.* New York: Teachers College Press, 1985.

Durkheim, Émile. *Moral Education: A Study in the Theory and Application of the Sociology of Education.* Translated by Everett K. Wilson and Herman Schnurer. Edited by Everett K. Wilson. New York: Free Press, 1961.

Kohlberg, Lawrence. *The Psychology of Moral Development.* San Francisco: Harper & Row, 1984.

Simon, Sidney B., and Sally W. Olds. *Helping Your Child Learn Right from Wrong: A Guide to Values Clarification.* New York: McGraw-Hill, 1977.

Wilson, John. *A New Introduction to Moral Education.* London: Cassell, 1990.

Moral luck

TYPE OF ETHICS: Theory of ethics

ASSOCIATED WITH: Beliefs and practices involving moral evaluations of people

DEFINITION: Cases of moral luck involve people who possess morally significant features over which they have no control

SIGNIFICANCE: The possibility of moral luck seems to threaten the commonsense idea that people can be held morally responsible for all of their morally significant features

Before considering the possibility of moral luck and its implications for ways of thinking about people, it is important to explain the notion of moral luck in some detail.

First, consider the notion of a morally significant feature. People have many features, but only some of them are morally significant. For example, the following features are clearly not morally significant: being six feet tall, being born on a Monday, and having brown eyes. By contrast, the following features are morally significant: being cruel, having murdered someone, being loving, having saved someone's life. These examples also illustrate the different kinds of morally significant features: some involve character traits, including beliefs and emotions, whereas others concern specific actions and ways of performing them.

The notion of having control over a feature is also important for explaining the notion of moral luck. Roughly speaking, people have control over a feature only if there is something that they can do to acquire it or something that they can do to get rid of it. For example, it seems clear that nobody has control over the following features: having been born during the night, having a body that is mostly water, and being unable to run faster than the speed of sound. By contrast, it is typically believed that most people have control over the following features: being excessively selfish, being very generous, being rude to a stranger on a particular occasion, and being patient with a child in a specific instance. Given these notions, it is possible to explain the concept of moral luck with some precision: Moral luck involves people possessing morally significant features over which they have no control.

Is moral luck possible? Are there any actual cases of moral luck? These questions are controversial. Before considering an apparent case of moral luck, it will be helpful to explore the significance of moral luck for ways of thinking about people.

One often holds people responsible for the morally significant features that they possess. For example, if one learns that certain people are greedy and have been caught stealing, typically one thinks of them (rather automatically) as being blameworthy for having these features. Similarly, upon discovering that people are generous and regularly help less fortunate people, typically one thinks of them (rather automatically) as being praiseworthy for having these features. (Besides evaluating other people, one often evaluates oneself in these same ways.)

These nearly automatic reactions to the morally significant features that people possess are called into question by the possibility of moral luck. If moral luck is possible, then it could turn out that some people possess morally significant features over which they have no control; therefore, it would be completely inappropriate to hold them morally responsible for those features. (After all, typically, one does not hold people morally responsible for features over which they have no control, such as the fact that they are unable to jump over the moon.) Therefore, the possibility of moral luck suggests that people's relatively automatic practices of evaluating others may be hasty and superficial.

Furthermore, the possibility of moral luck also seems to threaten people's conception of themselves as people who have control over their moral characters and actions. Although it is not surprising that there are some features over which one has no control, one's individual autonomy and self-determination seem to be undercut if one possesses morally significant features over which one has no control.

Given the significant implications of the possibility of moral luck, it is not surprising that questions concerning moral luck generate a great deal of controversy. Many people argue that moral luck is possible by appealing to the following kind of case: Imagine a truck driver who fails to stop at a stop sign and passes through an intersection without incident. Now imagine a second truck driver who does exactly what the first one does in similar circumstances but who also runs over and kills a small child who has darted into the street suddenly. This seems to be a case of moral luck, since it is a matter of luck that the second truck driver has a morally significant feature that the first truck driver lacks (namely, the feature of having killed a child).

Many people think that cases such as this demonstrate the possibility of moral luck. Some of them insist further that people's ways of evaluating others and their concepts of themselves as self-determining agents should be revised. Others simply deny the claim that a person must have control over a feature in order to be held morally responsible for possessing it. Still others, who are not persuaded by cases such as the one described above, reject the claim that moral luck is possible by restricting the notion of a morally significant feature in some way (for example, so that all such features are features over which persons have control). It is hard to say which approach to the question of the possibility of moral luck is best; reflective persons must decide themselves what to think. —*Scott A. Davison*

See also Autonomy; Determinism and freedom; Equality; Fairness; Freedom and liberty; Guilt and shame; Humility; Impartiality; Merit; Moral responsibility; Ought/can implication; Punishment; Responsibility.

BIBLIOGRAPHY

Feinberg, Joel. *Doing and Deserving*. Princeton, N.J.: Princeton University Press, 1970.

Fischer, John Martin, ed. *Moral Responsibility*. Ithaca, N.Y.: Cornell University Press, 1986.

Nagel, Thomas. *Mortal Questions*. Cambridge, England: Cambridge University Press, 1979.

Zimmerman, Michael J. "Luck and Moral Responsibility." *Ethics* 97 (January, 1987): 374-386.

Moral principles, rules, and imperatives

TYPE OF ETHICS: Theory of ethics
DATE: Fifth century B.C.E. to present
DEFINITION: Comprehensive, fundamental, and theoretical approaches to ethical behavior
SIGNIFICANCE: Morality raises the most fundamental questions about how one should live one's life

All people have a number of notions of right and wrong. These notions manifest themselves in a variety of ways. Some of these beliefs pertain to simple matters such as manners or taste, others pertain to more general matters such as customs and laws, and others guide the most fundamental aspects of human life: These are the beliefs that shape one's character and determine what others think about one as a human being. One's moral beliefs say more about one as an individual than does any other aspect of existence. Whether one is rich or poor, old or young, one's moral beliefs do more to define one's life than anything else.

The terms "morality" and "ethics" are often used interchangeably, but the distinction between the two is important to any serious study of ethical matters. The clearest distinction can be revealed by noting that there is a school of ethics called "situational ethics"; there is not, however, a moral school of thought that could be described as "situational." Morality can never be relative. What distinguishes morality from ethics is that morality is always universal and prescriptive. For this reason, the notions cited above about manners, taste, customs, and even laws may be considered ethical beliefs, but they are not part of a moral code. When ethical views and moral beliefs come into conflict, morality must prevail, because moral beliefs are universal and fundamental.

Looking at the negative connotations of these two terms is a helpful way to highlight their differences. A person who cheats at cards may be considered unethical, but that does not necessarily mean that the person is immoral. Being immoral is a much graver character flaw than is being unethical. A person may behave unethically on occasions and in certain circumstances, but to be immoral is to possess fundamental—if not permanent—character flaws that render one untrustworthy in most situations.

It must be noted that some people are amoral. They have no broad system of beliefs that guide their behavior. This does not mean that they have no notion of dos and don'ts in life, only that their beliefs are not guided by a universal system that provides justification for human actions.

Moral principles. The best example of moral principles continues to be the one articulated by Aristotle in his *Nicomachean Ethics*. Aristotle's moral principles were guided by a teleological concern. The teleological concern central to Aristotle was happiness. For Aristotle, morality meant doing what would provide a happy life as opposed to doing simply what one desired at the moment. Happiness, in this sense, has more to do with one's total lifestyle than it does with a few activities. It would be fair to say that Aristotle's understanding of happiness is more closely related to satisfaction or contentment than it is to simple pleasures. This is why reason plays such a large role in Aristotle's moral teachings.

Moral principles generally depend on reason. One must first understand the principle and then be able to apply it to different situations as they occur. Utilitarianism provides another good example of moral principles. The principle that guides utilitarianism is "the greatest good for the greatest number." One must understand this principle in order to exercise the judgment necessary to apply the principle.

The moral principles developed by Aristotle lead to a broad discussion of character. To him, morality is what determines who as well as what one is. Morality does much more than merely determine one's actions; it also determines one's thoughts and shapes one's soul.

Moral Rules. The Ten Commandments listed in the Old Testament of the Bible represent a clear set of moral rules. The prescribed and prohibited forms of behavior cited in the Ten Commandments provide more specific guides to human actions than do abstract principles. Moral rules place less emphasis on reason and more on authority or obedience. The "thou shalts" and "thou shalt nots" of the Ten Commandments do not leave as much room for judgment as one usually finds in moral principles.

It is much easier to provide children with moral rules than it is to describe moral principles. Children are often told to share their toys or not to hit one another. These are good rules, and children are often expected to follow these rules because they have been told by their parents or other adults to behave that way. People often assume that any further explanation would be beyond the reach of very small children.

In a similar manner, religious rules are often presented as rules that should be accepted as an article of faith. While this is true to some extent of all moral guides, rules tend to provide fewer opportunities for individual judgment than do principles. Rules tend to be more rigidly prescriptive than principles. Like the parental rules cited above, they rely on the authority of the rule givers—authority that the rule receiver is in no position to question or challenge.

Moral rules function in much the same way as laws: They spell out, in the most direct and detailed manner, what one should or should not do, and those who fall under their jurisdiction are expected to be obedient. When Moses came down from the mountain with the Ten Commandments, he

appeared in the capacity of a lawgiver, not that of a seminar leader. He appeared as a messenger from God with a strict set of specific orders that were intended to shape and guide the lives of the people. The only choice given to the people was obedience and salvation or disobedience and eternal damnation.

Moral rules are the simplest and most direct form of moral guide, but as people become more inquisitive about moral issues, certain moral rules may prove less clear and simple. Most often, moral rules are an effort to apply less tangible moral principles. When this occurs, the justification for the moral rules is found in the moral principles that guide them. When this is the justification for moral rules, it is important to remember that the rules are guided by the principles.

Moral Imperatives. Immanuel Kant established the most basic set of imperatives found in moral literature. Imperatives are commands or orders, so moral imperatives should be viewed as basic moral commandments or orders. Kant defines two distinct types of imperatives: hypothetical and categorical. Kant's hypothetical imperative is a means to some other end. If one desires a certain end, it is imperative that one employ a particular means. In contrast, a categorical imperative is an end with no reference to something beyond itself. Most ethical rules are hypothetical imperatives; morality, in contrast, consists of categorical imperatives. In the simplest terms, categorical imperatives are obeyed for their own sake.

Moral references to imperatives are generally considered to be references to what Kant defined as categorical imperatives, but it is important to keep the other alternative in mind when the general topic of moral imperatives arises. Kant further considered obligations and duties that accompany imperatives to be limited to rational creatures, for only rational beings can abide by such universal laws. If this is true, one might add that only rational beings are capable of moral considerations of any kind.

Moral Tensions. Alexis de Tocqueville, the nineteenth century French philosopher and social historian, once made a distinction between what he called "instinctive patriotism" and "reflective patriotism." While either might produce the same behavior in a person, the former was akin to a reflex reaction that required little or no thought; the latter was the result of careful consideration and extensive reflection.

Morality would seem to have a similar distinction. There is the morality that is so deeply ingrained in one from an early age that it guides one's actions without one's ever giving it a moment's thought. There is also morality that is the result of extensive study and careful analysis. Generally, there is a link between the two, but not everyone is curious enough to want to examine the basic moral assumptions. Some people feel that a careful examination or questioning of their moral beliefs is heresy. For this reason, certain moral beliefs are caught in a tug-of-war between reason and revelation.

The conflict between reason and revelation can be explained in the light of the realization that some moral beliefs are the result of factors that claim to be beyond human comprehension, while others are considered the result of human comprehension. Faith in a superior being who reveals moral laws through a person, persons, writings, or acts provides the clearest example of rules that must be accepted yet might never be understood.

The quest to understand moral matters encompasses a wide range of competing notions about how one comes to such an understanding. Ancient philosophers considered understanding to be a matter of discovery. The laws that should guide human behavior were determined by nature and preceded human existence. The task of understanding is one of using intellectual ability to learn the truths over which one has no control. Many modern philosophers believe that people can understand only what they themselves create. Existentialism is the philosophical school most often associated with this belief.

How Do People Acquire Moral Beliefs? In *A Question of Values,* Hunter Lewis describes six ways of acquiring moral beliefs: authority, logic, sense experience, emotion, intuition, and science. This is a good representative sample of the different ways in which people develop moral beliefs. If one is taught to obey parental authority in one's early years, one will generally find it easier to accept other authorities in later years. For most people, parental authority is their first exposure to subordinating bodily desires to some other influence. If one learns to control one's desires, one can then substitute other influences for parental authority in later years. One's ability to respond to any kind of moral guidance is dependent upon one's ability to control one's own actions.

The factors that influence beliefs usually change as people mature emotionally and intellectually. For this reason, simple rules provide people's first exposure to moral codes. As people grow older, these rules become more complex, and as people develop greater intellectual abilities, they become more likely to look to broader principles for moral guidance. Eventually, an individual should reach the point at which he or she can understand the most compelling and imperative moral guides. This moral maturation should lead from acceptance of authority or emotional considerations to more sophisticated guidance via logic or science.

Moral development need not, however, be linear in nature. David Hume argued that there is a moral sentiment that directs human moral behavior; reason does not have the authority to do so. Moral philosophers have never agreed on the main source of morality or on its final justification; they agree only that moral theories and moral actions are a necessary part of being human.

Conclusion. Since the days of Socrates, morality has played a central role in the battle between passion and reason. How people temper their most basic desires and behave in a moral manner has been one of the truly great questions of moral philosophy. This concern has produced many competing theories over justification. How can one convince an individual or a community of individuals to behave in ways that appear to contradict the most basic instincts?

Reason, salvation, and self-interest have all been used to explain why one might choose to combat these most basic and primitive drives. A society's ability to convince its population to adhere to a set of moral rules, principles, or imperatives is what has determined whether that society is judged to be civilized or barbaric. The United Nation's Universal Declaration of Human Rights has become the global barometer that is used to determine which nations are civilized and which are not. In fact, it refers to violations of its moral code as "barbarous acts." The assumption behind this declaration is there are some common and universal moral principles that should guide the activities of any nation or state.

To use the terminology of the United States of America's Declaration of Independence, there are certain "unalienable rights" that human beings naturally possess. These "unalienable rights" constitute the moral imperative that should guide all civilized nations. The general principles called "human rights" are a direct result of this moral imperative.

—Donald V. Weatherman

See also Ethics/morality distinction; Morality.

BIBLIOGRAPHY

Ashmore, Robert. *Building a Moral System.* Englewood Cliffs, N.J.: Prentice-Hall, 1987. An excellent, short introduction to the basic principles and concepts necessary to understand general ethics. This well-written work makes the most critical moral issues accessible to general readers.

Lewis, Hunter. *A Question of Values.* San Francisco: Harper & Row, 1990. A good introductory work that divides moral topics into a series of questions. Especially helpful is the way it breaks down the different approaches one can take in choosing a moral system. Contains a good mixture of theoretical issues and their behavioral applications.

Pojman, Louis, ed. *Ethical Theory: Classical and Contemporary Readings.* Belmont, Calif.: Wadsworth, 1989. As the title indicates, this volume contains both classical and contemporary writings on moral issues. A good reference work with very helpful reading lists at the end of each chapter.

Rachels, James. *The Elements of Moral Philosophy.* New York: Random House, 1986. One of the best topical introductions to morality in print. It examines religious and social approaches to moral theory in an objective manner. The suggestions for further reading are as good a guide to major writings on moral theory as can be found.

Solomon, Robert. *Ethics: A Short Introduction.* Dubuque, Iowa: Brown & Benchmark, 1993. This work is especially valuable because of the distinction it makes between ethics and morality. There is also a wonderful discussion on the tensions that can develop between community values and individual values.

_____. *Morality and the Good Life.* 2d ed. New York: McGraw-Hill, 1992. One of the best short anthologies of classical works on morality and ethics. This work has a helpful introductory chapter and provides a useful introduction to each of the readings. The readings are presented in chronological order, but the editor provides a convenient guide for a topical arrangement as well.

Moral realism

TYPE OF ETHICS: Theory of ethics

DATE: 1900 to present

ASSOCIATED WITH: G. E. Moore, W. D. Ross, John McDowell, and Simon Blackburn

DEFINITION: A theory that states that moral facts are independent of the individuals who come to know and recognize them

SIGNIFICANCE: Moral claims do not reflect what individuals feel about actions, events, and so forth; instead, they are real properties of such actions and events

Moral realism is a philosophical position that views moral facts such as good, right, and wrong in the same way that scientific realism views natural facts: that is, these facts are independent of and exist prior to their being thought, understood, and believed by individuals. G. E. Moore, in his book *Principia Ethica* (1903), was the first to formulate this position. Moore argues that beauty, goodness, right, wrong, and so forth are features of the world and actions that are true whether anyone recognizes them or not. When one claims that someone has done something good, for example, this does not reflect simply what one thinks of the action (as subjectivists argue), but reflects the intuition of a property that this action *really* has: goodness.

Moral properties, however, are not natural properties, or properties that one can recognize with one's natural faculties (senses). Moral properties are what Moore refers to instead as simple, unanalyzable, nonnatural properties. To clarify this idea, Moore compares the intuition of moral nonnatural properties to the intuition of mathematical axioms and proofs. One does not use one's senses to see that one step in a mathematical proof follows from another; likewise, one does not use one's senses to see that an act is good, but it is nevertheless seen to be good.

There are some problems with Moore's position, however, and much of the work in moral realism since Moore has been an effort to resolve these difficulties. For example, since moral properties are nonnatural and are not perceived by the senses, Moore must account for people's intuition of these properties by claiming that people have a moral intuition, a moral sense. The notion of a moral intuition or sense, however, is itself a rather mysterious notion that is left unexplained. Some proponents of moral realism, agreeing with Moore's claim that there are moral facts, have simply accepted this mystery. Philosophers such as W. D. Ross, in *The Right and the Good* (1930), accept the notion of moral intuition as a commonsense given. Just as many people would accept the use of intuition in mathematics as a given, so do Moore and those who follow him accept the use of moral intuition in making moral claims.

A more troubling problem with moral realism involves explaining the ontological status of moral facts. If, as moral realists argue, moral facts have a reality that is independent of thinking, desiring subjects, and if these facts can give direction to and place constraints on actions, then the question of what this independent reality is arises. The reality of moral facts is not the same as that of natural facts, yet they have the power to motivate individuals to place constraints upon themselves. How do they do this? Critics argue that in answering this question, moral realists must argue for an extravagant and unnecessary ontology. In short, they must unjustifiably attribute rather strange attributes to an equally strange entity called a moral fact if these facts are to do what the moral realist says they do.

There have been many attempts to resolve this apparent problem, but two are of particular note. Richard Boyd, in "How to be a Moral Realist" (1988), argues that moral properties can indeed be identified with physical properties, though in a sophisticated and peculiar way, and hence a moral realist need not be committed to the view that moral properties are nonnatural. The difficulty with Boyd's position lies in explaining this peculiar identification of moral properties with physical properties while avoiding what Moore calls the "naturalistic fallacy"—the fallacy of identifying simple, unanalyzable moral properties with identifiable natural properties. Boyd's response is to state that a moral realist can claim that moral properties are in some sense physical properties and also claim that these moral properties remain undefinable or unanalyzable. Precisely because moral properties are undefinable, the way in which the property of goodness is to be understood as physical will also always remain undefinable.

John McDowell, in "Values and Secondary Qualities" (1985), argues that moral properties are to be identified with physical properties (he avoids nonnaturalism in this way) but are to be identified in the same way that secondary qualities such as color are identified with physical things. Thus, in the same way that red, a secondary quality, emanates from a physical object (which is a primary quality) by means of this object's reflection of light at a certain wavelength, so too are moral properties to be understood as an emanation from a primary quality such as a physical action or an event. Secondary qualities are inseparable from primary qualities, and therefore moral properties are inseparable from physical properties, but they are not strictly identical to primary qualities. For example, one can turn off the light in one's room at night and the objects (primary qualities) in the room will still be there, but the colors (secondary qualities) will not. Secondary qualities and moral properties are real, but they are not real in the same sense, or in the same way, that primary qualities and physical properties are real.

There are many variations among those who argue for moral realism, but they are all agreed, following Moore, that moral facts are independent, real, and distinct from the individuals who know and are motivated to act on the basis of such facts.

—Jeff Bell

See also Moore, G. E.; Moral-sense theories; Naturalistic fallacy.

BIBLIOGRAPHY

Boyd, Richard. "How to Be a Moral Realist." In *Essays on Moral Realism*, edited by Geoffrey Sayre-McCord. Ithaca, N.Y.: Cornell University Press, 1988.

Kaufman, Frederik. "Moral Realism and Moral Judgments." *Erkenntnis* 36, no. 1 (1992): 103-112.

McDowell, John. "Values and Secondary Qualities." In *Morality and Objectivity*, edited by Ted Honderich. Boston: Routledge & Kegan Paul, 1985.

Moore, G. E. *Principia Ethica*. New York: Cambridge University Press, 1959.

Waller, Bruce. "Moral Conversion Without Moral Realism." *Southern Journal of Philosophy* 30, no. 3 (1992): 129-137.

Moral responsibility

TYPE OF ETHICS: Theory of ethics

DATE: Concept developed as early as the Egyptian *Book of the Dead*, c. 3500 B.C.E.

ASSOCIATED WITH: British philosophers Austin Duncan-Jones, P. H. Nowell-Smith, P. F. Strawson, and C. A. Campbell

DEFINITION: Being morally responsible can be being eligible for moral evaluation or being blameworthy or praiseworthy

SIGNIFICANCE: If determinism rules out moral responsibility, one never deserves praise or blame for anything one does

Many philosophers claim that determinism and moral responsibility are compatible. Austin Duncan-Jones claims that the statement, "He deserves blame for doing that wrong" simply means, "Blaming him for doing that wrong will favorably influence him and others." In that case, even if the man was causally determined to act as he did, blaming him could favorably influence him and others, and therefore determinism and moral responsibility are compatible.

Duncan-Jones's account cannot make good sense, however, of one person's being more blameworthy than another person. One person's deserving more blame than another person is not simply a matter of his being more favorably influenceable by blame. The person who is least blameworthy may be the person who is most favorably influenceable. Moreover, deserving blame and being overtly blamed to a good effect do not amount to the same thing. A wicked king on his deathbed may deserve blame for some wrong even if overtly blaming him for it will not favorably influence him or very many others.

P. H. Nowell-Smith defends the compatibility of determinism and desert as follows. "Finding the cause of a thing does not necessarily affect our evaluation of that thing. For instance, finding that Mozart's musical ability was due to his education, practice, and heredity would not diminish our admiration for his ability. Similarly, no matter how a person came to have his moral principles, they are his and he is judged for them. Explaining how one came to be as he is does not save the bad pianist who reveals his incompetence; nor does it save the bad man who reveals his wickedness."

Typically, people do ignore determinism when making judgments of praiseworthiness and blameworthiness. Yet if one cannot help being the way one is, can one really deserve credit or blame? This challenge to the typical approach is not adequately answered by merely redescribing that approach. Determinism would not rule out excellent qualities or the appreciation of them, but in spite of Nowell-Smith's argument, determinism might rule out the deserving of credit for such qualities.

In *Freedom and Resentment*, P. F. Strawson argues as follows that determinism would not rule out the rationality of blame. "Because of our human nature and our membership in society, we have a certain way of looking at human relationships. For instance, whether we feel grateful or resentful depends on what we think of other people's attitudes and behavior toward us. And we connect blame with wrongdoing. This way of looking at human relationships is part and parcel of being human and living in society. It is not something we choose or something that we can give up. It needs no further justification. But if we could give it up, our choice in this matter would not depend on whether determinism is true, but instead on whether giving up these attitudes would lead to an improved life in society. Therefore, whether we can give up blame or not, determinism would not rule out the rationality of blame."

Even if one cannot give up blame, however, that does not mean that blame is justified. If one cannot help feeling regret over something, it does not follow that one is adequately justified in having this feeling. If one had absolutely no control over what one did, it would make no sense to regret. It also might be possible to give up blame, since a society in which wrongs are viewed as illnesses beyond one's control is conceivable. If it is possible to give up blame, the question of whether it would be in the interests of society to do so is important. The main question at issue, however, is whether determinism would provide the kind of excuse that would rule out blame. It may be in the interests of society not to regard determinism as an excuse, even if, in all fairness, it is one.

In contrast to Strawson, Nowell-Smith, and Duncan-Jones, C. A. Campbell maintains that determinism is incompatible with moral responsibility. To support his position, Campbell cites the testimony of those he regards as being at an advanced stage of moral reflection. Such individuals are aware that everything may be causally determined and have wondered whether people really have a choice about what they do. They agree that one must have a choice in order to be morally responsible. For them, a person is blameworthy only if he or she could have chosen otherwise without being caused to do so. Campbell is making an appeal to moral authority. For it to succeed, there must be a consensus among the authorities. The problem for his argument is that such a consensus is lacking.

Even if the moral authorities agreed with Campbell, there would still be the following basis for maintaining the compatibility of determinism and moral responsibility. Making choices without being caused to do so would seem to be a matter of chance. If such choices are matters of chance, they seem to be things that simply happen to turn out well or ill and therefore are not things for which people deserve praise or blame. Thus, making choices without being caused to make them would seem to rule out moral responsibility. Also, if not being causally determined rules out being morally responsible, then being morally responsible requires being causally determined, in the same way that if being nonperfect rules out being God, then being God requires being perfect. Thus, it seems that moral responsibility is compatible with causal determination. A major question for this argument is, "Can making a choice without being caused to make it be plausibly construed as something besides a matter of chance?" —*Gregory P. Rich*

See also Determinism and freedom; Responsibility.

BIBLIOGRAPHY

Dworkin, Gerald, ed. *Determinism, Free Will, and Moral Responsibility*. Englewood Cliffs, N.J.: Prentice-Hall, 1970.

Fischer, John Martin, ed. *Moral Responsibility*. Ithaca, N.Y.: Cornell University Press, 1986.

French, Peter A., ed. *The Spectrum of Responsibility*. New York: St. Martin's Press, 1991.

Glover, Jonathan. *Responsibility*. London: Routledge & Kegan Paul, 1970.

Young, Robert. *Freedom, Responsibility, and God*. New York: Barnes & Noble, 1975.

Moral-sense theories

TYPE OF ETHICS: Theory of ethics
DATE: Eighteenth century
DEFINITION: An effort to find the basis of moral behavior within human nature, rather than in external codes of morality
SIGNIFICANCE: Many attempts have been made to ground morality not in revealed religion, but in the social nature of human beings; moral-sense theory is one such attempt

The best summary of moral-sense theory as a philosophical movement can be found in the Preface to James Bonar's book *Moral Sense* (1930):

The subject [of this book] is the rise, progress, and decline of a theory of moral philosophy which prevailed in this country [England] for the greater part of the eighteenth century.

Founded by Shaftesbury, and built up by Hutcheson, it derived our moral perceptions from a special Moral Sense, interpreted on the analogy of the Five Bodily Senses.

The book attempts an account of these two leaders, and of their principal followers and critics. The followers include the doubtful supporter David Hume; the critics Adam Smith and Immanuel Kant.

The movement had its origin in reaction, its growth in the positive statements of its principals, and its decline as much in changing fashions of explanation as in actual criticism.

Origin. By the end of the seventeenth century in England, conventional religious morality, with its imposed standards of behavior, had come into serious question for a number of reasons. First, the rise of Protestantism had introduced an antiauthoritarian note into much of the discussion of the subject. The rationalist-materialist philosopher Thomas Hobbes argued that the human organism was a mechanical object whose principal motivation was avoidance of pain and death, and that what passed for social morality was the calculating surrender of certain rights to avoid these unpleasantnesses; no positive source of morality existed. Second, Isaac Newton's mathematical demonstrations loosened God's hold on the physical universe, so to speak, as the motions of stars and planets and of microscopic particles were explained without recourse to divine intervention. The bodies of animals and humans had been found by Stephen Hales and William Harvey, among others, to be governed by mechanical principles; perhaps human spirit and morality might find a similar explanation. Finally, John Locke's relentless questioning of sources of knowledge—how can one truly know anything when the connection between the senses and brain impressions is so tenuous (a problem that continues to exist even in the present state of knowledge: Does translation of diverse stimuli into chemical-electrical impulses mean that one knows the world about one?)—suggested that new explanations were in order for morality and much else.

The Moral-Sense Answer. The man who proposed and named the "moral-sense" was Anthony Ashley Cooper, Third Earl of Shaftesbury. Principally in reaction to Hobbes's idea of the innate selfishness of man, Shaftesbury pointed out that, far from being selfish, humankind must necessarily possess a capacity for moral cooperation, or a successful society could not exist. Moral behavior, therefore, is that which works for the public interest, an argument later expanded by Hume. Francis Hutcheson developed the idea of the moral sense as a sense, explaining that good and bad actions arouse in people feelings of pleasure or revulsion, and feelings are the results of a sense like any other. The moral sense mediates between moral knowledge and moral behavior, and it is the motivation for the latter. It is also innate, not the result of moral education. One could not, in fact, be morally educated if one's moral sense were not present to identify virtuous and benevolent actions.

Criticism and Decline. Moral-sense theory was not without its critics even as it was being developed. At the lowest level, equating it with sight, hearing, and so forth was derided because there was no moral sense organ comparable with the eyes or ears. Hume answered this objection by sidestepping it: People know their senses through their characteristic perceptions, and it is clear that people perceive the morality of behavior. Other objections had to do with the nonuniversality of moral standards and the lack of symmetry between pleasure and virtuous action—that is, one recognizes a virtuous action by one's feeling of pleasure at it, but a feeling of pleasure by itself does not imply a virtuous action. In these matters Hume, as already noted, strengthened the argument that human morality is largely societal and the greatest good for the greatest number is therefore a primary moral principle. Other moral faculties were proposed: Samuel Clarke and others held that moral perception is the province of reason or understanding, not feeling. Adam Smith argued for "sympathy," which today people tend to call "empathy," the recognition of the passions or affections of others that leads to benevolent consideration of their welfare. The cleric Joseph Butler chose conscience as his implement of moral discrimination. Finally, Kant, in his monumental summation of the philosophy of reason at the end of the eighteenth century, rendered the question moot by stating that no logical or scientific demonstration was possible for God, freedom, or immortality, but that these were nevertheless logical necessities in a system that contained morality. Thus, a special moral sense or faculty was not necessary and efforts to demonstrate one gradually fell off.

Aftermath. Although identification of a moral faculty or sense is no longer considered a valid philosophical preoccupation, a number of the concerns of the moral-sense thinkers have persisted. Among these are the identification of morality as social in nature and the positions that feeling has a legitimate place in a system of morals, that there must be general rules for judging conduct, and that one of these rules should be the greatest good for the greatest number.

—*Robert M. Hawthorne, Jr.*

See also Butler, Joseph; Hobbes, Thomas; Hume, David; Kant, Immanuel; Kantian ethics; Shaftesbury, Earl of (Anthony Ashley Cooper).

BIBLIOGRAPHY

Bonar, James. *Moral Sense*. London: G. Allen & Unwin, 1930.

Raphael, David Daiches. *British Moralists, 1650-1800*. 2 vols. Oxford, England: Clarendon Press, 1969.

_____. *Moral Judgement*. London: George Allen & Unwin, 1955.

_____. *The Moral Sense*. London: Oxford University Press, 1947.

Selby-Bigge, L. A., ed. *British Moralists; Being Selections from Writers Principally of the Eighteenth Century*. 2 vols. *1897. Reprint. New York: Dover, 1965.*

Sprague, Elmer. "Moral sense." In *The Encyclopedia of Philosophy*, edited by Paul Edwards. Vol. 5. New York: Macmillan, 1967.

Willey, Basil. *The English Moralists*. New York: W. W. Norton, 1964.

Moral status of animals

TYPE OF ETHICS: Animal rights
DATE: From antiquity

ASSOCIATED WITH: Philosophers, scientists, and others who argue about the morally correct way to treat animals
DEFINITION: The philosophical concept underlying the question of whether humans have moral obligations to animals
SIGNIFICANCE: Moral obligations to other people arise from their having moral worth; if animals are morally similar to human beings, then people may have similar obligations to them

In many respects, nonhuman animals are treated as morally irrelevant. Humans eat them, conduct painful experiments on them, and use them for entertainment and sport; animals are seen as a part of the material world to be manipulated for the benefit of humankind. This attitude has its roots deep in Western culture. In Genesis 1:28, God says: "Be fruitful, multiply, and replenish the earth, and subdue it; and have dominion over the fish of the sea, and over the fowl of the air, and over every living thing that moveth upon the earth," and philosophers including Saint Thomas Aquinas and Immanuel Kant have echoed this attitude. John Locke, whose ideas helped to shape capitalist democracies, regarded the dominion over nature given to humankind by God as the source of human rights to property.

A number of arguments have been put forward against this "dominion position." The indirect-value argument holds that, although humans are the only morally relevant beings, other animals are essential for human well-being and are valuable as means to that end. A sophisticated version of this argument merges the need for human well-being with a recognition of the need for biodiversity. This view, however, gives animals only the most tenuous grip on moral relevance. If people found that the eradication of crocodiles had no effect on the integration and stability of the ecosystem, then crocodiles would suddenly become morally irrelevant. Furthermore, the worth of the animal in question still depends on its contribution to human welfare, and this misses an important part of what it means to have moral worth. No one wishes to be regarded merely as a means to an end, and any morality that regarded people as such would be fundamentally impoverished.

The second counterargument to the dominion position is utilitarian. Utilitarianism holds that the only morally relevant feature in any situation is the presence or absence of pain and pleasure, and that in moral calculations everyone's pain or pleasure counts for one and no one's for more than one. Concerning animals, Jeremy Bentham argued: "The question is not 'Can they reason?' nor 'Can they talk?' but 'Can they suffer?'" (*Principles of Morals and Legislation*, 1789).

The utilitarian argument is very powerful and for many people has proved decisive. Trips to a slaughterhouse, factory farm, or cosmetics testing laboratory, the utilitarian's visual aids, have often proved more powerful than a thousand academic discussions.

The third common route out of the dominion position is via a consideration of moral rights. A strong case for this approach is made by Tom Regan in *The Case for Animal Rights* (1983). Regan argues that, contrary to utilitarianism, in which value is attached simply to the pains and pleasures that people experience, individuals, as agents, have inherent value. This value is independent of gender, race, age, birthplace, or abilities and is founded on the fact that all people are "experiencing subjects of life." Each person is "a conscious creature having an individual welfare that has importance to us whatever our usefulness to others."

Regan then sets out to show that animals are just as much experiencing subjects of life as are humans and therefore also have inherent value, by showing that the differences postulated between humans and other animals are not significant. The primary supposed difference is reason—people are said to be the only rational animals. Regan argues that many animals have reasoning capacity and that although some humans don't have that capacity (infants, the comatose, and so forth), it is not assumed that they are less morally valuable than other humans.

In response to the utilitarian or rights argument, some people have tried to argue that animals do not feel pain or have interests. This is clearly vacuous. The question is really whether that pain and those interests count in the moral calculus in the same way that human pain and interests count. Someone who accepts that animals feel pain and have interests but claims that these features do not count in the same way that they do for humans may be immune to both the utilitarian and rights arguments. To argue that one should accept the moral significance of the pain of the animal on grounds of the pain of the animal, or the moral significance of its being an experiencing subject of life on the grounds of its being an experiencing subject of life, is clearly circular. Simply to argue on grounds of consistency and relevant similarity will not work, since the idea that those similarities are relevant in this case has already been rejected. This difficulty is experienced by all those who try to expand the circle of moral concern. It faced those who tried to abolish slavery and to extend full consideration to women and minorities.

Despite their difficulties, these three arguments have proved to be powerful and persuasive. International concern for the welfare of animals has led to the founding of groups campaigning for the ethical treatment of animals. The latter part of the twentieth century, in particular, has seen an intense focus on human attitudes toward animals and other elements of the natural world.   —Robert Halliday

See also Animal rights; Environmental ethics.

BIBLIOGRAPHY

Fox, Michael Allen. *The Case for Animal Experimentation.* Berkeley: University of California Press, 1986.

Midgley, Mary. *Animals and Why They Matter.* Harmondsworth, England: Penguin Books, 1983.

Regan, Tom. *A Case for Animal Rights.* Berkeley: University of California Press, 1983.

Rodd, Rosemary. *Biology, Ethics, and Animals.* Oxford, England: Clarendon Press, 1990.

Singer, Peter. *Animal Liberation.* New York: New York Review of Books, 1975.

Morality

TYPE OF ETHICS: Theory of ethics

DATE: Although the concept of morality is present by implication in ethical thought as early as the fifth century B.C.E., the term *moralitas* appears in the fourth century C.E. in the writings of St. Ambrose

ASSOCIATED WITH: Ethical theories that recognize obligations as a primary factor

DEFINITION: From the Latin *mores* (traditions, folkways), morality is especially concerned with personally held ethical beliefs, theories of obligation, and the social elements that reinforce ethical decisions

SIGNIFICANCE: Several of the most perplexing questions of ethical philosophy are found within the sphere of morality

Morality and Ethics. Although less inclusive than ethics, morality encompasses a wide variety of areas related to the field of ethics. Many but not all ethical theories come within the sphere of morality.

Ethical theories that lack a primary notion of obligation or duty, concern for the noninstrumental good of other persons, the demand for responsibility, and the recognition of the distinction between moral and nonmoral reasons cannot be accounted moral theories.

Morality includes within its scope far more than ethical theories, however, for it accounts for (or attempts to account for) the human mechanisms for the choice between good and evil. In addition, since there is a social aspect to human moral adherence, the structures of religion, law, and society are often examined from the perspective of the roles they play in promoting morality.

Varieties of Morality. Personal codes of morality and societal structures supportive of morality are an obvious reality in the world, but the theory of ethical nihilism (amoralism) holds that morality is based upon illusions and that moral enforcement by and the supportive structures of society serve other purposes. Friedrich Nietzsche, generally regarded as an ethical nihilist, denied the legitimacy of any objective theories of morality. Whether familiar with the original or not, Nietzsche seemed to have divined the truth of Hume's is/ought dichotomy and its implications for objective morality. Nietzsche claimed that the question left unanswered by all systems of morality was "Why be moral?"

Additionally, Nietzsche's hard determinism led him to the same conclusions about the impossibility of any objective moral order, with its necessary dependence upon moral responsibility. Interestingly, Nietzsche ascribed the institution of morality to the attempt of the weak and inferior members of the herd to restrain the strong and superior members. In doing so, the German philosopher was only elaborating and making more sophisticated the arguments put forward by Thrasymachus in Plato's *Republic*.

Immanuel Kant's critical philosophy was, in Nietzsche's view, an attempt of the class of the clerisy to retain its influence and power by mystification and mysticism, and this was especially true of the moral philosophy surrounding the doctrines of the categorical imperative. Nietzsche may be credited with further developing the sociological critique of morality, but Karl Marx, the father of communism, competed with him in that enterprise. The Marxian socioeconomic analysis of morality may be seen as the mirror image of the Nietzschean.

Karl Marx interpreted all history as the history of class conflict; particular forms of morality represented reflections of the economic orders out of which they arose. Thus, in the Marxian view, morality in general, along with religion, arose from the interests of the upper classes in controlling the proletariat—impeding both general uprisings and lesser depredation against property.

For many people, religion is inextricably associated with morality, and the taboo systems of primitive mythic religions bear a distant but discernible relationship to the more elaborate and sophisticated systems of philosophy-based morality.

Fear of vengeance by gods, demons, or animistic spirits for trespasses against sacred taboos may seem to be a long way from the Kantian categorical imperative or John Stuart Mill's act utilitarianism, but many moral systems—including many of great complexity—rely at least in part upon the fear of supernatural reprisals for violations against the moral law.

In Christian natural law ethics, acts done for the love of God, without fear of punishment and without desire for reward, are the most meritorious—the very embodiment of pure *caritas*. Despite this judgment, Saint Thomas Aquinas enthusiastically endorsed the biblical maxim that "Fear of God is the beginning of wisdom." Indeed, even Immanuel Kant declared posthumous rewards and punishments to be necessary so that the virtuous person not be proved a fool.

Historically, of course, the notion of after-death rewards and punishments seems to have developed slowly. Taboo violations were usually punished here and now, as in Greek mythology, where various wrongdoers were cursed and punished in this life by the gods and Furies. Hades—the underworld abode of the dead—was a place of universal assignment of the shades of the departed, where the good and bad alike enjoyed a fleshless, tepid existence, as portrayed in the eleventh book of Homer's *Odyssey*. Tartarus was a place of special torture for those who, like Tantalus and Sisyphus, had directly offended the gods, while certain heroes, such as Hercules, underwent apotheosis, becoming divine. Such extraordinary positive and negative sanctions were rare, however, and the ordinary mortal could expect neither.

In like manner, the divine justice recorded in the early books of the Old Testament seemed to stop at the grave. In both the Hebrew and the classical traditions, this incomplete vision of justice may finally have culminated in the supreme artistry of the Greek tragedy and the Hebrew Book of Job.

The unique tension in both forms arose from the development of full moral codes in the absence of a full theodic system at those times in those cultures.

In the *Republic* and elsewhere in the Platonic dialogues, Socrates spoke of souls that went before the lords of the underworld to be judged and suitably rewarded or punished for moral decisions made during their lives. Likewise, in Virgil's *Aeneid* (reflective of the ideas of the late Roman Republic and the early Roman Empire), the afterworld has become much more a place of reward, punishment, and purgation, and in Christianity, of course, the dogmas of Heaven, Hell, and purgatory combined with the doctrine of an all-loving, all-just God to provide a more thoroughgoing theodic system that served to reinforce the laws of morality.

In addition to promoting the idea of external reinforcement of the moral law, Christianity gave great prominence to the notion of *conscientia* ("conscience"), an interior faculty of the soul that aided the intellect in the recognition of the good. Medieval commentators attempted to relate the ancient Greek notion of *synderesis* to conscience, but although there were similarities between the two concepts, they were scarcely synonymous.

With the concept of conscience, late Judaism and early Christianity made the moral law an intimate and essential part of the individual person rather than a purely external constraint only. Natural law philosophers had to face the fact that many cultures did not conform to their moral teachings. If conscience were a natural faculty of soul, how could it be possible for diverse cultures to take such remarkably divergent positions regarding moral law? One society condemns cannibalism, while another condones it. In one nation, sexual libertinage is a punishable offence, while in another it is an unsanctioned common practice. In one land, slavery is an accepted practice; in another, it is the gravest of evils.

Natural law ethicians traditionally answered this problem by maintaining the position that although the conscience was a natural faculty of the soul that was not a social construct by one's culture, one's conscience could be perverted so that it would endorse evil. Such a perversion of conscience could be one of two kinds: Persons attracted to an evil action often indulge in elaborate self deception in order to pervert conscience in a culpable manner. The most common form of nonculpable perversion of conscience is by an invincible ignorance of the good that blinds a person to certain moral truths, often because of the training, education, and orientation provided by the person's culture.

Morality is often enforced by the external constraints of society as well as the influences of conscience and reason. The training and instruction of society—in the family, in the church, in formal education, and in the structuring of life experiences—reinforces or undermines the official moral codes promulgated by society.

Morality and Law. In regard to the legal codes of society, as viewed by natural law analysis, a distinction may be made between two types of relations to the moral law. First, not all moral law needs to be enforced by positive law. Even the most theocratic of societies usually leaves a space between moral law and positive law—not every vice is punishable by the state. Few societies, for example, punish gluttony or private drunkenness (if they permit the drinking of alcohol) or simply lying (as opposed to fraud, perjury, or libel).

Within the law, however, another distinction applies—that between intrinsic and extrinsic morality. Acts forbidden or commanded by intrinsic morality are held to be obligatory or, alternatively, morally wrong in themselves (*malum in se*). When positive law commands or forbids acts under intrinsic morality, it is merely recapitulating and sanctioning the moral law. Divine law, ecclesiastical law, and civil law all have aspects of intrinsic morality. God commands humankind not to steal, but in the natural law view, stealing is wrong in itself, apart from being forbidden in the Decalogue. In Catholic ecclesiastic law, priests are forbidden to perform the sacrament of matrimony in order to link a brother and a sister in marriage, but incest is wrong apart from this rule of canon law, and the positive law only recognized and articulates this inherent evil. Finally, the laws of New York State outlaw murder, but the wilful killing of the innocent is a moral wrong that is independent of any statute law against it.

In the case of extrinsic morality, the act commanded or proscribed by the positive law is morally neutral in itself but is made morally wrong or morally obligatory by being commanded by just authority. In divine law, God commands the observance of the sabbath, but a day of rest, let alone a particular day of rest, is scarcely obligatory by virtue of the moral law written in human nature. It is obligatory only because it is commanded by just authority. In Catholic ecclesiastical law, priests in the Latin Rite are forbidden to marry. This is simply a rule of the Church that could be altered at any time. A priest who violates this rule does wrong not in the act itself, but because the Church is presumed to have the right to make that morally neutral act impermissible (*malum prohibitum*). Finally, residents of the United Kingdom are instructed to drive on the left-hand side of roadways. A British subject who drives to the right is not directly violating a moral law but is doing wrong because he is defying the Queen-in-Parliament.

Extrinsic morality, furthermore, is held to have three clear relations to intrinsic morality. First, extrinsic morality can never contradict intrinsic morality but may only supplement it. Second, the purposes served by extrinsic moral commands are ones that ultimately would be endorsed by values inherent in intrinsic morality. To take an example, most traffic regulations are in the sphere of extrinsic morality, but saving innocent persons from death and injury and facilitating commerce relate to values of the intrinsic moral order. Finally, obedience to just authority is itself a principle of intrinsic morality.

Many of the particular moral rules and structures of society are of the extrinsic moral order, although tradition and long usage may lend them sacrosanctity in the eyes of the people.

Morality and Psychology. The psychological mechanisms of moral choice have also been a central concern of morality from the earliest days of ethical theory. In less-complex theories, such as hedonism, the mechanism of choice could be described simply. An individual instinctually pursues pleasure, and when he or she makes a choice that results in pain rather than pleasure, or in less pleasure than that which an alternative choice would have produced, that can be explained by ignorance. Even in the theory of the Cyrenaic (or irrationalist) school of hedonism, which clearly maintained the subjectivity of values, errors about consequences of actions or about one's own anticipated reaction to those consequences were still the source of "evil" actions.

In Immanuel Kant's deontology, there was, to a great extent, the assumption that freedom of the will, which itself was made central by the principle that "'Ought' implies 'can'," explained the selection of evil. In the *Groundwork of the Metaphysics of Morals* and the *Critique of Practical Reason*, Kant spoke as if there could be such a thing as freely chosen evil, but by the time of his last work, *Religion Within the Bounds of Reason Alone*, he had clearly abandoned that position as untenable. He took the Judeo-Christian story of the Fall in Eden and applied his own analysis. Did the tempter's wiles, or weakness of will, or the promptings of the first parents' lower natures cause the choice of evil? From the Kantian perspective, the problem in each of these explanations was that if they forced the will, then the will would not seem to be free. If the tempter's temptation was irresistible, then how could the Fall have been the moral fault of Adam and Eve, since they could not have acted otherwise, but if the serpent's seduction was resistible, why was it not resisted?

Given the full implications of Kant's moral psychology, there could be no such thing as freely chosen evil, and Kant ended by denying the possibility of "devilish minds"—that is, minds that freely and knowingly select evil over the good.

It is, perhaps, in Thomistic ethics that the most detailed and complex explanation of the agathokakological (containing good and evil) paradox appears. Thomas Aquinas explained that all human action arises from a desire (*appetitus*) in the subject. This desire aims at obtaining a good (*bonum*) that the subject lacks, as a state of being (*ens*). All action, therefore, seeks self-perfection (*perfectio*), which is only completely achieved in the state of blessedness in Heaven (*beatitudo*). For Thomism, problems arise because every good can be a personally held value (*bonum proprium*), but such personally held values may be truly good (*verum bonum*) or may be only an apparent good (*apparens bonum*). For Thomism, evil consists in the pursuit of a relative, apparent good in place of a true, absolute good.

Despite the sophistication of the Thomistic analysis of moral choice, serious questions remain unanswered: Why would the subject select an apparent good over a true good? If that choice had been made deliberately, how could the decision to pursue the apparent good over the true good have been made? If such a pursuit had not been deliberately chosen, how could the subject be morally responsible for that pursuit?

Another aspect of morality concerns the relationship of interior intentionality to exterior moral action. The subjective and objective elements in moral and immoral actions are necessarily related in all serious theories of moral philosophy. In the primitive taboo ethic, the simple act alone was sufficient. Speak the words, eat the substance, touch the object, and divine retribution followed, no matter what the motivation for the act, no matter what the subject's knowledge of the nature of the act.

Among libertarians and determinists alike, there is a recognition of the need for an interior disposition to the objective moral or immoral act for that act to make its perpetrator culpable. Habituation of vicious or virtuous actions eliminates the direct intentionality before particular acts of vice or virtue, but it is generally held to meet the standards for moral responsibility because the general intention in the course of habituating the action is held to replace the specific intention that would normally be present before each particular act.

Although much of the relationship between interior disposition and external act has been explored in moral philosophy, it has not all been sufficiently explained. Why do moral philosophy and the law alike regard the actual accomplishment of external, objective acts of evil as crucial to the degree of immorality or of criminality in the intention? It is clear that without the intention, killing is not murder, but the justification of the greater immorality and the greater criminality in murder over attempted murder is not so easily justified. If one clearly intended to kill an innocent person without justification and carried out the attempt, but the attempt failed through some technical flaw, how might one be said to be less blameworthy than if one had succeeded?

From the point of view of human positive law alone, the sharp distinction between the criminal act that has been completed and that which has been merely attempted may, in fact, rest upon no more than accident or chance. One attempted to shoot a man, but one's aim proved faulty, and the bullet missed. One's intention has been precisely the same as that of a successful murderer, and it is only a matter of moral luck that one is not guilty of murder, but only of attempted murder. Why should the fact that one is a bad shot excuse a degree of guilt for what one has both intended and attempted?

Since the civil law deals with the needs of society as well as the moral values of its citizens and since the law can only very imperfectly scan the intentions of the human heart, it may well be understandable that the law of the state differentiates between crimes attempted and crimes completed, but why should the moral order make such a distinction? Intuitively, such a distinction seems to be reasonable, but no carefully articulated justification of such a distinction has been successfully made.

Morality is at the core of the ethical sciences, and the most interesting problems in ethics are concentrated in the sphere of morality. The nature of obligation, the logic and mechanism of moral choice, and the relationship of intentionality to the objective factor in the blameworthiness and praiseworthiness of moral actions are among the most challenging areas for further intellectual investigation.

—Patrick M. O'Neil

See also Absolutes and absolutism; Ethics; Goodness; Intrinsic good; Natural law; Nihilism; Right and wrong; Universalizability; Values.

BIBLIOGRAPHY

Aristotle. "Nicomachean Ethics." In *The Basic Works of Aristotle*, edited by Richard McKeon. New York: Random House, 1941. The work demonstrates how all facets of human life relate to ethical choices.

Kant, Immanuel. *Grundlegung zur Metaphysik der Sitten*. Hamburg: F. Meiner, 1952. The good will (proper moral intention to obey the moral law) is seen as the source of all ethical good.

_____. *Religion Within the Limits of Reason Alone*. Translated by Theodore M. Greene and Hoyt H. Hudson. New York: Harper, 1960. Kant explores the possibility of freely chosen evil.

Katz, Leo. *Bad Acts and Guilty Minds—Conundrums of the Criminal Law*. Chicago: University of Chicago Press, 1987. The relation of interior intention to outward action is explored.

Plato. *The Collected Dialogues of Plato*. Edited by Edith Hamilton and Huntington Cairns. Translated by Lane Cooper et al. New York: Pantheon Books, 1966. The *Republic*, especially, deals with the role of social institutions in reinforcing moral values.

Thomas, Aquinas, Saint. *Summa Theologica*. Translated by Fathers of the English Dominican Province. Westminster, Md.: Christian Classics, 1981. Saint Thomas gives a detailed account of the moral psychology of the choice of good and evil.

Moses (c. 1300 B.C.E., near Memphis, Egypt—c. 1200 B.C.E., place unknown

TYPE OF ETHICS: Religious ethics

ACHIEVEMENTS: Delivered Hebrews from Egyptian slavery; traditionally regarded as the author of the Pentateuch

SIGNIFICANCE: Moses introduced the concept of ethical monotheism and provided the ancient Hebrews with a legal code based on the idea of holiness

Moses is best remembered for delivering the Hebrew people from Egyptian slavery and subsequently providing them with a legal code that he claimed he received from God. Questions of authenticity, dates, and other issues raised by critical scholarship are beyond this article's scope. Rather, it is assumed here that the books of Genesis, Exodus, Leviticus, Numbers, and Deuteronomy, sometimes referred to as "The Laws of Moses," or simply the Pentateuch, constitute a distinct body of literature. The latter four volumes contain specific directives that the ancient Hebrews believed to be a divinely sanctioned basis for their legal, political, religious, and social systems.

Divisions Within the Law. There are three primary divisions within the Hebrew Law. The first division is the Decalogue, or Ten Commandments (Exod. 20:1-17; Deut. 5:1-21). The first four commandments define the proper attitude that one should exhibit toward God. Commandments five and ten establish the sanctity of the family, while commandments six through nine establish individual rights. Each commandment is a moral injunction aimed at establishing a code of right conduct.

Civil legislation marks the second division in Moses' law. These laws focus mainly on Hebrew interpersonal relationships. For example, between Exodus 20:18 and Exodus 23:33 there are more than seventy specific statements delineating between accidental and premeditated acts. Hebrew civil law usually determined the appropriate compensation that one should receive in the event of property loss.

The third division in Moses' law involved ceremony (Exod. 24-34; Lev.). This was perhaps the most far-reaching element of the Hebrew legal code. Whereas the civil law concerned individual relationships, the ceremonial law focused on the relationship between God and humanity. These laws outlined every facet of Hebrew worship, ranging from the construction of a suitable place of worship to the role that priests played both in religious ritual and society in general. The ceremonial law also outlined an elaborate system of offerings that Hebrews were commanded to offer to God. In some cases, these offerings were animal sacrifices; in others, grain offerings. In any event, the ceremonial law was designed to keep the Hebrews' religion pure and free from pagan influence. Moreover, since Moses described God both as holy and as expecting the Hebrews also to be holy, the ceremonial law provided a means whereby they could express a wide variety of spiritual needs, ranging from ceremonial cleansing from sin to joy and thanksgiving.

Characteristics of Old Testament Ethics. Ancient legal codes, most notably the Babylonian Code of Hammurabi, addressed legal issues on a case-by-case basis and emphasized retribution—"an eye for an eye." Certain features of the Mosaic code also called for retribution, but Moses' Law was more far-reaching. In *Toward Old Testament Ethics*, Walter C. Kaiser, Jr., identifies five characteristics of Old Testament ethics. First, they were personal. Since God used himself as the standard of absolute righteousness, he expected his people to obey the law. Second, Old Testament ethics were theistic. In addition to believing that God had given that the law to Moses personally, the Hebrews also believed that the law reflected God's character. Third, Old Testament ethics were internal. Moses indicated that God's

law was not merely an external checklist. Rather, God was concerned about the Hebrew's internal spiritual condition. Additionally, these ethics were future oriented. Throughout the Old Testament, biblical writers indicate that a Messiah will ultimately fulfill the law perfectly. Hence, Old Testament ethics are rooted in hope. Jesus claimed to fulfill all requirements of the law (Matt. 5:17-18). Other New Testament writers likewise claimed that Jesus was the fulfillment of the law (Rom. 10:4; Gal. 3:24). Finally, Old Testament ethics are universal. Even though Moses delivered the law to the Hebrews, it is understood that God's standard of holiness was applicable to all nations (see Gen. 13:13, 18:25).

Significance. Moses' significance to ethics is that he introduced ethical monotheism. If the Hebrews were to be God's people, Moses explained, they were obligated to obey God's commandments. Yet the Hebrews were not to keep Moses' law simply to win God's favor. Rather, Moses said that God was infinitely holy and, hence, the law was a standard of personal rectitude. Moreover, since the Hebrews saw God as infinitely good, the law was good because God himself had given it. Moses, therefore, revealed God as an ethicist. Additionally, Moses' law revealed a God who was genuinely interested in humanity. True, he could be offended, but he also provided forgiveness. He likewise promised to bless the Hebrews and go with them wherever they went. This concept of a holy God who placed just expectations upon people and cared about them personally laid the foundation for the ethics of the Western world.

—Keith Harper

See also Christian ethics; Ethical monotheism; Jesus; Jewish ethics; Ten Commandments.

BIBLIOGRAPHY

Kaiser, Walter C., Jr. *Toward Old Testament Ethics*. Grand Rapids, Mich.: Zondervan, 1983.

Maston, Thomas Bufford. *Biblical Ethics: A Guide to the Ethical Message of Scriptures from Genesis through Revelation*. Macon, Ga.: Mercer University Press, 1982.

Muilenburg, James. *An Eye for An Eye: The Place of Old Testament Ethics Today*. Downers Grove, Ill.: InterVarsity Press, 1983.

_____. "Old Testament Ethics." In *A Dictionary of Christian Ethics*, edited by John Macquarrie. London: SCM Press, 1967.

Wright, Christopher J. H. *Living as the People of God: The Relevance of Old Testament Ethics*. Leicester, England: InterVarsity Press, 1983.

Motion picture ratings systems

TYPE OF ETHICS: Media ethics
DATE: 1968
ASSOCIATED WITH: Motion Picture Association of America (MPAA)
DEFINITION: Motion picture ratings systems classify films according to standards of content

SIGNIFICANCE: Motion picture ratings systems generally link film content with social values

The motion picture industry of the United States of America has long attempted to forestall government controls by observing self-imposed regulations. Originally, those regulations were proscriptive, intended to make a preponderance of exhibited films palatable to general audiences, but subsequent policy, using ratings to influence public exposure, enabled a wider range of material to appear in major releases. Regulatory systems have been established elsewhere, but the varying U.S. approaches provide excellent studies in the application of standards.

State and local government attempts to censor film date

itly presented" and "The treatment of bedrooms must be governed by good taste and delicacy").

Two major ratings systems originated during this period. In 1933, the Film Board of National Organizations formulated the MPPDA-supported Green Sheet, which used age and educational criteria to classify films as A (Adult), MY (Mature Young People), Y (Young People), GA (General Audience), C (Children, unaccompanied), or a combination of those ratings. The following year, a committee of bishops formed the influential Legion of Decency, which rated movies on a scale from A-I (morally unobjectionable for general audiences) to C (condemned).

THE VOLUNTARY MOVIE RATING SYSTEM MOTION PICTURE ASSOCIATION OF AMERICA, 1991		
Code	**Meaning**	**Potentially Offensive Material**
G	General Audiences. All ages admitted.	None. (Impolite language and minimal violence are allowed.)
PG	Parental Guidance Suggested. Some material may not be suitable for children.	Minimal amounts of nudity, sensuality, profanity, and violence.
PG-13	Parents Strongly Cautioned. Some material may be inappropriate for children under 13.	All of the above, plus drug use, nonsexual nudity, and/or one harsh sexually derived word used in a nonsexual context.[+]
R	Restricted. Children under 17* require adult guardian.	All of the above.
NC-17*	No Children Under 17* Admitted.	All of the above in a patently adult context.
[+]More potentially offensive language may be used if the Rating Board finds, through a special vote, that the resulting rating would better reflect the opinion of American parents.		
*Age varies in some jurisdictions.		

back to a 1907 Chicago ordinance that was upheld by the Illinois Supreme Court in 1909. The potential impact of such rulings was evident in the proliferation of state and local censor boards as well as a 1915 U.S. Supreme Court determination that cinema was not protected under the First Amendment. With the goal of curtailing widespread government censorship, from 1909 to 1921 the National Board of Censorship assumed some responsibility for the prerelease evaluation of film content. This citizens' group, supported by the film industry, was the nation's first voluntary censorship body.

In 1922, the major Hollywood studios appointed Will Hays the head of their newly formed association, the Motion Picture Producers and Distributors of America (MPPDA). Created to maintain industry sovereignty, the MPPDA in 1934 enacted a code of ethics known as the Production Code. Arising out of the Mae West era, the Code combined lofty statements of principle ("No picture shall be produced which will lower the moral standards of those who see it.") with a battery of specific regulations (for example, "*Methods of Crime* should not be explic-

Movies without the Production Code Seal were effectively banned from theaters. Code stipulations were, however, periodically amended and perennially subject to administrative give and take (intense lobbying won a place for Rhett Butler's "forbidden" last word in 1939's *Gone with the Wind*). The Code remained in place in the 1940's, as Eric Johnston replaced Hays, the MPPDA became the MPAA, and antitrust decisions forced studios to sell their theaters.

After the Supreme Court overturned its 1915 ruling in 1952, the newly opened theater market exhibited not only unapproved foreign features but also domestic productions such as *The Moon is Blue* (1953), which had been denied the Seal for its treatment of virginity. The commercial viability of such films, together with the precedent-setting releases of *Son of Sinbad* (1955) and *Baby Doll* (1956)—the first C films to receive the Seal—heralded further shifts in standard application. Additional Court decisions and jolting thrillers such as *Psycho* (1960) and *Cape Fear* (1962) built momentum for extensive Code revision in 1966, when Jack Valenti became the third MPAA president. Early frustrations with language in *Who's Afraid of Virginia Woolf* (1966) and nudity in *Blow-Up* (1966) influenced his replacement of proscription with a voluntary film rating system in 1968.

Officially intended to place responsibility for children's moviegoing with parents and guardians, the new system reflected contemporaneous rulings on children and obscenity. Overseen by the MPAA, the National Association of Theatre Owners (NATO), and the International Film Importers and Distributors of America, it classified submitted films according to their appropriateness for one of four possible audience groups. G for General Audiences, M for Mature Audiences (parental guidance suggested), and R for Restricted Audiences were trademarked; X (no one under 17 admitted), adopted at the urging of NATO, was not. M, which parents misinterpreted as being sterner than R, was initially replaced with GP (implying a "General Audience" film for which "Parental Guidance" was suggested) and later with PG. In 1984, the young audience categories were expanded to include PG-13.

Adult film classification also changed. At first, some X features won significant mainstream interest. Soon, however, the rating became identified with pornography, to which it was frequently self-applied. Excluding the young audience market by definition, the rating also precluded advertising in most outlets, leading many major producers to edit movies from X to R. (Some features, such as *Midnight Cowboy*, 1969, eventually made that transition without cutting.) Ongoing debate over film tailoring and the need for another "adults only" category sparked the creation of the MPAA's federally registered certification mark NC-17, first assigned to *Henry and June* (1990). In the early 1990's, the MPAA also began issuing explanations of specific ratings to theaters and critics.

Although criticized for representing an abandonment of moral and ethical responsibility, the shift from proscription to ratings has been praised for enabling major producers to exercise greater freedom of expression. Despite such increased license, the questions of the ratings system constituting a form of self-censorship remained.

Because ratings greatly influence a project's viability, films are not simply rated after completion; throughout the creative process there may be ratings-oriented interplay involving filmmakers, the Rating Board, and occasionally (after the code has been assigned) the Appeals Board. This process may receive wide public attention, often dwelling on potentially offensive material and sometimes leading to the creation of alternate versions aimed at different markets. Naturally, content not recognized as potentially offensive may be perceived as implicitly approved. The MPAA uses regular polling to establish that its standards represent the views of a majority of citizens.

Besides advising parents and guardians about film content, the ratings system, which encompasses trailers and film advertising, requires the cooperation of theater owners. At the box office, administrators discriminate according to age and appearance (sometimes requiring potential consumers to identify themselves by birth date), as well as geographic location. This approach reinforces and establishes taboos and hierarchies related to age, appearance, maturity, and media.

The ratings system has been endorsed by the Video Software Dealers Association. Similar systems of self-regulation have been adopted or proposed for recording, video games, and television programming. —*David Marc Fischer*

See also Art; Art and public policy; Censorship; Children; Children's rights; Consistency; Family values; First Amendment; Freedom of expression; Language; Pornography; Self-regulation; Taboos; Values clarification.

BIBLIOGRAPHY

De Grazia, Edward, and Roger K. Newman. *Banned Films.* New York: R. R. Bowker, 1982.

Farber, Stephen. *The Movie Rating Game.* Washington, D.C.: Public Affairs Press, 1972.

Leff, Leonard J., and Jerold L. Simmons. *The Dame in the Kimono.* New York: Grove Weidenfeld, 1990.

Randall, Richard S. *Censorship of the Movies.* Madison: University of Wisconsin Press, 1968.

Schumach, Murray. *The Face on the Cutting Room Floor.* New York: William Morrow, 1964.

Motivation

TYPE OF ETHICS: Theory of ethics
DATE: Third century B.C.E. to present
DEFINITION: An internal condition that arouses a person to behave in a particular way and to persist in that behavior until a particular goal is attained
SIGNIFICANCE: Raises the question of whether human motivation is basically good and peace-loving, evil and destructive, or amoral

Ethics deals with determining what is good and bad and with moral principles and values. These are all aspects of behavior. In order for behavior to occur, a person must be motivated. Without motivation, the person would do virtually nothing. Driven to action by a motive, however, the person engages in behavior that persists until the motive is satisfied. The word "motive" derives from the Latin *movere*, meaning "to move."

One of the prevailing issues of motivation is the nature of human motives and thus the nature of human nature. As Charles N. Cofer and Mortimer H. Apley have stated the issue in *Motivation: Theory and Research* (1964):

Is man—unfettered and untarnished by the experiences and constraints of society—essentially good, altruistic, brotherly, creative, peace loving? Or, alternatively, is he essentially evil, egocentric, aggressive, competitive, warlike, requiring the constraints of society in order to keep him from destroying his fellows and himself?

Early Conceptions. In Aristotelian ethics, as in ethics generally, the issue concerned the appropriate direction of desire and action (that is, motivation). Good or right action was a product of reason and a strong will. Practicing performing good or just acts caused those acts to become pleasurable and habitual, and the will then chose freely that which knowledge determined to be good. Through the ensuing centuries, this belief that the will controlled the animal side of humanity and guided it toward right virtue and salvation persisted. The philosopher Immanuel Kant believed that good actions originated from a sense of duty or moral law. The will is motivated to choose a course of good action in the light of moral law.

A different view was elaborated in the mid-nineteenth century by the philosopher Arthur Schopenhauer. Will was viewed as a basic force or striving and was evil. The impulses of the will brought no pleasure, only pain. Gratification of the will's impulses did not produce happiness, only satiety.

Contemporary Conceptions. These philosophical views have been carried into contemporary times by psychology. "Will" has been replaced by "motivation." The issue of whether human motivation is good or evil is addressed by three major theoretical systems, each of which provides a different answer: behavioral theory, psychodynamic theory, and humanistic theory.

Behavioral Theory. Behaviorism was founded by John B. Watson in 1913. Behaviorists viewed motives as internal stimuli that persist and dominate behavior until the person reacts to satisfy the motive. Human motives are, however, neither good nor evil. Good and evil depend on conditioning provided by the environment. One of Watson's most famous (and outrageous) statements says: "Give me a dozen healthy infants, well formed, and my own specified world to bring them up in and I'll guarantee to take any one at random and train him to become any type of specialist I might select—doctor, lawyer, artist, merchant-chief and, yes, even beggar-man and thief, regardless of his talents, penchants, tendencies, abilities, vocations, and race of his ancestors." Although contemporary behaviorists are no longer such extreme environmental determinists, they would agree with Watson that ethics is primarily a matter of environmental conditioning.

Psychodynamic Theory. To Sigmund Freud, the true purpose of life lay in the satisfaction of its innate motives. These motives derive from bodily needs, produce tension, and cause all activity. The two classes of motives are the life-sustaining motives (sex, hunger, and so forth) and the death or destructive motives (cruelty, sadism, violence, destruction, and murder).

The life and death motives arise from the oldest and most primitive part of the mutual apparatus: the id. The id is not conscious of reality; it is illogical, irrational, has no values, no concept of good or evil, no morality, and continually seeks instant discharge and pleasure. In part, the function of the other two divisions of the mental apparatus, the ego and the superego, was to control, regulate, and contain the id in a manner consistent with the demands of external reality. Acts of destruction and aggression, such as war, represent a failure to regulate and control the expression of the death motive.

The idea that the id knows no values and has no sense of good, evil or morality is similar to the behavioral view of neutrality about the nature of human nature. Psychodynamic theory, however, is essentially a pessimistic view of human nature. The true purpose of life is not some lofty or idealistic state, but the satisfaction of the motives of the id in a manner consistent with maintaining civilized society. World War I and other widespread acts of death and destruction convinced Freud of the primacy of aggression and that the ego and superego often lose the battle to effectively control and regulate it.

Humanistic Theory. According to the clinical psychologist Carl Rogers, "The basic nature of human beings when functioning fully is constructive, trustworthy, forward-looking, good and capable of perfection." In 1956, John Adelson stated: "Man is born without sin, aspiring to goodness, and capable of perfection; human evil is exogenous, the betrayal of man's nature by cruel circumstance." This motive of full functioning or self-actualization is part of an inherent process called syntropy, a movement toward growth, expansion, and realization of the self.

That self-actualization is difficult to achieve is a result of societal constraints and the false goals set by society. Society often rejects, punishes, ridicules, or threatens nonactualized individuals, rather than helping them.

Evidence. The nature of human nature has been debated since antiquity. Since humans are capable of both good and evil behaviors and amply exhibit both types, and since it is conceptually and ethically impossible to conduct an appropriate experiment to resolve the issue, the nature of human motivation will no doubt continue to be debated for many more centuries.
—*Laurence Miller*

See also Behaviorism; Freud, Sigmund; Psychology.

BIBLIOGRAPHY

Cofer, Charles N., and Mortimer H. Apley. *Motivation: Theory and Research*. New York: John Wiley & Sons, 1964.

Freud, Sigmund. *New Introductory Lectures on Psychoanalysis*. Translated and edited by James Strachey. New York: W. W. Norton, 1965.

Hampden-Turner, Charles. *Maps of the Mind*. New York: Macmillan, 1981.

Maslow, Abraham H. *Toward a Psychology of Being*. 2d ed. Princeton, N.J.: Van Nostrand, 1968.

Skinner, Burrhus F. *The Shaping of a Behaviorist*. New York: Knopf, 1979.

Muhammad al-Mustafâ (c. 570, Mecca, Arabia—June 8, 632, Medina, Arabia): Prophet

TYPE OF ETHICS: Religious ethics

ACHIEVEMENTS: Received the revelation of the Qur'ân and founded Islam

SIGNIFICANCE: In addition to the Qur'ân, the traditions of the life of the Prophet, who is seen as an exemplary human, are regulative in Islamic ethics

Muhammad's role in Islam is that of the Seal of the Prophets:

He is *al-Muṣṭafâ*, the "Chosen One" who completed the line of the prophets and received the perfect revelation, the Qur'ân. Since God chose Muḥammad al-Muṣṭafa for this supreme human task, Muḥammad is seen as the exemplary or even perfect human. Muḥammad put forth a pure monotheism, in which all facets of life are to be submitted to and are to remind one of the will of God. (*Al-Islâm* means, literally, "submission" or "surrender"—in this context, to the Divine Will.) Communal life, too, is to be dedicated to God: Since all sovereignty resides with God, the separation of church and state is alien to Islam.

Role of Ḥadîth. The Qur'ân (*sûra* 33:21) states, "Verily, in the messenger of Allah ye have a good example for him who looketh unto Allah and the Last Day, and remembereth Allah much" (Pickthall's translation). Since the specific prescriptions and proscriptions in the Qur'ân cannot cover all particulars of situations in which one might find oneself, the traditions (*ḥadîth*) of the life and sayings of the Prophet (the "good example") are looked to for further guidance in the conduct of daily life.

Veneration of Muḥammad. It is incorrect to say that Muḥammad is *worshipped* in Islam: Muslims worship only God. Muḥammad and his family are, however, deeply revered. Pilgrimage to the Rauḍa (Muḥammad's mausoleum in Medina) is common, and the image of Muḥammad as merciful intercessor on behalf of the faithful emerged early in the history of Islam. Popular songs and poetry celebrate Muḥammad's life, and numerous stories of miracles have grown up around Muḥammad's biography. Intellectuals who are skeptical of many of the popular tales, nevertheless have profound respect for the Prophet and his guidance of the Muslim community.

Mystical Meaning of Muḥammad's Life. Muḥammad's life often has been interpreted in Sufism as having mystical and allegorical meaning. The *Isrâ'* and *Miʿrâj* (the traditions of Muḥammad's nocturnal tours through Hell and through Paradise, respectively), in particular, have been fecund sources of Sufi literature, in which those journeys are seen as allegories representing the journey of the soul from worldly attachments, along the path of spiritual development, to the state of final mystical bliss. The Prophet is also seen by some philosophers, such as Ibn ʿArabî, as having an eternal essence that exemplifies Divine Reason and is manifested in the Prophet's temporal life and teachings.

Biography. Muḥammad was born into the Quraysh, a large trading clan who ruled Mecca. He was orphaned at six, and his grandfather died when Muḥammad was about eight. His care was then assumed by his uncle, Abû Ṭâlib, whose son ʿAlî became a close companion of Muḥammad (and later would be among the first to embrace Islam). At age twenty-five, Muḥammad married Khadîja, who was somewhat his senior. She bore him four daughters in a happy marriage and is widely revered for her steadfast comfort and support of Muḥammad.

Arabia was religiously eclectic: There were various Christian influences, widespread polytheism (including the veneration of many deities enshrined in the Kaʿba in Mecca), and, at least among the Bedouins, animism. Unsatisfied with prevalent religion, Muḥammad often retreated for contemplation to the cave at Hira, where, in 609, he began receiving the revelations that constitute the Qur'ân.

Although the monotheism of the Qur'ân was resented by most Meccans, Muḥammad and the other Muslims were invited to migrate to Yathrib and to mediate communal disputes there. Muḥammad left Mecca in June, 622: The *hijra* (departure) for Yathrib marks the beginning of the Islamic era, when Muḥammad's efforts turned away from worldly Mecca and toward building a new Muslim community. Muḥammad devised a constitution for Yathrib, which later became known as *Madînat al-nabî* (the City of the Prophet), or Medina. The constitution of Medina would be used often as a paradigm of proper Islamic political organization.

The Qur'ân states that Islam is continuous with and the fulfillment of the partial revelations that were given to Jesus and the major figures in Judaism; and the early Muslims prayed toward Jerusalem. A revelation that occurred circa 623 (Qur'ân 2:144-145), however, commanded Muslims to pray toward the Kaʿba, which is supposed to have been built by Abraham and Ishmael but corrupted by later polytheists. Muslim protection of the Kaʿba was thus a high priority. Military confrontations with the Meccans ensued between 624 and 630, when Muḥammad conquered his ancestral home without resistance. The Kaʿba was cleansed of idols, and pilgrimage to the Kaʿba (the *hajj*) has since been obligatory for Muslims. Muḥammad made his final pilgrimage to the Kaʿba in 632. Upon his return to Medina, Muḥammad died.

The ease of the final conquest of Mecca would exact a price later, since many Meccans had converted to Islam for their own convenience and gain when they saw conquest by the Muslims as inevitable. Because there was no clear procedure for succession to leadership of the Islamic community, debates erupted almost immediately about who had been the true companions of the Prophet and who had been mere associates of convenience. —*Thomas Gaskill*

See also ʿAlî ibn Abî Ṭâlib; Fâṭima; Ḥadîth; Islamic ethics; Qur'ân; Sharîʿa; Sufism.

BIBLIOGRAPHY

Armstrong, Karen. *Muḥammad: A Biography of The Prophet*. San Francisco: HarperSanFrancisco, 1992.

Dashti, Ali. *Twenty Three Years: A Study of the Prophetic Career of Muḥammad*. Translated by F. R. C. Bagley. London: Allen & Unwin, 1985.

Schimmel, Annemarie. *And Muḥammad Is His Messenger: The Veneration of the Prophet in Islamic Piety*. Chapel Hill, N.C.: University of North Carolina Press, 1985.

Muir, John (Apr. 21, 1828, Dunbar, Scotland—Dec. 24, 1914, Los Angeles, Calif.): Writer

TYPE OF ETHICS: Environmental ethics

ACHIEVEMENTS: Lobbied for the establishment of Yosemite, Sequoia, and General Grant National Parks;

was a founder of the Sierra Club

SIGNIFICANCE: Increased public interest in preservationism

Muir moved to a Wisconsin homestead when he was eleven and attended the University of Wisconsin from 1858 to 1863. After a year of farming while waiting for a draft call, he decamped to stay in Canada from 1863 to 1864. In 1867, he began a full-time career in nature study, starting with a projected thousand-mile walk to the Gulf of Mexico on his way to South America. Frustrated by serious illness, he went to California and lived in the Yosemite Valley for five years. In 1873, he began a full-time career as a nature writer and preservationist, spending summers hiking and observing natural phenomena in the mountains. In 1889, Muir began writing and lobbying to preserve Yosemite Valley as a National Park. In 1896, as one of its founders, he became the first president of the Sierra Club; remaining in that position until 1914. He was preeminent in publicity and lobbying (1905-1913) against San Francisco's Hetch Hetchy water project. Although unsuccessful, this effort broadcast the preservationist ethic nationwide. Muir's contributions to glaciology and geomorphology give him minor scientific status. He published more than 500 articles and essays, many of which were based on his mountaineering journals. His books include *Mountains of California* (1894), *My First Summer in the Sierra* (1911) and *The Yosemite* (1912).

See also National Park System, U.S.; Sierra Club.

John Muir (Library of Congress)

Multiculturalism

TYPE OF ETHICS: Race and ethnicity

DATE: Twentieth century

DEFINITION: The position that education should reflect various cultures, ethnic backgrounds, and traditions, not merely the culture and traditions of the dominant segment of society

SIGNIFICANCE: One of the most controversial issues in American education in the 1980's and beyond, multiculturalism challenged on political and moral grounds the traditional focus on the male-oriented, European-American cultural tradition in education and public policy

Although the concept of multiculturalism is as old as the ancient Greeks and Hebrews, its advent as a major issue in American education in the 1980's brought it into the mainstream of public debate. Questions about multiculturalism and the related "political correctness" movement were among the most widely discussed and divisive in the United States in the late 1980's and early 1990's. Particularly on college and university campuses, clashes over alleged sexism, racism, and insensitivity attracted extensive media attention. In public schools, where ethnic and racial diversity was a fact of life, parents, students, and public officials struggled with the complicated question of how to balance the broader community's interests with those of Native American, Mexican American, African American, and other minority groups.

The rights and dignity of women, homosexuals, and others not adequately represented, in the multiculturalist perspective, in American education or in the use of resources were basic concerns of the movement. Advocates of multiculturalism argued that traditional education ignored, and even distorted, the contributions of people outside the European-American mainstream.

Conflicting Ethical Views. Both advocates and critics of multiculturalism have appealed to ethical principles to justify their perspectives. Supporters have generally emphasized the need to correct the alleged harmful effects of traditional policies on the grounds that these policies have distorted the truth and have encouraged isolation and self-doubt. Growing evidence that many ethnic minority children were losing self-confidence and falling behind in their education seemed to substantiate the claims of multiculturalists that something was seriously wrong with the American educational process. As the proportion of minority children in American schools climbed from 21 percent in 1970 to more than 26 percent in 1984, public awareness of cultural diversity and related problems significantly increased. To many multiculturalists, it seemed obvious that inherent bias, especially in schools and colleges, was a major cause of inequality and its many socially harmful effects.

Critics, however, argued that the real causes of inequities lay elsewhere—in social history rather than the educational system and its support mechanisms—and that multiculturalism actually made matters worse by heightening tensions and group identity at the expense of community. Historian Arthur M. Schlesinger, Jr., wrote that multiculturalism encouraged the fragmentation of American society into "a quarrelsome spatter of enclaves, ghettos, tribes." Former secretary of education William J. Bennett dismissed multiculturalism as a symptom of the "disuniting of America."

Political Correctness and Cultural Pluralism. Complicating the quest for an ethical consensus on multiculturalism in the early 1990's was the "political correctness," or PC movement, which sought to eradicate racist, sexist, and ethnocentric language from the classroom and public forums. When political correctness first appeared in public discussion around the turn of the twentieth century, it was a slogan among Marxists and certain other ideology-intensive groups indicating adherence to accepted party principles and interpretations. In the later environment of the multiculturalist movement, it was applied to the treatment of minorities, women, and ethnic groups. This added to the task of defining common ethical and political ground by subtly transforming the issue of community into one of words about community and symbolic behavior that might offend or discourage a particular group or individual within it.

Supporters of multiculturalism insisted that sensitivity to the feelings and positions of all people is not only ethically compelling but also politically and economically essential for the effective functioning of a democratic society. Without it, larger numbers of people drop out in one sense or another, to the detriment of the entire society. The art, historical contributions, and personal worth of all people, it is argued, augment the traditional culture with creative new elements that benefit all. If they are ignored, a potential enrichment of the culture is lost, and tragic consequences can result in regard to the ability of those left out to find a productive place in society.

Implications for Ethics. In his *Civilization and Ethics* (1923), Albert Schweitzer observed that "ordinary ethics" seek accommodation and compromise. That is, "they try to dictate how much of my existence and of my happiness I must sacrifice, and how much I may preserve at the cost of the existence and happiness of other lives." In essence, that is the pivotal issue in current multiculturalist theory. Its ethical norms are centered in the need to balance the individual's interests with those of the larger community. For Schweitzer, the solution lay in envisioning a higher ethic that he called "reverence for life"; that is, an absolute regard for all life in a broadly inclusive ethic. The ethical challenge of multiculturalism is to find ways to avoid violating basic individual rights such as freedom of speech and conscience while protecting the rights of all segments of society and incorporating their identity and contributions into the whole. This thrusts it inevitably into the realm of politics, where moral vision is often blurred by considerations of resources, the need for competent personnel to lead multicultural educational programs in schools and elsewhere, and the development of cooperative undertakings that give substance to theory.

In that sense, multiculturalism, to be meaningful, must defy the image that it is merely a buzzword or a new kind of oppression and ground itself in its most basic ethical principles of responsibility and cooperation to assure both justice and respect for all. —*Thomas R. Peake*

See also Comparative ethics; Justice; Political correctness.

BIBLIOGRAPHY

Banks, J.A., and McGee Banks, eds. *Multicultural Education: Issues and Perspectives.* Boston: Allyn & Bacon, 1989.

D'Souza, Dinesh. *Illiberal Education: The Politics of Race and Sex on Campus.* New York: Vintage, 1992.

Graff, Gerald. *Beyond the Culture Wars: How Teaching the Conflicts Can Revitalize American Education.* New York: W. W. Norton, 1992.

Hughes, Robert. *Culture of Complaint: The Fraying of America.* New York: Oxford University Press, 1993.

Sykes, Charles J. *A Nation of Victims: The Decay of the American Character.* New York: St. Martin's Press, 1992.

Yates, Steven A. "Multiculturalism and Epistemology." *Public Affairs Quarterly* 6 (October, 1992): 435-456.

Mutually Assured Destruction (MAD)

TYPE OF ETHICS: Military ethics
DATE: Coined in the 1960's
ASSOCIATED WITH: Nuclear arms
DEFINITION: Each of two potential combatants is deterred from attacking the other by the realization that, ultimately, its own destruction would be assured in retaliation
SIGNIFICANCE: Its emphasis on killing millions of innocent people in retaliation to a nuclear attack is morally repugnant to many people

To protect and preserve values is the only justifying cause for the use of force that is admitted in civilized moral tradition. The defense and protection of the innocent is one of the cardinal points of those values. Counterpopulation destruction deterrence—that is, the threat to destroy civilian population as retaliation against a nuclear strike—is thus immoral, even when this threat is part of a strategy to prevent war. MAD defies one of the most fundamental traditional ethics of warfare, the principle of noncombatant immunity, which has been in operation since World War II, and which requires that deliberate physical harm be limited to military targets. Others will argue, however, that even if it is morally wrong under any circumstances to deliberately kill innocent civilians, it is not necessarily wrong to threaten (or intend to risk) such killings, provided that such threats are necessary to deter greater evils. Nevertheless, it is virtually impossible to untangle the good and the evil elements in this concept; the good is an aspect of the evil, and the evil is both the source and the possible outcome of the good it seeks to achieve.

See also Arms race; Cold war; Deterrence.

Mysticism

TYPE OF ETHICS: Religious ethics

DATE: 800-400 B.C.E.

DEFINITION: Belief in experience that cannot be explained or understood exclusively in rational or scientific terms

SIGNIFICANCE: Controversy exists about the relationship of mysticism and ethics. Some claim that mystical experience supports ethical behavior, while others claim that it can lead to indifference to ethical issues

Some religious thinkers and philosophers condemn mysticism because they view it as an attempt to escape from the duties and responsibilities of life. Ethical behavior presupposes a concern for self and others. Mystical experience occurs when a person directly perceives an undifferentiated unity that is beyond the deepest center of the individual self. While in the grip of mystical experience, one forgets everything else, including oneself and the world. Apologists for mysticism assert that although mystical experience involves a temporary withdrawal from the world and its problems, it is not intrinsically escapist. Mystical experience supports better ethical choices by expanding and sharpening awareness, making the person who has such an experience better able to assess the ethical ramifications of conduct.

Definition of Mystical Experience. Mystical experience is best defined first in terms of what it is not. Mysticism does not seek experience of the occult, such as that of ghosts or disembodied spirits. It does not include parapsychological phenomena, such as telepathy (communication at a distance), clairvoyance (perception beyond natural range of the senses), or precognition (knowledge of an event in advance of its occurrence). Mystical experience does not necessarily involve seeing visions or hearing voices. Individuals who are not mystics may possess supernormal powers or experience visions. Mystical experience is not necessarily associated with religion, although it is often sought for religious reasons and described in religious language.

The core of mystical experience involves an apprehension of an ultimate nonsensuous unity beyond all created things. Extrovertive mysticism finds the fundamental Unity manifesting itself in the diversity of the world, while introvertive mysticism finds the One beyond the deepest center of the individual self. The *Upaniṣads* of India, spiritual treatises that date from 800 to 400 B.C.E. and provide some of the oldest descriptions of mystical experience in the world, record experiences of both extrovertive and introvertive mysticism. The *Upaniṣads* claim that the Ultimate Reality is both inside and outside creation. The person who beholds all beings in the Ultimate Reality and the Ultimate Reality in all beings is truly wise and free.

The extrovertive mystic perceives the One by looking outward. While appreciating the diversity of the created world, the extrovertive mystic perceives the objects of perception in such a way that the One shines through them. The medieval German mystic Johann Eckhart described an experience in which he found the grass, wood, and stone that he observed to be distinct and yet One. The extrovertive mystic perceives the One in all things. It is a type of experience that tends toward pantheism, the view that God and creation are identical.

Extrovertive mysticism is not the predominant way of experiencing the Unity beyond the multiplicity of the created universe. Introvertive mysticism is the most common kind of mystical experience. The introvertive mystic finds the One beyond the deepest center of the self in an experience of pure consciousness. Conscious but not conscious *of* anything, the mystic is absorbed in a state of alertness that does not contain any concept, thought, or sensation. The mystic's individuality seems to melt away into infinity. This oneness, encountered beyond the deepest level of the self, is often identified with God because it is experienced as being eternal and infinite, beyond space and time. Saint John of the Cross, the sixteenth century Spanish poet and mystic, described pure consciousness as a state in which the person is so united to the simplicity and purity of God that the awareness is pure and simple, devoid of all objects of perception.

The actual experience of undifferentiated unity is said to be independent of the interpretation given to it. Religious people associate the experience with God. The Jewish tradition identifies pure consciousness with the apprehension of divine glory, not with God's being; while the Christian and Islamic traditions identify it as an experience of union with God. Other philosophies and religious traditions, such as Hinduism, tend to view pure consciousness as an experience of the impersonal Absolute in which the individual self merges with the Ultimate Reality.

Evidence of mystical experience is found in religious and philosophical traditions all over the world and in all periods of history. Mystical experience is usually incorporated into a religious or philosophical tradition the purpose of which is to secure full knowledge, salvation, or liberation for the people who participate in it. Each tradition recommends ascetical practices to prepare a person for mystical experience. These include the practice of virtue and right action, the removal of sin and inclinations toward evil, and the renunciation of personal desires. Ascetical disciplines are practiced to remove obstacles between self and the Ultimate Reality and to prepare the person to enjoy direct contact with the One beyond all created things.

Objections to Mysticism on Moral Grounds. Although virtuous behavior is usually considered to be a prerequisite for mystical experience, some philosophers and religious thinkers have objected to mysticism on the basis of their belief that it undermines the basis for ethical decision making. The experience of a fundamental undifferentiated unity beyond perception causes the experiencer's awareness to transcend all distinctions, including the duality of good and evil. Mystical experience implies that the separation of the individual self, the created world, and the Absolute are illusions and that the eternal One is the only reality. All these ideas about the nature of mystical experience and the Ultimate Reality have implications for the mystic's approach to ethical issues.

The twentieth century theologian Paul Tillich objects on moral grounds to the experience of pure consciousness because individual identity seems to disappear when the mystic's awareness transcends all objects of perception. The experiencing individual, who is involved in relationships with self, others, and the wider environment, is necessary for morality. If all contents of consciousness disappear in mystical experience, the mystic steps outside of both the positive and the negative elements of concrete experience. Those who transcend experience altogether allow themselves to forget about the existence of evil and problems in themselves and in the world. A truly moral person cannot withdraw from life, from relationships with others, or from involvement with the community. By retreating into oneself in search of a private experience of union with Ultimate Reality, the mystic neglects ethics and social obligations.

Another twentieth century theologian, Martin Buber, objects to mysticism because the loss of awareness of individuality in pure consciousness leaves open to doubt the reality of each individual self and each thing in the world of ordinary experience. Ethical values and obligations can be applied only to real selves and real things. In addition, a relationship between real selves and real things is a prerequisite for moral and ethical activity.

Mysticism is also attacked on the ground that morality has no basis if the phenomenal world is considered to be an expression of the infinite and eternal One beyond space and time. If individuals are not really separate beings, then the mystic might conclude that the wrong perpetrated by one person against another is an illusion. There is no reason to intervene to stop injustice if the person who is being wronged and the offender are two aspects of one reality. In transcending all differentiation in pure consciousness, the mystic also transcends the distinction between good and evil. A person who considers evil to be an illusion may be apathetic in the face of it, choosing to accept it rather than change it or fight it. Since the mystic makes no moral distinctions while united with the Ultimate Reality, one might conclude that mysticism is amoral at best.

In early Christianity contemplation of the divine essence was valued more highly than action. Since the ultimate goal of moral action in the world is salvation or the contemplation of God in heaven, life's highest aspiration is to gain pure consciousness, which prefigures life in heaven. When the would-be mystic is advised to reject all love and attraction for created things in order to direct all love toward God, he or she is encouraged to neglect social and moral obligations. The pursuit of mystical experience seems to undercut morality when it is considered to be superior to ethical action. Work in the world is downgraded to second-class status.

Hinduism and Buddhism are especially criticized on moral grounds for emphasizing contemplation of the Ultimate Reality over action. Both traditions define salvation as *mokṣa*, or liberation from ignorance about the true nature of the self. Enlightenment or salvation means the direct experiential knowledge that the individual self is in reality the Cosmic Self, the Ultimate Reality. The pursuit of *moksha* involves efforts to transform one's own state of consciousness and thereby change the quality of one's experience. The person is not primarily concerned with changing the world or fulfilling personal and social duties.

Mysticism's Contribution to Ethics. While apparently selfish reasons, such as the desire to escape personal suffering or gain eternal happiness, do inspire people to seek mystical experience; most mystics come to realize that mystical experience is not an end in itself. Supporters of mysticism on ethical grounds point out that the mystic prepares for mystical experience by concentrating on growing in virtue, developing self-discipline, and acting in accord with moral principles. In turn, mystical experience accelerates the growth of virtue and brings greater ethical effectiveness to the mystic's activity. Direct contact with the Ultimate Reality in pure consciousness has very direct and beneficial ethical consequences. Rather than a selfish and self-centered withdrawal from the world of action, the experience of pure consciousness is considered to be a most effective means of fostering right action.

The arguments against mysticism on moral grounds take the description of pure consciousness out of context. They disregard the ethical frameworks surrounding mystical experience, which demand moral conduct to prepare for it and consider moral conduct to be its fruition. They conclude that the experience of pure consciousness can have negative consequences for morality only in the sense that all distinctions are transcended within it. Although pure consciousness is an experience of undifferentiated unity, it does not necessarily lead the mystic to conclude that multiplicity and distinction are inconsequential. It does not make the mystic apathetic in the face of suffering and evil in the world. Mystics do not abandon ethical action because their enlightened state allows their awareness to go beyond distinctions between good and evil.

Such conclusions reflect a one-sided judgment of the impact of the experience of pure consciousness on the lives of the people who experience it. Advocates of mystical experience counter the objections to mystical experience on moral grounds by pointing to the descriptions of enlightened individuals found in different traditions and the testimony of the lives of great mystics. It is a paradox that the experience of pure consciousness in which individual identity seems to dissolve into absolute nothingness can improve the quality of the person's action. Critics of mysticism fail to recognize that the experience of unity can provide a basis for ethical decision making and conduct that is as good as or better than that provided by the experience of the separateness.

Mystics are described as friends of God whose extraordinary virtues follow from the powerful intimacy with God that union with God in pure consciousness creates. They are held up as models for others to emulate. In the Christian tradition, a person's spiritual attainment is found lacking if that person claims to enjoy mystical experience but does not lead a life of exemplary virtue. The Christian tradition considers charity or love of self and others because of God to be the most important virtue. Charity requires the mystic to tend to the needs of others and not only focus on mystical experience. Gregory the Great, a sixth century pope and theologian, maintained that mystical experience reinforces morality. He advocated a lifestyle that combined the cultivation of mystical experience (the contemplative life) with active service to others. According to Richard of St. Victor, a twelfth century Scottish mystic, after enjoying the heights of mystical experience, the contemplative goes out on God's behalf in compassion to others.

The Advaita Vedānta tradition, founded by the ninth century Indian philosopher Śhankara, maintains that Brahman, the Ultimate Reality, is all that exists. The person who views Brahman as the only Reality does not engage in immoral acts. The enlightened person works for the benefit of others.

According to Buddhism, the goal of mystical experience is nirvana, the annihilation of desire in pure consciousness. Four virtues grace the person who experiences nirvana: friendliness toward all creatures, compassion for all sentient beings and the desire to remove their suffering, joy in the happiness of all creatures, and impartiality toward them all. Since an enlightened person is no longer governed by egocentric considerations, he or she acts for the benefit of others. The *bodhisattva* exemplifies the highest example of virtue and enlightenment in the Buddhist tradition. Just as the Buddha worked in compassion to relieve the suffering in the world by making known the experience of nirvana, the bodhisattva renounces nirvana out of compassion for all created things, vowing not to step out of time into eternity until all other created things have entered nirvana first.

In Buddhism the emptiness of nirvana is said to manifest as infinite compassion toward all created beings. The goal of the bodhisattva is to lose all ego-consciousness through expanding in boundless giving to others. Separateness of individual persons and things from each other and from the Ultimate Reality is not necessary to motivate virtuous behavior. The compassionate conduct of the bodhisattva exemplifies this fact. Oneness can also serve as the basis for ethical conduct.

Christian mystics especially emphasize that mystical experience overflows into love for others and action for the benefit of others. Pure consciousness in the form of the secret infusion of God's love into the soul is the source of moral activity. When the person loses the awareness of the boundaries of the individual self in pure consciousness, the once-separate self is aligned with the Ultimate Reality. The love that flows out of mystical experience has its basis in the realization of the One, which eliminates the separation between one's neighbor and oneself. All selfishness, cruelty, and evil originate in alienation from self and others.

The relationship between mystical experience and ethics is also explained by the paradoxical assertion that absolute fullness and virtue is located in unmanifest form in the apparent nothingness of pure consciousness. Saint John of the Cross, a sixteenth century Spanish poet and perhaps the most important European mystic, describes pure consciousness as the nothingness (*nada*) that contains everything (*todo*). Every experience of pure consciousness infuses absolute divine attributes into its recipient. The process of personal development through mystical experience involves the progressive infusion of these divine qualities. The infusion of divine attributes implies a corresponding process of purification, the removal of personal limitations that disallow that infusion to be complete. The Upaniṣads call the Ultimate Reality the source of all virtue and the destroyer of sin. The mystic's transformation through this dual process of illumination and purification improves his or her activity. The mystic performs action with a more finely tuned appreciation of right and virtue because contact with pure consciousness results in greater alertness and freedom from personal limitation.

Although initially a person might shun worldly concerns in order to concentrate on acquiring mystical experience, at some point, the mystic becomes concerned about moral issues. The life of Thomas Merton, the twentieth century writer and mystic, unfolded in this way. After seeking refuge from worldly life by entering a Trappist monastery near Louisville, Kentucky, he became increasingly concerned with the world he thought he had left behind. He called himself a guilty bystander who was implicated along with the rest of humanity in the crises and problems of society. His physical withdrawal from the world outside the monastery walls did not prevent him from trying to change the world. He attacked racism, the existence of nuclear weapons, and U.S. participation in the war in Vietnam. Merton exemplifies the contemplative who by withdrawing from the world and devoting time to cultivating mystical experience creates a certain distance between himself and the rest of the world that allows him to perceive evil more clearly. Merton became the prophet whose voice was heard in the wilderness, demanding the end to the madness of the nuclear threat and the injustice of racial discrimination. As prophet, the contemplative becomes involved and tries to communicate a vision of what God wants for society and for the world.

Personal limitations in the would-be mystic might initially motivate the person to seek mystical experience in order to avoid problems or find personal salvation. Since mystical experience fosters increased awareness and removes personal limitations, however, at some point the mystic renounces such selfishness. The mystic's personal growth eventually translates itself into love and concern for others, two virtues that are fundamental for ethical decision making.

Mysticism does support ethics. The personal development that results from mystical experience provides the mystic with the means to reflect and to act in greater harmony with ethical and moral principles. Those who attack mysticism on moral grounds seem to disregard the evidence of the experience of the great mystics, who inspire others to emulate such high levels of personal integration and moral conduct that their admirers are tempted to proclaim them to be nothing less than perfect reflections of the divine on Earth.

—*Evelyn Toft*

See also Asceticism.

BIBLIOGRAPHY

Horne, James R. *The Moral Mystic*. Waterloo, Canada: Wilfrid Laurier University Press, 1983. A thorough exploration for the nonspecialist of the relationship among mysticism, religion, and morality.

Huxley, Aldous. *The Perennial Philosophy*. New York: Harper, 1945. An anthology with commentary organized by topic that identifies the features common to mystical philosophy and experience in the world's major philosophical and religious traditions.

Wainwright, William J. *Mysticism: A Study of Its Nature, Cognitive Value, and Moral Implications*. Madison: University of Wisconsin Press, 1981. A philosophical critique of the various definitions and theoretical frameworks for understanding mystical experience. Includes an analysis of the relationship of mysticism and morality.

Nader, Ralph (b. Feb. 27, 1934, Winsted, Connecticut): Activist

Type of ethics: Business and labor ethics

Achievements: Founder of various citizen activist groups; author of *Unsafe at Any Speed* (1965) and many other books and articles

Significance: Nader has focused attention on the abuse of power by corporations and government bureaucracy; he has campaigned for individual rights in the areas of the economy and politics

A graduate of Princeton University and Harvard Law School, Ralph Nader first attracted national attention in 1965 with the publication of his book *Unsafe at Any Speed*, which described the engineering flaws of the Chevrolet Corvair and criticized General Motors (GM) for emphasizing design at the expense of safety. GM hired a private investigator in an attempt to discredit Nader, but eventually Chairman James Roche was forced to apologize to Nader in front of a Senate subcommittee. Nader has founded numerous organizations, including the Public Interest Research Group, Center for Auto Safety, Center for Study of Responsive Law, and Public Citizen. Among the books that Nader has authored or edited are *Taming the Giant Corporation*, *The Lemon Book*, and *Who's Poisoning America?* He has been instrumental in the passage of scores of laws, such as the National Traffic and Motor Vehicle Safety Act and the Freedom of Information Act, and he helped to pass a California ballot initiative in 1988 that rolled back automobile insurance rates. Nader has consistently called for more accountability on the part of corporations and government agencies as well as a shift of power to citizens in their roles as voters, taxpayers, consumers, workers, and shareholders.

See also Consumerism.

Nāgārjuna (c. 150-c. 250, India): Buddhist philosopher

Type of ethics: Religious ethics

Achievements: Indian Buddhist thinker who developed the Mādhyamaka school of Mahāyāna Buddhism

Significance: Developed the philosophy of *śūnyatā*, or "emptiness"

Nāgārjuna was an Indian Buddhist thinker central to the Mādhyamaka school of Mahāyāna Buddhism. He lived from approximately 150 to 250 and continued the classic Buddhist approach to liberation from suffering through mental discipline.

Nāgārjuna's innovation was the concept of "emptiness," or *śūnyatā*. This is a recognition that things have no meaning in themselves; instead, they derive significance from their relationship to other things. (For example, "day" has no meaning apart from "night.") This contextual understanding of meaning is called *pratītya-samutpāda*, or "dependent co-arising."

Despite the essential emptiness of the categories that people employ to understand the world, on a pragmatic level people have to use those categories in order to live. In terms of ethics, Nāgārjuna's contribution was to separate ultimate from conventional truths, so that although people should live fully aware of the basic illusoriness of reality, they should

Consumer rights activist Ralph Nader.

also uphold a moral path in their daily lives. Rather than release from this world (*nirvāṇa*), Nāgārjuna believed the ideal to be that of the *bodhisattva*, or "enlightened being": living in the world but being aware of its insubstantiality, and working for the benefit of all beings.

Nāgārjuna's thought has influenced Buddhism in Tibet, China, Korea, and Japan for the nearly two millennia since his death, particularly in the Zen tradition.

See also Bodhisattva ideal; Buddha; Buddhist ethics; Zen.

Nagasaki. *See* **Hiroshima and Nagasaki, bombing of.**

Nānak, Guru (Rāi Bhoi dī Talvandī; 1469, Talwandi, Punjab—1539, Kartārpur, Punjab, Mughal Empire): Religious leader

Type of ethics: Religious ethics

Achievements: Founder of the Sikh faith

Significance: Espoused the equality of all people, a moral code of behavior, and the defense of religious truth

Nānak, who was born in Punjab, in what is now Pakistan, founded the faith known as Sikhism. Nānak was called *guru,* or spiritual teacher, and his followers were called *Sikhs,* or disciples. The religious system established by Guru Nānak was firmly monotheistic, rejecting idolatry and ritualism of all kinds. The Sikh community, called the *Panth,* was egalitarian in its social life, emphasizing rejection of the Hindu caste system through its tradition of eating at community kitchens. Charity toward the poor and defense of the weak characterized the Sikhs. After Guru Nānak's death, there were nine successor gurus who led the Sikh *Panth* in turn. Various innovations were introduced, most notably involving greater militancy in the face of persecution, but all of them continued to build on the ideals established by Guru Nānak. After the death of the last guru, Guru Gobind Singh, leadership passed to the holy book of the Sikhs, the *Guru Granth Sahib.* It is housed in *gurdwaras,* Sikh shrines where people gather to worship, eat together, and discuss community events. There are currently about 16 million Sikhs in the world today who claim the heritage of Guru Nānak, most of them in the state of Punjab in India. The Sikhs are currently experiencing a great deal of turmoil, since many of them seek to develop an independent state in which Sikhism could flourish.

See also Hindu ethics; Sikh ethics.

Narcissism

TYPE OF ETHICS: Personal and social ethics
DATE: The myth of Narcissus dates to ancient times, with its most famous expression in the poetry of Ovid (first century); although the poet Samuel Coleridge used the term "narcissism" in a letter in 1822, public use seems to have begun with the British psychologist-sexologist Havelock Ellis in 1898 and the psychotherapist Sigmund Freud in 1905
ASSOCIATED WITH: Self-love, selfishness, self-absorption, and the failure to mature emotionally
DEFINITION: The neurotic, pathological love of self and fascination with self
SIGNIFICANCE: Narcissism raises interesting questions about duties in regard to maintaining certain attitudes of mind quite apart from external actions that may arise from those attitudes

Narcissism is a complex vice and a neurotic complex. The narcissus complex, identified by Havelock Ellis and by Sigmund Freud, involves an inordinate fascination with one's self—one's body, one's mind, one's actions.

Narcissism was named for Narcissus, a beautiful youth in Greek mythology who spurned all lovers. Nemesis, the avenger of *hubris* (inordinate pride), punished Narcissus by causing him to fall in love with his own reflection in the water, rendering him unable to move away. He was transformed into a flower by the gods.

Selfishness and immoderate self-love may be a part of the effects of narcissism, but there is a core that is unique to the vice. In some ethical systems, only the effects of narcissism could be judged culpable, but in natural-law analysis, at least, narcissism would itself be blameworthy as an "occasion of sin" and as an orientation of will and intellect whereby one denies the appropriate concern owed to one's fellow humans and the appropriate worship owed to God.

The neurotic complex might seem to be outside the considerations of ethics, but to the extent to which the complex developed as the result of freely chosen actions and freely entertained dispositions, it is blameworthy. To the extent that the proclivities of the complex could be resisted but are not, the complex is subject to ethical analysis.

Finally, narcissism must not be viewed only as an endangerment to one's relationship to God and to fellow humans but also as a warping of the proper development of the self. Narcissism causes the aesthetic judgment, the intellectual faculty, and the power of the will to be perverted from their proper outward orientation, stunted, and turned inward.

See also Egoism; Egotist; Golden rule; Humility; Individualism; Love; Pride; Self-love; Selfishness; Vice.

Nation of Islam

TYPE OF ETHICS: Race and ethnicity
DATE: Founded 1931
ASSOCIATED WITH: Wallace D. Fard, Elijah Muhammad, Malcolm X, Warith Deen Muhammad, Louis Farrakhan, African Americans, and Islamic religion
DEFINITION: The Nation of Islam is an African American religious and social movement that proclaims adherence to Islamic faith and practices as the way to achieve equality, justice, and freedom in all spheres of life
SIGNIFICANCE: Its use of Islam to proclaim a millennium in which white racist supremacy would be supplanted by black supremacy was unprecedented; advocated separatism if religious, social, economic, and political concerns were not met

Variously referred to as Black Muslims, the Black Muslim Movement, the World Community of Al-Islam in the West, and the American Muslim Movement, the Nation of Islam is heir to the separatist and self-improvement ethics of Marcus Garvey's Universal Negro Improvement Association and the each-race-for-each-religion philosophy and strict ethical behavior of Noble Drew Ali's Moorish Science Temple. It is both a religious movement and a social movement. As part of the worldwide Islamic religion and as an African American expression of Islam, the Nation of Islam has evolved some uniquely radical ethics vis-à-vis the American racial problem.

History. The Great Depression of the 1930's was particularly difficult for African Americans. Living in overcrowded slums, laid off and displaced by white workers as jobs became scarce, culturally marginalized and insulted by welfare officials, most African American workers and their dependents began to have bitter feelings about the power and control wielded by white Americans. Noble Drew Ali had died and Marcus Garvey had been deported in 1927. A leadership vacuum among African Americans was thus created as the Great Depression arrived. It was the destiny of Wallace D. Fard to fill this leadership role by shaping the frustrations, anger, and energy of marginalized African Americans into an Islamic redemptionist religious movement that taught Afro-Asiatic history in house-to-house meetings and fiercely proclaimed a divinely ordained future era in which black supremacy would replace white supremacy and blacks would rule the earth. Such was the beginning of the Nation of Islam in Detroit, where it built its first temple as African Americans became members in large numbers. Fard was succeeded by Elijah (Poole) Muhammad, and under the latter the Nation of Islam moved its headquarters to Chicago and spread to other states, building temples, schools, farms, apartment complexes, restaurants, and grocery stores. It developed a security force called the Fruit of Islam (FOI) and began its own publications. As it grew, the movement experienced some internal problems, and in the course of its years has had prominent leaders such as Malcolm X, Warith Deen Muhammad, and Louis Farrakhan.

Polarities. Though changing social circumstances have resulted in its changing or modifying its views and beliefs, especially as it moves toward orthodox Islam, the Nation of Islam has tended to see things in racial polarities to counteract what it sees as the racist ideology of the dominant American culture. In place of the Magnolia myth (the stereotype of music-making servile African Americans "lounging peacefully under the sweet-scented magnolias behind the big house—happy and contented in their station" as loyal servants to the generous master), which is the foundation of the idea that the African American is naturally docile, inherently imbecilic, and instinctively servile, the Nation of Islam created the myth of Yakub, which states that the "original man" to whom Allah (God) gave the earth to rule was the black man and his race, and that a rebellious scientist named Yakub performed a genetic experiment from which an inferior white race emerged. White supremacy is thus counteracted by black supremacy, and in this polarity it is the unnaturally white devils versus naturally divine blacks, and the white religion (Christianity) versus the black religion (Islam). The black Zion is where the white man is absent. Thus, there seems to be a strong determination by the Nation of Islam to belie white myths and beliefs.

Ethics. The Nation of Islam adheres to strict moral behavior in private and social life. Its religious practices include praying five times a day, facing east toward Mecca and making proper ablutions (for the Muslim must be clean inwardly and outwardly) before praying. It is morally binding on members to attend temple activities; defaulters are suspended. The religion forbids certain foods, such as pork, both for religious reasons and to denigrate white supremacy (because the hog is "dirty, brutal, quarrelsome, greedy, ugly, a scavenger which thrives on filth . . . [and] has all the characteristics of a white man!"); in addition, black-eyed peas, cornbread, and chitlins must be avoided because they are not easily digestible and are a "slave diet"—and there are "no slaves in Islam." Fresh lamb, chicken, fish, and beef are approved. Moderation in eating is encouraged. Members are also forbidden to gamble, use drugs, smoke, or consume alcohol.

Members of the Nation of Islam are encouraged to marry within the movement; those who marry outside the movement are pressured to bring their spouses to join it. Interracial marriages and liaisons may bring severe punishment, if not expulsion, and male members are expected constantly to watch and protect their women against the white man's alleged degrading sexual obsession. Divorce is discouraged, though not prohibited. Sexual morality is strictly enforced under the puritanical vigilance of FOI. The use of cosmetics and the wearing of revealing and provocative clothes are forbidden. It is unethical for a married woman to be alone in a room with a man other than her husband.

Long before social and governmental agencies in America took seriously the relationship between crime and drugs, the Nation of Islam had developed and perfected a method for ferreting out and rehabilitating drug addicts so that they could remain themselves and stay away from crimes. It introduced a six-point drug therapy: making the patient admit his drug addiction; making him realize why he is an addict; telling him how to overcome this by joining the Nation of Islam; exposing him to the religious and social habits of the clean and proud members of the movement; making him voluntarily initiate a break from drug addiction with the full support and charity of the Muslim fraternity during the agony of the withdrawal period; and, finally, sending him out, when cured, to seek out other drug addicts for rehabilitation. Under the watchful and caring eyes of the Nation of Islam, an ex-drug addict also becomes an ex-criminal, since the drug habit that requires stealing, killing, or engaging in prostitution to support it is eliminated.

The Nation of Islam believes that territorial, political, and economic separation of blacks and whites is necessary to the mutual progress, peace, and respect of the two races in North America; the alternative is for them to leave America—the blacks to Africa and the whites to Europe. It urges peace among brothers, including whites, but points out that peace with whites is impossible because the white man "can only be a brother to himself." Members should be willing to die for dignity and justice if that becomes necessary, and should never hesitate to defend themselves and retaliate when attacked. The movement warns that "an eye for an eye and a tooth for a tooth" is the most effective manner to resolve racism, and that members should "fight with those who fight against [them]."

While respecting the "original" Bible, the Nation of Islam teaches that the Bible dedicated to the white man called King James has been corrupted and used by the Christian religion to enslave African Americans. Christianity thus becomes a "slave religion" teaching the oppressed to love and pray for the oppressor and the enemy; it further teaches the oppressed to offer both cheeks to be repeatedly slapped by the oppressor without retaliation, even offering the oppressor the cloak after the oppressor has taken away the coat of the oppressed. Christianity in this view is a "religion organized and backed by the devils for the purpose of making slaves of black mankind."

The Nation of Islam encourages thrift and discourages buying on credit because "debt is slavery." Members are discouraged from living beyond their means and wasting money. Hard work is extolled, and honesty, competence, cleanliness, and respect for authority, self, and others are expected of all members. The movement operates numerous businesses and encourages members to buy goods made by African Americans.

Conclusion. The dynamism of the Nation of Islam is in its ability to modify some of its views to changing circumstances. Though it asks for a separate nation, it did not hesitate to support Jesse Jackson's attempt to run for the presidency of the Untied States in 1984. Keeping ethical behavior in perspective, Louis Farrakhan challenged Ronald Reagan's 1986 order that banned American citizens from visiting Libya and rebuked Michael Jackson for corrupting American youths by means of his female-like behavior. Members of the movement have castigated Michael Jackson for unethically disclaiming his blackness by bleaching his skin to a "leprous" color that is neither white nor black nor brown, and for destroying, through plastic surgery, the face that Allah gave him. The Nation of Islam makes strong demands on its adherents and draws attention to race relations in America.   —*I. Peter Ukpokodu*

See also Civil rights movement; Discrimination; Islamic ethics; Malcolm X; Racial prejudice; Segregation.

BIBLIOGRAPHY

Lee, Martha F. *The Nation of Islam, An American Millenarian Movement.* Lewiston, N.Y.: Edwin Mellen Press, 1988.

Lincoln, C. Eric. *The Black Muslims in America.* Rev. ed. Westport, Conn.: Greenwood Press, 1982.

Malcolm X. *The Autobiography of Malcolm X.* New York: Ballantine Books, 1992.

_____. *By Any Means Necessary: Speeches, Interviews and a Letter by Malcolm X.* Edited by George Breitman. New York: Pathfinder, 1970.

_____. *Malcolm X: The Last Speeches.* Edited by Bruce Perry. New York: Pathfinder, 1989.

Marsh, Clifton E. *From Black Muslims to Muslims: The Transition From Separatism to Islam, 1930-1980.* Metuchen, N.J.: Scarecrow Press, 1984.

National Anti-Vivisection Society

TYPE OF ETHICS: Animal rights
DATE: Founded 1929
DEFINITION: The NAVS was established to abolish live animal experimentation entailing surgical cutting
SIGNIFICANCE: The NAVS questions the validity of human domination over animals, believing in the fundamental equality of animals and humans

As one of several national and international humanitarian organizations dedicated to the elimination of biomedical research using animals, The National Anti-Vivisection Society (NAVS) was formed as a reaction against more conservative animal welfare organizations such as the Humane Society of the United States and the American Society for the Prevention

of Cruelty to Animals. While these societies are dedicated to the prevention of cruelty and improvement of conditions for all animals, unlike the NAVS, they are not officially committed to the total elimination of animal experimentation for human gain. While vivisection narrowly refers to the surgical cutting of animals, with or without anesthesia, the term has been broadened to include any experimentation on animals. The anti-vivisection movement challenges the utilitarian notion that the sacrifice of animals for the greater good of humanity is acceptable and desirable, thereby condemning speciesism— the belief that humans have the right of domination over nature and are superior to animals. On a pragmatic level, the organization also challenges the usefulness and applicability of animal experimentation to human medical science.

See also Animal research; Dominion over nature, human; Moral status of animals; Sentience; Vivisection.

National Association for the Advancement of Colored People (NAACP)

TYPE OF ETHICS: Race and ethnicity
DATE: Founded 1910
ASSOCIATED WITH: The civil rights movement
DEFINITION: The NAACP was established to fight for legal rights for minority groups in the United States
SIGNIFICANCE: The NAACP was the first group to seek legislation at the national, state, and local levels banning racial discrimination

The NAACP, with more than 500,000 members and 1,600 local chapters, promotes equality of rights for all Americans and continues to fight against racial discrimination in employment and education. Founded in 1910, it is an interracial organization seeking, through "litigation, legislation and education," a complete end to racial prejudice and discrimination. Its most important victory came in *Brown v. Board of Education of Topeka* (1954), when Thurgood Marshall, chief counsel for the NAACP and a future Supreme Court justice, successfully argued that the "separate but equal" doctrine established by the Court in 1896 was unconstitutional. Segregation by law was declared illegal, and school districts that separated students by race would have to begin to desegregate "with all deliberate speed."

The National Negro Committee, out of which came the NAACP, was organized in 1909 in response to a bloody race riot in Springfield, Illinois, in 1908. Two African Americans were murdered by a white mob and seventy more were injured. The state militia eventually restored order, but only after many homes in the black community were burned by a white mob and two thousand African Americans were forced to flee the city. No white rioters were punished. William English Walling, a white southern journalist, was appalled by the death and destruction and called for "a large and powerful body of citizens" to come to the assistance of the African Americans in Springfield. At a national conference, the Committee called for an end to "caste and race prejudice" and for "complete equality before the law." W. E. B. Du Bois, the famous black scholar and future editor of the NAACP's magazine *The Crisis*, along with Jane Addams, founder of Hull House in Chicago and a leading white advocate of equality, were among the early members.

Lawyers for the NAACP first appeared before the Supreme Court in 1915 and decided to seek out cases that violated the Constitution, especially the Fourteenth Amendment's protection of equal rights for all citizens of the United States. In their first successful case in 1927, NAACP lawyers convinced the court that a state law denying people

can who had "reached the highest achievement in his field of activity." Named for Joel E. Spingarn, a white professor of literature at Columbia University and longtime chairman of the Board of Directors of the National Association, the medal became the group's highest tribute. Among the winners of the Spingarn Medal were Thurgood Marshall; W. E. B. Du Bois; George Washington Carver, the famous scientist; James Weldon Johnson, the poet; Carter Woodson, the historian; educator Mary McLeod Bethune; soprano Marian Anderson; novelist Richard Wright; labor leader A. Philip Randolph;

Roy Wilkins (second from right), who led the NAACP during the 1960's, is shown here with (from left) Attorney General Robert Kennedy, Martin Luther King, Jr., and union leader A. Philip Randolph. (National Archives)

the right to vote unless their grandfathers had been registered to vote was unconstitutional. Without the NAACP's litigation and successful pursuit of justice for all, equality of rights would have continued to be denied and segregation might still be the law of many states.

In 1915, the NAACP established a prize, the Spingarn Medal, to be given annually to the African Ameri-

chemist Percy Julian; U.N. diplomat Ralph J. Bunche; Jack Roosevelt "Jackie" Robinson, the baseball player; poet Langston Hughes; and social scientist Kenneth Clark, for his work on the *Brown* decision.

See also *Brown v. Board of Education of Topeka*; Civil rights movement; Discrimination; Segregation.

National Gay and Lesbian Task Force

TYPE OF ETHICS: Sex and gender issues
DATE: Founded 1973
ASSOCIATED WITH: The civil rights movement of the 1960's and the 1970's
DEFINITION: The NGLTF was established to fight for freedom and full equality for gay men and lesbian women
SIGNIFICANCE: The NGLTF is the first national activist organization established on behalf of gay/lesbian rights; its adjunct, the NGLTF Policy Institute, is the only national information clearinghouse and resource center dedicated to educating and organizing around gay/lesbian issues throughout the world

The National Gay and Lesbian Task Force (NGLTF) represents the estimated 25 million homosexual Americans and fights to secure full civil rights, freedom, and equality for these citizens. Its activities involve strengthening and supporting grassroots groups; promoting research, education, and outreach; and providing activist leadership training to foster public policies to advance gay rights and end discrimination based on sexual orientation. The NGLTF also compiles and publishes statistics on hate crimes (which increased 172 percent between 1988 and 1992), discrimination (the NGLTF has been working since 1975 to ensure passage of a federal civil rights bill that would end discrimination for reasons of sexual orientation in the areas of housing, employment, public accommodations, credit, and federally assisted programs), health care (including AIDS-HIV concerns), and family issues (including domestic partnerships, foster and adoptive parenting, and child custody and visitation questions) and the impact of these problems on the gay community. The NGLTF lobby helped to secure the passage of the Federal Hate Crimes Statistics Act, the Americans with Disabilities Act, and AIDS emergency relief funding.

See also Bigotry; Civil rights; Gay rights; Homosexuality; Sexual stereotypes.

National Labor Relations Act

TYPE OF ETHICS: Business and labor ethics
DATE: Enacted July 5, 1935
ASSOCIATED WITH: U.S. Congress
DEFINITION: Labor law designed to eliminate strikes by making illegal unfair practices by employers and by legalizing important labor practices, including collective bargaining and the closed shop
SIGNIFICANCE: During the Great Depression, the federal government attempted to help provide for the general welfare of the people by granting labor concessions that would promote industrial harmony between labor and management

Within months of the Supreme Court's invalidation of the National Industrial Recovery Act, Congress, led by Senator Robert Wagner of New York, passed legislation to assist employees and at the same time attempt to cure industrial strife by eliminating its chief cause: strikes. The law (known as the Magna Carta of labor) would eradicate the underlying cause of strikes, unfair employer practices, by encouraging collective bargaining, thereby granting employees equal bargaining power with their employers. Using the National Labor Relations Board to administer its provisions, the act, which applies to all employers engaged in interstate commerce, provides governmental processes for the selection of employee bargaining representatives. The act prohibits employers from interfering with union formation, establishing a "company" union, discriminating against union workers, refusing collective bargaining, or retaliating against workers who file charges under this act. Congress amended the act in 1947 to forbid the closed shop and again in 1959 to monitor union officials' activities.

See also Labor-Management Relations Act.

National Labor Union

TYPE OF ETHICS: Business and labor ethics
DATE: Established August 20, 1866
ASSOCIATED WITH: International Industrial Assembly (1864), Ira Steward and the Grand Eight-Hour League, and local and state trades' assemblies
DEFINITION: A national federation of trade unions organized to utilize producers' cooperatives and national political action to secure workers' rights
SIGNIFICANCE: During the mid-nineteenth century, organized labor sought economic equality with business to accompany earlier national movements toward political and religious equality

Fearing the widening economic gap between employer and worker, William H. Sylvis led the Molders' Union and other

Senator Robert F. Wagner, the foremost proponent of the National Labor Relations Act. (Library of Congress)

national labor (craft) unions to join forces to organize the National Labor Union (NLU) to lobby for the rights of labor. The platform of the highly political NLU provided a plan to maintain its laborers' freedom, equality, and stature in American life. The NLU advocated higher wages, an eight-hour day, cooperative stores, and government action to assist labor. Women and African Americans were encouraged to organize and participate in the NLU. Upon President Sylvis' death in 1869, the NLU split over such ethical issues as women's rights, labor party involvement, and monetary expansion. By 1872, the NLU had become essentially a labor party, and after its lack of success in the election of 1872, both the NLU and the labor party collapsed. The NLU established the first truly national association of labor unions and succeeded in lobbying Congress in 1868 to establish an eight-hour day for federal laborers and artisans.

See also Knights of Labor.

National Organization for Women (NOW)

TYPE OF ETHICS: Sex and gender issues
DATE: Founded 1966
DEFINITION: NOW encourages state and national legislatures to make laws guaranteeing women's rights
SIGNIFICANCE: NOW asserts that discrimination against women should be illegal, not merely immoral

NOW's activities are based on the assumption that women have been denied the opportunity for professional achievement because practices that discriminate against them are not illegal. Since the United States is committed to equality, NOW believes, its laws should prohibit practices that impede women's climb to success. The years of NOW's existence have been marked by controversy over what sorts of rights require legal protection if women are to advance. For example, most members of NOW believe that reproductive rights, including the right to abortion, must be protected by law if women are to be free to make career choices. Many anti-abortionists support women's rights but criticize NOW for condoning killing. Some members of NOW have argued that NOW must lobby to protect the rights of homosexuals and minorities if it is to help the advancement of women in those categories. Other members have responded that the organization can best serve the majority of women if it maintains a narrow focus on employment rights, as it did in its early years when it was headed by its founder, Betty Freidan, author of *The Feminine Mystique*.

See also Equal pay for equal work; *Feminine Mystique, The*; Feminism; Wage discrimination; Women's liberation movement.

National Park System, U.S.

TYPE OF ETHICS: Environmental ethics
DATE: First park established in 1872
ASSOCIATED WITH: The U.S. conservation and preservation movement
DEFINITION: More than three hundred parks that are administered by the Department of the Interior

SIGNIFICANCE: Implementation of the land ethic

In 1870, members of the Washburn survey decided, around a campfire in the geyser region, to recommend public ownership and preservation of scenic features in the Yellowstone region rather than claiming them for themselves. This led Ferdinand Vandiveer Hayden, director of the U.S. Geographical and Geological Survey of the Territories, to lobby Congress, which established Yellowstone National Park in 1872. In 1886, the park was organized under the Army. In 1916, the National Park Service was established in the Department of the Interior, with Stephen Mather as its first director. Mather organized the system, emphasizing preservation and display. In the mid-1960's, Congress responded to the land ethic by directing the establishment of wilderness areas within existing parks. The park system also has broadened its scope from preserving spectacular scenic areas such as the Grand Canyon to include significant historical sites, outstanding recreational areas, and areas designed to preserve viable examples of important ecosystems, such as the Florida Everglades. National Parks are established by acts of Congress that define their areas and control their operation. Some national monuments, such as Death Valley National Monument, are of the same character as national parks but are established and controlled by Executive Order.

See also Conservation; Leopold, Aldo; Muir, John.

Nationalism

TYPE OF ETHICS: Politico-economic ethics
DATE: Coined eighteenth century
ASSOCIATED WITH: The Enlightenment; the French Revolution
DEFINITION: A state of mind in which the supreme loyalty of the individual is felt to be owed to the nation
SIGNIFICANCE: Places an excessive and exclusive emphasis upon the nation at the expense of moral and ethical values by encouraging the overestimation of one's own nation and the simultaneous denigration of others

Nationalism is usually manifested in two forms: as a sentiment and as a movement. Nationalist sentiment is the feeling of anger aroused by the violation of the nationalist principle or the feeling of satisfaction aroused by its fulfillment. A nationalist movement is one that is actuated by a sentiment of this kind. There are various ways in which the nationalist principle can be violated. The political boundary of the state can fail to include all members of the nation or it can include them all but also be host to a substantial number of foreigners. A nation may even exist in a multiplicity of states with no distinct political boundary, as in the case of the Jews before the creation of Israel in 1948. Another violation of the nationalist principle to which the nationalist sentiment is very sensitive and often hostile occurs when the political rulers of the nation belong to a nation other than that of the majority of people over whom they rule, a fact that explains the violent resistance encountered by some imperialist and colonial regimes.

Historical Origin. The roots of modern nationalism have been traced to what was for perhaps a hundred thousand

Park	Location	Date Established	Park	Location	Date Established
Acadia	Maine	1919	Katmai	Alaska	1980
Arches	Utah	1971	Kenai Fjords	Alaska	1980
Badlands	South Dakota	1978	Kings Canyon	California	1890
Big Bend	Texas	1944	Kobuk Valley	Alaska	1980
Biscayne	Florida	1980	Lake Clark	Alaska	1980
Bryce Canyon	Utah	1928	Lassen Volcanic	California	1916
Canyonlands	Utah	1964	Mammoth Cave	Kentucky	1941
Capitol Reef	Utah	1971	Mesa Verde	Colorado	1906
Carlsbad Caverns	New Mexico	1930	Mount Ranier	Washington	1899
Channel Islands	California	1980	North Cascades	Washington	1968
Crater Lake	Oregon	1902	Olympic	Washington	1938
Denali	Alaska	1980	Petrified Forest	Arizona	1962
Everglades	Florida	1914	Redwood	California	1968
Gates of the Arctic	Alaska	1980	Rocky Mountain	Colorado	1915
Glacier	Montana	1920	Sequoia	California	1890
Glacier Bay	Alaska	1980	Shenandoah	Virginia	1935
Grand Canyon	Arizona	1919	Theodore Roosevelt	North Dakota	1947
Grand Teton	Wyoming	1929	Virgin Islands	Virgin Islands	1947
Great Basin	Nevada	1987	Voyageurs	Minnesota	1975
Great Smoky Mountains	Tennessee and North Carolina	1930	Wind Cave	South Dakota	1903
Guadalupe Mountains	Texas	1972	Wrangell-Saint Elias	Alaska	1980
Haleakala	Hawaii	1960	Yellowstone	Wyoming, Montana, and Idaho	1872
Hawaii Volcanoes	Hawaii	1916	Yosemite	California	1890
Hot Springs	Arkansas	1921	Zion	Utah	1919
Isle Royale	Michigan	1931			

Title: U.S. NATIONAL PARKS

years the basic social institution of humankind: the tribe. Out of this institution grew a sentiment of union that was nurtured and reinforced by common traditions and customs, by legends and myths, and, most important, by a common language. Prior to the sixteenth century, military conquests, commercial activities, and certain religions overflowed tribal barriers and imposed "international" loyalty in place of tribal loyalties. Tribal nationalism was thus systematically replaced by a form of internationalism, which meant the subjection of local group feeling to the claims of a great empire or the demands of an inclusive church.

During the sixteenth and seventeenth centuries, this traditional internationalism would also crumble as the Catholic church was wrecked by the rise of Protestantism and empires fell one after the other. Out of the ruins of the empires and the wreckage of the church emerged a new system for Europe. This system involved an agglomeration of peoples with diverse languages, dialects, and traditions, whose purpose was more to increase the wealth, prestige, and power of reigning families than to build up homogeneous nationalities. In France and England, and later in Spain, Germany, Italy, and Russia, the strongest noble families won the territory and, with their supporters, created monarchical governments that by the early eighteenth century had started evolving steadily into modern-day national states.

Evolution. The evolution from monarchical governments to national states was catalyzed in the eighteenth century by the advent of the philosophers of the Enlightenment, who did more than anybody else to convert people's loyalty from the royal families and the church to the service of the nation. Prior to the eighteenth century, wars were usually dynastic and religious in origin and had nothing to do with individual rights. European peoples were bartered from one reigning family to another, sometimes as a marriage dowry, sometimes as the booty of conquest. In the same manner, overseas peoples were exploited by rival sets of European tradesmen and soldiers, and there were great commercial wars to determine whether natives of America, Asia, and Africa should belong to Spain, France, Belgium, Holland, Germany, or England. The so-called national frontiers, which were ironically referred to then as "natural," had been acquired by any means other than natural: force, guile, marriage, inheritance, purchase, diplomacy, and illegal confiscation, for example. Individuals (or subjects) could not choose to whom they wanted to give their loyalty.

Through the efforts of the Enlightenment philosophers, this status quo was challenged. Religion, which had hitherto been untouchable, was substantially demystified. The natural was substituted for the supernatural, and science for religion. The philosophers held that Christianity, be it Catholic or Protestant, was a tissue of myths and superstitions. In place of religion and the church, human reason was exalted and almost deified. Perhaps the greatest contribution of the Enlightenment philosophers to modern nationalism was their insistence on the natural rights of the individual, and in particular the right of national self-determination, which allows the individual to choose the sovereign state to which to belong and the form of government under which to serve. Furthermore, they insisted that all governments should be for the good of the governed and that the prince should be the servant of the people. The first outbursts of modern nationalism (the French Revolution of 1789) were directly inspired and fanned by these principles.

The Spread of Nationalism. After the French Revolution, believing themselves to be the benefactors of the human race, the French were eager to impose their newly found liberty and their superior national institutions upon all of Europe and perhaps the world. That most of Europe and the world were not ready or willing to accept liberty *à la française* made little difference. French expansionism took precedence over its revolutionary messianism; what had been supposed to be a support for national liberation became a pretext for territorial expansion. Reacting to this turn of events, the rest of Europe became animated by the desire to resist the French. The name of France became not only feared but also hated. That fear and hate would later become fundamental in spreading the sentiment of modern nationalism, for it was in a bid to stop French expansionist

aggression that the rest of Europe started appealing to national sentiment.

From that point on, nationalism was well on its way to becoming the dominant religion. For many people, the nation became the chief object of worship. The loyalty and devotion once given to old dynasties and the church were now given to the fatherland. The defense of the fatherland had become the end of most people's endeavors and almost the sole object, other than immediate family, for which they would willingly die.

Ethics Versus Realpolitik. In the same way that the realization of a common culture and destiny as well as the instinct to survive induced a group to believe itself a nation, so they also made that group aware of the differences that set it apart from other groups. As these differences sharpened, so did feelings of national exclusiveness and the national dislike of others.

Friedrich Hertz's *Nationality in History and Politics* (1957) identifies two aspects of the spirit of nationalism: its positive and constructive side, which promotes national solidarity and freedom; and its negative and destructive side, which promotes the mental seclusion of the nation, leading to mutual distrust and prejudice, and culminating in a striving for superiority and domination. In the latter case, nationalist sentiment is often accompanied by a show of national aggressiveness, in which, more often than not, the primary aim is the quest for national honor, which in turn is expressed in terms of power, superiority, a higher rank among nations, prestige, and domination. In other words (to echo the thoughts of Niccolò Machiavelli), the aims of politics in the national interest became ultimately centered on the acquisition of land, human energy and resources, and the relative weakening of other powers.

By the beginning of the nineteenth century, realpolitik nationalism had become the new religion of the people. Boyd C. Shafer, in *Nationalism: Myth and Reality* (1955), finds a number of parallels between the "new faith" and many of the distinguishing marks of the "old religions." According to him, like the traditional religions, nationalism developed a morality that had its own rewards and punishments, virtues and sins, and missionary zeal. There were many similarities, even in the fanaticism with which those of contrary opinions were persecuted in the name of the new "divinities": liberty and fatherland. The similarity with religion did not end there.

Like the Christians, "good" nationalists were zealous in spreading their gospel, as indicated by the national imperialistic and colonial ventures of the nineteenth century, although behind the new national will for expansion, the motives were mixed and sometimes contradictory. Bourgeois entrepreneurs coveted trade and profit, politicians sought popularity, military men wanted glory, some hoped to propagate liberty and the Christian faith, and others were simply looking for adventure. That this might mean a denial of other people's right to a fatherland made no difference.

Nationalism became more and more violent and exclusive as people began to show an absolute faith in their superiority over other nationalities. National egoism, becoming more and more intensified, came to be accepted as moral and therefore desirable. Thus, most Western European powers, particularly France and Britain, acquired huge colonial empires to serve their national interests and bolster their national power. Germany, Italy, and Japan, all in the name of the nation, embarked on a series of expansionist aggressions that later culminated in World War II. After the war, in order to consolidate its national power, the Soviet Union pushed westward in Europe to absorb the Baltic states, making Poland, Czechoslovakia, Hungary, Romania, and Bulgaria into satellite nations. Finally, the United States, in an effort to propagate its own form of democracy abroad and thereby ensure its national security, "fought" the Cold War.

Nationalism also comes in other forms besides that of aggression against other nations. In some cases, it is manifested in the form of intolerance and aggression against internal opposition (totalitarian regimes), minorities (such as the Iraqi Kurds), or a racial segment of the population (as in South Africa). When this happens, more often than not, nationalism becomes a disruptive force, tending to destabilize rather than enhance social order. It may even come in a form of economic egotism, such as protectionism. In the early stages, political considerations dominated nationalism, but over the years, a tendency developed to regard the state as an economic as well as a political unit. Economic nationalism merged with imperialism to become one of the driving forces of contemporary history.

Thus, over time, nationalism had evolved from its original phase of liberalism as conceived by the Enlightenment philosophers, when reason, tolerance, and humanitarianism were the watchwords, and had become inevitably tied to the realpolitik that had begun with the rivalries of earlier tribal groups. In its process of transformation from a positive to negative force, liberal nationalism gradually deteriorated until it lost most, if not all, of its earlier moral character. Just as Machiavelli excluded morality from politics, so did Georg W. F. Hegel in the early nineteenth century place the nation-state above morality, a legacy that continued well into the twentieth century.

The Imperialist/Colonial Legacy. In *Macro-Nationalisms: A History of the Pan-Movements* (1984), Louis L. Snyder identifies two lesser-known but important satellite movements running concurrently with established modern nationalisms.

The first movement involves the many mini-nationalisms that are seeking to break away from the established nation-states. The disadvantage of modern nationalism as it emerged from the European model in the eighteenth century is that it presupposes a common language and a reasonably homogeneous society. By the middle of the twentieth century, however, few states could claim to be "pure" nations with a completely homogeneous ethnic composition. Thus emerged the problem of minorities, their rights, their dubious loyalties, and their mistreatment by the majorities. Expansionism, which was begun in the eighteenth and nineteenth centuries and which hitherto had been an attribute of national power, eventually became a Pandora's box for the imperialist powers, as problems of homogeneity and self-determination forced issues of nationalism into the forefront of global politics. This is particularly true of some Western European states, in which many mini-nationalisms inside the established nation-states seek to break away from larger units; for example, France (Corsica), Spain (Basque), and Britain (Catholic Ireland). Meanwhile, in the East, for similar reasons, the Soviet Union completely disintegrated, giving way to a multiplicity of new nations; Czechoslovakia gave birth to two autonomous states, while the former Yugoslavia, which is terribly divided along ethnic lines, engaged in a bitter civil war to determine the fate of the newly created "nations."

The second movement involves the many macro-nationalisms that seek to expand the established nation-state to a supranational form. According to Snyder, macro-nationalisms, or pan-movements, seek to promote the solidarity of peoples united by common or kindred languages, group identification, traditions, or characteristics such as geographical proximity. Like established nationalisms, they reveal an aggressive impulse that seeks to control contiguous or noncontiguous territory. In addition to this power syndrome, they are also animated by specific elements: for Pan-Slavism, it was messianic zeal; for Pan-Germanism, territorial expansion; for Pan-Arabism, religious zeal; for Pan-Africanism, racial unity; for Pan-Asianism, anticolonialism; for Pan-Americanism hemispheric solidarity; and, finally, for Pan-Europeanism, economic unity.

The moral issues involved in the nationalism of Europe are different from those that operate in other parts of the world—especially in Asia and Africa—principally because, from the onset, the liberal values of the Enlightenment were not applied to the colonial possessions. Anticolonial nationalism was an intellectual response to this contradiction. Most of the peoples in these two continents were initially united in their struggle to gain national independence and to secure better standards of living for their people. Almost everywhere in the Third World, the ideology of nationalism was firmly linked to the ideology of development. Unfortunately, in some of these cases, nationalism and self-determination have had to be settled not by votes but by armed conflicts.

In Africa, the situation became particularly delicate when colonialism bestowed on the new states administrative structures that were anything but ethnically homogeneous. To preserve or attain national independence, African people have had to resort to civil wars (Belgian Congo, Nigeria, Sudan, Ethiopia), terrorism and guerrilla warfare (South Africa); or even full-scale war (Morocco).

The Moral Legacy. In conclusion, it could be said that during the course of the twentieth century, the nationalist process matured into a real cult of superiority in which nationalism assumes the role of a "political religion," with prestige and power as its "supreme gods," as was the case in Nazi Germany and Benito Mussolini's Italy. Governments acted as they pleased, in their own national interest, and were limited only by superior strength, although in almost all cases elaborate efforts were made to cloak all acts of nationalism in moralism. Even the superpowers had to resort to the moral crusade to identify their own standards with general humanitarian principles to legitimize nationalistic endeavors. Thus, in the Cold War, the United States and the Soviet Union not only challenged each other along political and economic lines but also presented themselves as bearers of universal moral systems, proclaiming standards that they recommended for all nations.   —*Olusoji A. Akomolafe*

See also Fascism.

BIBLIOGRAPHY

Gellner, Ernest. *Nations and Nationalism*. Ithaca, N.Y.: Cornell University Press, 1983. Demonstrates how political units that do not conform to the principle "one state, one culture" feel the strain in the form of nationalistic activity. Although it is addressed to political scientists, sociologists, and historians, this book should appeal to anyone who is seriously concerned with human society.

Hertz, Friedrich O. *Nationality in History and Politics*. London: Routledge & Kegan Paul, 1957. A multidisciplinary study of nationalism that deals with the psychology, sociology, and politics of national sentiment. Provides an excellent analysis of the relationships among nationalism, religion, language, and race.

Shafer, Boyd C. *Nationalism: Myth and Reality*. New York: Harcourt, Brace & World, 1955. This book offers the reader in nationalism a valuable starting point. It includes a chronological account of the history of nationalism.

Snyder, Louis L. *Macro-Nationalisms: A History of the Pan-Movements*. Westport, Conn.: Greenwood Press, 1984. This is the second of two volumes that deal with two aspects of nationalism: mini-nationalism and macro-nationalism. Students of macro-nationalism will find it particularly useful, because it discusses in detail all the established pan-movements.

——————. *The New Nationalism*. Ithaca, N.Y., Cornell University Press, 1968. A comprehensive account of post-1945 nationalism that includes detailed studies of Arab, African, Asian, and Latin American nationalisms.

Native American ethics

TYPE OF ETHICS: Beliefs and practices

DATE: Fifteenth century to present

DEFINITION: The ethical systems and moral codes of the tribal peoples of native North America

SIGNIFICANCE: Native American cultural traditions and worldviews differ significantly from those of Western traditions

Several problems attend to any overview of Native American ethics. First, students of Native American cultural traditions have rarely focused on the topic of ethics, and therefore the amount of material available is minimal. Introductory texts on Native American religions typically fail to consider the topic. For example, Åke Hultkrantz's *The Study of American Indian Religions* (1983) and *Native Religions of North America* (1987), Sam D. Gill's *Native American Religions: An Introduction* (1982), and Lawrence E. Sullivan's *Native American Religions: North America* (1989) have no entries for "ethics" or "morality."

Second, the few scholars who did give some consideration to the manners, customs, and moral codes of Native American peoples generally had no formal training in ethics. Those who did tended to assume that the moral categories defined by the Western philosophic and religious traditions could be transferred to Native American cultures without any fear of misrepresentation. Thus, these scholars were preoccupied with questions of sexuality and general social structures, whether or not these were considered of prime importance by the natives.

Finally, the phrase "Native American ethics" suggests historical fiction. Only in the last four decades of the twentieth century has any pan-Indian identity emerged for Native Americans. The reality is that each tribal tradition considers itself to be a unique entity with a specific identity and cultural web.

Travelers and Missionaries. Historically, Western discussions of the moral condition of Native American peoples date from the fifteenth century. For the next four centuries, materials relating to the ethics of Native American peoples primarily were recorded in the accounts of early travelers and missionaries. Typically, the debate centered on the question of the status of Native Americans as moral beings.

The earliest example dates from 1550, when Charles V of Spain summoned Juan Gines de Sepúlveda and Bartolomé de Las Casas to Valladolid to hear arguments on the nature of the beings discovered in the New World. Sepúlveda argued that the "Indians" were natural slaves. His evaluation provided justification for the Spanish system of *encomiendaro*. Las Casas, having spent four decades in the New World, provided broad evidence for a contrary view that the natives were highly developed and possessed natural virtues. New England Calvinists and romantics in the tradition of Jean-Jacques Rousseau carried forth the ignoble-noble savage debate into the twentieth century.

Anthropological and Ethnological Studies. In the mid-nineteenth century, Max Müller, Edward Tylor, Herbert Spencer, and other evolutionary positivists used the existing materials on Native American cultures to serve their universal theories of human development. Spencer, for example, concluded that "savages" lacked the necessary mental capacities to make moral distinctions, while Tylor argued that primitive peoples had not risen to the stage of ethical development that is characteristic of higher religions. These ethnocentric appraisals of "primitive" peoples in general, and Native Americans specifically, continued to inform the study of Native American peoples through the first half of the twentieth century.

Native American ethics are expressed in religious rituals such as this Ghost Dance. (Smithsonian Institution)

Led by Franz Boas and Clark Wissler, twentieth century anthropological and ethnological studies of Native American cultures tended to ignore religious topics except as they contributed to cultural or diffusionist theories. Discussions of social relations focused on kinship patterns and formal social organization. Franz Boas's *Kwakiutl Ethnography* (1966), for example, contains no references to ethics, moral codes, or values. Paul Radin's *The Winnebago Tribe* (1923) and *The Trickster* (1956), Ruth Benedict's *Patterns of Culture* (1934), and Gladys Reichard's *Navaho Religion* (1950) use psychological approaches that reduce moral values to the satisfaction of human needs. Religion, when considered, focuses on topics such as the supernatural, sorcery, and witchcraft to the exclusion of ethical matters. Ruth Landes' *Ojibwa Religion and the Midéwiwin* (1968), for example, limits the term "ethics" to a distinction between "good" and "evil" in the context of sorcery and witchcraft, with no discussion of the ethical principles that might inform those evaluations.

Philosophic Studies. Richard Brandt's *Hopi Ethics* (1954) and John Ladd's *The Structure of a Moral Code* (1957) provide the only published formal theoretical studies of Native American ethics. Brandt and Ladd conclude that pragmatism best characterized Hopi and Navaho ethics. Brandt's methodology uses native interviews about ethical issues defined by Brandt rather than by the Hopi. Ladd's methodology is aimed at hypothetical reconstruction of Navaho ethics from the native point of view. Both Brandt and Ladd assume that ethics is concerned exclusively with social relations and therefore give little consideration to religious issues.

Emic Studies. A. Irving Hallowell's *Ojib-wa Ontology, Behavior, and World View* (1960) marks a turning point in the study of the ethics of Native American peoples. Hallowell concluded that the key to Ojibwa behavior and worldview is found in a distinctive ontology that, on the one hand, expands the category of person to include "other-than-human persons," and, on the other hand, defines moral behavior relationally. N. Scott Momaday's "A Man Made of Words" (1970) suggests that the idea of appropriation and the related concepts of appropriateness and propriety guide Native American relationships. Dorothy Lee's *Freedom and Culture* (1959), Howard Harrod's *Renewing the World* (1987), and Fritz Detwiler's "'All My Relatives'" (1992) further argue for the relational nature of the ethics of Native American peoples based on the expanded notion of "person." Harrod's work, in particular, grounds ethics in ritual experience. Through ritual, the ethical bonds that sustain a relational world-view are renewed and enhanced. If a relational ontology is fundamental to Native American world-views, then further investigation of Native American ethics from a relational perspective is required. —*Fritz Detwiler*

See also Environmental ethics; Native American genocide.

BIBLIOGRAPHY

Brandt, Richard B. *Hopi Ethics: A Theoretical Analysis.* Chicago: University of Chicago Press, 1954.

Detwiler, Fritz. "'All My Relatives': Persons in Oglala Religion." *Religion* 22 (July, 1992): 235-246.

Hallowell, A. Irving. *Ojibwa Ontology, Behavior, and World View.* Indianapolis: Bobbs-Merrill, 1960.

Harrod, Howard. *Renewing the World: Plains Indian Religion and Morality.* Tucson: University of Arizona Press, 1987.

Ladd, John. *The Structure of a Moral Code: A Philosophical Analysis of Ethical Discourse Applied to the Ethics of the Navaho Indians.* Cambridge, Mass.: Harvard University Press, 1957.

Momaday, N. Scott. "The Man Made of Words." In *The First Convocation of Indian Scholars,* edited by Rupert Costo. San Francisco: Indian Historian Press, 1970.

Tedlock, Dennis, and Barbara Tedlock, eds. *Teachings from the American Earth: Indian Religion and Philosophy.* New York: Liveright, 1975.

Native American genocide

TYPE OF ETHICS: Race and ethnicity

DATE: 1492-1916

DEFINITION: Native American genocide refers to the long, slow destruction of peoples and their ways of life

NATIVE AMERICAN TRIBES THAT HAVE BEEN COMPLETELY EXTERMINATED			
Tribe	Region Inhabited	Years Exterminated	By Whom/ What
Calusa	Florida	1513-1530	Spanish/war
Massachusetts	New England	1617-1633	Smallpox
Pequot	New England	1637-1638	English/war
Powhatan	Virginia	1637-1705	English/war
Narraganset	Rhode Island	1675-1676	English/war
Susquehannock	New York	1675-1763	Disease/war
Chitimacha	Louisiana	1706-1717	French/war
Natchez	Mississippi	1716-1731	French/war
Chinook	Columbia River region	1782-1853	Smallpox
Yavapai	Arizona	1873-1905	Tuberculosis

SIGNIFICANCE: European Americans justified the extermination of millions of Native Americans by declaring them unfit for civilized living

The European discovery of the New World had devastating consequences for the native population. Within a century of Christopher Columbus' landing in 1492, the number of people living in the Americas had declined from 25 million to 1 million. Whole societies in Mexico and South America died within weeks of initial contact with Spanish explorers and adventurers. The major cause of the devastation was disease. Native Americans had lived in total isolation from the rest of the world since first arriving in the New World from Central Asia around 20,000 B.C.E.; hence, they had escaped the devastating epidemics and diseases, such as smallpox and the plague, that had afflicted the rest of humankind for generations. Such diseases normally required human carriers to pass them on to others, and such conditions did not exist in the New World until after 1492.

Columbus and his crew made four separate voyages to the New World between 1492 and 1510, and on each of those voyages sailors brought new diseases with them. Even the common flu had devastating consequences for defenseless Native American babies and children. Other people of the world had built up immunities to these killers, but Native Americans had none, so they died in massive numbers. In the 1500's, most of the dying took place from Mexico south, since the Spanish appeared to be uninterested in colonizing North America. Only after the English settled Jamestown in 1607-1608 and Plymouth in Massachusetts in 1620 did the epidemics affect Native Americans in that region.

The first major tribe to be exterminated in North America was the Massachusetts of New England, whose population died out completely between 1619 and 1633 from a smallpox epidemic. Yet other things besides disease were killing Native Americans. Most Europeans believed that the people they came across in their explorations were not human at all, but instead savage, inferior beings who had no law and order, no cities, no wealth, and no idea of God or progress. When they died from "white man's diseases," this offered further proof of the weakness and helplessness of the population. They could not even make good slaves because they died so quickly from "minor" illnesses. That is why the Europeans turned to Africa for their supply of slave laborers; Africans, who had had a much longer history of contact with other peoples of the world, had built up immunities to the killing diseases. Native Americans were not so lucky.

As time passed, immunities were built up by native peoples, and fewer tribes were extinguished by diseases. Warfare, however, continued to take its toll. Thousands of Native Americans died defending their homelands from American settlers in the aftermath of the War for Independence. Native Americans were not made citizens by the Constitution of 1787 but were legally defined as residents of foreign nations living in the United States. Wars and conflicts over territory devastated many tribes by 1830. In that year, president Andrew Jackson and Congress adopted a program, the Indian Removal Act, that they hoped would put an end to wars with the Native Americans. Under this new act, the American government would trade land west of the Mississippi River for land owned by the tribes in the east. Land in the west, acquired from France in 1803 as part of the Louisiana Purchase, was deemed unsuitable for farming by Europeans. Native Americans, on the other hand, would be able to survive on the Great Plains, called the "Great American Desert" by most whites, by hunting buffalo and other game.

Congress authorized the president to exchange land beginning in 1831. Three years later, a permanent Indian Country was created in the West and settlement by whites was declared illegal. By 1840, Indian Removal was complete, though it took the Black Hawk War in Illinois, the Seminole War in Florida, and the terrible march forcing the Cherokee from Georgia to the Indian Territory, to complete the process. At least three thousand Native American women and children died at the hands of the U.S. Army on the Cherokee "Trail of Tears." Indian Removal meant death and disaster for many eastern tribes.

Conflict was reduced by the program only until whites began moving into the West in the 1860's. During the Civil War (1861-1865), several Indian Wars were fought in Minnesota and Iowa, and the infamous Chivington Massacre took place in Colorado in 1864. In this incident, 450 Native Americans were slaughtered without warning in a predawn raid by the Colorado militia. To prevent massacres in the West, Congress enacted a "reservation policy," setting aside several million acres of western lands for "permanent" Indian settlement. The Army had the job of keeping the tribes on their reservations. Frequent wars resulted as Great Plains tribes attempted to leave their reservations to hunt buffalo and the army drove them back.

Problems increased with the coming of railroads. The first transcontinental railroad began carrying passengers in 1869. Huge buffalo herds presented the railroads with a major problem, however, because they took hours and sometimes days to cross the tracks. To keep trains running on time, railroads hired hunters to kill the buffalo. By the late 1880's, they nearly accomplished their goal of killing off all the herds. Buffalo had once numbered 100 million, but by 1888, there were fewer than 1,000. With the destruction of the buffalo came the end of the Native American way of life. The final war was fought in 1890 in the Black Hills of South Dakota on the Pine Ridge Reservation. An Indian holy man claimed that the whites would disappear and the buffalo would return if Native Americans danced a Ghost Dance. Magical shirts were given to the dancers that were supposed to protect them from white men's bullets. When the white Indian agent asked Washington for help to put down the Ghost Dancers, the Army responded by killing hundreds of the Native Americans, whose magical shirts did not work.

Native Americans did not become American citizens until 1924 and were required to live on reservations. Not until 1934 was self-government granted to the tribes, and by that time the reservations had become the poorest communities in the entire United States. The reservations continue to have the highest levels of unemployment, alcoholism, crime, and drug addiction found in U.S. communities. These signals of social disintegration and disruption are the final results of a policy of extermination that began in 1492. The long, slow death of Native American culture and society continues.   —Leslie V. Tischauser

See also Bigotry; Genocide; Genocide, cultural; Racial prejudice; Racism.

BIBLIOGRAPHY

Debo, Angie. A History of the Indians of the United States. Norman: University of Oklahoma Press, 1970.

Deloria, Vine, Jr. Custer Died for Your Sins: An Indian Manifesto. New York: Macmillan, 1969.

Farb, Peter. Man's Rise to Civilization as Shown by the Indians of North America from Primeval Times to the Coming of the Industrial State. New York: Dutton, 1968.

Josephy, Alvin M., Jr. The Indian Heritage of America. New York: Alfred A. Knopf, 1968.

Washburn, Wilcomb E. The Indian in America. New York: Harper & Row, 1975.

Natural law

TYPE OF ETHICS: Theory of ethics
DATE: First century B.C.E. to present
ASSOCIATED WITH: Cicero, Saint Thomas Aquinas, and John Finnis

DEFINITION: The theory that the rightness of actions is determined by the laws of human nature instead of the customs or laws of society
SIGNIFICANCE: The natural law theory was a predominant view of law and morality until the seventeenth century and still has many supporters

Antecedents of Natural Law Theory. The natural law theory of morality has its roots in classical Greek and Roman philosophy. Greek thinkers such as Aristotle (384-322 B.C.E.) emphasized the teleological nature of humanity. In other words, each human being has a fixed human nature and a certain "function"; namely, the capacity for rational thought. It is implied in Aristotle's philosophy that moral actions are those that fulfill one's nature as a rational human being. Furthermore, in the *Rhetoric* (c. 335 B.C.E.) Aristotle differentiates between positive or "particular" laws and laws "according to nature." Aristotle described the latter as a "common" law; that is, one that was common or natural to all humanity.

The notion of natural law is even more explicit in the writings of the Roman philosopher and statesman Cicero (106-43 B.C.E.), who is usually associated with the Stoic school of philosophy. Cicero argued in his essays for an eternal and immutable law that prevailed for all people at all times. Moreover, this law is grounded in human nature. According to Cicero, "Law is the highest reason, implanted in Nature, which commands what ought to be done and forbids the opposite." In general, this notion of a natural law (*ius naturale*) permeated the Stoic philosophy, which emphasized the equality of all persons according to the law of nature. Moreover, this idea of a natural law was not foreign to Roman jurists; hence, it affected the development and application of actual laws in Roman society.

One finds intimations of the presence of this natural law in several other classical writers, such as Augustine (354-430 C.E.) and Boethius (480-523 C.E.). Augustine, for example, contended that the only valid temporal laws were those that were consonant with the eternal and immutable law of God. Other laws were simply unjust and hence lacked any authority. Even Saint Paul concludes in one of his epistles that we find a morality that conscience discerns naturally inscribed in our hearts (Romans 2:14-16).

Saint Thomas Aquinas. The philosopher who is most closely associated with the natural law ethic is Saint Thomas Aquinas (c. 1225-1274). Aquinas developed an elaborate philosophical system based in large part on the philosophy of Aristotle. His most famous work is known as the *Summa Theologica* (1266-1273). The *Summa* is a lengthy treatise in which Aquinas presents and defends his complete philosophical system. In a major section of this work known as "The Treatise on Law," he articulated his conception of natural law morality. This brief work has been extremely influential in the history of moral and political philosophy.

Aquinas begins from what he calls the "eternal law," which is the law of God's creative work by which He directs everything to the fulfillment He has in mind. All true laws are derived from and related to this eternal, unchanging law of God. According to Aquinas, the natural law that governs the lives of human beings is a participation in this eternal law. God created humans and gave them a definite nature that is subject to certain laws; specifically, the laws of its own development. Moreover, each nature is oriented intrinsically toward the goal of developing and realizing all of its vast potential. Hence, the primary obligation placed on humans by God is simply *self-fulfillment*. In other words, a human being's fundamental moral obligation is to fulfill his or her nature, to actualize his or her potencies, to develop in a fully human way. This obligation comes from God the creator but it is also written or inscribed ontologically into each human nature and clearly manifests itself to any intelligence that discerns this nature.

Given that human nature is oriented toward its own fulfillment, the first principle of morality is simple to deduce: "Good is to be done and promoted and evil is to be avoided." All other precepts of the natural law are based on this principle. It is important to note that the word "good" here refers to the final end of self-realization or self-fulfillment. Thus, the first precept of the natural law could be expressed as follows: "Fulfill your true nature as a person," or simply "Follow nature."

How exactly can one fulfill one's nature and actualize one's potential in order to become more fully human? In Aquinas' view, one must merely follow one's *natural inclinations*. These inclinations are a deep-seated and innate part of human nature, and they provide the general specifications of the first precept, "Do good," as applied to human nature. The natural inclinations derive from three levels. As beings (or substances), humans are naturally inclined toward self-preservation; hence, whatever is a means of preserving life and avoiding death belongs to the natural law. As animals, humans are naturally inclined to take in food, to reproduce through sexual intercourse, and so forth. As rational human beings, humans are naturally inclined toward a life of reason (that is, the acquisition of knowledge), toward friendship and a social life, and toward a life of virtue and the love of God. Unfortunately, Aquinas does not provide a very extensive list of these inclinations, he lists only a few primary precepts of the natural law.

The main point, however, is clear: If one follows these natural inclinations, one will attain genuine self-fulfillment and happiness. Indeed, one is *obliged* to follow these inclinations and not to oppose one's own nature. The natural inclinations are not known by means of conceptual reasoning or logical analysis. Instead, they are known intuitively and naturally by anyone possessing a properly functioning practical reason. Hence, one's practical reason both knows these natural inclinations and directs their implementation in particular circumstances. In this sense then, reason—or what Aquinas calls "right reason" (*recta ratio*)—is indisputably the ultimate norm of morality.

Since, as Aquinas points out, people grasp as goods the fulfillments to which they are naturally inclined, it follows that there is a basic precept of the natural law that corresponds to each natural inclination. In other words, the natural inclinations as intuited or known by reason become the natural laws that bind one from within. They become the basic principles of morality—the so-called primary precepts of the natural law. These principles are immutable because they emanate from the fixed human nature. Also, these laws are universal, since all humans share a common nature. It becomes clear, therefore, that these primary precepts of the natural law, which are universal and immutable, serve as a fixed and unshakable basis for all morality and law.

Aquinas stresses that there are also secondary precepts of the natural law. These are derived from applying the primary precepts to more particular kinds of situations. Unlike the primary precepts, the secondary ones are not infallibly or intuitively known, may be disputed at times, and often hold only as a general rule or "for the most part." Many civil laws and other moral mandates fall into this category. Aquinas' treatment of these secondary precepts reveals that he does allow for some flexibility in the development of law and morality.

The final issue considered in Aquinas' discussion of natural law is the relationship between human law and the natural law. Human law, according to Aquinas, is a further application of the natural law in a particular community and historical epoch. The necessity of such laws emanates from the unwillingness of some people to follow their own natural aptitude for virtue. Aquinas insists that every *genuine* human law must be derived from and based on the natural law. He argues that the force of law depends on its justice and rightness, which in turn depends on the rule of reason. Since the first rule of reason is the law of nature, every law must be based on this law of nature. Many laws will be established by tyrannical or inept rulers and legislators that will depart from the natural law and will be neither right nor just. When such laws deviate from the natural law, they are a corruption of law and have no binding force. Aquinas maintains that laws can be unjust or illegitimate in two ways: They are opposed to either the human good or the divine good. Clearly, then, any law that violates the common good, that is not just and does not participate in the natural law, is no law at all. All human law must, therefore, yield to the higher law of nature. It should be pointed out that even laws passed by good and upright rulers, laws perhaps good in themselves, might be poorly adapted to a particular situation. Hence, one might be justified in not following such a law under such circumstances.

Thus, there is an explicit hierarchy in Aquinas' philosophy of law. The natural law participates in and derives from the eternal law, and human law is subservient to the natural law. Whenever it conflicts with that law, it is null and void. The natural law, then, should be the ultimate guide and moral compass for all legislators and leaders.

Natural Law and Natural Rights Theory. A related but conceptually different approach to morality is the *natural rights* theory, which was developed by English philosophers such as Thomas Hobbes (1588-1679) and John Locke (1632-1704). Locke, for example, argues for various natural rights such as the right to life, liberty, and property. According to Locke, these natural rights should be the basis for the laws and rules of civil society. The similarity between this viewpoint and the natural law ethic of Aquinas is the grounding of morality in rights that emanate from the nature of human beings. Locke, however, detaches his limited natural law theory from the metaphysical and theological underpinnings used by Aquinas. He also rejects the idea of natural hierarchies. Like Aquinas and other natural law philosophers, however, he claims that there is something higher than civil laws. In other words, the ultimate standards of law and morality are the natural human rights of life, liberty, and property. Moreover, the state exists to secure and guarantee those fundamental rights. Thus, strictly speaking, Locke did not adopt a traditional view of morality based on natural law, but he did infer certain natural rights in the same manner as natural law philosophers such as Aquinas. Also, like traditional natural law theories, Locke's philosophy argues from the facts of human nature to the values that ground morality and law.

The School of Natural Law. During the seventeenth and eighteenth centuries, there were many further developments in the evolution of natural law theory. What came to be known as the school of natural law was dominated by thinkers such as Hugo Grotius and Samuel von Pufendorf, along with Johann Gottlieb Fichte and Immanuel Kant. These philosophers discussed natural law in purely secular terms; hence, they too disassociated natural law from its metaphysical and theological suppositions. They regarded the law of nature as manifest to anyone through the natural light of human reason. This school also focused on different types of associations that form in society—particularly those regulated by law. They developed theories of the state, society at large, and associations and their relation to the state. Grotius, for example, developed a natural law conception of the state. Beyond any doubt, even these obscure works have had a notable impact on the evolution of legal and political theory.

Contemporary Versions of the Natural Law Philosophy. There are several insightful contemporary versions of natural law morality that for the most part have been inspired by the philosophy of Saint Thomas Aquinas. For example, legal philosophers such as John Finnis have attempted to build on and advance the work of Aquinas. In Finnis' version of natural law morality, there is a fuller and more elaborate articulation of human goods. Like Aquinas, Finnis contends that the end of each human being is self-fulfillment, or what he calls "human flourishing." In his seminal work *Natural Law and Natural Rights* (1980), Finnis argues for seven basic goods, or aspects of human well-being that contribute to this flourishing: life, knowledge, play, aesthetic experience, sociability and friendships, practicable reasonableness, and religion. Human flourishing is

realized by actualizing these basic goods. Finnis also contends that practical reasonableness directs and guides the way in which people actualize the other goods. It is a critical intermediate principle that guides the transition from human goods to judgments about right and wrong actions. According to Finnis, one is practically reasonable when one participates in all human goods *well*. Thus, the bedrock moral principle for Finnis can be summed up as follows: "Make one's choices open to human fulfillment; that is, avoid unnecessary limitations of human potentialities." In other words, the moral law holds that one should promote human flourishing by respecting these basic human goods in one's own actions and in the actions of others.

Finally, it is worth noting that the notion of a natural law grounded in human nature is implicit in the writings of many other contemporary thinkers. Consider, for example, the writings of Martin Luther King, Jr.; specifically, his famous "Letter from a Birmingham Jail," which was written in 1963. In this letter, he explains his rationale for disobeying the law by claiming that an unjust law is not really a law at all. Citing Saint Augustine, King invoked a higher "natural" law as a standard for judging the unjust discriminatory laws that could be found in some states in the early 1960's. King's writings raise the question of how one is to judge the laws of civil society if one does not have this higher standard cited by Aristotle, Cicero, Augustine, Aquinas, and many others.

Criticisms. Critics have identified many problems associated with the natural law approach to morality. Some of the strongest criticism has been directed against Saint Thomas Aquinas, since he is regarded as the most noted systematizer of natural law theory. To begin with, the critics argue that Aquinas' discussion is seriously deficient in that he does not enumerate more primary precepts of natural law. Aquinas mentions only a few such precepts and should have given much more attention to the actual content of the natural law. Thus, the famous question 94 of the *Summa* in which these precepts are articulated under the form of natural inclinations is one of the most disappointing sections in the whole "Treatise on Law." It is difficult, then, to arrive at a comprehensive list of specific and definable duties that should be followed in the light of the natural law.

In addition, Aquinas and other natural law advocates perhaps place too much emphasis on the immutability of human nature, which in turn accounts for the remarkable stability of the law. A more adequate moral theory must focus more explicitly on *possible* and future human fulfillment. In other words, more attention must be given to humanity's continual evolution and to possible forms of human fulfillment that have not yet been defined.

Still another criticism that is directed against Aquinas and his followers is the dependence of his natural law theory on the metaphysical assumptions of his philosophy. One such assumption is that the universe is organized in a teleological fashion and that all beings are ordained a certain end. Without this assumption, Aquinas' version of natural law becomes somewhat problematic, since it is predicated on the notion that human nature is oriented intrinsically toward self-realization. Science, however, specifically physics and biology, has rejected this teleological view of nature. For example, the biologist would argue that the development and growth of organisms is not caused by some inner teleology, but by the presence of genetic information that controls the process of growth. Thus, modern science and reason do not support the teleological assumptions of Aristotle and Aquinas. It is possible, of course, to revise the natural law framework so that it is not dependent on a foundation of teleology. In other words, the absence of a teleological assumption does not preclude a coherent natural law ethic.

Relevance of Natural Law. The natural law tradition has had a significant influence on the development of law and political theory in Western civilization. First of all, it represents the viewpoint that there are *objective moral principles* that can be discerned by reason. It has also influenced the emphasis on natural rights that is expressed in constitutional laws. Natural law theory seeks to justify these rights and other moral requirements that should serve as the basis of any legal system. Unless a system adheres to this natural law, it cannot be considered legitimate or justified. Thus, the rules of any society are not valid if they come into conflict with the demands of the natural law. In short, a valid law must be a moral law; that is, one that is consistent with the natural law.

The natural law tradition stands in unequivocal opposition to the tradition of positivism that distinguishes between law and morality. In addition, legal positivists stress that an unjust law is still a law. They hold that natural law theory confuses what law is with what it ought to be. Obviously, the debate between positivists and natural law proponents is a spirited one that will not be resolved easily. It is also clear, however, that the framework of natural law, despite its flaws, has many merits, since it accounts for the authority of law and provides a general guideline for judging the worth and quality of diverse legal rules.

—*Richard A. Spinello*

See also Augustine, Saint; Hobbes, Thomas; Kant, Immanuel; King, Martin Luther, Jr.; Locke, John; Stoic ethics; *Summa Theologica*; Thomas Aquinas.

BIBLIOGRAPHY

Finnis, John. *Natural Law and Natural Rights.* New York: Oxford University Press, 1980. A modern and comprehensive treatment of natural law in the tradition of Aristotle and Aquinas.

Grisez, Germain G., and Russell B. Shaw. *Beyond the New Morality: The Responsibilities of Freedom.* 3d ed. Notre Dame, Ind.: University of Notre Dame Press, 1988. A perceptive account of natural law theory that offers some practical guidance for implementing this theory in one's everyday moral decisions.

King, Martin Luther, Jr. "Letter from Birmingham Jail." In *Why We Can't Wait.* New York: New American Library, 1968. This letter was written to "My Dear Fellow Clergymen" during King's incarceration in Birmingham in the heyday of the civil rights movement. It is a clear and nontheoretical discussion of a "natural law" that governs all humanity.

O'Connor, D. J. *Aquinas and Natural Law.* London: MacMillan, 1967. This short book is a lucid account of Aquinas' ethical doctrines. It considers his philosophical presuppositions, along with the influence of Aristotle. The book also offers a critical assessment of Aquinas from the perspective of contemporary analytical philosophy.

Passerin d'Entreves, Alessandro. *Natural Law.* London: Hutchinson University Library, 1970. A brilliant and accessible discussion of the general spirit and aim of Aquinas' ethical thought and the entire natural law tradition.

Thomas Aquinas. *On Law, Morality, and Politics.* Edited by William P. Baumgarth and Richard J. Regan. Indianapolis: Hackett, 1988. Extended selections from Aquinas' writings on natural law and other areas of morality. Contains a useful introduction that helps to illuminate the main lines of Aquinas' complex writings.

Natural rights

TYPE OF ETHICS: Human rights

DATE: Natural rights date back to fifth century Greece, with subsequent development throughout the Middle Ages and the Enlightenment

ASSOCIATED WITH: Sophocles (469-406 B.C.E.), Aristotle (384-322 B.C.E.), Cicero (106-43 B.C.E.), Hugo Grotius (1585-1645), and Saint Thomas Aquinas (1225-1274); all contributed to the development of natural law and natural rights

DEFINITION: Natural rights are those rights that are based on the concepts of natural law, rather than on moral, legal, religious, political, rational, or other concepts

SIGNIFICANCE: Human rights concepts were originally an extension of natural law principles; concepts of human rights have expanded from the realm of individual rights to include areas of international law, economic development, and foreign policy

Historical Development of Human Rights. From 1945 to 1948, aghast at the systematic violations of human rights committed during World War II, especially the Holocaust, and aware of the lack of enforcement mechanisms to hold persons accountable for such behavior, the countries of the United Nations initiated the process of developing legally binding international standards of conduct. In 1948, the United Nations General Assembly universally adopted the Universal Declaration of Human Rights (UDHR), marking the introduction of a basic canon of civil, political, economic, social, and cultural rights into the international forum.

The Universal Declaration of Human Rights consists of thirty articles that declare, among others, the rights to life; liberty; property; nationality; education; thought; religion;

HUMAN RIGHTS THAT EVOLVED OUT OF NATURAL RIGHTS CONCEPTS	
Natural Rights Concept	Human Rights
Freedom	Self-deterimination: rights to food, shelter, education, medical care, and social security
Liberty: freedoms of expression and religion	Liberty: freedoms of assembly, expression, religion, thought, culture, nationality, and movement; right to asylum
Equality	Equality: equality before the law, equal education, equal employment
Property	Property: right to employment, equal pay
Self-government	Representative government: fair elections, participatory government, equal suffrage, equal access to public service.
Freedom from arbitrary arrest	Due process: presumption of innocence, right to fair trial; freedoms from torture, detention, and exile
Personal privacy	Right to privacy: domestic privacy, privacy of correspondence; rights to family, marriage, honor, reputation, and leisure

and freedom from torture, arbitrary arrest, and detention. Because of its ties with natural law, the UDHR has been criticized for being Eurocentric, giving rise to claims that its standards are not applicable to non-Western nations. Indeed, several pillars of the UDHR and subsequent international human rights instruments (the Covenant on Civil and Political Rights, the Covenant on Economic, Social and Cultural Rights, the Convention on the Elimination of All Forms of Racial Discrimination, and the Convention Against Torture) are rooted in the early ideas of justice that derive from Western civilization.

Ideas of Justice in Ancient Greece. The Greek idea of justice was one that both guided individual behavior and served as a blueprint for the organization of society. The ethical beliefs of prominent Greek thinkers—Sophocles and Aristotle, in particular—were grounded in the belief that the higher laws of the gods transcended the obligations and duties dictated by the rulers of society. Like Plato and Socrates, Aristotle believed that adherence to ethics creates an ideal society, one in which hereditary class status does not determine one's social rank.

Roman and Catholic Doctrine of the Middle Ages. Influenced by classical Greek philosophy, the Roman Emperor Justinian (502-565) distinguished among Roman natural law (*jus civile*), the common law of all nations (*jus gentium*), and natural law (*jus naturale*). The Romans emphasized the necessity for a proper trial, the presentation of evidence and proof, and the illegality of bribery in judicial proceedings.

The ideas proposed by Marcus Tullius Cicero (106-43 B.C.E.) further cultivated a theory of natural law (*jus naturale*). Cicero's

Brotherhood of Man made no distinction between what is legally right and morally right, and he promoted the idea that Roman law should be filled with "natural reason" (fair, equitable solutions) instead of reliance upon positive legal provisions. Natural law was God-given, eternal, and immutable, and it could be applied to all people at all times.

The emphasis on natural reason as the foundation of law continues with the Catholic doctrine of the Middle Ages and the writings of Saint Thomas Aquinas. Hugo Grotius (1585-1645) clearly breaks from the older doctrine of natural rights by maintaining that natural law originates in pure reason, not the scriptures. For Grotius, even nature and mathematics are unchangeable by God.

The Enlightenment. The basis of the Enlightenment was a belief in the perfectibility and decency of humankind. John Locke's essay on civil government (1689) contends that in the original state of nature all persons have the same rights and obligations and are entitled to defend their rights to life, freedom, and property. Rousseau's *Social Contract* (1712-1778) argued that the presence of evil cannot be blamed on humankind's natural tendencies, but must be ascribed to social injustice and inequality; like Locke, Rousseau believed in a natural state of existence in which all are equal. Voltaire (1694-1778), another eighteenth century natural law theoretician, advocated for the rights still demanded today, including the freedoms of person, press, and religion.

Eighteenth Century Revolutions. The basic documents of the American Revolution, which reveal the evolution of natural law theory during the Enlightenment, influenced the French struggle for freedom. The rights of man, the social contract, popular sovereignty, separation of government powers, right to property, religious freedom, and freedom of thought all are contained in the Declaration of Independence and the Bill of Rights.

Parallel to constitutional developments in America, the French Declaration of the Rights of Man and the Citizen (1789) recognized the rights to liberty, property, equality before the law, repudiation of all hereditary privilege, national sovereignty, accountability of public officials, freedom of speech and press, separation of government powers, personal safety, and the right to resist oppression. Subsequently, in 1793, a new French constitution was developed that went beyond the document of 1789 in providing for the rights to work, to mass education, and to rise in insurrection.

Generations of Human Rights. France's development of the 1793 constitution is a historical example in which the dichotomy between civil, political rights and economic, social, and cultural rights is visible. Just as the 1793 French document linked economic status and opportunity to the attainment of basic human rights, elements of current human rights discourse maintain that human rights are indivisible. Poor nonwestern countries assert that civil and political rights (referred to as first-generation rights because they are readily attainable) cannot be given priority over economic, social, and cultural rights (second generation rights, inclusive of the rights to education, housing, employment, and social security). Amid diverse global conditions, the development of an international code of ethics, which began in ancient times, has been broadened by the demand for economic, social, and cultural justice.

Natural Law and Applicability of Human Rights. The natural-law origins of the Universal Declaration of Human Rights fuel the conflict over the global application of human rights. Countries not rooted in the Western tradition of natural law agree that although human beings are born free and equal in dignity, the source of this higher order is dependent upon cultural protocol. Adherence to tradition and desire for its maintenance have given rise to the development of human rights documents that reflect differing social, cultural, and religious realities. Examples of such documents are the African (Banjul) Charter on Human and Peoples' Rights and the Islamic Declaration of Human Rights.

Conclusion. Since 1948, an extensive register of international human rights has been developed. For example, feminism has extended human rights arguments to the defense of women and their protection against male-biased social, religious, and legal norms. The continuous articulation of human rights is both an extension of natural-law doctrine and an effort to respond to varying cultural perceptions of human rights and differing global economies, religions, and political conditions. The 1948 Universal Declaration of Human Rights (UDHR), with its mixture of first- and second-generation rights—civil and political rights with economic, social, and cultural rights—is testimony to the merging of tradition and modernity in the effort to develop an international collection of ethics. While the first twenty articles of the UDHR cover the rights to life, liberty, property, equality, and justice, subsequent articles proclaim the rights to education, equal pay, an adequate standard of living, nationality, and the cultural life of one's community.

The loss of natural rights as the major authority for human rights has led to two problematic results. The creation of seemingly unlimited and unattainable economic, social, and environmental rights, as well as the justification for the proliferation of many other rights; and the relativism of rights when each culture claims its own unique rights for itself and opposes any universal (natural rights) claim for human rights. —*Richard C. Kagan* and *Kerrie Workman*

See also Civil rights; Human rights; Universal Declaration of Human Rights.

BIBLIOGRAPHY

Castberg, Frede. "Natural Law and Human Rights: An Idea-Historical Survey." In *International Protection of Human Rights*, edited by Asbjorn Eide and August Schou. New York: Interscience, 1968. Professor Eide is one of the great European (Norwegian) experts on human rights and natural rights law.

Palumbo, Michael. *Human Rights: Meaning and History*. Malabar, Fla.: Robert E. Krieger, 1982. This basic reader on the history of human rights contains general readings from the works of philosophers and politicians. Provides a general overview of the development of human rights concepts.

Pollack, Ervin H. *Human Rights*. Buffalo, N.Y.: Jay Steuart, 1971. A collection of works by legal philosophers on such topics as the definition of human rights, the identification of human rights, and the relevance of international standards to morality.

Schwab, Peter, and Adamantia Pollis, eds. *Toward a Human Rights Framework*. New York: Praeger, 1982. The central theme of this volume is the universality of human rights. The work supports the idea that human rights are products of history and are dynamic. Argues for the indivisibility of human rights.

Naturalistic fallacy

TYPE OF ETHICS: Theory of ethics
DATE: Coined 1903
ASSOCIATED WITH: English philosopher G. E. Moore
DEFINITION: The mistaken attempt to define a moral entity such as good in terms of a natural one such as pleasure
SIGNIFICANCE: If the attempt to define a moral entity in terms of a natural entity is indeed fallacious, there are negative implications for naturalistic ethics and positive ones for intuitionistic ethics

G. E. Moore (1873-1958), a Cambridge philosopher, argued in his *Principia Ethica* (1903) that ethical naturalism should be rejected because it commits the naturalistic fallacy. Moore said that the naturalistic fallacy "consists in the contention that good *means* nothing but some simple or complex notion, that can be defined in terms of natural qualities." To the contrary, Moore maintained that good is simple and indefinable in any terms, natural or otherwise. Thus, he sometimes seemed to apply the "naturalistic fallacy" designation to *any* attempt to define good.

Moore did not object to saying that pleasure is good. In fact, it is the business of ethics to determine what things are good. His objection was against those who would claim that pleasure *means* good, that good and pleasure are the same thing. He would claim that people rightly say that a lemon is yellow, but they do not mean by that that lemon and yellow are the same.

The "Open Question Argument." To support his claims about a fallacy, Moore offered what has been called the "open question argument." For any definition that might be proposed for "good," it can always be meaningfully asked whether that thing really is good; whereas, with a legitimate definition, such a question would not be meaningful. For example, if "mother" means "female parent," then these terms are interchangeable. It would make no sense to inquire whether your mother were really your female parent, since this would be asking whether your mother were really your mother. Moore maintained, however, that it will always make sense to ask whether pleasure (or any other proposed definition) is really good.

John Stuart Mill and the Fallacy. Moore stated that John Stuart "Mill has made as naive and artless a use of the naturalistic fallacy as anybody could desire." According to Moore, Mill claimed that good meant desirable and that what was desirable was to be discovered by looking at what was desired. Since pleasure is what is desired, it is the good. Moore accused Mill of slipping fallaciously from what *is* desired to what *ought* to be desired, from the *fact* of desired to the *value* of desirable.

In a summary of what he had said about Mill, Moore said, "if his contention that 'I ought to desire' means nothing but 'I do desire' were true, then he is only entitled to say, 'we do desire so and so because we do desire it'; and that is not an ethical proposition at all; it is a mere tautology." Thus, it can be seen that Moore was concerned not only with the naturalistic element of Mill's definition but also with his attempt at any sort of definition.

Criticism of Moore. There have been numerous critiques of Moore's fallacy claims. Some have pointed out that it is a misnomer, since the objection is to all definitions, not only naturalistic ones, and that it should perhaps be called the "definition fallacy." These critics have gone on to propose answers to the "open question argument." Some have suggested that perhaps "good" has several meanings and thus an examination of any one of these might seem to leave an open question. Perhaps, alternatively, the term is extremely difficult to define, as Socrates found with moral terms, but this difficulty does not prove that *no* definition is possible.

Other critics have denied that Mill and other naturalists were making any attempt at definition. In response to these critics, however, it has been argued that whether the naturalist appeals to a definition or to a principle, one always turns out to be grounded in the other, and in neither case can the moral element be logically deduced from the nature of things.

In further support of Moore, it has been said that if indeed a definition of "good" in some natural (or even metaphysical) term could be established, then this would rob moral judgments of their prescriptive force. That is, a judgment of "X is good" would become purely descriptive and would elicit a "so what?" response, just as might a judgment of "That apple is red." Put another way, although Moore's discussion of the naturalistic fallacy may be confusingly presented, it nevertheless testifies to the special character of moral terms as evaluative and action-guiding elements that cannot be captured by any descriptive substitution.

—Ruth B. Heizer

See also Fact/value distinction; Intuitionist ethics; Is/ought distinction; Moore, G. E.

BIBLIOGRAPHY

Binkley, Luther J. *Contemporary Ethical Theories*. New York: Philosophical Library, 1961.

Frankena, William K. *Ethics*. Englewood Cliffs, N.J.: Prentice-Hall, 1963.

Harrison, Jonathan. "Ethical Naturalism." In *The Encyclopedia of Philosophy*, edited by Paul Edwards. New York: Macmillan, 1967.

Schilpp, Paul Arthur, ed. *The Philosophy of G. E. Moore*. La Salle, Ill.: Open Court, 1968.

Taylor, Paul. *Principles of Ethics*. Encino, Calif.: Dickenson, 1975.

Warnock, Mary. *Ethics Since 1900*. London: Oxford University Press, 1960.

Nature, rights of

TYPE OF ETHICS: Environmental ethics

DATE: 1700 to present

DEFINITION: An attempt to reconcile the human ability to destroy and manipulate the environment with the needs of other species

SIGNIFICANCE: Helps to provide a framework within which humans and other species can exist and develop

Western thought, being greatly influenced by Christianity, has historically assumed the dominance of humans over all plant and animal species. The ability to destroy, domesticate, and alter other species has been seen as an inherent argument for human dominance of the natural world. Until the latter part of the twentieth century, little regard was given to the rights of nature to exist within a framework beneficial to species other than humans. The development of environmental crises such as global warming, extinction, and the depletion of natural resources has led philosophers to consider the rights of nature.

When Thomas Jefferson wrote the Declaration of Independence, he declared that all men were created with unalienable rights that allowed them to be treated with equality. Jefferson's ideal, while extended to all humans, was not at the time the reality for all humans. Approximately one hundred years after Jefferson wrote the Declaration of Independence, Charles Darwin presented the idea of the evolution of species. Darwin's idea suggested that those species that currently exist do so because they were best able to adapt to the changing environment in which they live. It is important to note that Darwin did not put forth the idea that the strongest species survived, but rather that the most adaptable species survived. Darwin's theory was slightly distorted and generally believed to be survival of the fittest or strongest. This distortion of Darwin's theory, coupled with Jefferson's emphasis on the unalienable rights of humankind, led to a popular belief that humans had the right to regard nature as simply a resource to use and dominate without regard for any rights that nature might possess.

As a result of the idea of dispensable natural resources, be they inanimate or animate, human technological development and industrialization led to several ecological problems during the latter half of the twentieth century. Global warming, depletion of the earth's protective ozone layer, increases in harmful gases in the atmosphere, and the extinction of plant and animal species are a few of these problems. The burgeoning ecological crisis began to illustrate the intricate and dependent relationship of humans with the natural world. As a result, philosophers and other thinkers began to reevaluate the rights of nature and the role of humans. It became clear that all species on the planet were interconnected and that the environment had forced all species into a subtle compact for survival.

Initially, nature was not viewed as possessing inalienable rights. Instead, the argument was made to protect nature for the benefit of human existence. Nature was important only insofar as it provided what was needful for human existence; if a human activity infringed upon nature in a way that was not viewed as destructive to human existence, then the activity was morally acceptable. Indeed, this view is still held; however, a deeper view of nature began to develop from this perspective. This deeper view argued that humans are only a percentage of an ecological whole, and that each part of this whole is dependent upon the other parts. The interdependence of the parts means that the rights of any one part are not greater than the rights of other parts of the ecological whole. Each species acts upon the society of other species and is acted upon by this society. This fact is commonly illustrated by such concepts as the food chain. In fact, all species, as a result of their existence in the environment, are involved in a social contract with one another. Those who argue from this perspective point out that humans as well as other animals perceive and react to the environment; therefore, humans and other animals have equal value in an environmental context.

The interdependence of species is the cornerstone for the rights-of-nature argument. The theory of evolution supports the idea that all species are created equal because all species have evolved from common ancestors. The species currently residing on the planet are not historically the strongest or most fit but the descendants of the most adaptable species. It is an error to use one species' ability to manipulate the environment as a sanction to disregard the rights of other species. Furthermore, the fact that humans are able to know many of the details about how nature works as a result of biological science does not mean that humans have the right to disregard the rights of nature. Jefferson's unalienable rights for men do not discriminate upon the basis of intelligence; thus, the argument is applied to nature and humans. Humans are capable of knowing the workings of other species, but this should not justify disregard for these species' rights.

If it is held that nature has rights and that human rights are rights that should be accorded to the entire community of species, then how should actions be judged to be right or wrong? Perhaps the best definition is that of Aldo Leopold, who defines an action as being right when it preserves the integrity, stability, and beauty of the biotic community. If nature is accorded an ethical status that is equal to human ethical status, a benchmark such as Leopold's will be needed to make judgments about the actions that humans take. —*Tod Murphy*

See also Animal rights; Dominion over nature, human; Leopold, Aldo; Moral status of animals; *Silent Spring*.

BIBLIOGRAPHY

Attfield, Robin. *The Ethics of Environmental Concern.* New York: Columbia University Press, 1983.

Brennan, Andrew. *Thinking About Nature: An Investigation of Nature, Value, and Ecology.* Athens: University of Georgia Press, 1988.

Day, David. *The Eco Wars: A Layman's Guide to the Ecology Movement.* London: Harrap, 1989.

Miller, G. Tyler, Jr. *Living in the Environment: An Introduction to Environmental Science.* 6th ed. Belmont, Calif.: Wadsworth, 1990.

Pimm, Stuart. *The Balance of Nature? Ecological Issues in the Conservation of Species and Communities.* Chicago: University of Chicago Press, 1991.

Spellerberg, Ian. *Evaluation and Assessment for Conservation: Ecological Guidelines for Determining Priorities for Nature Conservation.* London: Chapman & Hall, 1992.

Nature Conservancy Council

TYPE OF ETHICS: Environmental ethics
DATE: Chartered 1949
ASSOCIATED WITH: Society for the Promotion of Nature Reserves
DEFINITION: The NCC was established to promote the conservation of natural environments
SIGNIFICANCE: The NCC establishes and conducts research on national nature reserves and sites of special scientific interest

The Nature Conservancy Council was established "to provide scientific advice on the conservation and control of the natural flora and fauna of Great Britain; to establish, maintain and manage nature reserves in Great Britain; and to organize and develop the research and scientific services related thereto." While the NCC was not the only conservation organization in the United Kingdom, its mission of scientific research combined with conservation was unique. Some national nature reserves are owned by the Conservancy; others are privately or publicly owned lands that are subject to reserve agreements. The Conservancy was given the power to acquire land compulsorily when necessary. Through its land acquisition activities, it provides an alternative to development and plays an important role in habitat preservation. The NCC works with voluntary organizations, universities, and other government organizations in its conservation and scientific efforts. It has increased public awareness of ecological processes and support for conservation. The NCC provided a model for The Nature Conservancy in the United States. The latter is a private organization that conserves critical habitats by acquiring land through purchases or gifts, manages the sanctuaries, and supports research.

See also Biodiversity; Conservation; Endangered species.

Nazi science

TYPE OF ETHICS: Scientific ethics

DATE: 1933-1945

DEFINITION: Experiments conducted by the German scientific establishment during the period when Adolf Hitler and the Nazi party dominated Germany

SIGNIFICANCE: Graphically illustrates the need for a code of ethics among scientists from all disciplines by depicting the human catastrophe that occurred when able scientists were not guided by such a code

For more than twelve years (January 31, 1933-May 2, 1945), Germany was dominated by a political movement called the *Nationalsozialistische Deutsche Arbeiterpartei* (NSDAP or Nazis, for short). Upon becoming the chancellor of Germany, Nazi leader Adolf Hitler launched the twin programs of *Machtergreifung* and *Gleichschaltung* (the former term meaning "seizure of power" and the latter meaning "coordination"). The Nazis first installed members of their own party or party sympathizers into positions of authority in every government organization in Germany—schools and universities, scientific research institutes, medical facilities, youth groups, women's organizations, museums, philharmonic orchestras, art galleries, and virtually everything else in Germany. Nazis or Nazi sympathizers in those organizations then "coordinated" the activities of the people they controlled with Hitler's view of what all Germans should do and think. German scientists also had to coordinate their experiments with Hitler's own peculiar view of the universe and humanity's place in it. The ultimate result was the destruction of human lives on a scale so massive as to defy understanding.

History. Hitler's understanding of human society represented a vulgarized form of ideas that evolved from scientific experiments and theories in Western Europe and the United States during the nineteenth century. Evolutionists,

NAZI SCIENTIFIC EXPERIMENTS	
Physics	Research program to produce a nuclear bomb
Optics	Research program to establish a giant mirror in low earth orbit, the object being to focus the sun's energy on enemy targets on Earth to incinerate them.
Chemistry	Experiments that succeeded in producing synthetic rubber and synthetic gasoline; development of several new types of poison gases, including nerve gas
Aeronautics	Development of aircraft powered by jet and rocket engines; development of ballistic missiles
Medicine	Experiments on unwilling human subjects, including mass sterilization utilizing X rays, experiments in reviving persons subjected to extremely low temperatures, and experiments in the medical killing of terminally ill and incurably insane patients
Biology	Selective breeding of human beings (the *Lebensborn* program); biological warfare experiments

geneticists, and eugenicists from the so-called "hard" sciences, along with psychologists and Social Darwinists from the "soft" sciences, contributed to the construction in the minds of Hitler and many other people of an essentially racial interpretation of human history.

Evolutionists taught that all members of a species of living organisms are involved in a constant struggle for survival. Those organisms that have inherited characteristics from their ancestors that are best suited for survival will outcompete their less genetically blessed rivals and thus pass along those beneficial traits to their offspring. When scientists rediscovered Mendelian genetics immediately after 1900, many of them began to realize that breeding a superior stock of human beings poses no more of a scientific problem than does the selective breeding of plants and animals. A program of selective human breeding would assure that only desirable characteristics would pass from one generation to the next.

Social Darwinists argued that human races (or nations) are engaged in a struggle for survival, as are the members of individual species. If a nation or race does not possess or adopt the physical and intellectual qualities necessary to allow it to outcompete its rivals, it will be swept into the dustbin of history and become extinct or its members will become subservient to superior nations or races. Social Darwinists combined with advocates of selective human breeding to form the international eugenics movement.

Eugenicists included scientists from every discipline, but especially anthropology, medicine, and psychology. They argued that governments should adopt regulations to assure that future generations would enjoy the best physical and intellectual constitutions that their gene pools could supply. Eugenicists advocated that individuals with congenital diseases of the mind or body should undergo mandatory sterilization to prevent their disabilities from being passed along to future generations. During the 1920's and 1930's, governments in many Western European countries and several state legislatures in the United States adopted laws mandating sterilization for persons with inheritable infirmities.

Some of the eugenicists advocated that enlightened governments should adopt euthanasia programs to eliminate persons with mental or physical disabilities that were of a terminal nature or that rendered them incapable of enjoying an ill-defined "quality of life" acceptable to the euthanasists. The euthanasists tried to convince governments that the inmates of medical clinics, hospitals, and insane asylums should be screened by qualified physicians who would determine whether their lives were of any further value to themselves or to society. Those inmates deemed by screening physicians to be incurably ill (mentally or physically) or as "useless eaters" should, according to the euthanasists, be granted "mercy deaths." Only in Nazi Germany did the government adopt euthanasia. The German euthanasia program led directly to mass murders in Nazi concentration camps.

The Nazi government also coopted all the other sciences in Germany to advance its own view of how Germany and the world should be organized. The sciences of aeronautical engineering, chemistry, and physics in particular became integral parts of a huge military-industrial complex designed to make advanced weapons of war. In Hitler's Social Darwinistic worldview, war was a natural and necessary condition of human evolution. In his semiautobiographical *Mein Kampf* (1926), Hitler clearly expressed his intent to conquer territory in the Soviet Union into which the German race could expand. As one of his earliest actions after attaining dictatorial power in Germany, Hitler began a massive expansion of the German armed forces. German scientists from every discipline began to devote their research to areas that would further Hitler's military intentions.

Some German scientists began programs that led to the development of the world's first operational jet fighter aircraft. Others began developing experiments in rocketry that culminated in the V-2, a ballistic missile that wreaked great havoc among civilians in Britain. German chemists developed toxic gases (never used) that were more deadly than any that had been used in World War I. Chemists also discovered how to make synthetic rubber as well as synthetic gasoline derived from coal, in an effort to assure that the German war machine could continue to function even if it were cut off from supplies of petroleum and rubber by an enemy blockade. German physicists began research designed to produce revolutionary new weapons of war, including a program that almost produced a nuclear bomb. Other exotic weapons-systems research included plans for a giant mirror that, when placed in low Earth orbit, could focus the sun's rays on any spot on Earth with devastating results.

Perhaps the most flagrant violations of accepted scientific ethical principles in Germany during the Nazi era occurred in medical science. Medical researchers in some concentration camps routinely used unwilling human subjects in macabre experiments that often resulted in the death or disfigurement of the subjects. Physicians in concentration camps, medical clinics, and insane asylums willingly participated in "selections" (determining whether individuals were fit for work or should be summarily executed). In the case of some of the concentration camps, physicians made these selections without conducting even cursory medical examinations. The physicians also extracted organs from the cadavers of those who had been killed and sent them to medical research institutes throughout Germany for experimentation. Physicians perpetrated this dismemberment without the knowledge or approval of the victims or the victims' families.

Many scientists presently condemn the atrocities that were committed in the name of science in Germany during the Nazi era. They believe that German scientists of the period abandoned all accepted ethical principles while they were caught up in a national madness brought on by extraordinary circumstances. A number of the German scientists involved, however, maintained that their actions were entirely ethical, because they were all intended to serve the highest good—

the improvement of the human condition. In the long view of history, they maintained, the human race will benefit enormously from their actions—materially, physically, and intellectually. The Nazi scientists adopted the position that, in science, the end justifies the means. Many scientists in all countries today accept that position, at least to some degree. Perhaps more than any other event in history, the Nazi era underscores the absolute necessity of a universally accepted code of scientific ethics if any semblance of humanity is to be maintained in the wake of an increasingly technological and scientific society. —*Paul Madden*

See also Experimentation, ethics of; Hitler, Adolf; Holocaust; Nazism.

BIBLIOGRAPHY

Beyerchen, Alan D. *Scientists under Hitler: Politics and the Physics Community in the Third Reich*. New Haven, Conn.: Yale University Press, 1977.

Bracher, Karl Dietrich. *The German Dictatorship: The Origins, Structure, and Effects of National Socialism*. Translated by Jean Steinberg. New York: Praeger, 1970.

Cecil, Robert. *The Myth of the Master Race: Alfred Rosenberg and Nazi Ideology*. New York: Dodd, Mead, 1972.

Lifton, Robert Jay. *The Nazi Doctors: Medical Killing and the Psychology of Genocide*. New York: Basic Books, 1986.

Muller-Hill, Benno. *Murderous Science: Elimination by Scientific Selection of Jews, Gypsies, and Others, Germany 1933-1945*. New York: Oxford University Press, 1988.

Nazism

TYPE OF ETHICS: Modern history
DATE: 1919-1945
ASSOCIATED WITH: Adolf Hitler and Germany
DEFINITION: A German political movement that advocated racial nationalism, including anti-Semitism, dictatorial government, and expansion into eastern Europe by means of war
SIGNIFICANCE: Nazism denied Western liberalism and democracy by denying human and civil rights and by committing ruthless aggression in international relations

Nazism, a contraction of the term "National Socialism," was a German political movement that emerged in the aftermath of World War I with Adolf Hitler as its leader. From the very start, it espoused ideas that rejected Western values of humanitarianism, rationalism, liberalism, democracy, and socialism in favor of extreme nationalism, racism, and a political system of single-party dictatorship. Nazi policies and practices violated human and civil rights, first in Germany and later in conquered Europe, and resorted to violent power politics in international affairs.

The forerunner of Nazism as a political party was the German Workers' Party, which was organized in Munich early in 1919. Adolf Hitler, a lower-middle-class Austrian by birth and a corporal in the German army during World War I, joined the German Workers' Party later in the year. It soon was renamed the National Socialist German Workers'

Party, and Hitler, showing oratorical and organizational talent, became its undisputed leader in 1921.

The main tenets of Nazism were drawn from the party program of 1920, Hitler's speeches and writings (especially his ponderous two-volume *Mein Kampf* [*My Struggle*], published in 1925 and 1926), and other Nazi publications. They attacked liberalism and parliamentarianism, including democracy, as inherently weak political systems and branded the early leaders of the Weimar Republic, liberals, socialists, and Jews as "November criminals" of 1918, who had overthrown the imperial government. In place of the failed parliamentary democracy, Nazism offered authoritarian rule rooted in a solid hierarchical system of leaders and followers. At the head would be a *Führer*, or "leader," who, with the support of the Nazi party, would exercise total control over the society and mobilize it for the achievement of the political and social goals that he postulated.

Nazism, above all, extolled racial nationalism, which was derived from the nineteenth century racial theories of the Frenchman Joseph-Arthur de Gobineau, the Germanized Englishman Houston Chamberlain, and the German Paul de Lagarde. Proponents of Nazism contended that human races were divided into culture-creating and culture-destroying groups, which were engaged in a Social Darwinian struggle of survival of the fittest. At the top of the culture-creating races stood the Nordic-Aryan-Germanic group, the "master race," which was destined to dominate inferior races. At Hitler's instigation, Nazism singled out the Jews as the greatest threat to the pure Aryans because the Jews, the leading culture-destroying race, were conspiring to gain domination over the world. In Nazi foreign policy, the idea of the primacy of the Aryan race was combined with a Great German nationalism or imperialism, whose aim it was to create a Great German empire far beyond the borders of the German nation. Such an expansion was to give the German people the *Lebensraum*, or "living space," that it needed to ensure its security and economic independence.

The Nazis did not conceal that they would attain power legally, but once in office they would destroy the constitutional system. Within one month after Hitler was appointed chancellor early in 1933, he had communists and many socialists confined to quickly established concentration camps and suspended civil rights. Through cajolery, pressure, and terror, he prevailed upon the Reichstag ("parliament") to give him dictatorial powers, which he used to eliminate trade unions and all political parties except the Nazi party. In 1934, he murdered the top leadership of the Storm Troopers, or S.A., and some non-Nazis, when he felt threatened by a rival from within his own ranks. He justified these acts of criminality by declaring: "I was responsible for the fate of the German people and thereby I became the Supreme Judge of the German people."

The Nazi practices of eliminating opponents by sending them to concentration camps or murdering them, persecuting Jews purely on racial grounds, maintaining a police state,

Nazi leader Adolf Hitler is saluted after announcing the annexation of Austria at the Reichstag. (National Archives)

and pursuing an aggressive foreign policy left no room for the observance of ethical principles in politics. It is important to realize, however, that liberal democratic governments also generally do not feel bound by ethical constraints if the national interest is at stake. Though idealists among philosophers and scholars argue that, for example, foreign policy must be based on prudence and ethical principle, realists on the order of George Kennan (and they are a majority) maintain that in world politics moral or ethical concerns must be subordinated to national interest. Given the absence of accepted international standards of morality and effective bodies of enforcement when violations occur, each government, being concerned with military security, the integrity of its political life, and the well-being of its citizens, must act on its own to protect its national interests. Implied in this stance, however, is a sense of moderation and responsibility when pursuing the national interest in international relations.

The Nazi regime under Hitler's direction defined national interest in the most expansive terms. Hitler once characterized Germany's foreign policy by declaring: "Germany will become a world power or it will not exist at all." In the early years of Nazi dictatorship, he and his associates constantly proclaimed the German Reich's "sincere desire for peace," while unilaterally abrogating the restrictions of the Treaty of Versailles, rearming Germany, and then, in 1938, annexing Austria and the German-speaking Sudetenland of Czechoslovakia. In 1939, Nazi Germany unleashed World War II through aggression against Poland, followed by campaigns into France and other European countries in 1940. One year later, Hitler attacked the Soviet Union, waging an unparalleled brutal ideological war in the quest for *Lebensraum* in the East.

While worldwide violence was raging as a result of war, the Nazi regime also prepared for the elimination of "racially inferior" populaces and "those of lesser value" in society. The persecution of German Jews culminated in the violence against Jewish property and people of the *Kristallnacht* of 1938. With the outbreak of the war in

1939, a euthanasia program was begun, resulting in the killing by injection or by gassing of almost 100,000 mentally and physically handicapped persons, most of whom were German. Finally, the plan to liquidate all European Jews in Nazi hands—the Final Solution—was implemented by Hitler and some of his immediate associates in 1941. It claimed the lives of almost six million people. In addition, Nazi actions led to the murder of millions of Gypsies, Slavs, homosexuals, and other racial and political "enemies." This unprecedented mechanized genocide was only stopped by the defeat of Nazi Germany and the suicide of Adolf Hitler in 1945.

After the total defeat of Germany and the inglorious death of the *Führer*, Nazism never revived as a significant force. Following the establishment of the Federal Republic of Germany in 1949, its Federal Constitutional Court outlawed the noisy but unimportant Socialist Reich party in 1952 as a neo-Nazi organization. In the 1960's and 1980's, two right-wing parties were formed: the National Democratic Party and the Republicans. Both have shown some neo-Nazi features but have achieved little influence. More noteworthy have been a number of small neo-Nazi groups formed since the 1970's, whose racist hate propaganda and violence, directed not primarily against Jews but against foreigners, especially Turks, have aroused consternation since the unification of Germany in 1990. These groups cannot, however, be viewed as the forerunners of an organized neo-Nazi movement.

—George P. Blum

See also Anti-Semitism; Ethnic cleansing; Hitler, Adolf; Holocaust; Nuremberg Trials.

BIBLIOGRAPHY

Bracher, K. D. *The German Dictatorship: The Origins, Structure, and Effects of National Socialism.* Translated by Jean Steinberg. New York: Praeger, 1970.

Bullock, Alan. *Hitler: A Study in Tyranny.* Rev. ed. New York: Harper & Row, 1962.

Donahue, Anne Marie, ed. *Ethics in Politics and Government.* New York: H. W. Wilson, 1989.

Fleming, Gerald. *Hitler and the Final Solution.* Berkeley: University of California Press, 1984.

Hitler, Adolf. *Mein Kampf.* Translated by Ralph Manheim. Boston: Houghton Mifflin, 1971.

Jackel, Eberhard. *Hitler's Weltanschauung: A Blueprint for Power.* Translated by Herbert Arnold. Middletown, Conn.: Wesleyan University Press, 1972.

Spielvogel, Jackson J. *Hitler and Nazi Germany: A History.* 2d ed. Englewood Cliffs, N.J.: Prentice-Hall, 1992.

Negligence

TYPE OF ETHICS: Business and labor ethics
DATE: Entered English in twelfth century; present in ancient Roman law as *necligentia*
ASSOCIATED WITH: Commerce and law
DEFINITION: The failure to maintain due standards of care in one's actions, whether in general or in those specific duties one has undertaken by office or profession, thereby causing or potentially causing harm to another
SIGNIFICANCE: Negligence raises interesting and unique questions about the relationship of intentionality to guilt; virtually all moral relations have a potential for negligence

Negligence has long been an important concept in both ethics and law. In ethics, the notion of negligence arises out of the conception that one owes a duty of a degree of care toward one's fellow humans in all one's activities and that under given circumstances, one may owe even greater degrees of care arising out of special duties that one takes upon oneself in virtue of the public office or profession one has assumed.

Law and morality both recognize a distinction between advertent negligence, which involves the wrongdoer's proceeding with acts after recognizing the dangerous nature of those actions or omissions, and inadvertent negligence, which involves the wrongdoer's undertaking dangerous acts (or omissions) without having recognized the risk that they impose upon others. The former, which is often called recklessness, is generally regarded as the more culpable form, while the latter raises complex theoretical difficulties for ethicians and legal scholars.

The primary problem with inadvertent negligence both in ethics and in law arises from the seeming contradiction between the nature of such negligence and the deliberate intentionality requisite for an act to be culpable. In moral theory, the problem is easily resolved by linking the inadvertent negligence to the idea of culpable ignorance.

The wrongdoer behaved unsafely because he did not know the potential consequences of his actions, but this ignorance does not exculpate him because he should have known. At some time in his past, he failed to acquire the knowledge necessary to recognize the character of his acts. If this failure resulted from deliberate neglect on the part of the wrongdoer—for example, skipping sessions of his job training—then this was culpable ignorance and the wrongs which flowed from it were blameworthy.

In the case of legal negligence, both civil and criminal, more difficult problems seem to present themselves. Criminal guilt usually involves both an *actus reus*, or guilty act, and a *mens rea*, or guilty mind (criminal intention). H. L. A. Hart, the noted British legal philosopher, wrestled with this problem without reaching a conclusive solution: How can inadvertent negligence have a *mens rea*? If one were to recognize the nature and potential consequences of one's act(s), would one not be guilty of advertent negligence, or worse?

The answer to this puzzle may lie in a nonproximate *mens rea* that the law may be seen as assuming to exist in the absence of plausible proof to the contrary. Take, for example, the case of a roofer who has been carefully dropping waste materials from a roof into a dumpster several floors below. Suddenly, after such care, he hurls a bucket off the roof without checking its trajectory and injures a pedestrian below.

The roofer testifies at his trial that he does not know why he threw the bucket as he did and that he gave no thought to the dangers involved in such an act. If he is believed, he will be convicted of an offense connected with inadvertent negligence. If the roofer could provide a plausible explanation of his action that could trace its origins to a cause ultimately outside the roofer's control, however, he might expect acquittal.

Assume that the roofer produces proof that the tar he employed—a new variety on the market—emitted hallucinogenic fumes and that he was working with that tar just before the allegedly negligent incident. If his proofs were accepted, he would doubtlessly be exonerated, because he had indicated a cause for his actions that lay outside his control.

In the absence of such proof, however, the unstated assumption of the law must be that at some earlier time—perhaps even years before—the defendant developed (by omission or commission) habits of mind that were likely ultimately to lead to negligent actions in the future and that in the acquisition of these habits lay the culpability.

The acceptance of those habits of mind constitutes a nonproximate *mens rea* for any negligent acts that might later be done as a result. This interpretation demonstrates that the law of negligence is not a strict liability statute—that is, one enforced without regard to intentionality—as some have maintained.

Another difficulty that has perplexed legal theorists involves whether the standard of negligence should be objective or subjective. H. L. A. Hart stated that the objective standard attributes fault to an agent who failed "to take those precautions which any reasonable man with normal capacities would in the circumstances have taken." A subjective standard would give greater weight to the particular circumstances and capacities of the subject.

Finally, there is the question of the relationship of the degree of blameworthiness in negligent acts to the actual results that flow from them. A negligent driver (for example, one using excessive speed) might injure somebody or might not. Under one theory, his blameworthiness remains the same despite the external circumstances, but others have asserted that effects in the extramental world are a factor in guilt, as a result of so-called "moral luck."

—*Patrick M. O'Neil*

See also Business ethics; Duty; Employees, safety and treatment of; Professional ethics; Prudence.

BIBLIOGRAPHY

Feinberg, Joel. *Doing & Deserving*. Princeton, N.J.: Princeton University Press, 1970.

Hart, H. L. A. *Punishment and Responsibility*. Oxford: Clarendon Press, 1968.

Milo, Ronald D. *Immorality*. Princeton, N.J.: Princeton University Press, 1984.

Morris, Herbert. *Freedom and Responsibility*. Stanford, Calif.: Stanford University Press, 1961.

Smith, Holly. "Culpable Ignorance." *Philosophical Review* 92 (October, 1983): 543-572.

New York Times Co. v. Sullivan

TYPE OF ETHICS: Media ethics

DATE: 1964

ASSOCIATED WITH: U.S. Supreme Court

DEFINITION: The Court's decision limited states' authority to award libel damages based on their own laws and established "actual malice" as the standard for cases involving public officials, later expanded to include "public figures"

SIGNIFICANCE: This case represents an advance in personal and press freedom of speech by preventing legitimate social criticism and commentary from being repressed by the threat of lawsuits

New York Times Co. v. Sullivan was sparked by an advertisement placed in *The New York Times* in 1960 by the Committee to Defend Martin Luther King and the Struggle for Freedom in the South. The advertisement, which was meant to raise support for King's civil rights movement, criticized several Southern jurisdictions, including Montgomery, Alabama, although it did not name any individuals. In response, Montgomery City Commissioner L. B. Sullivan sued the *Times* for libel in circuit court, which found the newspaper guilty under Alabama law. After the Alabama Supreme Court affirmed this judgment, the *Times* appealed to the Supreme Court, claiming violations of its rights of free speech and due process under the First and Fourteenth Amendments to the Constitution. The Court held unanimously that Alabama law failed to protect adequately freedom of speech and of the press, and that "actual malice" would henceforth be the national standard for determining libel actions involving public officials.

See also Due process; First Amendment; Libel.

Nicomachean Ethics: Book

TYPE OF ETHICS: Classical history

DATE: Probably between 335 and 323 B.C.E.

AUTHOR: Aristotle; recorded by Aristotle's son Nicomachus

SIGNIFICANCE: Defines a virtuous person as one who desires the good that the intellect discerns; such a good is usually a mean between the extremes of too much and too little

Aristotle assumes that all things, human beings included, have a good, a purpose or end, which it is their nature to fulfill. To understand the virtue of human nature, one must discover the specific good that is its purpose. Human nature, in Aristotle's analysis, has two levels: the nonrational and the rational. Each level has its good and corresponding virtue.

The virtue of the rational level is to recognize and contemplate truth. This purely intellectual virtue has value in itself but is not sufficient for morality. Morality is only possible when both levels of human nature work together.

The nonrational level of human nature includes vegetative functions, such as biological growth, over which reason has no control, and appetitive functions, such as hunger and sexual desire, which can be guided by reason. The virtue of this level of human nature occurs when the "appetite" comes to desire the good that the intellect discerns. This is moral virtue. It requires not only insight but also practice that cultivates moral behavior into habit.

In most cases, Aristotle says, the good is a mean between two extremes. Courage, for example, is the good that lies between rashness (too much) and cowardice (too little).

See also Aristotelian ethics; Aristotle.

Niebuhr, H. Richard (Sept. 3, 1894, Wright City, Mo.—July 5, 1962, Greenfield, Mass.): Theologian

TYPE OF ETHICS: Religious ethics

ACHIEVEMENTS: The author of important books such as *The Meaning of Revelation* (1941) and *Christ and Culture* (1951), Niebuhr became one of the leading Christian ethicists of the twentieth century

SIGNIFICANCE: Niebuhr used insights from history, sociology, psychology, and philosophy to explore ways in which the Christian faith could help to transform and redeem the world

H. Richard Niebuhr taught and wrote in the heyday of Christian theology in the twentieth century. Karl Barth, Paul Tillich, and his own brother Reinhold were his contemporaries. Niebuhr's ethics emphasized perpetual reformation. His evaluation of Christianity in the United States convinced him that Christian faith everywhere had to keep attuned to the God who could free it from cultural enslavement. To the degree that Christian communities made the "fitting response," they could spark a transformation that would bring the world closer to the kingdom of God. Niebuhr's greatest contribution may be his way of engaging in ethical reflection. His thought moved back and forth between society and human encounters with the ultimate. His ethics aimed at turning rigidity into openness, misplaced absoluteness into creative relativity, and the difficulties of history into movements of responsible faith. Thus, if adjectives such as existential, relativistic, and cultural are necessary to describe Niebuhr's ethics, no less accurate are terms such as theocentric, communal, and universalistic.

See also Christian ethics; Niebuhr, Reinhold.

Niebuhr, Reinhold (June 21, 1892, Wright City, Mo.—June 1, 1971, Stockbridge, Mass.): Theologian

TYPE OF ETHICS: Religious ethics

ACHIEVEMENTS: Revised and promoted the social gospel movement of the early twentieth century

SIGNIFICANCE: Niebuhr's political and social activism demonstrated that his brand of Christianity was relevant to the practical issues of his day

Reinhold Niebuhr, the son of an immigrant minister, was born in Wright City, Missouri, in 1892. After studying at Eden Theological Seminary and Yale Divinity School, he became in 1915 the pastor of the Bethel Evangelical Church in Detroit, where he took an active role combating racial prejudice and supporting labor's right to strike. In 1928, Henry Sloane Coffin offered Niebuhr a teaching position at Union Theological Seminary in New York; Niebuhr remained there until his retirement in 1960.

Although Niebuhr continued his social activism while at Union, he also became famous as a writer and as a professor of Applied Christianity. He wrote more than twenty books and 1,500 articles, reviews, and editorials. Among his important topics were liberalism and fundamentalism, and the nature of faith in the light of history and science. Perhaps his most significant contribution to American social ethics was in his rethinking of the social gospel, a religious movement prevalent in early twentieth century American theology that optimistically held that people, through their efforts to reform society, could help God bring his kingdom to Earth in the near future.

Niebuhr did not think that the problems of society could be easily solved, for to him, social decisions presented themselves as choices between relative evils. In his writings, he focused on the limitations imposed by evil. Niebuhr argued that, although individuals were capable of moral behavior and development, nations, corporations, labor unions, and other such collective entities were not, because pride more easily manifested itself in groups.

See also Christian ethics; Niebuhr, H. Richard.

Nietzsche, Friedrich (Oct. 15, 1844, Röcken, Saxony, Prussia—Aug. 25, 1900, Weimar, Germany): Philosopher

TYPE OF ETHICS: Modern history

ACHIEVEMENTS: Author of *Beyond Good and Evil* (1886) and *On the Genealogy of Morals* (1887)

SIGNIFICANCE: Interpreted ethics as an expression of humanity's "will to power"; encouraged moral relativism through reevaluation of traditional ethical theories and their absolute principles

Nietzsche attacked traditional ethical theories, especially those rooted in religion. He did so because he believed that human life has no moral purpose except for the meaning that human beings give it. His outlook encouraged moral relativism, but he also advocated a demanding personal ethical perspective of his own. It emphasized the individual will, excellence, and discipline. In both its critical and its affirmative dimensions, Nietzsche's philosophy continues to have profound effects on moral theory and practice.

The Will to Power. "We are unknown to ourselves, we men of knowledge—and with good reason." Thus begins Nietzsche's *On the Genealogy of Morals*. His theme was that even though people may regard themselves as well informed, sophisticated, and knowledgeable, their lack of courage keeps them from uncovering what is happening in human existence and morality. Nietzsche tried to check this plague of self-delusion.

Nietzsche contended that it is self-deception not to admit honestly that "life simply *is* will to power." He was no advocate of the democratic ideal of human equality. Such a doctrine, he thought, only levels the quality of life toward mediocrity. Individuals vary greatly in their talents and abilities, and there are basic qualitative differences that leave us unequal as persons. Nevertheless, each individual, according to Nietzsche, will do what he or she can do to assert power.

Beyond Good and Evil. As Nietzsche interpreted the course of human history, Western culture had been dominated by an unfortunate distinction between "good" and "evil," a distinction that the Christian religion in particular has done much to encourage. Spurred by a deep hatred of aristocratic ways they could not emulate, the masses of humanity, often supported by religious leaders, indulged in a revenge-motivated negation of the qualities of an aristocratic life. As Nietzsche saw things, the "good" of the good-evil distinction had emphasized equality, selflessness, meekness, humility, sympathy, pity, and other qualities of weakness. It had castigated the noble, aristocratic qualities—self-assertion, daring creativity, passion, and desire for conquest—by calling them evil. The prevalence of this concept of evil, Nietzsche contended, is responsible for weakness and mediocrity among those in dominant positions. It has annihilated the qualities that are essential for excellence in life.

Human existence, however, need not end on this dismal note. If Nietzsche sometimes regarded himself as a voice crying in the wilderness, he also thought human life could redeem itself by going "beyond good and evil": "Must not the ancient fire some day flare up much more terribly, after much longer preparation?" he wrote. "More: must one not desire it with all one's might? even will it? even promote it?" The spirit of nobility—affirmation of life, struggle, conquest, and a passionate desire to excel—these characteristics need to be uplifted. Nietzsche's aim, however, was not to duplicate the past but to put these essential qualities back into contemporary life.

God Is Dead. Nietzsche's proclamation of the death of God was a fundamental ingredient in the reevaluation of values Nietzsche advocated. This proclamation emerged from his conviction that the morality of mediocrity and affirmations of God's existence, especially as the latter are understood in Christianity, stand inextricably tied together. Nothing, argued Nietzsche, has done more than Christianity to entrench the morality of mediocrity in human consciousness. In Nietzsche's view, for example, the Christian emphasis on love extols qualities of weakness. Christianity urges that it is our responsibility to cultivate those attributes, not because of an abstract concept of duty but because it is God's will that we do so. As this conception developed, Nietzsche argued, it bound people in debilitating guilt. It also led them to an escapist tendency to seek for fulfillment beyond this world.

Arguably one-sided, Nietzsche's critique was loud and clear: Christianity, with its conception of a transcendent, omnipotent, omniscient, just, and loving God, denies and negates too much that is valuable in this world. Nietzsche did not deny that the long dominance of the Christian faith is a real manifestation of the will to power and that certain individuals have revealed unusual qualities of strength in establishing Christianity's authority. He was convinced, however, that the result has been to place an inferior breed in control of life. Nietzsche believed that,

by proclaiming that God is dead, he would eliminate the underpinning of Christian morality, thus making it less difficult to move beyond the conventional understanding of good and evil.

The issue of God's existence, believed Nietzsche, is more psychological than metaphysical. That is, Nietzsche thought that belief in God is an additional tool used to distort the facts of life and to attack and to bring to submission individuals of noble character. His aim was not so much to prove or disprove the existence of God as to show that belief in God can create a sickness. He wanted to convince people that the highest achievements in human life depend on the elimination of this belief.

Implications for Ethical Conduct. Nietzsche's philosophy places strong demands on those who would live by it. He urged such people to consider that life is an eternal recurrence. Therefore, one ought to choose so there is no need for regret. The goal is to act so that, if confronted by an identical situation an infinite number of times, one could honestly say that one would do nothing differently.

—John K. Roth

See also *Beyond Good and Evil*; Egoism; Individualism; Relativism; Selfishness; Will.

BIBLIOGRAPHY

Hayman, Ronald. *Nietzsche: A Critical Life*. New York: Oxford University Press, 1980.

Heller, Erich. *The Importance of Nietzsche: Ten Essays*. Chicago: University of Chicago Press, 1988.

Kaufmann, Walter. *Nietzsche: Philosopher, Psychologist, Antichrist*. Princeton, N.J.: Princeton University Press, 1950, 1974.

Koelb, Clayton, ed. *Nietzsche as Postmodernist: Essays Pro and Contra*. Albany: State University of New York Press, 1990.

Nehamas, Alexander. *Nietzsche: Life as Literature*. Cambridge, Mass.: Harvard University Press, 1985.

Nietzsche, Friedrich. *Beyond Good and Evil*. Translated by Walter Kaufmann. New York: Vintage Books, 1966.

_____. *On the Genealogy of Morals*. Translated by Walter Kaufmann and R. J. Hollingdale. New York: Vintage Books, 1967.

Schacht, Richard. *Nietzsche*. London: Routledge, 1983.

Nihilism

TYPE OF ETHICS: Modern history

DATE: First used in the 1780's; popularized in the mid-1800's

ASSOCIATED WITH: Russian novelists Ivan Turgenev and Fyodor Dostoevski; German philosopher Friedrich Nietzsche

DEFINITION: The doctrine that there is no rational foundation for truth and that existence is without meaning

SIGNIFICANCE: Results in an inability to make ethical judgments, to say what is right or wrong

Nihilism in general refers to the view that the world is without meaning. It is often used as a term of criticism, for if a philosophical position can be shown to result in nihilism, its assumptions may warrant reexamination. Other thinkers maintain that nihilism is a tenable position to hold.

Jacobi. The term "nihilism" was first used by the German philosopher Friedrich Jacobi. Jacobi criticized modern philosophy's faith in reason as the foundation of all knowledge. The rationalist doubts everything but what the mind can discover by itself. For Jacobi, this skeptical approach must culminate in the belief that nothing exists, for there is no rational foundation for belief in anything outside one's own mind. For Jacobi, reason affirmed nothing, and he called the belief in nothing "nihilism," from the Latin word *nihil*, meaning "nothing."

In his *David Hume on Belief: Or, Idealism and Realism* (1787), Jacobi argues that the radical skepticism of Hume is in fact nihilism. The nihilist, as epitomized for Jacobi by Hume, sees no justification for belief in the existence of the external world, other people, God, or even a self.

Nihilism, then, is primarily a problem with the theory of knowledge for Jacobi. The reliance of modern philosophy on reason as the source of all knowledge leads to an unacceptable outcome, and therefore the reliance on reason alone must be misguided.

Nihilism also has unacceptable ethical implications, according to Jacobi. If nothing exists outside one's own mind, there can be no ethical obligations to other beings. The nihilist is free to decide what is right or wrong. Whatever the nihilist wills is good, because there is no standard for goodness other than what the mind itself wills.

Russian Nihilism. Nihilism first came into popular use in Russia in the mid-1800's, as both a literary and a political term. In Ivan Turgenev's novel *Fathers and Sons* (1862), the character Bazarov proudly declares himself a nihilist. For Turgenev, nihilism entails rejecting tradition in favor of scientific rationalism and materialism.

As a political movement in Russia, nihilism was associated with belief in radical freedom, a questioning of all social conventions and authority. The nihilists saw themselves as the vanguard of social change, exposing tyranny and hypocrisy in the name of reason. Factions of the movement degenerated into advocating anarchism and terrorism.

For Fyodor Dostoevski, nihilism is associated with atheism. In *The Brothers Karamazov* (1880), Ivan Karamazov declares, "If God does not exist, then everything is permitted," exemplifying the destructive ethical consequences of nihilism. There is no basis on which to call any act right or wrong. The individual has complete freedom to follow all desires and impulses and to declare these desires good.

Nietzsche. The figure in philosophy with whom nihilism is most closely associated is the German philosopher Friedrich Nietzsche (1844-1900). He uses the term in both a negative and a positive sense. As a term of criticism, he uses it to describe the result of Western culture's search for truth. In Nietzsche's view, this search began with Socrates' dialectic method as seen in the dialogues of Plato. He sees the reliance on rational inquiry as undermining the healthy, noble, and artistic instincts typified by the ancient Greek tragedians.

In *The Will to Power* (1887), Nietzsche asks: "What does nihilism mean? That the highest values devaluate themselves." Western culture values truth most highly, but the very search for truth is destined for failure at the outset because, according to Nietzsche, there is in fact no truth to be discovered. He sees himself as the first person to fully grasp this insight, but he believes that the history of modern thought has increasingly moved toward the same realization and thus toward nihilism. The entire enterprise of truth-seeking is in fact nihilistic because it avoids the reality that there is no truth.

In *Thus Spoke Zarathustra* (1884), Nietzsche prophesies that Western civilization will culminate in the "last men," who are aware that there is no foundation for values or truth, but who are indifferent to this lack. The last men will live a life of pleasure, relieved of the burden of seeking truth and of any moral duties that an objective right or wrong might require. Nietzsche calls this attitude "passive nihilism."

Out of the last men will emerge an "overman," one who fully recognizes that there is no independent meaning or value in the world. The overman in this sense is a nihilist also. In contrast to the last men, however, he sees that the lack of independent meaning gives him the power to create his own truth. This realization enables him to create a world of significance in his own image, breaking free of the passive nihilism of the last men. Nietzsche calls the overman's creative response to nihilism "active nihilism," and sees this creation of meaning out of nothing as the highest, noblest task for humans.

The Twentieth Century. A number of twentieth century philosophers argue that it is impossible to justify moral judgments rationally. Nihilism is sometimes used as a critical term to describe these views. For example, the emotivist Charles Stevenson argues that moral judgments are merely aesthetic expressions of approval or disapproval and cannot be proved or disproved. Similarly, the existentialism of Jean-Paul Sartre and Albert Camus asserts that moral judgments are always simply the arbitrary decisions of individuals.

—Paul Gallagher

See also Anarchy; *Being and Nothingness*; *Beyond Good and Evil*; Camus, Albert; Dostoevski, Fyodor; Emotivist ethics; Sartre, Jean-Paul.

BIBLIOGRAPHY

Allison, David, ed. *The New Nietzsche*. Cambridge, Mass.: MIT University Press, 1985.

Beiser, Frederick. *The Fate of Reason*. Cambridge, Mass.: Harvard University Press, 1987.

Heidegger, Martin. *Nietzsche*. Translated by David F. Krell. San Francisco: Harper & Row, 1979-1987.

Rosen, Stanley. *Nihilism*. New Haven, Conn.: Yale University Press, 1969.

Yarmolinsky, Avrahm. *Road to Revolution*. Princeton, N.J.: Princeton University Press, 1986.

Nirvana

TYPE OF ETHICS: Religious ethics
DATE: Established c. 600 B.C.E.
ASSOCIATED WITH: Buddhism, Hinduism, and Jainism
DEFINITION: Nirvana is the highest good of Buddhism, but the way in which nirvana is understood varies from community to community and from epoch to epoch; the earliest interpretation, still held by Theravāda Buddhists, is that nirvana is the enlightenment of the individual leading to the cessation of desire and rebirth; later interpretations, developed especially in Mahāyāna and Vajrayāna Buddhism, emphasize the moral and physical significance of nirvana
SIGNIFICANCE: The understanding of nirvana governs the ethical practices of Buddhists, and ethical practices assist in the attainment of nirvana

The term "nirvana" (Sanskrit, *nirvāṇa*) is used to designate the ultimate reality in Buddhist traditions. While the Hindu and Jain traditions also employ this concept, nirvana has received its most distinctive formulations in the many varieties of Buddhism.

Early Interpretations. According to Buddhist tradition, Siddhārtha Gautama achieved enlightenment more than 2,500 years ago and came to see the true nature of existence. The Pali scriptures relate that in that moment Gautama, now referred to as the Buddha, or awakened one, realized both the fundamental problem of existence and its solution. The Buddha's message, based on this moment of insight, was that the basic quality of existence is *duḥkha*, which connotes suffering, illness, emptiness, unsatisfactoriness, and insubstantiality. In his analysis of this situation, the Buddha stated that the pervasive reality of *duḥkha* is predicated on a false understanding of the nature of the self. People suffer anguish because they believe in a permanent, substantial self or soul, a belief that generates obsessive craving *(tṛṣṇa)* for objects, experiences, ideals, or persons that will provide comfort, security, and enrichment for the "self." Transient reality, however, is unable to fulfill human desires. Those things that people expect to satisfy their cravings for permanence and happiness are unable to do so because they are insubstantial and evanescent. The more people grasp, the more they suffer and, according to Buddhist teaching, the more they are reborn into the world of *saṃsāra*. (The Buddhist traditions accept many of the Hindu assumptions about the nature of reincarnation.)

The Buddha then offered a practical solution to the problem of *duḥkha*. If the cause of anguish is a mistaken belief, then its resolution lies in gaining wisdom, or enlightenment. Enlightenment reveals the insubstantiality of the self (*anātman*) and shows that what is called "self" (Buddhists often use the term "ego" to designate this construction) is merely a constantly changing constellation of energies (aggregates of being). The deep existential appropriation of this insight has profound behavioral and moral consequences, beginning with the cessation of craving. The *arhat* (one who has achieved enlightenment) has realized nirvana, the absolute state of perfect wisdom and

release from the cycle of rebirth.

Nirvana is most often described in negative terms, not because it designates a negative state, but because it names a reality that is beyond ordinary experience and hence beyond the limitations of language. Nirvana is "the eradication of ignorance," "the elimination of suffering," and the "end of desire." Translated literally, nirvana is "extinction." Unfortunately, this meaning has often conveyed to the Western mind the misleading impression that Buddhism is a nihilistic religious tradition. Nirvana does not mean extinction of the self—since in Buddhism there is no real self—but rather the extinction of the illusion of self. Referred to in more positive terms, nirvana is bliss, absolute happiness, and unconditioned tranquillity.

Tradition distinguishes between two modes of nirvana: nirvana with substrate (*sopadhiśeṣa nirvāṇa*) and nirvana without substrate (*nirupadhiśeṣa nirvāṇa*). The distinction names the difference between the arhat who lives and the one who is dead, or the difference between nirvana and final nirvana (*parinirvāṇa*). As a living person, the arhat may still experience physical pain and other forms of karmic fruition (the consequences of previous actions). At *parinirvāṇa*, however, all karmic energies are dissipated and the arhat is released from rebirth. The Buddha refused to answer his disciples' questions about the nature of final nirvana. At most, he would say that final nirvana is neither nothingness nor not-nothingness, a paradoxical way of stating that the unconditional is beyond ordinary comprehension.

Nirvana is intrinsically related to the ethical outlook of Buddhism. The path to nirvana is in great measure an ethical one. The Buddha prescribed for his followers a regimen that included study, meditation practice, and moral behavior (the eightfold noble path). He encouraged his followers to live by specific precepts, which were to be accepted not as commandments but as principles for striving to live a compassionate and egoless existence. Among these precepts were abstaining from false speech, not harming sentient beings (*ahiṃsā*), not taking that which is not offered, abstaining from sexual misconduct, not consuming alcohol or other drugs, and earning one's living in a way that helps rather than harms other beings. The Buddha also counseled the cultivation of wholesome characteristics such as friendliness, patience, and compassion. Each aspect of the Buddhist path is intended to enable the individual to overcome the ego's tendency to become attached (or addicted) to things, persons, and ideas. The path fosters nonattachment and egolessness, which advances one's progress toward enlightenment. Wisdom and morality therefore are inextricably connected. To behave in a purely selfless way, one must grasp the truth about the nature of existence, especially the nonexistence of the self; and to realize this truth, one must follow the precepts that help remove the obstacles that hinder awareness.

Later Interpretations. In subsequent development of the Buddhist traditions (particularly in the Mahāyāna and Vajrayāna), greater emphasis was placed on the element of compassion, and nirvana came to be interpreted in more corporate terms. Because of his compassionate and selfless nature, the Buddha, it was believed, would not abandon those who had not yet attained nirvana. Spurred by his conviction, the Mahāyāna Buddhist communities began to venerate the ideal of the *bodhisattva*. The bodhisattva was regarded as a great being who postponed final nirvana to assist all beings in the alleviation of suffering and the realization of nirvana. Since Buddhahood was now considered an ontological reality attainable in principle by anyone, the Buddhist universe came to be populated by countless bodhisattvas, all working to bring about the simultaneous nirvana of all beings.

—*Mark William Muesse*

See also Ahiṃsā; Bodhisattva ideal; Buddha; Buddhist ethics; Four noble truths.

BIBLIOGRAPHY

Corless, Roger J. *The Vision of Buddhism: The Space Under the Tree*. New York: Paragon House, 1989.

Harvey, Peter. *An Introduction to Buddhism: Teachings, History and Practices*. New York: Cambridge University Press, 1990.

Kalupahana, David J. *Buddhist Philosophy: A Historical Analysis*. Honolulu: University of Hawaii Press, 1976.

Nyanaponika Mahathera. *The Road to Inner Freedom*. Kandy, Sri Lanka: Buddhist Publication Society, 1982.

Rahula, Walpola. *What the Buddha Taught*. Rev. ed. New York: Grove Press, 1974.

Nobel Peace Prize

TYPE OF ETHICS: Modern history

DATE: Nobel Foundation established June, 1900

ASSOCIATED WITH: Swedish chemist and industrialist Alfred Bernhard Nobel

DEFINITION: The yearly Nobel Peace Prize is awarded to "those who, during the preceding year, shall have conferred the greatest benefit on mankind"

SIGNIFICANCE: By honoring those people who have furthered the cause of world peace, the Nobel Peace Prize has served to publicize and promote good works

Alfred Bernhard Nobel, a Swedish chemist and industrialist, was initially noted for his invention of dynamite. In 1867, Nobel received a patent for this work. It should be noted, however, that the applications of nitroglycerine and dynamite that Nobel had in mind were for peaceful purposes such as the construction of rail systems and highways. His industrial research also contributed toward the production of a variety of materials, including artificial textiles and rubber. As a consequence, Nobel had amassed a considerable fortune by the time of his death in 1896.

Establishment of the Nobel awards was based on Nobel's will, which was written in November, 1895. Nobel directed that the major portion of his fortune, some $9 million, should be set aside for a fund, invested in safe securities, "the interest on which shall be annually distributed in the form of prizes to those who, during the preceding year, shall have conferred the greatest benefit on mankind." The awards were to be given in the fields of chemistry, literature, physics, physiology or medicine, and peace. The Peace Prize was to be administered by a committee of five persons elected by the Norwegian *Storting* (Parliament). The Nobel Foundation, which was to supervise the investments, was established and approved by His Majesty Oscar II, King of Sweden, in June, 1900.

Nobel's attitude toward peace evolved from his interest in literature. Beginning in 1887, he carried on a regular correspondence with the Austrian writer, Bertha von Suttner. The wife of an Austrian Baron, von Suttner was among the first notable female writers to establish a pacifist view. Her 1889 novel *Die Waffen nieder* (*Against Arms*) was a bitter denunciation of war and its consequences, and its title became the slogan for the peace movement. In 1905, von Suttner was awarded the Nobel Peace Prize.

Though the extent to which Nobel was directly influenced by the baroness is in dispute, there is no question that he admired both her writings and her work on behalf of pacifism. Nobel had few illusions about the attitude of the peace movements toward immediate disarmament and compulsory arbitration. It was Nobel's view that movement toward these worthy goals could only proceed gradually. For example, he believed that governments should develop agreements for the peaceful settlement of disputes but that these agreements should be limited to a single year.

During the early 1890's, Nobel evolved the idea of an economic support for peace. Several concepts contributed to this idea. In a letter that Nobel wrote to von Suttner in 1892, he argued that if nations could establish mutual military agreements, the "atmosphere of security" would ease the transition to disarmament. In addition, the very horror of war itself, particularly in the light of the development of new and more destructive weapons, would cause "all civilized nations . . . to recoil from war and discharge their troops."

It remains unclear why Nobel rejected Swedish academies for the Peace Prize Committee in favor of the Norwegian Storting. The Swedish media were, in fact, quite indignant when the "rejection" became known. Several theories have been proposed. The explanation that seems most credible reflects on the Norwegian Storting's strong support for international cooperation and arbitration. In addition, during the period in which Nobel was clarifying his will, the Norwegian poet Bjørnstjerne Bjørnson was playing a major role in the peace movement.

The procedure for determining the honoree for the Peace Prize is similar to that established for awarding the other prizes. Nominations are requested in September of the year preceding the award, and the deadline is the end of January in the year of the award. Individuals eligible to tender nominations include both current and former members of the Storting, their advisers, members of international committees relevant to the peace process (for example, the International Arbitration Court in The Hague), and previous recipients of the Peace Prize.

The decision on the Peace Prize is determined by the Norwegian Nobel Committee. Members on the Committee are picked by the Storting and are chosen on the basis of their expertise in any of three areas: international law, political history, and political economy. The field of nominees is narrowed between February and September, and the final decision is usually announced during the latter months of the year.

The awarding of the first Peace Prize was announced on December 10, 1901. The first recipients of the award were Jean Henri Dunant and Frederic Passy. Born in Geneva in 1828, Dunant had spent his life in the pursuit of morality and peace. It was his vision that led to the establishment of the International Red Cross in 1864. During the Franco-Prussian War in the 1870's, Dunant pushed for an international court of arbitration through his association Alliance Universelle de l'Ordre et de la Civilisation. Among the speakers before the alliance was Passy. Dunant also worked for more humane treatment for prisoners of war, views that eventually came to a measure of fruition.

Passy, too, was a strong advocate for peace societies. As a member of the French Chamber of Deputies, Passy was instrumental in creating a variety of treaties of arbitration.

Over the course of decades since the first awards, a wide variety of both individuals and institutions have been honored with the Prize. Winners have been international, from the Americas and Europe, but also from Asia and Africa. During the first five decades of the award, the basis for the honor was generally international in scope. For example, beginning in 1902, individuals associated with the International Peace Bureau were honored several times. After World War II, however, honorees tended to be more parochial, in that awards were based on initiative for changes in more localized areas. In 1952, Albert Schweitzer was honored for his humanitarian work in Africa. In 1960, Albert John Lutuli received the Peace Prize for his peaceful campaign to end apartheid, legal segregation, in South Africa. Lutuli's award represented a watershed for the Prize Committee in that it was the first time a black African was so honored. —*Richard Adler*

See also Peace studies.

BIBLIOGRAPHY

Abrams, Irwin. *The Nobel Peace Prize and the Laureates: An Illustrated Biographical History, 1901-1987.* Boston: G. K. Hall, 1987.

Chatfield, Charles, and Peter van den Dungen, eds. *Peace Movements and Political Cultures.* Knoxville: University of Tennessee Press, 1988.

Evianoff, Michael, and Marjorie Fluor. *Alfred Nobel: The Loneliest Millionaire.* Los Angeles: Ward Ritchie Press, 1969.

\multicolumn{3}{c}{NOBEL PEACE PRIZE WINNERS}		
Year	**Winner(s)**	**Reason**
1901	Henri Dunant (Swiss)	Founding of International Red Cross and Geneva Convention
	Frédéric Passy (French)	Founding of first French peace society
1902	Élie Ducommun (Swiss)	Work with Permanent International Peace Bureau
	Charles Albert Gobat (Swiss)	Administration of Inter-Parliamentary Union and International Peace Bureau
1903	Sir William Cremer (British)	Founder and secretary of International Arbitration League
1904	Institute of International Law	Development of international law and studies of laws of neutrality
1905	Bertha von Suttner (Austrian)	Support of pacifist societies; founding of Austrian peace society
1906	Theodore Roosevelt (American)	Negotiations to end Russo-Japanese War
1907	Ernesto Teodoro Moneta (Italian)	Work with Lombard League for Peace
	Louis Renault (French)	Organization of peace conferences
1908	Klas Pontus Arnoldson (Swedish)	Founding of Swedish Society for Arbitration and Peace
	Fredrik Bajer (Danish)	Work with International Peace Bureau
1909	Auguste Beernaert (Belgian)	Work with Permanent Court of Arbitration
	Paul d'Estournelles de Constant (French)	Founding and direction of French Parliamentary Arbitration Committee
1910	Permanent International Peace Bureau	Promotion of international peace and arbitration
1911	Tobias Asser (Dutch)	Conferences on international law
	Alfred Fried (Austrian)	Writings on peace; editor of *Die Friedenswarte*
1912	Elihu Root (American)	Organization of Central American Peace Conference; settlement of problem of Japanese immigration into California
1913	Henri Lafontaine (Belgian)	President of International Peace Bureau
1914-1916	No awards	

(Continued)

Year	Winner(s)	Reason
1917	International Committee of the Red Cross	War relief
1918	No award	
1919	Woodrow Wilson (American)	Support for League of Nations
1920	Léon Bourgeois (French)	President, Council of League of Nations
1921	Karl Hjalmar Branting (Swedish)	Promotion of Swedish social reforms
	Christian Lous Lange (Norwegian)	Secretary-general, Inter-Parliamentary Union
1922	Fridtjof Nansen (Norwegian)	Russian relief work; originated "Nansen passports" for refugees
1923-1924	No awards	
1925	Sir Austen Chamberlain (British)	Locarno Peace Pact
	Charles G. Dawes (American)	Plan for German reparations
1926	Aristide Briand (French)	Locarno Peace Pact
	Gustav Stresemann (German)	German acceptance of reparation plan; development of Locarno Peace Pact
1927	Ferdinand Buisson (French)	President, League of Human Rights
	Ludwig Quidde (German)	Writings on peace; participation in peace conferences
1928	No award	
1929	Frank B. Kellogg (American)	Negotiations for Kellogg-Briand Peace Pact condemning war as means of solving international problems
1930	Nathan Söderblom (Swedish)	Writings on peace; association with ecumenical movement
1931	Jane Addams (American)	Work for international peace; president, Women's International League for Peace and Freedom
	Nicholas Murray Butler (American)	Work with Carnegie Endowment for International Peace; promoter of Kellogg-Briand Pact
1932	No award	
1933	Norman Angell (British)	Work for international peace; author of *The Great Illusion*
1934	Arthur Henderson (British)	President, World Disarmament Conference of 1932
1935	Carl von Ossietzky (German)	Promotion of international disarmament; pacifist writings
1936	Carlos Saavedra Lamas (Argentine)	Negotiation of peace settlement between Bolivia and Paraguay
1937	Lord Robert Cecil (British)	Working with peace movements; founding of International Peace Campaign
1938	Nansen International Office for Refugees	Relief work among refugees
1939-1943	No awards	
1944	International Committee of the Red Cross	War relief
1945	Cordell Hull (American)	Work for peace as United States secretary of state; work on formation of United Nations
1946	John R. Mott (American)	YMCA work/relief for displaced persons
	Emily Greene Balch (American)	President, Women's International League for Peace and Freedom
1947	Friends Service Council and the American Friends Service Committee	Humanitarian work
1948	No award	
1949	Lord John Boyd-Orr (British)	Directing United Nations Food and Agriculture Organization
1950	Ralphe Bunche (American)	Mediation of Israeli War for Independence; director, Division of Trusteeship of the United Nations
1951	Léon Jouhaux (French)	Organization of national and international labor unions
1952	Albert Schweitzer (German)	Humanitarian work in Africa
1953	George C. Marshall (American)	Promotion of European Recovery Program

| \multicolumn{3}{c}{**NOBEL PEACE PRIZE WINNERS**} |

Year	Winner(s)	Reason
1954	Office of the United Nations High Commissioner for Refugees	Work on refugee problems
1955-1956	No awards	
1957	Lester B. Pearson (Canadian)	Organization of United Nations' Egyptian force; president, United Nations General Assembly
1958	Georges Pire (Belgian)	Settlement of displaced persons
1959	Philip Noel-Baker (British)	Promotion of peace; author of *The Arms Race, A Program for World Disarmament*
1960	Albert Lutuli (South African)	Campaign against South African racial segregation
1961	Dag Hammarskjöld (Swedish)	Work for peace in Congo; secretary general of United Nations
1962	Linus Pauling (American)	Work for elimination of nuclear weapons
1963	International Committee of the Red Cross and the League of Red Cross Societies	Humanitarian work
1964	Martin Luther King, Jr. (American)	Nonviolent protests in support of civil rights for blacks
1965	United Nations Children's Fund (UNICEF)	Worldwide aid for children
1966-1967	No awards	
1968	René Cassin (French)	Promotion of human rights; drafter of United Nations Declaration of Human Rights
1969	International Labour Organisation	Improvement of working conditions
1970	Norman E. Borlaug (American)	Increases in food production through development of high-yield grains of wheat and rice
1971	Willy Brandt (German)	Improvement of East-West relations and promotion of European unity
1972	No award	
1973	Henry Kissinger (American)	Negotiation of Vietnam War cease-fire
	Le Duc Tho (Vietnamese) (Declined award)	
1974	Seán MacBride (Irish)	Work for human rights
	Eisaku Satō (Japanese)	Work to improve international relations; work toward limitation of nuclear weapons
1975	Andrei Sakharov (Soviet)	Promotion of peace and respect for human rights for the individual
1976	Mairead Corrigan (Irish)	Organization of movement to end sectarian violence in Northern Ireland
	Betty Williams (Irish)	
1977	Amnesty International	Aid for political prisoners
1978	Menachem Begin (Israeli)	Efforts in settling Middle East conflict
	Anwar el-Sadat (Egyptian)	
1979	Mother Teresa (Agnes Bojaxhiu) (Indian)	Aid and service to India's poor
1980	Adolfo Pérez Esquivel (Argentine)	Promotion of human rights and nonviolence
1981	Office of the United Nations High Commissioner for Refugees	Support for refugees
1982	Alva Myrdal (Swedish)	United Nations disarmament negotiations
	Alfonso García Robles (Mexican)	
1983	Lech Wałesa (Polish)	Nonviolent campaign for workers' rights in Poland
1984	Desmond Tutu (South African)	Nonviolent campaign against South African racial separation
1985	International Physicians for the Prevention of Nuclear War	Campaign on potential effects of nuclear war

(Continued)

(Continued)	NOBEL PEACE PRIZE WINNERS	
Year	**Winner(s)**	**Reason**
1986	Elie Wiesel (American)	Efforts on behalf of victims of repression and racial discrimination
1987	Oscar Arias Sánchez (Costa Rican)	Attempts to end wars in Central America
1988	United Nations peacekeeping forces	Prevention of military conflicts
1989	The Dalai Lama (Tibetan)	Nonviolent efforts opposing Chinese occupation of Tibet
1990	Mikhail Gorbachev (Soviet)	Promotion of world peace by reducing East-West tension
1991	Aung San Suu Kyi (Burmese)	Nonviolent promotion of human rights and democracy in Burma
1992	Rigoberta Menchú (Guatemalan)	Work for social justice and recognition of the cultures of indigenous peoples
1993	Nelson Mandela (South African)	Work for a negotiated end to apartheid
	F. W. de Klerk (South African)	

Gray, Tony. *Champions of Peace: The Story of Alfred Nobel, the Peace Prize, and the Laureates*. New York: Paddington Press, 1976.

Lipsky, Mortimer. *The Quest for Peace: The Story of the Nobel Award*. South Brunswick, N.J.: A. S. Barnes, 1966.

Nobelstiftelsen. *Nobel: The Man and His Prizes*. 2d ed. Amsterdam: Elsevier, 1962.

Pauli, Hertha. *Toward Peace: The Nobel Prize and Man's Struggle for Peace*. New York: Ives Washburn, 1969.

Nonviolence

TYPE OF ETHICS: Politico-economic ethics
DATE: Mid-twentieth century
ASSOCIATED WITH: Mohandas K. Gandhi and Martin Luther King, Jr.
DEFINITION: Refusal to use violence to resolve conflict and/or the use of nonviolent forms of power to promote just social change
SIGNIFICANCE: Grounded in the religious recognition of the sacredness of each human life and in the humanist belief in the equal worth of all persons, nonviolence witnesses to the power of love in transforming personal and institutional relationships

Nonviolence, as Robert L. Holmes has documented, has roots in a variety of cultures and historical documents, including the Bible, the Talmud, the Bhagavad Gītā, *Lao Tzu*, and Sophocles' *Antigone*. In certain periods and traditions, such as early Christianity (pre-fourth century) and Jainism (a religion related to Hinduism), the prohibition against violence takes an absolute form. Based on the recognition of the sacredness of all human life, nonviolence stands as a continuing protest to the wanton destruction of life evidenced in the collective histories of warfare, crime and punishment, and economic and political oppression.

History. Throughout most of its history, nonviolence has been expressed as nonresistance, the refusal to use violence to combat evil even for purposes of self-defense. In the nineteenth century, in the work of persons such as Henry David Thoreau and Leo Tolstoy, strategies of passive resistance were developed whose purpose was to point out social injustice with the hope of generating a consensus for positive social change. Such theorists advocated noncompliance with unjust laws and resistance against unjust social policies.

The practice of nonviolence was further developed in the twentieth century, particularly in the work of Mohandas K. Gandhi (1869-1948) in freeing India from British rule and that of Martin Luther King, Jr. (1929-1968), in struggling to end racial inequality in the United States. Both developed strategies of nonviolent resistance that emphasized the active confrontation of injustice for purposes of social transformation. Both emphasized that true nonviolence is not passivity in the face of evil, but the active confrontation of evil and injustice wherever they exist. Central to these religious philosophies is the belief in personal as well as social transformation. The practitioner of nonviolence must, as Gandhi notes, renounce the "internal violence of the spirit" and truly love the opponent. Also central is the recognition of the ineffectiveness of violence, which only creates more hatred and more violence in a never-ending spiral. Only nonviolent suffering acting as witness to truth and justice can break the spiral. Nonviolentists must, then, according to Gandhi, learn "the art of dying" just as violentists have learned the "art of killing."

Following the partial success of Gandhi's and King's movements, political theorists began to analyze nonviolence as a political rather than a religious strategy. Here the emphasis is placed on organizing nonviolent forms of power as a means of forcing social change rather than upon personal transformation and the use of the power of love. As analysts recognized, the exercise of power requires the consent of the governed. Organized withdrawal of that consent on a large scale can lead to the collapse or transformation of social systems (such as the collapse of Communism in Eastern Europe). Such theorists explore the use of various forms of nonviolent power in such areas as labor (strikes and slowdowns), buying (boycotts), noncompliance with laws, and moral suasion. Much analysis has focused on situations in which nonviolent strategies have been employed. Theorists have unearthed a rich tradition of historical applications of nonviolence. Although nonviolence is often viewed as a tool for oppressed, powerless groups, advocates have developed plans for the total nonviolent civilian defense of nations against external aggression. Confronted with nuclear weapons, against which military defense may mean self-annihilation, nonviolent civilian defense is presented as the only sane alternative.

As a theory and a practice, nonviolence continues to develop and be refined. Important developments include an expansion of the concept of violence that is to be transformed by nonviolent means to include psychological violence (for example, racism, sexism, terrorism), institutional violence, the violence caused by the structure of existing social institutions (such as hunger, poverty, political oppression), and violence against the natural environment. Feminists have developed connections between feminist theory and nonviolence pertaining to women's issues and the development of nonhierarchical social structures. Nonviolence continues as an important strategy in a variety of Third World settings in which the resort to violence by oppressed groups is regarded as futile.

Ethical Arguments Employed. (1) All human life is sacred and all persons have equal worth. People do not have the right to take a life, not even in self-defense. (2) The recognition of the sacredness of persons requires people to intervene nonviolently wherever people suffer from war, political oppression, poverty, or discrimination. (3) Violence breeds more violence and does not provide lasting solutions to conflicts. One must, then, love one's opponent, accept the opponent's violence, and return love. Love, however, requires that one recognize truth and injustice, demanding change. Only such love can break the cycle of violence and create just social structures and renewed relationships. (4) There are many nonviolent means that may be employed. Moral action requires the development of an effective strategy for social change. (5) Although the practice of nonviolence may lead to suffering and death for its practitioners and will sometimes fail, the suffering caused will be much less than it would have been if violent means had been employed. In addition, the likelihood of lasting success is much greater. —*Charles L. Kammer III*

See also Ahiṃsā; Civil disobedience; Gandhi, Mohandas Karamchand; King, Martin Luther, Jr.; Pacifism; Thoreau, Henry David.

BIBLIOGRAPHY

Cooney, Robert, and Helen Michalowski, eds. *The Power of the People: Active Nonviolence in the United States.* Philadelphia: New Society, 1987.

Holmes, Robert L., ed. *Nonviolence in Theory and Practice.* Belmont, Calif.: Wadsworth, 1990.

McAllister, Pam, ed. *Reweaving the Web of Life: Feminism and Nonviolence.* Philadelphia: New Society, 1982.

Merton, Thomas. *The Nonviolent Alternative.* Edited by Gordon Zahn. New York: Farrar, Straus and Giroux, 1980.

Sharp, Gene. *The Politics of Nonviolent Action.* 3 vols. Boston: Porter Sargent, 1973.

Normative vs. descriptive ethics

TYPE OF ETHICS: Theory of ethics
DATE: 1740
ASSOCIATED WITH: David Hume, G. E. Moore, and analytical philosophy
DEFINITION: Normative ethics attempts to formulate prescriptive moral utterances, whereas descriptive ethics deals with the meaning and nature of moral utterances
SIGNIFICANCE: It is a matter of great importance to be able to distinguish between prescriptive and descriptive kinds of moral utterances

Normative ethics deals with the formulation of ethical codes of behavior and moral paradigms of evaluative decision making. Normative ethics prescribes moral principles defining the good, the right, duty, obligation, law, and justice. A normative approach assumes the universality of its ethical principles and attempts to justify them on a rational basis. Christian ethics is a classic example of normative ethics. The following are normative moral utterances: "All promises ought to be kept." "Killing another human being is wrong." "Capital punishment is just because it deters crime." "A father has a duty to provide physical support for his children." In all these examples, the common element is the prescription of a certain course of action or its evalu-

Mohandas Gandhi leads a nonviolent march opposing British policies in India. (Library of Congress)

ation. The most famous example of normative ethics is found in the Ten Commandments.

In this article, the terms "descriptive ethics" and "meta-ethics" will be used synonymously. Descriptive ethics is ethics shorn free of prescriptive or evaluative elements. Descriptive ethics deals with the meanings of moral utterances, the relationships between them and moral actors, and the nature of moral argumentation. Descriptive ethics may take a sociological, psychological, ethnographic, or philosophic approach. A sociological analysis of ethics may concern itself with the relationship between moral behavior and social coercion. Psychology may deal with the relationships between moral behavior and the different stages of human growth and development. Ethnography may study the relationships between ethical beliefs and culture and tradition. Philosophical analysis will tend to concern itself with the semantic meaning of moral utterances, their sense and pragmatic context.

Thomas Hobbes (1588-1679) treated ethics as a descriptive science of the aversions and appetites of the human organism. The good, according to Hobbes, is any object of human desire and appetite. Human behavior, in this view, is motivated by aversion to fear and want and appetites for security and gain. Hobbes's descriptive approach is made possible by his mechanistic view of the universe and human nature.

The descriptive approach that finds a natural cause for moral behavior is known as naturalism. One famous advocate of naturalism was David Hume (1711-1776), who, more than any other philosopher, thoroughly modernized and secularized ethics and philosophy. In *A Treatise of Human Nature* and *An Enquiry Concerning the Principles of Morals*, Hume attempts to answer the metaethical questions of the meanings of ethical terms such as "good," "right," "justice," "virtue," and "vice." Hume concludes that ethical terms are not qualities of a special moral sense or predicates of ethical objects. Instead, they only convey sentiments of approbation or approval; therefore, ethical judgments are entirely subjective. Whenever an object is judged to be good, it means that it is either pleasant or useful. Thus, moral judgments are really judgments of taste.

Naturalistic analysis claims that the good and the right are determined by human appetites. Naturalism holds that an object is valued as good because it is desirable. The proposition "X is good" means "I desire X." One form of naturalism is emotivism, which holds that ethical judgments are only expressions of personal feelings of approval or distaste. This could lead to subjectivism and ethical relativism. In fact, there can be no real ethical disagreements. Ethical judgments only express the attitudes of speakers.

Hedonism is another form of naturalism. Hedonism equates good and evil with pleasure and pain. Whatever produces pleasure is equivalent to the good. Utilitarianism in the hands of Jeremy Bentham maintained a vulgar view that overvalued the quantitative aspects of pleasure. John Stuart Mill, in *Utilitarianism*, distinguished between good and bad pleasures. Intellectual and cultural pleasures are superior to mere physical pleasures. As Mill put it, "I would rather be Socrates dissatisfied than a pig satisfied." One of the most formidable challenges to naturalism came from G. E. Moore. Moore's critique of naturalism is known as the naturalistic fallacy. This fallacy involves defining good in terms of something else, such as pleasure. For Moore, good was an indefinable quality.

As Karl-Otto Apel points out, normative ethics seems to have been made obsolete by Hume's distinction—norms cannot be derived from facts; an "ought" statement cannot be derived from an "is" statement. The scientific grounding of ethics is impossible. Science deals only with facts. In effect, Hume relegated moral norms to the subjective domain. As a result, modern science will accept objectivity only in the mathematical and empirical sciences—not in morality. Morality is purely subjective, from the point of view of modern science. Since Hume and Max Weber, science has claimed to be value free, only positing technological goals, but one can only ask with Apel: What about the criteria for and desirability of technological goals? Can science really free itself from ethics?

As Apel claims, scientific claims involve arguments. Arguments occur in speech situations, in contexts of communication in which certain ethical norms are, in fact, presupposed. Other persons are recognized as genuine subjects of communication. Involvement in argumentation implies ethical claims such as truthfulness and sincerity. Thus, if Apel is correct, science is not value free and there cannot ever be a purely descriptive ethics.

—Michael R. Candelaria

See also Hedonism; Hobbes, Thomas; Hume, David; Metaethics; Mill, John Stuart; Moore, G. E.; Naturalistic fallacy; Ten Commandments; Utilitarianism.

BIBLIOGRAPHY

Apel, Karl-Otto. *Towards a Transformation of Philosophy*. Translated by Glyn Adey and David Frisby. London: Routledge & Kegan Paul, 1980.

Ayer, Alfred Jules. *Language, Truth, and Logic*. New York: Dover, 1952.

Hume, David. "A Treatise of Human Nature." In *Berkeley, Hume, and Kant*, edited by T. V. Smith and Marjorie Grene. Chicago: University of Chicago Press, 1957.

Moore, G. E. *Principia Ethica*. Cambridge: Cambridge University Press, 1971.

North Atlantic Treaty Organization (NATO)

TYPE OF ETHICS: International relations

DATE: Founded April 4, 1949

DEFINITION: NATO was formed to provide security to Western European nations against the perceived Soviet threat; the alliance has achieved its original purpose and is searching for a new sense of mission in the post-Cold War period

SIGNIFICANCE: NATO's posture of deterrence, which included the threat to use nuclear weapons against the Soviet Union during the Cold War era, has been questioned on moral and ethical grounds

The North Atlantic Treaty Organization (NATO) is a defensive and political alliance among sixteen Western nations. The alliance, which was created when twelve nations (Belgium, Canada, Denmark, France, Iceland, Italy, Luxembourg, The Netherlands, Norway, Portugal, the United Kingdom, and the United States) signed the North Atlantic Treaty in Washington, D.C., on April 4, 1949, was joined by Greece and Turkey in February, 1952, West Germany in May, 1955, and Spain in May, 1982. The treaty is a military alliance designed to prevent aggression or to repel it should it occur. It also provides for continuous consultation and cooperation among member nations in political and economic matters.

The United States was instrumental in creating NATO and has enjoyed hegemonic status within the alliance; the alliance's commitments consume about 50 percent of the U.S. defense budget each year. American commitment to NATO marked a fundamental transformation of the guiding principles of U.S. foreign policy; it caused the United States to depart from its traditional policy against entanglement in permanent alliances and from its isolationist foreign policy.

Historical Background. NATO has provided the basic framework for the political and military structure of the West during the postwar period. The idea of a permanent peacetime alliance among North Atlantic nations was conceived when "Cold War" conflict was developing between the United States and the Soviet Union. The Truman Doctrine of March, 1947, for example, acknowledged the disharmony of interests with the Soviet Union and underlined the need to contain the expansion of Soviet communism. The events of 1948—the communist coup in Prague in spring of 1948 and the Soviet blockade of Berlin in June, 1948—further convinced the United States and its allies that the Soviet Union was an expansionist power and that it was willing to use force and subversion to become involved in the affairs of Western Europe.

NATO, which was a response to the perceived Soviet threat to Western Europe, became the keystone of America's security commitments. NATO had two main goals. Its short-term goal was to rehabilitate the war-shattered economies of Western European nations and to maintain their political stability by countering communist-inspired subversions in Europe. NATO's long-term goal was to re-create a European balance of power against the Soviet Union by making Europe strong militarily as well as politically and economically. NATO has succeeded in accomplishing both goals.

Structure of NATO. The North Atlantic Council, which is composed of ministerial representatives of member countries, is the chief policy-making body of NATO; it meets at least twice a year. The Council is assisted by several committees. The Military Committee is the highest military authority in NATO. It is composed of the chiefs of staff of all member countries except France (Iceland, having no military forces, is represented by a civilian), and it makes rec-

ommendations to the Council and to the Defense Planning Committee on military matters. NATO forces are divided into three commands: Allied Command Europe, the Atlantic Ocean Command, and the Channel Command.

NATO's First Forty Years. Though the alliance has survived for more than a generation, NATO's solidarity has varied over time. In the early 1950's, West Germany's participation in NATO became an issue and was settled in the Paris Agreements of 1954; West Germany joined the alliance in 1955. The withdrawal of the French forces from the integrated military command structure of NATO in 1966 weakened the alliance (France remains a member of the North Atlantic alliance). As a result of the French action, NATO headquarters had to be moved from Paris to Brussels. In 1974, Greece withdrew (until 1980) from the NATO military command because of Turkish military actions in Cyprus. Yet the political cohesion of NATO has been quite remarkable.

NATO members agreed from the beginning that the primary purpose of the alliance was to be prepared militarily to counter Soviet attack. Their strategy rested in credible deterrence of threats to Western security. For protection against possible Soviet attack on Europe, NATO has relied on the U.S. nuclear umbrella. American nuclear weapons have been deployed in Western Europe, though they have always remained under U.S. command. The deployment of intermediate-range nuclear weapons (Cruise and Pershing II missiles) in 1983 and 1984, however, brought strong opposition from intellectuals, political leaders, and peace activists who feared that the presence of the intermediate-range nuclear weapons in Europe would increase the likelihood of a nuclear confrontation with the Soviet Union. NATO's strategy of deterrence has also been questioned on moral and ethical grounds, since it uses civilian populations as potential nuclear targets. Yet, the developments of the late 1980's—the 1987 Soviet-American INF treaty (supported by all NATO members) on the elimination of a class of intermediate- and short-range nuclear missiles based in Europe, the breaking down of the Berlin Wall in 1989 followed by the reunification of two Germanys in 1990, and the disintegration of the Soviet Union and of the Warsaw Pact (NATO's communist counterpart)—have radically transformed the political and strategical environment in which NATO operates.

NATO and the New World Order. Major international changes of historical proportion that took place between 1989 and 1991 have called into question the relevance of NATO in the post-Cold War world. With the collapse of Soviet threat, NATO lost its principal *raison d'être*. It is therefore in a state of disarray. For example, in October, 1991, France and Germany proposed the creation of a corps-strength Western European army of 30,000 troops aimed at giving the region a defense capability independent of NATO. The idea was challenged by Britain, however, as being a potential threat to NATO. NATO members also disagree over security problems arising outside the area covered by the treaty. In May, 1993, when President Clinton proposed to expand the involvement of NATO in the Bosnian conflict by sending 50,000 NATO troops (of which 20,000 to 25,000 troops would have been American) to Bosnia and Herzegovina as part of a peace-keeping force, he met stiff resistance from European allies. New issues such as the admission of former communist countries (Russia, Poland, and other countries in Eastern Europe) to the alliance and out-of-area problems (the Bosnian conflict, for example) have yet to be resolved by NATO. In view of the changed reality of world politics in the post-Cold War era, NATO must redefine its purpose. The future of NATO is quite uncertain.   —*Sunil K. Sahu*

See also Cold War; International law.

BIBLIOGRAPHY

Carpenter, Ted Galen, ed. *NATO at Forty: Confronting a Changing World*. Lexington, Mass.: Lexington Books, 1990.

Cerutti, Furio, and Rodolfo Ragionieri, ed. *Rethinking European Security*. New York: Crane Russak, 1990.

Golden, James, ed. *NATO at Forty: Change, Continuity, and Prospects*. Boulder, Colo.: Westview Press, 1989.

Hyde-Price, Adrian. *European Security Beyond the Cold War*. Newbury Park, Calif.: Sage, 1991.

Ireland, Timothy P. *Creating the Entangling Alliance: The Origins of the North Atlantic Treaty Organization*. Westport, Conn.: Greenwood Press, 1981.

Kaplan, Lawrence S. *NATO and the United States: The Enduring Alliance*. Boston: Twayne, 1988.

Sloan, Stanley R., ed. *NATO in the 1990s*. Washington, D.C.: Pergamon-Brassey's, 1989.

Steinbruner, John D., and Leon V. Sigal, eds. *Alliance Security: NATO and the No-First-Use Question*. Washington, D.C.: Brookings Institution, 1983.

Nuclear energy

TYPE OF ETHICS: Environmental ethics

DATE: Mid-twentieth century to present

DEFINITION: The production of energy via processes that affect the nucleus of the atom

SIGNIFICANCE: There is no consensus regarding whether the benefit derived from nuclear energy production is worth its present and future cost to the biosphere

The invention and utilization of devices to convert energy from natural forms into readily accessible forms has accompanied the technological progress of humans. Humans are continuously searching for methods that efficiently meet their rapidly increasing energy demands.

The "nuclear age" began in 1938 with the discovery by Otto Hahn and Fritz Strassmann that substantial amounts of energy are released when heavy atoms such as uranium are broken into smaller atomic fragments. This process of nuclear fission is one of three types of nuclear reactions that release substantial amounts of energy. The fission of one gram of uranium 235 can keep a 100-watt light bulb continuously lit for twenty-three years, whereas only eight minutes of light can be generated by burning one gram of gaso-

An antinuclear rally. (National Archives)

line. When controlled, the fission process can be used to generate electric power; uncontrolled, it becomes the destructive power of atomic bombs.

Although the peaceful uses of nuclear power cannot be morally equated with the military uses, events such as the accidents at Three Mile Island and Chernobyl demonstrate the conflict between basic ecological priorities and technological accomplishments. Ethical considerations in the past have focused mainly on human beings. People tend to regard themselves as the only beings of inherent value, with the remainder of the natural world being a resource valued only for its usefulness to humans. While the limitations of past technologies have allowed the survival of the natural biosphere, modern technology, with its potential for impact on future generations, requires an ethics of long-range responsibility.

When Hiroshima was bombed, little was known about radioactive fallout. In the 1950's, it was discovered that the above-ground testing of nuclear weapons introduced radioactive materials into the upper atmosphere to be transported by the winds for deposition in distant places. The strontium 90 produced in these explosions became a concern in 1954. Chemically, it behaves like calcium and is incorporated into the food chain via plants, cows, and milk, ultimately ending up in children's bones. Another radioactive by-product, iodine 131, incorporates itself into the thyroid gland. The radioactive

NUCLEAR ENERGY TIME LINE	
1896	Radioactivity is discovered by Antoine-Henri Becquerel.
1938	The nuclear fission process is discovered by Otto Hahn and Fritz Strassman.
1940	Nuclear chain reaction experiments are begun at Columbia University in New York.
1942	The first controlled, sustainable nuclear fission chain reaction is produced at the University of Chicago by Enrico Fermi's research team.
1945	Nuclear bombs are dropped on Hiroshima and Nagasaki, causing massive destruction.
1957	The reactor core of the Windscale reactor in England overheats, releasing a significant amount of radiation into the environment.
1957	Nuclear waste at a top-secret nuclear-weapons production facility in Russia's Chelyabinsk province explodes, causing wholesale environmental destruction in the area. This disaster is kept a secret from the world until 1976.
1979	A major environmental disaster is averted when the fuel core of Pennsylvania's Three Mile Island reactor becomes overheated to near meltdown conditions. Decontamination of the facility for reuse becomes a long-term process.
1986	Human error results in a massive fire at the Chernobyl nuclear reactor in the Ukraine, releasing massive quantities of radioactive material into the atmosphere, leading to contamination in many areas of Europe.

emissions from these incorporated elements can lead to the development of cancer. Humans can thrive only in the particular environmental niche to which they are adapted. The fact that human bodies cannot discriminate between species such as radioactive iodine and safe iodine shows that damaging the environment jeopardizes the survival of the human race. Radioactive pollutants are particularly insidious because they remain in the environment for long periods of time—it takes almost 400 years for the radioactivity of a sample of strontium 90 to degrade to a negligible level. These problems led the United States and the Soviet Union to prohibit the atmospheric testing of nuclear weapons in 1963.

On December 2, 1942, a team of scientists at the University of Chicago produced the first controlled nuclear chain reaction, the experiment that led to the harnessing of the atom for peaceful purposes. Nuclear reactors have since been used to generate electricity, to power ships and rockets, and to power water desalination plants.

Although a modern nuclear reactor is not a bomb, because its concentration of radioactive fuel is too low, environmental safety is still an issue. Major accidents, such as the 1957 Windscale, England, disaster in which the reactor core overheated and a significant amount of radiation was released into the atmosphere and the 1986 Chernobyl catastrophe in which 90,000 people had to be evacuated from a nineteen-mile danger zone and a large amount of radioactive material was ejected into the atmosphere, are examples of the destructive potential of nuclear energy production. Although absolute safety at nuclear reactors cannot be guaranteed, modern safeguards have decreased the likelihood of such disasters.

Little attention was paid to the disposal of nuclear wastes in the early days of nuclear power generation. Nuclear waste includes all by-products generated in either routine operations or accidents at any point along the nuclear fuel trail (uranium mining, enrichment, fuel fabrication, spent fuel, and so forth). Since these wastes cannot be detoxified, they must be completely isolated from human contact until they have decayed to negligible levels. For plutonium, the most dangerous species in nuclear waste, this time period is at least 240,000 years.

Is it possible to store such materials in isolation for thousands of centuries? Historically, nuclear waste has not been adequately contained. While scientists predicted that the plutonium stored at Maxey Flats, Kentucky, the world's largest plutonium waste facility, would migrate only one-half inch on-site over a 24,000-year period, it actually migrated two miles offsite within ten years. More than 500,000 gallons of waste stored at Hanford, Washington, leaked into the soil, introducing radioactive pollutants into the Columbia River and the Pacific Ocean. The worst example of breached storage occurred in the Ural Mountains of the Soviet Union in the late 1950's, when an unexpected and uncontrolled nuclear reaction occurred in stored waste, rendering more than twenty square miles uninhabitable to humans and other species. Thus, the ethics of using nuclear energy until the technology exists for safe storage repositories must be questioned.

Even if safe storage technology can be developed, storing waste for thousands of centuries remains a gamble. Disposal sites must remain undisturbed by acts of war, terrorism, and natural processes such as ice sheets and geological folding, while storage conditions must not allow the waste to become reactive. History discounts the ability of humans to protect their "treasures" for extended periods of time; for example, the tombs of Egypt were left undisturbed for less than four thousand years.

How humanity generates the energy needed by its technology is a complex issue. The elimination of nuclear energy generation without a concomitant reduction in humanity's energy requirements would only result in the burning of more fossil fuel. Although this occurrence would avoid future nuclear disasters and end the accumulation of radioactive waste, it would also exacerbate the "greenhouse effect" and the resultant global warming, which also puts the biosphere at risk for future generations. Ultimately, the chance of disaster in the present and the legacy of toxic waste that humans neither have the knowledge to make safe nor the ability to contain must be compared to the risks posed by alternative methods of energy production to present and future generations.

—Arlene R. Courtney

See also Atom bomb; Global warming; Greenhouse effect; Nuclear Regulatory Commission, U.S.

Bibliography

Barlett, Donald L., and James B. Steele. *Forevermore: Nuclear Waste in America.* New York: W. W. Norton, 1985.

Cohen, Bernard L. *Nuclear Science and Society.* Garden City, N.Y.: Anchor Press, 1974.

Irwin, Michael. *Nuclear Energy: Good or Bad?.* New York: Public Affairs Committee, 1984.

Medvedev, Zhores A. *Nuclear Disaster in the Urals.* New York: W. W. Norton, 1979.

Nye, Joseph S. *Nuclear Ethics.* New York: Free Press, 1986.

Nuclear Regulatory Commission, U.S.

Type of ethics: Environmental ethics

Date: Established 1974

Associated with: The Energy Reorganization Act

Definition: The NRC is an independent agency of the U.S. government that licenses and regulates the civilian uses of nuclear energy and materials

Significance: One NRC responsibility is ensuring the protection of environmental quality; this had not been a responsibility of the Atomic Energy Commission

The Energy Reorganization Act of 1974 established the Energy Research and Development Administration (ERDA) and the Nuclear Regulatory Commission (NRC) and abolished the Atomic Energy Commission (AEC). One purpose of the Act was "to enhance the goals of restoring, protecting, and enhancing environmental quality." The Act separated the licensing and regulation of civilian nuclear energy and materials from their development and promotion. These functions had been joined under the AEC. The Act directed the NRC to identify possible nuclear-energy sites and to evaluate potential environmental impacts from their construction and operation. In 1977, the ERDA was abolished and its responsibilities were transferred to the Department of Energy. The NRC regulates the processing, transport, handling, and disposal of nuclear materials and is responsible for protecting public health and safety and the environment. It licenses and oversees the construction and operation of nuclear reactors that generate electricity. Before licensing reactors, the NRC holds hearings to enable public participation in the process. It also inspects facilities for violations of safety standards and investigates nuclear accidents.

See also Atomic Energy Commission (AEC); Nuclear energy.

Nuremberg Trials

Type of ethics: International relations

Date: 1945 to 1949

Associated with: Nazi leaders and the Allied Powers in World War II (Great Britain, France, the United States, and the Soviet Union)

Definition: In a main trial, Nazi leaders were tried for conspiracy, crimes against peace, war crimes, and crimes against humanity; twelve subsequent trials dealt with doctors, SS officers, and other Nazis

Significance: The Nuremberg principle holds that, because of duties higher than obligation to the state, an individual can be held criminally accountable under international law

Following the end of World War II, twenty-four Nazi leaders were charged before the International Military Tribunal as war criminals on the following charges: (1) conspiracy; (2) crimes against peace—planning or waging a war of aggression; (3) war crimes—"violations of the laws or customs of war," including murder or ill-treatment of civilians and prisoners of war, killing hostages, plundering property, wanton destruction of cities, and "devastation not justified by military necessity"; (4) crimes against humanity—"murder, extermination, enslavement, deportation, and other inhumane acts committed against any civilian population, before or during the war, or persecutions on political, racial, or religious grounds in execution of or in connection with any crime within the jurisdiction of the Tribunal, whether or not in violation of domestic law of the country where perpetrated" (Charter of the International Military Tribunal, Article 6).

The tribunal tried twenty-two of the indicted. Hermann Goering, first the head of the Gestapo and later the commander-in-chief of the Air Force, was considered the major defendant. Rudolf Hess had been deputy leader; in 1941, he flew to Scotland and was imprisoned. Joachim von Ribbentrop served as foreign minister. Wilhelm Keitel took over as the chief of staff of the High Command of the Armed Forces after Hitler abolished the War Ministry in 1938. Ernst Kaltenbrunner headed the Reich Security Police, including the Gestapo and the security service of the SS. Alfred Rosenberg was the minister for the Occupied Eastern Territories. Hans Frank, the Nazi party lawyer, was the governor-general of occupied Poland. Wilhelm Frick was the minister of the interior. Julius Streicher was the leading anti-Semite propagandist. Walter Funk was president of the Reichbank. Hjalmar Schacht headed the Reichbank prior to Funk and the Ministry of Economics prior to the war, where he piloted the financing of war production. Karl Doenitz, as admiral, directed the U-boat battle in the Atlantic and succeeded Erich Raeder as commander-in-chief of the Navy. Raeder was commander-in-chief of the Navy until 1943, when he resigned in a disagreement with Hitler. Baldur von Schirach built the Hitler Youth organization and later was made governor of Vienna. Fritz Sauckel headed the forced-labor mobilization. Alfred Jodl was chief of the Operations Staff of the Armed Forces. Franz van Papen served as vice chancellor after Hitler came to power. Arthur Seyss-Inquart, an Austrian who assisted in the Nazi takeover of Austria, was Reich governor of Austria, assisted in the Nazi takeover of Czechoslovakia and Poland, and was Reich commissioner for The Netherlands. Albert Speer was Hitler's architect and minister of armaments. Constantin von Neurath, a diplomat, was made the Reich protector of occupied Czechoslovakia. Hans Fritzsche headed the radio division of the Propaganda Ministry. Martin Bormann, Hitler's secretary and head of the party Chancellery after Hess fled, had not been captured but was tried in absentia. Robert Ley, leader of the Labor Front,

NUREMBERG WAR CRIMINALS: CHARGES AND VERDICTS				
Defendant	Count 1	Count 2	Count 3	Count 4
Hermann Goering	Guilty	Guilty	Guilty	Guilty
Rudolf Hess	Guilty	Guilty	Not Guilty	Not Guilty
Joachim von Ribbentrop	Guilty	Guilty	Guilty	Guilty
Wilhelm Keitel	Guilty	Guilty	Guilty	Guilty
Ernst Kaltenbrunner	Not Guilty	—	Guilty	Guilty
Alfred Rosenberg	Guilty	Guilty	Guilty	Guilty
Hans Frank	Not Guilty	—	Guilty	Guilty
Wilhelm Frick	Not Guilty	Guilty	Guilty	Guilty
Julius Streicher	Not Guilty	—	—	Guilty
Walter Funk	Not Guilty	Guilty	Guilty	Guilty
Hjalmar Schacht	Not Guilty	Not Guilty	—	—
Karl Doenitz	Not Guilty	Guilty	Guilty	—
Erich Raeder	Guilty	Guilty	Guilty	—
Baldur von Schirach	Not Guilty	—	—	Guilty
Fritz Sauckel	Not Guilty	Not Guilty	Guilty	Guilty
Alfred Jodl	Guilty	Guilty	Guilty	Guilty
Franz von Papen	Not Guilty	Not Guilty	—	—
Arthur Seyss-Inquart	Not Guilty	Guilty	Guilty	Guilty
Albert Speer	Not Guilty	Not Guilty	Guilty	Guilty
Constantin von Neurath	Guilty	Guilty	Guilty	Guilty
Hans Fritzsche	Not Guilty	—	Not Guilty	Not Guilty
Martin Bormann (in absentia)	Not Guilty	—	Guilty	Guilty

committed suicide before the trial began, and industrialist Gustav Krupp was found to be too senile to stand trial.

The Charter (Articles 9, 10, and 11) provided that the Tribunal could declare organizations criminal and that individuals could be tried before national, military, or occupation courts of the four powers for membership in such organizations. The indictment charged that the following organizations were criminal in character: the Reich Cabinet, the leadership corps of the Nazi Party, the SS (*Schutzstaffeln*, or Black Shirts), the SD (*Sicherheitsdienst*), the SA (*Sturmabteilungen*, or Stormtroopers), the Gestapo (secret state police), and the General Staff and High Command of the Armed Forces.

Each of the four Allied powers named a judge and an alternate judge to the International Military Tribunal: Lord Justice Geoffrey Lawrence and Justice Norman Birkett (Great Britain); Attorney General Francis Biddle and Judge John J. Parker (United States); Professor Henri Donnedieu de Vabres and Conseiller Robert Falco (France); and Major General I. T. Nikitchenko and Lieutenant Colonel A. F. Volchkov (Soviet Union).

The trial began on November 20, 1945, and, after 216 trial days, concluded on October 1, 1946, when the Tribunal delivered its judgment. Justice Robert Jackson of the Supreme Court led the prosecution counsel for the United States; Attorney General Hartley Shawcross and David Maxwell-Fyfe for Great Britain; François del Menthon, Auguste Champetier de Ribes, Charles Dubost, and Edgar Fauré for France; and General R. A. Rudenko and Colonel Y. V. Pokrovsky for the Soviet Union. Each defendant was represented by the counsel of his choice.

The Tribunal acquitted three defendants (Schacht, von Papen, and Fritzsche). Twelve were sentenced to death by hanging (Goering, von Ribbentrop, Keitel, Kaltenbrunner, Rosenberg, Frank, Frick, Streicher, Sauckel, Jodl, Bormann, and Seyss-Inquart) and were hanged on October 16, 1946. Three were sentenced to life imprisonment (Hess, Funk, and Raeder); two to twenty-year terms (von Schirach and Speer), one to fifteen years (von Neurath), and one to ten years (Doenitz). Goering committed suicide the evening before the scheduled executions. Four Nazi organizations were declared criminal: the leadership corps of the Nazi Party, the SS, the SD, and the Gestapo.

Between October, 1946, and April, 1949, twelve subsequent trials, conducted by American judges primarily from state supreme courts, were held at Nuremberg. In the Doctors' Trial, twenty-three physicians were tried; all but seven were found guilty of experiments on human subjects. Other trials involved judges who were SS members, SS officers who operated concentration camps and committed mass murders, industrialists—including Alfred Krupp (son of Gustav) and the directors of I. G. Farben—who used slave labor, and army leaders who took hostages, destroyed villages, and shot prisoners.

—*Ron Christenson*

See also Aggression; Anti-Semitism; Geneva conventions; Genocide; Hitler, Adolf; International justice; International law; Law; Nazism.

BIBLIOGRAPHY

Conot, Robert E. *Justice at Nuremberg*. New York: Harper & Row, 1983.

Lifton, Robert Jay. *The Nazi Doctors*. New York: Basic Books, 1986.

Smith, Bradley F. *Reaching Judgment at Nuremberg*. New York: Basic Books, 1977.

Taylor, Telford. *The Anatomy of the Nuremberg Trials*. New York: Knopf, 1992.

Tusa, Ann, and John Tusa. *The Nuremberg Trial*. London: Macmillan, 1983.

Obedience

TYPE OF ETHICS: Personal and social ethics
DATE: 1960's
ASSOCIATED WITH: Stanley Milgram
DEFINITION: The tendency for people to follow commands, real or implied, from someone in a position of authority
SIGNIFICANCE: Human behavior is affected by subtle but strong social influences; people are obedient to others in authority, even when it is psychologically difficult to comply with their requests

Obedience is not necessarily bad or good. A sinister example of obedience occurred in World War II, when more than six million innocent people were tortured and killed by Nazis who claimed that they were only following the orders of their superiors. A positive example of obedience is a three-year-old who obeys her parents' commands to play in the yard rather than the road. A sinister example of disobedience is a criminal who disobeys laws. A positive example of disobedience is Rosa Parks, who was arrested in 1955 for disobeying laws that segregated seats on public buses in Montgomery, Alabama. Her disobedience of the law that stated that she must sit in the back of the bus was a major landmark in the civil rights revolution in the United States. Whether obedience is right or wrong is determined by the individual, the situation, and others' or history's evaluation of the obedience or disobedience.

Some obedience is necessary. Social groups of any size depend on a reasonable amount of obedience to function smoothly. Society would be chaotic if orders from police, parents, physicians, bosses, generals, and presidents were routinely ignored or disobeyed. The division of labor in a society requires that individuals have the capacity to subordinate and coordinate their own independent actions to serve the goals and purposes of the larger social organization.

Obedience results because people do not feel responsible for the actions they perform under orders from an authority figure. They believe that the person giving the orders has the responsibility for the results of the actions. At the Nuremberg trials after World War II, many of the Nazi war criminals stated that they believed their actions were wrong but did not feel personally responsible for them, because they were merely following orders.

The feeling of not being responsible, however, is insufficient to explain why people so readily follow orders, especially in cases in which the behavior far exceeds the scope of the order. For example, the cruelty and savagery of some of the soldiers in the infamous My Lai incident (in which U.S. soldiers killed innocent Vietnamese villagers) was not necessarily demanded in their orders to "pacify the village."

A personal factor that may underlie the willingness to follow orders is ideological zeal, the belief that the required actions are right or in support of a good cause. Another personal factor is gratification; people feel powerful and free upon carrying out the orders. Furthermore, individuals sometimes believe that they will reap material gain or personal advancement by following the specified orders. Another personal factor that influences whether people obey is the role that they are filling. Roles often include rules that people obey the orders of certain others.

Situational factors that influence obedience are prestige, proximity, the presence of others who disobey, and reminders of personal responsibility. Prestige means that it is easier to obey the commands of a high-ranking (prestigious) officer than those of a low-ranking officer. Proximity has to do with both the person giving the orders and the victim. Thus, it is easier for soldiers to follow orders given in person rather than over the phone, and it is easier to follow orders to kill others by high-altitude bombing than to follow orders to kill others by stabbing. Also, it is easier to disobey when others present are disobeying than it is if others are obeying. Finally, obedience diminishes when a person is reminded that he or she will be held personally responsible for any harm that results from his or her actions.

Several other factors may affect disobedience. First, embarrassment hinders disobedience. Many people do not want to rock the boat, make a scene, or be rude. Second, lacking a language of protest hinders disobedience. Many people literally have no words with which to disobey. Third, people may be entrapped into obedience. The first steps of entrapment pose no difficult choices. One step leads to another, however, and the person is ultimately committed to a course of obedience.

Obedience can result from five types of power that individuals and groups can exercise over others. First, coercive power arises from the potential to deliver punishment to force another to change his or her behavior. For example, parents who punish their children for putting their hands into cookie jars are exercising coercive power to induce their children to obey their directives to stay out of the cookie jar. Second, reward power arises from the potential to deliver positive reinforcement to induce another to change his or her behavior. For example, parents who give their children cookies for doing their homework are exercising reward power to induce their children to obey their directives to do their homework. Third, legitimate power arises from being in a particular role or position. Generals, for example, have the authority to give orders to underlings because of their rank. Fourth, expert power arises because others see the person as particularly knowledgeable. Physicians, for example, induce others to obey their directives to quit smoking because they are seen as health care experts. Fifth, referent power arises because others admire the person giving the orders. For example, Mother Teresa could probably get others to obey her commands because she is greatly admired.

—Lillian M. Range

See also Milgram experiment; Psychology.

BIBLIOGRAPHY

Hamilton, V. Lee. "Obedience and Responsibility: A Jury Simulation." *Journal of Personality and Social Psychology 36, no. 2 (February, 1978): 126-146.*

Kelman, Herbert C., and V. Lee Hamilton. *Crimes of Obe-*

dience. New Haven, Conn.: Yale University Press, 1989.

Milgram, Stanley. *Obedience to Authority*. New York: Harper & Row, 1974.

Sabini, Jon, and Maury Silver. "Critical Thinking and Obedience to Authority." In *Thinking Critically*, edited by John Chaffee. 2d ed. Boston: Houghton Mifflin, 1988.

Objectivism

TYPE OF ETHICS: Theory of ethics

DATE: Mid-twentieth century to present

ASSOCIATED WITH: Twentieth century American novelist and philosopher Ayn Rand

DEFINITION: Objectivism is the philosophical system of Ayn Rand; it claims that there are objective facts about the world and human beings that should be the basis for philosophical speculations

SIGNIFICANCE: Objectivism, as it applies to ethics, is a version of ethical egoism that claims that human beings, since they are of intrinsic value and incomparable worth, are obligated to act only in their own interest

There is an initial problem with explaining objectivism. Its major developer and proponent, Ayn Rand, did not write a well-reasoned philosophical treatise on her worldview, but used objectivism as a backdrop for the characters in her novels and offered glimpses of it in her frequent lectures. One must be a bit of a detective to piece together her position. Compounding the problem is the fact that a significant segment of the philosophical community does not take her work seriously, because she was not a professional philosopher. It should be said at the outset that objectivism is not only an ethical theory but also an overarching integrated worldview with ethical, metaphysical, epistemological, political, social, and aesthetic elements. What follows is an account of the ethical component of her thought.

Rejection of Altruism. Ayn Rand begins by rejecting traditional ethical theory, which she labels "the ethics of altruism." Whether utilitarian or deontological in nature, the ethics of altruism requires a moral agent sometimes to set her or his interests aside and act for the interests of others. It is even possible, in this view, to be obligated to give up one's life for the sake of others. To put it another way, the ethics of altruism may require a moral agent to think of herself or himself as without value as compared to others. Individuals can become merely means to others' ends. Rand finds this result absolutely abhorrent. At the core of her theory is the fact of the absolute moral worth of the individual. Each human being has intrinsic value, and any theory that requires someone to negate that value is wrong.

Egoism, on the other hand, embraces the intrinsic worth of the individual and places the individual's interests at the heart of the ethical theory. Because it claims that a right action is one that is in the best interest of the individual who is acting, it will never require that an agent sacrifice her or his interests for the interests of others. The worth of the individual is intact.

Rand's Version of Egoism. Egoism as an ethical theory has been around at least since the time of Plato. Rand takes the basic framework of the egoistic principle and reworks it in the light of certain moral facts about human beings that she takes as fundamental. These facts can be ascertained by reflecting on the answers to the following questions. What is the end for which a human should live? On what principle shall a human act to achieve this end? Who should benefit from the actions? In other words, what is the ultimate value? What is the ultimate virtue? Who is the primary beneficiary?

According to Rand, life itself is the goal of life. People live in order to live. This is why she says that human life has intrinsic value. A human life is always an end in itself. The principle on which to act is rationality. It is that aspect of human nature that distinguishes humans from other living things. Therefore, it must be the primary virtue. One lives life to the fullest by being rational. Finally, the only beneficiary of an agent's actions that would meet the criterion of rationality would be the agent. It is this last condition that permits the marriage of these moral facts with egoism. It follows, then, that for a human being to achieve an end, she or he must live according to the ethical principle of rational self-interest. Human beings are under an ethical obligation to do whatever would promote the interests of that individual.

Reaction. Needless to say, objectivism caused quite a stir. Critics were quick to point out that Rand's ethical claims were tantamount to selfishness and, since selfishness is not a desirable character trait, ought to be dismissed summarily. Ayn Rand did little to dispel this association with selfishness and, in fact, tried to exploit this identification (and hysteria) for her own gain. Witness the title of her 1964 book: *The Virtue of Selfishness*.

In point of fact, however, though she did use the word "selfishness" quite often, her theory is much more sophisticated than her critics allow. She gives selfishness a precise definition, which turns out to be nothing like the imprecise understanding of the term in common usage. For Rand, selfishness is merely the rational pursuit of self-interest. Certainly, it would be in one's rational self-interest to take into consideration, sometimes, the interests of others. The common understanding of selfishness embodies the idea of pursuit of one's interests exclusively without regard to the interests of others. Therefore, Rand's use of the term is different from the common usage. Rand admits that she chose the term "selfishness" deliberately for its shock value and uses the above equivocation for the twofold purpose of undermining the ethics of altruism and championing her brand of ethical egoism.

This ethical component of objectivism, then, stands or falls with ethical egoism. There is nothing inherently wrong with Rand's version. The other components of objectivism, however, do not stand up well to philosophical criticism, and this is another reason objectivism is held in low regard.

—John H. Serembus

See also Altruism; Egoism; Self-interest; Selfishness.

BIBLIOGRAPHY

Peikoff, Leonard. *Objectivism: The Philosophy of Ayn Rand*. New York: Dutton, 1991.

Rand, Ayn. *Atlas Shrugged*. New York: Random House, 1957.

_____. *For the New Intellectual*. New York: Random House, 1961.

_____. *The Fountainhead*. Indianapolis: Bobbs-Merrill, 1943.

_____. *The Virtue of Selfishness*. New York: New American Library, 1964.

Obligation. *See* Duty.

On Liberty: Book

TYPE OF ETHICS: Modern history
DATE: Published 1859
AUTHOR: John Stuart Mill
SIGNIFICANCE: *On Liberty* has been a central focus of liberal ethics and philosophy for more than one hundred years, and it continues to be a major work for those interested in questions of individual freedom

In *On Liberty,* John Stuart Mill provided a powerful defense of individual freedom of thought and action. Mill's ideas have been a source of inspiration for those concerned with civil liberty and individual freedom for more than one hundred years, but his assertions in this volume were not in accord with the rest of his substantial body of work. The popularity of *On Liberty* was the result of a combination of Mill's substantial reputation and the work's contents, which, while popular with the general reader, have been frequently criticized by professional scholars and reviewers.

Biographical Background. John Stuart Mill was the son of Scottish philosopher James Mill, who, under the influence of Jeremy Bentham, reared the boy to be a prodigy. At the age of three, the young Mill was studying Greek, and throughout his youth, childish pleasures were denied him in favor of intellectual activities. At twenty, he fell into clinical depression, apparently caused by the lack of emotional support in his upbringing, but he recovered and ultimately had a successful career as a bureaucrat in the India Office and as a philosopher. Among his important works are *System of Logic* (1843), *Principles of Political Economy* (1848), and *The Subjection of Women* (1869). In 1830 he met Harriet Taylor. They conducted an intense though, according to themselves, chaste courtship until 1851, when, Taylor's husband being two years dead, they married. Harriet Taylor proved to be an important influence on Mill's thought. It was thanks to his wife that Mill came to regard "the woman question"—that is, women's social, political, and economic equality—as one of the most important issues of the mid-nineteenth century. This attitude appears to have been decisive in the development of *On Liberty* (1859), Mill's most popular work.

On Liberty. Mill opened his consideration of the question of liberty by asserting that he was making one simple, straightforward proposition: Society had no warrant by legal sanction or moral suasion to limit the individual's freedom of thought or action for any reason except to prevent harm to another person or property. Even should an action be clearly shown to be harmful to the individual, Mill insisted, any restriction other than fair warning was wrong.

In the realm of ideas, Mill believed that free discussion was necessary if the truth was to be determined. To deny any idea currency was to deny the possibility, however faint, that it might be true and to deny it the opportunity of challenging other ideas to test their truthfulness. To set standards of logic or taste or scholarship or of any kind was to set up a censor. Who was to set the standard and enforce it? One of Mill's great fears was that the community might attempt to do so, thus establishing a tyranny of the majority.

While certainly extreme, Mill's position concerning freedom of expression was far from unprecedented, though he did not take the case so far in any of his other writings. His argument that action too should be unfettered as long as it posed no threat to anyone but the actor, however, was quite unusual. In *On Liberty,* it is clear, though not really explicit, that Mill was concerned much more with physical and material harm than with moral or spiritual harm when he asserted that society might restrain the individual from harming others. As truth emerged from the forum of free debate, the development of truly individualistic character in a person arose from the process of choosing types of conduct. For many of Mill's contemporaries, this was little more than advocacy of anarchy. Within the liberal tradition, freedom of action was regarded as good but not without limits. Free speech would lead to changes in those limits (laws, custom, and so forth) so that acceptable behaviors might be enlarged. Mill's emphasis on diversity and individual, unfettered, development was one of his significant contributions to liberalism.

The absolute nature of Mill's view of liberty left him with a number of difficult questions to confront. For example, what about indirect harm such as that caused by a drunk to his or her dependents? Does experience ever establish a moral truth so clearly that society should insist that it be observed? Mill insisted that beyond teaching rationality to children (the principle of liberty did not apply until an individual reached maturity), society had no right to require a standard of conduct. When society tried to do so, it usually simply insisted on the standard of the majority. Unfortunately, the examples provided in *On Liberty* tend to be issues such as religious beliefs, which had already been largely agreed upon as inappropriate for society to impose.

Another problem for Mill was the source of individual morality. He had long since rejected the possibility that mankind's moral sense was intuitive or innate. In the end, he asserted that moral sense was "natural" in that it was a "natural outgrowth" of human nature. Although this conclusion was not very satisfactory, Mill went further with the question.

Not only did the ideas in *On Liberty* not coincide with those contained in Mill's other work, but there were two issues that Mill was unwilling to leave to the workings of the principle of liberty: education and population control. He was willing to insist that parents be required to educate their children and that the growth of population be restrained. These matters were too critical for the welfare of humankind to be left to be developed, like truth, from debate; therefore, the state should intervene. This lack of consistency within his complete oeuvre and even within *On Liberty* itself seems to have been a result of the influence of Harriet Taylor Mill. Not only was she more inclined toward single-issue, simplistic thought than was Mill, but she also pressed Mill to pursue the issue of women's equality ever more vigorously. *On Liberty* reads as if it came from an extremely repressive society, but aside from what was called the "woman question," nineteenth century England was not such a society. Part of the purpose of *On Liberty* seems to have been to universalize the issue of feminine equality so that men had a stake in it and would take it seriously. This purpose apparently led Mill into a position more extreme than the one that he generally took.

Implications for Ethical Conduct. Mill's established reputation meant that *On Liberty* had an immediate and large audience. Although many reviewers and scholars took issue with some of its ideas, the book was enormously popular with undergraduates and the general reading public. Not only did it broaden the liberal attitude about freedom of speech, but it also led to a much greater support for freedom of action. Its influence continues to be strong in the late twentieth century. —*Fred R. van Hartesveldt*

See also Mill, John Stuart; Utilitarianism.

BIBLIOGRAPHY

Cowling, Maurice. *Mill and Liberalism.* Cambridge, England: Cambridge University Press, 1963.

Hamburger, Joseph. *Intellectuals in Politics: John Stuart Mill and the Philosophic Radicals.* New Haven, Conn.: Yale University Press, 1965.

Himmelfarb, Gertrude. *On Liberty and Liberalism: The Case of John Stuart Mill.* New York: Alfred A. Knopf, 1974.

Packe, Michael St. John. *The Life of John Stuart Mill.* London: Secker & Warburg, 1954.

On War: Book

TYPE OF ETHICS: Military ethics
DATE: Published 1832 as *Vom Kriege*
AUTHOR: Carl von Clausewitz (1780-1831)
SIGNIFICANCE: War is an extreme but natural extension of politics by violent means; therefore, from the standpoint of ethics, war is connected with the ethics of politics and has nothing to do with the military; grave moral powers do, however, exist within the military

Carl von Clausewitz's purpose in analyzing war is purely theoretical and not prescriptive. To the question "What is war?" he answers: "War is an act of violence to compel our opponent to fulfill our will" ("*Der Krieg ist . . . ein Akt der Gewalt, um den Gegner zur Erfüllung unseres Willens zu zwingen*"). War is not an isolated act; it is an extension of *Politik*—a blatant instrument of such policy. The decision to go to war and the proposed goal beyond victory are political, not military. Theory must, however, be analyzed in the context of real events. A paper war is not a real war; a real war is subject to influence by chance and circumstance. Real war is dangerous for its participants and is a test of their exertion.

War is not only "an elaborate duel" ("*ein erweiterter Zweikampf*"), a vast drama—a comedy for the victor, a tragedy for the loser. From another point of view, war is a game ("*ein Spiel*") and a "gamble" ("*ein Glücksspiel*"), both objectively and subjectively. A theory of war must be an analytical investigation that later might prove beneficial to reason and judgment. It must consider the ends and means of warfare, which consist of strategy and tactics. Tactics are the uses to which the army is put to achieve victory. Strategy has to do with the plan for achieving victory. The real activity of war lies in the tactical aspect of battle, since tactics govern fighting. The immediate object of battle is to destroy or overcome the enemy, but the ultimate object is to subject the enemy to one's will in a political sense. Toward this end a combatant may desire to enforce whatever peace it pleases; it may occupy the enemy's frontier districts and use them to make satisfactory bargains at the peace settlements.

See also *Art of War, The*; Military ethics.

Oppression

TYPE OF ETHICS: Human rights
ASSOCIATED WITH: Intergroup relations and the unjust exercise of power
DEFINITION: From the Latin root *oppressus* ("to press against or down upon"), "oppression" is the systematic subjugation or domination of a relatively disempowered social group by a group with more access to social power
SIGNIFICANCE: Has implications for conflict resolution, the distribution of resources, and multiculturalism

Within a given society or subculture, groups are often either accorded or denied access to rights and privileges, relative to other groups, based on specific socially constructed categories. This system is based on a belief in the inherent superiority of one group over all others and its right to dominate. While it is true that one individual can harass, intimidate, violate, molest, and brutalize another, in the broadest sense, "oppression" as a concept is generally discussed within a larger historical, social, and political context.

Oppression is composed of two key elements: prejudice and social power. "Prejudice"—from the Latin *praejudicium* ("previous judgment")—involves holding an adverse opinion or belief without just ground or before acquiring sufficient valid information. "Social power" can be defined as the ability to get what one wants and to influence others. "Target group" is the term given to those oppressed groups that are denied access to the rights and privileges enjoyed by other groups. Group members are oppressed simply on the basis of their target group status. (Synonyms for "target group" include "minority group," "oppressed group," "disenfranchised group," "subordinate group," and "stigmatized group," among others.) Examples of target groups in the United States are people of color—African Americans, Asian Americans, Latinos, Native Americans or "Indians" (race); immigrants (ethnicity or national origin); Jews, Muslims, atheists (religion); women (biological sex); gay, lesbian, and bisexual people (sexual orientation or identity); transgenderists (gender identity); working class and poor people (class); the very old and the very young (age); people with mental and physical disabilities (ability); and fat people (appearance). "Dominant group" is the term given to groups with access to rights and privileges that are denied to target groups. (Synonyms for "dominant group" include "majority group" and "oppressor group.") Examples of dominant groups in the United States are white people, or "Caucasians" (race); people of European, especially Anglo-Saxon, ancestry (race, ethnicity, national origin); Christians, and especially Protestant sects (religion); males (biological sex); heterosexuals (sexual orientation or identity); middle and "owning" class (class); people generally between the ages of twenty-one and fifty (age); and people considered "able bodied" physically and mentally (ability, appearance).

Most people find themselves both in groups targeted for oppression and in those dominant groups that are granted relatively higher degrees of power and prestige. Some examples of such situations are a white middle-class woman, a Jewish man, an African American Christian man, a white lesbian, and a white blind thirty-five-year-old man.

Forms of Oppression. There are as many names for the varieties of oppression as there are for the categories of target and dominant groups based, for example, on race (racism), ethnicity or patriotism (ethnocentrism, chauvinism, imperialism, xenophobia), religious affiliation (religious prejudice, anti-Semitism), biological sex (sexism, misogyny), sexual orientation or identity (homophobia, biphobia, heterosexism), economic status (classism), age (ageism), and mental and physical ability (ableism).

This does not mean that all groups experience forms of oppression similarly. The experiences of victims of racism, for example, are not identical to those of the victims of homophobia. The forms of oppression, however, run parallel and at points intersect. All involve negative prejudgments whose purpose is to maintain control or power over others. Oppression can be the result of a deliberate, conscious act, or it may be unconscious and unintentional yet still have oppressive consequences.

Manifestations of Oppression. Oppression involves negative beliefs (that may or may not be expressed), exclusion, denial of civil and legal protections, and, in some cases, overt acts of violence directed against target groups. The many forms of oppression can be said to operate on four distinct but interrelated levels: the personal, the inter-

This Tibetan refugee left his homeland to escape from the oppressive rule of the Chinese, who overran Tibet in 1950. (National Archives)

personal, the institutional, and the societal (or cultural). The personal level refers to an individual's belief (bias or prejudice) that members of target groups are inferior psychologically or physically. The interpersonal level is manifested when a bias affects relations among individuals, transforming prejudice into its active component—discrimination. The institutional level refers to the ways in which governmental agencies; businesses; and educational, religious, and professional organizations systematically discriminate against target groups. Sometimes laws, codes, or policies actually enforce discrimination. The societal (or cultural) level refers to social norms or codes of behavior that, although not expressly written into law or policy, nevertheless work within a society to legitimize prejudice and discrimination. This often involves epithets and stereotypes directed against target groups. Oppression is said to be "internalized" when target group members take on the shame that is associated with their target group status.

Functions of Oppression. Dominant groups maintain oppression over target groups for a number of reasons: to gain or enhance economic, political, or personal rewards or to avoid the potential loss of such; to protect self-esteem against psychological doubts or conflicts; to promote and enhance dominant group value systems; to better comprehend a complex world by categorizing or stereotyping others.

Though oppression clearly serves many functions, it can also be said to hurt members of the dominant group. Frederick Douglass, a former slave and an abolitionist, said at a civil rights meeting in Washington, D.C., on October 22, 1883: "No [person] can put a chain about the ankle of [another person] without at last finding the other end fastened about his [or her] neck." His words are also relevant today, for everyone is diminished when anyone is demeaned.

—*Warren J. Blumenfeld*

See also Ageism; Anti-Semitism; Bigotry; Disability rights; Discrimination; Ethnocentrism; Homophobia; Racial prejudice; Racism; Segregation; Sexism.

BIBLIOGRAPHY

Allport, Gordon. *The Nature of Prejudice*. Reading, Mass.: Addison-Wesley, 1954.

Blumenfeld, Warren J., ed. *Homophobia: How We All Pay the Price*. Boston: Beacon Press, 1992.

Daly, Mary. *Gynecology: The Metaethics of Radical Feminism*. Boston: Beacon Press, 1978.

Goffman, Erving. *Stigma: Notes on the Management of Spoiled Identity*. New York: Simon & Schuster, 1963.

Kovel, Joel. *White Racism*. New York: Columbia University Press, 1984.

Smith, Barbara, ed. *Home Girls: A Black Feminist Anthology*. New York: Kitchen Table Press, 1983.

Wistrich, Robert S. *Anti-Semitism: The Longest Hatred*. New York: Pantheon Books, 1991.

Zinn, Howard. *A People's History of the United States*. New York: Harper & Row, 1980.

Ortega y Gasset, José (May 9, 1883, Madrid, Spain— Oct. 18, 1955, Madrid, Spain): Philosopher

TYPE OF ETHICS: Modern history

ACHIEVEMENTS: Author of *La rebelión de las masas* (1929; *The Revolt of the Masses*, 1930) and many volumes of essays and articles

SIGNIFICANCE: A metaphysics professor and existentialist, Ortega y Gasset helped to bring Spain into contact with the thought and culture of the rest of Europe

José Ortega y Gasset was a professor of metaphysics at the University of Madrid from 1910 until 1936. He had traveled and studied in Europe, especially in Germany, and when he returned, he brought European philosophy and political thought that had been ignored in Spain for centuries. An excellent and prolific writer, he wrote scores of newspaper and magazine essays and articles on philosophy and on general cultural topics. He studied and taught metaphysics, because he was interested in questions about the fundamental nature of reality. His quest for an ultimate reality led him to questions about the nature of knowledge and the nature of society. It was his social theories that made Ortega y Gasset an international figure. In *La rebelión de las masas*, he argued that society is always ready to topple and that humankind is always ready to slip back into barbarism. Only by bowing to an elite class can people keep their societies going. This small, elite group thinks and plans and holds the power—it gets things done. So long as everyone else is willing to accept this leadership, human societies can stand firm.

See also Elitism; Existentialism.

Ought/can implication

TYPE OF ETHICS: Theory of ethics

DATE: Expressed in Aristotle's *Nicomachean Ethics* in the late fourth century B.C.E.

ASSOCIATED WITH: Italian philosopher Saint Thomas Aquinas, German philosopher Immanuel Kant, and British philosopher R. M. Hare

DEFINITION: "Ought" signifies moral obligation and "can" signifies ability or possibility; according to the "ought-implies-can" principle, if one is morally obligated to do a thing, it is possible for one to do it

SIGNIFICANCE: If one is charged with failing to fulfill an obligation to do *x*, and if doing *x* was not possible, one can use the principle to say that one was not really obligated to do *x*

The "ought-implies-can" principle has practical and theoretical importance in ethics. In particular cases, it provides a defense against the charge of wrongdoing, not by providing an excuse for the wrong, but by denying that any wrong was committed. Assuming the principle to be true, if one can never act otherwise, then any time one thinks that one did not act in such a way as to fulfill an obligation is really a time when one did not have that obligation. In other words, assuming the truth of the principle and that one can never act otherwise, one can never do wrong.

The root idea of the moral "ought" seems to be that something is morally necessary or morally owed. "Ought" is supposed to imply "can" in the sense that if it is not true that one can do *x*, then it is not true that one is obligated to do it. Some people think that the principle is, like the statement "Bachelors are males," true simply because of the meanings of the words. It is self-contradictory, however, to say "Bachelors are not males," and it is not self-contradictory to say "I know what I ought to do, but I cannot do it." Therefore, the principle does not seem to be a conceptual truth.

R. M. Hare, in chapter 4 of his *Freedom and Reason* (1963), claims that people use "ought" in moral contexts to prescribe or advise, and that it makes no sense to advise one to do something that is impossible. Even if such advice is pointless, however, it does not follow that the principle is true. One does not show that "believing x" implies that "x is true" by pointing out that in certain contexts it makes no sense to advise one to believe something that is false.

A defender of the principle may say that people do not blame a person for failing to do something once they realize that it was impossible for that person to do it. The suggestion is that people do not blame in such cases because the person's inability to do something meant that the person or she was not, after all, obligated to do it. It seems, however, that people might not blame in such a case because they accept the person's inability as an excuse for failing to fulfill the obligation, not because they accept the inability as a reason for saying that the person was not obligated.

A person may have inappropriate feelings and be unable to control them. Even then, it may be reasonable to say that that person ought to feel ashamed, grateful, disturbed, or remorseful, and that there is something wrong with anyone who cannot have these feelings. One may say that the "ought" in such cases expresses an ideal, as does the "ought" in the statement "Everyone ought to be able to live like a king." An "ought" that expresses an ideal does not imply "can," but not every case in which "ought" does not imply "can" seems to involve an ideal "ought."

Consider, for example, cases of culpable powerlessness. Imagine that Smith promises to meet Jones in two hours, then changes his mind and takes a powerful sedative. At the time of the promised meeting, Smith cannot be there, but it still seems that he ought to be there. Defenders of the principle may say that Smith's obligation to be there ceased once he could not be there, but that he did wrong in making it impossible for himself to be there. If people should be blamed for failing to fulfill an obligation, however, then Smith was obligated to be there, since one would blame him for not being there as well as for making it impossible for himself to be there. To hold to the principle in cases of culpable powerlessness seems to make it too easy for people to cancel their obligations.

Alvin I. Goldman, in chapter 7 of his *A Theory of Human Action* (1970), considers rewriting the principle as follows to avoid such cases: If a person ought to do x at time t, then there is some time, at or before t, at which he is able to do x at t. In that case, there is no reason to say that Smith is not obligated to keep his appointment, since before he took the sedative he was able to keep the appointment he had made for time t.

Now, however, cases of powerlessness that should rule out obligation will not do so. For example, if before Smith could take the sedative he was struck with complete paralysis while alone in his apartment, his obligation should terminate. It will not terminate given the revised principle, however, since according to it, he *can* still keep his appointment.

There is, however, the following basis for believing that at least one interpretation of the principle is true. If a person ought to do x, he is properly subject to moral judgment if he fails to do it. If he is properly subject to moral judgment if he fails to do x, then it is physically possible for him to do it. (Something is physically possible if it is consistent with the laws of nature. Being able to fly is inconsistent with those laws, and that is why not being able to fly is not properly subject to moral judgment.) Therefore, if a person ought to do x, it is physically possible for him to do it. If "ought" also implies a sense of "can" that rules out causal determination, the principle provides some reason for believing that determinism is incompatible with freedom and moral responsibility.
—*Gregory P. Rich*

See also Determinism and freedom; Moral responsibility; Responsibility.

BIBLIOGRAPHY

Goldman, Alvin I. *A Theory of Human Action*. Englewood Cliffs, N.J.: Prentice-Hall, 1970.

Henderson, G. P. "'Ought' Implies 'Can.'" *Philosophy* 41 (April, 1966): 101-112.

Montefiore, Alan. "'Ought' and 'Can.'" *Philosophical Quarterly* 8 (January, 1958): 24-40.

O'Connor, D. J. *Free Will*. Garden City, N.Y.: Anchor Books, 1971.

Stocker, Michael. "'Ought' and 'Can.'" *Australasian Journal of Philosophy* 49, no. 3 (December, 1971): 303-317.

White, Alan R. *Modal Thinking*. Ithaca, N.Y.: Cornell University Press, 1975.

Pacifism

TYPE OF ETHICS: Politico-economic ethics

DATE: First century to present

ASSOCIATED WITH: Antiwar movements, Jainism, Buddhism, Historic Peace Churches, A. J. Muste, John Howard Yoder, Mohandas Gandhi, and Martin Luther King, Jr.

DEFINITION: Refers to moral opposition to war in particular or violence in general; the literal meaning of pacifism is peacemaking

SIGNIFICANCE: Pacifism raises questions about the morality of war itself, beyond the issue of whether a specific war is just or unjust; it also offers individuals a possible basis for nonviolent resistance to the state

One of the most ethically troubling aspects of human existence is the problem of war, because of its connection with killing. Given the moral aversion to killing found in most ethical theories, war has been the subject of much ethical reflection and analysis in an attempt to provide either a justification for or a critique of war. Pacifism results from the belief that war can never be justified and is always immoral. Although pacifism may take different forms, moral opposition to war is a common theme. One of the questions that pacifists have tried to answer is whether pacifism also implies opposition to all forms of violence in addition to war.

History and Sources. While pacifism has a philosophical grounding, its main source is religion. The Jain tradition in India practices pacifism by avoiding killing even insects. Buddhism also has a pacifist dimension. The dominant source for pacifism in Western culture, however, has been the Christian tradition.

Employing elements of the Hebrew scriptures, such as peace, righteousness, and compassion, along with an image of Jesus as nonviolent, early Christians began to raise ethical

Pacifist Jeanette Rankin, who was also the first woman member of Congress (1932). (AP/Wide World Photos)

questions about war and participation in the military. The basis for these concerns centered on two factors. First, the Roman army had its own gods and religious rituals that contradicted both the Christian emphasis on one God and Christian forms of worship. Participation in the Roman army for a Christian would therefore be equivalent to idolatry or false worship. The second factor was based on more explicit ethical concerns about the morality of killing. Using the statements of Jesus, especially those taken from the Sermon on the Mount, some early Christians developed a moral framework that opposed the shedding of blood and, by extension, participation in war. Warfare was seen as a denial of the message of Jesus regarding love of enemies as well as a rejection of the kind of life that Jesus demanded of his disciples. The question thus arose whether a person could be both a Christian and a warrior.

This ethical issue of Christian participation in war increased as Christianity came more and more to be the established religion of the state following the proclamation of toleration by Constantine in 313. Christians faced the dual changes of subsiding persecution and more direct involvement in the affairs of state, including war.

The ethical concern over war turned on the conflict between two principles: not harming others and protecting the innocent. Sometimes protecting the innocent might entail harming others, even killing them. War also became a matter of loyalty to the state. Moral qualms about killing were often resolved by means of a separation between public and private ethics. Christians could kill and participate in war as a consequence of the public duty of being soldiers, but not as private individuals. In addition, the development of the just war theory began to be the dominant ethical perspective on war in Christianity. There was still a strong pacifist element within the Christian tradition, however, and it surfaced most dramatically in the Protestant Reformation during the sixteenth century.

The Radical Reformation, or the Anabaptists, viewed war as directly antithetical to the Christian message. The Anabaptists sought a return to what was described as the New Testament Church, which they understood to be completely opposed to war and violence. One of the major documents of the Anabaptist movement, the Schleitheim Confession of 1527, holds that the use of the sword is outside the perfection of Christ. The Anabaptists thus rejected the distinction between public and private ethics and the justification that it provided for war. As a consequence, they also sought to limit the demands of the state and to call into question the claims of value made on behalf of the state. The Anabaptists are the ancestors of the Historic Peace Churches, such as those of the Mennonites, Quakers, and Amish. Pacifism is a central component of their views of Christian ethics.

Pacifism was also defended on humanistic and philosophical grounds. Desiderius Erasmus, the sixteenth century Christian humanist, argued that war was wasteful and impractical. It offered nothing from which humanity could benefit and only revealed the horrors that human beings could visit upon one another. The eighteenth century philosopher Immanuel Kant emphasized the impracticality and irrationality of war. His famous dictum to treat people as ends and never as means also created a strong argument against the morality of war, since it seemed that war did treat people as a means. These religious and philosophical views have combined to give pacifism its focus and variety. John Howard Yoder lists eighteen types of pacifism in his book *Nevertheless* (1976).

Moral Foundations. The moral basis of pacifism usually has several dimensions: a view of God, a normative understanding of humanity, and the importance of love. A philosophically based pacifism may not fully develop a view of God. If God is part of the pacifist ethic, God is seen as underlying creation, which imparts a moral structure to the world in the direction of sustaining creation. War, which is destructive, denies the divine relationship to creation and becomes immoral. Humanity is characterized by a fundamental unity. Beneath the differences that qualify human existence is an explicit humanness that extends beyond differences such as race, religion, or ethnic origin. Pacifism seeks to uphold the basic unity by refusing to allow the differences to become justifications for war and killing. As a result, love is often the central moral feature of pacifism in a practical sense. A pacifist would claim that love, as the basis for human actions, entails the rejection of war and possibly even all forms of violence. For this reason, the goals of pacifism are more than simple opposition to war; they involve finding alternatives to the use of violence to resolve conflicts and an emphasis on peace research and education.   —*Ron Large*

See also Ahimsā; Conscientious objection; Gandhi, Mohandas Karamchand; Jain ethics; Jesus; King, Martin Luther, Jr.; Nonviolence; Peace studies; War and peace.

BIBLIOGRAPHY

Brock, Peter. *Freedom from Violence: Sectarian Nonresistance from the Middle Ages to the Great War*. Toronto: University of Toronto Press, 1991.

Cady, Duane. *From Warism to Pacifism: A Moral Continuum*. Philadelphia: Temple University Press, 1989.

Hauerwas, Stanley. *The Peaceable Kingdom*. Notre Dame, Ind.: University of Notre Dame Press, 1983.

Helgeland, John, R. J. Daly, and J. Patout Burns. *Christians and the Military: The Early Experience*. Edited by R. J. Daly. Philadelphia: Fortress Press, 1985.

Mayer, Peter, ed. *The Pacifist Conscience*. Chicago: Regnery, 1967.

Miller, Richard. *Interpretation of Conflict: Ethics, Pacifism, and the Just-War Tradition*. Chicago: University of Chicago Press, 1990.

Teichman, Jenny. *Pacifism and the Just War*. New York: Basil Blackwell, 1986.

Yoder, John Howard. *Nevertheless: The Varieties and Shortcomings of Religious Pacifism*. Scottdale, Pa.: Herald Press, 1976.

Passive resistance. *See* **Nonviolence.**

Pain

TYPE OF ETHICS: Bioethics

DEFINITION: A sensory and emotional experience associated with injury, illness, and suffering

SIGNIFICANCE: Perceptions of pain and attitudes toward those in pain are shaped by culture and must be examined to determine ethical responses and treatments

The treatment and relief of pain is often considered to be a central goal of the medical profession, at least by those who seek care. People usually think of pain as a warning sign that something has gone wrong in the body's systems; however, not all pain serves this function, and not all pain is indicative of physical malfunction.

Physiology. Pain is usually separated (somewhat arbitrarily) into two diagnoses: acute and chronic. While chronic pain is often defined clinically as acute pain persisting longer than six months, there are differences in perception and meaning that go beyond merely temporal distinctions.

Acute pain is also of two types, classified by the speed with which the actual nerve impulses reach the brain. When an event, such as a burn, triggers signals to be sent to the brain, one set of signals travels much faster. These are the initial impulses, "fast" pain, that travel on myelinated (sheathed in a protein-lipid layer) A delta fibers. These impulses reach the brain in a fraction of a second, while the "slow" pain, which travels on unmyelinated C fibers, takes up to a couple of seconds to register in a person's consciousness. The further the site of stimulus is from the brain, the greater the difference in the times these signals register. Fast pain is sharp and bright. Slow pain is dull and aching, and ultimately more unpleasant.

In addition to the nerve impulses sent to the brain, for which the chemical neurotransmitter seems to be substance P (for pain), chemicals are released at the site of stimulus. Prostaglandins draw blood to the area to gain the healing and infection-fighting power of white blood cells. Prostaglandins also increase the sensitivity of the nerves in the immediate vicinity of the injury, as do bradykinins and leukotrienes, which are also released.

Psychological Components of Pain. Pain cannot, however, be relegated to mere physical perception. The knowledge of the consequences of pain is inextricably entwined with the feeling and assessment of pain. In a now-famous study published in 1946, Henry K. Beecher found that men who were severely wounded in battle reported far less pain (and some no pain at all) than did civilian patients with comparable wounds caused by surgery. The reason for this seems clear: For men in battle, severe wounds are the ticket home. Pain cannot be separated from the personal and social consequences of its presence.

Pain Versus Suffering. Many people take pain and suffering to be synonymous, yet they are different and distinct. Pain can occur without causing suffering, as does the pain that athletes endure during competition. There can certainly be suffering without pain, either physical, such as severe itching, or mental, as in grief. (Some authorities do not distinguish between physical and mental suffering, believing them to be so linked as to be inseparable.) Pain is usually taken to be a physical perception, while suffering is psychological distress. Intrinsic to suffering is a threat to the integrity of a person as a whole. The anticipation of pain and loss can cause as much suffering as the actuality thereof.

Meanings of Pain. Pain has had different interpretations in different cultures and periods of history. While today Western culture ostensibly reaches toward the eradication of pain, this has by no means always been the case. Aside from medical inability to eliminate pain in the past, pain and suffering have themselves been considered valuable in many cultures. The Christian religion, in particular, has traditionally deemed experiencing pain, in some circumstances, a virtue. Suffering, especially suffering for others, is considered one of the highest forms of sanctity, as can be seen from the litany of saints by martyrdom throughout the ages. In other religious traditions, pain and suffering are, or can be, due punishment for sins or wrong actions committed either in this life, as in Judaism and Islam, or in past lives, as in Hinduism and Buddhism. The word "pain" in English is derived from the Latin word *poena*, meaning "punishment." The English word for one who seeks medical care, "patient," also comes from the Latin. Its root, *pati*, means "the one who suffers." Underlying these derivations, and extending beyond the words themselves, is the cultural acceptance that pain and suffering are an inevitable part of life and as such are not intrinsically evil. This attitude is the basis for medical hesitancy to consider pain a problem to be treated in and of itself, rather than simply as a symptom of other disease or injury.

Treatment of Pain. Because of these deep-rooted cultural attitudes toward pain and those who suffer, only recently has aggressive treatment of pain become an issue in medical ethics. Studies have shown surprising underutilization of pain-relieving medication for sufferers of severe pain, especially among terminal cancer patients. This seems to be because of fears of addiction to narcotics and a lack of knowledge of proper use. The use of heroin for terminal patients has long been accepted in Great Britain but continues to be prohibited in the United States.

Alternative forms of treatment are becoming more acceptable, although the efficacy of some remains to be substantiated. Biofeedback techniques, chiropractic, hypnosis, and TENS (transcutaneous electrical nerve stimulation) are generally accepted to be of value for many patients. Acupuncture is gaining ground in the United States. For millions of people, however, effective pain relief is still a phenomenon of the future.

—*Margaret Hawthorne*

See also Biofeedback; Hypnosis; Illness.

BIBLIOGRAPHY

Bowker, John W. "Pain and Suffering: Religious Perspectives." In *Encyclopedia of Bioethics*, edited by Warren T. Reich. New York: Free Press, 1978.

Ganong, William F. *Review of Medical Physiology*. 14th ed. Norwalk, Conn.: Appleton & Lange, 1989.

Morris, David B. *The Culture of Pain*. Berkeley: University of California Press, 1991.

Pan-Africanism

TYPE OF ETHICS: Race and ethnicity

DATE: Coined 1900

DEFINITION: A macronationalist movement aimed at uniting peoples of African descent

SIGNIFICANCE: Seeks through racial unity to find solutions to the problems of flagrant injustice, economic deprivation, and discrimination based on skin color

The so-called discovery and partitioning of Africa was a classic story of gold, glory and God, compounded by greed, adventure, and missionary zeal. In the process, imperialist invaders squeezed the continent of its wealth, while announcing to the world that they were bringing the benefits of civilization to backward peoples. Pan-Africanism awakened a new spirit that rejected patience and the acceptance of suffering and inferiority. The emotional impetus for its concepts flowed from the experience of a widely dispersed people—those of African descent—who believed themselves either physically, through dispossession or slavery, or socially, economically, politically, and mentally, through colonialism, to have lost their homeland. With this loss came enslavement, persecution, inferiority, discrimination, and dependency. It involved a loss of freedom and dignity. This realization, bolstered by an awareness of their common heritage, led to a desire among black people for some link with their African origins. It became a vehicle for the struggle of black people to regain their wealth, pride, strength, and independence as emotions were converted into ideas and ideas into slogans. Above all, however, the ideals of Pan-Africanism grew from the desire to regain dignity and equality for all black people.

Growth in Diaspora. Originally, Pan-Africanism was dominated by the leadership of the blacks residing in the United States and the West Indies. During the late 1870's, following the era of Reconstruction, blacks in the United States were alienated by growing racism and economic depression. Some among them began to think in terms of returning to Africa. Marcus Garvey, who was of Jamaican origin, would later exploit this discontent by preaching a back-to-Africa message to the blacks of the New World. His idea of exodus to Africa was embedded in the prospective creation of an exclusively black race, an idea that earned him the endorsement and eventually the open support of the Ku Klux Klan, who, although for different reasons, welcomed his desire to expatriate all blacks to Africa. Another pioneer spokesman for Pan-Africanism in the diaspora was

PAN-AFRICANISM TIME LINE		
Time	**Place**	**Event**
1900	London	Henry Sylvester Williams calls the first-ever Pan-African Conference.
1920	New York	Declaration of the Rights of the Negro Peoples of the World is read at a conference held in New York. During the conference, Marcus Garvey is elected Provisional President of Africa.
1919-1927	Europe and the United States	W. E. B. Du Bois calls four Pan-African Congresses.
1945	Manchester, England	The Fifth Pan-African Congress, which is organized by Africans, is held.
1958	Accra, Ghana	The first conference of Independent African States is held.
1959	Ghana	The Ghana-Guinea Union is established. It is declared by its signatories to be the beginning of a Union of Independent African States.
1960	Addis Ababa, Ethiopia	The second conference of Independent African States is held. The Pan-African movement splits into two major factions because of ideological rifts.
1960	Brazzaville, Congo	The Brazzaville Group (otherwise known as the Union of African States and Madagascar) convenes and makes public its moderate views on African unity and related issues.
January 3-7, 1961	Casablanca, Morocco	The Casablanca Conference announces that it favors a political union that would eventually lead to a "United States of Africa."
May 8-12, 1961	Monrovia, Liberia	Taking its cue from the Brazzaville Group, the Monrovia Conference announces that it favors a form of unity that allows for the preservation of national sovereignty.
July 1, 1961	Accra, Ghana	In response to the Brazzaville Group, Ghana, Guinea, and Mali issue the Charter for the Union of African States.
May 25, 1963	Addis Ababa, Ethiopia	The Organization for African Unity, which unites the two camps, is founded.

W. E. B. Du Bois. His main concern was achieving absolute equality for the entire black race, an idea that had been born out of his conviction that the "favored few" had no moral right to prosper at the expense of the toil of the "tortured many."

The Nationalist Dimension. The second stage of Pan-Africanism began with the gradual decolonization of Africa after World War II, when the character and leadership of the movement became more Africanized. Educated Africans who had come to study in universities in Europe and America had come to know firsthand about racial intolerance and the economic subjugation of blacks. Three of those students, Kwame Nkrumah (Ghana), Nnamdi Azikiwe (Nigeria), and Hastings Banda (Malawi), all of whom had been exposed to the Pan-Africanist movement of the diaspora, would later become presidents of their respective countries at independence.

The African nationalist leaders gave a new meaning to Pan-Africanism—African solidarity and unity—for it was believed then (and now) that the process of political and economic emancipation that had begun during the nationalist days could only be consolidated through a cohesive and united continental Africa. The dreams of African unity that they had so nurtured and cherished would run into all kinds of problems, however, and by 1960, ideological differences had sharply divided the newly independent nations into rival camps, a division that was further aggravated by superpower rivalry. While some insisted on a political union that would require giving up some sovereignty, others favored a simple association of states. This proved to be harmful for the continent's much-needed economic development and political stability, and it was not until 1963 that they finally found a common ground with the establishment of the Organization of African Unity (OAU).

The OAU's charter sought to "promote unity and solidarity of African states" through "political, economic and scientific cooperation." Ever since, the continent has been plagued by a series of problems ranging from political instability to outright economic disasters. Allegations of human rights abuse are widespread, and in many cases, the prospects for majority rule have been dampened by the installation of military regimes, which usually are corrupt and morally bankrupt. Civil wars and cases of mass starvation are rampant, while the whole continent continues to be haunted by the discriminatory policies of South Africa. Many of these problems have been blamed on, among other things, the lack of a sound guiding philosophy for development as well as the absence of a leadership code of ethics.

—*Olusoji Akomolafe*

See also Integration; Nationalism.

BIBLIOGRAPHY

Ajala, Adekunle. *Pan-Africanism: Evolution, Progress and Prospects*. London: A. Deutsch, 1973.

Dias, Joffre P. F. *Le Panafricanisme et l'Organisation de l'Unité Africaine: Synthèse historique et bibliographique*. Geneva: J. P. F. Dias, 1988.

Mathurin, Owen Charles. *Henry Sylvester Williams and the Origins of the Pan-African Movement, 1869-1911*. Westport, Conn.: Greenwood Press, 1976.

Rimmer, Douglas, ed. *Africa Thirty Years On*. Portsmouth, N.H.: Heinemann, 1992.

Tokareva, Zinaida. *Organization of African Unity: Twenty-five Years of Struggle*. Translated by Clance Nsiah Jaybex. Moscow: Progress, 1989.

Panentheism

TYPE OF ETHICS: Beliefs and practices
DATE: From antiquity
DEFINITION: A religious/philosophical belief system that attempts to mediate between theism and pantheism
SIGNIFICANCE: Attempts to explain the relationship between God and the universe

To understand panentheism, one must also become familiar with pantheism, for both philosophies consider God, this world, and the universe, and both try to explain how the three are related. The older of the two is pantheism, which posits that God and the universe are one and the same. Despite apparent diversity and disorder in the cosmos, the universe is ordered and unified, and that order and that unification are expressions of God. Because pantheists give no place to the transcendence of God, however, that philosophical position eventually gave rise to panentheism, whose advocates hold that all reality is part of the being of God and that God transcends all reality. God is the universe, but he is also much more. Although the philosopher who first coined and defined the term "panentheism" was the German Karl Christian Friederich Krause (1791-1832), various early Greek philosophers (such as Thales, Xenophanes, and Parmenides) held many views that were consistent with panentheism.

Panentheism. In developing their philosophical "system," modern panentheists usually follow Krause, who attempted to mediate between theism and pantheism. Panentheists believe that God (absolute being) is primordial, a being without contrariety who is one with the universe but is not exhausted by it (God is bigger than the universe). All individuals are part of a spiritual whole, a league of humanity. For the human being, self-consciousness provides the starting point of panentheism, for it allowed, Krause held, the ego to learn that it was both mind and body and also to learn that it was part of God.

Because God is good, human-kind should share in the goodness, and humankind's inner union with God becomes the foundation of ethics, with ethics becoming the heart of religion. Just as a living cell has certain freedom within a living body, however, so, too, do humans have a degree of freedom. Krause viewed all individuals as part of the divine, and he became a crusading reformer who, for example, argued against capital punishment; he also believed that republican government was the only political system that was worthy of the divine. Regarding all "organized" religion as oppressive, he criticized theocracy, religious censorship, and religionists' disdain for the world.

Closely related to both pantheism and panentheism is the doctrine of "emanation," which asserts that an overflowing superabundance of the divine God resulted in the production of the universe. All reality, then, flows from a perfect and transcendent principle. The first gift of the divine overflow was intelligence, which allowed humans to understand their world, their reality. Opposed to evolutionism, emanationism is timeless, and its source (God) remains undiminished.

Panentheism: Its Critics and Its Supporters. Most critics hold that both pantheism and panentheism fail to account for the individuality, the personality, and the freedom of each human being. Likewise, both beliefs fail to account for evil, ignorance, and error on the part of some people. Thus, negatives exist in the world and the universe—negatives that could not emanate from a perfectly good God. Using acquired knowledge and the powers of observation, critics also deny that the universe contains total unity. Indeed, the idea of a unified universe is actually devoid of content, because diversity obviously exists. Likewise, modern scientific progress is not in accord with a unity theory. Darwin's evolutionary theory, for example, stands opposed to both pantheism and panentheism. Organized religion also remained most critical of both pantheism and panentheism; one religionist called both beliefs "worms" of heretical "perversity" and inventions of the devil.

Some critics of panentheism attack the philosophic reputation of Krause, who gave the doctrine its most complete explanation. During his lifetime, for example, his ideas were so suspect that he was denied professorships at such prestigious universities as Göttingen and Munich. Furthermore, he coined many words that had meaning only for him (and that confused later scholars). Likewise, he also produced bizarre neologisms that were too much for the German language, as well as being untranslatable.

Over time, supporters of panentheism—such as Krause's disciples Julian Sanz del Rio of Spain, Heinrich Ahrens of Belgium, and Hermann von Leohardi of Germany—attempted to answer the critics, but in doing so they raised more questions. For example, while grappling with the problem of evil, some supporters argued that evil resulted only when an individual organism—because of ego—tried to tear itself away from the harmony of the whole (which is part of God). Yet such a defense actually raises the question about the goodness of God. Why would God create organisms that ultimately try to tear away?

Although panentheism has shown a remarkable ability to survive, such survival is no indication that—especially in view of the criticisms—it has any basis in fact.

—*James Smallwood*

See also God; Pantheism.

BIBLIOGRAPHY
Aiken, Alfred. *That Which Is, a Book on the Absolute.* New York: Hiller Press, 1955.

Hegel, G. W. F. *Lectures on the Philosophy of Religion.* Translated by E. B. Speirs and J. B. Sanderson. 3 vols. London: K. Paul, Trench, Trubner, 1895.

Jacob, Margaret C. *The Radical Enlightenment: Pantheists, Freemasons, and Republicans. London: Allen & Unwin, 1981.*

Piper, H. W. *The Active Universe.* London: University of London Press, 1962.

Spinoza, Benedictus de. *The Collected Works of Spinoza.* Edited and translated by Edwin Curley. Princeton, N.J.: Princeton University Press, 1985-present.

Wolfson, Harry A. *The Philosophy of Spinoza.* Cambridge, Mass.: Harvard University Press, 1983.

Pantheism

TYPE OF ETHICS: Beliefs and practices
DATE: From antiquity; popularized in the eighteenth century
ASSOCIATED WITH: Found in many religious and philosophical systems from antiquity to the present
DEFINITION: The belief that God is synonymous with the universe; God is everything, and everything is God
SIGNIFICANCE: This affirmation of the immanence of God within nature encourages an ethical stance of "reverence for life" and the goal of "harmony with the universe"

Pantheism is older than civilization. Some see its origins in animism, the primal religious conviction that everything has a soul or spirit. Popularized during the Enlightenment, the English word "pantheism" is from two Greek roots, *pan* ("all") and *theos* ("god"), meaning that "God is everything." This term suggests that God is the totality of all things—real and imagined, actual or potential. As a being "apart" or "separate" from nature, God does not "exist." Within the Western tradition, Pantheism was a powerful moral force for the Stoics, the Neoplatonists, and such modern thinkers as Baruch Spinoza. Within the Eastern traditions, Pantheism is evident in Islamic mysticism (Sufism), certain types of Taoism (urging conformity to the *Tao*, or "rhythm of the world"), and Hinduism.

See also *Ethics*; God; Marcus Aurelius; Panentheism; Spinoza, Baruch; Stoic ethics; Taoist ethics.

Paradoxes in ethics

TYPE OF ETHICS: Theory of ethics
DATES: Problems originated 1950 (collective action) and 1951 (cyclical preferences in Arrow's problem)
ASSOCIATED WITH: Brian Barry, Russell Hardin, Kenneth Arrow, and others
DEFINITION: Ethical theorists have attempted to promote rationality as a basis for value consensus to solve collective action and decision-making problems
SIGNIFICANCE: Two paradoxes illustrate that rationality alone is insufficient to generate an ethical consensus that makes action or decision making possible in many cases

Ethical questions deal with the correct values one should use in making individual and collective decisions. The dilemma for recent ethical thinkers has been to agree upon a set of values that may form the basis for collective decisions, given the increasing pluralism of many societies and the global environment. A common response has been that even though all individuals may not agree on value issues, if all individuals agree to behave *rationally*—that is, to act in a consistent manner in pursuing their individual self-interests—then collective goals can be reached and collective decisions can be made. Unfortunately, two problems show that ethical paradoxes arise even when the only assumption one makes about individual motivations is that all individuals are acting to maximize their own utilities. These paradoxes cast doubt on the idea that rationality is a sufficient means of reaching collective decisions or goals.

Definition—Logic of Collective Action. Two political theorists, Brian Barry and Russell Hardin, define a paradox as a set of conflicting or contradictory arguments to which one is led by apparently sound arguments. The first paradox of rationality to be discussed is the problem of collective action. This problem states that a self-interested individual may not be able to work with others toward a collective good even when all individuals involved realize that their individual interests would be served if all cooperated in the venture. A "collective good" is defined as a benefit in which all in a group may share, even if all do not contribute to its creation or maintenance. Examples of collective goods include clean air, which all may breathe even if all individuals did not help clean up the environment, or public television, which all may watch even if all did not send in contributions during a pledge drive.

It has been generally assumed in the social sciences that self-interested individuals will contribute to collective goods if they feel that they receive more in benefits than the cost of contribution; hence, the common appeal from public television that "if you feel the entertainment on PBS is worth more than $100 a year, please pledge this amount to the station." The logic of collective action, however, disputes this claim.

Assume that one individual does believe that the benefits received will outweigh the costs of contributing. If the individual contributes to the goal and the goal is reached, that individual's profit is the worth of a share of the collective good minus the cost of contribution. If the individual does not contribute to the goal, however, and the goal is reached, that individual's profit is the worth of his share of the collective good with no deductions. Under these circumstances, the self-interested individual should "free-ride" on the work of others and not contribute. If the individual contributes to the goal and the goal is not reached, the individual's profit is negative and is equal to the cost of contribution, since there is no collective good to share. If the individual does not contribute to the goal and the goal is not reached, the individual's profit is zero. Under these circumstances, the self-interested individual should once again not contribute. Hence, the individual should not contribute regardless of whether the goal is reached; the only exception to this rule occurs when one individual's contribution will make the difference between success or failure in the venture. Given that the chances of such a situation are very small in large groups, no large-scale collective action should be possible. One may ask, of course, "what if all persons acted that way?" The sting of the problem is that all self-interested persons should be expected to act this way, so that goods such as clean air, public television, and others should not be created by voluntary contributions.

Proposed Solutions. Some people have argued that a sense of altruism might lead individuals to contribute to a collective good. There are two problems with this argument. First, even if one is motivated by humanitarian concerns, it still might not be reasonable to contribute to a large-scale collective effort if that effort might not succeed because of the logic of collective action; one would be better off giving the money to a homeless person. Second, there remains a great deal of behavior that humanitarian motives cannot explain. Individuals do not join interest groups such as the National Organization for Women or the National Rifle Association out of altruism; they join out of self-interest. It is there that the paradox of collective action arises: An individual's self-interest may prevent him or her from participating in collective action that would serve his or her self-interest if all individuals participated in it. Furthermore, all persons involved may realize that this situation exists and still be unable to do anything about it.

Definition—Cyclical Voting Patterns. The second paradox involves cyclical voting patterns. It shows how three individuals, ranking three alternative choices, may not be able to assemble a transitive ranking for the whole group. Consider three individuals, A, B, and C, and three policy choices, x, y, and z. Assume that the three individuals rank these choices in the following manner.

	A	B	C
First preference	x	y	z
Second preference	y	z	x
Third preference	z	x	y

Note that all individuals' preference orderings are transitive—that is, if x is preferred to y, and y is preferred to z, then x is preferred to z. How does the group rank these preferences, using majority rule? Since A and C prefer x to y, the group prefers x to y by majority rule. Since A and B prefer y to z, the group prefers y to z by majority rule. Since the group prefers x to y and y to z, one would assume that the group prefers x to z. B and C prefer z to x, however, so by majority rule, the group prefers z to x. One arrives at two results, one in which the group prefers x to z, and another in which the group prefers z to x.

Proposed Solutions. Several solutions to this problem have been advanced, but none is entirely satisfactory. One answer states that all three choices are equally preferred by the group, but that is not true; in fact, any given choice may be beaten by another choice as the top preference. Another answer suggests changing the voting rules so that more than a majority is needed to reach a group preference. Kenneth Arrow has shown in a general proof, however, that *any* decision rule based upon individual choices may fall victim to this problem, if three or more choices and three or more individuals are involved. Another answer suggests that one should merely use the first result derived, but this solution leaves the result dependent upon the order in which alternatives are considered. For example, if the group considers x and y first, x is preferred to y; if the group then considers y and z, y is preferred to z, and hence, the group prefers x to y and y to z. If the group considers z and x first, however, z is preferred to x; if the group then considers x and y, x is preferred to y, and hence, the group prefers z to x and x to y. The ordering of these alternatives has been changed entirely simply by changing the sequence in which the alternatives were considered. For those who value majority rule as an ethical means of reaching decisions, this problem gives dictatorial power over voting results to the individuals who decide the sequence for voting on alternatives.

Finally, one may simply say that it is impossible to reach a decision. One may then, however, define this as alternative w and rank it as the least preferred alternative for all three members. Hence, all three persons would wind up with gridlock, their last choice. Majority rule thus may prevent individuals from reaching a majority decision; indeed, if one goes back to the original three-person problem, any given ordering of x, y, and z would mean that one of the three individuals (A, B, or C) will get his or her way despite the disapproval of a majority of the other group members.

Problems as "Paradoxes." The paradox in both of these problems is evident. In the first case, self-interested action prevents the creation of collective goods that would serve all individuals' self-interests. In the second case, majority rule may result in decisions that violate the majority will or in gridlock, which is the alternative least preferred by all. By pursuing self-interest or majority rule, one arrives at conclusions in both cases that contradict one's original rules. The ethical problem here is evident: In both cases, individuals follow the rational pursuit of their own self-interests and discover that rationality alone is insufficient grounds for taking group action or reaching a group decision. These paradoxes illustrate that rationality alone cannot bear the burden of generating an ethical consensus about the correct forms of action or decisions in a society.

—*Frank Louis Rusciano*

See also Prisoner's dilemma.

BIBLIOGRAPHY
Abrams, Robert. *Foundations of Political Analysis: An Introduction to the Theory of Collective Choice.* New York: Columbia University Press, 1980.
Arrow, Kenneth J. *Social Choice and Individual Values.* New York: John Wiley & Sons, 1963.
Barry, Brian. *Economics, Sociologists, and Democracy.* Chicago: University of Chicago Press, 1978.
Barry, Brian, and Russell Hardin, eds. *Rational Man and Irrational Society?* Beverly Hills: Sage Publications, 1982.
Downs, Anthony. *An Economic Theory of Democracy.* New York: Harper & Row, 1957.
Falletta, Nicholas. *The Paradoxicon.* New York: John Wiley & Sons, 1990.
Hofstadter, Douglas R. *Gödel, Escher, Bach: An Eternal Golden Braid.* New York: Random House, 1983.
Rusciano, Frank Louis. *Isolation and Paradox: Defining "the Public" in Modern Political Analysis.* Westport, Conn.: Greenwood Press, 1989.
Schelling, Thomas. *Micromotives and Macrobehavior.* New York: W. W. Norton, 1977.

Pascal, Blaise

Pascal, Blaise (June 19, 1623, Clermont-Ferrand, France—Aug. 19, 1662, Paris, France): Philosopher
TYPE OF ETHICS: Renaissance and Restoration history
ACHIEVEMENTS: Author of *Lettres provinciales* (1656-1657; *The Provincial Letters*, 1657) and *Pensées* (1670; *Monsieur Pascal's Thoughts, Meditations, and Prayers*, 1688)
SIGNIFICANCE: Developed very persuasive arguments against all efforts to compromise moral values in order to attain political or social influence; encouraged readers to recognize the essential "grandeur" of each individual even under the most difficult circumstances

Although Blaise Pascal was a very important mathematician and physicist, he has remained famous above all for his eloquent writings on the moral obligations that accompany a commitment to Christianity. Pascal believed that an acceptance of divine authority enables people to develop an objective foundation for moral values. The problem of ethical subjectivity disappears once one accepts the revealed and liberating truths to be found in the Bible and in the exegetical works of respected Church Fathers such as Saint Jerome and Saint Augustine. Because of the clarity and the depth of his analysis of ethical questions, Blaise Pascal has remained one of the most influential and controversial French writers, even several centuries after his death in 1662.

The Provincial Letters. Beginning in 1646, Pascal and his sister Jacqueline Périer became very interested in the Catholic religious movement associated with the monastery, convent, and school at Port-Royal. The priests and nuns at Port-Royal were referred to as Jansenists because a major influence on their view of Christian spirituality had been a 1640 book on Saint Augustine by a Dutch theologian named Cornelius Jansen. The Jansenists encouraged personal spiritual development and denounced all attempts to allow worldly values to interfere with the purity of a total commitment to Christian values. Books by such important Jansenist theologians as Antoine Arnauld and Pierre Nicole provoked an intense controversy with French Jesuits, who were then very influential at the court of King Louis XIV and with French bishops and priests. The basic disagreements between the Jesuits and the Jansenists dealt with the theological concept of grace and the use of casuistry, which is the practice by which a priest applies general moral standards to individual cases in order to determine if a specific action was sinful or if a repentance was sincere.

Between January, 1656, and March, 1657, Pascal published eighteen anonymous letters that were addressed "to a Jesuit provincial by one of his friends." Ever since its creation in the 1540's by Saint Ignatius Loyola, the Jesuit order has been administratively divided into broad geographical areas called provinces whose spiritual leaders are called provincials. The eighteen *Provincial Letters* are masterpieces of polemic rhetoric. Pascal sought to diminish the growing influence of French Jesuits by attributing to the entire order rather extreme positions taken by certain Jesuit theologians such as Antonio Escobar y Mendoza and Luis de Molina, who had argued that specific actions that most Christians would consider to be patently wrong would not be considered sinful if the motivations of the people who did those things were taken into account. Pascal believed that such an approach to ethics was very dangerous because it could lead people to justify actions that were clearly incompatible with God's teachings. In his seventh Provincial Letter, for example, Pascal denounced efforts by Escobar y Mendoza and Molina to justify dueling. A duelist might well claim that his intention was not to kill his adversary but to defend his own honor, but Pascal ridiculed such convenient and insincere excuses designed to disregard God's straightforward commandment: "Thou shalt not kill." Although Pascal was clearly unfair in associating all Jesuits with the radical positions of such theologians, his *Provincial Letters* did denounce very effectively the danger of moral laxism and the pernicious belief that "the end justifies the means."

Thoughts. During the last few years of his life, Pascal was writing "an apology for the Christian religion," but extremely poor health required him to rest frequently and this prevented him from writing for extended periods of time. He was, however, able to compose eight hundred fragments that were discovered and edited after his death by his nephew Étienne Périer, who called these fragments *Thoughts* (*Pensées*). Despite the uncompleted nature of *Thoughts*, it contains profound insights into the myriad relationships between ethical and religious problems. Unlike his fellow mathematician and philosopher René Descartes, who had argued in his 1637 book *Discourse on Method* that logic alone sufficed to explore moral problems, Pascal was convinced that only an acceptance of the revealed truths of Christianity could enable him to recognize the moral foundation for a just society.

Pascal stated that there were basically two ways of dealing with moral problems. By means of "the spirit of geometry" ("*l'esprit de géométrie*") one examines in a purely logical manner the many steps that are involved in resolving ethical questions. "The spirit of insight" ("*l'esprit de finesse*") helps

Blaise Pascal (Library of Congress)

one to recognize intuitively that certain actions are morally wrong whereas others are morally correct. Although he did not deny the importance of logical reasoning for discussions of ethical problems, Pascal sensed that most moral decisions are inspired by intuitive feelings that are formed by one's religious training and by the diversity of one's experiences. In *Thoughts*, Pascal appealed to the deep emotional and psychological reactions of his readers in order to persuade them that an acceptance of "the grandeur of man with God" and "the misery of man without God" will lead people to embrace those religious and ethical values that are presented in the Bible.

—*Edmund J. Campion*

See also Calvin, John; Christian ethics; God; Jesus; Justice; Revelation; Ten Commandments.

BIBLIOGRAPHY

Davidson, Hugh. *Blaise Pascal*. Boston: Twayne, 1983.

Krailsheimer, A. J. *Pascal*. New York: Hill & Wang, 1980.

MacKenzie, Charles. *Pascal's Anguish and Joy*. New York: Philosophical Library, 1973.

Mortimer, Ernest. *Blaise Pascal*. New York: Harper, 1959.

Nelson, Robert. *Pascal, Adversary and Advocate*. Cambridge, Mass.: Harvard University Press, 1981.

Pascal, Blaise. *Pensées and The Provincial Letters*. Translated by W. F. Trotter and Thomas M'Crie. New York: Modern Library, 1941.

Topliss, Patricia. *The Rhetoric of Pascal*. Leicester, England: Leicester University Press, 1966.

Passions and emotions

Type of ethics: Personal and social ethics
Associated with: Charles Darwin and William James
Definition: Emotion refers to a wide range of subjective states (love, fear, and so forth) that are evoked when important things happen; emotions are changes from the steady, level flow of normal consciousness; passions are emotions that attract one person to another
Significance: Emotions have a behavioral component and may cause people to act in ways that are ethical or unethical

Emotions add color to the world of experience. They motivate people to approach or avoid something, generally in an energetic way. They are made up of four components: conscious or subjective experience, bodily or physiological arousal, characteristics or overt behavior, and changes in thoughts or cognitions.

On the feeling or subjective level, emotions have elements of pleasure (or displeasure), intensity, and complexity. Pleasant or positive emotions tend to enhance an individual's sense of well-being and promote constructive relationships with others. Unpleasant or negative emotions, in contrast, tend to decrease an individual's sense of well-being and create disturbed relationships with others. Intensity is often reflected in the words used to describe emotions; for example, uneasy, fretful, tense, apprehensive, tremulous, agitated, panicky, and terrified. The complexity of emotions means that one person's sense of joy is different from another's. Thus, emotions have a private, personal, and unique component. They are complex subjective feelings.

On the physiological level, emotions are accompanied by bodily sensations or physiological arousal. The physiological arousal occurs mainly through the actions of the autonomic nervous system, which regulates the activity of glands, smooth muscles, and blood vessels. The autonomic responses that accompany emotions are ultimately controlled in the brain by the hypothalamus, the amygdala, and the adjacent structures in the limbic system.

There are several different types of physiological changes that accompany emotions. One change is in galvanic skin response, the electrical conductivity of the skin that occurs when sweat glands increase their activity. A second change is in the pulse rate. When a person is very angry or afraid, for example, his or her heart may accelerate from about 72 beats per minute to as many as 180 beats per minute. A third change is in the blood pressure, which may rise alarmingly when a person is angry or afraid. A fourth change is in the breathing rate, which typically becomes rapid and uneven when a person is experiencing strong emotion. A fifth change is in muscular tension, which is particularly prominent when the emotion is intense fear or anger. Other changes that accompany emotions include inhibition of salivation, pupil dilation, and inhibition of digestive processes.

The physiological changes that accompany love, joy, or other emotions may be smaller and more subtle than those accompanying anger and fear.

On the behavioral level, people reveal their emotions through characteristic overt expressions, such as smiles, frowns, furrowed brows, clenched fists, slumped shoulders, and changes in posture and tone of voice. When people are sad, for example, they tend to slouch and to speak in a lower, less variable pitch than the one they use when they are angry or afraid. People reveal their emotions in their body language, or nonverbal behavior. Some researchers argue that no body movement is accidental or meaningless. Rather, one communicates something in the slightest movement, even though one may be unaware of it.

On the cognitive level, emotions are accompanied by changes in thoughts, beliefs, and expectations. When happy, people become more optimistic; when sad, they are likely to see the negative sides of situations. In general, people's thoughts are guided by and consistent with their emotions.

Like colors, emotions cover a wide spectrum. There are six basic emotions: love, joy, surprise, anger, sadness, and fear. Three dimensions on which these basic emotions vary are evaluation (positive or negative), potency (strong or weak), and activity (relatively high or low in arousal). Some theorists include disgust and contempt as primary emotions. Others add shame, contempt, interest, guilt, anticipation, acceptance, and distress as primary emotions. Still other theorists reject the concept of basic emotions altogether. Of course, people experience many different emotions. Some theorists propose that many emotions are produced by blends and variations in intensity of primary emotions, like colors on a color wheel.

What causes emotions? Several theories have been developed to answer this question. One theory is that they result from specific physiological changes, with each emotion having a different physiological basis. Proposed independently in the late 1800's by William James and Carl Lange, this theory stood common sense on its head. Everyday logic suggests that when a person stumbles onto a rattlesnake in the woods, the conscious experience of fear leads to visceral arousal (the fight-or-flight response). This theory, in contrast, asserts the opposite: the perception of visceral arousal leads to the conscious experience of fear. Thus, this theory asserts that the person becomes afraid because the sight of the rattlesnake causes muscles, skin, and internal organs to undergo changes. Fear is simply the awareness of these changes. The James-Lange theory of emotions emphasizes the physiological determinants of emotion.

The James-Lange theory of emotions has two overall criticisms. First, anger, fear, and sadness seem to share similar physiological patterns of arousal, although recent research has detected some subtle differences in the patterns of visceral arousal that accompany basic emotions. Second, people with severe spinal cord injuries are deprived of most feedback from their autonomic nervous systems, yet they still experience emotions. Physiologists generally agree that physiological arousal influences the intensity of emotions, but not the emotions themselves.

A second theory of emotions asserts that when a person is emotional, two areas of the brain, the thalamus and the cerebral cortex, are stimulated simultaneously. Stimulation of the cortex produces the emotional component of the experience, whereas stimulation of the thalamus produces physiological changes in the sympathetic nervous system. Accordingly, emotional feelings accompany physiological changes, they do not produce them. This theory of emotions holds that they are physiologically similar to, and occur sooner than, changes in the internal organs.

Proposed by physiologists Walter Cannon and Philip Bard (1927), this theory has two criticisms. First, physiological changes in the brain do not happen exactly simultaneously. Second, people often report that they have an experience and then later have physiological and emotional reactions to it. For example, they have a near-accident in a car, and only later become very frightened.

A third theory of emotions is that they are caused by facial feedback. The idea is that sensations from the movement of facial muscles and skin are interpreted by the brain and result in emotion. According to this somatic view, smiles, frowns, and furrowed brows help to create the subjective experience of various emotions. Consistent with this view, research shows that if people are induced to frown, they tend to report that they feel angry. Furthermore, people who have been blind since birth smile and frown much like everyone else, even though they have never seen a smile or frown. Also, infants only a few hours old show distinct expressions of emotions that closely match those of adults, and infants recognize facial expressions in others at a very young age. Thus, infant and cross-cultural similarities in emotional expression support the facial feedback or evolutionary theory of emotions.

Originally proposed by Charles Darwin, this theory asserts that emotions developed because they have adaptive value. They signal an intent to act and prepare the individual to act. Fear, for example, would help an organism avoid danger and thus would aid in survival. This view of emotions is that they are a product of the evolution of facial expressions, which were our ancestors' primary mode of communication before language developed.

This facial feedback theory of emotions suffers from the criticism that there is little evidence that specific facial feedback initiates specific emotions. Researchers generally agree that facial feedback and physiological arousal influence the intensity of emotions, but not the emotions themselves.

A fourth theory of emotions is that interpreting or appraising a situation as having a positive or negative impact on one's life results in a subjective feeling that is called emotion. The idea is that a stimulus causes physiological arousal. The arousal creates a need for an explanation of some kind, which the person makes from the situational cues available and from his or her cognitive processes, such as thoughts, interpretations, and appraisals. This explanation results in emotion. This theory of emotion stresses that there are two components to emotions: a cognitive component and a situational component.

This theory of emotion, which can be traced to psychologists Stanley Schachter and Jerome Singer (1962), has been revised by Arnold Lazarus (1991) to recognize the fact that emotions may initially occur without physiological arousal. Lazarus also believed that each emotion has its own specific relational theme, or person-environment relation, which involves benefit in the case of positive emotions and harm in the case of negative ones.

To test this theory of emotion, Schachter and Singer conducted an experiment in which they told volunteers that they were testing the effects of a vitamin supplement. Instead, these volunteers were injected with epinephrine, a powerful stimulant that increases physiological arousal. The volunteer students were unaware of the typical bodily effects of the adrenaline. To see if the setting in which the volunteers experienced their arousal influenced how they interpreted their emotions, Schachter and Singer hired undergraduates and paid them to act either happy and relaxed or sad, depressed, and angry. These hired students, called stooges, pretended that they were volunteers in the same drug study. Instead, they were given injections of saltwater, not epinephrine. Their emotional behavior was strictly an act. The happy stooges shot wads of paper into a wastepaper basket and flew airplanes around the room. The unhappy stooges complained about the questionnaire they had to fill out and voiced their dissatisfaction with the experiment. All the volunteers showed increased physiological arousal. Those with happy stooges reported that the drug made them feel good; those with the sad, angry stooges reported that the drug made them feel anger. Schachter and Singer concluded that the physiological feelings that accompanied both joy and anger were the same, but the label attached to the emotion depended on the person's situation.

These theories of emotions may all be partly right, but no one theory fits all the data. Physiological and cognitive influences interact in complex ways to produce emotional experiences.

Emotions have three main functions. One function of emotions is that they help people adapt and survive. For example, crying alerts others that one is in pain or discomfort, and being in love fosters social interactions. A second function of emotions is that they signal that something important is happening and rouse one to action. In an evolutionary sense, some emotions are part of an emergency arousal system that increases the chances of survival by energizing, directing, and sustaining adaptive behaviors. For example, being afraid may motivate one to run away from a dangerous bear that is running toward one, and being angry may cause one to work harder to reach one's goals.

Other emotions, such as sadness, relief, and contentment, may involve an integrated pattern that includes a decrease in arousal and behavioral intensity.

Though rousing people to action may be positive, it may also be negative, so that emotions may disrupt behavior. The relationship between physiological arousal that accompanies an emotion and task performance is known as the Yerkes-Dodson law, which states that performance on a task depends on the amount of physiological arousal and the difficulty of the task. In general, for many tasks, moderate arousal helps performance. For new or difficult tasks, low arousal facilitates performance; for easy or well-learned tasks, high arousal facilitates performance. For example, high arousal would interfere with performance on a difficult test, but it facilitates signing one's own name legibly. In contrast, low to medium arousal would result in better performance on a difficult test, but it might lead one to sign one's name illegibly.

Emotions rouse people to action in another sense as well: The expectation of pleasant emotions serves as an incentive. Many purposeful, motivated behaviors are designed to induce feelings of happiness, joy, excitement, or pride.

A third function of emotions is to help people communicate by sending social signals. They inform others about one's internal state and intentions. Many facial expressions, such as happiness, anger, sadness, fear, disgust, and surprise, are recognized as emotional expressions by people in widely varying cultures. In fact, emotional facial expressions are strikingly similar in different cultures. Yet different cultures encourage or discourage the expression of some emotions more than others. Adults in all societies learn to suppress some of their emotional responses or to mask them with voluntary control of facial muscles. This masking is never perfect, and other facial muscles can give away true feelings.

Different factors influence emotion. Personality and motivational factors affect emotion by influencing what situations people expose themselves to and how they think about those situations, as well as physiological and behavioral responses. Therefore, personality variables can predispose people to experience certain kinds of emotions. For example, extroverted people are likely to experience strong positive emotions in response to positive events but less-intense reactions to negative events. In contrast, people who are high in neuroticism experience weak positive emotional responses to positive events but strong negative responses to negative events.

Learning also influences emotion. Cultures have different standards for defining the good, the bad, and the ugly. For example, physical features that provoke sexual arousal and feelings of infatuation in one culture (such as scars) may elicit feelings of disgust in another culture.

Biological factors also influence emotion. The concept of preparedness suggests that people may be biologically primed to experience fear in response to certain stimuli, such as heights or snakes.

Intrapsychic factors may also predispose people to certain emotions. For example, anger that has been stored up since childhood may be released if a situation reminds one of that internal conflict. Also, psychological defenses sometimes predispose people to transform one emotional response into another, more acceptable one. Thus, anger may be transformed into sadness, or sexual feelings into fear.

Emotions do not occur in a vacuum. Rather, they always have objects. People are not simply angry, afraid, proud, or in love. They are angry at something or someone, afraid of something or someone, and so forth. Furthermore, the stimuli that trigger emotional responses are not always external. Sometimes they are internal, occurring in the form of images and memories. Usually, people can identify the eliciting stimuli, but not always.

Emotions are shaped by one's biological and psychological predispositions, by what one learns in one's environment, and by one's personality and motivations. One experiences them in response to internal or external objects. They give life color.

—Lillian M. Range

See also Evolution, theory of; James, William; Psychology; Self-control.

BIBLIOGRAPHY

Carlson, John G., and Elaine Hatfield. *Psychology of Emotion*. Fort Worth, Tex.: Harcourt Brace Jovanovich, 1992. This text is an outstanding summary of theory and research on emotion. It has a readable and informative description of the biology and psychology of emotion. Contains many interesting examples and practical applications.

Darwin, Charles. *The Expression of Emotions in Man and Animals*. Chicago: University of Chicago Press, 1965. Darwin's original statement of the evolutionary model of emotion, this text holds that emotional expressions are biological traits that are shaped by evolutionary history, stressing that emotions perform an extremely useful function for survival. Darwin also points out that animals and humans share a great number of similar facial expressions. He describes in minute detail the facial expressions of different emotions in humans and animals, naming the particular muscles that come into play in each instance.

Ekman, P. *Telling Lies: Clues to Deceit in the Marketplace, Politics, and Marriage*. New York: W. W. Norton, 1985. Describes the evidence on complex nonverbal patterns that reveal emotions that are different from what people may be saying. Attempts to explain how to accomplish the very difficult task of detecting deceit in business and in life.

Izard, C. E. "The Structure and Functions of Emotions: Implications for Cognition, Motivation, and Personality." In *The G. Stanley Hall Lecture Series*, edited by I. S. Cohen. Washington, D.C.: American Psychological Association, 1989. Provides an overview of current issues in research on emotions, including Izard's theory, facial feedback theory, and the development of emotions in children.

Lazarus, R. S. *Emotion and Adaptation*. New York: Oxford University Press, 1991. This monumental work contains reviews and distillations of Lazarus' work and that of others.

It arrives at a new statement of cognitive appraisal theory.

McNaughton, N. *Biology and Emotion*. Cambridge, England: Cambridge University Press, 1989. A thoughtful, highly readable, up-to-date integration of evolutionary and physiological approaches to the understanding of emotion.

Plutchik, R., and H. Kellerman, eds. *Emotion: Theory, Research, and Experience*. Vol. 1. San Diego, Calif.: Academic Press, 1990. Offers up-to-date and comprehensive reviews of the scientific literature for the field of emotion.

Stein, N. L., B. Leventhal, and T. Trabasso, eds. *Psychological and Biological Approaches to Emotion*. Hillsdale, N.J.: Lawrence Erlbaum, 1990. Contains chapters written by experts in the field of emotion.

Strongman, K. T. *The Psychology of Emotion*. 3d ed. New York: Wiley, 1987. Offers a historic overview of theories of emotion, written at a level appropriate for advanced undergraduates. Also includes information on the role of cognition in emotion.

Tomkins, S. S. *Anger and Fear*. Vol. 3 in *Affect, Imagery, and Consciousness*. New York: Springer, 1991. Contains a fascinating account of the evolutionary origins of anger and fear, and tells how they can be modified by cognitive and experiential factors.

Peace Corps

TYPE OF ETHICS: Human rights
DATE: Founded 1961
ASSOCIATED WITH: John F. Kennedy
DEFINITION: The Peace Corps promotes international friendship by supplying trained personnel to other countries
SIGNIFICANCE: The Peace Corps assists developing nations and helps Americans focus on issues of what kind of assistance to other nations is useful and appropriate

The Peace Corps of the United States is an independent agency of the federal government, with an annual budget of some $186 million. It sends volunteers to eighty-six foreign countries to help staff schools and hospitals, and to share agricultural and technical knowledge. The Peace Corps was founded in 1961 while John F. Kennedy was president. He asked young people to volunteer for two-year terms, and many recent college graduates seeking adventure and a chance to serve accepted the offer. At first, anyone who was willing to volunteer was accepted and given something to do. By the 1980's, however, Peace Corps volunteers tended to be older and more highly trained in technical areas. In the wake of the Vietnam War and Watergate, a growing cynicism about the government caused fewer volunteers to join. In 1983, the Ronald Reagan Administration revived the program, hoping to use the volunteers to spread conservative ideas worldwide. By the 1990's, opinion about the Peace Corps was divided. Many people believed that the Peace Corps was primarily a means for a wealthy nation to share its prosperity, and to promote world harmony. Others saw an insidious form of interventionism in the program.

See also Intervention.

Peace studies

TYPE OF ETHICS: Theory of ethics
DATE: World Peace Foundation established in 1910
ASSOCIATED WITH: World Peace Foundation, Peacemaking for Families, League of Nations, the United Nations, and the United States Institute for Peace
DEFINITION: Education that explores alternatives to war; makes connections among issues of human justice, development, and ecological balance; supports conflict resolution at all levels; and encourages the transformation of individuals and institutions
SIGNIFICANCE: The study of peace encourages awareness of people's common humanity, their interconnectedness with one another and the universe, and personal, professional, and political choices that reflect that awareness

Peace studies is an emerging discipline that affirms that peace is more than the absence of war; peace is harmony among people and countries based on respect for oneself and others. The study of peace weaves together three major threads. *Peace studies* as an academic discipline examines war, relations among nations, conflicts and their resolution, and proposals for peace; *peace education* identifies effective methods used to teach peace in a family, a classroom, or a community setting in order to develop civic and global citizenship and world peace; and *peacemaking* focuses on the values by which one lives one's life and cares for others in the family, for the community, and for the planet. Unless these three threads are woven together in theory and practice, the goal and meaning of peace studies are lost.

Desire for peace and the elimination of war can be traced to the ancient oral and written histories and literature of diverse peoples from all continents. A modern study of peace can be traced to the establishment of the World Peace Foundation in 1910. The advent of atomic warfare in World War II increased the demand for the study of foreign policy, development, international conflict, and alternatives to war. Early in U.S. history, George Washington called for the establishment of a United States Academy for Peace, a proposal that was reconsidered by every Congress until 1986, when the United States Institute for Peace was established.

Peace studies emerged slowly as an academic discipline. In the 1960's, there were few courses in higher education that addressed peace issues, although peace studies formed the basis of education in several colleges run by the historic Peace Churches, notably the Brethren, Quaker, and Mennonite churches. Peace studies received an impetus during the Vietnam War, when growing numbers of war protesters raised issues of war and alternatives to war in classrooms and institutions of higher learning around the world. The Institute for World Order (now the World Policy Institute) was among the first organizations (1966) to link and address issues of war, development, gender and racial inequality, human rights, and ecological balance with issues of world peace. As terrorist activities and the nuclear threat escalated in the late 1970's, the leaders of most of the world's reli-

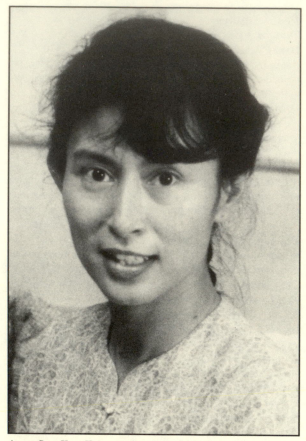

Aung San Kuu Kyi, winner of the 1991 Nobel Peace Prize. (Nobel Foundation)

gions added their voices to the call for the study of peace and justice issues. By 1983, at the peak of the International Nuclear Freeze Campaign, public and private campuses worldwide began including one or more courses related to the study of war, the nuclear threat, conflict management, global cooperation, and world peace in their curriculums. Ten years later, hundreds of campuses worldwide offered peace studies programs. Students can now receive a minor or major at the undergraduate level, a Master's degree, and, at several universities, a doctoral degree in peace studies.

Academic programs in higher education, which often focus on the historical or theoretical, hold an important place in peace studies, for it is in the academy that the various disciplines provide for the examination of diverse topics that are related to war and peace. Two acknowledged dangers in the academy include the failure to study issues of peace from a cross-cultural or interdisciplinary perspective and the failure to link the theoretical and historical perspectives of peace with personal, family, and community lifestyle choices. A growing number of scholars have suggested that peace studies must move beyond theory; it must be values based, address domestic and global issues, be relevant to all age groups, and lead to education for re-

sponsible global citizenship.

Peace education programs at the elementary and secondary levels, developed during the Vietnam era, do promote values, as well as attitudes and skills related to affirmation, communication, cooperation, respect for diversity, nonviolent resolution of conflict, and skills for critical thinking and decision making. Three of the most notable in the United States are the Children and Non-Violence, Children's Creative Response to Conflict, and Peacemaking for Children: Alternatives to Violence programs. The Nuclear Freeze Campaign of 1982 expanded international awareness of the nuclear threat and generated new calls for peace education. The Milwaukee Public Schools became the first major school system in the United States to respond to this call, implementing a K-12 peace education curriculum in 1985.

Peacemaking for Families educational programs, developed in 1976 by Jacqueline Haessly, evolved from a belief that the values, attitudes, and skills of peacemaking are first shaped in the home. Five years later, the National Parenting for Peace and Justice Education Network was established by James and Kathleen McGinnis. Family Life Education for Peace, initiated by Nona and Carroll Cannon, is an emerging field in the academy. All three programs link peace with values education.

Peacemaking as a way of life occurs when individuals and societies make the link between the personal and the political. Julia Sweig and Sharon Boggs are among those who remind peace educators that issues of domestic and community violence must be addressed and skills for community building must be taught if peace is to be achieved in a community and the world.

Organizations that promote peace studies in the United States include Children's Creative Responses to Conflict; Council for Peace and Conflict Studies; Consortium for Peace Education, Research, and Development; Educators for Social Responsibility; Fellowship of Reconciliation; Global Education Associates; Jane Addams Peace Association; the Milwaukee Peace Education Resource Center; Parenting for Peace and Justice Network; the United Nations University for Peace—San Diego; the United States Institute for Peace; and the World Policy Institute (formerly the Institute for World Order). Many of these organizations also have international affiliations. —*Jacqueline Haessly*

See also International justice; International law; War and peace.

BIBLIOGRAPHY

Freire, Paulo. *Education for Critical Consciousness*. New York: Seabury Press, 1973.

Haessly, Jacqueline. *Peacemaking: Family Activities for Justice and Peace*. New York: Paulist Press, 1980.

McGinnis, James, and Kathleen McGinnis. *Parenting for Peace and Justice*. Maryknoll, N.Y.: Orbis Books, 1981.

Mendlovitz, Saul, ed. *On the Creation of a Just World Order*. New York: Free Press, 1975.

Meyer, Robert S. *Peace Organizations, Past and Present: A Survey and Directory.* Jefferson, N.C.: McFarland, 1988.

Mische, Gerald, and Patricia Mische. *Toward a Human World Order.* New York: Paulist Press, 1977.

Montessori, Maria. *Education and Peace.* Chicago: Regnery, 1972.

Reardon, Betty. *Comprehensive Peace Education: Educating for Global Responsibility.* New York: Teachers College Press, 1988.

Shuman, Michael, and Julia Sweig, eds. *Conditions of Peace: An Inquiry.* Washington, D.C.: EXPRO Press, 1991.

Thomas, Daniel C., and Michael T. Klare, eds. *Peace and World Order Studies: A Curriculum Guide.* 5th ed. Boulder, Colo.: Westview Press, 1989.

Peirce, Charles Sanders (Sept. 10, 1839, Cambridge, Mass.—Apr. 19, 1914, Milford, Pa): Philosopher

TYPE OF ETHICS: Modern history

ACHIEVEMENTS: Author of *Photometric Researches* (1878)

SIGNIFICANCE: America's greatest logician and most original nineteenth century philosopher, Peirce utilized scientific and progressive thought to challenge immutable beliefs by emphasizing the pragmatic nature of truth

From 1864 to 1907, Peirce served as an occasional lecturer at Harvard and The Johns Hopkins University on the topics of logic and pragmatism. His genius and potential on pragmatic theory were never fully realized or publicly appreciated, however, because of his personal difficulties, eccentricity, and opposition to traditional philosophical thought. Peirce believed that it was a mistake to accept a priori reasoning, or absolute truth, without first examining its results. In an article published in *Popular Science Monthly* in January, 1878, he attempted to answer the question "How to Make Our Ideas Clear" by stating that an idea's utility and results or effects give it meaning, not some inherent absolute truth or a priori reasoning. One's conception of these effects becomes one's conception of the object. Peirce interpreted every subject, including philosophy, almost entirely from a logical (pragmatic) perspective. Peirce emphasized that pragmatism is a principle of method—not of metaphysics. Using this principle, he claimed that scientific laws were statements of probabilities only and subject to evolutionary change. Unlike his disciple and benefactor William James, however, Peirce never discarded his beliefs in an Absolute or in universals. Scholars consider Peirce's work an important intellectual foundation for twentieth century progressivism.

See also James, William; Pragmatism; Progressivism.

Peltier, Leonard

TYPE OF ETHICS: Race and ethnicity

DATE: 1977

ASSOCIATED WITH: American Indian Movement (AIM); Federal Bureau of Investigation

DEFINITION: Leonard Peltier was convicted in the 1975 shooting deaths of two FBI agents

SIGNIFICANCE: The case raises the question of whether it is right for a government to bend the law to convict someone believed to be guilty of a serious crime

On June 26, 1975, two FBI agents were killed in a shoot-out on the Lakota Indian Reservation in Pine Ridge, South Dakota. Leonard Peltier, a member of the American Indian Movement (AIM), was found guilty of the killings. Peltier declared himself innocent. Peltier appealed his conviction many times. During the appeals, the court found that the government had acted improperly in arresting and trying him. Federal authorities admitted to falsifying affidavits used to extradite Peltier from Canada. Witnesses in the original trial had been coerced, and evidence supporting Peltier's claims was suppressed. In spite of these irregularities, the courts refused to overturn Peltier's conviction. Peltier's case became known throughout the world. Many people believed that, even if he were guilty, he had not been granted a fair trial. Amnesty International declared him a political prisoner, and important religious leaders spoke out on his behalf. A book and three films were made about the case. In 1992, a "Mr. X" confessed to the killings. Peltier's supporters continued to hope that they could win him a new trial.

See also Amnesty International; Due process; Native American genocide.

Pentagon Papers

TYPE OF ETHICS: Media ethics

DATE: 1971

ASSOCIATED WITH: U.S. Supreme Court

DEFINITION: The Supreme Court held, in *U.S. v. New York Times Company, that the federal government could not restrain The New York Times* from publishing certain Vietnam War era documents known as the "Pentagon Papers"

SIGNIFICANCE: The Court's ruling meant that in cases involving national security, the government must meet a heavy burden of justification before it can prevent the press from exercising its First Amendment rights

Popular sentiment against the Vietnam War was on the rise in the spring of 1971, when Daniel Ellsberg, a former U.S. Department of Defense employee, and his friend, Anthony Russo, Jr., stole copies of two massive volumes that have come to be known as the Pentagon Papers. These volumes, "History of U.S. Decision-Making Process on Vietnam Policy" and "Command and Control Study of the Gulf of Tonkin Incident"—which were classified "Top Secret-Sensitive" and "Top Secret," respectively—together constituted a history of American involvement in Vietnam since World War II.

Ellsberg and Russo passed the filched documents on to *The New York Times* and *The Washington Post*. In its June 13, 1971, edition, the *Times* began publishing a series of excerpts from the government studies.

Government Attempts Prior Restraint. After the *Times* had published two more excerpts on June 14 and 15, 1971, the federal government filed a motion in the U.S. District

Court for the Southern District of New York requesting that the court restrain the *Times* from publishing more passages from the Pentagon Papers. Although the court refused to issue an injunction against the paper, it did grant the government a temporary restraining order, which prevented the *Times* from publishing portions of the Pentagon Papers while the government prepared its case. On June 18, *The Washington Post* also began publishing excerpts from the Pentagon Papers, and the government moved to restrain it, too, in federal court in the District of Columbia. The legal action in the case, however, remained focused on New York City.

On June 18, the district court in New York heard the case, in which the government claimed that the publication of the documents in question would compromise the nation's war effort. Nevertheless, the government's request for an injunction was denied, although the temporary restraining order was extended until the government's appeal to a higher court could be heard. This appeal also was rejected, and on June 24, the government filed a petition with the Supreme Court.

Supreme Court Rejects Government's Case. The parties appeared before the Court on June 26, 1971, and the Court delivered its opinion on June 30: The entire litigation had lasted slightly longer than two weeks. Like the lower courts, the Supreme Court rejected the government's attempts to rationalize prior restraint of the press by appealing to national security, dismissing the cases against both the *Times* and the *Post*. The Court was not unanimous in its decision, voting six to three, but writing for the majority, Justice Hugo L. Black delivered a stinging rebuke to the administration of President Richard M. Nixon: "the Solicitor General argues . . . that the general powers of the Government adopted in the original Constitution should be interpreted to limit and restrict the specific and emphatic guarantees of the Bill of Rights. . . . I can imagine no greater perversion of history."

Although the dissenters, Chief Justice Warren E. Burger, Justice Harry A. Blackmun, and Justice John M. Harlan, argued that the Court should defer to the executive branch's concerns, Justice Black's opinion reaffirmed the Court's role as interpreter of the Constitution and guardian of individual rights: "Madison and the other Framers of the First Amendment . . . wrote in language they earnestly believed could never be misunderstood: 'Congress shall make no law . . . abridging the freedom . . . of the press. . . .'"

Government Continues Prosecution of Ellsberg and Russo. The government continued, nevertheless, to prosecute Ellsberg and Russo, gaining indictments against them for theft of federal property and violations of the federal Espionage Act. The two defendants were tried in U.S. District Court for the Central District of California, where the Pentagon Papers were allegedly stolen.

Unlike the original Pentagon Papers litigation, the Ellsberg and Russo prosecution dragged on for many months. Although the government had first obtained a preliminary indictment against Ellsberg in June, 1971, the trial of the two defendants did not commence until more than a year later.

The trial was halted almost immediately after it began, however, when it was revealed that the government had been secretly taping the defendants' confidential communications. After the parties had gone through the process of selecting a new jury, the trial recommenced in January, 1973. Shortly thereafter, however, the entire Pentagon Papers case was colored by news of the Watergate imbroglio, which began with the September, 1971, government-sponsored burglary of the offices of Lewis Fielding, Ellsberg's psychoanalyst, committed in an effort to uncover other Ellsberg accomplices. When further revelations of the government's continuing illegal wiretaps of Ellsberg's conversations reached the court, the entire criminal prosecution of Ellsberg and Russo was dismissed. The Nixon Administration had not only undermined its reputation and its case against the defendants but had also ensured that future administrative attempts to restrain the press from exercising its First Amendment rights would be more difficult. —*Lisa Paddock*

See also First Amendment; Journalistic ethics; Privacy, invasion of; Watergate break-in.

BIBLIOGRAPHY

French, Peter A. *Conscientious Actions: The Revelation of the Pentagon Papers*. Cambridge, Mass.: Schenkman, 1974.

Meiklejohn Civil Liberties Institute. *Pentagon Papers Case Collection: Annotated Procedural Guide and Index*. Berkeley, Calif.: Author, 1975.

Salter, Kenneth W. *The Pentagon Papers Trial*. Berkeley, Calif.: Editorial Justa, 1975.

Schrag, Peter. *Test of Loyalty: Daniel Ellsberg and the Rituals of Secret Government*. New York: Simon & Schuster, 1974.

Ungar, Sanford J. *The Papers and the Papers: An Account of the Legal and Political Battle Over the Pentagon Papers*. New York: Columbia University Press, 1989.

People for the Ethical Treatment of Animals

TYPE OF ETHICS: Animal rights

DATE: Founded 1980

DEFINITION: PETA was incorporated to educate policy makers and the public about issues involving the abuse of animals, and to promote the rights of animals

SIGNIFICANCE: In its struggle for the protection of animals, PETA has opened minds to the ethical rights of all living creatures

PETA, which has more than 400,000 members, is the largest and fastest growing animal rights organization in the country. PETA unites scientists, lawyers, and intellectuals in opposition to animal abuse. In 1981, Alex Pacheco, the head of PETA, as an undercover worker, exposed cruelty to monkeys in a Silver Springs, Maryland, laboratory. PETA was responsible for the closing down of the largest horse-slaughtering operation in the United States in Marlin, Texas, in 1984. PETA also disclosed a Defense Department plan to use animals in gunshot wound research. A landmark achievement in exposing unethical animal experimentation occurred in 1984, when PETA publicized the extremely cruel treatment of primates in head injury experiments carried out at the University of Pennsylvania. In education and activism, PETA has articulated the ethical worth of animals and the sanctity of all life, and by speaking for those who cannot speak has made clear humanity's ethical obligations to other creatures.

See also Animal research; Cruelty to animals; Humane Society of the United States; Moral status of animals; Singer, Peter; Vivisection; World Society for the Protection of Animals.

Perfectionism

TYPE OF ETHICS: Theory of ethics
DATE: Late 1980's and early 1990's
ASSOCIATED WITH: Paul Hewitt and Gordon Flett
DEFINITION: The tendency to set unrealistically high standards for oneself or others
SIGNIFICANCE: Perfectionism has personal as well as social aspects, both of which may influence ethical beliefs and behaviors

Although originally believed to be a unidimensional concept involving only the self, perfectionism is now thought to be a multidimensional construct that has three components: self-oriented perfectionism, other-oriented perfectionism, and socially prescribed perfectionism. Self-oriented perfectionism is intrapersonal (within the self) and involves being strongly motivated to be perfect, setting and holding unrealistically high goals for oneself, striving compulsively, thinking in an all-or-nothing manner in which only total success or total failure exist as outcomes, focusing on flaws and past failures, and generalizing unrealistic self-standards across behavioral domains. For example, self-oriented perfectionism is expecting oneself to be Atlas and hold up the world without dropping anything, and thinking of oneself as a failure if one errs in any way.

Other-oriented perfectionism is interpersonal and involves beliefs and expectations about significant others. It entails setting unrealistically high standards for others, placing great importance on whether they attain these standards, and rewarding them only if they meet these standards. For example, other-oriented perfectionism is expecting a significant other to be Atlas and hold up the world and giving no positive reinforcement if anything at all is dropped. Socially prescribed perfectionism is also interpersonal and involves the need to meet the standards and expectations that are perceived by significant others. Its essence is the belief that significant others have unrealistic standards and perfectionistic motives for their behaviors, and that they will be satisfied only when these standards are met. For example, socially prescribed perfectionism is thinking that significant others expect one to be Atlas and hold up the world and believing that they will be utterly disappointed if one fails in any way. Self-oriented, other-oriented, and socially prescribed perfectionism are three separate but related aspects of perfectionism.

Perfectionism may be positive or negative. On the positive side, most employers would rather have employees who take pride in their work, who consistently work to the best of their ability, and who try to make their results as perfect as possible. Likewise, most teachers would rather have students who are exact and precise in their work, who do all their assignments as instructed, and who consistently operate at their maximum capacity. In other life situations as well, perfectionism can be a very positive quality. On the negative side, there are intrapersonal and interpersonal costs associated with perfectionism. Intrapersonally, perfectionists are never satisfied with their efforts, no matter how hard they try. They consistently fail to meet their goals, so their lives can be quite frustrating and their self-esteem quite low. They can fail to produce a whole picture of the forest because they are so thoroughly examining the trees. They fail to understand that there are times when an adequate job is all that is required. Interpersonally, perfectionists can be difficult persons with whom to live, work, and interact. Their exacting standards can lead to rigidity and make interpersonal relationships fraught with disappointments and recriminations. Therefore, perfectionism may be a positive or negative personal characteristic.

In the late 1980's and early 1990's, Paul Hewitt and Gordon Flett and colleagues in Winnipeg, Canada, developed the Multidimensional Perfectionism Scale, a forty-five-item measure of self-oriented, other-oriented, and socially prescribed perfectionism. Respondents rate such statements as "When I am working on something, I cannot relax until it is perfect" (self-oriented perfectionism), "I have high expectations for the people who are important to me" (other-oriented perfectionism), and "People expect nothing less than perfection from me" (socially prescribed perfectionism) on a seven-point Likert scale from 1 = Strongly Disagree to 7 = Strongly Agree. Respondents receive scores for all three dimensions of perfectionism.

The Multidimensional Perfectionism Scale (MPS) is a strong instrument. In terms of reliability, the MPS is internally consistent as well as consistent over time. In terms of validity, the MPS is correlated with related concepts such as high self-standards, self-criticism, fear of negative evaluation, and social importance goals. In terms of multidimensionality, factor analysis has produced results that are consistent with the three dimensions of the MPS. Furthermore, it is not substantially influenced by response biases. Thus, the Multidimensional Perfectionism Scale is an experimentally sound instrument.

Using the Multidimensional Perfectionism Scale, researchers have shown that perfectionism is correlated with anxiety, suicide, alcoholism, eating disorders, and personality disorders. It is also correlated with feelings of failure, guilt, indecisiveness, procrastination, shame, and low self-esteem. Thus, perfectionism is associated with psychopathology. General research on perfectionism has adopted a diathesis-stress approach that highlights the role of mediators between perfectionism and adjustment. According to this approach, problems of adjustment are elevated considerably when self-oriented perfectionism is combined with such mediating variables as negative life stressors, an internal attributional style, emotion-focused coping, and ego-involving conditions. — *Lillian M. Range*

See also Psychology; Self-control; Self-respect.

BIBLIOGRAPHY

Hewitt, Paul L., and Gordon L. Flett. "Perfectionism in the Self and Social Contexts: Conceptualization, Assessment, and Association with Psychopathology." *Journal of Personality and Social Psychology* 60 (March, 1991): 456-470.

Hewitt, Paul L., Gordon L. Flett, and Samuel F. Mikail. "The Multidimensional Perfectionism Scale: Reliability, Validity, and Psychometric Properties in Psychiatric Samples." *Psychological Assessment: A Journal of Consulting and Clinical Psychology* 3 (September, 1991): 464-480.

Mosher, Shawn W. "Perfectionism, Self-Actualization, and Personal Adjustment." *Journal of Social Behavior and Personality* 6, no. 5 (1991): 147-160.

Perjury

TYPE OF ETHICS: Legal and judicial ethics
DATE: Defined sixteenth century
ASSOCIATED WITH: Criminal law
DEFINITION: The crime of falsely testifying in a material matter while under oath
SIGNIFICANCE: Perjury originated as a spiritual violation; it is especially immoral to call upon God to witness that false testimony is true; the community's interest in the integrity and accuracy of sworn statements in judicial or other official proceedings is substantial

The essence of the crime of perjury is giving false testimony under oath regarding a matter that is being considered by a court or other tribunal. "False" does not mean mistaken, however great the error; it means that the witness believes his or her own testimony to be false and makes false statements willfully in spite of taking an oath to tell the truth. Perjury is a very serious crime. It was punishable by death in England in ancient times; later, the punishment became banishment or mutilation of the tongue. The penalty is still very severe; in the United States in the 1990's, perjury was still punishable by life imprisonment in one or two states and by a long term of years in all the others. There are few perjury prosecutions. It is a difficult crime to prove, because the prosecution has to show that the witness knew the testimony to be false. A person who has been acquitted of a criminal offense is now protected by the double-jeopardy clause from being charged with perjury for testimony given in his or her own defense.

See also Lying.

Permissible acts

TYPE OF ETHICS: Theory of ethics
DATE: From antiquity
ASSOCIATED WITH: Absolutism and relativism
DEFINITION: Acts whose performance does not constitute a violation of moral duty
SIGNIFICANCE: The highest priority in all of ethics is to know one's duty and attempt to fulfill it. The way to do this is by restricting one's acts to the realm of the permissible

The concept of a permissible act is one that is typically learned very early in life. One learns that there are certain requirements that are binding upon one's behavior, and permissible acts are recognized as those acts that do not violate any of these requirements. Because most of these requirements are actually requirements to refrain from certain types of acts, one quickly identifies certain courses of action as being impermissible. Permissible acts, then, are acts one knows one can perform without violating these requirements.

More precisely, the relation between permissibility and duty is the following: If one has a moral duty to perform a particular act, then it is permissible for one to perform the act but not permissible for one to refrain from performing the act. If one has a moral duty to refrain from a particular act, then it is permissible for one to refrain from the act but not permissible for one to perform the act. If one does not have a moral duty either to perform or refrain from a particular act, then it is permissible for one to perform the act and permissible for one to refrain from the act.

Ethicists have distinguished four different categories of morally permissible acts. First, some morally permissible acts are neither morally praiseworthy nor morally blameworthy. These acts tend to be somewhat inconsequential as far as morality is concerned. For example, raising one's hand in the air or clearing one's throat is a morally neutral act (under most circumstances). It is neither praiseworthy nor blameworthy, and hence it cannot be the violation of duty.

Second, there are morally permissible acts that one has a moral duty to perform. Indeed, all instances of carrying out one's moral duty are permissible; it can never be impermissible to carry out one's duty.

Third, some morally permissible acts are morally praiseworthy but not the fulfillment of duty. That is, it is sometimes possible to act in a way that goes beyond moral duty, and it is always permissible to perform such acts. This category includes so-called acts of supererogation, acts whose performance is praiseworthy but not obligatory and whose omission is not blameworthy.

Fourth, some morally permissible acts are morally blameworthy. These acts, known as acts of offence, are blameworthy without constituting a violation of duty. They are bad enough to warrant blame but not bad enough to be classified as forbidden. Of all the acts that are permissible, these are the only ones whose performance has a negative ethical status. A significant number of moralists are skeptical as to whether acts of this type are possible.

There is considerable disagreement in ethics between those who defend an absolutist approach and those who defend a relativist approach. The concept of permissibility is thought of quite differently by the defenders of these two approaches.

Defenders of an absolutist approach follow Plato in thinking that there are standards of morality that are eternal, absolute, and unchanging. They are the same for everyone and are discovered, not made. From this it follows that what is morally permissible is also the same for everyone in relevantly similar circumstances. What is permissible does not depend upon one's culture or the period of history in which one lives.

Defenders of a relativist approach believe that people draw up standards of morality to govern their lives; before there were any people, there were no standards of morality. Different cultures have different conceptions of what is permissible, and that is exactly what one should expect. Someone from one culture might become quite alarmed at discovering that adultery, for example, is considered permissible in a different culture. That is not to say, however, that one culture is right and another is wrong, for in this view there are no moral absolutes. All that one can say is that different things are permissible in different cultures, and there is no question of one culture's being better or more correct than another.

Some ethical traditions place such emphasis upon duty as to virtually eliminate the possibility of permissible acts other than those that consist in doing one's duty. For example, in certain theological traditions, the demands of God or of other deities are so all-encompassing as to leave few occasions in which, with respect to the same act, it is both permissible to perform it and permissible to omit it. One is virtually always in a position of having a duty either to perform an act or to refrain from performing it, depending upon the will of God.

Another example is act utilitarianism. Roughly speaking, act utilitarianism is the view that one ought always act in such a way as to bring about the greatest benefits for the greatest number of persons. Thus, at any given time, one has a duty to choose the act that maximizes benefits and a corresponding duty not to choose any act that does not. In this view, it is hard to see how there can ever be an act that is both permissible to perform and permissible to omit.

Other ethical traditions place a high premium on the possibility of permissible acts and of the importance of learning how to choose between two or more permissible acts. Learning to make such choices is not possible within the confines of act utilitarianism. There is good reason to believe, however, that people attain moral maturity in situations in which decision making is more than following the stark demands of duty. Sooner or later, people must learn how to make wise decisions regarding courses of action that are permissible but not uniformly prudent from a moral point of view. This is especially true with respect to acts that are blameworthy but permissible;

moral maturity will teach one to avoid these when possible, even though they violate no moral duties.

—Gregory Mellema

See also Duty.

BIBLIOGRAPHY

Baier, Kurt. *The Moral Point of View.* Ithaca, N.Y.: Cornell University Press, 1958.

Donagan, Alan. *The Theory of Morality.* Chicago: University of Chicago Press, 1977.

Kovesi, Julius. *Moral Notions.* London: Routledge & Kegan Paul, 1967.

Singer, Marcus. *Generalization in Ethics.* New York: Russell & Russell, 1971.

Stob, Henry. *Ethical Reflections.* Grand Rapids, Mich.: Wm. B. Eerdmans, 1978.

Personal relationships

TYPE OF ETHICS: Personal and social ethics
DEFINITION: Intimate associations between two persons that define their lifestyles and mold their character
SIGNIFICANCE: Ideals and standards of conduct are needed to make relationships beneficial to their participants and consonant with harmony and justice in society

The Old Testament tale of Adam and Eve's expulsion from the Garden of Eden opens the theme of a personal relationship that leads to disaster for both parties. Philosophy, religion, law, and social institutions have sought to structure personal relationships in marriage and the family to bring the conduct of individuals in line with the good of others and social stability. Monogamous marriage and a nuclear family are believed to have conferred an evolutionary advantage on the human race by increasing the probability of survival for children born and reared in such unions.

The family is not only a biological survival unit, a haven, and a refuge. It is also a school for moral sentiments: Parents experience moral growth and socialize children according to community norms, and natural affection among family members generates altruistic emotions. The traditional duties of a husband and father were to furnish security and economic support and to exercise moral authority within the family. The wife and mother managed the household, nurtured children, and owed her husband fidelity. Children were to obey and respect parents and elders, and to help and be loyal to one another.

Ancient Greece and Christianity. Plato (fourth century B.C.E.) questioned the ethical value of marriage and the family and championed other forms of personal relationships. Athenian women were often uneducated and did not move in society, even in the company of their husbands. Wealthy aristocrats enjoyed the company of cultivated women prostitutes, and some courted male adolescents as protégés. In the *Symposium*, Plato maintains that an erotic relationship between a mature and a younger man, when inspired by philosophy, enables each to progress to the highest levels of human moral and intellectual development and creativity.

Since the first step in moral progress is to admire another for qualities of mind and character, rather than physical attractiveness, "Platonic love" has come to mean nonsexual friendship between any two persons with shared ideals of beauty, truth, and goodness. This nonsexual Platonic ideal enriches many teacher-student relationships and associations between those who dedicate themselves to science, art, and philanthropic activities.

In *Republic*, Plato's ideal state abolishes marriage and the family because they constitute "exclusive centers of private joys and sorrows" that distract citizens from the common good and prevent women from developing their talents and serving the whole community. Plato proposes eugenic matches between men and women of reproductive age and the communal rearing of children, so that neither parents nor children know their biological relationships. By law, all children call one another brother or sister and all adults father or mother; adults call each child son or daughter. In this way, Plato theorized, each person would develop for others in the community the bonds of affection and loyalty ordinarily limited to a few.

Aristotle (fourth century B.C.E.) claimed that *Republic*'s personal ties would be "watery" and morally ineffectual. He insisted that the friendly relationships of private life should promote both individual happiness and communal harmony. There is friendship when two persons mutually desire the good of the other for the other's own sake and each does some kind of good for the other. He distinguishes more transient "imperfect" friendships, in which the good achieved is pleasure or utility, from permanent "perfect" friendships based on appreciation of each other's character, in which the two join in pursuing noble goals, as in Platonic love. By maintaining that perfect friendship may exist between husband and wife, Aristotle defended the moral potential of marriage, whose family life combines daily virtuous activities, pleasure, and utility.

Christianity introduced new moral elements into personal relationships: It demanded love for those without attractive or useful qualities and love for those who do wrong or offend one. Being modeled on divine love, Christian love is generous, compassionate, and forgiving; it chastises but does not abandon a wrongdoer, seeking instead the person's moral regeneration.

Viewing sexual appetite as a source of evil, Christian ethics required fidelity of both husband and wife and prohibited both premarital and extramarital sex. The relationship of Dante Alighieri (1265-1321) to Beatrice in Dante's *Divine Comedy* reflects the medieval ideal of noble love, a model for the Christian relationship of man and woman. Dante's vision of the beautiful young Beatrice draws him heavenward: She personifies divine, loving concern for his weakness and inspires him to transcend carnal desires in order to achieve a loving union with her.

Romantic Love, Sexual Revolution, Male Bonding, and Feminism. The plays of William Shakespeare portray the popular modern ideal of romantic love. In them, a man and a woman feel erotic passion for each other and believe that they are perfectly suited for life together. Shakespeare is realistic in depicting the ambivalent potential of romantic love for happiness or misery: In the comedies, the lovers' ingenuity and constancy enable them to overcome obstacles, including the objections of kin, and they end in socially approved marriages. Impulsiveness, jealousy, or imprudence, however, lead to tragedy for the naive adolescent lovers of *Romeo and Juliet* (1595), the military hero of *Othello* (1622) and his bride Desdemona, and the sophisticated older lovers of *Antony and Cleopatra* (1623).

The romantic ideal of marriage based on mutual attraction prevails in American society. When romance fails or attends a third party, divorce is a resort. In the case of a couple with young children, remarriage and custody arrangements alter the tenor of family life and complicate parent-child and sibling relationships. The sexual revolution of the 1960's and 1970's liberalized sexual morality and legitimated various consensual forms of personal relationships. Premarital and extramarital sex, children born out of wedlock, homosexuality, lesbianism, and abortion no longer have the social stigma that once was attached to them. In common speech, a "relationship" connotes two unmarried persons who engage in consensual sex and are constant companions. The social norms of "recreational sex" are mutual consent and avoidance of pregnancy and sexually transmitted diseases. These limited norms do not address romantic feelings, which may exist on one side but not the other, and the consequent dangers of misunderstanding, deception, and exploitation of one by the other.

Films such as *The Deer Hunter* (1978) celebrate the phenomenon of "male bonding." Men who come together in often arduous activities of war, sports, work, leisure, or even crime develop comradeship that leads them to undertake dangerous tasks for the sake of one or more of their number. Male bonding is a source of strength and mutual support; it is ennobling and useful to society when it inspires men to behave courageously and selflessly. In the absence of moralizing influences such as the family, however, male bonding in urban gangs incites violent behavior and often is destructive to the individuals themselves. Gang members rely on money, power, and intimidation in relationships with outsiders and sometimes with intimates as well.

Some feminists consider male bonding, marriage, the family, and romantic love stratagems as elements of a patriarchal social organization that is designed to keep men in positions of power and women in subordination. Feminism has profoundly affected all forms of personal relationships by attacking the ideal of feminine submissiveness: Instead, feminism promotes self-assertion and independence for women both within and outside marriage and the family; it has opposed male domination in sexual harassment and employment practices. Some feminists condemn pornography on the grounds that it leads men to view and treat women as sex objects.

Contemporary Ethics. Contemporary "justice" ethics, represented by John Rawls's *Justice and Fairness* (1971), confers on consensual personal relationships equal legitimacy with marriage and family ties. Rawls does not accord marriage and family their traditional status of objective values to be endorsed by the moral principles of a just society; he categorizes them as subjective preferences, optional elements in an individual's life plan. Family partiality for the economic security of its members impedes a more egalitarian distribution of wealth. The assignment of special moral weight to the needs and well-being of family members is improper, for the moral attitude in justice ethics is one of rational impartiality toward individuals.

The morality of personal relationships in justice ethics is rights-based and contractual: Since autonomy, the power of the individual to act in accordance with his or her life plan without interference from others, is an objective value, intimates may not intrude upon it. One is obliged to respect the autonomy of all others and not to violate their basic human rights; other ideals or duties are matters of mutual agreement or subjective preference. Impartiality requires one to translate legal bans against racial, ethnic, and sexist discrimination into personal conduct by not showing bias in personal relationships with others.

Psychologist Carol Gilligan, in *In a Different Voice* (1977), theorizes that justice ethics embodies a masculine ethical perspective: Men value autonomy for the freedom it affords them to pursue power and prestige in the social organization without the burden of personal relationships. Women articulate a different ethical voice that reflects the nurturing functions that they fulfill in human life and values "relatedness." In ethical dilemmas, men apply universal moral principles impartially in order to secure justice in society; women seek a detailed narrative of the situation in order to resolve it without impairing valued relationships.

Other philosophical critics of justice ethics say that it overlooks the moral power of friendship and family ties. They formulate a "care" ethic in which the well-being of particular persons has independent moral weight. Their ethical attitude is one of attentive solicitude to particular persons. A person's moral responsibility is to be sensitive to the needs of intimates and anticipate threats to their well-being, to be receptive to their interpretation of a situation, and through dialogue to seek resolutions that respect each person's integrity. Some feminists hear the feminine ethical voice as calling them to lives of self-abnegation and devotion to others, threatening the gains of women's liberation.

Existentialist philosophers Martin Heidegger and Jean-Paul Sartre see personal relationships as being inextricably connected with personal identity and social structure. One's personal identity depends on what one is to others and what they are to one; these interpretations of self and other in turn are determined by how each plays his or her social role, which is defined by the social organization.

According to Heidegger's *Being and Time* (1927), one's everyday mentality is so task-oriented that one tends to lose sight of the particular human beings for whose sake one does the work. Individuals relate to others in three different ways: The prevalent way is to distance oneself from others, hiding oneself or putting on a disguise in order to get along smoothly with them and get on with one's work. When another's affairs demand attention, one steps into the other's life, managing matters for the other so as to "remove" the other's own care. This way makes one dominant and the other dependent; both lose their freedom. In authentic solicitude, one stands by the other, looks to what the future has in store for both, and helps the other to understand the shared situation and to be resolute in making his or her own place in the world. In this way, each gains authentic selfhood without losing freedom.

According to Sartre in *Being and Nothingness* (1943), sexual relationships model all personal relationships in a capitalist society, which values power and promotes competition among individuals. The "battle of the sexes" reflects the battle of egos in all forms of personal relationships. One seeks to inveigle or force the other to surrender freedom and acknowledge one's own superiority. This incessant struggle for domination is self-defeating and turns into masochism and sadism. Personal relationships cannot be self-affirming, Sartre suggests, until a restructuring of society enables each to will the freedom of all others.

Heidegger's and Sartre's theories point out undesirable ways of caring for others, which render personal relationships mutually self-destructive. Personal sexual relationships involve power, not only pleasure. Evils in personal relationships are the sort-sighted, callous, or cruel exercise of power and authority, and the manipulation and exploitation of another for personal advantage. Contemporary ethics stresses the evils of sexual harassment and the violation of another's rights, autonomy, and dignity.

It is agreed that each person in a relationship should be honest, sincere, and compassionate toward the other, respecting the other's individuality and integrity. Although a relationship should foster moral development, there is debate regarding whether one should be "the conscience of others," in Heidegger's phrase, or withhold forgiveness from an intimate on moral grounds. Most controversial is the primacy of autonomy, especially in close personal relationships. Joint decision making by spouses, for example, on matters of common interest is desirable yet may compromise autonomy; on occasion, one's own good, the good of another, or the preservation of the relationship itself may involve some yielding of autonomy. Because autonomy honors commitments based on rational choice and can change according to circumstances, it does not support biological family ties, and every personal loyalty, including marriage, is revocable. Yet constancy amid changing circumstances is the ethical and emotional heart of enduring personal relationships.

Unfinished Business. Anglo-American ethics, with its

emphasis on individual rights and autonomy, has largely neglected the philosophy of personal relationships. Social changes since World War I—such as the entry of women of child-bearing age into the work force, the liberalization of sexual relationships, divorce and remarriage of those with young children, increase in life span, and government social programs—have altered traditional forms of personal relationships and created new ones. The dynamics of intimacy and personal moral character for traditional relationships in these changed social conditions and for newer forms of relationships require further study.

A major issue is the reevaluation of the social importance of the family. The disintegration of the family contributes to, or makes intractable, social problems of drug addiction, child abuse and neglect, learning and educational deficiencies, juvenile crime, and homelessness. It is estimated that 40 percent of violent crimes take place between persons who know each other—often, between family members or persons with consensual relationships. Training and support in family life help an individual to deal with anger and frustration toward intimates and to develop the self-discipline needed to succeed in education and employment.

A second issue is the reexamination of ideals and standards of conduct in marriage, the family, and consensual relationships. Family life needs not only to embody justice but also to be fulfilling to adults and attentive to the well-being and moral development of children. Although fear of AIDS has led to more circumspection in sexual relationships and negative features of the "single-parent" family prompt measures to prevent pregnancy among teenagers, attention should go beyond health to the impact of consensual personal relationships on the characters and overall well-being of the individuals concerned and others caught in their relationships.

Gender differences in personal relationships make a difference. Whether women and men have divergent ethical perspectives is still being debated, but there is agreement that the goals and expectations of men and women differ in heterosexual relationships: Women usually look for trust, security, and companionship, while men more often seek immediate pleasure and are content with less emotional involvement. Gender differences also operate in problems of sexual harassment in and out of the workplace.

Finally, there are ethical differences between parity and nonparity personal relationships. In relationships between friends, spouses, coworkers, and siblings, there is rough parity between two persons in terms of power, knowledge, talents, and moral authority. In contrast, parent-child, employer-employee, doctor-patient, and teacher-student relationships involve an imbalance so that the obligations, ideals, and goals of one are in some respects not the same or commensurate with those of the other. Achieving the ideals of the relationship and the avoidance of manipulation and destructive dependency may take different forms in parity and nonparity relationships.

The doctor-patient relationship provides a model of how contemporary ethics has changed ideals in interpersonal relationships. In traditional medical paternalism, a doctor made decisions about how to treat and what to tell a patient and often withheld from a patient knowledge of the seriousness of his or her medical condition. Biomedical ethics has modified this nonparity relationship: A physician is now required by law to obtain informed consent for treatment from a competent patient; a patient has the moral obligation to participate in decision making and to take into account interests of his or her intimates. A patient needs to know the truth about his or her future prospects, in part because they affect the lives of his or her intimates. By extending and applying the insights and ideals of justice and care ethics, the philosophy of personal relationships may analyze and reform more intimate one-on-one intercourse.

—*Evelyn M. Barker*

See also Family; Family values; Friendship; Marriage; Women's ethics.

BIBLIOGRAPHY

Badinter, Elisabeth. *L'Un est l'autre*. Paris: Editions Odile Jacob, 1986. A lively anthropological account of heterosexual relationships from prehistory onward, with speculation on the impact of new reproductive technologies.

Blum, Lawrence A. *Friendship, Altruism, and Morality*. London: Routledge & Kegan Paul, 1980. Argues the reliability of altruistic emotions for moral motivation and the consistency of friendship with ethical impartiality.

Gilligan, Carol. *In a Different Voice*. Cambridge, Mass.: Harvard University Press, 1982. An eloquent description of psychological studies supporting the theory of two different courses of moral development in men and women.

Murphy, Jeffrie G., and Jean Hampton. *Forgiveness and Mercy*. Cambridge, England: Cambridge University Press, 1988. A revealing debate on the justice ethics proposition that forgiveness is sometimes morally wrong.

Noddings, Nel. *Caring: A Feminine Approach to Ethics and Moral Education*. Berkeley: University of California Press, 1984. A readable exposition of an ethics based on caring rather than on principles, showing how ethical care develops from natural care experienced in childhood.

Thomas, Laurence. *Living Morally: A Psychology of Moral Character*. Philadelphia: Temple University Press, 1989. An insightful analysis of parental love that compares it to friendship and romantic love.

LIST OF ENTRIES BY CATEGORY

HISTORY, RENAISSANCE AND RESTORATION

HUMAN RIGHTS

INTERNATIONAL RELATIONS

LEGAL AND JUDICIAL ETHICS

MEDIA ETHICS

MILITARY ETHICS